INDIAN GIVEN

A BOOK IN THE SERIES
Latin America Otherwise: Languages, Empires, Nations

SERIES EDITORS
Walter D. Mignolo, Duke University Irene Silverblatt, Duke University
Sonia Saldívar-Hull, University of Texas, San Antonio

MARÍA JOSEFINA SALDAÑA-PORTILLO

INDIAN GIVEN

Racial Geographies across Mexico and the United States

Duke University Press   Durham and London   2016

© 2016 Duke University Press
All rights reserved
Printed and bound by CPI Group (UK) Ltd, Croydon, CR0 4YY
Designed by Courtney Leigh Baker
Typeset in Arno Pro by Westchester
Library of Congress Cataloging-in-Publication Data
Saldaña-Portillo, María Josefina, [date]
Indian given : racial geographies across Mexico and the United States / María Josefina
Saldaña-Portillo.
pages cm—(Latin America otherwise)
Includes bibliographical references and index.
ISBN 978-0-8223-5988-3 (hardcover : alk. paper)
ISBN 978-0-8223-6014-8 (pbk. : alk. paper)
ISBN 978-0-8223-7492-3 (e-book)
1. Mestizos—Race identity—History. 2. Mexican-American Border Region—Race
relations—Political aspects—History. 3. Indians, Treatment of—Mexican-American
Border Region—History. I. Title. II. Series: Latin America otherwise.
F790.M47S25 2016
305.800972'1—dc23
2015025420

Cover art: Photograph of a mural by Curiot, *El Retorno de Akhankutti.*

For María Elena Martínez
your work inspired and challenged my own

For María Elizabeth Macías
and the thousands of Mexicans killed in the drug war

For Juan Flores
camarada, amigo, hermano

CONTENTS

Acknowledgments ix

INTRODUCTION. It Remains to Be Seen
Indians in the Landscape of America 1

1 SAVAGES WELCOMED
Imputations of Indigenous Humanity in Early Colonialisms 33

2 AFFECT IN THE ARCHIVE
Apostates, Profligates, Petty Thieves, and the
Indians of the Spanish and U.S. Borderlands 66

3 MAPPING ECONOMIES OF DEATH
From Mexican Independence to the Treaty
of Guadalupe Hidalgo 108

4 ADJUDICATING EXCEPTION
The Fate of the *Indio Bárbaro* in the U.S. Courts (1869–1954) 154

5 LOSING IT!
Melancholic Incorporations in Aztlán 195

CONCLUSION. The Afterlives of the *Indio Bárbaro* 233

Notes 259   Bibliography 299   Index 319

ACKNOWLEDGMENTS

It is a pleasure to have the opportunity to thank all the people and places that made this book possible. I have enjoyed every minute of researching and writing this book, and this is in large part because of the many collaborators who have helped me develop my ideas along the way. I would like to begin by thanking the staff at the Archivo General de Indias (AGI) for their assistance with my archival research and for the access they provide to the wealth of information in the colonial record. I would also like to thank the Benson Latin American Collection at the University of Texas for access to their holdings and for their extraordinary helpfulness.

Several institutions supported me financially and intellectually in the writing of this book. I thank the Fulbright U.S. Scholars Program for awarding me a Fulbright García-Robles (FGR) fellowship for Mexico City in 2010–2011, as well as the FGR staff who welcomed me to their city. While on the fellowship, I was a visiting scholar with the Programa Universitario de Estudios de Género (PUEG) at the Universidad Nacional Autónoma de México. I would like to thank Marisa Belausteguigoitia, then director of the PUEG, as well as her outstanding staff. Under her leadership, the PUEG provided a rich intellectual environment during my year in Mexico and fomented collaborative research. The discussions at the PUEG have left their mark on the book and I am very grateful. I thank the Recovering the U.S. Hispanic Literary Heritage Project for their 2010 Research Grant for transcription of the archival manuscripts retrieved from the AGI. I want to thank Edith Betancourt for her assistance with the transcription of some of these eighteenth-century documents. And I thank Oscar Marquez for his excellent work on compiling the bibliography for this book.

Many thanks to David Eng, David Kazanjian, Teemu Ruskola, and Priscilla Wald for the manuscript workshop they participated in that launched this book project. These four brilliant people helped me to realize the project's full potential, providing key guidance in imagining its contours and continuing to challenge me with their insight since then. I am ever in their debt. Over the course of the last five years, several centers, programs, and departments have invited me to workshop chapters from this book; I learned so much in these exchanges and the book is so much better for them. I thank María Elena Martínez for so many things, among them her early invitation to present my work at the Department (then Program) of American Studies and Ethnicity at the University of Southern California (USC). Thanks to Ira Livingston and Jonathan Beller for inviting me to the Aesthetics and Politics Initiative at Pratt University, trailblazing just around the corner from my house. I thank Alex Lubin for inviting me to the Center for American Studies and Research (CASAR) at the American University of Beirut. Debra Castillo invited me to the Counterstories of Greater Mexico Conference on behalf of the Latin American and Latino Studies programs at Cornell University. I thank her and the programs for facilitating this vibrant and lasting intellectual exchange. I thank Lisa Marie Cacho, Jodi Byrd, and Karen Flynn at the University of Illinois, Urbana-Champaign, for their organization of the "Affinities and Assemblages" symposium where those two words were made operative. José Antonio Lucero at the University of Washington invited me to the Simpson Center for the Humanities there for a fantastic conversation with Adam Warren and Marisa Duarte as part of their Mellon Sawyer Seminar Series: thanks all around. I also thank Valentina Napoletano for her invitation on behalf of the Latin American Studies Working Group at the University of Toronto. I thank Andrew Friedman and the Faculty Working Group in American Studies at Haverford College. Many thanks to Rodrigo Laguarda for his invitation to the "Historia en Distinctos Registros" colloquium at the Instituto Mora, as well as for the many exciting conversations we shared on borderlands history. Together, all the participants of these many discussions left an indelible imprint on this book.

And now to those friends and allies who are smart and playful and made this book possible with their intellectual support, but also with those much-needed fun breaks in and around New York and Mexico City: Roopali Mukherjee, Ed Cohen, Ardele Lister, Jean Franco, Ira Livingston, Iona Man-Cheong, Rob Miotke, Eric Taylor, Gayatri Gopinath, Tei Okamoto, Claudia Urey, Catherine Zimmer, Jennifer Portnof, Sara Pursley, Emma Bianchi, Ito Romo, David Eng, Teemu Ruskola, Mary Louise Pratt, Renato Rosaldo, Maria Damon, Mayra Guillén, Ana María López Dzib, Frida Gorbach, Rodrigo Laguardia, Guadalupe Avendaño Portillo (*y toda tu familia*), Licha Portillo (*y toda tu familia*), Mayté Portillo (*y toda tu familia*): you rock, you make me happy, thank you! And always, always Juan Flores and José Muñoz. I miss you. Then there are those dear comrades who go one step beyond offering deep friendship and intellection and are involved in the book's production. Shay Brawn. Where would I be without you? Thank you for your fine editorial eye and for making this book a much easier read. Livia Tenzer, how far we have traveled. Thank you for all your expertise and assistance in procuring permissions and in proofing the proofs. David Sartorius, in your nerdy historian voice, always looking out for me and making me giggle, thank you. Madhu Dubey, you will always be my go-to second set of eyes, chapter after chapter. Thank you and no rest for the weary. Ken Wissoker, you are a gem of an editor. From the first discussion we had regarding the structure for this book to the last bit of advice on the title and everything in between, you are always able to discern the significance of my project and distill it for me. I thank you for your patience and guidance but also for your singular vision— on the last book, on this book, and on the next. I am also grateful to Jade Brooks for your hand in producing this final product.

Finally, I would like to thank the Tepoztlán Institute for Transnational History of the Americas and my chosen academic family, the international collective that makes the institute and my brain hum. I am especially grateful to Marisa Belausteguigoitia Ruis, Geraldo Cadava, Natti Golubov, Nicole Guidotti-Hernández, Laura Gutiérrez, David Kazanjian, María Elena Martínez, Bethany Moreton, Alexandra Puerto, Yolanda Martínez San Miguel, Mario Rufer, David Sartorius, Ben Sifuentes-Jáuregui, Freddy Vilches, Pamela Voekel, Adam Warren, and *papi chulo* Elliot Young. Lisbeth Haas and Reiko Hillyer, honorary collective members, you too are part of this family. This group of friends and intellectual interlocutors is why this book exists. It is a product of the institute's yearly conferences, of its vision and care. I love everything about our collective—our joy but also our fights. Thank you all for your engagement and generosity. We lost our dear friend María Elena last year. I hope this book lives up to your standard, *querida*, because I couldn't have written it without your shining example, or without your trampoline dream. You will always be the leading lady in my cabaret!

Finally for real this time, once again, I thank David Kazanjian. You're a pretty smart cookie. And a sweet one.

INTRODUCTION

IT REMAINS TO BE SEEN
Indians in the Landscape of America

"Ah," sighed Dean, "the end of Texas, the end of America, we don't know no more."... Laredo
was a sinister town that morning. All kinds of cab-drivers and border rats wandered around,
looking for opportunities. There weren't many; *it was too late*. It was the bottom and dregs
of America where all the heavy villains sink, where disoriented people have to be near *a
specific elsewhere* they can slip into unnoticed.... Just beyond, you could feel the enormous
presence of whole great Mexico and almost smell the billion tortillas frying and smoking in
the night. We had no idea what Mexico would really be like.... We felt awful and sad. But
everything changed when we crossed the mysterious bridge over the river and our wheels
rolled on official Mexican soil, though it wasn't anything but a carway for border inspection.
Just across the street Mexico began. We looked with wonder. *To our amazement it looked
exactly like Mexico.*... fellows in straw hats and white pants were lounging by the dozen
against battered pocky storefronts....

Old men sat on chairs in the night and looked like *Oriental junkies and oracles.*...

These people were unmistakably Indians and were not at all like the Pedros and Pan-
chos of silly civilized American lore—they had high cheekbones, and slanted eyes, and soft
ways; they were not fools, they were not clowns; they were great, grave Indians and they
were the source of mankind and the fathers of it. —**Jack Kerouac**, *On the Road*

What enables Jack Kerouac's protagonist, Sal Paradise, to visualize the
southwestern landscape of Laredo, Texas, as sinister and villainous?[1] As
teeming with rats seeking out criminal opportunities but also anxious to slip
away, undetected, across the border, presumably to a forgiving Mexico? Meanwhile, the "enormous presence" of the Mexican landscape enters through the
senses as well, anticipating the arrival of Sal and his iconic sidekick Dean
Moriarty with the *smell* and *feel* of its racial difference, the billion fried tortillas, hovering across the bridge like atmosphere, enticing them to come and

partake. Sal and Dean have no idea what Mexico "would really be like," and yet their eyes discover, to their amazement, that it "looked *exactly* like Mexico." How do they know, before they see, what their vision will apprehend: a nation of "great, grave Indians"? The sharp edges of the Indians' high cheekbones and slanted eyes cut and divide Mexico from the United States just as decisively as the Rio Grande, and just as "naturally" their racial difference gives Mexican geography its meaning: soft, inviting, lounging, ancestral, wise (oracles), and stoned (junkies). Mexico is a "*specific* elsewhere," a prearranged space of indigenous peasantry, in iconic white garb and sombreros, who sit in and against landscape, becoming one with the environment they inhabit. The racial character of the United States represented by Laredo is, by contrast, melancholic ("awful," "sad") and exhausted by its own civilization, at the "end" of knowing.[2]

Sal perceives a racial geography, a racial divide along the border—on one side Indians, on the other side not; on one side Oriental enchantment, on the other western (white) banality. Conventionally, Kerouac overlays an east–west axis onto a south–north cartography, and even the way in which Kerouac positions Laredo and Nuevo Laredo connotes a well-worn geographical imagination mediated by racial difference. Rather than positioning the twin cities horizontally, he has one sit atop the other vertically, as villainous dregs "sink" down to "the bottom" of the United States to seep into a receptive Mexico. Although Kerouac privileges subordinate Mexico as more authentic and good than "America," moral characteristics wrought from its indigeneity, the geographically given hierarchy between Mexico and the United States remains intact.

Indian Given: Racial Geographies across Mexico and the United States is about the power of racialized "ways of seeing" national geographies as presumably natural, especially as they are visualized along the divide of the Mexico–U.S. border. As John Berger pithily put it in his paradigm-shaping *Ways of Seeing*, "The way we see things is affected by what we know or what we believe" (8). While concerned with how Mexico and the United States are visualized and known as nations, *across* in the title indexes a relationship between these two geographies rather than an exhaustive account of either, suggesting a process that is ongoing rather than a settled state. These visualized geographies cross each other, they work at cross-purposes, conflicting and constituting each other. They are interactional and intermixed. They exist *entre dos países*—between two countries—and because of each other. Laredo and Nuevo Laredo are ideal cities to foreground this crossing—this *entre*— and the constructed aspect of Kerouac's emblematic geographic vision of the border, because historically, economically, ecologically, and socially these cities form *one* cultural landscape. Advertising signs, city slogans, newspapers, cultural events, radio programs, and bumper stickers still today bill the twin cities as "LareDOS" or "Los Dos Laredos" (figs. I.1–I.4). Architecturally, the two cities mirror each other as well, with each urban center organized in the traditional Spanish colonial pattern, with a uniform street grid emanating from a central plaza surrounded by administrative offices, hotels, and places of commerce.

The two cities share an architectural heritage because they share a colonial heritage. The founding of Laredo, Texas, preceded Nuevo Laredo, Tamaulipas, but both were effects of colonial intrusions. As part of the viceroyalty of New Spain, San Agustín de Laredo was founded on the northern bank of the Rio Bravo (or Rio Grande) by a handful of families in 1755 on a land grant issued by the Spanish Crown to Capítan Don Tomás Sánchez de Barrera y Gallardo. The city was strategically positioned adjacent to a river crossing frequented by indigenous peoples of the region. An epicenter of indigenous life along the river long before 1755, this place was named by the colonists after its function, "paso de los indios" (Indian Pass). Less than one hundred years later, after the conclusion of the U.S. expansionist war against Mexico in 1848 and the annexation of its northern territory, seventeen Laredo families decamped across the river to establish Nuevo Laredo on the other side of the newly drawn, neocolonial border, anxious as they were to remain under Mexican sovereignty. I elaborate on this history here because it underscores the power of Kerouac's constructed vision of the border as a stark divide between two distinct racial geographies ("Just across the street Mexico began"). Situated along corresponding sides of the river, these arid towns are geologically, architecturally, and "racially" far more similar than dissimilar. Today, as in 1955 when Kerouac published his autobiographical novel, Laredo's population (like its architecture and environs) looks quite similar, if not identical, to the population of Nuevo Laredo: mestizos, Indian, and light skinned, 90 percent of the city's inhabitants are still of Mexican descent. Nevertheless, Sal *saw* radically different *racial* geographies on either side of the "mysterious bridge" rather than overlapped or crossed ones.

Indian Given: Racial Geographies across Mexico and the United States elucidates how Kerouac arrived at his rather commonplace representation of the visual landscape of the border region (dangerous/accommodating, reckless/passive, maleficent/virtuous: adjoining but distinct national spaces), how his conventional iteration of the racial difference between the United States and Mexico enters as if naturally through the senses: the United

INTRODUCTION 3

FIG. 1.1. Los 2 Laredos boxing gym, Laredo, Texas.

FIG. 1.2. Team logo for the Tecolotes de Los Dos Laredos, Nuevo Laredo, Tamaulipas, baseball team.

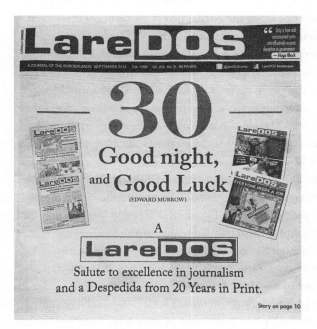

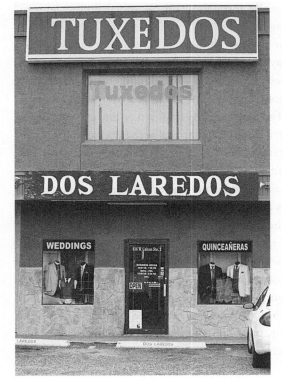

FIG. 1.3. Last issue of *LareDOS: A Journal of the Borderlands*, a monthly periodical published in Laredo, Texas, 1994–2014.

FIG. 1.4. Storefront, Laredo, Texas.

States as nonindigenous space atop Mexico as indigenous space. Contemporary perceptions of violence along the border invert the terms of these racialized landscapes, underscoring their reiterative force. Mexico, still indigenous, is now the scene of barbarous crime, while the United States, still nonindigenous, is the passive recipient of its drugs and immigrants. That this is a *geographical* rendering of the two nations' racial character (barbarous Mexico/noble United States) is further underscored by the proliferation of maps of "drug cartel" territories in Mexico. An internet search brings up maps representing the boundaries of the Sinaloa cartel, the Gulf cartel, the Zeta cartel, and others—their boundaries discretely cut across Mexican geography but always stop abruptly, reassuringly, but unrealistically, at the border of the United States.[3] It is my contention in this book that perceptions like these—of natural landscapes and landscapes of cultural difference—are racially derived, the national geographies and the geography of the border region meticulously produced through the colonial encounters with indigeneity. The way we perceive natural landscape, the way we have mapped national and regional geographies out of it—particularly along the Mexico–U.S. border—are the result of a complex history of encounter with indigeneity. Succinctly put, the geographies of the United States and Mexico have been produced, materially and representationally, through historical, social, and racial relation with indigenous subjects.

Springboarding off of the last two decades of scholarship in critical geography, I argue that the ways in which national geographies are perceived, imagined, lived, and mapped are supremely racial, and that these racially produced geographies cannot be understood without a thorough investigation of the colonial modes of governmentality imposed on and engaged by indigenous people. If our contemporary geographies of the Hispanophone and Anglophone Americas are racially derived, the only way to understand this derivation is through a transnational study of the colonial records of Spanish and British colonization. *Indian Given* is not just or primarily a comparative study, though comparison is a necessary component of its endeavor. Rather *Indian Given* seeks to move beyond comparison, as recent colonial and postcolonial studies scholars of race have urged.[4] Scholars of comparison have demonstrated that the method developed in tandem with European imperialism, U.S. neocolonial expansion, and Cold War containment. Comparative scholarship often used its purported empiricism to demonstrate the superiority or greater development of Anglo-American and Northern European geographical areas.[5] Certainly, most contemporary comparative scholarship no longer plays handmaiden to teleological or developmentalist political

6   INTRODUCTION

projects. Nevertheless, I consider this work transnational (for all of its own freighted legacy) because I am less interested in even value-neutral comparison than in demonstrating the ways in which the racial geographies of Mexico and the United States were mutually constituted and imbricated in their colonial legacies.[6]

Spanish and British colonialism in North America were space-making endeavors, and I argue that they created space through the careful placing (and displacing) of indigenous subjects in landscape. As such, they produced distinct, indeed divergent, racial geographies: colonial places apparently replete with Indians or bereft of them, despite the actual presence or absence of Indians. In moving beyond comparison, *Indian Given* investigates not only how and why these colonial space-making enterprises produced such dissimilar racial geographies but also the instances in which these colonial enterprises conspired in their construction of racialized spaces, in their placement and displacement of indigenous subjects. Spanish and British colonial missions, in other words, were competitive enterprises but they were also at times complicit in their creation of their racial geographies and the types of Indians therein.

Indian Given investigates these complicities, examining the historical conjunctures during which these distinct racial geographies were mutually constituted. It pays particular attention to the region where these geographies productively overlapped, along the border of what would become Mexico and the United States. Contemporary cultural phenomena like Chicano Aztlán and white vigilantism, like the "Muslim jihadist" and the "narco-terrorist," are also explored in *Indian Given,* and I argue that they are the effects of these overlapping racial geographies along the Mexico–U.S. border. In fact, these phenomena can only be properly understood as political and cultural formations when considered within the context of colonial space-making enterprises, as they are genealogically derived from the historical juxtaposition of these competing and complicit racial geographies. The construction of "the border" itself as a political demarcation and as an ecology of meaning, as a drug economy and as a source of psychic anxiety and distress (materialized, for example, in Arizona's passage of SB 1070, the Support Our Law Enforcement and Safe Neighborhoods Act) are effects of these overlapping racial geographies that engage each other with productive force. In order to properly understand the contemporary ramifications of these racialized geographies, the urgency of the present if you will, it is necessary to reconstruct the genealogies of our divergent yet shared Mexican and U.S. racial geographies. Thus, *Indian Given* necessarily spans a vast chronological period in its analysis, from the sixteenth to the twenty-first century, each chapter organized around a historical flashpoint that illuminates moments of crisis in the mapping of colonial and national spaces.[7]

If the ways we perceive American landscapes are mediated by "Indianness," if the racial geographies we currently inhabit in the Americas are saturated with it, as I contend, then it is equally true that the generic categories of "the Indian" and "el indio" are the result of this colonial production of space as well.[8] The invention of "the Indian" by colonialism is a well-rehearsed idea, especially in Latin American historical and anthropological scholarship.[9] *Indian Given* adds to this scholarship by demonstrating the manner in which Indians and *indios* were spatially produced (as effects and progenitors of European colonialisms), especially in their generic guises. The colonial, generic constructs of Indians and indios, I contend, were derived in part from the perception of Indians and indios in and as landscape. By approaching these generic categories geographically, as mapped phenomena that appear, disappear, and reappear at strategic moments over the long arc of colonial and national encounter, we see that there is not one singular idea of the Indian or indio operating at any particular historical juncture, much less over the centuries since 1492. "Indians" and "indios" are not transhistorical phenomena, in other words. The point is not simply that the terms *Indian* and *indio* fail to index the rich heterogeneity of the thousands of indigenous peoples in the United States and Mexico, but rather, that there were multiple *generic* "Indians" and "indios" deployed over time, with these generic concepts morphing as required by the acquisition of space by Spanish and Anglo-American colonialism, especially during moments of colonial or national crisis. Even the two terms were and are imperfect translations of each other, as "Indian" in the contours of U.S. racial geography means very different things than "indio" in the contours of Mexican racial geography. *Indian Given* is an exploration of the *untranslatability* of these two terms, the incommensurability of Indian and indio. The purpose of this book is to trace these generic categories over time, elucidating how articulations, reiterations, and transformations of Indians and indios produced racialized space, and in turn, to trace how the exigencies of the production of colonial and national spaces gave us Indians and indios. I offer the reader two distinct but complicit genealogies of Indian difference as produced in colonial and national geographies.

To say that Indians produced Mexican space, produced its national character, is not a particularly contentious claim. To the contrary, Mexico prides itself on its indigenous past and present. "México se folkloriza solo" (Mexico folklorizes itself), as a friend and colleague is fond of saying, and it does so

8 INTRODUCTION

through the deployment of its indigenous cultures. Everywhere in Mexico, the state monumentalizes its indigenous past and present in the service of nationalism and as a condition of its revolutionary character.[10] Mexico locates its mestizo present in its indigenous past. Nevertheless, it is my hope to defamiliarize the manner in which Mexican nationalism claims its indigeneity and to defamiliarize the place of indigenous peoples in Mexican society by demonstrating how both New Spain and Mexico were graphed through the political project of plotting indios in space for instrumentalizing and universalizing purposes. On the other hand, to suggest that the geography and national character of the United States were produced by a similar process of indigenous emplotment is still a relatively new and contentious claim.[11]

In both popular and academic historiography of the United States, indigenous peoples as first inhabitants are scripted to disappear, either fortuitously or tragically, while the physical territory of the United States is scripted as *terra nullius* in waiting. *Indian Given* defamiliarizes this historiography as well, by demonstrating the centrality to the development of a U.S. racial geography of locating Indians in landscape. The dominance of the trope of the disappearing Indian in open landscape is in part attributable to the "frontier thesis" school of U.S. historiography created by Fredrick Jackson Turner at the turn of the twentieth century. Turner represented the Great Plains and the Southwest as an expanse of "free land" available for (white) settlement and U.S. development. The frontier thesis is profoundly Lockian in its construction of land as freely available due to its improper possession by indigenous peoples, but Turner also follows Kant's climate determinism and association of moral value with race when he derives Anglo-American *character* from the encounter with geography.[12] For Turner, the "peculiar institutions" of democratic and egalitarian political life in the United States are derived from settlers' compulsory innovation in the face of an ever-receding frontier as they were "compelled to adapt themselves to the changes of an expanding people—to the changes involved in crossing a continent, in winning a wilderness, and in developing at each area of this progress out of the primitive economic and political conditions of the frontier into the complexity of city life" (Turner 1893, 2). The *specificity* of the continent's wilderness gives mimetic shape to "American" character and culture.

Certainly, indigenous peoples appear in Turner's historiography only to eventually cede ground and vanish from the landscape in the face of white settlement's superior order. And yet even in this quintessential tale of American conquest and character, indigenous peoples do much more than simply disappear. Turner locates Indians in landscape so that "Americans" may acquire their proper "Americanness." Indians give "American ingenuity" its unique character:

> The wilderness masters the colonist. It finds him a European in dress, industries, tools, modes of travel, and thought. It takes him from the railroad car and puts him in the birch canoe. It strips off the garments of civilization and arrays him in the hunting shirt and the moccasin. It puts him in the log cabin of the Cherokee and Iroquois and runs an Indian palisade around him. Before long he has gone to planting Indian corn and plowing with a sharp stick; he shouts the war cry and takes the scalp in orthodox Indian fashion. In short, at the frontier the environment is at first too strong for the man. He must accept the conditions which it furnishes, or perish, and so he fits himself into the Indian clearings and follows the Indian trails. Little by little he transforms the wilderness, but the outcome is not the old Europe . . . here is a new product that is American. At first, the frontier was the Atlantic coast. It was the frontier of Europe in a very real sense. Moving westward, the frontier became more and more American. (4)

It is not only the wilderness that masters the colonist, but the Indian. The colonist abandons European industries and adopts indigenous technologies— modes of transportation (birch canoe), agriculture (planting corn), architecture (palisades, log cabin) and dress (hunting shirt, moccasin).[13] Indeed, for Americans to emerge out of the "primitive . . . conditions of the frontier," the Indian must first primitivize the effeminate colonist, who becomes Indian from the inside out, uttering a guttural "war cry" and in an "orthodox fashion" opening the Indian's head to appropriate his knowing ways. It is of key significance that the gender of the Indian and colonist alike is masculine, because U.S. (and Mexican) racial geography is a highly gendered space. The American wilderness is the condition of possibility for colonial and indigenous masculinity, as the male Indian teaches the male colonist how to survive and thrive in the "too strong" environment. Colonial masculinity is achieved *through* indigenous adroitness in landscape, an adroitness that in turn authors colonial savagery (scalping). The wilderness and masculinity become one in the frontier thesis, as American geography embodies a muscular Indianness.[14]

Thirty years after Turner, frontier historian Walter Prescott Webb offered a similar analysis of "American character" derived from a gendered and gendering environment mediated by Indian embodiment in his opus *The Great Plains*. As much a geographical primer as a history, *The Great Plains* begins with an analysis of the topography, climate, plant, and animal life of

10 INTRODUCTION

the Plains, all key factors in the development of Native American culture and subsequently U.S. culture for Webb. In his account, the flat landscape and arid climate of the Plains, so different from the "humid timber region" of the Eastern seaboard, determined the differences between the nomadic Plains Indians and the settled civilized Eastern Indians (Webb 1931, 47). Moreover, as in Turner, the landscape-derived characteristics of the Plains Indians were transmitted to the "white man" through contact:

> The Plains Indians were by nature more ferocious, implacable, and cruel than other tribes. . . . Historians in the nineteenth century distinguished clearly between "civilized" Indians, or the Eastern tribes, and "wild" Indians, or the Plains tribes. . . . the frontiersmen on the Plains soon learned that one could not surrender to an Indian. The Indians rarely, if ever, surrendered themselves, and they had no concept of the white man's generosity to a vanquished foe. If one cannot surrender, then one must flee or fight, and in the end must die rather than fall alive into the hands of the enemy. (59)

Leaving aside Webb's unsustainable assertion of the "white man's generosity," the frontiersmen learned to withstand the harsh landscape by learning not to surrender to the ferociousness of the Plains Indians. Once again, in other words, the conquering of environment is accomplished through the Indians, whom the colonists must mime in order to succeed on the Plains. Colonial space-making is again a gendered and gendering experience, as the graphing of its seemingly inhospitable environment into habitable space is mediated by the encounter with active, muscular Indians. Indeed, Webb described extensively and with great admiration the specific skills of the Apache and Comanche in battle, skills that were developed due to the nature of the landscape and climate of the Plains, and were eventually transferred to the white man, who mimes the Indian in learning to flee or fight rather than to surrender. Throughout Webb's analysis, as in this passage, American masculine character, implacable and intrepid, is wrought from the encounter with implacable and intrepid Plains Indians, like the Apache and Comanche.[15]

Indian Given, then, seeks to defamiliarize this historiography of the Indian who is vanished or reduced to reservation by plumbing the depths of the colonial archive for the various types of gendered Indians who were necessarily located in space for the constitution of a national geography. In sundry ways, Indians and indios are the condition of possibility for the emergence of the United States as well as Mexico. It is in this sense that the racial geographies of these two countries are indeed Indian given, and that the book arrives at its

FIG. I.5. Plaza de las Tres Culturas, commemorative stone plaque, Tlatelolco, Mexico City. The inscription reads: "August 13, 1521 / Heroically defended by Cuauhtemoc / Tlatelolco fell under the power of Hernán Cortés / Neither triumph nor defeat / [It] was the painful birth of the mestizo people / That today is Mexico."

title. *Indian Given* is intentionally a play on the derogatory term "Indian giver." An "Indian giver" is someone who takes back something they have willingly given or sold, and the slur derives its meaning from another popular myth of U.S. history, that the Indians gifted colonists their land, fair and square, and now they unjustly demand its return. By contrast, Mexican historiography openly recognizes the violence and injustice of indigenous dispossession at the hands of Spanish conquistadors. Indeed, public culture memorializes the injustice in Mexico City, whether in the Diego Rivera murals that adorn the walls of the National Palace or on the plaque outside Tlatelolco in the Plaza de las Tres Culturas commemorating the armed encounter of the Nahuas and Spaniards as neither a victory nor a defeat ("No fue triunfo ni derrota"), but as the "doloroso nacimiento del pueblo mestizo" (the painful birth of the mestizo people) (fig. I.5). The violence and suffering of indigenous people in the conquest is constantly, reiteratively affirmed and projected onto landscape.

Nobel Prize winner Octavio Paz most famously nationalized the violence of indigenous conquest in his chapter "Hijos de La Malinche" from *El laberinto de la soledad*. Mexicans are *all* the sons of mother-Malinche (Cortés's translator), who is characterized by Paz as the victim of a violation, of a fraud:

¿quién es la Chingada? La Chingada es la Madre abierta violada o burlada por la fuerza. El "hijo de la Chingada" es el engendro de la violación, del rapto o de la burla. Si se compara esta expresión con la española, "hijo de puta", se advierte inmediatamente la diferencia. Para el español la deshonra consiste en ser hijo de una mujer que voluntariamente se entrega, una prostituta; para el mexicano, en ser fruto de una violación.

[Who is the fucked one? The fucked one is the mother who is opened, violated, or tricked by force. The "son of the fucked one" is the product of a rape, of a kidnapping, or a mockery. If we compare this expression with the Spanish "son of a whore" we immediately perceive the difference. For the Spaniard the dishonor consists of being the son of one who voluntarily offers herself, a prostitute; for the Mexican, it is in being the fruit of a violation.] (Paz 1994, 33)

In comparing the Mexican colloquialism "hijo de la chingada" (son of the fucked one) with the Spanish colloquialism "hijo de puta" (son of a whore), Paz underscores that the indigenous victims of colonialism ceded nothing "voluntarily" or for a fair price. Rather they were the victims of an injurious fraud. As in Turner, the terms of becoming Mexican are highly gendered: Malinche, mother-as-territory, is ripped open by the masculine agency of the Spaniard, and the products of this rape are consequently engendered as humiliated, enraged, and brutish male subjects (sons). Paz *generalizes* the violence against and the defrauding of indigenous peoples by colonialism—*all* Mexicans are *hijos de la chingada*/sons of the fucked one—and he accomplishes this through the open female indigenous body. At the same time, because all Mexicans are also engendered by the Spaniards who raped and conquered, the hijo de la chingada also contains within himself the one who rapes, the *chingón*. The chingón is "activo, agresivo y cerrado . . . el que abre" (active, aggressive and closed . . . the one who opens) (32). The act of colonizing is still enabled through the territorial embodiment of the indigenous woman, but it is paradoxically the offspring of the rape that is now the one who colonizes, as the chingón aggressively opens not only the female indigenous body of his mother, but also the territory of the future nation. *Mestizaje* contains multitudes: aggression and passivity, culpability and victimage.[16]

For our purposes, what it significant and suggestive about Paz's analysis is that it reveals the "pained birth" of Mexico's *racial* citizenship (mestizaje) to be Indian given, accomplished by casting the Malinche-mother and the chingón father (now also part indigenous) as progenitors of the entirety of

Mexican territory, and by situating this original wound in stone at the heart of Mexico's Plaza de las Tres Culturas ("meeting place of three cultures") within the capital (fig. I.5). At first glance it appears difficult to reconcile the Mexican colloquialism of hijo de la chingada with the U.S. colloquialism "Indian giver," but by juxtaposing these national space-making projects we defamiliarize both and make visible the relationships between them. The generalization of indigenous injury to the entire Mexican population by the popular phrase "hijo de la chingada" (indeed as source of the population) paradoxically renders contemporary indigenous grievance impossible, just as the slur "Indian giver" renders contemporary indigenous redress unnecessary (because U.S. Indians presumably gave up their land voluntarily). If all Mexicans are equally injured by/responsible for/born of colonialism, then all were equally defrauded and defrauder, and in a manner that is similar though not identical to Indian giver, hijo de la chingada deflects national culpability. The dispersal of injury, its location in a generalized territory and a distant past, renders contemporary indigenous claims for restitution of governmentality and respect for territorial integrity more difficult to make in Mexico, just as the term *Indian giver* makes indigenous claims for full sovereignty and territorial integrity appear not only impractical but unjust in the United States. The slur from which this book takes its title reveals a deep historical anxiety on both sides of the border: the indigenous peoples rightfully demand their land back! Evoking this historical anxiety, the title *Indian Given* indexes the ongoing, legitimate claims of indigenous peoples to their colonized territories. Indigenous peoples did not cede their lands willingly, but insofar as they were constituted as the objects of colonial and then national gazes, they became unwilling participants in historical, discursive, and geographical constructions that facilitated the conquest of their territories and continues to facilitate their ongoing dispossession.[17]

My investigation into the colonial origins of the racial geographies of Mexico and the United States is informed and indeed inspired by contemporary indigenous movements for rights and territory on both sides of the Mexico–U.S. border. Mexican and U.S. indigenous rights movements often coalesce in political endeavors at a global level, but they do not align in their political aims or models of subjectivity at the national level. Mexican indigenous movements most often express political demands in the guise of regional or communal autonomy, while U.S. indigenous activists express political demands in the guise of national sovereignty. These two political formations register very different ideas of nationhood and citizenship.

In *Indian Given*, I elucidate the similarities and differences between these movements and their forms of political subjectivity by suggesting how they emerged within and correspond to distinct racial geographies. *Indian Given* does not focus on autonomy and sovereignty, but it was in part motivated by a desire to understand the differences between these political formations and the colonial and national histories that engendered them. Over the course of my career, I have participated in several scholarly and activist meetings between U.S. and Mexican indigenous peoples, sometimes serving as linguistic (and cultural) translator. I have witnessed U.S. indigenous scholar/activists lecture their Mexican counterparts on the inefficacy of autonomy as a vehicle for expressing their political demands, and I have had to explain to bemused Mexican indigenous scholar/activists that sovereignty in the United States entitles indigenous peoples to their respective nation's passport. I have heard U.S. indigenous scholar/activists deride Mexican indigenous culture as an effect of the "tourist industry" and I have overheard Mexican indigenous scholar/activists deride U.S. indigenous peoples as too light skinned to be authentically Indian. This book approaches these hostilities and differences as problems of historical as well as linguistic and cultural translation. Just as racial geographies produced historical differences in the meanings of Indian and indio, so too they produced different modes of indigenous political engagement.

By excavating colonial and national pasts, *Indian Given* seeks to elucidate the political formations of autonomy and sovereignty as they developed in relationship to these transformative space-making projects. Neither autonomy nor sovereignty mirror pre-Colombian lifeways though both express modes of political, social, and economic organization that survived, in altered form, brutal colonial and national projects. While not the specific focus of the book, I nevertheless hope that *Indian Given* clarifies the ways in which autonomy and sovereignty emerged, respectively, out of processes of indigenous negotiation and struggle with the space-making projects of their conquering national and colonial powers. This is not to suggest that these political formations lack authenticity, but rather to explain the specificity and efficacy of sovereignty and autonomy within their corresponding racial geographies.

Indian Given is primarily, though not exclusively, an interrogation of the representations of Indians in the archives of colonial conquest and national dominion. Substantively different racial geographies emerged from the Spanish and Anglo-American colonial projects, but in each case these geographies were consolidated around the repeated and ritualistic location, expulsion, or inclusion of imaginary Indians. Indigenous subjects did not sit idly by, and their engagements, interventions, negotiations, and struggles with and in national and colonial space-making projects are discussed accordingly in *Indian Given*, but indigenous protagonism is not the main focus of this book. The role of indigenous protagonism in colonial and national history is amply documented in the archival record, often by indigenous peoples themselves, and many worthy historical and anthropological accounts of such protagonism have emerged—especially over the last twenty years—on the basis of this record. I borrow extensively from these scholars of Mexican indigenous studies and U.S. Native American studies to provide context for my own supplementary history. In addition, chapter 2 of *Indian Given* uncovers some new archival material that contributes to the history of the Spanish settlement of Nuevo Santander and the Provincia de Tejas, and as such also contains the trace of indigenous protagonism. Nevertheless, my focus is on hegemonic genealogies of racial difference, and the language and terminology of *Indian Given* reflect this. I use terms such as *the figure of the Indian, imagined Indians,* or *indios bárbaros* not to refer to actual indigenous peoples, but to index colonial and historical constructions of indigenous humanity as graphed on space by nonindigenous protagonists.[18]

Racial Geographies

Colonial occupation was a matter of seizing, delimiting, and asserting control over a physical geographical area and *of writing on the ground* a new set of social and spatial relations. This was, ultimately, tantamount to the production of boundaries and hierarchies, zones and enclaves; the subversion of existing property arrangements; the classification of people according to different categories; resource extraction; and finally the manufacturing of a large reservoir of cultural imaginaries. These imaginaries gave meaning to the enactment of differential rights to differing categories of people for different purposes within the same space. —**Achille Mbembe,** "Necropolitics"

[Landscape's] usage has varied from reference to the tangible, measurable ensemble of material forms in a given graphical area, to the representation of those forms in various media such as paintings, texts, photographs or performances, to the desired, remembered and somatic spaces of the imagination and the senses.... Indeed, the connections between the morphology of a territorially bounded region, and the identity of a community whose social reproduction is tied to usufruct rights and obligations over that area, lie at the root of the German *Landschaft* and its derivatives. But there is a profound connection, forged over half a millennium, between the modern usage of landscape to denote a bounded geographical space and the exercise of sight or vision as a principal means of associating that space with human concerns. —**Denis Cosgrove,** "Landscape and the European Sense of Sight: Eyeing Nature"

It is my contention that Mexican and U.S. national geographies are neither merely natural nor strictly politically derived.[19] Rather, they are the effect of visualizing indios and Indians in landscape. If both national boundaries and the way in which we visualize national geographies are derived from the racializing of space through the figure of the Indian, then "racial geography" is not simply a term for describing a given effect in space in racial terms. Racial geography is a technology of power, and when used as an analytic and theory of spatial production, it indexes the series of techniques used to produce space in racial terms. Visualizing spaces as racial geographies is not just about discussing a manner of seeing, in other words; racial geography theorizes a way of envisioning, of mapping, of accounting for and representing space as Indian given. Thus racial geography as an analytic necessarily builds on the recent disciplinary critiques of the role geography played in colonialisms and augments these critiques.

During the era of colonial explorations, the language of geographic inquiry became the language of Enlightenment knowledge production itself: "charting" fields of knowledge; exploring the "terrain" of the human mind; "mapping" the stages of mankind.[20] Modern geography provided the material knowledge of colonial exploration: the cartographic renderings and the detailed descriptions of spectacular peoples and places previously unknown to Europeans. However, geography also provided the metaphorical representation of the entire world as a spectacle of humankind available for description and knowledge production, for comparison of the principal differences between "the West" and the "non-West" (Gregory 1994, 15–69, cited in Withers and Livingstone 1999, 14).

Spanish and British colonialisms were certainly European, but were they uniformly "Western"? My study suggests not. The Spanish and British perceived indigenous peoples in landscape differently and settlers interpolated themselves into landscapes accordingly, producing distinct Enlightenments despite shared European origins—a Catholic and a Protestant Enlightenment, if you will. Moreover, both these Enlightenments were fully shaped by the encounter with "non-Western" peoples. Historicizing the relationship between modern geography and these Enlightenments brings to the fore two aspects of modern geography that will be central to my analysis. First, geographic knowledge production is a visual and visualizing enterprise, one that in the era of colonial exploration "brought all the world into *view*" (Livingstone and Withers 1999, 14, italics mine). Second, modern geography is *representational* in the broadest sense of the word.[21] Geographic knowledge production in these distinct Enlightenments not only offered Europeans

INTRODUCTION 17

"realistic" descriptions, classifications, and comparisons of colonized people and places; it also was foundational in the metaphorical production of a modern geography of human (racial) difference. Thus I suggest that colonial exploration produced geographies of the "new world" that were fundamentally ocular experiences—as mediums for seeing landscapes as full or devoid of barbarous life—and that these geographies-as-ocular-experiences were themselves productive of racial differences through metaphorical and philosophical representation. Geography is not only a discipline for mapping the world to be seen: it is also a way of disciplining what we see, of disciplining us into seeing (and knowing) mapped space as racialized place.[22]

While the discipline of geography played a decisive role in colonialism, it is the deconstructive turn in social geography over the last thirty years that enables *Indian Given*'s critique of Mexican and U.S. racial geographies. How did shared "cultural imaginaries" of race get "manufactured," as Mbembe suggests, in the American context? How did they specifically get dispersed through space and *on* geographical landscapes through the "classification" of America's Indians and indios? How did the "production of boundaries and hierarchies" along the Mexico–U.S. border take shape not only through the "subversion of existing property arrangements," but through the establishment of new spatial relationships between indigenous and nonindigenous peoples? Feminist and critical imperial geographers help me to take up these questions for the United States and Mexico as matters of spatial practice and not simply of historiography. Their engagement with "the spatiality of colonialism and empire" over the last thirty years enables a visioning of colonial occupation as a *physical* "writing on the ground," as a practice of power that gave meaning *and materiality* to colonized spaces through indigeneity and not in spite of indigenous presence (Clayton 2003, 354).[23] Colonialisms produced not only large reservoirs of cultural meaning attached to race but also new spaces and modes of apprehending landscapes.

The terms of analysis offered by feminist and critical imperial geographers make it possible for us to discern how Spanish and British colonialism etched a new set of spatial and racial relations onto the landscape of the "New World" and onto the "morphology of a territorially bounded region" (Cosgrove 2003, 249). British and Spanish colonists were economically motivated in usurping the "usufruct rights and obligations" of indigenous peoples in particular landscapes in the service of forming new communities of identity, but this usurpation was never merely economic. Dispossession was also an ocular experience that created shared space, as Cosgrove underscores; it was an "exercise of sight or vision" that reassembled the association of particular human

18 INTRODUCTION

concerns with particular spaces. In *Indian Given* I trace how Spanish and Anglo-American colonial concerns re-placed or removed indigenous concerns in/from certain places. Eventually, colonial concerns became national ones, and an ensemble of tangible and measurable geographical forms became "national landscapes," those "desired, remembered and somatic spaces" that imaginatively relied on the visioning and emplotment of Indians and indios. I use "vision" in both its hallucinatory ("having a vision") and entrepreneurial guises ("to have vision"), rather than simply as the act of seeing. In both guises, vision implies a movement from interiority to exteriority.[24] As suggested by Cosgrove's language (and Kerouac's), apprehending landscape visually is an interiorized experience projected onto space. The eye anticipates what the psyche desires, recursively turning landscapes into remembered (representational) and somatic (physical) spaces of becoming "American" or Mexican.

To say that envisioning landscapes is an interiorized experience does not, however, imply that the apprehension of landscape is an individual and individuating experience. To the contrary, "While it is obvious that much of learned seeing is personal, much too is social, governed by conventions about what may be seen, by whom, when and in what context, about associations and meanings attributed to a given scene, and about its form and compositional properties" (Cosgrove 2003, 252). The racial geographies of Mexico and the United States are *shared* perceptions of space, governed by learned conventions that have developed over more than five hundred years of locating and imagining indigenous peoples, and that continue to produce and reproduce space. Because they developed palimpsestically over centuries, through learned, shared conventions, racial geographies have what Henri Lefebvre has called the "illusion of transparency . . . a view of space as innocent, as free of traps or secrets" (1991, 28). Racial geographies are anything but innocent, though they do masquerade, as Lefebvre suggests, as the "as it really is" of visual landscape (Blunt and Rose 1994, 4).

In his study of the changes wrought by NAFTA on the physical environment of the Canadian-U.S. border, Matthew Sparke reminds us that the term *geography* is derived from the Greek words for "earth-writing" (*geo* and *graphein*). Geography, then, implies a *process*—"the inherently unfinished and multilayered 'graphing of the geo'"—rather than a given representation of a cartographically fixed place (Sparke 2005, xii). Understanding racial geography as an unfinished geo-graphing defamiliarizes the maps of Mexico and the United States as well, allowing us to see these maps not as the given cartography of closed and settled nations, but as *ongoing* palimpsests of spatial negotiation amongst colonial, national, and indigenous populations.[25] If

INTRODUCTION 19

geography is the "graphing of the geo," a more precise way of phrasing the questions driving this book might be to ask how the geo of northern Mexico and southwestern U.S. has been graphed and re-graphed in racial terms over time. *Indian Given* charts the writing and re-writing of these particular earth-spaces as the "visible scene/seen" of Indians and indios. I borrow this concept of the "visible scene/seen" of race from Richard H. Schein's work elucidating cultural landscape as built racial environment. Any cultural landscape, for Schein, encompasses both the material scene and the perceptual seen of a history of racial relations: "Because of its qualities as tangible, visible scene/seen, it follows that not only can we interrogate the historical and geographical dimensions of the landscape as an object in and of itself (as a material thing, or set of things), we can also read and interpret cultural landscapes for what they might tell us more broadly about social worlds of the past" (Schein 2006, 5). *Indian Given* interprets the racial geographies of the United States and Mexico as both material and perceptual scenes/seens of social worlds past.

In the introduction to their *Handbook of Cultural Geography*, Kay Anderson et al. insist on the necessity of "uniting the historical and geographic imagination" in any "serious study of 'taken for granted' ethnogeographical terms," and *Indian Given* answers this call in its historical and spatial discernment of the ways in which ethnogeographical terms such as *Indians* and *indios*, *mestizos* and *whites*, gained meaning along the Mexico–U.S. border (2003a, 302). Racial geographies are not only representational practices, as iterated and reiterated by Turner, Webb, Paz, and Kerouac; they are also spatial practices that must be decoded and interpreted. Allison Blunt and Gillian Rose have argued that the gendering of geography was less an effect of imposed patriarchal structures and more the result of a "social process of symbolic encoding and decoding that produces . . . some spaces as women's and others as men's" (1994, 3). In a similar vein, *Indian Given* analyzes the racial geographies of Mexico and the United States less as the effects of imposed unitary structures of colonial or neocolonial power—of pillaging, extermination, and dispossession; of Black Legend and Manifest Destiny (as colonialism and neocolonialism are frequently narrated)—and more as social processes that unfolded and enfolded over time. With their discrete origins in Spanish and British colonialisms, these racial geographies are an encoding and decoding of national, regional, and local spaces as symbolically indigenous and nonindigenous, as symbolically mestizo and white.

It is this symbolic encoding and decoding of spaces as indigenous and nonindigenous, as mestizo and white, as Mexican and "American," that enables us, for example, to envision the United States as a pristine and expansive landscape from "sea to shining sea," devoid of habitation for wide swaths, despite its intense urbanization and pollution. On the other hand, such coding and decoding of space is also what enables us to envision Mexico as a landscape crowded with Indians and tropical vegetation, littered with the ruins of pyramids, despite its intense urbanization and pollution. In both countries and in both cases, a handful of Europeans encountered multitudes of indigenous peoples, and millions of indigenous people continue to live in their own modern territories, and yet it is the encoding and decoding of spaces through time that produced such distinct "ethnogeographical" imaginations of these contiguous countries as indigenous and nonindigenous, as mestizo and white.

Linda Peake has insisted that "space and identities are co-produced; the places people occupy . . . are constitutive of identities, and spaces are given meaning through the social practices of groups that repeatedly occupy them" (2010, 65). Racial geography as an analytical category focuses our attention on the spatial practices that produced Mexico and the United States as transparent spaces occupied by primarily mestizo and white identities respectively, but it also enables us to discern how indigenous places and people were "co-produced" by colonialism and nationalism.[26] Racial geography enables us to decode how Indians and indios were coproduced as human bodies in contradistinction to colonists as human bodies, all within the landscapes of "encounter," and to deduce how indigenous peoples were subsequently coproduced in and by the confined spaces of the *ejido* and the reservation within landscapes of nationalism. If racial geography as an analytical category enables us to "recognize configurations of power that have situated indigenous peoples spatially in specific ways" (Kobayashi and Leeuw 2010, 123), it also enables us to see how it is that the generic categories of Indians and indios are reiteratively deployed for the purposes of producing space elsewhere.

There is an uncanny persistence of the conventional racial graphings of Indians and indios in the neoliberal present of an increasingly unified and militarized economic geography of northern Mexico and southwestern United States, but the graphing of the figure of the Indian exceeds this regional space as well. As Sparke suggests, "Every geography, whether assumed or explicitly elaborated as such, every mapping, picturing, visualization, landscaping, theorization, and metaphorization of space becomes *rereadable* in this sense not just for what it includes, but also for what it *overwrites* and *covers up* in the moment of representing spatially the always already unfinished historical-geographical process and power relations of its spatial production" (Sparke

2005, xvi, emphasis mine). Thus, for example, we can reread the indio bárbaro in the pervasive picturing of northern Mexico as the space of barbarous *narcos,* or in the academic theorizing of Mexico as ungovernable. Similarly, the picturing of landscapes in Afghanistan and Iraq as liberated by U.S. intervention overwrites the landscapes of manifest destiny on the Great Plains; "nation building" in desert climes rereads U.S. exceptionalism, far away from the geographical origins of the U.S. "frontier" but still derived from it. Furthermore, all of this metaphorization is made possible by the image of Islamic jihadists covering up images of implacable Comanche and Apache foes. All these contemporary visualizations draw on rich colonial and postcolonial inscriptions of indigeneity in the landscapes of the border region. They register the persistent *hetero*temporality of the region, revealing, even as they overwrite, the traces of barbarous Indians in "historical-geographical process[es]" of intimate spatial production and relation. *Indian Given* offers a historical-geographical comparison of the heterotemporal spatial production of Indians, Mexicans, whites, and mestizos in intimate relation along, across, and beyond national borders. These racialized geographies are "Indian given" not because indigenous people have themselves graphed the geo thusly (though indigenous peoples have intervened in these processes), but because the U.S. and Mexican geos-as-nation were and are graphed around the troublesome trace of the Indian.

To arrive at the multilayered and fluctuating history of the production of the racialized geographies condensed along the border of the United States and Mexico, the chapters assembled in *Indian Given* consider a series of *spatial practices* that graphed the geo of the Mexico–U.S. border: the sixteenth-century colonial emplotment of indigenous humanity in the "New World" by the Spanish and British; the eighteenth-century practice of Spanish settlement among the indigenous populations of Texas, with its *encomiendas,* missions, and presidios; the nineteenth-century scalping posses commissioned by Mexico's northern states but formed by U.S. citizens; the nineteenth-century negotiation of the Treaty of Guadalupe Hidalgo, with its creation of new national borders and forms of citizenship; the early twentieth-century legal cases that redrew the boundaries of U.S. (white) citizenship; the late twentieth-century emergence of Chicano nationalism and the geographically imagined formation of Aztlán as homeland in the aftermath of the civil rights era; and finally, the drug trade and the drug war in northern Mexico, as the latest reiteration of racial space.

As Lefebvre reminds us in his foundational theory of the production of space, spatial practices—those concerned with production and reproduction of life (and death) and of social relation—do not by themselves produce space. Rather, the production of space also entails the *representation of space* by scientists, urban planners, social engineers, and artists, among others, who "identify what is lived and what is perceived [in spatial practice] with what is conceived."[27] Thus, *Indian Given* also takes up the *representations* of space that go hand-in-hand with spatial *practices* in geo-graphing: by those social engineers of the place of Indian humanity within colonialisms; by the *vecinos,* settlers, priests, and soldiers of the colonial archive; by the civil rights activists in the U.S. Southwest who envisioned utopic alternatives to their segregated landscapes; by the authors of literary chronicles of travel, borders, and crossings; by the directors of films about dystopic cultural landscapes in both Mexico and the United States. These spatial practices and representations of space together produce ever-fluctuating racial cartographies of the Mexico–U.S. border: of the Indian as denizen, of the Mexican as mestizo, of the Mexican American as white, of the Anglo-American as citizen, of the Mexican Indian as exceptional, of the U.S. Indian as anachronism. Even beyond these shifting racial categories, however, spatial practices and the representations of space produce racial geographies as *representational space*; together producing the borderlands as that "dominated—and hence passively experienced—space which the imagination seeks to change and appropriate. [Representational space] overlays physical space, making symbolic use of its objects" (Lefebvre 1991, 39). The borderlands were and continue to be representational space in the colonial and national imaginaries of both Mexico and the United States. The "symbolic use" of the vast expanses of the border, of its heterotemporal cities and towns, today creates our shared imaginary of its lived racial relations. Together, the spatial practices of early colonial settlement and of U.S. expansionism conjoined with the representation of space in historiography, literature, and film to produce a shared set of conventions for envisioning of the border region and its racial geographies.

Temporal, Legal, and Psychic Mappings

Rights were for those who had the capacity to exercise them, a capacity denoted by racial identity. This conception of rights was contingent on race—on whether one could claim whiteness—as a form of property. —**Cheryl Harris**, "Whiteness as Property"

Colonialism is not simply an application of particular notions of law and territory; it is the active positioning of people on a massive scale. —**Audrey Kobayashi and Sarah de Leeuw**, "Colonialism and the Tensioned Landscapes of Indigeneity"

Racial geography as a theory of the production of space enables us to arrive at a different way of graphing history as well, a graphing that is not contingent on causal or derivative relationships through time. Thus my analysis in *Indian Given* of the multiple layers of racial formation mapped onto a given cartography of the border is not an argument for the ways in which the Spanish and Anglo-American colonization of Indians and mestizos in the region led inevitably or directly to the drug war or the militarization of the border; nor is it an argument about how complicities of racial geographies may have led to the inevitable integration of the region through the drug economy and free trade. Dipesh Chakrabarty has described this form of historicist thinking as a "one way flow of time" (Chakrabarty 2000, 243). The reader will not find in these pages an argument about how representations of narcos, undocumented immigrants, and terrorists are derived from Spanish and Anglo-American colonial representations of Indians and Mexicans, respectively or together. Such explanations of the relationship between "past" and "present" would reduce the colonial reverberations in the present to mere anachronisms. Rather, the uncanny persistence of the barbarous Indian of the colonial record is emblematic of the persistence of racial geographies through time, emblematic of the "timeknot" of history, of the heterotemporality described by Chakrabarty as "the plurality that inheres in the 'now,' the lack of totality, the constant fragmentariness, that constitutes one's present" (Chakrabarty 2000, 243).[28]

An investigation into the spatial production of the racial geographies of the region allows us to see how colonial and contemporary geographies are related palimpsestically, as a plurality that exists in the heterotemporality of the present. The figure of the Indian produced in colonialism persists not as anachronism but as an ongoing historical-geographical process in the (b)ordering of space. Put another way, the figure of the Indian constituted by colonial spatial practices and representations of space continues to affect our contemporary production of racial geographies, although not in direct casual relation. The (Spanish or Anglo-American) figure of the Indian is recursively available for the continual (re)production of racially bordered spaces beyond the confines of the physical border that divides Mexico and the United States. Moreover, our paranoid apprehension of the racialized geography of the border today depends—however unwittingly—on these colonially given figures of the Indian. This palimpsestic relationship then is not exactly historicist, although it is temporal and historical; it requires a spatialized understanding of time, rather than a developmentalist or teleological notion of history.

The heterotemporality of the present in both Mexico and the United States is expressed in the multiple racial geographies that are overlain in this "multi-

24 INTRODUCTION

cultural" border region, informing subject formation and models of citizenship. On one hand, there is the Mexican racial geography of mestizaje that, in the nineteenth and twentieth centuries, privileged admixture even while maintaining mestizo and indigenous racial categories in hierarchical relation.[29] On the other, there is the polarized geography of race in the United States that, in the nineteenth and twentieth centuries, privileged racial separation and a stark white/black binary of racial relation.[30] Both of these racial geographies, however distinct from each other, were produced through settlement, war, genocide, custom, negotiation, representation, and jurisprudence. As such, *Indian Given* does not advance an argument for the heterotemporality of mestizaje against the singular temporality of binarism. Rather I am arguing that heterotemporality is an effect of the racial geographies of mestizaje and binary white/black relations colliding in the same vexed space.

Each of these geographies, in turn, is traced over the previous temporalities of colonial racial orders with their erasures and/or inscriptions of the figure of the Indian and over indigenous temporalities of social relation.[31] If the Spanish summoned the Indian to appear before the Crown as grist for the mill of their colonial project, Anglo-American colonists also required the presence of Indians to secure their own expansionist enterprises and to consolidate their "exceptionalist" white character. In both racial geographies, in other words, the figure of the Indian was/is sometimes rallied and sometimes banished. The fate of the Spanish colonial mission—even along the distant northern frontier of New Spain—was intimately tied to the fate of the Indians' souls, and as such the bellicose apostates were as essential to the colonial production of space as the most docile of converts, if not more so. It is not until the nineteenth century that the fate of Anglo-American immigrants to the frontier was tied to the disappearance of the Indian, literally and figuratively, to the dispossession of the indigenous inhabitants of their claim to the land and to their banishment from the historical scene of proprietary claim.[32] Racial geography as a theory of space and heterotemporality as a theory of history allow us to graph the various scenes/seens at once: the legal/cultural/psychic landscape of the border is full of Indians; the legal/cultural/psychic landscape of the border is devoid of Indians. Heterotemporality and racial geography as a theory of the present offer a model for understanding the clash of the multiple racial epistemologies of coloniality and postcoloniality transpiring in one region, one citizen-subject at a time.

For a crucial dimension of this vexed scene of heterotemporality is the legal formation of citizen-subjects in the distinct yet interlinked racial geographies of the United States and Mexico. Critical race scholars and U.S.

ethnic studies scholars have demonstrated that the racial composition of the United States is neither accidental nor preordained; rather it is the effect of a programmatic colonial and postcolonial effort to use the law to calculate whiteness as the principal property of full citizenship and to enhance perpetually the life chances of this racial category against all others (Acuña 1972, Padilla 1980, Williams 1990, Takaki 1990, Harris 1993, Haney López 1996, Foley 1997, Delgado and Stefancic 2001, Gómez 2007, Gross 2008). The United States' long legal history of distributing and withholding the full rights of citizenship according to race (including the rights to self-determination, to property, to liberty, to mobility, and to suffrage) is a history of the production of a racialized national space: of a "white" majority population living, predominantly, in exclusive spaces on the one hand (suburbs, gentrified urban areas, rural retreats) and of a series of minoritized populations limited, predominantly, to marginalized spaces on the other (bedroom communities, "ghettos," work camps, reservations). This legal engineering produced the patterns of rural and urban settlement we occupy in the United States today, still largely divided along racial lines. Racial legislation engineered not simply a white propertied class but a racial majority with an investment in their whiteness as a form of property that protects them against the kind of discrimination, segregation, immiseration, and death reserved for peoples of color (Harris 1993). This production of racialized national spaces through discriminatory practices paradoxically produced the U.S. nation as *the* representational space for normative republicanism and for unrestricted individual freedom, facilitated in large part by associating whiteness, as a form of exclusive property, with meritorious good character.

In contradistinction to the United States' history of segregation and discrimination in the guise of republicanism and liberty, Mexico's history of legislation privileged racial inclusiveness through assimilation, producing the nation as the representational space of mestizaje and of presumptive racial democracy. The eradication of New Spain's caste system, with its gradation of privileges and obligations, and the abolition of slavery figured prominently in the Mexican independence movement. Articles abolishing castes and slavery, and explicitly declaring the equality of all Mexicans regardless of race, appeared in several iterations of Mexico's nineteenth-century constitutions and declarations of independence (the 1812 Elementos Constitucionales, arts. 24 and 25; the 1813 Sentimientos de la Nación, arts. 12, 15, and 22; the 1821 Plan de Iguala, art. 11; the 1857 Constitución Política, arts. 2 and 5).[33] While Mexico has no legal or paralegal history of limiting suffrage, intermarriage, settlement, or access to employment according to race, this equality before the law does not imply that Mexico's indigenous and *afromestizo* populations have been historically free of racial discrimination. However, the form of this racial discrimination in Mexico is significantly different from that in the United States. Nineteenth-century liberal leaders made a concerted legal effort to deracinate the indigenous population through assimilation policies. Though these policies largely failed and many were reversed after the 1910 revolution, the presumptive logic of mestizaje persists, especially with regard to indigenous peoples and afromestizos. Nevertheless, the *representation* of the space of the nation as inclusive of racial difference is not merely symbolic. Indigenous peoples and afromestizos participated actively in the wars of independence (1810) and revolution (1910), and in the social, political, and economic life of the nation in the postrevolutionary period. Indigenous peoples especially figure prominently in the historiography of these iconic events. In other words, the representation of the Indian as the foundation of the country is a key element in the graphing of the national geo. At the same time, the rhetoric of admixture making the nation stronger—of forging nationhood out of the mixture of Spanish and Indian cultures—has been the dominant mythos since the 1910 revolution. As a consequence of these seemingly contradictory ideals in the racial geography of Mexican nationalism, the Indian is at once summoned to appear everywhere as the *foundation* of Mexican character and instructed to disappear into the more perfect union of mestizaje.

Indian Given does not seek to adjudicate which of these legal mappings of racialized citizen-subjects, the Mexican or the United States, is more "modern" or "democratic." It is not, in other words, an account of Mexican mestizaje as a more "user friendly" racial geography than the U.S. white/black binarism, as a "third space" of more capacious psychic inclusion. Rather, the heterotemporality of this region is vexing for the inhabitants therein because of the complex and incongruent demands of racial formation and allegiance issued by *both* of these geographies at once. And as such, *Indian Given* offers an account of subjects forged in the competing temporalities of U.S. and Mexican racial geographies. The citizen-subject inhabits heterotemporal racial geographies, but these heterotemporal demands also inhabit the psyche. Mexican American and Chicana/o subject formation offers a particularly fruitful site for the analysis of the psyche constituted in the time and space of competing racial demands. However, all subjects forged in this space are vexed by its racial heterotemporality, whether white, black, afromestizo, mestizo, Native American, or *indigena*. Because *Indian Given* offers us an analysis of the transnational production of these racial geographies, it enables us to see these vexed psychic spaces as mutually produced in the overlapping, heterotemporal space of the border.

INTRODUCTION   27

Indian Given stages heterotemporality in each chapter as well, placing colonial and postcolonial documents in dialogue with each other in order to trace the figure of the Indian as it appears and disappears from sight. I stage these conversations between colonial and postcolonial texts to interrupt the teleological progression of history that sweeps us ever forward from colonial subjection to anticolonial revolution to postcolonial nationhood to neoliberal postnationalism (Scott 2004). If we refuse to respect this progressive temporality—if each chapter of time does not hinge on the passing away of the previous order—we can not only ask different kinds of questions of colonial and postcolonial texts, we can also imagine the possibility of different futurities. By exploring the relationship between colonial and postcolonial texts, *Indian Given* demonstrates how the past is enjoined with the present and theorizes the psychic consequences of these articulations between past and present.

The Indians given in the Spanish and Anglo-American colonial archives, I contend, respectively enabled the postcolonial forms of mestizo and white subjectivity in Mexico and the United States today, but *Indian Given* also offers an account of the trauma of possibilities foreclosed or repressed by these layered racial formations. What were the costs, I ask, of a fictive whiteness and a fictive mestizaje in the psychic life of U.S. and Mexican citizen-subjects, indigenous and nonindigenous alike? What was the psychic toll of banishing given Indians from the scene of white subjectivity and citizenship, as in the case of the United States? Or of summoning her forth as the mother of a mestizo subjectivity and citizenship, as in the case of Mexico? And in the borderlands, where U.S. and Mexican racial geographies overlap, intersect, and collide, what were/are the psychic costs to Mexican American and Chicana/o subjects who were/are multiply hailed by fictive forms of racial citizenship, fraught with the foreclosure and repression of indigenous pasts? What was/is the psychic toll, in other words, of being "white by law"?[34] Of being forced to denounce first one's indigenous ancestry and then the nationalist and masculinist identity associated with mestizaje in order to claim the rights of (white) U.S. citizenship?

If the Indians imagined in the Spanish and Anglo-American colonial archives indexed the repression or foreclosure of indigenous particularity, then they also indexed a history of violence denied or deemed necessary by contemporary nationalisms. Qualities and virtues were propped onto these imagined Indians, engaged in fictive scenes of ushering in the nation; and when moments of national crisis threatened the loss of these given Indians, then these national qualities and virtues were also threatened. Or, more precisely

28 INTRODUCTION

put, when moments of national crisis revealed the indigenous particularity that was repressed and/or foreclosed in the foundation of the nation, the violence of foundational origins disrupted the seemingly transparent and innocent racial geographies of the United States, Mexico, *and* Aztlán. National imaginaries of foundational justice, fairness, and democracy (in the U.S. case), or of inclusion, anti-imperialism, and sovereignty (in the Mexican case) are interrupted, disturbed. *Indian Given* theorizes these disturbances in the national imaginary as *psychic effects* on particular citizen-subjects who are/were particularly affected by these seismic shifts in racial geographies colliding and colluding along the border.

Literature and film are vital to this project of theorizing the effects of racial foreclosure and repression on the psyche, offering insight into the racial unconscious of history by concerning themselves precisely with the inevitable silences in the historical record, with the necessary exclusions of the law. Literature and film enable us to take account of the psychic toll of racial geographies on the citizens of the national imaginaries considered here, by affording us theoretical speculation and fictive accounts of the silences in the archive. Moreover, the method of literary analysis when applied to the archive offers us a glimpse into the racial unconscious of history. *Indian Given* advances the argument that the historical and geographical archives also have an unconscious and seeks to elaborate its contours. Psychoanalytic theory, and particularly the recent contributions of psychoanalytic scholars of race, also allows me to elaborate a theory of the formation of a racial unconscious of history that is heterotemporal, rather than universal or eternal. If the historical and legal archive has a racial unconscious then psychoanalysis coupled with literary analysis allows me to discern the psychic disturbances that are repressed but also documented in the archives over the course of colonial and national histories. The palimpsestic Indians and indios in the historical and legal archives record the racial repressions necessary for the construction of given racial geographies, in other words.

Recent studies of the psychoanalysis of race offer a hermeneutic for apprehending the fraught racial geographies considered here and provide a theory for interpreting the citizen-subjects produced by these racial geographies, for analyzing the psychic terrain of those subjects forced to live by the racial repressions and foreclosures imposed on them by the fictions of whiteness and mestizaje, by the fictions of imagined Indians. Literary and filmic texts help in this endeavor because they do not simply "represent" racialized subjects who have been written into (not only out of) history and the law, but they also elucidate the complex processes of psychic formation

INTRODUCTION   29

entailed by racialization, offering an account of the ways in which the psyche is interdicted by race. In what ways might the psyche of a subject be shaped by the foreclosure and repression of indigenous "lost objects"? How might the Indian-as-lost-object—banned or repressed not only from space but from psychic life—nevertheless remain with the psyche? How might the foreclosed, lost, or repressed racialized Indian not only remain but also animate the subject formed by fictive notions of whiteness or mestizaje? It is through literature and film, placed in dialogue with history and the law, that we find adequate answers for these questions and begin to elaborate a theory of the racial unconscious of heterotemporal history and space.

The first chapter of *Indian Given* compares the religious disquisitions on indigenous humanity of Bartolomé de Las Casas and Juan Ginés de Sepúlveda with the sermons and political treatises of religious and revolutionary elites in the thirteen colonies to contrast the manner in which Indians were interpellated into empires, and the distinct racial coordinates of Spanish and British settlement that ensued as a consequence. Each of the subsequent chapters pairs historical and legal documents with literary, epistolary, or filmic texts that respond or correspond to these documents. In chapter 2, I pair eighteenth-century documents from the Spanish colonial archive on settlement and war in Texas with the film *No Country for Old Men* to discern the heterotemporal function of the indio bárbaro from early conquest to the war on terror, and to consider the psychic consequences of this conquest through the film's Texas lawman who allegorically fights a "war on terror" of his own. Chapter 3 pairs the Treaty of Guadalupe Hidalgo and nineteenth-century Mexican scalping laws with Américo Paredes's novel *George Washington Gómez*, following the spatial practices of the Apaches and Comanche who refused to vanish into mestizaje or onto reservations in the newly annexed territory of the U.S. Southwest, but also tracing the violent "resolution" of these racial confrontations in the psychic geography of the novel's Mexican American protagonist.

In chapter 4, I pair a set of neocolonial legal opinions from naturalization, discrimination, and segregation cases brought in the first half of the twentieth century with the personal letters and public speeches of the Mexican American activists who participated in this early civil rights campaign to achieve justice through the courts. While Mexican Americans' ambiguous racial status within U.S. jurisprudence demonstrated the incommensurability of U.S. and Mexican racial geographies, it was also essential to the spatial production of a (white) political democracy. In the letters and speeches of the activists, we discern Mexican Americans grappling with these incommensurate geographies, attempting to map livable spaces out of unlivable ones.

30   INTRODUCTION

In chapter 5, I consider two cases brought against Mexican American youth activists in the aftermath of the civil rights era. In the trial transcripts, we witness the emergence of Chicana/o consciousness as a critique of racially produced spaces in California. These cases index not only the birth of a consciousness of a movement and a people, they also index the emergence of the geographic imaginary of Aztlán. These cases are paired with a reading of Oscar Zeta Acosta's postcolonial *The Autobiography of a Brown Buffalo,* which deconstructs the racial geography of the Southwest while also shedding light on the Chicana/o consciousness as not only a historical formation but also a psychic one that melancholically incorporates the figure of the Indian in its geographic, cultural, and political enunciation. Finally, the coda considers the heterotemporal indio bárbaro's appearance in the figures of the narco-terrorist and the Islamic jihadist by analyzing the political speech of presidents Felipe Calderón and Barack Obama.

Indian Given brings together the theoretical perspectives offered by postcolonial and Latin American studies with those offered by American studies and U.S. ethnic studies not only to achieve a fuller understanding of the racial geographies we continue to occupy in our contemporary lives but also in the hopes of interrupting the violent effects these geographies continue to have on the vast majority of the population of the heterotemporal Americas. When we consider the colonial history of the United States alongside the colonial history of Mexico, we also disrupt prevalent scholarly accounts of white settler colonialism. For all of their insightful contributions to the study of empire, Marxist and anti-imperialist scholars have consistently excluded Latin America from the paradigm of white settler colonialism. Consequently, this book asks, what is occluded in that exclusion? Is this occlusion of Latin America in general, and Mexico in particular, the effect of privileging one racial geography above all others? Examining Mexico as a crucial site of white settler colonialism moves us toward a much more complex understanding of the relationship between colonizer and colonized, between indigeneity and whiteness, than that of genocidal elimination and absorption (Wolfe 2012).

1

SAVAGES WELCOMED
Imputations of Indigenous Humanity in Early Colonialisms

The debate between these two outstanding figures of sixteenth-century Spain was one of the most curious episodes in the history of the Western world. For the first time, and probably for the last, a colonizing nation organized a formal inquiry into the justice of the methods used to extend its empire. For the first time, too, in the modern world, we see an attempt to stigmatize an entire race as inferior, as born slaves according to the theory elaborated by Aristotle. —**Lewis Hanke**, *All Mankind Is One*

In the chapters that follow, *Indian Given* considers defining instances in the formation of the racial geographies of the United States and Mexico as recorded in the historical and legislative archive, in literature and film, and in political speech. I trace the emergence of these two representational and material *national* spaces from their respective colonial mappings of the figure of the Indian from the eighteenth through the twenty-first centuries. Before proceeding to these spatial productions of racial nationalism, however, it behooves us to consider the early colonial geo-graphings of the American continent in the face of its original inhabitants, as these mappings are constitutive of modern humanism in both its liberatory and brutal guises. Too often the birth of humanism is narrated as a *northern* European development of the Enlightenment. By revisiting these early colonial mappings through the critical eye of racial geography, we see not only that the origins of humanism are to be found much earlier in southern Europe, but that the encounter with the native inhabitants of the Americas itself determined humanism's form. By revisiting these early iterations of indigenous absence/presence, we can not merely tell a different origin story but more importantly understand the ongoing political ramifications and spatial consequences of these early humanist imaginings for both indigenous and nonindigenous Americans.

Specifically, two flashpoints of the early colonial period illuminate the question of the Indian-as-property in the case of New Spain, and of Indian property in the case of New England and the thirteen colonies; I will analyze both in this chapter. The first flashpoint is the historically unprecedented debate between Bartolomé de Las Casas and Juan Ginés de Sepúlveda on the just methods of conquest in the "New World," referred to by colonial historian Lewis Hanke in the opening epigraph. Convened by the Holy Roman Emperor Carlos V in 1550, the Junta de Valladolid, a specially appointed panel of fourteen learned jurists charged with adjudicating the proper method of colonial conquest, listened to these two men present their scholarly evaluations of indigenous humanity. Acts of Spanish conquest were clearly space-making enterprises, often accomplished by the grafting of Spanish colonial cities over indigenous ones. Underscoring the importance of the Valladolid proceedings in determining the racial coordinates of these space-making enterprises, all expeditions of conquests were officially suspended pending its outcome. Though this was an exceptional event in the history of European empire, as suggested by Hanke, the Junta de Valladolid was only the apogee of a debate amongst Spanish friars, jurists, scholars, colonists, administrators, and royal advisors on the nature of indigenous humanity that began in the fifteenth century with Columbus's letters to Queen Isabel after initial contact and continued through the eighteenth century with the "settlement" of New Mexico, Texas, and Alta California. If the self-reflection and autocritique of the Spanish empire at Valladolid is remarkable and noteworthy, Hanke reminds us that it was the freedom of Spanish colonists to turn Indians into property *as a race* that was at stake.

The second colonial flashpoint transpired more than two centuries later, but was no less foundational for the British colonies along the mid-Atlantic seaboard. With the Proclamation of 1763, the British Crown declared the Indian territories west of the Appalachian and Allegany mountain ranges closed to new settlement in the interest of protecting indigenous territories from further colonial encroachment. As in the case of the Junta de Valladolid, this proclamation was in the interest of implementing a more just means of conquest, in this case an effort to recognize and respect indigenous domains. The Royal Proclamation of 1763 unleashed a torrent of political speech by elites like Thomas Jefferson and Benjamin Franklin on the impropriety of the British Crown placing indigenous property out of reach of the colonists. As in the Valladolid debate, this elite political speech con-

34   CHAPTER ONE

tained its own assessment of indigenous humanity, which was subsequently instrumental in the construction of U.S. revolutionary identity and the drafting of the constitution in 1787. Like Sepúlveda and Las Casas, revolutionary elites positioned themselves as authorities on indigenous character, and their speech had material consequences for the racial geography of the Americas. The proclamation and the revolutionary feud that ensued represented less the endpoint of political debate on the nature of indigenous humanity than a pivotal moment in a process of mapping the continent that would continue well into the period of nineteenth-century expansion into the Great Plains and the Southwest.

Once again, we should not discount these efforts to revisit and revise policy toward indigenous populations by Spanish and British imperial powers as merely cynical and duplicitous justifications for rapacious conquest. The story of European colonialism in the American theater is most often narrated as such, but to do so misses an important avenue of critique. These juridical encounters with indigeneity prodigiously produced new terms for interpreting all of humanity, and by examining them with a critical eye we glean the absence/presence of the Indian at the heart of the human.

These preliminary debates in New Spain and the thirteen colonies produced colonial and national space by establishing the racial coordinates *in the landscape* of what Jodi Byrd (2011) has called "Indianness." In *The Transit of Empire* Byrd proposes the *idea* of Indianness as the "ontological ground" of U.S. settler colonialism, as the site "through which U.S. empire orients and replicates itself by transforming those to be colonized into 'Indians' through continual reiterations of pioneer logics" (xiii). In her deconstructive analysis, Byrd demonstrates how "Indianness"—its reiterative signification as ethnographic savagery, pathological sovereignty, and "lamentable and tragic loss"—enables the "transit" of empire as the U.S. imperial project proceeds by seeing Indians everywhere it casts its acquisitive eye (xviii). As suggested in my introduction, there was not a single transhistorical iteration of the Indian or *indio,* and thus I offer the friendly rejoinder that there was not *a* singular "Indianness" but multiple ones—as least as many as there were European colonial ventures in the Americas—each with its own set of human-making and space-making imperatives. This chapter investigates early Spanish and British iterations of Indianness, not as singular ontologies but as distinct epistemologies that enabled the racial geographies of Mexico and the United States, that enabled the seeing of Indians in landscape in multiple, useful guises. As Byrd suggests, Indianness serves the ontological purpose of constituting the colonizer, not the native. Nevertheless, colonial Indianness*es* (plural) continue to resonate in the twenty-first century, deeply impacting indigenous politics of the present.

In her meticulous comparison of British and Spanish colonialism, *American Pentimento,* Patricia Seed (2001) argues that the two contemporary expressions of indigenous political identity in the Americas—as subjects desiring rights in Latin America versus subjects desiring land in the United States—correspond to the imperial imperatives of labor versus land. Spanish settlers' appetite for indigenous labor produced abject indigenous subjects stripped of dignity who now demand rights as full members of Latin American nation-states, while British settlers' appetite for land produced displaced indigenous subjects stripped of autochthonous domains who now demand self-determination in separate sovereignties from the United States. I sympathetically suggest that Seed's exemplary materialist analysis provides us with an incomplete explanation not only of the long life of the distinct iterations of Indianness in the United States and Latin America, but also of the actual unfolding of Spanish and British colonialism. After all, Spanish settlers also desired and acquired indigenous land while British settlers also indentured and enslaved indigenous labor. The "land versus labor" dichotomy in comparative colonial historiography—itself an iteration of the rapacious-colonizer narrative—is symptomatic of the deeper cartographies of racialization, of seeing Indians in and as landscape. The dispossession and indenture dichotomy, in other words, is an *effect* of racial geography and not its cause, an effect of how colonial powers visualized and produced the absence/presence of actual indigenous peoples, of how indigenous peoples were made useful in the visual and cartographic production of space, and as such, racial geography offers a supplement to Seed's analysis.

"Though They Be Outside the Faith of Jesus Christ"

The historical context for the debate at Valladolid is twofold.[1] On one hand, the debate took place within the context of the conquest as it transpired in the theater of the Americas and within the chambers of the Council of the Indies. On the other hand, the debate also took place within the theater of Europe during Christianity's epic confrontation with the Ottoman Empire. Spain was at the center of both theaters in the aftermath of the *Reconquista,* as the ascendant empire and as the defender of Christian orthodoxy. In the American theater the 1550 debate was neither the first time expeditions were suspended while inquiries were conducted into the conditions of conquest, nor the first time that a Spanish king and the Council of the Indies sought

36   CHAPTER ONE

expert opinions from juries of scholars and ecclesiastics. In 1514, King Ferdinand suspended an expedition while he considered its legitimacy, and in 1532–1533 the Council of the Indies solicited opinions from the first ecclesiastical junta convened to ascertain indigenous capacity for self-government and for Christian instruction. That junta, comprised of bishops and friars who had served as evangelizers in the New World, advised that the Indians were rational beings capable of conversion (Hanke 1974, 12–13). Rather than settling the debate, the official council statement to this effect precipitated declamations from detractors of indigenous character followed by statements from its defenders.

In the context of this furious battle over the proper treatment of the indigenous peoples, Pope Paul III issued the papal bull *Sublimis Deus* in 1537. The bull defended indigenous capacity, stating that any detractors were clearly under the influence of "the enemy of the human race [Satan]," as they hindered "the preaching of God's word of Salvation" by insisting Indians be "treated as dumb brutes created for our service." The wording of the bull underscores the intertwining of indigenous capacity for conversion with the colonial treatment merited by them: "The Indians are truly men and . . . they are not only capable of understanding the catholic faith, but . . . they desire exceedingly to receive it. . . . Notwithstanding whatever may have been or may be said to the contrary . . . [they] are by no means to be deprived of their liberty or the possession of their property, even though they be outside the faith of Jesus Christ" (cited in Hanke 1974, 21).[2] The bull did not settle the debate, but in the ensuing years the defenders of indigenous capacity and freedom held sway over Carlos V. In 1542 a reform movement led by Dominican missionaries (including Las Casas), jurists at the Escuela de Salamanca (School of Salamanca), and other prominent theologians prevailed on Carlos V to issue the Nuevas leyes para la governación de las Indias y buen tratamiento y conservación de los Indios (New Laws for Governing the Indies and for the Good Treatment and Preservation of the Indians).[3] During the initial wave of conquest, the Spanish Crown had rewarded conquistadors with individual *encomiendas*, granting them the right to access, without payment, the labor (or goods) of entire communities of Indians, presumably in exchange for their Christian conversion and education in the Spanish language.[4] The New Laws of 1542 affirmed the freedom of the Indians, prohibited their enslavement under any circumstances, required remuneration for their services, and, most importantly, abolished the notorious encomienda system by making it nonhereditary.[5]

Predictably, a rebellion among the *encomenderos* ensued. In 1544 in Peru, Gonzalo Pizarro (brother of conquistador Francisco Pizarro) led a rebellion that deposed (and eventually killed) Spain's Viceroy Blasco Núñez Vela for attempting to implement the New Laws. The rebellion was deemed so threatening to royal authority that in 1545 Carlos V suspended several stipulations of the New Laws, including the nonhereditary clause that would have phased out the encomienda. Boosted by their success in postponing these provisions, encomenderos throughout the Spanish empire began a campaign to make their encomiendas perpetual. This in turn spurred Las Casas, then bishop of Chiapa, to set sail for Spain in 1547 for the last time to lobby for the reenactment of the suspended provisions. The Indians of Oaxaca and colonial Chiapa had granted Las Casas and his lifelong companion Friar Rodrigo de Andrada the legal authority to represent them before the Council of the Indies. The Indians of Peru subsequently authorized Las Casas to offer Felipe II as much money as necessary to end the encomienda (Hanke 1959, 29). It was in part Las Casas's indefatigable efforts that brought Sepúlveda into the fray. In the aftermath of the 1542 New Laws, and in response to Las Casas and his allies' ongoing efforts to persuade the Court of Castile to prohibit *any* private control of indigenous peoples, the president of the Council of the Indies, Cardinal García Jofre de Loaysa, invited Sepúlveda to prepare a treatise defending the mode of Spain's conquest and specifically indigenous indenture (Adorno 2007, 114).

Dominican theologian Juan Ginés de Sepúlveda was a renowned Renaissance scholar; as a translator of Aristotle, a philosopher, and a royal historian, Sepúlveda had already proven his ability to defend just war and Christian orthodoxy in the face of internal and external threats (Hanke 1974, 61). This brings us to the second historical context of the Valladolid debate: the rise of Lutheran reformation and the Ottoman Empire in the European theater. Sepúlveda is the joint that brought the American and European theaters together. In the second half of the 1520s, the Ottomans had amassed 100,000 troops on the eastern edge of Austria, preparing to lay siege to Vienna. By 1529, under the leadership of Suleiman I they had routed the Hungarian army and were poised to invade Europe. Sepúlveda wrote to Carlos V imploring him to come to the defense of the city, as otherwise "all Catholics, whose salvation and freedom are mainly in your hands, will be at risk and in great danger" (Losado, 9, cited in Mariscal 2006, 261). Carlos V had already banned Islamic practices and the speaking of Arabic among Morisco communities in Spain by 1526 in response to Europe's generalized preoccupation with Islamic incursions and fear of domestic collaboration.[6]

"Collaboration" took a different guise, however. In the 1530s, students at the prestigious Colegio de San Clemente de Los Españoles in Bologna, organized a pacifist, antiwar movement in response to the threat of Islamic inva-

38   CHAPTER ONE

sion. Under the influence of Luther and Erasmus, these students questioned the very concept of just war, as "all war, including defensive war, was contrary to the Catholic religion" (Hanke 1974, 61).[7] Sepúlveda had studied Aristotle in Bologna as a student, and Pope Clement VII dispatched him to the city to quell the student rebellion. In his capacity as "visitor general," Sepúlveda published a treatise against the pacifist students in 1535 entitled, *Demócrates primer o De la compatibilidad entre la milicia y la religión cristiana* (The first Democrates or On the compatibility of military action and the Christian faith). *Demócrates primer* is staged as a Socratic dialogue between Democrates, a philosopher who explains the concordance of Christian principles and war, and Alfonso, an ex-soldier who espouses the views of the antiwar students.

When the Council of the Indies solicited Sepúlveda opinions on just war in the American theater, then, it did so knowing his positions and within this context of Islamic war and Christian dissent in the European theater. Sepúlveda himself understood his position on the conquest in the Americas as a continuation of his views on just war in *Demócrates primer*, as indicated by the mimetic title of his treatise prepared for Valladolid, *Demócrates segundo o De las justas causas de la guerra contra los indios* (The second Democrates or On the just causes of war against the Indians, hereafter *Demócrates II*). *Demócrates II* was similarly staged as a Socratic dialogue, this time between Democrates and a neophyte named Leopoldo who, according to Hanke, was based on Martin Luther as a further critique of Luther's vocal opposition to the anti-Islamic campaigns (1974, 91). As Spanish literary scholar George Mariscal aptly states, the "transfer of discursive fields related to the construction of 'the enemy' from one group to another" was "relatively easy"; "for Sepúlveda, this act of transference extended from the Islamic threat in Europe directly to Amerindian societies in the colonies" (2006, 263–264).

My point in foregrounding this twofold historical context for the 1550 Valladolid debate is to point out the inevitable conflation of—indeed the genealogical affiliation among—the Islamic infidel, the Morisco and converso collaborator, the Christian heretic, and the New World barbarian. This is a key aspect in the racial graphing of the colonial geo for Spain, for the indios the Spanish encountered for the first time at the end of the fifteenth century were not cut from a new cloth. Rather, the ideas expressed about their nature, particularly by their detractors, emerged out of this deeper history of Spain's encounter with Islam and with the Protestant reformation. The American racial geography of Indianness in New Spain shares a genealogy with the European geography of Islamic infidel and Christian traitor, and we will see these iterations of what it means to be Indian throughout the Spanish colonial record of settlement in chapters 2 and 3. The indio was always potentially the enemy; his loyalty was always being tested; his faith, once it occurred, needed always to be protected. Most important, the Indian is the horizon of inclusion. He existed in landscape, as we shall see, not to be obliterated, but to be convinced, cajoled, coerced, and included, by force if necessary.

The "Council of Fourteen" at the Junta de Valladolid was comprised of the most learned theologians and jurists in Spain, including several former members of both the Council of Castile and the Council of the Indies. These judges would hear from Sepúlveda and Las Casas in turn, and then make a decision on a rather circumscribed, if consequential, question: Was it lawful for the Spanish Crown to wage war against the indigenous populations of the New World in order to first bring them under Spanish rule and then instruct them in the Christian faith (Hanke 1959, 38)? Sepúlveda reoriented the debate from a disquisition on the proper method of bringing indigenous peoples to the faith to a disquisition on the quality of indigenous humanity. Given that the papal bull *Sublimis Deus* recognized the indigenous as humans with souls who were rational and free, Sepúlveda's option was to focus on the quality of that rationality and freedom, to establish that the moral turpitude of the indigenous required their enslavement. Sepúlveda was not the first to impugn indigenous character in this way, but his argument was not just an exercise in rhetorical cunning. Neither was Valladolid just an exercise in semantics. Rather, the encounter with indigenous peoples required a new calculation of the human.

Sepúlveda and Las Casas, in fact, were forging a new doctrine of Catholic humanity. It was a doctrine derived in part from the medieval legal reasoning that had justified the crusades against Jewish and Muslim infidels on the basis of the unity and hierarchy of Christ's dominion over the entire world.[8] This medieval geography of humanity—predicated on the mandatory unity of all beings through Christ—had sanctioned the wars of Crusade in the Holy Lands for more than two hundred years by establishing the European doctrine of Petrine responsibility over Christ's flock. As legal scholar Robert Williams (1990) explains, "Christian princes could be called on by Rome . . . to bring the heathen and infidel sheep of Christ's universal flock, living 'as if in barbarism,' to civilization as understood by Eurocentric and Christocentric norms" (73). Because the inhabitants of the Holy Land had been exposed to Christ, according to this doctrine, they denied him at their own peril. Civil slavery had long existed in Europe, but it was restricted to infidels (Muslims and Jews) captured in "just wars" and crusades. Indigenous peoples, by contrast, had never been exposed to Christ and thus had not *denied* him. They

40 CHAPTER ONE

could not be classified by this medieval logic. They existed in a unique category outside the history of belief that had long defined and divided humanity. For many of the Spanish theologians and missionaries, this was precisely what made the New World a utopic space for conversion. Just as the Indians had never been exposed to Christ, so too they had never been exposed to the false faiths of Judaism or Islam, or to the heretical Christianity of Protestantism (Adorno 2007, 234). The New World was the perfect geography, in other words, for mapping the *one* true Catholic faith onto its landscape; but the mapping of this unity depended on the indios the Spaniards encountered. They were the condition of utopic possibility.

As the representatives of the Catholic Church, the monarchy of Castile and Aragon derived dominion over the New World through the medieval principles of Christian unity and Petrine responsibility, but the encounter with the unique humanity of these indigenous peoples rendered the methods of achieving these principles deeply suspect. As Renaissance scholars, Sepúlveda and Las Casas had been trained in classical philosophy and both enlisted Aristotle to buttress their opposing positions. Sepúlveda turned to Aristotle's theory of natural slavery to supplement natural and canon law, laying out four reasons requiring wars of conquest in the New World: to end indigenous idolatry, cannibalism, and lascivious sexuality/sodomy; to defend the weak who were subject to these "sins"; to insure the safety of those missionaries who went to spread the Gospel; and most important, to govern the Indians because they were "natural slaves," too debased to properly rule themselves (Hanke 1959, 41; Adorno 2007, 114). The first three reasons for war against Indians were well rehearsed, but Aristotle's theory of natural slavery allowed Sepúlveda to introduce the presumed inferiority of indigenous *rationality*, adding a twist to the deliberations. While slavery on *religious* grounds was well codified in medieval Europe,[9] Sepúlveda argued the legitimacy of mass enslavement on the grounds of inferior *reason* before a formal panel vested with the power to advise the king on royal policy.

After Sepúlveda's protagonist Demócrates has enumerated the recognized causes for war based on "natural and divine law" (punishment for injuries inflicted by persons or nations, self-defense, justice for the weak), he insists on another "less clear and less frequented" but no less legitimate cause.[10] "The greatest philosophers" all agreed on the justice of "subjugating by force of arms, when no other road is possible, those who due to their natural condition should obey others, and yet reject their [i.e., Spain's] rule" (*Demócrates II*, 289). The student Leopoldo expresses surprise at this "extraordinary" opinion, so outside the bounds of common sense (*común sentir de los hombres*) and asks Demócrates not only who would be born under such an unfortunate star as to be by nature condemned to servitude, but if all the learned councils of jurists (*jurisconsulatas*) jest "when they teach that all men are initially born free, and that slavery was introduced against nature" (290). Demócrates assures Leopoldo that these jurists deliberate with "seriousness" and "prudence." And yet, not having passed through the "threshold of philosophy," when these jurists speak of slavery they speak of an artificial condition that is imposed by the superiority of force (*fuerza mayor*) or by civil right or law (*derecho civil*). When philosophers speak of slavery, they refer to the "inherent slowness of understanding and to inhumane and barbarous customs" (291).[11] Slavery is thus transformed from a condition imposed on a person from the outside to a condition emerging from within a people. As the dialogue progresses, Demócrates often makes the former (the inhumane custom of slavery) into a condition of the latter (slavery as the consequence of incompetent understanding). Idolatry, "nefarious lust," and a rudeness or indolence of the mind are strung together in evident relation for Sepúlveda (315, 317, 319, 323).[12] And thus we see an insidious reversal. Reasonable people are not barbarous because of their customs (i.e., nonbelief); rather their customs are barbarous because of their impaired reason.

For Aristotle, all men and women possessed rationality, as this was a universal condition of humanity. Women and natural slaves possessed inferior reason because they lacked the capacity for deliberation and decisiveness. In what is perhaps the most notorious passage from *Demócrates II,* Sepúlveda begins by miming Aristotle's position:

> It is certain and without doubt, as affirmed by intelligent/discerning authors, that it is just and natural for wise, esteemed, and humane men to have dominion over those who are not so.... You can well understand, Leopoldo, if you know the customs and manners of different peoples, that the Spanish have a perfect right to rule these barbarians of the New World and the adjacent islands, who in wisdom, skill, virtues, and humanity are as inferior to the Spanish as children to adults, or women to men, for there exists between the two as great a difference as between savage and cruel races and the most merciful, between the most intemperate and the moderate and temperate and, I am on the verge of saying, between monkeys and men. (305)

As in Aristotle, "wise" men enjoy dominion over those whose intellectual capacity is "inferior," and consequently, in this analogy, indigenous people are to Spaniards as children are to adults, and women are to men. But Sepúlveda

42 CHAPTER ONE

goes further than Aristotle, for indigenous people's reason was so "intemperate," so imperfect, so "torpid," as to place them in close proximity to beasts. Democrates broaches this boundary between humanity and animality through simile and analogy, in direct contradiction to the *Sublimis Deus*. Sepúlveda was on the verge of saying that Indians were on the verge of being beasts. Simile saved Sepúlveda from committing heresy against the papal bull, but in his rhetorical turn of phrase, we bear witness *with* Sepúlveda to a category of the Indian that was still epistemologically in flux. What was the nature of this thing-being Indian, and did this nature permit Indian labor to become the property of others?

For Sepúlveda the answer was undoubtedly yes, not only because Indians were pagan infidels, but, more significantly, because their impaired reason made them natural slaves, placing them in proximity to beasts of burden. Importantly for Sepúlveda, the indigenous people, as natural slaves, received the greater benefit from their enslavement by the Spaniards: "It would be a great good for those depraved, barbarous, and impious ones to obey those who are good, who are humane and observe the true faith, so that through their laws, council, and communion, they might be returned to humanity and piety, which would be to the great benefit of Christian charity" (325). Indigenous people are restored (*redujesen*) to their own humanity through Christian enslavement.

Sepúlveda compared Indians with Middle Eastern infidels (Saracens, Moors, and Jews); offered analogies among the Indians, antediluvian mankind, and Sodomites; and repeatedly associated the Indians with bestiality and a bestial reason, a slowness and clumsiness of thought.[13] War against barbarians was always justified when—human though they may be—"their sins, impieties, and wickedness are so repulsive and hateful to God" (315). God sent a flood against Jews, after all, for "they were cannibals, practitioners of abortion, slept with their mothers, daughters, sisters and with beasts of burden" (317). Similarly, God was justified in sending fire and brimstone against the Sodomites for their "nefarious torpidity" (317). These analogies seek to interpret these new people within the religious-based divisions of medieval humanity and belonging, but they also demonstrate the instability and fungibility of the very category of the human at this moment of crisis. If the unity of humanity was necessarily established through Christ, what might be the status of humans who had never known Christ? Sepúlveda switched registers from religion to reason in order to render indios natural slaves—a remedial humanity in need of Christian correction. From Sepúlveda's Aristotelian perspective, their enslavement was a remediation, a virtue imposed on them to rectify their wayward status *and* their inferior reason.

Thus it was not merely the savage and cruel nature of the Indian human that associated him with beasts and infidels. Rather, repeatedly for Sepúlveda, it was the Indians' nefarious torpidity that *required* the Spaniards to conquer them through just war and to reduce them to a condition of servitude that would facilitate their conversion to a more *rational* humanity. Both natural law and biblical law required it:

> The man rules over the woman, the adult over the child. . . . That is to say, the most powerful and most perfect rule over the weakest and most imperfect. . . . We even see it sanctioned in divine law itself, for it is written in the Book of Proverbs: "He who is stupid [*necio*] will serve the wise man." And so it is with the barbarous and inhuman peoples who have no civil life and peaceful customs. It will always be just and in conformity with natural law that such people submit to the rule of more cultured and humane princes and nations. . . . And if the latter reject such rule, it can be imposed upon them by force of arms. Such a war will be just according to natural law. (293)

The Indians were idolaters and resembled Middle Eastern infidels, but this would not have been sufficient cause for their subordination even by medieval standards, as they had never rejected Christianity. Rather, a "repugnant stupidity" (*torpezas nefandas*) was at the root of the indio's evil and required their indoctrination into rational Christian humanism (317, 319). It was their own condition of natural slavery that imprisoned their full humanity, in other words, a humanity that could only be restored through patrician Christianity. Thus their inferior rationality motivated licentiousness so extreme as to lead them to indulge in human sacrifice, cannibalism, abortion, incest, and adultery.[14] On the principle of the unity of humanity, now based on reason as well as faith, Sepúlveda used the parable of the Good Samaritan as a further evidence *for* Spanish conquest: just as the Samaritan helped the Israelite who had been beaten by thieves, so must the Spaniard come to the aid of those indigenous "innocents" who were the victims of nefarious indios, "sacrificed by the impious beings of the barbarians" (329, 331). In this analogy the Indians are *both* Israelite and thief; they are usefully both victim and culprit, the saving of the one requiring the vanquishing of the other. Savage, servile, cruel, but worst of all dimwitted, the Indians required the Spaniards, as good Christians, to continue their wars of conquest and the encomienda as a means of conversion to both reason and faith, now united in a Catholic Enlightenment. Sepúlveda, through an argument about the gradations of human rationality, defined indigenous humanity in terms that reiterated the dichotomous mandate of the 1510 Requerimiento: all *rational* Indians would meekly submit to Christian faith and the Spanish Crown willingly (the *inocentes*), but those of limited rationality would refuse to submit (the *bárbaros*) and thus must prepare for a war of justified murder, pillaging, and plunder.[15]

At Valladolid, Sepúlveda read from notes prepared from his *Demócrates II*. He read for three hours. Meanwhile, Las Casas read in its entirety an apologia that would later be published under the title *En defensa de los indios* (*In defense of the Indians*; from here on, *Defense*). He read to the council for five days. Las Casas had clearly studied a manuscript version of Sepúlveda's *Demócrates II*, because he came prepared to use Aristotle's theory of natural slavery to dispute Sepúlveda's account of Indian character, specifically of indigenous rationality. In the first chapters of the *Defense*, Las Casas (1992) summarizes the four kinds of barbarism derived from his own interpretation of Aristotle's *Politics* and *Ethics*.[16] To the first class of barbarians belong the individual men of any nation "who, aroused by anger, hatred, or some other strong feeling, violently defend something, completely forgetful of reason and virtue" (Las Casas 1992, 29). Las Casas gives examples from European and religious history, including, perhaps in an allusion to Sepúlveda himself, "our Spaniards" who "in the absolutely inhuman things they have done to [indigenous] nations... have surpassed all other barbarians" (Las Casas 1992, 29). The second class of barbarians includes those peoples who do not have a written language that corresponds to a spoken one.

To the third class belong the "proper" barbarians, according to Las Casas's interpretation of Aristotle: "[Those] who, either because of their evil and wicked character or the barrenness of the region in which they live, are cruel, savage, sottish, stupid, and strangers to reason. They are not governed by law or right, do not cultivate friendships, and have no state or politically organized community. Rather they are without ruler, laws, and institutions" (Las Casas 1992, 32). Barbarous peoples from this third class are the only ones "the Philosopher" considers "slaves by nature," Las Casas insists, and they "are rarely found in any part of the world and are few in number when compared with the rest of mankind, as Aristotle notes at the beginning of the seventh book of *Ethics*" (Las Casas 1992, 33–34). They are rare because nature always seeks perfection, as Aristotle himself acknowledged according to Las Casas, and because "the works of nature are the works of the Supreme Intellect who is God" (Las Casas 1992, 34). Las Casas followed Sepúlveda's lead, tying natural slavery to impaired rationality, for *true* barbarians are "sottish, stupid, and strangers to reason." Due to this lack of reason, they lack sociality (friendship, community).

Las Casas insisted that indigenous peoples did not belong in either the first or third class of barbarians, and to prove this he spent the rest of the *Defense* providing evidence of indigenous rationality. Even before enumerating the wise merits of indigenous customs (and the heinous barbarism of Spanish conquest), though, Las Casas established early on that their rationality was due to Christian love:

> For the Creator of *every* being has not so despised these peoples of the New World that he willed them to lack reason and made them like brute animals, so that they should be called barbarians, savages, wild men, and brutes, as they [Sepúlveda et al.] think or imagine. On the contrary they [the Indians] are of such gentleness and decency that they are, more than the other nations of the *entire world*, supremely fitted and prepared to abandon their worship of idols and to accept . . . the word of God. (28)

Throughout the *Defense*, Las Casas is categorical in his argument: the Creator would not create some human beings to be despised brutes, and others to be wise masters. Las Casas insisted on the unchangeable and uniformly rational nature of *all* humans, as ordained by God. Nevertheless, to cover his bases, Las Casas again enlisted Aristotle to prove particularly the freedom of the indigenous people of the New World.

While Aristotle described those barbarians who were natural slaves in book 1 of *Politics*, in the third book of the same work, Las Casas explained, Aristotle described barbarians who

> have a lawful, just, and natural government. Even though they lack the art and use of writing, they are not wanting in the capacity and skill to rule and govern themselves, both publicly and privately. Thus they have kingdoms, communities, and cities that they govern wisely according to their laws and customs. Thus their government is legitimate and natural, even though it has some resemblance to tyranny. From these statements we have no choice but to conclude that the rulers of such nations enjoy the use of reason. (Las Casas 1992, 42)

The indigenous peoples of the New World fell into this category of Aristotelian barbarian according to Las Casas, a category that in no way precluded their freedom, but to the contrary ordained it. From this *use of reason* derived various rights, according to Las Casas's interpretation of ancient philosophy. As a consequence of their indisputable rationality, Las Casas argued, the Junta had "no choice" but to acknowledge that Indians (whether Christian or infidel) had a natural right to their possessions; that they could not be disposed of their goods or territories by Christian conquerors. They had the right to self-government, to freely elect their kings, lords, and dignitaries.[17] Furthermore, Indians had the right to depose those leaders when they failed to rule in the people's best interest. As rational beings, Indians were free from enforced servitude of any kind or duration. Most significantly, on the principle of the Christian unity of the world, Las Casas argued that Christ had given all men free will, and as such, Indians could not be compelled to accept the Christian faith under any circumstances, but rather must be persuaded to the faith. Meanwhile, the Petrine responsibility of the Spanish Crown as representatives of the papacy in the New World required the council to wholeheartedly protect these indigenous rights from being trammeled by Spanish colonists and conquistadors.

Las Casas's theorization of these rights—and his partial success in getting the Spanish Crown to acknowledge and defend these rights for the indigenous peoples in the New World—have justly earned him a reputation as the precursor of Enlightenment concepts of equality, self-determination, and freedom. As Luis N. Rivera (1992) explains in *A Violent Evangelism: The Political and Religious Conquest of the Americas,* Las Casas combined "the ontological definition of the rational unity of the human species from classic Greco-Roman philosophy, and the medieval ideal of the universality of divine grace" (141). In so doing, he espoused a universal theory of humanity based on the divine nature of human reason. While Catholicism's redemptive mission was the basis for this, Las Casas nevertheless placed indigenous capacity and culture *at the center* of his theory of universal humanity. As Mariscal (2006) points out, his religious indoctrination prevents us from considering this a modern, secular theory of the human (273). Nevertheless, Las Casas's arguments at Valladolid index an origin of the universalization of the human, one required by the indigenous encounter. Indigenous peoples—their customs, their cultures, their modes of reason—were central to the theorization of modern humanism the Valladolid debate initiated and portends. Indeed, the quality of indigenous reason—Las Casas's zealous affirmation of its resemblance to God's own reason—portends a secular humanism with indigeneity at its core, not at its margins. However, the Sepúlveda–Las Casas debate also indexed the brutal counterface of modern humanism, for reason, divinely endowed, comes to substitute for faith as the secular calculus of racial slavery. The debate at Valladolid, occasioned by the encounter with indigenous peoples in the utopian landscape of America, indexes the inauguration of Eurocentric reason as the new unit of measurement for a secular humanity.

For the purposes of discerning the representational logic used to map this newfound indigenous humanity racially onto the geography of the New World, I draw the reader's attention to the terms in which indigenous rationality is evidenced for Las Casas. The Indians' divine rationality is evidenced for Las Casas at once by their gentleness, by their docility, but most importantly by their "preparedness" to receive the Christian faith. Combining biblical orthodoxy and Aristotelian philosophy, Las Casas argued that indigenous peoples—idolaters and infidels though they may be—had a right to their freedom and self-determination due to their divinely derived reason. Divine rationality notwithstanding, Las Casas also stressed their openness to assimilation:

> From the fact that the Indians are barbarians [in the fourth Aristotelian sense] it does not necessarily follow that they are incapable of government and have to be ruled by others, except to be taught about the Catholic faith and to be admitted to the sacraments. They are not ignorant, inhuman, or bestial. Rather, long before they had heard the word Spaniard they had properly organized states, wisely ordered by excellent laws, religion, and custom. *They cultivated friendship and, bound together in common fellowship,* lived in populous cities in which they wisely administered the affairs of both peace and war justly and equitably, truly governed by the laws that at very many points surpass ours, and could have won the admiration of the sages of Athens. (42–43)[18]

There are two points to emphasize in this passage. First, the rationality of the Indians is underscored by their *sociality*. To prove that the Indians had reason, Las Casas repeatedly demonstrated that they were not as a mass of individuals indifferently gathered together, but a community with joint purpose. This sociality alone, under natural law and Aristotelian philosophy (hence the reference to Athens), gave Indians the right to have their own dignitaries and keep their own possessions, Las Casas argued. Furthermore, it was evident that these men adhered to natural law, because natural law dictated that some men were superior to others, and accordingly indigenous peoples had everywhere elected superior men to lead them in their "wisely" ordered governments (Peña 1989, 407).

This brings me to my second point. In Las Casas's model of Indian barbarism, sociality and self-government were easily assimilated *within* the hierarchical unity of European Christian dominion in the New World, and indeed facilitated the graphing of that hierarchy onto the American landscape. With Christ at its pinnacle, Las Casas fitted indigenous kingdoms into the pyramid

48 CHAPTER ONE

of Christian orthodoxy, transposing it onto the their geography: following in descending order from Christ were the Catholic Church, the Spanish monarchy, the secular and ecclesiastic colonial authorities, and the indigenous kings; each realm presided *over* the other, with each realm maintaining its appropriate temporal dominion over its own affairs. Thus we see in the emerging racial geography of Spanish colonial space-making endeavor, the indios are the very base of Christian unity in the Americas, their "cultivated friendship" and "common fellowship" emblematic of Christian community and unity. Indeed, Christian community is transposed onto American geography through the reasoned sociality of indigenous peoples.

If "space and identities are co-produced" as Linda Peake has argued, and "spaces . . . given meaning through the social practices of groups that repeatedly occupy them," then Las Casas gave meaning to the "New World" through his interpretation of the social practices he witnesses among indigenous peoples (Peake 2010, 65). This pushes Peake in a different direction than she intends, but my point is to underscore that the visioning of spatial practice among the indios by Las Casas in turn produced spatial meaning and identity in landscape; Indians were made to produce the American geography as utopian. The Christian unity of humanity was always already present in indigenous communities, ready to be brought forth by evangelical persuasion ("the sacraments") and easily assimilated within Spanish dominion ("Catholic faith"). At one point in the *Defense*, Las Casas described the Indians as being so "meek" that "when the Spaniards first penetrated their territories an enormous number of them quickly boarded the ships of the Christians with a sincere attitude and [later], entertaining the Spaniards in their homes, they paid them the highest honor as godlike men sent from heaven" (327). Again, indigenous reason recognized the divine order of the universe—Indians already anticipated Christian unity—by recognizing the Spaniards as representatives of Christ.

Although both Las Casas and Sepúlveda claimed to have won the debate in Valladolid, the Council of Fourteen never issued a ruling, or at least no record of any decision has surfaced in the colonial archive.[19] Though the council's decision remains lost to history, the Crown appears to have split the difference, according to the exigencies of colonial management. The Spanish Crown repealed the Requerimiento in 1556, ending any pretext for just wars against the Indians and any further grants of encomiendas.[20] However, the suspension of the nonhereditary clause of the encomienda remained in effect until 1573. In that year, new laws were issued that formally nullified the encomiendas and dictated that all new discoveries must follow Las Casas's recommendation that Indians be brought to the faith by persuasion and not warfare.[21] All this handwringing by the Spanish Crown regarding the legitimacy of their dominion—all of these councils, debates, revisions to the Laws of the Indians, censorships—was more than just rhetorical posturing, more than just the instrumentalized use of legal reasoning to further justify the pillaging of conquered lands. The status of the Christian in relationship to the newly discovered peoples was of great consequence to the Roman papacy (at this moment held by the Spanish king Carlos V) and to the Spanish monarchy under Prince Felipe II (Carlos's son), both as part of the reassertion of Catholic orthodoxy and repelling Islamic incursion in the European theater, and as part of the larger project of becoming one global (racialized) humanity *through* the American theater.

Christian Europe's relationship to the infidel, since medieval times, was based on scripture, on Christ's order to Peter to protect his flock. There was compunction in Christian scripture to look after the infidel because of the necessary unity of God's creation. However, the encounter with the indigenous inhabitants of the Americas transformed this Petrine responsibility by individuating it, by extending this responsibility to every Spaniard in the New World. "Never before," as Hanke points out, "had the indoctrination of non-Christians who were living in Christian kingdoms been considered the duty of all Spaniards.... Henceforth the *people*, not merely ecclesiastics, were expected to participate actively and responsibly in the conversion of the heathen" (1974, 4, 8). This new, shared responsibility of converting the indigenous "heathens" dispersed sovereign and divine power among the colonists, democratizing it, as colonists were required to internalize this Petrine compunction. Indeed, the modern origins of international law—which during this same era were elaborated by another Spanish Enlightenment jurist, Francisco de Vitoria—were similarly based on this unity of humanity and democratization of responsibility.

The discovery of indigenous reason enabled the theorization of an *international* modern law. As legal scholar Antony Anghie has argued, "The essential point is that international law, such as it existed in Vitoria's time, did not *precede* and thereby effortlessly resolve the problem of Spanish-Indian relations, rather international law was created out of the unique issues generated by the encounter between cultures" (1999, 90). In seeking a justification for Spanish conquest that was *not* based on divine law, Vitoria theorized secular unity of humanity established by the shared capacity for reason, evinced by well-ordered cities and well-reasoned governments of indigenous peoples, and from this evidence theorized the rights entailed by international sovereignty among nations. For Vitoria, as for Las Casas, the indio's shared capacity for

50   CHAPTER ONE

reason was proven to exist precisely by the Spanish visioning of the Indians and their kingdoms, in other words.[22] All nations, though differentiated between Christian and heathen, were equal under international law if they possessed reason and governmentality (Anghie 1999, 94). However, while it was the Indians' capacity for reason that granted them the right to their dominion and freedom under secular international law for Vitoria, it was this same rationality that *required them* to welcome the Spaniards with open arms.

By virtue of the *unity* (singularity?) of rational humanity and the universality of sovereignty, Indian nations were compelled to allow Spaniards into their dominions. The sovereignty enjoyed by Indian kings in turn required them to grant their equals in sovereignty, the Spaniards, all the rights their own subjects enjoyed, including the right to settle, trade, and proselytize in their indigenous dominions (Anghie 1999, 95, 97). The spatiality of indigenous sovereignty, confirmed by their reasoned sociality, required from indigenous peoples the recognition of the rights of the colonist.[23] But Vitoria goes even beyond these enumerated rights the Spaniards must be allowed to enjoy in Indian dominions on the basis of universal sovereignty and international law. When Vitoria theorizes the law of nations, he argues that the Indians were also compelled to "love" the Spaniards (his words) as they would love any other neighbor, revealing once more the Christian trace within secular reasoning.[24] The Valladolid controversy was emblematic of a period in early modern law in which the emergent Catholic Enlightenment grappled with this imperative of Christian unity: Christians and infidels—especially these peoples who were previously unbeknownst to them—must occupy *one* world, *one* dominion, *one* geography of humanity, different though they may be. Thus it was not only the Indian that must be made human before Europeans, but the European who must be made human before the Indian. *Love* thy neighbor. Indigenous peoples enjoying usufruct over the spaces they occupied, and producing meaning therein—possessing it with well-reasoned sociality—paradoxically produced Christian identity in the New World in accordance with the visioning of Las Casas, Vitoria, and even Sepúlveda. Locating Indian community in the American landscape presaged Christian unity and secular humanity.

Much has been written on the radically different positions taken in the Valladolid controversy by the "devil's advocate" and the "protector of the Indians." But the scholarly focus on elucidating Sepúlveda's and Las Casas's opinions—the differences between their interpretations of Aristotle as well as their other disagreements—distracts us from the underlying collusion of their stances. Sepúlveda's and Las Casas's Christian reasoning led both of them to compel the Spaniards to act on behalf of the Indian. The Indian infidel compelled the Spaniards' compunction as Christians. Indeed the very fact of the debate about *how* to act on their behalf enabled the discursivity of the event, enabled the proliferation of statements about the Indian. Even the fact of the debate remaining undecided is indicative of this ongoing discursivity. The debate proliferated statements about the Indian—they were savage, they were not savage; they had good government, they were tyrannical; they had capacious reason, they had limited reason—making them into not only the objects of conversion, but into objects of a study.

For Las Casas *and* for Sepúlveda, the Indian was central to the project of colonialism. Indeed, the Indians *required* the presence of the Spaniards in America in both their arguments. Clearly, the potential for vast economic gain motivated the Crown, church, and conquistadors in the New World, but the Valladolid debate was not a sheer ideological cover. Rather, through the legal and philosophical reasoning of early modern Spain—represented by Sepúlveda, Las Casas, and Vitoria among others—the Indian was made into the reason for the Spanish colonial mission, its condition of possibility as either exemplary humanity or humanity in need of remediation. Moreover, the Spanish colonist was made more fully human to the Indian through the injunction to love him. This had very important consequences for the long-term place of indigenous peoples in the racial geography of Latin America. They were brought under the Spanish Crown at the lowest rung as Spanish subjects and servants and thus were placed *within* the papacy's spiritual dominion. Their compelling infidelity placed them under the Petrine and paternal responsibility of colonial authorities. Indians were part of Spain's geographical empire, not apart from it.

Thus, in the nineteenth century, Indians would be brought into the newly independent nations of Latin America under terms like those laid out by the Valladolid controversy. Indians provided the aboriginal claims to sovereignty for each Latin American nation that sought self-determination and equality on the world scene. Indigenous people's millennial occupation of the American landscape not only produced indigenous identity in the manner suggested by Peake, indios' occupation of American landscape as visioned by colonialism also produced national identities, coding and decoding space in the service of independence movements. Once these nations were established, indigenous citizens became the most compelling obstacles to modernity for nationalist and revolutionary leaders. According to this discursive logic, Indians would always be brought within the geographical and epistemological boundaries of Latin American nations as origin and obstacle, as the condition of possibility for reiterative nationalisms and nationalist modernities, rather than set

52   CHAPTER ONE

apart from them. In both of these senses, then, Latin American nationalism is *Indian given.*

The Sepúlveda and Las Casas debate was not merely an adjudication of the humanity of the Indian. It was also a way of perceiving the geography of the new world in racial terms; not race in its modern biological sense but as an index of a difference that was coterminously religious and somatic.[25] The debate offered a discursive axis for graphing indigenous formations onto the colonial geography of New Spain as recognizable and reiterable plot points or racial coordinates. Rather than any Indians being either docile converts or rebellious infidels, it was most important that they always be potentially both. Thus they were never discretely designated points in the landscape, but rather they are constantly shifting along the dual axis of fidelity and infidelity. For the duration of Spanish colonialism, as long as Indians are so ambivalently positioned—not either/or but both/and—the raison d'être of the Spanish colonial project continued to exist. Thus, as late as the eighteenth century, colonists in New Spain who petitioned the Spanish Crown for the rights of settlement in Texas went to great lengths to describe *both* docile Indians who were ready to convert to Christianity *and* the barbarous Indians who refused conversion. In 1738, the petitioner Don Antonio Ladrón de Guevara gave detailed descriptions of the territory he wanted to settle, plotting docile Indians he intended to convert on a map of what is today south Texas and northern Tamaulipas, as well as plotting the warring factions of Indian infidels that encircled the would-be converts.[26] The docile Indians apparently awaited Ladrón de Guevara and his compatriots to come to them, in his account, both to save their souls and to protect those souls from the Indian infidels who resisted Christian unity. The American geography in the Spanish colonial archive was teeming with Indians, both hostile and docile, beckoning the Spaniard to come toward them in an attitude of brotherly love.

"The Wandering Savage Who Traverses the Wilds of America"

The representation of faithful and unfaithful Indians before the law that developed under early Spanish colonial judicial thought shaped the racial geography of New Spain by determining both the perception of the landscape in the eyes of settlers, and the settlement patterns and practices of the colonists among the indigenous populations, as we shall see in the next chapter.[27] If the Indian was the condition of possibility for Spanish settlement of New Spain, then the landscape was necessarily full of Indians who were either potential converts, malingering infidels, or both. Similarly, spatial practices of settlement were dependent on the willingness of certain indigenous populations to allow Spaniards to settle among or near them, to the potential detriment of other indigenous populations. These colonial tropes of faithful and unfaithful indios continue to inform, heterotemporally, the contemporary Mexican national scene/seen, as evident, for example, in the government and civil responses to indigenous autonomy movements in Chiapas, Guerrero, and Oaxaca over the last twenty years. Indigenous demands for autonomy are perceived as barbarous acts of infidelity, as flagrant unfaithfulness to national sentiment. Similarly, so too do the racial tropes of the "wandering savage" and the "vanishing Indian" continue to inform, heterotemporally, the U.S. national scene/seen in popular and public culture (O'Brien 2010; Deloria 1998).[28]

As historians and legal scholars have argued, this trope of the nomadic "savage" who traversed the landscape referenced in the above quote by Minister Frisbie—the Indian who occupied territory but did not own it—and the related trope of the vanishing Indian became the dominant modes of representing Indians in the nineteenth century (Banner 2005; Williams 1990; Blackhawk 2006). Both representations of the Indian were also representations of space: a racialized mode of envisioning the North American landscape as empty or emptying of its indigenous inhabitants. These tropes developed in tandem during the early colonial period of British settlement; however, they only became the dominant tactics for recognizing the Indian in the United States in the nineteenth century during western expansion. Together these dominant tropes ushered in a specific spatial practice of the U.S. *nation*: the massive dispossession of indigenous lands by nineteenth and twentieth century policies of removal, reservation, and allotment, in the interest of white European immigrant settlement. As rhetorically useful as these tropes were to remaking the racial geography of North America for a young, imperial U.S. by removing an obstacle to white settlement, and as persistent as they remain today, the tropes of the vanished/vanquished Indian and the nomadic Indian were only two of the representational tactics in the political repertoire of recognizing Indians in the North American landscape, and they were by no means the dominant ones in the colonial or revolutionary periods.

Scholarly arguments regarding the importance of these two representational tactics in the nineteenth and twentieth centuries have eclipsed a wider array of tactics for the emplotment of Indians in space during the colonial and revolutionary periods that played a definitive role in constituting (white) colonial and revolutionary subjectivity. During these periods, tactics for recognizing Indians in colonial spaces emerged among the colonists who imputed degrees of savagery or humanity to them for the purposes of waging war or

54 CHAPTER ONE

justifying dispossession and theft, but also for the purposes of facilitating negotiation, mediation, conversion, and the acquisition of lands by seemingly peaceful and just means.[29] Among those tactics for imputing savagery as a justification for seizing Indian lands were the assertions that heathens had no property rights Christian colonists need respect (Indian infidel); that the weaker, uncivilized Indians were required to succumb to the just conquest of the stronger, civilized European (vanquished Indian); that the Indian, in an early stage of civilization, claimed no rights in property, or held all property in common (nomadic Indian).[30] These tactics of imputing savagery did not go unchallenged or exist in isolation from other tactics during the early colonial period, however.[31]

Rather, in the face of the overwhelming evidence of indigenous settlement and agricultural production throughout the Atlantic seaboard in the early colonial period, these tactics temporarily ceded dominance to seemingly more benign tactics of imputing a full humanity to the Indians that were profoundly place based. British settlers ascribed humanity to indigenous peoples in recognition of their spatially produced identities, but this humanity nevertheless deepened the subjection of indigenous peoples and their "voluntary" alienation of territory. Colonists recognized the Indian by ascribing a liberal agency and a British notion of property holding to them. In the late seventeenth century Cotton Mather recognized the Indians as "infinitely barbarous" but nevertheless held that "the *Indians* had not by their Paganism so forfeited all Right unto any of their Possessions." Mather insisted settlers could not take indigenous lands "without *a fair Purchase* and *Consent* from the Natives" (Mather 1691, 72, 117–118; cited in Banner 2005, 16, emphasis mine).

Other renowned English colonists, like John Smith of Jamestown, William Penn of Pennsylvania, and John Lawson of North Carolina, contended that the Indians not only observed property rights but also allocated *individuated* property in land. Although an advocate of just conquest, Smith nevertheless described the Indians around Jamestown as individual property owners in his 1612 *A Map of Virginia*: "Each household knoweth their owne lands & gardens and must live of their own labours." Later in his description, Smith specifies, "they all know their severall landes, and habitations, and limits, to fish, fowle, or hunt in" (107, 184). In the late seventeenth century Penn insisted that the Indians were "exact Observers of Property" to London's Free Society of Traders, while in the early eighteenth century, Lawson explained that the Indians they encountered "have no Fence to part one anothers Lots in their Corn-Fields; but every Man knows his own, and it scarce ever happens, that they rob one another of so much as an Ear of Corn" (Penn and Lawson, cited in Banner 2005, 20). As early as 1609, William Crashaw, minister for the Virginia Company, sermonized about the morally correct way of acquiring Indian lands by analogizing the Christian colonist to Abraham: "A Christian may take nothing from a Heathen against his will, but in a faire and lawfull bargaine." He continues, "*Abraham* wanted a place to burie in, and liked a peece of land and being a great man, and therefore *feared,* a just and meek man, and therefore *loved* of the heathen, they bad him *chuse where hee would, and take it.* No, saith *Abraham,* but *I will buie it,* and so he paide the price of it: so must all the children of *Abraham* doe" (cited in Banner 2005, 13; emphasis in the original). These colonists are envisioning the landscape *through* the eyes of the Indian who knows *his* own property therein. It is not sufficient that the Indians hold property; they must do so by encoding the geography in the same gendered space-making terms as colonist—private, individuated holdings that only men can alienate and heir.

My purpose is neither to adjudicate the ethics of these tactics of recognition, nor to parse the incongruent meanings of "property" among settlers and Indians. Rather my purpose is to note, once again, the *similarity of effect* occasioned by the tactics of vision and recognition that imputed nomadic savagery and those that imputed propertied civilization; both rendered the land held by indigenous peoples alienable. If on one hand innumerable settlers justified their unlawful invasion and settlement of Indian lands by attributing savagery to the Indian, on the other the vast majority of colonial governments and individual colonists in the seventeenth and eighteenth centuries obtained Indian land in "a faire Purchase," in a "lawfull bargaine," with the "Consent" of these "exact Observers of property." And as "every Man knows his *own,*" this tactic of recognizing a comparable humanity in the Indian through the envisioning of "objective" relations of property made every native available to "the children of Abraham" as the potential seller of his lands, so long as the colonist "paide the price of it." Thus the effect of imputing humanity by recognizing the usufruct rights of indigenous peoples is not only to render the Indians as competent and free human agents capable of selling their lands and participating at a bargaining table on equal footing with the colonists but also to render the *colonist* as lawful and just, as hunting for a bargain but paying a fair price for their purchases. The colonist was, like Abraham, "feared" and "loved" by the heathen-human because though the colonist could merely take the land according to the right of first discovery or because of his superior humanity, instead he "saith . . . I will buie it." As in the Spanish case, once again we see that the identity of the colonist and the Indian are coproduced in this emerging colonial geography: the colonist encounters the Indians in a particular landscape and the Indian embraces the colonist in an attitude of love as well as fear.

In *How the Indians Lost Their Land*, legal scholar Stuart Banner (2005) argues that most early colonial governments and individual colonists purchased their lands from Indians in meticulously recorded transactions that involved the drawing up of contracts and the conveyance of deeds, despite the fact that Royal Charters "almost uniformly purported to convey property right to their recipients, without any hesitation over the possibility that Indians might already possess property rights in the same land" (2005, 15, 26). The reasons for purchasing land from the Indians, as opposed to conquering it, according to Banner, were straightforward and self-explanatory. Purchasing land from Indians willing to sell was easier and cheaper than fighting wars of conquest. Beyond this simple balance of forces argument, Banner stipulates that, while the right of first discovery purportedly gave England sovereignty over the Atlantic eastern seaboard, this sovereignty was not necessarily construed as conveying property rights to the lands already owned by Indians. Anglo-American self-serving theories regarding the just and unjust rights to settlement proliferated in the murky gap between English "sovereignty" over North American territory and the actual possession of it by the indigenous inhabits. As evidence of this gap, the formal, published documents explaining the legal rights to settle *specific* colonies—for example, those of Virginia, Plymouth, and New Jersey—would list a remarkable, even haphazard range of justifications for land acquisition, including the right of discovery, the need to convert the natives to Christianity, the miserable conditions of the heathens, the heathens' lack of proper title to the lands, the emptiness of the territory. Nevertheless, these documents would inevitably also list the *purchase* of said lands from particular Indian "kings" and "chiefs" as the primary justification for acquisition (Banner 2005, 20–22).

It behooved the early colonists to render the Indians as properly holding property rights out of sheer self-interest, according to Banner. This enabled the purchase of lands in the easiest and most immediate fashion, and in the most familiar form of exchange for the seventeenth- and eighteenth-century Englishman, the contract. While the governments of each colony required the colonists to attain formal permission from the Crown to make individual or collective purchases from Indians, these permissions were rarely denied.[32] Respect for English sovereignty required that the colonists obtain permission from the proper colonial officials, but their rights as Englishmen to enter contracts directly with Indians were not to be curtailed.[33] It is important to underscore that these "lawful" contract purchases coexisted with acquisition and appropriation of land by other means, some deemed lawful and others unlawful by colonial authorities. And certainly, these contractual purchases of land for money or goods between presumably consensual parties were riddled with fraud. Indeed, Banner documents in scrupulous detail multiple accounts of fraud that frequently accompanied these "voluntary" contractual transactions between Indians and colonists throughout the colonial period. Fraud most frequently entailed the use of alcohol or implicit force to induce Indians to sell their land; the knowing purchase of tribal lands from Indians who lacked the capacity to sell the land; the bribing of notaries to change the quantity of land sold on the written document from the quantity verbally agreed on; the bribing of chiefs to sell tribal lands without consultation of the tribe. Legal scholar Robert Williams refers to these land transactions that bore the form of legality, though they were fraught with bribery and trickery, as "fraudulent inducement[s]" (1990, 227).

Extending Williams (1990), I suggest that "fraud" was not simply a failure of the contract—a temporal aberration that should not have occurred—but was a constitutive element of the contract form. Whether there was fraud involved in these transactions or not, a great importance was placed on the performance of the contract. In both the cases that involved clear fraudulent inducements and those that did not, British colonials insisted that the contract be performed as if it were a fair exchange between two parties enjoying equivalent rights.[34] This performance of the contractual exchange, in other words, was a central tactic for the recognition of Indians as capable human agents, but the performance was as well the evidence of its constitutive fraudulence: a purely formal participation in the contract process made the contract substantive, regardless of the unequal power relations that mediated the meaning of the contract's content. The contract became a concept metaphor for "just practice," obfuscating its unjust ends. Moreover, the performance of the contract itself was a mechanism for imputing humanity to the Indians in their capacity first to own property and then to freely alienate it. Importantly, the performance of the contract imputed humanity to the colonist as well, as the fair-dealing, Christian recipient of voluntarily ceded lands. The contract, then, was a way of "legally" remapping the racial geography of the Atlantic seaboard, as white settlement replaced Indian settlement "justly," "fairly," and swiftly.

In whatever other quotidian ways these colonists might regularly have recognized the Indian as savage in their daily Christian lives, when it came to purchasing their lands, the Indian was righteously and perniciously recognized

58   CHAPTER ONE

as the possessor of property and free will. This compulsory performance of free will remained as a tactic in the recognition of Indian humanity throughout colonial *and* postcolonial U.S. history, as Indians would repeatedly be required to "voluntarily" sign treaties of removal and reservation with the U.S. government in the eighteenth and nineteenth centuries. In other words, the most persistent sign of the Indian's imputed humanity was, in the British colonial and later in the U.S. national framework, the ability to willingly sign away their rights to territory. Thus colonists encoded the newly forming colonial geography not with Indians who were nomadic and inconstant, but with Indians who were rooted in the landscape and possessed land they were willing to sell. As such, Indians were made into the coproducers of British colonial space and British colonial identity, for the colonist and the Indian met as equals in the exchange of land. As Cheryl Harris (1993) clarifies in her foundational article "Whiteness as Property," "Rights were for those who had the capacity to exercise them, a capacity denoted by racial identity" (1745). Harris's argument underscores the degree to which whiteness was the condition for exercising rights, and to such a degree that whiteness itself became a property "this conception of rights was contingent on race—on whether one could claim whiteness—as a form of property" (1745). Extending Harris, I suggest that the capacity to exercise the right to alienate one's property came to denote indigenous racial identity in this early colonial period as well. If the property of whiteness was emblemized by the capacity to buy and hold property, then the property of indigeneity was emblemized by the capacity to hold and relinquish land.[35]

This early colonial dispossession of indigenous lands through contractual agreement involved the location of a multitude of Indians encoded within the landscape as willingly ceding their property, and it set the stage for the second flashpoint in the constitution of colonial subjectivity. The combination of legal and extralegal acquisition of land by the colonists caused a major transformation in land tenure along the Atlantic seaboard, with indigenous tribes from the east pushed farther and farther west toward and over the Appalachian and Allegany mountain ranges. Though indigenous tribes consistently appealed to the British Crown to intercede on their behalf, both to halt the invasion by settlers into their hunting grounds and to invalidate those contractual arrangements where trickery and bribery had been used, the Crown had just as consistently been unwilling or unable to intercede. The result of this inaction by the British Crown in the face of land-hungry colonists was the French and Indian War (1754–63). The majority of Indian peoples sided with the French in its imperial war against the British, in the hope of stemming the tide of British encroachment on Indian lands west of the Appalachian and Allegany mountain ranges.

Although the British won the war, the British government at Whitehall decided the political and economic costs of fraudulent land transactions with Indians, as well as the outright settler invasions, were unsustainable. King George III issued the Royal Proclamation of 1763, banning *all* private land transactions between colonists and Indians (including purchases by local colonial governments) and all settlement west of the eastern mountain ranges. The proclamation explicitly addressed the many fraudulent means used to coerce or trick Indian tribes out of their territory:

> And whereas great frauds and abuses have been committed in purchasing lands of the Indians, to the great prejudice of our interests, and to the great dissatisfaction of the said Indians; in order, therefore, to prevent such irregularities for the future, and to the end that the Indians may be convinced of our justice and determined resolution to remove all reasonable cause of discontent, we strictly enjoin and require, that no private person do presume to make any purchase from the said Indians of any lands reserved but that if at any time any of the said Indians should be inclined to dispose of the said lands, the same shall be purchased only for us, in our name, at some public meeting or assembly of the said Indians.[36]

The Crown interpreted fraud here in a limited way, as "irregularities" that could be remediated by the proper exercise of the contract. Like the Valladolid debate, the proclamation was an attempt by a European imperial power to rectify methods of indigenous conquest. The Crown's solution to fraudulent contracts was to monopolize the right to purchase Indian lands. All purchases of Indian lands were to be conducted by the Crown's Indian superintendents, in public, with the proper Indian tribal authorities. Despite the intentions of the British government, the effect of the proclamation on Indian land tenure was, paradoxically, disastrous.

The Proclamation of 1763 sparked a revolutionary fervor among the colonists, who condemned the Crown for its attempts to impose "feudal" land policies in the colonies. Williams aptly describes the colonists' reactions to the proclamation thusly: "Such extensions of . . . imperial power were perceived by the radicals as striking directly at their particular vision of America. The English had come to the New World in search of plentiful and cheap lands free of the feudal burdens that made land dear and unavailable in England" (1990, 245). The freedom to acquire frontier Indian lands became analogous to freedom from feudal tyranny. The proclamation inspired colonial elites like Thomas Jefferson and James Otis, a Boston lawyer and pamphleteer, to write treatises about the "Norman" kings' usurpation of "true" English property rights in America and to associate American colonists with the pre-1066 Anglo-Saxons of England, who they claimed lived as free and equal citizens and enjoyed unimpeded rights to individual property and representative government before the coming of the Norman kings (Williams 1990, 262–271, 252–254). Paradoxically, the obstacle to American freedom in these antifeudal screeds took the shape of the rights of Indians to maintain their territories, as protected under the proclamation. Conversely, encoding the geography of the revolutionary United States as the land "of freedom" occurred through the location in landscape of sovereign Indians capable of freely selling their lands. Indian freedom engendered U.S. freedom, and imagined Indian identity coproduced the identity of colonist as true "Anglo-Saxon."

Colonial elites necessarily extended the antifeudal arguments against the proclamation to the Indians as well. Land speculators like George Washington, Benjamin Franklin, and Samuel Wharton, for example, had a financial incentive for arguing that the proclamation trampled the property rights of Indians and colonists alike. Prominent colonial elites like Washington, Franklin, and Wharton had continued to purchase extensive tracts of western lands from Indians even after the proclamation took effect, and thus they became lively defenders of Indian property rights as absolutely paramount to all other rights. A member of the Continental Congress, Wharton published an unsigned pamphlet titled, *Plain Facts: Being an Examination into the Rights of Indian Nations of America, to Their Respective Countries* in 1781. In it he argued against the European right of discovery entailing any property rights for white settlers:

> But if the princes and people of Europe, in more ignorant and superstitious ages, were so far misled by the emotions of avarice, ambition, or religious pride, as to believe it justifiable for them to cross the Atlantic, and usurp the possessions of unoffending nations . . . yet the pervading liberal influence of philosophy, reason, and truth, has since given us better notions of the rights of mankind, as well as of the obligations of morality and justice, which certainly are not confined to particular modes of faith, but extend universally to Jews and Gentiles, to Christians and infidels. (Wharton 1781, 5–6; cited in Williams 1990, 299–300)

Once again European Enlightenment thought (liberal "philosophy, reason and truth") is advanced *through* the encounter with indigenous peoples ("unoffending nations"), as it is their sovereignty that requires the universalization of *private* property rights. Wharton did not mince words. Indians had the right to their territories "according to the laws of nature and nations" and as "the original and first occupants and possessors of the country." He targeted King George and his proclamation as unlawful, in that "no European prince could derive a title to the soil of America from discovery, because that . . . can only give a right to lands and things, which have either never been owned and possessed" (Wharton 10–11, cited in Williams 1990, 303). The logical extension of antifeudal discourses, as Williams points out, would have been the extension of natural law rights of property to all Indian tribes. And it was the speculators in western Indian lands who "assumed the mantle of zealous advocate[s] of the Indians' natural-law right to engage in unregulated real-estate transactions" (Williams 1990, 272). In all the variants of the antifeudal arguments articulated by colonial elites, the role played by the tactics of recognizing Indians as the proper owners of the landscape was a constant and became a central mechanism in the constitution of a "revolutionary" American subjectivity as well. Ultimately, it was the status of *Indian property* as visualized within the landscape that determined the properties of a revolutionary "American" identity: the freedom of colonists to exert their right to acquire freely ceded Indian property became tantamount to freedom from feudal tyranny, unrepresentative government, abusive centralized authority, excessive taxation, and most importantly, the freedom to individual property and to profit from land speculation.

These anticolonial speech acts by colonial elites actively involved in land speculation were central to fomenting revolutionary sentiments in the mideighteenth century, especially among those colonists still hungry for homesteads. And yet the newly formed U.S. Congress refused to recognize the logical conclusion of these successful antifeudal arguments against British colonialism by failing to recognize Indian sovereignty over their lands. Instead, in 1790 the Congress passed the Indian Intercourse Act, declaring that "no sale of lands made by any Indians, or any nation or tribe of Indians within the United States, shall be valid to any person or persons, or to any state . . . unless the same shall be made and duly executed at some public treaty, held under the authority of the United States." Without irony, the Congress deftly appropriated for the U.S. government the exact same Norman-derived feudal right to Indian lands that the Crown had asserted in its Proclamation of 1763.[37] The Intercourse Act marks the transition from contract to treaty as the

62 CHAPTER ONE

medium for acquiring land from Indians "voluntarily." These treaties were no less fraudulent in their use of coercive inducements to pressure Indians to surrender their lands. Nevertheless, once again, the *performance* of the treaty between the U.S. government and the various Indian peoples became the new fraudulent tactic for recognizing Indians as human agents fully capable of freely alienating their property for the greater good of U.S. freedom: the expansion of democracy as individual property, the expression of (white) property as liberty.[38]

The Intercourse Act was the culmination of a series of compromises and legal provisions by which the U.S. Congress devolved the right of discovery from the British Crown onto the U.S. federal government. As such, it set the stage for the 1830 ruling by the U.S. Supreme Court in the ubiquitous case of *Johnson v. McIntosh*. In this case, the court ruled in favor of the federal and state governments' exclusive right to grant fee simple ownership of Indian lands to settlers. In his notorious opinion, Justice John Marshall not only asserted the United States derived the right of discovery from the British, but also that this right of discovery granted the United States "ultimate dominion" over land, including the "power to grant the soil, while yet in possession of the natives." Marshall went further, reducing the property rights of American Indians to a newly invented "right of occupancy." According to Marshall's legal reasoning, Indians "were admitted to be the rightful occupants of the soil, with a legal as well as just claim to retain possession of it," but they were not, nor had ever been, its owners. To justify this claim, Marshall negated the long history of colonial recognition of the property rights of the agriculturally based eastern Indians, and instead returned to the use of a long dormant tactic of recognizing Indians by imputing nomadic savagery. From Marshall's opinion: "The tribes of Indians inhabiting this country . . . were fierce savages, whose occupation was war, and whose subsistence was drawn chiefly from the forest. To leave them in possession of their country, was to leave the country a wilderness." And again contradicting recorded colonial history, Marshall asserted that the Indian inevitably vanished before superior whiteness: "European policy, numbers, and skill, prevailed. As the white population advanced, that of the Indians necessarily receded."[39]

This decision marked a major transformation in the concept of indigenous property rights, one that assuredly reflected the shift in military and political power between Native Americans and imperial U.S. citizens in the nineteenth century. Not only were Indians denied sovereignty over their territories by the court's decision, they were also denied basic property rights over their lands. They held only the right to occupy the land, and this at the discretion

SAVAGES WELCOMED   63

of the U.S. government. The Marshall decision ushered in the ascendance of those tactics of recognition that imputed savagery to the Indian with which I began this section: the nomadic, vanquished, and vanishing Indians. Even these savage Indians were nevertheless required to *voluntarily* recede from the scene of the nation by formally agreeing to sign treaties for their removal and/or placement on reservations. Over the long history of the United States, tactics for recognizing the Indian by imputing degrees of propertied humanity or nomadic savagery to them worked at times in tandem and at other times in conflict, as we will see in chapters 3 and 4. If the emerging category of race in the Spanish context indexed the transit from religious to secular humanity, in the Anglo-American case it indexed the fraught and limited transit of indigenous free will. These various tactics produced a racial geography of the United States in which the Indian—be they sovereign or savage—is nonetheless voluntarily receding from the democratic scene of the nation.

If the Indian was the condition of possibility for Spanish colonialism, the Indian was also the condition of possibility for settlement by British colonists. The faithful Indian, the unfaithful Indian, the Indian who holds ground, the Indian who cedes ground, the Indian who willingly relinquished the landscape, the Indian who willfully traverses American landscapes: the remaining chapters of *Indian Given* trace the heterotemporal effects of these legal mappings of indigenous subjects for the ways in which they have continued to graph the racial geographies of the United States and Mexico (and subsequently Aztlán). All these legal fictions for mapping Indians had profound geographical effects, permitting the graphing of the American geo by *criollo* and white European settlers, and subsequently by nation-building elites. These legal fictions for mapping Indians were certainly not timeless, as the Indian-humans found themselves reconfigured before the law of the United States and Mexico on several occasions. *Indian Given* attends to these legal re-mappings with an eye always on the reiterative, heterotemporal effect of early colonial modes of imagining the Indian across centuries, "tracing how racial struggles are reburied in a widening palimpsest of memory, only to be disinterred once again in another historical moment, reconstructed yet again and redeployed" (Mallon 2011, 322). These palimsestic configurations of the Indian as faithful or unfaithful, as voluntarily ceding ground or merely traversing it before vanishing, all had profound effects on the national imaginaries of the United States, Mexico, and Aztlán, as well as on the psychic lives and political projects of their citizens.

The imagined Indians of these early humanist mappings register for us the possibilities and foreclosures of the primal scenes of colonial encounter be-

64   CHAPTER ONE

tween British and Spanish settlers and the Indian inhabitants of America. The following chapters offer an account of the psychic toll of this legal and geographical history of repression, of the trauma and loss associated with these primal scenes. Each colonial and national interpretation of imagined Indians (British, Spanish, U.S., Mexican, and Chicana/o) that I examine indexes a foreclosure, repression, or loss, not only of the rich particularity of historical indigenous peoples, but of the possibility of different national geographies. Given Indians in the colonial and postcolonial eras foreclosed or repressed unimaginable forms of American citizen-subjects, even as they generated other forms of citizen-subjects (Indian and non-Indian); they foreclosed or repressed unimaginable forms of political, social, and economic association, even as they enabled the troubled national forms we inhabit today.

2

AFFECT IN THE ARCHIVE
Apostates, Profligates, Petty Thieves, and the Indians
of the Spanish and U.S. Borderlands

The *places* of social space are very different from those of natural space in that they are not simply juxtaposed: they may be intercalated, combined, superimposed—they may even sometimes collide. Consequently the local (or 'punctual' in the sense of 'determined by a particular point') does not disappear, for it is never absorbed by the regional, national or even worldwide level. The national and regional levels take in innumerable 'places'; national space embraces the regions; and world space does not merely subsume national spaces, but even (for the time being at least) precipitates the formation of new national spaces through a remarkable process of fission. —**Henri Lefebvre**, *The Production of Space*

Racial geography as a critical category enables us to discern the divergent genealogies of Indian difference that emerged in the early colonial period of New Spain and the thirteen original Anglo-American colonies. As suggested in chapter 1, imagined indios and Indians were put to distinct uses in distinct places for the graphing of the racial geographies of the two colonial regimes. This chapter moves us to the northern frontier of eighteenth-century New Spain, to the area that would eventually become the border region between Mexico and the United States. Especially in the archive of the early stages of Spanish colonization, we find the region becoming an "intercalated, combined, superimposed" landscape. As suggested by Lefebvre, the local—the punctual—determined by the particular point of indigenous settlement "does not disappear" into Spanish colonial settlement (Lefebvre 1991). Rather, Spanish colonial settlement as a regional space-making practice is superimposed and intercalated onto/with the punctual indigenous space-making practices. Indigenous production of space is never simply absorbed, as we shall see, but heterotemporally remains, haunting but also producing space up to the present. In the last section of the chapter we examine yet another intercalation and superimposition, that of U.S. national space onto the punctual and regional spaces of the Spanish colonial period. Using Lefebvre, racial geography enables us to challenge the model of white settler colonialism predicated on the theoretical presumption that white settlement practices displaced, eliminated, and absorbed indigenous spaces. Rather, with Lefebvre we witness how indigenous punctual practices and identities remain, actively producing space, even as the racial geographies of the United States and Mexico massively and raucously collide along the border.

Although nearly two hundred years of Spanish colonial practice separated them from the Valladolid controversy of 1550–1552, the Spanish colonists who petitioned the Crown for the rights to *poblar*, "to people," the territory between Nuevo León and Texas pictured the geography they wished to fill in terms remarkably similar to those laid out by Bartolomé de Las Casas and Juan Ginés de Sepúlveda. Each petitioner—Antonio Ladrón de Guevara, José de Escandón, Josseph Antonio Fernández de Jáuregui, Narciso Barquín y Montecuesta—visualized the landscape as an ensemble of tangible material forms, but also as the scene/seen of racial difference (Cosgrove 2003; Schein 2006). Though each petitioner mapped the terrain according to the cardinal coordinates, they also mapped it according to the racial coordinates established by the Valladolid debate: the landscape was filled with imagined Indians, both those whose docility beckoned the Spaniard to come forth in an attitude of brotherly love, and those whose hostility provoked the Spaniard to come forth waging a "good Samaritan" war in defense of the innocents. Indeed, the official petitions of all four men, as well as their subsequent published accounts of their exploits along the northern frontier, adhere to an almost formulaic coupling of docile with hostile Indians. Petitions by Guevara and Escandón privileged the figure of the errant Indian who only needed the proper guidance of gentle persuasion, while those by Jáuregui and Montecuesta privileged the figure of the savage bárbaro whose despicable and unwarranted crimes required military expeditions to force their proper submission.

In either case, these petitions teemed with Indians. For example, as governor of the Nuevo Reino de León (Nuevo León), Jáuregui wrote a letter to the king dated September 16, 1736, urging the settlement of the troublesome northern territory. In his description of this territory, as yet unpopulated by Spanish subjects, Jáuregui filled the margins of his narratives with lists of

Indian nations, names that presumably corresponded to what he was describing in each paragraph. Alongside one such paragraph, he wrote "Malincheños, Sarnosos, Amiyayas, Bocas prietas, Chapulines, Serranos, Cadimas, Borrados, Pamoranos, Janambres, Salineros."[1] In several paragraphs Jáuregui described the damages various indios had caused the good people of Nuevo León, in others he described the customs they practiced in their territories. The list of Indian names is visually overwhelming, and although the names are meant to supplement the central narrative of petition, they threaten to displace it. The pages are an apt visual metaphor for the emergent scene/seen of Spanish racial geography on the northern frontier, as it is the Indians' presence in the landscape that matters most, threatening to crowd out or encircle Spanish presence. Just as the list of Indian names are plot points in Jáuregui's narrative, so too are the actual Indians plot points in the landscape. They encode the space and embody it. Even the names Jáuregui assigns to some of these groups reflect the places in which they reside: "Indians of the mountains" (Serranos); "Indians of the salt lands" (Salineros); "Indians of the grasshopper lands" (Chapulines). And although not indicated in Jáuregui's narrative, one wonders if the "Malincheños" might not have acted as guides and translators through the landscape, after their namesake Malinche.

In the first section of this chapter, I examine Antonio Ladrón de Guevara's original, unpublished petition for the rights of settlement that I retrieved from the Archivo General de Indias (AGI) in Seville, Spain. Ladrón de Guevara envisioned the spatial embodiment and emplotment of indios in landscape in terms that would have been recognizable to the Crown in his petition for settlement, but he also recorded the punctual practices of multiple Indian peoples that produced space and identity according to their own social relations. These punctual geographies remain in the petition not as mere traces of the subaltern resistance, but as in turn productive of intercalated spaces of Spanish colonialism.

On the basis of his petition, the Spanish Crown initially awarded Ladrón de Guevara the right to populate the region over his rivals. Indeed, a notary annotated the petition in the margin of the final page, indicating that the king had approved the petition, authorizing the financing of his venture.[2] The Crown changed its mind, rescinding the rights, probably for economic reasons, as Guevara's pacifist plan depended entirely on the Crown's treasury for the establishment of Spanish missions and pueblos. Instead, the Crown ultimately awarded these rights to José de Escandón, renowned today for establishing Nuevo Santander (now south Texas and Tamaulipas) through a self-financing group of *vecinos* (neighbors), which included Ladrón de Gue-

68   CHAPTER TWO

vara.[3] However, it is in Guevara's petition to convert the indigenous populations of the "Seno Mexicano" (the Gulf Coast region) that we find not only his visceral apprehension of the populations he travels among—his seen/ scene of indigenous embodiment—but also the carefully rehearsed terms of colonial space-making. More precisely put, in the petition we discern the manner in which Guevara decoded the terms of *indigenous* space-making for the king, and recoded these practices in the recognizable terms of Spanish settlement. Guevara's rivals also decoded and encoded space in familiar racial coordinates, but Guevara's unpublished petition is the first recorded account of his travels through the Gulf Coast region and retains the unedited freshness and exuberance of a travel diary, recording a plethora of indigenous spatial practices he encountered in extensive, even joyful, detail.[4] Nevertheless, it is also a *practiced* account, as Ladrón de Guevara reiterates the proper coordinates of indigenous humanity, mapping them accordingly for the Crown's entrance onto the scene/seen, for colonial graphing of the geo.

After the analysis of Ladrón de Guevara's 1738 petition and the racial geography it encoded, I turn our attention northward to the Provincia de Tejas of 1758. The province was established in the second half of the seventeenth century, but by the mid-eighteenth century the Spanish and Indian pueblos therein were under siege. With Spanish dominion seriously challenged, I examine a set of unpublished letters also retrieved from the AGI concerning the 1758–59 Comanche attacks on the San Saba presidio and mission in Texas. If Ladrón de Guevara's petition reiterated indigenous racial coordinates in the landscape for the purposes of settlement, then these letters demonstrate the fluctuation and transformation of these coordinates when indigenous people refused Spanish spatial emplotment. The letters offer us a historical representation of indigenous peoples refusing their predictable emplotment in the most spectacular of ways: attacks, raids, killings, and war. However they also provide evidence that the production of space in Spanish colonialism was never a simple top-down affair. Rather than an imposition of Spanish hegemonic space on indigenous punctual spaces, the letters attest to an ongoing and complex negotiation between various indigenous peoples and colonial powers. The indios were not only writing back to the empire in blood, they were dictating the manner in which Spanish colonialism produced "settled" space.

In the final section of the chapter, I stage a conversation between the San Saba letters and the 2007 Cohen brother's film *No Country for Old Men* (a studiously faithful adaptation of the Cormac McCarthy novel by the same title) in order to foreground the transnational legacy of Spanish and Anglo-American racial graphing of the Southwest. As contemporary geographers have established, space is not simply an empty landscape waiting to be filled, but created through social relations over time. Though separated by over more than two hundred years, both the letters and the film offer us a representation of what is today central Texas as a landscape produced by relations of racial conflict. Going further, the film represents the landscape itself as productive of racial conflict. In this staged conversation, we witness how the Spanish and Anglo-American colonial coordinates of emplotment are reiterated, reconsidered, and revised, both in the historical archive of letters on Spanish-Indian wars, and in a fictional film about an ostensive drug feud in the 1980s. As *No Country for Old Men* also provides us with a *visual* archive of the contemporary war on terror, this staged conversation foregrounds the centrality of the figure of the Indian in consolidating both Spain and the United States at a moment of imperial crisis.

In staging this conversation, I am not suggesting that a twenty-first-century postcolonial representation of racialized bodies derives formulaically from colonial racial geographies, Spanish or Anglo-American. Rather, this conversation between the letters and the film stages a conversation between Dipesh Chakrabarty's concept of heterotemporality in the border region and Lefebvre's concept of the "innumerable places" taken in by national and regional space (Chakrabarty 2000, 243). The colonial documents considered here illuminate the innumerable places that heterotemporally occupy the U.S. Southwest today, "the plurality that inheres in the 'now.'" By returning the film to the rich Spanish, French, and Anglo-American colonial histories of the region, the intercalated, superimposed, and heterotemporal racial geographies of the region are also illuminated. It is this heterotemporal palimpsest, I suggest, that provides the film with its rich racial registry of geographical space. Meanwhile, *No Country* is also mediating the colonial encounter for the viewer, revisiting it as a way of interpreting U.S. imperial violence in the Middle East today. Through a 1980s drug exchange gone wrong, the film allegorically asks the viewer to weigh who is the barbarian terrorist *today*, and where has *he* wandered off to?

Geographical Primers of Faith, Love, and Grief

Los parajes que habitan los Indios gentiles que se pretende Poblar, se hallan circunvalados de las provincias que por el Mapa se Manifestan y por la frente de ellos la costa del Mar del Norte Ensenada Mexican y corre su orilla de Tampico, a la Bahía de San Joseph de los Texas, Nueva Philipinas. (The places where the pagan Indians live which we intend to populate are circumscribed by the provinces indicated on the map, and in front of them by the northern

70 CHAPTER TWO

sea of the Gulf of Mexico, and run from the border of Tampico to the bay of Saint Joseph of Texas, New Philippines.) —**Antonio Ladrón de Guevara**, "Noticias sobre los indios bárbaros y sus costumbres"

With his 1738 document, "Noticias sobre los indios bárbaros y sus costumbres" (News on the Barbarous Indians and Their Customs), Don Antonio Ladrón de Guevara petitioned the Spanish Crown and New Spain's viceroy for permission to "poblar" (to populate with both Spanish and Indian towns) the territory situated "from the border of [the coastal city of] Tampico to the northern Bay of San Joseph [Goliad, Texas]," from the inland city of Monterrey to the inland mission of San Antonio de Bexar, and from these all the way to the "northern sea of the Gulf of Mexico" (Ladrón de Guevara 1738).[5] Guevara is careful to predicate his cartographic designation (cities, provinces, and the Gulf Coast) of the area he intends to colonize with the mention of the fact that it corresponds to the "parajes que habitan los Indios gentiles" ([the] places where the pagan Indians live). His petition to populate the area would entail not only the coming of Spanish subjects to the area (Spaniards, criollos, mestizos, afromestizos, and indigenous peoples from the south), but also the moving of these independent *Indios gentiles* (pagan nations) into pueblos or onto missions. Guevara's use of the term *parajes* is significant and poorly translated as "place" for its meaning in Spanish is more complex. A paraje is not just *any* place (*lugar*), but a pleasing place. Paraje implies a habitable and inviting area or vista. Underscoring this usage, paraje can also refer to a pleasing detail of landscape in a painting. Thus, while Guevara's use of the term *inhabit* might suggest something less than proper ownership, the use of paraje suggests it is precisely the presence of the Indians that encodes the area he wants to poblar as habitable. The indios on their parajes confirm for Guevara that the area is habitable and moreover, their very presence in the territory invites him to this particularly pleasing place.

Like the petitions of his rivals, Guevara's takes the form of a geographical primer. Narrated chronologically as a travelogue of his exploratory journey, it provides the king with an introduction to a region as yet unconquered. Guevara is the eyes and ears on the ground of Spanish colonialism. His petition must demonstrate adequate knowledge of the natural space he intends to conquer—its resources, tributaries, mountain ranges, flora, and fauna—and Guevara diligently records the physical attributes of the territory according to its production value: the location of its rivers and potential agricultural valleys, of its salt flats and potential silver mines, of the grasslands potentially available for ranching. These geographical primers, however, must also contain an adequate account of the social space of the Indian nations that inhabit the region. Guevara diligently complies with a detailed account of Indian customs, as promised by the document's title. More than mere description, these petitions produce geographical knowledge and graph the geo through the already existing indigenous social relations in the area. They are a form of geographical emplotment for Spanish dominion to come. As it is a specifically *Spanish* dominion, the geographical emplotment of the indigenous social formations in the landscape becomes central, as the Spanish narrative of historical events will unfold alongside these indigenous formations, not in place of them. Guevara's geographical primer accordingly offers a visual accounting of the places and *the people* that await Spanish dominion.

Guevara describes the hunting, fishing, gathering, and cooking practices of the dexterous "heathen nations" that live "far from the Spanish frontier" along the fertile planes of the Rio Grande. He describes the "plenitude" enjoyed by them, enumerating the kinds of game, fish, plants, nuts, and fruits, noting "y así se mantienen sin sembrar ni otro ejercicio unos tiempos en unos parajes y otras a las orillas de los Ríos y Costa de Mar que regularmente se retiran a ellas por el invierno que para este tiempo ya se le han acabado las frutas frescas" (they maintain themselves without farming or any other enterprise, sometimes on their lands and other times at the edges of the rivers or along the gulf coast where they retire for the winter once fresh fruits are no longer available). Guevara's description of the eating habits of the indios may render them as lacking in enterprise, but their habits also provide an analysis of the seasonal productivity of the land capitalized on by them. Indeed, just prior to this evaluative reflection, Guevara describes the many uses of the cactus fruit, how it is cultivated, picked, prepared, and turned into flour by the women. The indios and their spatialized eating practices teach Guevara how to see the landscape, how to decode its meaning, learning what is edible and what is not, where to live and where not to live.

Guevara refers to the various bands of indigenous people who enjoy this plentitude simply as "Indios Grandes," most probably naming them after the Rio Grande, adhering to the Spanish practice in the northern frontier of designating indigenous peoples according to their location, as in Jáuregui's petition. Guevara not only identifies the people with the landscape, but following the logic of Spanish nomenclature, the Indian *becomes* landscape, and the landscape correspondingly becomes Indian, as the Indians-as-location cartographic structure determines the future emplotment of Spanish pueblos as centers of evangelization. Alternately, Guevara perhaps names the Indios Grandes according to their physical characteristics, literally "the big Indians."

Naming indigenous groups according to their supposed physical attributes encodes space in a different sort of way, this time according to phenotype. This reflects an ocular experience of indigenous peoples that produced a pro-toracial difference in landscape through metaphorical representation of the scene/seen of encounter: Sarnosos (scabby), Bocas prietas (dark mouths), Narises chicas (small noses).

According to Guevara, these Indios Grandes—barbarous though they may be—posed no threat to the Spaniards along the northern frontier, as their exemplary fishing skills allow them to live honestly if lazily:

> Los que usan esto [redes] con mas prolijidad son los indios que se allan retirados de las fronteras españolas[,] porque los que se estan fron-terizos[,] como se allan de continuo opuestos con las otras naciones que gozan de esta amplitude, para poderse substentar tienen por mas conveniente, pasar a robar los ganados y caballos de los españoles que no ir a introducirse en los terminos de otra nacion[,] temerosos de las crueles guerras que por ello se le originan, y no poder surtirse de lo que mas nesesitan para su mantenimiento sin poderse inculcar como lo hazen cuando el robo lo han executado en los bienes de los españoles de cuyo refugio se allan impedidos.

> [Those who use these [fishing nets] with the greatest dexterity are the Indians who are found far from the Spanish frontier, because those who live along the border [of the Spanish frontier], as they find themselves continually opposed to other nations that enjoy this plenitude, in order to sustain themselves find it more convenient to rob the livestock and horses of the Spaniards than to intrude upon the territory of another Nation, terrified of the cruel wars that such [a transgression] might cause, and unable to avail themselves of what they most need for their sustenance without infiltrating as they do when they rob goods from the Spaniards, from whose refuge they find themselves impeded.]
> (Ladrón de Guevara 1738)

Although it might seem incongruous, it is the Indians living in closest prox-imity to the Spanish towns of the northern frontier, penned in on one side by "cruel" nations who block their access to the sea, who become incapable of providing for themselves and must steal from the Spaniards to survive. Gue-vara is designing the space so that it requires maximum intervention by Span-iards, who must provide succor, as "good Samaritans," for these indios from the "cruel wars" waged by other dexterous indigenous nations, on one hand.

On the other, the Spanish *must* populate the land to protect the existing vecinos on the Spanish frontier from thieving incursions of the penned in indios.

Guevara's observation that these Indians rob from the Spanish because they "find it more convenient" is remarkably consonant with conclusions of anthropologists and historians who attribute the increased indigenous appropriation of Spanish livestock in the eighteenth century to the disruptions brought about by the spatial practices of Spanish pueblos in the northern territories.[6] Unaware of the economies of exchange and forms of territoriality among these "nomadic" hunting and gathering groups that already existed in the region, the Spanish established ranches, farms, and towns in their territories, and introduced domesticated livestock into the northern frontier.[7] The introduction of domesticated livestock impaired the ability of the Apache and other indigenous groups devoted to hunting bison and deer to continue their trading practices in these goods with the agriculturally based, indigenous communities of the region.[8]

According to historians Salvador Álvarez (2010) and Cecilia Sheridan Prieto (2002), the Spanish spatial practice of expanding the grazing lands of livestock depleted the stock of wild game and disrupted the patterns of trade among the different indigenous peoples of this area. Indigenous peoples of the northern frontier had well-established, cyclical patterns of trade before the coming of the Spaniards. By the sixteenth century, various groups of "nomadic" Indians camped on the outskirts of indigenous agricultural communities for the duration of the winter months, trading buffalo hides, fat, meat, and captive slaves—used by agricultural communities as labor—for the food crops these hunting-based peoples did not produce for themselves.[9] In other words, the seemingly innocuous spatial practice of introducing livestock production, practiced by the Spanish without fencing and enclosure, fundamentally reinscribed the geography of the northern frontier. It changed both the natural and the social organization of space in the region: where there was game, there was now livestock, and thus where there was hunting for exchange, there was now appropriation for exchange.

More significantly, the practice of Spanish ranching created an insatiable market for horses, cattle, and sheep not only among their own ranches, farms and towns in the far-flung provinces of New Mexico, Texas, Nuevo León, and Nueva Viscaya,[10] but also among indigenous agricultural communities that developed a taste for these new kinds of meat. Indeed, the contiguous indigenous and Spanish pueblos became the largest market for stolen livestock.[11] As the Apache, Comanche, and other groups involved in such trade competed to feed this growing demand, it did indeed become more "convenient" for them

74 CHAPTER TWO

to appropriate Spanish livestock than to hunt the depleted stocks of deer and bison. The irony was that they did so only to sell to other Spaniards and old trading partners.[12]

Guevara's suggestion that contact with Spanish towns had "corrupted" those Indians closest to them is accurate when viewed through this larger prism of indigenous economies of exchange, but also serves his political purposes by impugning his rivals.[13] Jáuregui was after all the governor of the Province of El Nuevo Reino de León, while Montecuesta was the ex-mayor of the Villa de los Valles in the Province of San Luis Potosí.[14] Guevara implied that Jáuregui and Montecuesta had both already failed in the proper method of colonization and indigenous instruction, since Potosí and Nuevo León formed part of New Spain's northern frontier "from whose refuge" these borderland Indians somehow "find themselves impeded."[15] Instead of properly protecting these docile indigenous peoples under the succor of the Crown and the church, Montecuesto and Jáuregui left them exposed to and terrorized by the fierce northern Indian nations. Significantly, on the previous page of the petition, Guevara described himself as peacefully partaking in many delicious meals of barbecued venison and maguey with these very "fierce" northern nations, leaving the reader to wonder just how threatening these nations were. He would be capable of making peace through Christian community (breaking bread), where his rivals will only make war.

A few lines later, oblivious to his argument's internal contradictions, Guevara blithely goes on to describe *both* the indigenous peoples on the margin of Spanish settlement *and* the independent northern nations as possessing "cowardly spirits" (*cobardes ánimos*) and as being divided amongst themselves. This contradiction is convenient, as they would be easily reduced into Spanish pueblos.[16] Guevara assured the king that the Spaniards would "alleviate" (*sobrellevándolos*) their suffering at each other's hands, as long as such settlement goes forth "in a particular fashion and with the experience required, experience which I have of one and another [Indian nations] from the many entries I have made to their habitats."[17] Recognizable in Guevara's petition are both Sepúlveda's Good-Samaritan-Spaniard *and* Las Casas's self-governing and docile Indians.

In *Noticias* Guevara proved himself adept at iterating and reiterating the terms of Spanish racial cartography onto the borderlands throughout his geographic description of the territory. Guevara repeatedly maps docile Indians who are potentially troublesome onto this geography of future Spanish dominion and surrounds them with troublesome Indians who are potentially peaceful. Skilled in the science of Spanish colonial map-making, Guevara is careful never to place any Indians entirely beyond the reach of Catholic persuasion, while nevertheless insisting on the need for immediate action to protect good Indians from bad. It is a delicate if confusing balancing act, a spatial practice of populating the territory that requires someone like himself, capable of distinguishing and dividing one kind of Indian from the other, so that evangelization may proceed apace.

A key example of this balancing act occurs in Guevara's extended discussion of the causes of war between the Spanish and the Indians along the northern frontier. As it is the poorest amongst the Spanish vecinos who are charged with protecting communities, Guevara explains, they inevitably drag their feet when sent in pursuit of Indian thieves. By the time these men gather to follow the offending Indians, often more than a month has passed,

> and this is the reason why the Indian aggressors are never punished and become more audacious[,] bad mouthing the Spanish government[.] Well [,] punishing those responsible for these invasions requires promptitude[,] rather than any number of poorly equipped soldiers[,] to reach them [the offending Indians] before they can join and confuse themselves with other innocent nations that often times and continuously find themselves paying for these aggressions at the hands of the Spaniards, [who] with sadness take the lives of their wives and children[.] And not the least of the prejudicial consequences of this is that the aggrieved seek vengeance and as they are so hurt, the perverse ones who have caused all this damage count on this to cajole and convince them [the innocent Indians] to commit even greater invasions, lying to them to rally their spirits, saying they [the Indian aggressors] have also been mistreated and abused in the same way. And this is the reason for so much agitation and volatile relations between Indians and Spaniards, proceeding all from the humiliating offenses by bad *Naturales* that [are paid for] by the others.[18] (Ladrón de Guevara 1738)

Guevara is explaining the disastrous confusion that ensued after an incident of livestock appropriation, when "Indian aggressors" breach the borders of the "innocent nations" and confuse themselves therein, making it impossible to distinguish guilty from innocent. However, in his language we are also privy to the confusion that necessarily ensued from the given categories of imagined Indians available to Guevara for reiteration. For in this passage, categories blend and boundaries are transgressed, as "aggrieved" Indians become linguistically confused with Indian "aggressors" seeking vengeance, and Indian aggressors become aggrieved Indians testifying to their own abuse at the hands of Spanish soldiers. Guevara's lack of punctuation, his ambivalent syntax, only serves to underscore the confusion entailed when attempting to distinguish aggressive Indians from innocent ones, to differentiate bad Indians and good. This confusion generated in Guevara's account, however, is not somehow outside of the discursive terms of colonial settlement, in excess of them. Rather, the shifting coordinates of indigeneity *enabled* the colonial mission to continue: the Spanish must continuously sort and classify indigenous difference, determining good Indians from bad, and bringing difference into Christian unity.

If Guevara's self-interested *Noticias* belie the political intrigue among Spanish elites competing to populate this area, as well as his visceral imagining of the racial geography in the making, his testimony also bore witness to the larger processes of spatial reorganization transpiring at the northern frontier of empire. The punctual indigenous geographies of the region coexist, heterotemporally, with the emergent Spanish racial geography. In other words, the *time* of Spanish settlement does not simply impose itself on indigenous time, usurping it. Indigenous time persisted, intercalated with Spanish colonial time. Guevara's *Noticias* registers the disparate and at times violent spatial practices of competing communities, each in turn attempting to reinscribe, maintain, or adapt the *meaning* of the geography of this northern frontier to match their worldview—to (re)signify the geography according to the requirements of their particular economic, social, political, religious, and protoracial relations.[19] Guevara's *Noticias* documents the frustrated efforts by Spanish colonizers to reinscribe the geography of this frontier according to the requirements of Spanish dominion by properly pacifying the indios of the region, reducing them to delimited, discrete Indian pueblos or missions alongside Spanish pueblos. To poblar was not to eliminate the indigenous but to imbue the spatial relation between Spanish and Indian pueblos with an appropriate hierarchical meaning. Accordingly, Guevara imagined the Indians he mapped for the Crown as alternately heathen and adversarial, heathen and friendly, or heathen and indifferent; all categories were amenable to the exigencies of Spanish colonization. As Mexican historian José R. de la Torre Curiel states: "Frente a naciones como los apaches, la corona española ensayó variados intentos de asimilación, alíanza, subyución y exterminio según cambianan las cicunstancias de la frontera septentrional novohispana" (When confronted with nations like the Apache, the Spanish Crown tried various strategies of assimilation, alliance, subjection, and extermination depending on the changing circumstances on the northern frontier.) (De la Torre 2011, 3). Guevara's flexible ascription, then, corresponded to the ever-changing strategies and exigencies of Spanish governmentality toward the indios bárbaros of the frontier: assimilation, alliance, subordination, or extermination.

In Guevara's ethnographic detail we glimpse the punctual practices of indigenous people determined by the particular point of their geographical articulation, but at times these punctual practices had been transformed by colonial incursion. As already suggested, the "robos" committed by both friendly and hostile Indians combined a punctual practice of trade amongst indigenous communities with a new mode of production introduced by the Spanish pueblos.[20] The appropriation of livestock enabled the Apache and the Comanche, for example, to adapt in the face of the Spaniards' persistent spatial reorganization of the northern frontier, however appropriation as a spatial practice was also *contingent* on Spanish presence, as Spaniards were both the purveyors and the consumers of stolen livestock (Ortelli 2010). Thus "Indian aggressors" were successfully *triangulating* the relationship of exchange that existed between Spaniards and "innocent" indigenous agricultural communities, maintaining the *centrality* of their economic function as the purveyors of meat, fat, and hides. Moreover, whereas the Spaniards insisted on representing this spatial practice by indios like the Apache and Comanche as a treasonous act against Spanish dominion, we may speculate that the appropriation of livestock enabled indigenous peoples to represent the Spanish practice of settlement in their territories in the most advantageous light: as a means of augmenting their trade. The practice of appropriating Spanish livestock enabled the Indian aggressors like the Apache and Comanche to maintain and expand their own territories as *representational spaces*, by turning the area into coherent economic and political formations that they commanded, as we shall see in the next section and in the next chapter.

The spatial practices of livestock appropriation and trade, which entailed the transportation of herds of cattle or horses across thousands of miles along Spain's northern frontier and beyond, became more and more intricate as Spanish settlement evolved. As both Ortelli and De la Torre document in their articles on the Sonora and Nueva Vizcaya regions during the decades of 1770 and 1780, Spanish authorities discovered that a "motley crew" of its own denizens were masquerading as Apache for the purposes of rustling cattle and horses. These multiethnic groups of "ociosos, vagabundos, viciosos y gente de mal vivir" (bums, vagabonds, addicts, and people dedicated to bad living), as the Spanish referred to them, did include some disaffected Indians who had abandoned life in the pueblos or on the missions (apostates in the eyes of the Spaniards) (Felip Arispe de Neve; cited in De la Torre 2011, 5). However, they were primarily made up of mestizos, afromestizos, and even

Spaniards from the lower rungs of economic life in the towns. Sometimes these disaffected members of Spanish and Indian towns joined Apache bands outright, foreswearing their previous familial allegiances (De la Torre 2011, 4).[21] More often, they formed their own groups that, in addition to their day jobs, rustled livestock from their home communities and then traded their booty to Apache and Comanche bands. Agricultural workers joined these multiethnic groups, and as they migrated for work from one pueblo to another, they would provide reconnaissance for the "gente de mal vivir" (De la Torre 2011, 6).

In these accounts of the "enemigos dómesticos encubiertos" and the "gente de mal vivir" we witness the obverse effects of the Spanish racial geography. The very fungibility of the given categories of indio necessary for the colonial mission to proceed—the ever-shifting coordinates of faithful and faithless Indians—created a paranoid apprehension of *every* Indian as potentially the enemy. Moreover, this fungibility contaminates *all* racialized others involved in the caste system and colonizing process, those caught in the vexing psychic space of subordinate racial formations. Mestizos, afromestizos, and poor Spaniards were called on by the Spanish racial geography to identify with the interests of Spanish Crown and criollo elites as part of a hierarchical caste system. Instead, a motley crew of subalterns identified their economic, political, *and caste* interests with the bárbaros, this identification pulling them into alliance with the unfaithful indigenous subjects of the northern frontier.

Beyond the spectacular accounts of *robos* and raids discussed in Guevara's petition, we witness quotidian forms of indigenous space-making. In Guevara's protoethnographic rendering of rituals of mourning, marriage, peace, and war, he captured the coproduction of indigenous identity and space. We glean the punctual spatial practices of indigenous peoples in their inviting parajes, indexing a local temporality that contradicts any idea of unsettled or wandering Indians. The rituals described by Guevara offer the reader a meticulous set of spatiotemporal practices that embedded everyday and cyclical life in the landscapes:

> The manner these heathen nations have of maintaining themselves is that each acknowledges the limits of its territory. Within it they establish their homes which are thatched huts or adobe structures they build so that they may maintain them without much effort[.] They divide themselves in three or four groups and at a distance of 8 to 10 *leguas* from each other build their homes[,] and the Indios Grandes go into the country to hunt deer, turkeys, rabbits, turtles, and wild boar all of

which exists in abundance in the fields and in the afternoon each one returns with what they were able to kill and to cook it they make a hole in the ground in which they put coal until it is as hot as an oven and in it they will even put a whole deer, leaving the skin to protect the meat from dirt . . . after two or three hours they take it out so tender that it is falling off the bone, without having been burned or any other defect, and very delicious. (Ladrón de Guevara 1738)[22]

Guevara is describing the indigenous method of pit barbecuing, entirely new to him, in meticulous detail, as well as the mouth-watering results: the venison is tender and delicious. Again, indigenous peoples not only teach Guevara what is edible in landscape, they teach him *how* it is edible in landscape, how they encode space with the meaning of social reproduction. Thus each nation recognized and respected the limits of its territory, perhaps important in maintaining the abundance of game for hunting for each nation and peace among them. This offers the reader an alternate interpretation of the "cowardly" attitude of the borderland Indians who refused to trespass onto the territories of other "cruel" nations, one of respect rather than fear. Within their territorial limits, these nations divided themselves into smaller groups—kinship clusters of some sort—leaving a copious amount of space between each. Guevara recognized the spatial encoding for what it was: not a haphazard organization or a failure to use space properly, but a form of spatial organization requiring a strict respect of territorial limits that allow for the sustaining of game and the reproduction of peaceful social relations necessary for each nation's reproduction as a whole. While the different groups comprising a single nation may live at great distances from each other (twenty-eight to thirty-five miles), each separate group shares the evening meal together, cooking communally. The simplicity of their housing, meanwhile, is attributable to their migration pattern. The Indios Grandes remain in their homes for the duration of the prickly pear season, Guevara informs us, from June to the beginning of December. Together, women from each group gather the fruit daily, drying part of it for the winter, during which they decamp to the coasts of rivers and the gulf to live from stores of dried fruits and nuts, and from fishing.

Rather than a random wandering across the northern frontier or terra nullius, Guevara depicted a rational and rigorous spatiotemporal order composed of regular transmigrations of the nations of the Rio Grande valleys. Though the kinship clusters maintained themselves at a great distance from each other in their daily life, Guevara informs the reader that they gathered regularly, according to the cycles of the moon. Another spatiotemporal practice kept them in constant contact as well: "The general signal they use and observe to communicate with each other is the burning of dry grass that exists in the country side[,] and because the smoke rises so high, it doesn't matter how far away they are from each other, they see it, and respond in the same fashion, and *this is how they communicate and keep each other apprised of where they are*" (Ladrón de Guevara 1738; emphasis added).[23]

Both the Indios Grandes' spatial *practices* of settlement and migration and their *representation* of space (the smoke signals that map these practices for each other) indicate a complex production of geographical space for use value and for social relation. Moreover, indigenous punctual practices mediated the uses of this particular and pleasing landscape for the Spaniards on the northern frontier, as made evident in Guevara's description. Indigenous punctual practices interpret the landscape for Guevara, enabling him to envision it as habitable in innumerable ways. Throughout his representation of their punctual spatial practices, Guevara adheres to protocols established by Las Casas in *In Defense of the Indians*. Guevara repeatedly underscores the *sociality* and *polity* of the Indios Grandes, rendering them amenable to Christian unity. Earlier on in *Noticias*, Guevara describes in detail the leadership structure of the Indios Grandes: their criteria for choosing political leaders, chief hunters, treasurers, and historians. And again, like Las Casas, Guevara also repeatedly reminds us that "the docility of these infidels is great and the more remote they are the more docile and simple they tend to be," and that "the honesty they demonstrate is natural and without malice or any other type of attitude" (Ladrón de Guevara 1738).[24]

Other punctual, spatiotemporal practices also render the Indios Grandes human in the model of Catholic Christian unity. Guevara discusses the manner in which they marry—voluntarily and with the approval of the parents and elders—and the necessary migration of the groom to the kinship cluster of the bride. And he describes the manner in which their deaths are honored in spatiotemporal terms as well:

> And if [a sick person] dies they bury him/her and inside his/her grave they put his/her bow, his/her arrow, and the other things s/he might have used and they will not stop even for an instant in the place where s/he died and after a year has passed[,] during the fruit season[,] they return to where they buried him/her and they throw him/her a party that lasts all day and the party finishes with singing and dancing in the style they practice and they say that the deceased comes down from up high and tells them that up above there are better deer and fruits to

eat. . . . the form of mourning a parent observes for a child or child for the parents is to shave their whole head, for siblings half [their head], and for uncles and cousins they mix ashes with the juice of prickly pears and rub this over their face and bodies, and they will do so every time they remember the deceased. (Ladrón de Guevara 1738)[25]

If the placement of their homes and their patterns of migration organized their landscape according to the reproduction of material and social relations, their grief organized it according to symbolic relation and sacred time. They *will not* pass where a member of their nation has died for a fixed period of time; they *will* return in celebration to a burial place after a year has passed, during the "fruit season." The Indios Grandes encode the landscape with the time and space of their punctual mourning practices. Likewise, the parajes encode the grieving practices of the Indios Grandes with calendric cycle of fruit production. The indigenous peoples encode the landscape with their memories of and desires for the dead, but the landscape also encodes their identity through somatic embodiment of their grief—the Indios Grandes shave their heads or cover themselves in ashes and the juice of the local cactus fruit *whenever they remember*. Allowing for Guevara's misapprehension of what he observed, we nevertheless glean a punctual spatial organization of the geography as *representational space*, corresponding to the complex material needs *and* spiritual beliefs of these indigenous peoples. Guevara has good reason for rendering the complexity of this indigenous representational space. Though Guevara never explicitly compares Spanish rituals and those of the Indios Grandes, the spatiotemporal organization of the indigenous group's geography around rituals of marriage, death, and bereavement is nevertheless easily incorporated into Christian unity, with its own sacramental spatiotemporal order of marriage, death, and bereavement. Guevara's primer produces a visual scene/ seen of racial difference in the specificity of his detail, but it is a difference that can and should, his text implies, be brought under Spanish dominion *as* difference. In Guevara's rendering the Indians *are* different, as they need be to require the coming of the Spanish, but they are also the same, welcoming the Spanish in an attitude of brotherly love.

Apaches in the Archive, Real and Imagined

In *The Comanche Empire*, Pekka Hämäläinen (2008) argues that the Comanche were the dominant empire in what is today the U.S. Southwest and lower Great Plains from 1750 to 1850. The Comanche did not merely keep Spanish,

French, and British-American settlers at bay, Hämäläinen argues they relegated these representatives of European imperial power to the very margins of their expansive territorial empire, subjugating them militarily, exacting economic tribute, and regulating all commerce among them and neighboring Indian tribes. A similar argument could be made for Apache military dominance in the eighteenth century farther south, in the provinces of Sonora, Nuevo León, Nuevo Mexico, Texas, and Nueva Vizcaya. In line with such an argument, the title of a second collection of eighteenth-century documents from the region retrieved from the AGI, *Las Invaciones de los Apaches en el territorio de Tejas* (*Invaciones*), might suggest to the reader Ranajit Guha's "prose of counterinsurgency," with the word *invasions* indexing its obverse—the trace of the Apache subalterns' successful, even expansive, armed resistance to the brutal, overwhelming force of Spanish colonization in their homeland (1998b).[26] The trace of the anticolonial subaltern, however, is not so predictably discernible in this archive. As Mexican historiography of the period has established, it was the Comanche's success in colonizing western New Mexico and northern Texas during the second half of the eighteenth century that forced the Apache out of their established homelands into the Provincia de Texas (Ortelli 2006; González 2002; Sheridan Prieto 2002). Thus the "invasions" in the document's title registered the obverse of Apache resistance or expansion. It registered instead a period of territorial loss and forced migration for the Apache at the hands of the Comanche, into territories of central and south Texas held by *other* indigenous populations and their Spanish allies.

The event that precipitated the epistolary documentation of these Apache "invasions" was, accordingly, the first *Comanche* attack on the San Saba presidio and mission in central Texas on March 16, 1758. The attack marked a turning point for Spanish colonialism along its northern frontier. The presidio and mission were originally established by the Spaniards on the San Saba River in 1756 at the behest of the Lipan Apache, who agreed to be Christianized on missions in exchange for Spanish protection against the Comanche's systematic offensive into their territories.[27] This mission project was the culmination of a ten-year effort by the Spanish Crown and the Franciscan order to persuade the Apache in Texas onto missions or into Spanish pueblos. The Crown believed the settlement of the Apache would lead by example to the pacification of *all* the northern tribes. These missions would provide an important bridge between Spanish pueblos in Texas and New Mexico, as well as a wall against French colonial encroachment (Romero de Terreros 2004, 618). Exhausted by war with both the Spaniards and the Comanche, the Lipan Apache finally acquiesced to the terms of Spanish recognition as *pacified*

AFFECT IN THE ARCHIVE   83

Indians, their request for Christian settlement a tacit acceptance of Spain's imposed racial geography in their territory. However, Spanish efforts to graph central Texas in the hierarchical, racialized terms of Spanish and Christian dominion—to succor the Lipan Apache in pueblos and protect them from the barbarous Comanche—failed miserably. For almost twenty years, the Comanche and their allies launched repeated attacks on the presidio and its environs, until the Spanish were forced to abandon San Saba in 1772. These attacks, an expression of Comanche dominion, halted the expansion of Spaniards in Texas, indeed forcing a strategic retreat to their already established missions and presidios, such as San Antonio de Bexar and Los Adaes. After the attacks on San Saba, Spanish efforts to build missions to pacify the Apache stopped entirely. The Spanish failure to protect the Christianized Apache effectively in the San Saba and San Antonio valleys permanently tipped the military scales in favor of the Comanche over the Apache, forcing the Apache's further migration southward into New Spain.

The rivalry between the Apache and the Comanche surrounding the San Saba mission and presidio complicates any simple progressive account of previous indigenous geographies inevitably ceding ground to Spanish racial geography, as well as any straightforward account of subaltern resistance to Spanish colonization. Instead, what transpired over the course of two years of attack makes evident the heterotemporal organization of space that persisted during this period. As with the Apache robos, the Comanche attacks on the mission were not a clear and definitive strike against the Spanish colonial order. Rather, the Comanche attacked the San Saba mission and presidio because of "what they saw [as] the Spaniards' unjust support of their traditional enemy," according to Franciscan historian Juan M. Romero de Terreros (617). And because of these attacks, the Comanche succeeded in eventually bringing the Spanish into a lasting alliance with them against the Apache. Hämäläinen interprets the subsequent Apache attacks on Spanish settlements as retaliatory, attributable to Apache anger at the Spaniards' betrayal of their alliance in favor of the Comanche (2008, 61).[28] Rather than representing resistance to Spanish settlements in northern New Spain, Apache and Comanche attacks represent orchestrated efforts to alternately lure the Spanish into allegiance or punish them for their betrayal. The Spanish had intended the San Saba mission and presidio to unite all the northern "naciones indias" (Indian nations) under Christian dominion. Instead, it was the Comanche, well armed by the French, who succeeded in uniting an estimated two thousand warriors to attack the mission, representing over a dozen northern indigenous peoples. The Comanche succeeded in the spatial reorganization of dominion in the region where the Spaniards failed. And ultimately, Spanish peace with the Comanche in the region was brokered at the Apache's expense.

The contravening interests of the Comanche, the Apache, and the Spanish in the Province of Texas, their battles and negotiations over the spatial organization of the central region, attest to a lived heterotemporality that defies the progressivism of most Southwest historiography of the period. In Hämäläinen's revisionist history, he insists on a singular temporality of the Comanche "empire" that dictated the spatial organization of the region—its military, trade, and racial relations—to Europeans and other indigenous peoples for one hundred years. However, while Hämäläinen's account offers a refreshingly new set of protagonists and interpretation of events in the history of the Southwest, his historiography still adheres to a teleological progression from one spatiotemporal order to the next. Moreover, his representation adheres to what anthropologist and postcolonial scholar David Scott has called a "Romantic mode of emplotment."[29] Hämäläinen's representation of the Comanche Empire is so Romantic that Comanche's anticolonial resistance has perfectly reversed the colonial power relation: it is the Europeans who are subjected at their hands.

In *Conscripts of Modernity*, Scott (2004) explains that this mode of representing instances of anticolonial resistance has become too rehearsed in postcolonial studies. In the prologue to his book, Scott calls instead for self-reflection. He asks postcolonial scholars, including subaltern studies scholars, to consider if we have conditioned ourselves to ask formulaic questions of anticolonial texts and to demand formulaic answers:

> Does the political point of anticolonialism depend on constructing colonialism as a particular kind of conceptual and ideological object? Does the moral point of anticolonialism depend on constructing colonialism as a particular kind of obstacle to be overcome? Does the purchase or salience of anticolonialism depend on a certain narrative form, a certain rhythm, and a certain conception of temporality? Does the anticolonial demand for a kind of postcolonial future oblige its histories to produce certain kinds of pasts? (7)

By way of an answer to his rhetorical questions, Scott argues that postcolonial scholars, in their allegiance with anticolonial efforts, paint a one-dimensional picture of colonialism as degradation and exploitation. If colonialism is constructed as pure constraint, then anticolonial freedom must depend on completely overcoming it. A dichotomous representation persists in postcolonial study, Scott argues, of colonialism as abject subordination and anticolonialism as just revolt. The narrative emplotment of anticolonialism is reduced to a progressivist formula: first colonial subordination/abjection, then anticolonial awakening/struggle, finally revolutionary denouement/freedom. This representation not only limits the futures that are possible to imagine but also limits our historiography. We confront the colonial archive with predictable preconceptions, expecting, for example, an uncomplicated narrative of rapacious, genocidal colonization from the Spanish and imposing a postcolonial desire for anticolonial revolution upon the "invading" Apache.

Such a Romantic set of postcolonial expectations is frustrated by this colonial archive, as Apache invasions would wrongly reduce the complex geography of racialized relations forged in this sophisticated crossroads to a dichotomy. As Scott pithily summarizes later in his book, "picturing colonialism one way—as a system of totalizing degradation—enables (indeed obliges) the critical response to it to take the form of the longing for anticolonial overcoming or revolution" (2004, 95). Instead of this postcolonial hermeneutic Scott cautions us against, it is imperative to open the Spanish colonial archive of given Indians to a different set of questions. Thus I suggest that the events surrounding the San Saba attacks, the contestation and negotiation over the geographical inscription of this territory, present us with a picture of the rich heterotemporality of the region, a picture capturing again "the plurality that inheres in the 'now,' the lack of totality, the constant fragmentariness, that constitutes one's present" (Chakrabarty 2008, 243). The events surrounding San Saba suggest an eighteenth-century Texas in which Spanish and indigenous cultures were coterminous with each other rather than in hierarchical relation. Instead of a neat succession of events in which the Comanche and Apache were subsumed ultimately into the sequential narratives of Spanish Black Legend, Mexican ineptitude, and U.S. success, heterotemporality offers the reader a historiography in which all these positionalities—indigenous and settler, imperialist and subjugated, dominant and subaltern—are in constant, creative motion. The various actors occupying the geopolitical "now" of the late eighteenth and early nineteenth centuries constantly negotiated and adapted their cultural belief systems to each other's. The spatiotemporal orders that these heterogeneous populations inhabited were repeatedly fractured and reconstituted by alliances brokered and broken. As with the petitions for settlement in neighboring Nuevo Santander, the geographical space described in *Invaciones* disrupts our historiography of modernity, as well as our postcolonial accounts of resistive agency. Moreover, the figure of the Indian in this archive is "a memory [that] flashes up at a moment of danger . . . [in] the instant when it can be recognized . . . singled out by history," to il-

86   CHAPTER TWO

luminate a twenty-first-century "terrorist" that haunts the violent memory of the imperial U.S. citizen, suggesting contemporary U.S. imperialism against Muslim nations is also Indian given.

In 1759 Don Diego Orttiz Parrilla was a colonel in the Royal Army and the commander of the Royal Presidio San Luis de las Amarillas along the Rio San Saba, charged with protecting the nearby Santa Cruz de San Saba mission. One year after the first Comanche attack on the San Saba mission in 1758, Orttiz and his troops were at the presidio preparing for a counteroffensive against the Comanche.[30] But instead of properly protecting the faithful Apache by going on the offensive against the faithless Comanche, Orttiz had to summon the cavalry to protect him and his own troops. On March 30, 1759, a little more than a year after the first Comanche attack, Orttiz Parrilla penned this desperate note:

> I make it known that a little after sunrise, on the day of today, a large number of enemy Indians, armed with rifles, descended upon the squadron of cavalry of this Presidio and upon the largest herd of livestock, with so much intrepidness and great force of luck, that even though a major resistance was put up by our people, until well past ten in the morning, the sergeant and 19 soldiers were left dead in the same area where they took all the horses and mules, taking possession of them in their entirety, thus when our reinforcements arrived, with an officer I dispatched there immediately upon receiving news of the attack, they [the Indians] had already retreated with it [the herd], leaving only the cadavers, dispossessed of their arms, clothes, and saddles, and even as they were retreating, this officer was able *to see a multitude* of enemies, and *he heard that they wailed, as is their custom* when they lose people in battle, he decided not to attack them because of the superiority he *recognized* in them; well, the soldiers who escaped the fury of battle [reported] that the number of armed Indians was imperceptible.[31]

A racial-geography approach to the events represented in this passage allows us to notice that it is the *Spanish* who are resisting the Comanche, and whose resistance fails. Given the terms of Spanish inscription, it is not entirely surprising that the colonizer should represent his troops as resisting the "great force" of *intrepid* Indians, as the *enemy* Indian is always a savvy bárbaro. Nor is it necessarily surprising that Orttiz Parrilla reports his men faltering at the site of the enemy Indians' numerical superiority. This is, after all, the second substantial attack on the mission, with more than twice as many men killed as in the first. It is noteworthy, however, that the officer immediately dispatched

AFFECT IN THE ARCHIVE   87

by Orttiz to help the troops decides not to launch a counterattack. Colonel Orttiz describes the officer's reasoning thusly: "no se dettermino á atacarlos por la superioridad que reconcío en ellos" ("it was decided not to attack them because of the superiority he recognized in them"). The officer's *recognition* inverts the terms of Spanish racial dominion. It is suddenly the troops who need succor, protection from the superior dominion of the Comanche. Orttiz's troops are not simply taken by surprise, they are beleaguered and overwhelmed by the enemy.

The Indians in the passage are once again described in the striking terms of *visceral* perception, again indexing a form of landscape becoming Indian: a *multitude* of Indians, incalculable to the human eye in number, blankets the landscape, becomes horizon. Even more suggestive is the representation of the wailing of the enemy warriors over their dead. The officer *hears* the multitude wailing. One interpretation could be that the barbaric cry fills the officer with fear, causing him to pause rather than advance. However, his pause also suggests a more profound recognition: it is their mourning which predicates his decision not to go on the offensive against the retreating Indians. As with Ladrón de Guevara, it was their mourning that required recognition from the Spaniards and verged on identification. Certainly, the wailing marks the otherness of the Indians ("as is their custom") and graphs the landscape for the troops with exotic, barbaric sound. However, this wailing also allows for potential identification. There is a coeval nature of grief between Spaniard and Comanche suggested by this representation of the warriors' lament: at this moment, the officer recognizes the Comanche, like the Spaniards, are mourning their dead. This recognition of their bereavement in the letter registers something other than subalternity for the Comanche, I would suggest, both as historical agents in the event and as representations of otherness in Orttiz Parrilla's estimation. It would be anachronistic to suggest that the officer's (and subsequently Orttiz's) pause to recognize the Comanche recognizing their dead constituted a recognition of *equality*. However, there is an unexpected representation of the parity of the Comanche in this letter: parity in strength, feeling, and custom. The wailing indexes the heterotemporality of this racialized seen/scene of landscape in battle, at once alienating *and assimilating* the Spaniards into the graphing of Texas.

Orttiz Parilla describes a *muchedumbre de enemigos* retreating from the attack. This image of a "multitude" of enemy Indians, "imperceptible" in number is again in keeping with the coordinates of Indianness in Spanish racial geo-graphing. The letter is sent to the governor of Texas as an appeal for military aid, and thus exaggeration is in order. But even more so than in the

88   CHAPTER TWO

petitions for the settlement of Nuevo Santander, *Invaciones* documents a *multitude* of Indians filling the landscape. In *Invaciones*, eighteenth-century Texas is not a near empty natural space sparsely populated by marauding Indians, hapless Spaniards, or lazy "half-breeds," as it is most often represented in U.S. popular culture and historiography. The Province of Texas documented by the military and religious colonial agents is replete with various kinds of exceedingly competent Indians. The Spaniards endlessly taxonomize the Indians they encounter, splintering the category under the very weight of colonial precision. In *Invaciones* the military officers and Franciscan friars alike differentiate between indigenous peoples not only according to tribe and custom, but also according to demeanor and disposition. As in the petitions for settlement, the word *Indian* never appears alone in this archive. It is often followed by national affiliation: Indios Taguacanes, Zavayas, Iscanses, Hichitas, Ranitas (all comprising the Wichita peoples), Tamaces, Aranames, Atayeyes, Pampospas, Pastias, and Tejas. More often, the Indians are categorized as "Indios gentiles," "Indios apostates," "Apaches gentiles," "Apaches bárbaros," "Apaches enemigos," and most puzzling, "Indios indiferentes." In other words, as the letters document the pursuit of war and the attempts at peace in the San Saba and San Antonio valleys, it becomes increasingly important for the Spaniards to precisely calculate the exact loyalties of each group of indigenous peoples they encountered. This is no longer a theoretical emplotment of dominion to come, as in Ladrón de Guevara's geographical primer. Rather the letters function as an inventory of potential friends and deadly enemies. They attest to the reality of racial geography, as the Spanish were not simply imposing their racial perceptions, but constantly reevaluating, abandoning, or changing their perceptions of these indios who were presumably awaiting Christian unity.

The letters in *Invaciones* attest to a series of events that tested the loyalties of all these various kinds of Indians in the eyes of colonial administrators. They include a description of what appears to have been a summer spying campaign in preparation for the fall offensive against the Comanche. The spying documented in the military letters was meant to determine the location and disposition of all the indigenous people between the missions of San Antonio and Los Adaes (near what is now Natchitoches, Louisiana). Franciscan friars from the Colegio de Nuestra Señora de Guadalupe in Zacatecas sent Hispanized Indians to these missions to make contact with the indigenous groups in the region and determine if they were potential allies or likely foes. In the summer of 1758 "el Indio Sanchez" conducts a reconnaissance mission that functions as a traveling poll. He reports back that the first Comanche peoples he comes across are very well armed by the French and well situated, protected by the "montte" [tall brush] on one side and the Rio de la Trinidad (Trinity River) on the other. It would take more than a day, Sanchez assured, to traverse the area in which these Comanche reside. Although these particular Comanche claimed not to have participated in the first attack on San Saba, they did participate in the second, they said, because "they always make themselves available for battles against the Spanish" ("Carta Orttiz Parrilla," Foja 91V).[32]

After crossing the Comanche territory, Sanchez comes on the nations of the Yattasi, Caodachos, and Nadotes Indians along the Rio Brazos. There are at least twenty Frenchmen living among them, planting and harvesting fruits, and supplying these nations with gunpowder, bullets, and guns. Later, Tejas Indians report to Sanchez:

> The Spanish are not good, because they do not give them the same things the French give them which is why the Taguacanes have told them that once they finished off the Presidio at San Saba, they are going to finish off the two Missions at Natchitoches and Adaes, so that the French will come and populate these areas and from this source the other nations would be more promptly aided [against attacks by the Apache].[33]
> ("Carta Orttiz Parrilla," Foja 91R–91V)

Apparently, the French living among the Tejas had promised them that they would be able to win the war against the Apache where the Spanish had failed. In this eighteenth-century version of the telephone game, the reader discerns that the indigenous groups of northeast Texas are hailing the French, inviting them to come to them, not in the terms of Spanish dominion, as evangelizers, but as better trading partners and as smarter allies against the Apache. The indigenous groups of the region are plotting with each other and with the powerful Comanche to manage, if not control, colonial *and Apache* space-making. They vociferously switch allegiances between European powers, in the hopes of winning the war against—or at least establishing peace with— the Apache. In the very next passage Sanchez reports back that a French man has charged the Tejas Indians with the task of kidnapping Apache children so that they might sell them to him. The Indians also boast to Sanchez that when they asked the French what they should do if they come upon Spaniards hiding or defending the Apache, the French presumably told them that this is why the French have given them so many arms: so that the Indians may begin a war with Spanish.[34] Once again, the threat of the French is wielded, through the spy Sanchez, against the Spanish.

90   CHAPTER TWO

If these reports speak to the various indigenous populations brokering the terms of their inscription in the competing spatial orders of European, Comanche, and Apache geographies, the role of *el Indio Sanchez* itself indexes the nagging instability of Spanish racial coordinates for "Indianness" at this moment of crisis in Spanish geo-graphing. Presumably a Christianized Indian in the service of the Spanish, el Indio Sanchez benefited from the fungibility of the *meaning* of his Indian difference to travel safely among the various enemy tribes in northern Texas. The fungibility of his Indian difference is what enables his *betrayal* of these indigenous peoples as well, as he reports back to the Spanish what they tell him. In his hyperbolic description of these indigenous groups and of the threats posed by the French, however, Sanchez may betray his own ambivalence over his allegiance to the Spanish. Like the motley crew of multiracial vecinos who lived among the Spaniards in Nueva Vizcaya and Sonora, but nevertheless stole from them at night disguised as Apache, the "true" allegiance of el Indio Sanchez is impossible to discern. Where one might expect obsequious assurances to the Spaniards of their easy superiority, instead Sanchez repeatedly tells the Spaniards that the populations of the various indigenous nations are innumerable, fierce, and unwavering in their commitment to banish the Spaniards from their lands in favor of the French. Also, the French are clearly positioned by the Indio Sanchez as interested and capable of winning indigenous allegiance and in making war against the Spanish. Sanchez's scouting mission at once serves to caution the Spanish in taking action against the Indians, for fear of confronting a united front, and to poison the Spanish Crown's relationship with the French.

Pages and pages of these letters among Spanish officers are written in this vein: locating Indians and locating their loyalty, locating *extranjeros* (foreigners) and locating their motives. The spatial practices of the Spanish, French, English, Comanche, Apache, and innumerable other indigenous nations overlap in this heterotermporal, cosmopolitan contact zone.[35] Allegiances are being brokered and broken, bodily fluids are being exchanged, translations and transactions proliferate. In the spirit of Scott's call to postcolonial scholars to resist a Romantic emplotment in our study of colonial relations, it seems that the discourse of anticolonial "resistance" would provide too paltry a vocabulary for analyzing the complicated relationships that transpired at these metropolitan crossroads of empires (including the Comanche's) between indigenous subjects and colonial representatives. An interpretation of these indigenous peoples as specifically *subaltern* would as well place too rigid an anticolonial demand on them to perform a story line of "resistant overcoming" of Spanish colonialism, to paraphrase Scott. Instead, these scenes require an analysis of intimacy and alliance, of Christian love offered and betrayed, or of racial geographies graphed and re-graphed, in part according to indigenous desires and punctual practices.

The Spanish colonizer in these documents concerning the invasions is always trying to differentiate between los Indios gentiles (given various tribal names), los indios bárbaros or indios Apache (used interchangeably), and los indios indiferentes (also multiply named). Indeed, on such differentiation depended the very lives of the Spanish, afromestizo, mestizo, Hispanized Indians, soldiers, *subalternos*, and missionaries who are entering indigenous territories: it determines where the missionaries would go, how many troops (with their requisite subalternos) must accompany them, and when vecinos could follow. This military and Franciscan inventory of indios, in other words, did not simply chart where and what kind of Indians were in the landscape; Indians did not merely fill natural space with their social relations. Rather once again indigenous peoples *become* the spatial coordinates for mapping Spanish settlement, as everything depended on their potential allegiance, betrayal, or indifference. Indian *naciones*, named and accounted for, summoned the Spaniards forth, for settlement, peace, or war, not as the mere reiterative trace of the Valladolid controversy, but as invested, interested, and calculating agents. In *Invaciones*, even more so than in the petitions for settlement, the identities of the different indigenous peoples and the Spanish were coproduced vis-à-vis each other, and vis-à-vis a landscape that is literally coded and decoded by the multiple and shifting spaces of allegiance and conflict, but also cohabitation. This is not a scene/seen of Romantic emplotment, but a scene where everyone is busily emplotting others and themselves on the basis of where perceived interests and advantages may lie.

On first read, it appears as if there is an easy differentiation in accordance with the terms of Spanish racial geography: Indios gentiles are the heathens who allow the Spaniards to live amongst them and are open to conversion, whereas indios bárbaros are those who attack Spanish missions and settlements. The lines differentiating the indios from one another, however, are tenuous at best and are always dissolving. Like the gente de mal vivir to the south, Indios gentiles who initially join the Spaniards in Christian settlement in Texas too often "abandon" the Christian faith. These "profligates" and "apostates" then harbor Apache in their midst, or worst yet, are suspected of participating in raids and robberies. And there are also many groups of indios bárbaros—particular Apache bands—who maintain a strict policy of peace with the Spaniards, and at times are valued allies against other indigenous

92   CHAPTER TWO

peoples. Categories splinter: there are indios bárbaros on the verge of being assimilated and there are indios bárbaros who absolutely cannot be; indios gentiles who can be trusted and those who cannot be trusted; and this strange group of indios indiferentes who neither allow the Spanish to live among them nor make war against them. Thus the colonial record is permeated with Spanish anxiety, with Spanish fear, with Spanish trust betrayed, with Spanish trust rewarded, and oddly, again with love. What became clear from *Invaciones* of war and peace is how extraordinarily dependent the Spaniards were on los indios in Texas. The Spaniard appears to the reader as a thwarted lover, bitter, vengeful, violent, but sustained in the gaze of the other nonetheless. Whether or not the other completes the subject in any psychoanalytic sense remains a question; but the Spaniard *is* enthralled by the other. This imagined Indian is the Spaniard's intimate.

The imagined Indians in this rich archive are the very condition of possibility for Spanish colonialism in Texas, in a Foucaultian sense. Taxonomizing the Indians, dissecting their customs, diagnosing their tractability, inciting their loyalty, these are the motivations that emerge as the driving force in these letters and documents from *Invaciones*. Creating knowledge about the Indians, plotting them along the dual axis of faithfulness and unfaithfulness, attempting to discipline them into a recognizably proper or improper subject is the very crux of Spanish racial geography, especially at this moment of crisis concerning the limits of dominion. Salt mines, agricultural lands, and grazing pastures may provide the economic justification for settlement in Texas and Nuevo Santander, but it is the encounter with the Indian that provides the driving passion for the colonial endeavor. The Spanish settlers—whether military strategists planning attacks, missionary priests yearning for true signs of faith, or petitioners before the Crown for the right of settlement of new territories—desire to know the other intimately, in a manner akin to love.

This is a one-sided love story to be sure, as we are never privy to the sentiments of the various Indian nations except by proxy. Nevertheless, it is a story of profound entanglement that not only thwarts the Romantic emplotment of resistance that Scott argues so dominates the postcolonial imaginary, it also challenges Marxist interpretations of white settler colonialism as a singularly profit-driven project, creating racial differentiation in order to enable the dispossession and elimination of indigenous peoples for the sole purpose of primitive accumulation toward a capitalist mode of production. The accumulation made possible by the mines, the agricultural valleys, and the grazing lands—as well as indigenous labor—may well have been the economic motivation for Spanish spatial practice of empire, but representing the space in terms of a Spanish racial geography of Christian unity was of equal inducement. Imagining the landscape dotted with Spanish and indigenous towns living side-by-side, bound by brotherly love: this was the racialized *representational space* enabling Spanish colonialism. We are forced to recalibrate subaltern studies methodologies and assumptions about the inevitable abjection of the Indian, and their submission to the story of the empire.[36] Whether as historical agents or as imagined Indians, the indigenous peoples of the northern frontier were the protagonists in this history. Thus European Enlightenment and Spanish modernity emerge *from* the colonial endeavor, from the imputing of humanity on the Indians in racial terms of Christian unity. A global theory of humanity was required to mediate the colonial encounter. Indigenous humanity was endlessly calculated, named, and accounted for; and Indians were *not* simply thieves and bandits, they were more often allies and even co-conspirators. While the French enticed some indigenous peoples to their side, they also drove a number of the "indifferent" bands into the Spanish settlements. So many different kinds of intimate relations were forged in this place of contravening political interests. The Indian was never marginal to this thick archive as subaltern subject, but always at its very center.

If the imagined Indian was at the very center of this Spanish colonial archive—as ally, enemy, cook, spy, thief, wife, profligate, apostate, translator, and traitor—how is it that s/he has so completely vanished from the scene of the postcolonial U.S. nation?[37] The Spanish colonizers depended upon *their* assimilation *by* the Indians to assure their safety and comfort. In the Spanish colonial archive we find Texas and Nuevo Santander teeming with life, as rich in indigenous nations as in salt mines. The abundance of multilingual, multicultural life worlds is rarely represented as pure obstacle for either those directing military actions or those requesting rights of settlement from the Crown. To the contrary, the fact that this area is populated by indios gentiles and indios bárbaros is repeatedly represented as an opportunity—the condition of possibility—for Spanish space-making. In contemporary representations in the United States, such as *No Country for Old Men* (both novel and film), the area is represented as exactly the opposite, as a barren landscape of radical loneliness where white men tread. Recognizing the erasure of indigenous peoples from the representation of U.S. history, geography, and popular culture is certainly not new or surprising. However, this vanishing act, and the palimpsestic geographies of race that it obscures, inevitably recenters the indigenous presence and that centrality haunts the U.S. national imagination as hysterical symptom. The Indians given by these racial cartographies give back to the nation new ideological purposes for war that may well surprise us.

94   CHAPTER TWO

No Country for Old Mexicans

Hysterics suffer mainly from reminiscences. —**Sigmund Freud and Joseph Breuer,** "On the Physical Mechanism of Hysterical Phenomena"

The film *No Country for Old Men* (2007) unfolds on the central plains and in a border town of southwest Texas in the 1980s. Nevertheless, as much about the contemporary wars of U.S. empire as it is about a drug deal gone wrong, the film indexes a heterotemporality of the present U.S. racial geography and its global reach. The cinematography in the film reiterates the coordinates of a nineteenth-century U.S. racial geography: representing the southwestern landscape as bereft of indigenous presence. But the camera frames the pivotal moment in the film's action in terms that visually confuse this central Texas landscape with the landscape of U.S. war in the Middle East. This visual transposition of one landscape on the other is enabled by the figure of the nomadic, savage Indian. *No Country* functions as political allegory, representing U.S. imperial violence abroad as if it were an internal matter, a recent flaw in the otherwise ethical character of a nation. To do so, the visual language of *No Country* first enacts the psychic repression and incorporation of the contemporary U.S. global violence for the viewing audience through the character of Anton Chigurh, who functions as a collective hysterical symptom. Secondly, and unsuccessfully, the film attempts to repress the cosmopolitan intersection of Spanish colonial and indigenous geographies from the seen/scene of the film's landscape, the central Texas counties of San Saba and Comanche. Uncannily, the action of the film transpires in the very same geographical location as the "Apache invasions," but the Indians who filled the locations depicted in *Invaciones* appear to have vanished—or rather been banished—from the film's action. However, with attention to the heterotemporal racial geographies of the region, we can deconstruct the film's encoding of the landscape as emptied of Indians, finding instead the punctual Indian who refuses to cede ground, willingly or unwillingly. Whereas the area was a thoroughfare of settler and indigenous interaction in the colonial archive, in the film the Comanche and Apache have been reduced to a trace, a historical anachronism recalled at the film's end as a parable about the white sheriff's isolation: the vanished Indian interiorized as the loss at the heart of masculine melancholia. Beyond the sheriff's melancholia, heterotemporally haunting the racial scene/seen of the film, is the insistent presence of Chigurh, who embodies Frisbie's "wandering savage who traverses the wilds of America" from chapter 1.

The action in *No Country* revolves around a simple plot. While hunting pronghorn deer, Vietnam veteran Llewelyn Moss (Josh Brolin)—from San

Saba County—stumbles across a drug deal gone wrong on the Texas range. With every Mexican involved in the drug deal shot dead except for a dying man who begs for "agua," Llewelyn decides to keep a satchel he finds there containing $2 million. Chigurh (Javier Bardem), a professional assassin hired to retrieve the money, inexplicably kills every bystander in his path, including his own employers, in pursuit of Llewelyn. Marginal to this plotline, but central to the narrative of the film, the introspective county sheriff Ed Tom Bell (Tommy Lee Jones) follows the trail of dead bodies and clues. Ed Tom hopes to save Llewelyn and his wife from the assassin, but spends most of his time on screen in melancholic rumination about the changes sweeping over the Texas landscape. Indeed the film begins with a two-minute voiceover by Ed Tom reflecting on the lost times of his father and grandfather from whom he inherited his badge, while the camera offers the audience several wide-angle shots of a barren, isolated desert prairie. Ed Tom's voiceover comes to an end as the camera pans from the landscape to a deputy arresting Chigurh and placing him in a police car, "The crime you see now it's hard to even take its measure. It's not that I'm afraid of it. I always knew you had to be willing to die to even do this job. But I don't want to push my chips forward and go out and meet something I don't understand. *A man would have to put his soul at a hazard.* He'd have to say 'okay, *I'll be part of this world'*" (emphasis added).

This opening voiceover introduces the western landscape as a character in the film, depicted as an expansive, virtually empty horizon, somewhat tamed by its broken barbwire fences, leaning telephone poles, and old-time windmills (figs. 2.1 and 2.2). These opening scenes of virtually undisturbed landscape set the tone of the film as nostalgic for a simpler, peaceful time of ethical clarity. It is the landscape of Fredrick Jackson Turner's open frontier, one that awaits the coming of white masculinity to unleash its potential for democratic egalitarianism. But it is also evokes Walter Prescott Webb's Great Plains, with their ferocious and cunning equestrian tribes. The arrest of Chigurh at the close of the landscape scenes serves to associate him with the changing nature of evil that is descending on this familiar southwestern landscape, changes that are a "hazard to the soul." Finally, Ed Tom's voiceover leaves hanging for the duration of the film the open question: What world would the Sheriff have to be a part of? The geography of 1980s central and southwest Texas saturated with the drug trade and with the blood of its perpetrators and victims? Or is there another world, one that heterotemporally haunts the film from its narrative *future*? One toward which Ed Tom's voiceover provides a bridge? Ed Tom's voiceover throws into relief the psychic distress of the

FIGS. 2.1.–2.2. From the opening scenes of *No Country for Old Men*, directed by Ethan and Joel Coen.

protagonist, as the words "Okay, I'll be a part of this world" indicate his melancholic state; Ed Tom has *already* withdrawn his libidinal attachment from "this world" of which he refuses to be a part. The rest of the film may be read as his seeking after the lost objects that haunt white masculinity. In the psychic structure of melancholia, these lost objects are *already* incorporated into his racial unconscious.

With his odd pageboy haircut, his neutral accent, and his ambiguous name, Chigurh is quintessentially foreign, but his foreign origin is indecipherable. Mexicans, the other "foreigners," are the oddly familiar violent banditos and colorful mariachis of the western genre, their banal racist depiction hardly raises an eyebrow. But Bardem's character is inscrutable. And it is precisely on this inscrutability that the political allegory of the film hinges. Chigurh is the jihadist within. Like the September 11 Al Qaeda suicide bombers who surreptitiously learn how to fly and then fashion airplanes into missiles, Chigurh is stealthy, with an eerie ability to improvise weapons out of everyday technology. Chigurh chokes the deputy sheriff with the very handcuffs that are meant to imprison him; uses a cattle gun to kill instantly and to break the locks of any door in his way. While the loud and bombastic Mexicans might reiterate the indios bárbaros of Spanish colonialism, Chigurh appears to be the foreigner who cuts across the landscape undetected.

Chigurh, however, is inscrutable in another way tying him more closely to contemporary representations of Islamic jihadists. His rigid ethical system is repeatedly underscored for the viewer. Chigurh decides the fate of his victims according to an absolute set of principles that are as unfathomable to the victim as they are to the viewer. He spares the life of a gasoline station owner whom he finds despicable for inheriting the station from his wife but takes the life of Llewelyn's innocent widow Carla Jean, even though he has already recuperated the $2 million. The assassin hired in turn to stop Chigurh assures Llewelyn that there is no way to escape Chigurh's vengeful sense of justice, "He's a peculiar man. You might even say he has principles, principles that transcend money or drugs or anything like that. He's not like you, hell he's not even like me." Like Chigurh's justice, Islamic fundamentalism is represented in U.S. media as peculiar: extremist, incomprehensible, savage, yet self-avowedly ethical. Indeed, this constitutes it's "terror": it is terrifying not knowing why the nation is held to account by the jihadists. Though the film unfolds in the early 1980s, Chigurh embodies the jihadist terror that haunts the contemporary national imagination as he exacts his wrath across central and southwest Texas.

If Chigurh embodies the swift, irrational justice/terror of the jihadist in this political allegory, Sheriff Ed Tom Bell embodies rational, measured Judeo-Christian law. The parallelism suggested between Ed Tom and Anton begins with their homonymous names but continues as Ed Tom tracks Anton, mirroring his steps down to one of the last scenes, in which the camera captures the two men standing identically on either side of a motel door (figs. 2.3 and 2.4). In this parallelism Ed Tom represents the opposite of Anton: transparent, folksy, wise, and kind. His loving wife sends him on his way on horseback to the scene of the initial shootout between the drug dealers with the admonition not to get hurt and to "hurt no one."

The scene of Ed Tom and his deputy on horseback establishes the heterotemporality of the landscape. Not only did all the drug runners arrive at

98   CHAPTER TWO

FIG. 2.3. Javier Bardem as Anton Chigurh standing on opposite side of door from Tommy Lee Jones as Sheriff Ed Tom Bell.

FIG. 2.4. Tommy Lee Jones as Ed Tom Bell outside motel room door on opposite side from Bardem/Chigurh.

the scene in trucks, the audience has witnessed several trucks and cars arrive by Ed Tom's arrival. Thus the sheriff on horseback again elicits the "simpler times" of Turner and Webb's Western frontier justice alluded to in Ed Tom's initial voiceover, a time when white lawmen like the Texas Rangers brought order on horseback by ridding the landscape of inept Mexicans and savage Indians. Yet men on horseback also suggest an outdated system of U.S. law, outmatched and overwhelmed by the "war on terror" and the "war on drugs" conflated in the figure of Anton. The sheriff and his deputy always arrive after Anton or the *narcos* have struck and are incapable of saving Llewelyn and

AFFECT IN THE ARCHIVE 99

Carla Jean from either. From his initial voiceover to the scene in which he decides to let Chigurh escape, Ed Tom is incapable of paying the price this new war exacts on his principles, walking away from Anton because he knows he cannot win without "hazarding his soul." He retires as sheriff and spends the rest of the film contemplating his ethical system and relationship to the law. As an allegory of the political context of the film's release date, Ed Tom's crisis of faith suggests the United States should have walked away from the wars in Afghanistan and Iraq as the sinister tactics of the jihadist required the compromise of the United States' liberal principles.

Underscoring this political allegory, the film ends with Ed Tom recounting for his wife (Tess Harper) two melancholic dreams about his father. We hear the ticking of a clock getting louder, suggesting the urgency of the moment. In the first dream Ed Tom's father gives him "some money," which the son fears he has lost, representing his highly valuable inheritance as a lawman put at risk by the events that have just transpired. Allegorically, the dream emblemizes the loss of ethical principles by the illegal tactics used by the United States in the current war against "terror." In the second dream, Ed Tom is lost in a blizzard when the father appears bearing light in the darkness: "When he rode past I seen he was carrying fire in a horn, the way people used to do." This second dream suggests the "father's law"—the foundation of the U.S. ethical character—may ultimately provide the guiding light in this newfound wilderness. The father's law will prevail as a beacon over time, even if Ed Tom fears he may have failed those principles in the moment. But if Ed Tom fails to uphold ethical principles of modern international law, he is also unwilling to betray them. Like a true melancholic in response to the loss that he cannot mourn, Ed Tom is paralyzed into inaction, his retirement representing his libidinal withdrawal, his refusal "to be a part of this world."

As a political allegory the film interiorizes the U.S. global war on terror in the figure of Ed Tom, representing it as a crisis of conscience, as the soul searching of an otherwise law abiding nation: will we betray our principles and "hazard our souls" by policing the world through illegitimate means? Or should we simply retire from the "inherited" role as the global sheriff? The film's political allegory is contingent on the one-way view of U.S. historiography and historical time: from a nation that forged its exemplary liberal principles in the simple, ethical frontier landscape to one that *just now* finds itself provoked into betraying principles in a violent war perpetrated by "evildoers" outside the bounds of reason. Texan Tommy Lee Jones, with his morose but ultimately kindhearted masculinity, is key to the allegory. Ed Tom represents a white masculinity paralyzed by the melancholic loss of abstract principles of justice and fair dealing—that light in the horn—a loss projected onto the figure of his (founding) father (not as the eastern, revolutionary elite but as frontier everyman). Importantly, it is Chigurh who provokes this loss with *his* savage methods of war, of which "it's hard to even take [their] measure." While the *consequences* of the U.S. war on terror are entirely internalized as a crisis of conscience that brings on an isolationist state of national melancholia, the *causes* for the betrayal of principles are entirely externalized. It is the foreigners, both those familiar Mexican *narcos* and unfamiliar jihadists, who have instigated this war and this loss of principle.

The terms of the film's political allegory end with this introspective conclusion, an attempt to insulate an American audience from the global effect of the violence perpetrated by the United States in the name of freedom. The legacy of U.S. imperialism, however, erupts heterotemporally throughout the film's action through the figure of the Vietnam veteran Llewelyn Moss. The first time that Chigurh kills a man with his cattle gun, he politely asks him, "Would you hold still, please, sir?" Immediately after this killing, the camera cuts to Llewelyn hunting deer. As he looks through the sight on his rifle, and as we look with him holding the deer in his/our sight, we hear Llewelyn say to the deer "you hold still." Not only is the Vietnam veteran conflated with Anton and his dispassionate killing through the imperative to "hold still," so too is the audience, as our sight and sound is aligned with Llewelyn's. Whereas Ed Tom is Anton's antonym, Llewelyn is cast as his synonym, seeing and moving as he sees and moves. Indeed, he is the only character in the film who in any way equals Anton's ingenuity or who lands a shot on Anton. In the end, it is not Anton, but the Mexicans who kill Llewelyn, suggesting Anton meets his match in this Vietnam veteran. By pitting Llewelyn against Chigurh in this way, the film's allegory suggests the United States is once again pursuing a losing war of containment in its current policing of the Middle East. Llewelyn, though by no means represented as effeminate, is nonetheless feminized vis-à-vis Chigurh by his name, pronounced "Lu-Ellen," suggesting the loss of another war of containment again unmans the United States. Ed Tom's melancholic crisis of conscience over the loss of U.S. ethical principle and effective masculinity are propped onto Anton, but the origin of the film's melancholy is Vietnam, the first military intervention that the U.S. loses. Indeed, the history of U.S. global intervention casts a shadow onto the Texas/Middle Eastern landscape. As Anton says to another Vietnam veteran Carson Wells and to the audience before killing him, "If the rule you followed brought you to this, of what use was the rule?"

Visually, U.S. violence in Iraq and Afghanistan is transposed onto the southwestern landscape through the seen/scene of the shootout. As Llewelyn tracks the deer he shot but failed to kill, he comes on the drug deal gone wrong. Again, the perspective of the camera and viewer is aligned with Llewelyn's. He comes to the top of a hill that looks out onto the shot-up trucks, pools of blood, and several racialized dead bodies (figs. 2.5 and 2.6). The scene, staged in the middle of the sandy desert of central Texas, at once harkens forward and backward from the narrative time of the film. The bloated, brown bodies, the blood-stained sand, are visually reminiscent of television coverage of the Iraq and Afghanistan wars, of news screens filled with desert landscapes similarly plotted with discarded vehicles and brown, bloated bodies.

Enabling this superimposition of Texas and Middle Eastern landscapes of death are the racial geographies of the United States and Mexico. The expendability of the brown body in the Texas landscape represented on screen indexes an earlier expendability of the imagined Indian from the scene/seen of the U.S. frontier. The mestizo bodies of Mexicans also recall the less spectacular death of the indigenous peoples of the northern frontier through Spanish conversion and assimilation. When read in conjunction with the colonial archive, this key scene on the arid Texas plain allows us to recall the Comanche attacks on San Saba where bodies were also lost in battle and understand the manner in which the Comanche and the Spanish racial geographies continue to inform and enable the film's representational coding of space. But it also allows us to recall an even prior scene of indigenous space produced in the practice of bereavement, discussed in Guevara's petition. Indigenous bereavement heterotemporally haunts *and informs* the racialized landscape of San Saba and Comanche counties and the film. Meanwhile, imagined Indians enable the production of Iraq and Afghanistan as landscapes of liberation. Heterotemporal representations of implacable Plains Indians enable the U.S. theater of war by mediating the representation of the Islamic terrorist and projecting images of conquered indigenous territory onto the Middle East. The perspective of racial geography allows us to discern both the imagined Indian who will cede ground to U.S. liberation and the punctual Indian who refuses to cede ground in the film and in the landscape of Texas, the indigenous present that holds its ground even when it appears banished.

Psychoanalytically, this heterotemporal indigenous present refuses successful repression by the film's unconscious, living on in the melancholia of Ed Tom and the landscape. Toward the end of the film Ed Tom visits his cousin, a man named Ellis who had been his grandfather's deputy. This older cousin is wheelchair bound, having been shot and paralyzed by a criminal during an arrest. He has not only libidinally withdrawn from the world because of his paralysis, he is withdrawn from the world visually, as the scene,

102   CHAPTER TWO

FIG. 2.5. Burning car in a landscape, reminiscent of scenes of war in Iraq.

FIG. 2.6. Two sheriffs arriving on horseback, overlooking a crime scene.

shot in a tight frame, contains him. One glimpses the brightness of the exterior landscape through a window, but the kitchen is dark and withdrawn from light. Immediately Ellis throws out any bucolic vision of the past. Ed Tom comes in search of solace but instead Ellis tells the story of an event that transpired in 1909:

> Your uncle ever tell you how uncle Mac came to his reward? Gunned down on his own porch over in Hudspeth County. Seven or eight of them come up there, *wanting this, wanting that.* Uncle Mac went in the back in the house to get the shotgun. Well, they was ahead of him. Aunt

AFFECT IN THE ARCHIVE 103

Ella come out, tried to stop the bleeding. Uncle Mac all the while trying to get that shotgun. They sat on their horses watching him die. After a while, one of 'em said something in Indian and they turned. . . . What you got ain't nothing new. This country's hard on people. (emphasis added)

If the violence confronting Ed Tom is nothing new, its reiterative nature is peculiarly illuminated by what the emotionally crippled and melancholically withdrawn Ellis tells us. These men who come speaking "Indian," "wanting this, wanting that," reiterate the Spanish colonial archive, with its representation of the multiethnic racial geography replete with raids and "robos," but also with translation and trade. As in *Invaciones*, the Indians come *speaking* and *wanting* something, seeking social relation, reciprocity, and economies of exchange. By 1909, however, they are met with incomprehension, as a monolingual Uncle Mac instinctively reaches for the gun. The naming of San Saba and Comanche counties commemorates the event of initial Spanish incursion, as well as prior indigenous possession, but popular representations of Texas in historiography have erased this richly coproduced space from contemporary historical memory. By 2007, *No Country* has reduced the "multitude" of indigenous populations rendered with such specificity in the Spanish archive to a historical anachronism of men who came "speaking Indian."

Dipesh Chakrabarty (2000) offers insight into the investment in the representation of history as anachronism, one that illuminates the representational strategies at work in *No Country* as well:

What is invested in the practice of anachronism that allows us to reify the past into an object of study? . . . If the rise of modern historical consciousness speaks of the coming of a certain modern and political way of inhabiting the world, I suggest that it also speaks of a very particular relation to the past. This is the desire on the part of the subject of political modernity both to create the past as amenable to objectification and to be at the same time free of this object called "history." (244)

Ellis's anachronistic reference to the "Indians" expresses just such a desire. This "Indian killing" is offered to Ed Tom as an object lesson about the transhistorical problem of "foreign" evils to the landscape that is at once central Texas and the United States: whether Indian, Mexican, or Islamic, there will always be a foreigner uncomprehending of our democratic landscape, or so threatened by it that they attack without reason. Simultaneously, by objectifying the Indian as a relic of the past, the film frees the viewer from history,

104   CHAPTER TWO

from any responsibility in the genocidal history that founds the nation. The Indians have gone, there is nothing to be done. In objectifying the Indian as a monochromatic anachronism, the film not only evacuates the colonial archive of its punctual heterotemporality, more importantly, it evacuates the present of its heterotemporality as well. The film never allows the victor and the vanquished of the United States's expansionist past to occupy the present simultaneously. Instead they are reduced to anachronisms or caricatures. If the Indian is anachronism, confined to the past and ineligible for redress, the Mexican is caricature with no place in the future of Texas or the United States.

Ellis's soliloquy on violence in central Texas reminds the viewer of the turn of the century, when white and indigenous relations were at the heart of the violence in the region. The film reduces the taxonomical specificity of indigenous peoples in the Spanish archive to the U.S. generic term *Indian*. As represented by Ellis, in the U.S. national imaginary of this period between the vanquishing of a multitude of Indians militarily and the banishing of them from historical memory, there is no need for distinguishing allies or differentiating enemies. Instead of the multilingual geographies of racial and cultural difference in need of constant translation and negotiation we witnessed in the Spanish archives, in Ellis's speech there is only the anachronism of the bloodthirsty and cowardly Indians who incomprehensibly shoot unarmed men in the back. Nevertheless, within this anachronism we must locate the trace of the Comanche who speaks even when s/he has been erased from the historical record, of the Apache who speaks the violence of a historical erasure. The violence represented by the film is not just the allegorical violence of the jihadist who seeks retaliation for the U.S. imperial ventures abroad, but the repressed violence of the initial colonial encounter: the violent appropriation and expropriation by the United States of a "muchedumbre" of racial others, reduced to the singular talking Indian. In *this* reading of the film, the character of Chigurh does not represent the quintessential foreigner after all but the original indigenous inhabitants who refuse anachronistic reduction, who refuse to cede their territory even after dispossession has occurred. The imagined Indian who heterotemporally traverses the melancholic landscape haunts it as a loss that refuses to be mourned and forgotten: the Indians came wanting this land back! Incorporated into a melancholic historical unconscious represented by Ed Tom and the landscape, like all lost objects, indigenous people refuse to remain lost.

A country—a racial geography of nation—wrought by such origins is indeed "hard on people." Interpreting Chigurh as the heterotemporal reiteration of punctual indigenous presence in landscape allows another alternative interpretation of Ed Tom's melancholia as well. Rather than representing a recent loss of abstract principles brought on by the wars against Vietnam or against Iraq and Afghanistan, the elusive Chigurh stands in for the loss of these principles at the foundation of the nation. The "simpler time" of frontier historiography never existed. There was only the constitutive fraudulence of liberal ideals of self-determination and democratic inclusion.

Anton Chigurh is a hysterical symptom, somatizing the melancholic loss of abstract principles at the birth of the U.S. nation and the repression of the untimely Indian at once. His iterations of violence function as a hysterical symptom. Just as in the film he physically embodies Ed Tom's fear of losing his democratic principles in the face of violence, so too does he physically embody the U.S. public's fear provoked by the 9/11 attack. In "Mechanism of Hysterical Phenomena," Freud, with Joseph Breuer, explains the causes and expression of hysterical symptoms thusly:

> Our investigations reveal, for many, if not most, hysterical symptoms, precipitating causes which can only be described as psychical traumas. Any experience which calls up distressing affects—such as those of fright, anxiety, shame or physical pain—may operate as a trauma of this kind. . . . In the case of common hysteria it not infrequently happens that, instead of a single, major trauma, we find a number of partial traumas forming a group of provoking causes. These have only been able to exercise a traumatic effect by summation and they belong together in so far as they are in part components of a single story of suffering. (Freud and Breuer 1974, 56)

By "common hysteria" Freud refers to the most common expressions that hysterical symptoms may take: the cough, the twitch, the dead limb. Against the grain, I read "common hysteria" as the hysteria shared in common by the U.S. public in response to the trauma of 9/11. As the embodiment of psychical trauma—as trauma made matter—Chigurh is "traumatic effect by summation," bringing together the psychical trauma suffered by U.S. citizens on 9/11 because "they belong together [as] a single story of suffering." However, I would like to focus on the fourth distressing affect specified by Freud and Breuer: *shame.*

What if Chigurh is the embodiment of a repressed, national shame? A shame that is at once the consequence of the dispossession of indigenous peoples of their lands, and of the neocolonial interventions of the United States across the globe and across time that dispossess people of their resources. What if each neocolonial intervention exacted a psychic toll of shame on the national imaginary of a country presumably based on anticolonial, noninterventionist, democratic principles? Rather than embodying the major trauma of 9/11, the violence Chigurh exacts across the American landscape embodies the innumerable places taken in by U.S. empire, the racial geography of U.S. imperialism, graphed through the reduction of indigenous peoples to reservations. Chigurh registers the partial trauma of each and every U.S. illegal intervention since the nation's inception that has marked its growth. Together, the domestic racial graphing of the geo, and the extension of this racial geo onto the globe, "form . . . a group of provoking causes" of shame. The shameful trauma of U.S. racial geography domestically and its intervention across the globe belong together "in so far as they are . . . components of a single story of suffering" by a global population subjected to U.S. domination. In this reading of Chigurh as hysterical symptom—as the hysterical figure of the vanishing Indian who registers the cost of this erasure and exacts its cost psychically—he can function as a bridge out into the world, rather than as the cause for melancholic retreat from it and provides the occasion for reflection about the suffering of the millions of people who have suffered the consequences of U.S. (neo)colonial geo-graphing at home and abroad.

3

MAPPING ECONOMIES OF DEATH
From Mexican Independence to the Treaty of Guadalupe Hidalgo

The events of the first half of the nineteenth century radically redrew the map of North America. First, the United States created "Indian territory" west of the Mississippi through the 1830 Indian Removal Act, which required the expulsion of most indigenous peoples from the eastern seaboard. Subsequently, it appropriated half of Mexico's territory through the 1848 Treaty of Guadalupe Hidalgo, which required the annexation of a multiracial, formerly sovereign Mexican population. These two cartographic events were intricately if subtly related (Medina 2009; Delay 2008; Aboites Aguilar 1991; Adams 1991; Weber 1981). While Mexico and the United States vied for control over the spatial reorganization of what is today the U.S. Southwest, they were also necessarily vying for control with the powerful Comanche, Apache, Seri, and Kiowa peoples, whose own spatial organization of the central plains was transformed by—but was also transforming of—national spaces. The transformation of colonial spaces into national ones collided most spectacularly in 1846, with the U.S.–Mexico War. Consequently, Mexican and U.S. racial geographies— their liberal visions of the scene/seen of nation—were, in Lefebvre's terms, "intercalated, combined, superimposed" along the border. The incommensurability of the superimposed racial geographies of these two nations was most evident in the application of the Treaty of Guadalupe Hidalgo, particularly in those articles pertaining to the rights of citizenship that *all* annexed adult Mexican men *should* have enjoyed under the auspices of the U.S. government. However, these distinct racial geographies also at times combined and colluded, particularly in the construction of the nineteenth-century indio bárbaro beyond assimilation into either nation. This shared racial imaginary of a savage indigeneity at once inside *and* outside the nation determined the permissible forms of lived indigenous territoriality that persist today.

Genealogically, indios bárbaros emerged in the colonial record of New Spain as the term used interchangeably with the Náhuatl term *Chichimecas*, used to designate all the northern peoples outside the Aztec empire, who were subsequently outside New Spain. On one hand, the Spanish use of the term *bárbaros* to describe these outliers preserved the Greek origin of the word, indicating foreigners or strangers. On the other, *bárbaros*, like the term *Chichimecas* for the Nahuas, also indicated a nomadic incivility, a heathen recalcitrance. The Nahuas had considered these northern tribes who resisted incorporation into their empire too inferior even for sacrifice to the gods. Nevertheless, as previously discussed, for Spanish administrators and vecinos of the northern frontier, indios bárbaros existed on a continuum of Christian unity, of Catholic humanity, not outside of it. Indios bárbaros could be friends and allies, or mortal enemies, but the steadfast intent of Spanish Empire was to bring them (by persuasion or force) under the mantel of Christian dominion. When a particular group of indios bárbaros entered into peaceful relations with the Spanish they ceased to be designated as such. In keeping with the debate at Valladolid, the bárbaro's condition was considered remediable, capable of shifting from recalcitrant foreigner to intimate relation. This happened with several Apache clans in Nuevo Mexico, Texas, and Chihuahua who ceased to be indios bárbaros—undifferentiated Apache—becoming instead Lipan or Mescalero upon peace with the Spanish. Unlike their Anglo-American counterparts for whom Indian savagery came to signify an inevitable vanishing from the scene/seen of empire and nation, for the Spaniards the indios bárbaros filled the landscape with the promise of colonial mission. As discussed in chapters 1 and 2, every discursive manifestation of indios bárbaros was always also an opportunity for geographical production: for the spatial practice of settlement, the representation of landscape, the perception of indigenous places as fetchingly hospitable or temporarily inhospitable to vecinos.

In examining the nationalist transformations of the geography of "frontier" between two emerging countries, we must discern the spatio-temporality of the indio bárbaros, their discursive transformation, but also their displacement in and through geography. Mexican, Apache, Comanche, and U.S. forces mobilized competing, shifting, and at times combined modalities of spatial organization in the first half of the nineteenth century. Mexican racial geography at first encompassed the Apache and Comanche, but eventually relocated them firmly outside the space of the nation. Apache and

Comanche raiders played a part in regraphing the Mexican geo into a national space averse to their presence as indios bárbaros, as these raiders attempted to maintain and augment their forms of territoriality in the wake of U.S. and Mexican independence and in the aftermath of U.S Indian removal (Delay 2008). After the end of the U.S.–Mexico War and the United States' triumphant regraphing of the geo west of the Mississippi into its own national territory, these same Apaches and Comanche were removed from the scene/seen of both nations, forced to choose between assimilation or death in Mexico and confinement on reservations by an increasing professionalized military in the United States. The indios bárbaros of northern Mexico congealed into a fixed idea of barbarism at once *spatially inside* the national boundaries of both countries, but *temporally outside* the historical time of nationhood.

The fixity of the indio bárbaro in the nineteenth-century Mexican racial imagination marked the ossification of the fluid racial geography of Spanish colonialism into polarized and mutually exclusive forms of indigeneity: those capable of (national) reason and those entirely foreign to it. The indio bárbaro, incapable of reason, became the point of collusion between the U.S. and Mexican racial geographies, congealing into a figure of dangerous difference threatening territorial cohesion of both nations in the aftermath of the U.S.–Mexico War. This would have unforeseen consequences for annexed Mexicans after 1848, those kissing cousins of these imaginary indio bárbaros, as we shall see in chapter 4.

Mexican Liberalism in Indigenous Territories (1810–1870)

Que asi como sesaron sus antiguas cargos, han terminado sus pribilegios, quedando igual, unos y otros, a todos los demas ciudadanía que con ellos forman la gran familia Mejicana. (Just as all their ancient obligations have ceased, so too their privileges have ended, as they are left equal, one and another, to all other citizens that form part of the great Mexican family.) —On Indian rights as citizens, minutes from New Mexico's Land Commission, assigned the task of evaluating requests for privatization of underutilized Pueblo communal lands, March 3, 1825

Violence not only characterizes these histories; it also becomes a primary lens for accessing and analyzing them. **—Ned Blackhawk**, "The Displacement of Violence"

After years of oscillating between negotiation and war with the Apache and Comanche, Bernardo de Gálvez, Bourbon reformer and viceroy of the northern Provincias Internas, finally established peaceful relations with each nation on behalf of the Spanish Crown in the 1780s (Weber 2005, 183–186).[1] This peace required a significant transformation in Spanish missionary policy and colonial mapping of dominion, a transformation brought about by the successful evasion of *reducción* by generations of Apache and Comanche. Unlike other indigenous peoples of the Internal Provinces, Apache and Comanche clans were no longer required to move permanently onto Spanish missions or into Indian pueblos as a sign of their submission. Nor were they required to give up their extensive ranging and roaming practices in favor of agricultural cultivation and settlement.[2] Instead they were allowed to come onto Spanish missions as they saw fit, to alternate between staying with missionaries who were required to provide them with food, clothing, and supplies, and ranging throughout their territories to hunt and trade with Pueblo Indians of New Mexico and Texas. With this new, tactical mode of colonial governmentality, the Spanish were able to minimalize the economic and social effects of Apache and Comanche raids for livestock and slaves on the haciendas and pueblos of the northern frontier. Indeed, the governors of the northern provinces were under strict orders *not* to pursue Apache and Comanche raiders when they appropriated livestock. A low level of raiding was the price paid for peace, for, as Bernardo de Gálvez is said to have quipped, "A bad peace with all the [Indian] nations who may ask for it will be more beneficial to us than the efforts of a good war" (Weber 2005, 138).

Whether Gálvez actually said this or it is apocryphal, his policies ushered in forty years of unprecedented peace on the northern frontier. This accommodation, while not entirely new in Spanish governmentality, was a novel form of graphing the geo. The Spanish Crown had always ceded degrees of local authority to indigenous political leaders through the famous *republica de los indios*. Nevertheless, the republica de los indios existed in colonial law in vertical relation to Spanish dominion.[3] In accordance with Las Casas's hierarchy of Christian unity, Spanish authority geopolitically presided over indigenous authority as the representative of Petrine responsibility. Thus Spanish settlement, as many scholars have noted, mapped itself directly atop indigenous communities in central New Spain, formally replacing the centers of indigenous political and religious authority with their own. However, these spatial practices of substitution and vertical dominion were not possible on the northern frontier.[4] Instead, Spanish accommodation with the equestrian tribes suggests a horizontal spatial practice of contiguity and intercalation. This distinct late-colonial geo-graphing allowed for the penetration of Spanish settlement onto Apache and Comanche territory, but also allowed for the continuance of Apache and Comanche spatial practices of territory. In other words, this accommodated peace grafted *three* geographic practices of spatial organization onto each other: intercalating the geographies of Spanish settlement, of agricultural indigenous pueblos, and of Comanche, Apache, Seri, and Kiowa ranging and raiding, allowing each spatial code not only to coexist but to buttress the other two. As discussed in chapter 2, it was the denizens of Spanish and indigenous pueblos who purchased from the equestrian tribes the goods they raided from *other* indigenous and Spanish pueblos. These intercalated spatial practices index different modes of belonging at the fringes of empire, as the Apache and the Comanche engaged in episodic participation in New Spain, moving on and off mission lands at will. Spanish Catholic humanity expanded to include precisely the difference that marked their barbarous character—their inclination to roam and raid—while nevertheless extending to them the "privileges" of Spanish empire: Christian succor, but most importantly Spanish goods. Given this geopolitical accommodation between New Spain and the Apache and Comanche, it is unsurprising that these two "recalcitrant" nations sided with Spain in the War of Independence, adding their warriors to the Crown's military forces.

Though these indigenous nations had sided with the Crown, it is also not surprising that Mexican federal and state authorities wished to maintain peaceful relations with them after the War of Independence. Mexican government leaders were anxious to include these powerful peoples into the new nation rather than take retaliatory action against them. In 1825, four years after the formal end of the War of Independence, Mexico's first federalist president, Guadalupe Victoria, gave a tricolor flag as his personal gift to the Comanche leader Hoyoso from the Texas Rio Grande Valley. In addition, President Victoria made Hoyoso and two other Comanche leaders honorary officers of the Mexican militia. These two acts—presenting the newly decreed *national* flag and bestowing *national* military honors—performed a formal recognition of the Comanche peoples as a part of the emerging Mexican ethnos; they effectively inducted the Comanche bands, represented by their leaders, into the nation.[5] During this first decade of independence Comanche leaders regularly visited Mexico City as officially invited guests of the changing central administrations. In late 1826, these efforts at courting the Comanche leadership succeeded in convincing Comanche leaders representing both eastern and western branches into signing new peace treaties in Chihuahua City and Santa Fe, respectively (Delay 2008, 16–23; John 1985, 472). Meanwhile the Apache maintained peaceful relations with the governments of the northern departments of independent Mexico until the late 1830s. In 1834, the governor of Chihuahua, José J. Calvo, declared that "[el apache] es hijo de la gran familia mejicana y *disfruta los mismos derechos al suelo donde nació* que nosotros como hijos de los conquistadores" [the Apache] is the son of the great

Mexican family, and *enjoys the same rights to this land where he was born* as we do as the sons of *conquistadors*) (cited in Durazo Herrmann 2001, 95; emphasis mine). Apaches remained on the Spanish-founded *establecimientos* (peace camps) at Janos, Chihuahua, until 1831, for example, a full ten years after independence (Griffen 1985, 144).

Given these peaceful and promising beginnings, how is it that a mere fifteen years after Governor Calvo declared Apaches to be part of the "great Mexican family," the Chihuahuan state legislature passed a law authorizing and funding the hiring of U.S. nationals to fight and to scalp these very Indians? The 1849 bounty law was passed in the state legislature, overriding a veto by Governor Angel Trías, after heavy lobbying by ex-Texas Rangers (presumably traveling through Chihuahua en route to the California gold rush) (Smith 1984, 42).[6] The Chihuahuan legislature authorized a reward of fifty Mexican pesos for each dead Apache, Comanche, or Kiowa warrior, at a time when one Mexican peso equaled one silver U.S. dollar. Bounty hunters were free to bring either the scalp or the head of these dead warriors to commissions that were specifically established to verify that each head or scalp bore the defining marks of the designated tribes. Apparently cases of mistaken identity and the death of innocents would not be tolerated after the fact, though the establishment of these commissions, and their grisly task, speaks to the bureaucracy of death established in the northern states. Within a matter of years, the "reward" for each warrior's head or scalp would escalate to 250 pesos per "pieza" (piece), as these scalps or heads were commonly called (Smith, 1985–1986, 29–30).[7]

Between 1847 and 1850, four northern states passed laws authorizing rewards for the scalps or heads of Apache, Comanche, Kiowa, and Seri Indians: Durango, Sonora, and Chihuahua offered cash rewards, while Coahuila offered land, foodstuffs, access to education, as well as the right to keep war plunder recovered from dead raiders (Smith 1984, 44).[8] These laws would remain in effect in these states until the 1870s, despite being repeatedly condemned by the central authorities in Mexico City as unconstitutional and immoral (Delay 2008, 160).[9] It was not only Anglo-Americans who participated in this gruesome bounty hunting. Coahuila's land-granting program drew displaced eastern tribes like the Seminole and Cherokee from Indian Territory into the business of scalp-hunting, as well as the Kickapoo from Texas, and people escaping enslavement from the U.S. South (Durazo Hermann 2001, 97). Meanwhile, Pápagos from Sonora and Tarahumaras from Guerrero were among the Mexican indigenous groups who formed their own auxiliaries to pursue their traditional enemies. These bounty programs led to staggering outlays by state treasuries, in some years totalling tens of thousands of pesos (Adams 1991, 206–207; Smith 1991–1992, 110–120). The large sums of monies spent on bounties are particularly noteworthy as this expenditure occurred during a period of national reorganization after the U.S. war of invasion, when the northern state treasuries were severely depleted.

The business of scalping—involving promulgation of laws, the outlay of extraordinary sums, the constitution of commissions for evaluating *piezas,* the organization of celebratory parades and exhibitions of the scalps and heads— was also an early example of transnational alliance between Mexico and the United States and the collusion of their racial geographies.[10] Mexican elites from the northern states were all too willing to ally themselves with ex-soldiers from the country that had only recently dispossessed Mexico of the northern half of its national territory. But while U.S. mercenaries dominated the scalp business, these mercenaries hired as foot soldiers North American Indians, African Americans, Mexican mestizos, indios, and afromestizos, and even "friendly" Apache and Comanche (Smith 1963, 45; Delay 2008, 160–161). In other words, these bounty programs engendered a multiethnic and multiracial community engaged in a transnational economy of death that lasted forty years (1845–1885). It is tempting to interpret this economy as the raw expression of liberal Mexico's true racism toward indigenous peoples. The hunting of indios bárbaros *was* an explicit means of national and territorial consolidation—a form of representational and spatial mapping of the nation—but this consolidation was not based on simplistic racial othering. Rather, Apache, Comanche, Kiowa, and Seri peoples were reduced to a singular barbaric Indian difference around which an emphatically multiracial and multiethnic nation of racial differences could ally, not in the model of "e pluribus unum" on the U.S. Seal, but as *e pluribus plures.*

The flexible and inclusive racial parameters of the emerging Mexican nation were repeatedly drawn in contradistinction to these indios bárbaros, on the one hand, and to U.S. racism on the other. For Mexico *did* understand itself to be in competition with the United States, not only for territory along the northern frontier, but also in the fulfillment of the promise of liberal equality and national inclusion for its racially diverse citizens. After all, the foundational documents of Mexican independence extended the same rights and obligations to *all* male citizens, regardless of race or class status. There were no restrictions on *male* suffrage. And even at the onset of northern Mexico's panic over equestrian raids and the emergent bounty programs, the central government insisted on the inclusion of these Indian raiders within the racial geography of Mexico.[11] Our purpose is to discern how it is that these in-

114   CHAPTER THREE

dios bárbaros of the northern frontier, initially included in the *gran familia mejicana*, came to be placed outside the limits of Mexican citizenship not *despite* the rhetoric and policies forthcoming from Mexican liberalism, but in *conjunction* with its humanist inclusion of racial difference. Mexican liberals from the capital understood themselves as creating an inclusive national geography, one that realized the abstract equality of citizenship for all of its varied racial constituents, in contrast with its northern neighbor. Mexicans along the border, however, reconfigured the indio bárbaro in a way that coalesced with the "savage Indian" of the exclusionary racial geography of the nineteenth-century United States. The Mexican elites along the border may have brokered this transnational alliance with Anglo mercenaries as an expression of racial parity among themselves and in contradistinction to these savage Indians, however it was average citizens of all races and ethnicities who operationalized the alliance. Moreover, despite the vociferous objections from the central government, Mexican federal and state legislative policies were only seemingly contradictory. In the end, state-sponsored scalping programs supplemented federal nation-building policy, underscoring how a national, inclusive mestizaje was forged through a new spatial iteration of the indio bárbaro in a newly congealed border landscape.

Mapping through Miscegenation in Northern New Spain (1750–1821)

In 1848 the Mexican national government passed a new settlement law—coincident with the first bounty laws *and* the Treaty of Guadalupe Hidalgo—for the establishment of military and civilian colonies along its northern frontier as an explicit alternative to scalping. These settlements were meant to act as a buffer against the raiders, as a first line of defense. Cognizant of the growing anger in northern states over the increased raiding by Apache, Comanche, Seri, and Kiowa, but hamstrung by its limited military force, the federal government instead established several settlements along the northern frontier with mestizo and indigenous Mexicans from the interior. These new settlements also included groups of indigenous peoples from Florida, Texas, and the Great Plains, as well as escaped U.S. slaves. The Mexican government successfully lured U.S. Indians and enslaved blacks to the region with promises of freedom, land, and access to education. These migrants from the north perceived the gran familia mejicana as more amenable to their racial difference than the unfolding racial geography of the U.S. nation (Smith 1984, 43; Delay 2008, 298). When the federal Mexican government pursued this plan for establishing multiethnic and multiracial settlements along the northern frontier as a buffer against raids by equestrian tribes, it was pursuing a plan not unlike Spanish colonial settlement of the region.

While Spanish colonial settlement in the region had been organized under the sign of miscegenation, based on a hierarchical yet flexible caste system, newly independent Mexico forwarded the settlement plan under the sign of an inclusive liberalism, capable of embracing as equals indios, mestizos, afromestizos, Indians, and African Americans. Although as a political philosophy mestizaje explicitly emerged in opposition to the Spanish caste system, Mexico's mestizo racial order was derived from miscegenation as a form of Spanish colonial rule in multiple ways. Not only were key principles of mestizo citizenship a liberal reformulation of the Spanish notion of Christian unity, as spatial practice miscegenation had produced the territorial space and the racial geography on which mestizo liberal citizenship was mapped in the nineteenth century. Spanish colonialism was notorious for its promotion of miscegenation as a spatial practice of conquest. Larger land grants and encomiendas, for example, were awarded to those *peninsulares* (Spanish nobility, officers, soldiers) who married indigenous women, while the encomiendas of peninsulares who refused to marry their concubines were often revoked. Furthermore, Catholic priests regularly refused to baptize children born of unwed couples, thereby pressuring peninsulares and criollos to marry the mothers of their children (Menchaca 2001, 54–55). For the first seventy-five years of colonial rule in New Spain, the Spanish administration officially promoted intermarriage and childbearing as a form of governmentality—of distributing rights, privileges, and obligations—but also as a form of physically transforming the landscape, from one of indigenous territorial control to one of Spanish dominion.[12] As argued in chapter 2, graphing the geo of New Spain proceeded according to physical intimacy and alliance between the colonizer and the colonized, and nothing emblemized this intimacy more than early Spanish policies on intermarriage and miscegenation.[13] Intermarriage functioned not only as a spatial practice of settlement, redistributing lands and populations previously under Nahuas rule to Spaniards. It concomitantly graphed the geo racially, creating new *castas* to be sorted and managed efficiently under a model of Christian unity administered by the priests and colonial administrators: peninsulares, criollos, indios, mestizos, afromestizos, all existed in hierarchical, familial relation.[14]

As Herman Bennett has argued, the slave trade to New Spain operated under the auspices of Christian unity and intermarriage as well, shaping the way in which enslaved peoples were allowed to live their female and male sexuality, but also allowing them to "appropriate rights for themselves" (Bennett

116   CHAPTER THREE

2003, 46). Beginning in 1518, under the rule of King Carlos I (subsequently Carlos V, Holy Roman Emperor), slave traders were permitted to transport human chattel to New Spain, "both male and female, provided they were Christians" (41). While this generally implied cursory baptism of Africans as they boarded or disembarked slave ships, once on American soil, royal directives promoted the administration of Christian practices among the enslaved. It was one of the myriad of ways for the king to assert his authority over conquistadors on the ground. As Bennett argues in *Africans in Colonial Mexico*:

> In Spanish America, a person's subject status as the king's vassal prevailed over his or her identity as property largely because the fledgling polis necessitated the Crown's jurisdiction of all subjects, even the master's chattel. As paterfamilias of the realm, the king's interest reigned ascendant over others claiming authority as head of household. Jurisdictional conflicts magnified the slave's multiple identities—identities accompanied by discrete but competing obligations and rights. (45)

Bennett's archival research demonstrates that Africans in New Spain recognized the "jurisdictional contest between their status as slaves and their status as Christians," skillfully manipulating the imposition of the sacrament of matrimony, wielding it as a Christian right, as a means of attaining autonomy and agency in their daily lives and those of their children (46). As Christian converts their right to exogamous marriage could not be curtailed, lest their free will be violated (45). As Bennett argues, enslaved Africans used exogamous marriage as a principal means for ensuring rights and freedom for their families, as the condition of the child followed the condition of the mother under slavery. Slavery had a dramatic impact on the racial composition of New Spain (and on the formation of liberal mestizo citizenship in independent Mexico). The 1646 census in New Spain counted 130,000 enslaved blacks to 125,000 Spaniards. While enslaved Africans were certainly constrained in their reproductive practices in ways that Spaniards were not, they too contributed to mestizaje in New Spain (Menchaca 2001, 60–61). As a consequence of exogamous marriage with Spaniards, mestizos, and Indians, by the 1742 census— less than a hundred years later—there were more than a quarter million free afromestizos in the Mexican territory.

Although the Spanish casta system that evolved from Spanish, indigenous, and African miscegenation was strategically flexible, especially regarding Christian marriage and baptism, it was nevertheless rigidly hierarchical in the distribution of privileges and power. Only the peninsulares were eligible for the highest royal or ecclesiastic offices, while criollos were eligible for midlevel managerial positions, or high offices in the military and colleges. In turn, mestizos were restricted to the lower echelons of administrative positions and to the guilds, while afromestizos had no legislated positions reserved for them in either offices or in guilds. Indigenous populations at times enjoyed greater rights and privileges than either mestizo or afromestizos. Because they were considered of "pure blood" like the Spanish and as having their own aristocracy, indigenous peoples were organized into their separate and subordinate republica de los indios.[15] Although indigenous peoples were forced to render labor or taxes to the Spaniards regularly, they were organized into their own townships, under the leadership of their own *caciques,* with their own administrative offices and, most importantly, with ownership of their communal lands (Díaz Polanco 1997, 29–58). Mestizos and afromestizos, by contrast, were organized into multiple castas depending on their degree of racial admixture. Regardless of what social prestige mestizos and afromestizos may have enjoyed over indigenous commoners, indigenous peoples had greater access to material resources and to political autonomy than the castas who tended to occupy low-level jobs, military service, and wage labor (Menchaca 2001, 63, 154–56). The colonization of the northern frontier presented the expanding population of mestizos and afromestizos with a path to social and economic mobility.

Late eighteenth-century census records for Nuevo Santander and Texas (1777, 1779–80, 1783, 1789, 1793) confirm this prevalent northern migration. Twenty to 34 percent of the population of the principal towns of Laredo, San Antonio, La Bahía (Goliad), and Nacogdoches were afromestizos (inclusive of all castas), while between 4 and 20 percent of the population were mestizos.[16] Mestizos and afromestizos from the interior of New Spain traveled north as soldiers, servants, and in some cases as slaves. However, census records from this period indicate that the majority either arrived as or quickly became vecinos: those merchants, artisans, and landholding farmers and ranchers so central to the settlement project of the northern frontier, as demonstrated by the petitions for the settlement of Nuevo Santander in chapter 2. Though the casta system of government existed in the north, it afforded mestizos and afromestizos greater economic and political opportunities. From Alicia V. Tjarks's comprehensive gender and racial analysis of these censuses: "Creoles strongly identified with the 'aristocracy' of Texas [however] . . . access to the ownership of the land was opened also to the darker castes and the census of 1779–1780 reveals that several mestizo, coyote, and *mulatto* vecinos of Béxar and La Báhia were owners of farms, ranches, and cattle" (1974, 322).

118   CHAPTER THREE

Not only was the hierarchical distribution of rights and privileges among the castas less rigid on the frontier, the categories themselves were more permeable than in the interior of New Spain. Misrepresentations in the census records regarding casta affiliation evidence this increased flexibility of racial borders on the frontier: "In proportion to their actual number, mestizos were so classified very infrequently, probably because such a name still carried with it, at least in the popular mind, a meaning of illegitimacy" (Tjarks 1974, 323). The "mulatto" caste was even more notorious and thus less frequently invoked: "To use that name was an insult or sure defamation. Such a strong prejudice promoted repeated racial 'migrations' of mulatto settlers.... Over the years they became 'mestizos' and even 'Spaniards' in the military documents and parish books, an example of racial ambiguity which soon found many followers among the local colored castes" (325–26). In the 1779–80 census of Texas, for example, mestizo and mulatto soldiers serving in the presidios were simply listed as "Spanish," suggesting that military service in the northern frontier could mitigate or supersede casta distinctions, providing an avenue for casta migration (323). *Lobos, coyotes,* mulattos, mestizos: all were "whitened" over time in the Texas ecclesiastical and census records, particularly as members of these castas gained economic power or married into Spanish and Indian households.[17] The frontier not only facilitated an individual's move from one casta category to another, it allowed mestizos and afromestizos, as a class, access to economic resources customarily reserved for Spaniards and Indians. Along the northern frontier, the stratifying racial categories became less meaningful across time and space. On the eve of Mexican Independence, the northern frontier, once so difficult to poblar, more closely approximated the racial equality sought by liberal leaders determined to eliminate caste distinctions than did central New Spain.

By the end of the War of Independence in 1821, the Spanish census had stopped using racial categories altogether and simply divided those under colonial rule into two groups, a reflection of the Bourbon reforms. The dominant census category was the *gente de razón,* which included peninsulares, criollos, afromestizos, mestizos, and all Indians who recognized *solely* the sovereignty of Spain. The subordinate category was that of indio, including all Christianized or "pacified" Indians who recognized Spanish sovereignty but who also maintained their own separate governing and religious systems in their townships and tribes. This category included the Navajo, Apache, Comanche, and other equestrian peoples who maintained peaceful relations with the Crown. The new categories for enumerating subjects imply not only

MAPPING ECONOMIES OF DEATH   119

a change in the distribution of rights (according to one's casta on the one hand or purity of blood on the other), but a shift in the determination of one's *character*. Now *all* castas, Spaniards, criollos, and some Indians shared the characteristic of reason "because they practiced Spanish-Mexican traditions, they were Catholics, and they recognized only the sovereignty of the government of Spain" (Menchaca 2001, 167).[18] While it is possible to interpret the contravening census category of the indio as the "other within" that allowed the gente de razón to congeal as an emerging national ethnos, as theorized by Étienne Balibar, such a reading would not be entirely accurate.[19] Rather, as argued in chapter 1, Indians continued to be the raison d'être of the colonial mission. This designation in the 1821 census, while paternalistic and derogatory in relationship to those presumed to possess reason, did not exclude Indians from the empire, but rather designated their continued special status within the realm. Census indios during the late-colonial administration continued to enjoy special rights and corporate privileges not available to the gente de razón (such as the New Mexico Pueblo Indians' right to hold property in common or the Comanche and Apache right to range and raid).

Regardless of its privileged position within the Spanish kingdom, the category of indio in this late-colonial period trended toward an un-racing, precisely because it became subordinated to the characteristic of possessing reason, in congruence with the Bourbon reforms. At any point, pacified indios could become gente de razón by forgoing their aboriginal culture, language, and autonomy in favor of Spanish-Mexican culture, language, and sovereignty. Indeed, there was an inevitability to this *becoming* set up in the bifurcation of colonial census categories of being. Whereas casta proliferated categories of differences through miscegenation (which continued apace), the assimilationist logic of gente de razón suggests that all indios should lose their cultural specificity eventually and become enlightened, liberal subjects. However assimilative the bifurcated census categories of gente de razón and indios may have been, they still allowed for a more flexible incorporation of indigenous forms of autonomous government and territoriality than would the forthcoming national governments. Determining late-colonial character in New Spain was a series of identifiable politico-cultural traits (not simply racial ones), with the common denominator remaining submission to Spanish dominion. Within this submission, different modes of territorial expression were permitted to the category of indio, including those of the equestrian tribes of the Northern Provinces.

Even this late in the colonial period, the dual racial axis for plotting faithful and unfaithful Indian informed the racial geography of New Spain. Particu-

120   CHAPTER THREE

lar Indians or groups of Indians could shift their coordinates from faithful to unfaithful Indians and back again, but their singularity as indios remained a necessary constant for the colonial mission. The equality of Mexican liberalism placed indigenous difference under erasure in an entirely new way. In the period of transition from a colonial racial geography to a national one, Indian difference presented a powerful challenge to the abstraction of equality and a breach to Mexican liberalism, one that the scalping and beheading of Apache, Comanche, Seri and Kiowa Indians helped to bridge.

The Geography of Liberalism:
The Making and Unmaking of Indigenous Difference

This same voice that resonated in the people [pueblo] of Dolores in the year 1810 ... also established the public opinion regarding the general union amongst Europeans and Americans, Indians and indigenous, as the only solid basis upon which our common happiness rests. —Plan de Iguala

Art. 12. All the inhabitants of New Spain, without any distinction [of caste] amongst Europeans, Africans, or Indians, are citizens of this Monarchy, with the opportunity to pursue any and all employment, according to their merits and virtues. —Plan de Iguala

Promulgated on February 24, 1821, the Plan de Iguala marked a compromise between conservative royalists and liberal independence leaders, one that effectively ended Mexico's war for independence.[20] The royalist, criollo colonel Agustín de Iturbide, sent by the viceroy to Oaxaca to crush the republican forces lead by Vicente Guerrero, instead persuaded Guerrero to join forces with him behind a more conservative vision of national independence. This philosophical compromise between liberals and conservatives is evidenced by the plan's incongruent establishment of broad principles of equality and freedom *and* a "Mexican Empire" based on a traditional European-style monarchy. While the coups and countercoups between liberals and conservatives continued for more than twenty years, these principles of full equality and liberty, of freedom of expression, and of nondiscrimination in the areas of occupation and education were reiterated in most of the subsequent federal and state constitutions. Article 11 of the 1827 Constitution of the State of Coahuila and Texas, for example, guaranteed *every* person within state limits, even those there in transit, the "imprescriptible rights of liberty, security, property, and equality," declaring it the duty of the state "to preserve and protect . . . these universal rights of men."[21] While the state constitution failed to free the enslaved population therein, article 13 did prohibit the importation of any new slaves to the state and established the unconditional freedom of all children born in the state thereafter, regardless of the condition of the mother. This turned the state into a safe haven for those escaping slavery from the United States, also rendering illegal the trade in native captives by the Apache and Comanche.[22]

Mexico's first *federal* constitution of 1824 did not explicitly articulate these liberal principles of equality and liberty, though they were implied. Nevertheless, the 1857 Mexican Constitution explicitly recognized the equality and liberty of all people regardless of caste and remained in effect until the revolutionary constitution of 1917 supplanted it. Article 2 of the 1857 Constitution not only extended the right to freedom to all enslaved peoples who set foot in Mexico but committed the government to the protection of their freedom. But if this second article was addressed to the United States—as slavery had been abolished in Mexico since 1829—articles 4 and 5 were addressed to past colonial policies of rank and caste. Article 4 guaranteed that all men were free to exercise any profession, job, or industry, and to solely enjoy the fruits of their labor, a direct refutation of colonial appointments according to caste and the Crown's policies of indigenous tribute. Article 5 prohibited *all* forms of indentured servitude and unpaid labor, including any labor rendered for educational or religious reasons. Again, this article targeted all remnants of the Spanish encomienda that remained on *latifundios,* but was also aimed at the Catholic Church's use of indigenous labor on missions and *reducciones,* presumably in exchange for hispanicization and evangelization.

These liberal tenets of equality and liberty for all inhabitants of Mexican soil, regardless of nationality or race, were more expansive and capacious than their counterparts in the United States. They formed the basis for an incorporative logic of nationalism, for an inclusive racial imaginary. And yet, this liberal equality also extended and deepened the assimilative logic of the late-colonial category of gente de razón. These liberal tenets of equality and freedom certainly liberated indigenous peoples from paternalistic and exploitative practices of the colonial period, and thousands of indigenous peoples participated in the War of Independence (Mallon 1995). Mexican liberalism, however, emphasized the acculturation of indigenous peoples on the basis of each individual's "merits and virtues." In this sense Mexican liberalism was attempting to "liberate" Indians from their cultural, political, and territorial difference. Under Spanish colonialism, indigenous groups had enjoyed a degree of political and cultural autonomy because of their separate status as indios.[23] Eliminating their racial difference from other Mexican citizens also entailed eliminating the privileges they enjoyed by virtue of their difference.

122   CHAPTER THREE

To understand the negative consequences of liberal enfranchisement for indigenous peoples, a turn to Marx's "On the Jewish Question" is useful. For Marx ([1843] 1978), European liberalism purported to liberate the state from religious constraint and to offer national citizens political emancipation from religious distinction and aristocratic tyranny. Political emancipation presumably freed each citizen from feudal relations of power through the principle of abstract equality and the performance of democratic acts of enfranchisement (everyone is equal at the ballot box). Once the political machinations of the state were free from religion, a citizen's religious and sundry differences were no longer to impede her or his political freedom and participation in democracy. Marx insisted that liberal political emancipation entailed neither the elimination of religious differences nor of political subordination. Instead, political emancipation simply relegated religious difference, along with a sundry of other naturalized preferences and differences (ethnicity, race, wealth), to the private sphere. By relegating characteristics like ethnicity and class that have a powerful and limiting impact on one's material condition to a private sphere of "difference," political emancipation effectively removed the unequal structures of power that produce discriminatory effects from the public sphere, from what would be deemed a proper area of political concern. The state is not only thus free to ignore these structural differences and inequities of power, now naturalized as mere accretions of private cultural differences and chance, but is required to do so. To consider the structural reasons for and discriminatory effect of such differences would be a violation of political emancipation, understood as the abstraction from one's differences before the law; to consider the negative effect of structurally produced differences would violate an abstract principle of equality and would be tantamount to discrimination. It was this "through the looking glass" view of freedom that Marx critiqued as a false form of human emancipation.

With independence, the liberal Mexican state extended to indigenous peoples this form of political emancipation, an abstracted equality that vigorously insisted caste and racial differences would no longer impede opportunity or political enfranchisement. All that was required of them was the privatization of their differences, now deemed merely cultural, so that all paths would be opened to individual Indians according "to their merits and virtues." (This configuration of citizenship is not far afield from the Bourbon category of "gente de razón," which similarly required recognition of a singular form of political authority.) Indigeneity, however, is not reducible to the private cultural sphere, especially as it had been reconfigured by the Spanish colonial regime. Indios were a political category under Spanish colonialism;

while subject to legal forms of discrimination on the basis of this political identity, indigenous peoples also derived concrete rights and privileges from it. Most important, indigenous identity enjoyed a territorial and political expression. Indigenous peoples were not reduced to a set of cultural traits, in other words, but were considered political entities with the right to their own structures of authority.

In exchange for this new form of liberal enfranchisement under Mexican independence—and in contradistinction to colonial mapping—indigenous people were expected to subsume their particular differences to an idealized national character and public sphere. It was no longer enough simply to accept Mexican sovereignty, as indigenous groups had accepted Spanish sovereignty in order preserve some of their political autonomy and punctual practices. On one hand, indigenous difference was celebrated as part of the new national culture, as foundational to it. This was after all an incorporative model of nationalism; the gran familia mejicana was and is a miscegenated one.[24] On the other, the Plan de Iguala and later constitutional iterations of it insisted on an abstracted universal "merit" or "virtue" as the basis for egalitarian participation in the public sphere. Mexican liberalism privileged abstracted principles of citizenship, in the process reducing indigenous difference to an ethnic variation within Mexican character. Indigenous identity, however, did not consist of a set of quaint cultural practices. Rather, it was produced and reproduced through specific modes of indigenous territoriality, through punctual uses of space sanctioned, in whatever abridged form, under Spanish dominion. Indigenous identity, in other words, was also a geography: it was a territorial articulation of autonomous political and economic practices that enabled cultural reproduction. These indigenous spatial practices were intercalated with Spanish and mestizo geography, to be sure, but they also sustained an autonomous sphere of intraindigenous representational space.[25] Mexican liberalism's insistence on the subsuming of indigenous geographies to the national one provided the historical and political context for the reintroduction of equestrian raiding on the northern frontier.

Comanche and Apache raiding increased exponentially in the two decades following Mexican independence (1830s–1840s), suggesting a causal relationship not only between Indian removal policies in the United States and raiding practices, as historian Brian Delay (2008) has argued in *War of a Thousand Deserts,* but also between the practices of Mexican independence and raiding. Not only did the number of raids increase, they became more and more devastating. Raiding parties made off with tens of thousands of

124 CHAPTER THREE

heads of horse and cattle per raid; they took hundreds of women and children captive as well, selling them as slaves in the new northern territories of the United States.[26] By August 1, 1848, the U.S. Army estimated that there were eight hundred enslaved Mexicans north of the Rio Grande (Smith 1985/86, 26). Raids lasted up to a month and eventually reached as far south as Zacatecas and Jalisco. On these raids, Comanche and Apache not only took horses and captives, they often killed adult males and all the livestock they could not herd. Apache and Comanche raiders burned down entire ranches and towns. This new era of raiding was a transformation in kind from the raiding during the Spanish period discussed in chapter 2. In *War of a Thousand Deserts,* Delay provides us with a thorough analysis of the political economy of Apache and Comanche raiding and its transformation. Delay attributes the resumption of raiding to two concomitant factors: the relocation of large populations of East Coast Indians to the newly created "Indian Territory" after the 1830 Indian Removal Act, and the vast influx of U.S. and European migration into the Indiana, Missouri, and Iowa territories, north of Indian Territory. Significantly, the territory designated for Indian relocation by the U.S. federal government is precisely the same geography recognized and designated as the "Comanchería" within the Mexican national maps of the period. Indian Territory and the Comanchería precisely overlapped.

This massive influx of Eastern Indians to "Indian Territory," in addition to the European immigrants pouring into the Great Plains, had a dramatic effect on the living conditions of the Comanche, and consequently the Apache, their traditional competitors for territory and trade. Not only did the newly arrived indigenous peoples increase demands on the natural environment, creating greater competition for resources in the Central Basin, they also created a voracious market for Mexican livestock and slaves (Delay 2007a, 43). Forced to march thousands of miles with only what they could carry, displaced tribes arrived to their new homes with nothing and in need of everything. European immigrants were meanwhile hungry to build their farms with horses, domestic animals, and captives raided from Mexican ranches and towns. The Apache and Comanche, the most adept and experienced raiders and traders, were pursuing these lucrative economic opportunities in the north by expanding their ranging territory deeper and deeper south into Mexico. Indeed, Delay primarily attributes this new and intensified wave of raiding to the changed political economy in the Great Plains and the Central Basin. As a member of a new school of borderlands and Native American historiography, Delay returns agency to the native inhabitants of the Central Basin in the making of U.S. history, though one must question the value of restoring indigenous agency only to put it to the service of U.S. expansionism. Apache and Comanche raiders were neither merely reactive nor defensive in the face of U.S. expansionist policies according to Delay, but capitalized on them. These equestrian actors were savvy entrepreneurs who not only took quick advantage of expanded trading opportunities but also collaborated with U.S. expansionists in preparing the ground for invasion by devastating Mexico's northern frontier. Apache and Comanche raids became considerably more deadly in the mid-nineteenth century because they were trading livestock and slaves with U.S. settlers and soldiers for rifles and guns (a practice that had been strictly prohibited in the Provencias Internas during Spanish colonial rule). U.S. military personnel and filibusters in Texas expressly colluded with the Comanche and Apache on various occasions, providing guns and rifles that increased the devastation in the northern towns and ranches (Weber 1981, 124–133; Delay 2007a, 57–58; Adams 1991, 217). Given the severity of the raids, Delay interprets Mexican state bounty laws for scalps as motivated by a desire for vengeance as well as protection. The indignity of these laws in turn set in motion ever worsening cycles of violence and revenge killings.

The "cycle of revenge" interpretation of historical events is long established by Mexican and U.S. border historians. Delay's award-winning intervention lies in his argument that the Apache and Comanche were pursuing economic interests created by Indian removal, as well as their own political interests as nations. The Apache and Comanche coordinated raiding and trading among their own bands and with other tribes as an assertion of territorial sovereignty in the face of a consolidating Mexican nation and an expanding U.S. nation. Their raiding was an attempt to maintain and indeed grow their territories southward, as their territories north of the Rio Grande were encroached on by foreigners: Euro-American and Indian. Nevertheless, according to Delay (and in keeping with the teleology of frontier historiography), U.S. expansionists worked in concert with Apache and Comanche political interests to achieve their own ends of invading and annexing Mexico (2007a, 63). By 1846 the northern Mexican states were so beleaguered, their economies and defenses so devastated by Apache and Comanche attacks, that U.S. invasion forces faced little or no opposition from this front line of defense. This "cycle of revenge" explanation, even when augmented with restored political and economic indigenous agency, is at once a sufficient and insufficient explanation of *why* Apache and Comanche pursued their raids with such an excess of violence, as well as why Mexicans responded with an equally spectacular form of violence: scalping and beheading.

126   CHAPTER THREE

Revenge is a sufficient explanation in that this excess of violence was certainly *personal*. The degree of violence suggests a sense of betrayal by an intimate, betrayal amongst brothers. The Apache and the Comanche after all had been considered part of "la gran familia mejicana," and their return to raiding symbolized more than just a return to previous economic traditions practiced under late colonialism. Rather the nineteenth-century raiding practices were different in quality and quantity to eighteenth-century raiding and trading. To the Mexicans of the northern states who had fostered peaceful relations with the Apache and the Comanche both before and after independence, had lived among them, and engaged in trade relations with them for over a century, raiding of northern ranches and towns would have been a deep betrayal of a burgeoning national ethnos. These practices would have been seen as violating the new liberal model of abstract citizenship and of the very integrity of the nation, since that raiding happened under the shadow of U.S. imperialist ambitions. This sense of betrayal is evidenced by the fact that the bounties placed on individual Apache and Comanche warriors who had lived among the Mexicans, who were educated in Spanish, and who had converted to Catholicism, were set at two to three thousand pesos per scalp, ten times greater than the bounties for nonassimilated Indians (Smith 1985–1986, 36). These increased bounties for assimilated Apache and Comanche who joined raiding parties were commensurate with Spanish colonial policy, for the Crown had always punished more severely the crimes of apostate Indians than those of pagan Indians.

From the perspective of the Apache and the Comanche, the abandonment of the Crown's policy of preferential treatment of Indians in the name of a new principle of abstract equality after independence must have been perceived as a deep betrayal as well. For Indians from the interior of New Spain, indeed for the tens of thousands who fought on the side of independence, the imputation of their humanity in these new liberal terms signified a refutation of the degrading paternalism of colonialism. The Apache and Comanche had officially enjoyed a different mode of incorporation under late colonialism. The Bourbon reforms allowed the equestrian tribes to maintain their territorial practices, their political economy of regional trading in livestock, hides, fat, and captives, as long as they recognized Spanish sovereignty in a strictly formal sense. The requirements of liberal nationalism would have been perceived as a betrayal of the complementary geographies of control that had benefited equestrian tribes, pueblo Indians, and Spanish vecinos alike during the last decades of Spanish colonialism.

Some borderlands historians, like Weber and Delay, contend that Mexican states could not afford the price of peace with the Apache and Comanche. Their coffers were so reduced by the War for Independence that they could not sustain Spain's policy of gift giving to the Apache and Comanche who seasonally returned to missions and towns in recognition of their affiliation with New Spain. However, given the tens of thousands of pesos these northern states raised as bounty for scalps, it was not simply a matter of economics but of principle. Each northern state's constitution echoed the Plan de Iguala, declaring all men equal citizens before the law regardless of race and eliminating colonial privileges for the indigenous. For example, in 1825 a New Mexican Land Commission, charged by the state legislature with the task of evaluating requests from mestizo citizens for the privatization of Pueblo communal lands, decided in favor of the right to privatization. The commission declared that Pueblo Indians had no special protected right to communal lands, "just as all [the Indians'] ancient obligations have ceased, so too their privileges have ended, as they are left equal, one and another, to all the other citizens that form part of the great Mexican family" (Hall 1984, 28n41).[27] This equality of Indians before the law threatened the flexible and multiple systems of territoriality accommodated by a racial geography whereby civilized *and* barbarous Indians, one and another, were brought under Spanish dominion and within Catholic unity with their special rights and privileges.

Because several Apache and most Comanche bands remained indios bárbaros—potential converts to Christianity—they had enjoyed special rights and privileges before the Spanish Crown that mestizos and afromestizos had not: access to lands, to autonomous governing bodies, to alternative territorial economies. The geography of the new nation, however, while embracing of indigenous character, could not accommodate the distinct territorialities of these equestrian tribes. To the contrary, as a nation attempting to secure the insecure and porous borders of the northern frontier, Comanche and Apache expression of their territoriality by raiding and trading was perceived as a traitorous betrayal of the geography of nation.[28] The postcolonial racial geography taking shape in Mexico willingly incorporated indigenous cultural character, as long as it was cut off from spatial practice. The Mexican nation-state could accommodate Indians, but it could not accommodate indigenous political and economic spatial practices that required an alternate representation of the national space to itself. Simply put, Spanish colonial racial geography was flexible enough to accommodate and combine with indigenous modes of autonomous spatial organization, especially along the northern frontier where its hegemony was tenuous. New Spain incorporated

128 CHAPTER THREE

various indigenous punctual practices of political economy due to its racial geography. The dual axis of faithful and unfaithful Indians enabled the intercalation of Spanish and Indian spatial practices, as indigenous *difference* required Spanish presence. Meanwhile, Mexican liberal elites, both in the capital and in the northern states, were anxious to distinguish their practices from colonial practices and to consolidate a notion of abstract *Mexican* character.

Revenge is an insufficient explanation for the practice of bounty scalping, however, in that it indexes something *beyond* a desire for retaliation. The practice of scalping and beheading also indexes an important transformation in the racial geography of the region under the aegis of nation. Scalping was a spatial practice of statecraft. At a moment of postindependence anxiety over centralized authority, bounty laws enabled Chihuahua, Durango, Coahuila, and Sonora to appropriate for themselves the previously monarchical privilege of raising an army in defense of the realm. Thus scalping was a spatial practice that produced a national geography of race, by establishing the contours of Mexican territory and character at once. As a Foucaultian performance of the power of the monarch over the body politic, these state legislators appropriated for themselves the colonial sovereign's power to withdraw life. However, in their expression of this power they also appropriated the spectacular form of monarchal power, for scalping and beheading are tortures generally exacted on the body *after death*. Thus, at this foundational moment in the transition from colonialism to republican rule, these northern state legislatures appropriated the sovereign's exclusive right to enact excessive, public violence, for in scalping and beheading "justice pursues the body beyond all possible pain" (Foucault 1979, 34). At the same time as they invest themselves with sovereign power, these state legislatures do so in the "democratic" spirit of liberalism, as they invest every man with power to enact this violence on the bodies of dead Apache and Comanche warriors.

If these bounty laws function to constitute the states as sovereign entities of a sovereign nation, then their timing to coincide with the U.S. war against Mexico begins to make cartographical sense. They are early iterations of a transnational alliance. What better way to broker peace with the United States than to recognize U.S. nationals as coeval in a just war against a mutual and untimely enemy: the nations of indios bárbaros? In brokering this transnational alliance, Mexican elites of the northern states assert a racial parity between themselves and the ex-U.S. soldiers they hired as mercenaries to scalp Indians. After all, these bounty laws are a local manifestation of article 11 of the 1848 Treaty of Guadalupe Hidalgo, which formally assigned the task of policing and punishing the savage tribes for raids against Mexicans to the U.S. military, also on the grounds of racial parity.

If scalping and beheading were the expression of a newly constituted sovereign justice pursuing the body of the indio bárbaro beyond all possible pain, these were specifically marked bodies. As previously mentioned, commissions were established in all four states to inspect the scalps or heads of the dead for the signs and markings of *Apache* and *Comanche* male warriors: to check for telling tattoos, for the correct shaving of the head, for the proper war regalia (Smith 1991–1992, 114). It was very important that this violence be directed against the *proper* Indian bodies, those of the indios bárbaros and none other. There were gross violations of this principle to be sure, involving the killing and scalping of peaceful Apache, mestizos, women and children, and Indians from other tribes. Nevertheless, scalpers scrupulously presented all scalps for inspection before bounties could be rewarded. In this sense, scalping and beheading performed an important internal function for the consolidation of the nation-state bureaucracy and of Mexican character.

While U.S. mercenaries dominated the bounty business, they were by no means the only ones. Numerous bounty posses were led by and made up of Mexican mestizos and afromestizos, Mexican Indians, and even North American Indians and African Americans who acquired Mexican citizenship through their participation in these posses (like a nineteenth-century DREAM Act for U.S. immigrants in Mexico). As a spatial practice, bounty programs engendered a multiethnic and multiracial demos within Mexico by having *proper* citizens enact sovereign justice against the specifically targeted bodies of the *improper* indios bárbaros. Successful bounty hunting was celebrated in towns all over the north with parades, with spectacles not unlike the feudal spectacle of the scaffold (Smith 1991–1992, 112; Smith 1985–1986, 26). It is all too appropriate that the word commonly used for Apache and Comanche scalps was *pieza* because *pieza* is also the word for a theatrical or musical performance. For on display at these parades and celebrations were not only the heads and scalps of dead warriors; also on display were the performances of proper *Indian* citizenship in and for the Mexican nation. Scalping was theatrics of national embodiment.

In 1874 August Santleben, a Texas merchant passing through Chihuahua City, described one such parade in precisely the theatrical terms of national embodiment:

> The *friendly* Indians on the reservations, influenced by this reward, made a regular business of waging war on the wild tribes, and they

would absent themselves from their villages *for months,* seeking opportunities to secure scalps, by *waylaying* their victims in favorable localities; but frequently their object was effected by surprises which resulted in *the extermination of entire settlements.* The State did not concern itself with reference to their plan of warfare, and it approved their destruction by any method that might be adopted because the hostilities were a constant menace. A natural enmity existed between the peaceable and warlike tribes and it was easy to excite the cupidity of the former by offering liberal rewards. By such means the State rid itself of a large number of uncontrollable savages and gave protection to its citizens.

The celebration I witnessed was not only approved by the city officials, but the programme was, evidently, arranged by them beforehand. The procession entered the city about ten o'clock in the morning, and a brass band in front discoursed appropriate music. The warriors followed on horseback, *in their war-paint* and *decked out in all their finery,* about fifteen of whom had long poles to which were secured the scalps of their victims killed in battle, *together with the bows and other trophies necessary* to prove their valor. The women and children of the tribe came next, on horses, in single file, and their *oddity* added an attraction to the display. I was really impressed by the significance of the occasion, which had the appearance of a great festival, on account of the interest manifested by the citizens. (Santleben [1874] 1910, 165–166, emphasis added)

This dramatic performance is not only orchestrated by city officials, it is *literally* orchestrated, though the reader is left to ponder what would be "appropriate music" for such an event. Santleben incorrectly mapped the coordinates of a U.S. racial geography onto Chihuahua when he envisioned the friendly Indian bounty hunters as coming from "reservations." These self-evidently peaceful Indians nevertheless harbor a "natural enmity" for their brethren and find it within themselves to butcher them. Moreover, friendly Indians "hunt down" savages on settlements like the one at Janos, established by the Spanish in the eighteenth century to gather the peaceful Apache in Chihuahua. It is during one such attack on Janos that Geronimo's wife and children were massacred, turning him into the fiercest Apache warrior in Mexican and U.S. history. All the while, the state of Chihuahua imagines itself as giving succor, giving "protection to its citizens" *through* the friendly Indians. Even as new racial geographies get mapped onto this terrain, the terms of Spanish racial geography palimpsestically persist, differentiating "peaceable Indians" from "warlike tribes." And yet the meaning of these racial coordinates for Indianness are being transformed under liberalism at this very juncture. Mexican liberalism reiterates colonial coordinates with a new deadly difference in its new racial geography.

These friendly Indians paraded the scalps of the vanquished, but it was their own living Indian difference that was on display. As spectator, Santleben's eye focused on the parading Indians' war paint, on their finery, on the *oddity* of their women and children. Presumably their oddity is due to the indigenous accouterments of their femininity, but it stands in for the indigenous character of the entire parade, and yet these citizens celebrated them in their oddity. These friendly warriors were paid for the scalps, but it was they who purchased inclusion for their entire village into the great Mexican family *as Indians* with their bounty of Apache and Comanche scalps. With their indigenous finery and oddity, they were protagonists of this theatrics of a national embodiment. After three hundred years of Spain's hierarchical caste system, the newly independent northern states fulfilled the promise of liberal equality for the nation. Through these bounty laws, rather than in spite them, these states forged an abstracted multiracial national constituency proud of its indigenous constituents, performed paradoxically through the act of scalping and beheading Indians. According to the unironic, brutal logic of abstract liberal equality, then, permissible barbarity, with all its cultural accouterments, was folded into the formation of nation, while impermissible barbarity was "properly" excised. The Mexican *nation,* more anxious of its territorial boundaries than the Spanish Empire, simply could not accommodate the multiple modes of geographical organization entailed by inducting the Apache and Comanche into la gran familia mejicana. Moreover, the *spatial* practices of Apache and Comanche raiding and trading were spectacular representations of the geography they traversed as under their own jurisdiction. This sharing of territory as political spaces—as complementary representational spaces of governance—was beyond the imagination even of Mexico's incorporative racial geography. Many Indians were called to the crucible of Mexican nationality, with their merits, virtues, and cupidity, but only some would enter. Apache and Comanche scalps opened the door of advancement for other Indians to step into the nation.

A Geography of Loss Part I: The Treaty of Guadalupe Hidalgo

The 1848 Treaty of Guadalupe Hidalgo ended the conflict between Mexico and the United States, but as Mexican and indigenous scholarship of the nineteenth century makes evident, the two-year U.S. war of aggression against Mexico was deeply entangled with this longer war between the mercenaries hired by Mexico's northern states and the equestrian tribes. Even if we disregard the teleological argument that U.S. federal and state agents fomented the Apache and Comanche raids to prepare the way for a U.S. invasion of Mexico, it is nevertheless evident that Mexico, the United States, and the equestrian tribes were triangulated in these wars, with alliances among these parties shifting dramatically over time from 1810 to 1870. The space-making practices of these three powers were intercalated, combined, and superimposed in these wars (Lefebvre 1991, 88); their racial geographies competed but were also often in complicity with each other in drawing and redrawing the boundaries of permissible citizenship in Mexico and the United States. In the first half of this chapter I focused on the space-making practice of war involved in the constitution of la gran familia mejicana. The war between Mexico and the equestrian raiders was a space-making project in at least two ways. On one level, these were wars of territorial boundary making: the Apache and Comanche defended and expanded their territory while Mexico sought to establish and secure the boundaries of the new nation against U.S. imperial expansion. At another level, Mexico's scalping war against the equestrian tribes entailed the production of the nation as a Lefebvrian representational space: the laws, commissions, parades, and newspaper articles sought to represent the contested space of the nation as one composed of a multiracial demos, as a model of civic kinship (mestizaje) protecting itself from the savage outside.

For the second half of this chapter I focus on the production of the U.S. nation as a representational space in the aftermath of the U.S.–Mexico War. Specifically, I analyze the Treaty of Guadalupe Hidalgo for how it produced the annexed territory as a representational space as well. The treaty set the terms for the incorporation of the annexed population by racializing annexed Mexicans in relation to Anglo-Americans, but also in relation to the Mexican indigenous populations, who suddenly found themselves firmly cast out of the national boundaries of an entirely new imperial power—the United States. The treaty re-graphed the geo of the former northern Mexican region into the U.S. Southwest, establishing not only new boundaries of nation but an infelicitous boundary between indigenous and Mexican racial identity. The bifurcation of indigenous and mestizo identities was required by the racial geography of the United States, and this ontological boundary-making necessarily was implicated in and affected by the coterminous war against barbarous Indians happening in the northern Mexican states.

From the U.S. perspective, the racial logic of the treaty established the terms for enfranchising former Mexican citizens as U.S. citizens by requiring *some* Mexicans (and subsequent Mexican American generations) to repress or deny their indigenous and afromestizo heritage, while requiring other Mexicans—indigenous, afromestizos, and too-dark mestizos—to excise themselves from the geography of citizenship altogether. The effect of this requirement for the denial, repression, or expulsion of racialized and Indian difference immediately found expression in early Mexican American literary production, with the figure of the indio bárbaro claiming psychic space in a protonationalist imaginary. "Mexican," "white," "Indian," and "black" identities were graphed—summoned to appear or disappear from the U.S. racial geography of the region—by the treaty's legacy of representing and differentiating proper citizens from improper ones in what today constitutes the U.S. Southwest.

Legal scholar Christopher David Ruiz Cameron contends that historians of the Treaty of Guadalupe Hidalgo are primarily concerned with the legacy of just two of its twenty-three articles, articles 8 and 9 because these two articles enabled rather than curtailed the dispossession of annexed Mexicans ("One Hundred Fifty Years of Solitude" 2000). These two articles presumably guaranteed the land and civil rights of the newly annexed population. From article 8:

> Mexicans now established in territories previously belonging to Mexico, and which remain for the future within the limits of the United States, as defined by the present treaty, shall be free to continue where they now reside, or to remove at any time to the Mexican Republic, retaining the property which they possess in the said territories, or disposing thereof, and removing the proceeds wherever they please, without their being subjected, on this account, to any contribution, tax, or charge whatever.[29]

It would appear there is little room for interpretation: annexed Mexicans are entitled to the preservation of their property, whether or not they elect to become U.S. citizens. Similarly, article 9 seems straightforward in its extension of civil rights to those who chose U.S. citizenship:

> The Mexicans who, in the territories aforesaid, *shall not preserve the character* of citizens of the Mexican Republic . . . shall be incorporated

134   CHAPTER THREE

into the Union of the United States and be admitted, at the proper time (to be judged of by the Congress of the United States) *to the enjoyment of all the rights of the citizens of the United States* according to the principles of the Constitution; and in the meantime shall be maintained and protected in the free enjoyment of their liberty and property, and secured in the free exercise of their religion without restriction. (emphasis added)

U.S. and Mexican historians uniformly agree on the failure of the U.S. government to have delivered on this promise of the "enjoyment of all the rights of citizens of the United States" to the newly annexed Mexicans or to have protected their property rights. They differ only in their attribution of responsibility for this failure. Again, according to Ruiz Cameron, most historians interpret the treaty as the "recorded deed of the biggest 'land grab' in American history," as nothing more than the codification of the U.S. interests in Mexico that led to war (Ruiz Cameron 2000, 1–2). Thus U.S. courts *necessarily* interpreted the treaty in favor of U.S. claimants and against annexed Mexicans. Another school of treaty scholarship insists the treaty provided real protections for Mexicans, but argues they were culturally ill equipped for navigating the U.S. common-law legal system, placing the burden of Mexicans losses on their "culture." Reclamationist scholars and activists interpret the treaty as a living document guaranteeing the civil and human rights of Mexicans from 1848 through today. Hence, these rights remain to be (re)claimed by Mexican Americans through the courts (Ruiz Cameron 2000). All three camps of historical scholarship locate the failure in the *execution* of the treaty, rather than in the content of the articles, reading the meaning of the articles as self-evident.

This widespread agreement among U.S. historians and Chicana/o scholars on the *failure* of the treaty to deliver on its promise to annexed Mexicans has led Early American scholar David Kazanjian to read the treaty against the grain, to ask what it would mean to fulfill the treaty's promise. Rather than consider the cornucopia of rights that go tantalizingly unfulfilled in the treaty, Kazanjian argues that the fulfillment of the promise of article 9 formally required Mexicans to give up, to relinquish, the "character" of Mexicanness in order to enjoy "all the rights of the citizens of the United States" promised by the treaty. As the first sentence of article 9 stipulates in the prohibition "shall not preserve the character," Kazanjian suggests, "the first step on the road to becoming a U.S. citizen is a negation, a becoming un-preserved, disposed of, lost, wasted" (2003, 207). Becoming a U.S. citizen required the loss of a

Mexican character that is at once national *and* racial, as the vernacular use of "character" underscores. By the mid-nineteenth century, the transformation of the term *race* from a taxonomic category under Spanish colonialism into a biological category under liberal nationalism was well underway. "Character," according to the *Oxford English Dictionary*, linked race and nation, referring to "the sum of the moral and mental qualities which distinguish an individual or a race, viewed as a homogeneous whole," as well as to "the individuality impressed by nature and habit on man or nation."[30] As a word indexing both the "moral and mental qualities" of a race and the individuality "impressed by nature" on man or nation, "character" is used interchangeably in the treaty with "citizenship." If the use of "character" in the treaty underscored the intertwined nature of race and nation, this imbrication of racial, national, *and* moral character was not inexorable. To the contrary, article 9 suggests that at least some Mexicans might shed ["shall not preserve"] their racial as well as national characteristics. Indeed, U.S. citizenship required this loss, this unbecoming Mexican.

How might this "unbecoming" proceed, according to the terms of the treaty itself? The U.S. Senate struck article 10 from the treaty, so article 11 directly follows article 9.[31]

> Considering that a great part of the territories, which, by the present treaty, are to be comprehended for the future within the limits of the United States, *is now occupied by savage tribes* [*actualmente ocupada por tribus salvajes*], who will hereafter be under the exclusive control of the Government of the United States, and whose incursions within the territory of Mexico *would be prejudicial in the extreme*, it is solemnly agreed that all such incursions shall be forcibly restrained by the Government of the United States whensoever this may be necessary; and that when they cannot be prevented, they shall be punished by the said Government, and satisfaction for the same shall be exacted *all in the same way*, and with *equal* diligence and energy, *as if* the same incursions were meditated or committed within its own territory, *against its own citizens*. (emphasis added)[32]

The article then lists the various circumstances under which the U.S. government must protect Mexican citizens and their property from enslavement and theft at the hands of these "savage tribes" that *occupy* the newly annexed territories. This article registered the profound transformation in the terms for imputing indigenous humanity in Mexico during the midcentury wars with some of the equestrian tribes. The *tribus salvajes* referenced here are no longer a simple iteration (without difference) of the indios bárbaros of the Spanish colonial archive, those potential converts, allies, and coconspirators of chapter 2. Nor are they the Apache and Comanche members of the gran familia mejicana, who rightfully possessed (*disfruta los mismos derechos al suelo donde nacio*) the territories they traversed for the purposes of hunting and trade at the dawn of Mexican independence. Rather by the midcentury, the particular indigenous groups once referenced as indios bárbaros—Apache, Comanche, Kiowa, Seri—lacked all singularity, having been reduced to a *transnationally* self-evident savagery, as the change in nomenclature underscores. These tribus salvajes now merely occupied space, without any terms of possession or customary use that needed be respected. Whether the Mexican citizens referenced in article 11 found themselves in northern Mexico or in the southwestern United States, it was incumbent on the U.S. government to protect *proper* Mexicans from the savage indios—"equally," "in the same way," "as if" they were protecting their own citizens. Article 11 posited equality between Mexican character and U.S. character. However, this equality—this sameness before the law—was purchased through the *transnational* economy of death based on the scalping and beheading of the "savage tribes," who now established the true border between civilized and uncivilized (racial) character.

Article 11 deftly placed U.S. and Mexican citizens on one side of a liberal divide of equality and fraternity, shielded by its terms, while placing these Indians on the other side, their savagery precluding recourse for them to inclusive national racial geographies. Indeed, the "savage tribes" *enabled* similitude among some mestizo Mexicans and white U.S. citizens in the aftermath of an expansionist war that was waged by the United States on purely racial grounds and for the purposes of the racial subordination of Mexicans. The pretext used by U.S. imperialists for invading Mexico was that Mexicans were unfit to govern their own territory, precisely as a direct consequence of their "half-breed" racial/national character. Meanwhile proslavery expansionists considered the acquisition of Mexican territory a way of extending their economic and political power.

Even as the treaty formalized the most pernicious violation of Mexican national territory ("the biggest land grab in history"), it designated the *indigenous incursions* as that which "would be prejudicial in the extreme." As a spatial practice, the treaty instituted the most dramatic remapping of the geography of North America since the invasion of the Europeans and until the promulgation of NAFTA. This spatial practice was a racial geo-graphing, representationally contingent on the institution of a new racial order on the landscape as well. The border between Mexico and the United States was remapped, moved south- and westward to encompass 900,000 square miles of annexed territory. Yet in the treaty's representation of space, it was the savage Indians who violated the newly graphed spatial boundaries of *both* nations. Establishing new national boundaries and national characters therein became contingent on the exclusion of "savage tribes" from the racial geographies of both nations. The article was more than just a spatial practice that ceded the territory of one nation to another, in other words. It was also a representational practice that attempted to align the liberal visions of two distinct racial geographies of citizenship—mestizo and white rule—that were about to collide spectacularly on the ceded lands. This attempt at alignment of racial geographies was facilitated by the signification of "savage tribes" as marauders-in-landscape. "Tribus salvajes" became the trope of *noncitizenship* for the racial geographies of both the United States and Mexico. This treaty, then, enacts the nation as representational space as well. Mexico and the United States had very distinct racial visions of what constituted liberal citizenship at this juncture—Mexico's broadly incorporative, the U.S.'s broadly exclusionary. The treaty attempted to align these two conceptions of racialized citizenship in the annexed territory by triangulating them through a homogenized savage Indian marauder who endangered both nations. This attempt to align modes of racial citizenship failed miserably for those annexed populations that had previously been included under the liberal terms of mestizo Mexican citizenship, and especially for the Apache and Comanche, persecuted by both U.S. and Mexican militaries.

The article ends by stipulating "*the sacredness of this obligation* shall never be lost sight of by the said Government" (*"tendrá muy presente la santidad de esta obligación"*). The language of article 11 varies from the narrowly legalistic language of negotiated settlement in the rest of the treaty. Clearly inserted at the behest of the Mexican government, the "sacredness" of the obligation alludes to a colonial model of domination through Christian unity discussed in chapter 1. However, the terms of this Christian unity have shifted to encompass proper Mexicans and U.S. citizens, rather than indios bárbaros, Spaniards, and mestizos. Christian unity is now proposed between the citizens of two nations. While article 11 purportedly guaranteed the protection of Mexicans *in Mexico* from the savage tribes, annexed Mexicans remaining on the U.S. side of the new geographical divide were left in perilous proximity to Indian savagery. This proximate danger between "savage tribes" and proper Mexicans was consistently and repeatedly elided in the execution of the treaty; indeed, the treaty enabled this elision with its requirement for disavowal. For

138   CHAPTER THREE

the religious inflection of article 11 bespeaks a psychic anxiety over the United States' ability to discern the exact nature of the Mexican racial character alluded to in article 9, a psychic anxiety reminiscent of the anxiety expressed by eighteenth-century Spanish settlers trying to discern good allies from bad enemies, as discussed in chapter 2. The tribus salvajes were the "bad Indians" against which annexed Mexicans—gente de razón composed of "good" Indians and mestizos—should attain social visibility in the new geopolitical landscape of the Southwest. But if the language of article 11 alluded to a Christian unity requiring the fine discernment of enemies and friends as discussed in chapter 1, the ground for that discernment had shifted from behaviors of proper submission and subjugation to Spanish Empire and Mexican nation, to the color of one's skin in the United States.

Careful consideration of articles 9 and 11 enables us to cull the treaty for layers of racial geographies that left their traces therein: the colonial, the national, the neocolonial. If the representational space produced in articles 9 and 11 must be gleaned from the intertext of these multiple geographies, the sacredness of the U.S. obligation to Mexico was tied directly to Mexico's and the United States' *other* ongoing wars: Mexico's war with the Apache and Comanche in the north; the United States wars of removal against the Cherokee, Creek, Choctaw, Chickasaw, and Seminole nations in the Southeast. Indeed, it is these wars that are alluded to in article 11 and that facilitated the United States war against Mexico in the first place. From the last paragraph of the treaty:

> And, finally, the sacredness of this obligation shall never be lost sight of by the said Government, *when providing for the removal of the Indians from any portion of the said territories,* or for its being settled by citizens of the United States; but, on the contrary, special care shall then be taken *not to place its Indian occupants under the necessity of seeking new homes,* by committing those invasions which the United States have solemnly obliged themselves to restrain.

The damaging consequences of the Indian Removal Act and Euro-American expansion on the integrity of the Mexican nation were explicitly recognized in the treaty. Not only did the treaty prepare the way for future Indian removal in the United States ("when providing for"), it recognized that the United States had previously usurped Comanche and Apache territory in creating "Indian Territory": "shall ... not ... place its Indian occupants under the *necessity* of seeking new homes." The creation of "Indian Territory" created the exigency of looking for new homes, avenues of trade, and sites for raiding among the Apache, Comanche, and other equestrian tribes originally from the greater Great Plains. Even as the treaty creates a category of "savage tribes" so foreign to nationalist reason that they must be eliminated, it also recognizes that even these most "unreasonable" of indios bárbaros had very good reasons for their actions of raiding and trading.

The Treaty of Guadalupe Hidalgo maps a series of usurpations. Chicano scholarship and popular culture uniformly represent the U.S. war with Mexico as the usurpation of Chicana/o territory and rights.[33] Certainly, the U.S. usurped a quarter of a continent and Euro-American settlers usurped the property of tens of thousands of former multiracial vecinos by violence and fraud. But was this a usurpation of *Mexican* territory? The Mexican nation tried and failed to usurp the equestrian tribes of their territories because it refused to recognize the flexible modes of Spanish incorporation, modes of incorporation initially captured in the early mappings of the Mexican nation.[34] Just as certainly, the narrow racial terms of U.S. citizenship usurped Chicana/os of their indigenous and afromestizo heritage by requiring that they become purely white to maintain their rights and property, as discussed further in chapter 4. Nevertheless, when Chicana/os position themselves as the inheritors of the Southwest (Aztlán) from specifically *Aztec* ancestors, as examined in chapter 5, they misidentify not only the nature of their loss required by the treaty, they also usurp the territorial claims of the indigenous inhabitants of the Southwest, including those of the Comanche who are part of the Uto-Aztecan linguistic family. What is lost in the racial geography imposed by the treaty onto the annexed Mexicans is not this ancestral tie to the Aztec Empire. Rather, lost is this rich and changing history of Spanish and Mexican racial geographies: the "purity" of Spaniards and Indians *and* the miscegenation of caste; the accommodation of various forms of spatial practices in one shared place; the rise of mestizo liberalism which at once universalizes indigenous character for all its population, yet requires the "acculturation" of indigenous peoples; the complicated and nuanced technologies for dispersing and withholding liberal equality and reason. On the other side of the coin, U.S. Native American scholars have also lost this rich, complex history of Spanish and Mexican racial space that was required to disappear by the United States' interpretation of the Treaty of Guadalupe Hidalgo.

The popular analogy of Chicana/os as *los Aztecas del norte* occludes both the requirement to repress or deny indigenous heritage as enshrined in article

140   CHAPTER THREE

9 and the history of this anxious repudiation of savage Indian character—of indios bárbaros—by the Mexican government recorded in article 11. By representing Chicana/os as los Aztecas del norte, the Aztlán analogy forgets the historical differences drawn by the Mexican government between the equestrian tribes as the quintessential indios bárbaros, and gente de razón as the "civilized" pueblo Indians, mestizos, and afromestizos. The Mexicans who negotiated the treaty tried to signal the differences between good Indians and bad to the U.S. government that would annex the northern territories. Proper Mexicans—Indian, mestizos, and afromestizos annexed by the United States—were to be rigorously differentiated from those tribus salvajes indicated in article 11, who then became the target of joint Mexican and U.S. extermination efforts.[35] The U.S. racial geography proved incapable of mapping such fine differences among the general annexed population. Instead, it drew other distinctions. No Indians in the annexed territories, "civilized" or not, would be treated as full citizens, nor would they be allowed to keep and manage the lands designated them by the Spanish Crown. Afromestizos were also ineligible for citizenship, and indeed faced enslavement in most of the newly annexed territory.[36] Meanwhile, mestizos would be required to forswear their mixed racial heritage or be judged accordingly by U.S. law.

The annexed Mexicans were given two choices by the treaty articles. They could either retain their Mexican character, eventually relocating to the southern side of the border, or they could relinquish their Mexican character and remain on the northern side of the divide. Article 9 suggests Mexicans relinquish their character in implicit exchange for U.S. character. And yet article 11 reveals a prescient anxiety among Mexicans that their racial character might be mistaken as Indian savagery that would require removal. And indeed, the U.S. government repeatedly read annexed Mexicans as rebellious, barbaric, and incapable of properly holding landed property. Neither black nor white, the majority of annexed Mexicans lingered in dangerous proximity to an imputed savage Indian difference. Thus annexed Mexicans were pulled into an ambivalent identification with their indigenous heritage—ambivalent because on the one hand they were required to relinquish their miscegenated racial heritage, privileged by Spanish colonialism and by Mexican nationalism; on the other, the identification was repeatedly thrust on them as they were "mistaken" for Indian before a law that prohibited Indians from proper citizenship and from maintaining their territories. The treaty indexes this ambivalent identification in the racial geography of the Southwest as it was transformed from Mexican to U.S.

Geography of Loss Part II: A Literary Reckoning

To analyze fully the psychic consequences of this structure of ambivalent identification with and disavowal of indigeneity, it is necessary to move from the historical register to the literary one. As I suggest in the introduction, it is only by moving to the aesthetic register that we are able to discern the psychic consequences of this legal geo-graphing, as the interiority of those affected by it is rarely captured in the historical or legal archive. *George Washington Gómez* (*GWG*) is one of the earliest examples of Chicana/o literature and part of the Chicana/o literary canon. Américo Paredes wrote most of *GWG* between 1936 and 1940, a time when the combining of the racial geographies of Mexico and the United States in the borderlands had devastating consequences on the lives of annexed Mexicans. A native of Texas himself, Paredes wrote *GWG* while living in his hometown of Brownsville, in the heart of the segregated Rio Grande Valley where Jim Crow laws applied equally to Mexicans and blacks. Thus he was well acquainted with the U.S. interpretation of the treaty's imposition of disavowal of Indian and afromestizo identity, a disavowal that played an integral role in the formation of the racial geography of the segregated Southwest. Indeed, the novel documents the life of a man fatefully named George Washington Gómez, born in the Rio Grande Valley and trapped in a devastating psychic structure of identification with and disavowal of his indigenous ancestry, of his "Indian difference." The novel traces his psychic development in a region where the overlapping and conflicting racial geographies afflict his psychic formation to such a degree that a psychosis is triggered. The novel follows the protagonist from the moment of his birth during a multiracial, seditious insurrection in southwest Texas to the moment of his adult return to the Rio Grande Valley as a U.S. army spy during World War II, a twentieth-century reiteration of the "Indio Sanchez" spy during the eighteenth century discussed in chapter 2.

Part 1 of the novel takes as its historical backdrop an important event in the history of south Texas. In 1915, almost sixty years after the Treaty of Guadalupe Hidalgo, a multiracial coalition of insurgents led by Mexicans and Mexican Americans from both sides of the Rio Grande staged a two-year campaign to overthrow the U.S. government and establish an independent republic along the river. Aniceto Pizaña and Luis de la Rosa led the insurgency, launching hundreds of armed attacks against Anglo farms and businesses. The motto on the seditionists' flag read "igualdad e independencia" (equality and independence), and their army was called the Liberating Army for Races and Peoples. The novel begins by immediately returning the reader to the moment of this insurgent movement, thereby reasserting a Mexican geography of racial inclusion and equality. The novel opens with four Texas Rangers patrolling the Texas *llano* (the plain) in search of a fictional character named Anacleto de la Peña, a "bandit" who leads a fictionalized version of this historical movement. De la Peña's name is an amalgamation of Pizaña and de la Rosa, and like these two historical actors, he leads his men in a war to separate from Texas and to establish a multiracial "Republic of the Southwest."[37]

This fictionalized representation of the multiracial seditionist movement provides not only a historical backdrop for the action of the novel but also a psychological backdrop for the protagonist's psychic development. By citing this particular moment, the novel posits as the political horizon a utopian structure of identification in which mestizo, afromestizo, and indigenous identity remain unalienated from each other and where national, racial, and moral character coalesce in the Republic of the Southwest. Indeed, the seditionists' call for "equality" and for the liberation of all races harkens back to Mexican liberalism and the pernicious effects of its abstraction from difference. And yet, the fact that the novel posits a separate seditionist state— rather than a return to the fold of the Mexican nation—indicates that central to the seditionist's cause was a desire to reinterpret the meaning of Mexico's mixed racial character in the face of a segregationist U.S. racial geography. United States racial geography after all misinterpreted and discriminated against miscegenated bodies, reducing them to the biological signification of "bad moral character." However, as this seditionist revolt fails, the utopian ideal of unalienated racial/moral character remains just that: an ideal that recedes into nostalgia. By choosing this historical context, Paredes citationally sets the birth of the novel's protagonist within the nostalgic but lost possibility of unalienated racial subjectivity.

The novel opens with four rangers who have just encountered a seditionist named Lupe García. They dismiss him, indicating in their dialogue that he is nothing more than a savage bandit, an indio bárbaro incapable of expressing national allegiance to any republic, even to the Republic of the Southwest. Meanwhile, the third-person narrative voice informs us that the rangers actually let him pass because they recognized him and feared the deadly aim of García's rifle. The rangers immediately associate this dark-skinned Mexican with abjection (banditry) and danger (deadly accuracy), both attributes of the residual Indian savagery associated with the Apache and Comanche. The rangers dismiss the dark-skinned García as an indio bárbaro outside the space/time of the nation, for loyalty to the nation presumably unfolds across a linear, teleological time. The cupidity of the indios bárbaros precludes such developmental reason. Instead, as the indio bárbaro, the character of Lupe García haunts the narrative as a ghostly apparition, incapable of duration over the narrative time of the novel, but capable of appearing and disappearing across the Southwest landscape sporadically and strategically at will. In other words, in a novel about the protagonist George Washington Gómez, his uncle Lupe García nevertheless punctually erupts onto the narrative landscape, alternately precluding and enabling the Mexican American protagonist's assimilation in the new racial landscape.

The Mexican Lupe García as the indio bárbaro gets dismissed from the chronological time of the novel as the Apache and Comanche were dismissed from the scene/seen of the twentieth-century U.S. nation. Consequently, the policing of seditious acts gets displaced within the text onto the adjudication of Mexican American (racial) character. In the very next scene, the rangers find themselves at a loss when they encounter a light-skinned Gumersindo Gómez, the expectant father of the novel's protagonist who is traveling with the Anglo Doc Berry en route to the birth of his child. The rangers are incapable of adjudicating Gumersindo's moral character because they are confused by his racial attributes:

> The two sour-faced Rangers were staring at the red-haired man, *as though trying to place him.* The man fidgeted in his seat and avoided their eyes. Finally one of the Rangers spoke, "What's your name, feller?"
>
> "He doesn't speak much English," Doc Berry said.
>
> "Mexican, eh?" said MacDougal. "For a minute there I thought he was a white man." He looked steadily at the man, who began to show signs of nervousness.
>
> "He's a good Mexican," Doc said. "I can vouch for him."
>
> "He's okay if you say so Doc," MacDougal answered. "But it's getting kinda hard these days to tell the good ones from the bad ones. Can't take any chances these days. But he's all right if you say so." (*GWG*, 5–6, emphasis added)

Gumersindo's racial formation is indecipherable to the rangers because he is light skinned and red haired but clearly not Anglo. They can't place him within the racial taxonomy of the U.S. nation. His race is ambiguous and therefore dangerously deceiving. It is clear to the rangers that he is not a black man, and yet it is not at all clear that he is a white man—a certainty that would immediately clarify any concern over his moral character. Thus the Rangers are forced to move to a register other than race, and they ask him his name. Once Doc Berry clarifies that the passenger, though redheaded, is

144   CHAPTER THREE

in fact a Mexican, the question of Gumersindo's character comes sharply into focus. Doc Berry must immediately vouch for him or his life will be in danger: "He's a *good* Mexican." An annexed Mexican's racial formation is always ambiguous and dangerous, no matter how white s/he may appear, and racial ambiguity indexes an ambiguous moral character before the law as well. Thus the ambiguity over the nature of Gumersindo's character must remain unresolved. He is never fully assimilated into "good" moral character, as the rangers' response of "if you say so Doc" is hardly a resounding acceptance of Doc Berry's appraisal. Instead, it continues to be hard to "tell the good ones from the bad ones." And indeed, in retaliation for this short-lived, multiracial revolt of 1915–17, the Texas Rangers indiscriminately killed thousands of innocent Mexican Americans under the pretext of the sedition. The Texas Rangers retaliation was so indiscriminate that even the apologist Texas Rangers historian Walter Prescott Webb was forced to concede "many innocent Mexicans were made to suffer," in "the orgy of bloodshed" (Webb, *The Texas Rangers*, [1935] 1965, 478).

In the very next scene of the novel, the Gómez family decides on the name of the couple's first son. The boy's grandmother initiates the naming process by insisting that he needs to be baptized in the Catholic Church, representing the old racial geography of Spanish dominion. Christianization through baptism was the paramount determinant of character in New Spain, not racial difference. Gumersindo enthusiastically suggests "Crisósforo!" But Feliciano, the boy's uncle and a member of the seditionist movement, belittles his brother-in-law's aristocratic pretensions: "Sounds like *fósforo* to me. . . . Who wants to be named after a safety match?" Instead, the uncle tries to hail the boy into the subjection of Mexican revolutionary nationalism, suggesting the name "Venustiano," after Venustiano Carranza, the iconic, corrupt leader of the 1910 Mexican Revolution. Feliciano's very interest in the Mexican Revolution makes evident his inability to relinquish the character of Mexican citizenship, as required by the treaty. He cannot but be interested in the politics of a revolution transpiring right across the border from his home. Indeed, the porous nature of the Rio Grande border is precisely what preserves this character, as many exiled revolutionary leaders, including Ricardo Flores Magón, were headquartered in the Mexican American towns along the border. Feliciano explicitly identifies with revolutionary Mexico in the novel, and while this identification would seem to underscore the unreliable nature of annexed Mexicans' nationalist sentiment, it more poignantly underscores Feliciano's yearning for a national identification that does not depend on his racial whitening. For Feliciano yokes the Mexican Revolution to the Texas multiracial seditionist movement when he next suggests the name Cleto, after the fictionalized local seditionist hero Anacleto de la Peña. Feliciano's easy elision from one revolutionary movement to another underscores that the Mexican Revolution, like the seditionist movement, held the promise of encompassing the mixed racial character of all the nation's citizens. And it is certainly true that the twentieth-century Mexican revolution embraced indigenous difference to a degree unimaginable to the nineteenth-century liberal independence leaders who, for all their pronouncements of inclusivity, were unable to incorporate Apache and Comanche forms of territoriality into "la gran familia mejicana."

In response to Feliciano's suggestions of revolutionary names, "Gumersindo smiled absently and shook his head" (15). The phrasing of this response is particularly compelling. It suggests that by "smiling absently," Gumersindo absents himself from the revolutionary nationalism so powerful in defining Mexican character during the period represented in the novel. Furthermore, with an almost reflexive shaking of his head, Gumersindo rejects this interpellation for his child as well. When Feliciano insists the boy would "do fine if he's half as good as Anacleto," the text continues, "'It isn't that,' answered Gumersindo in a soft voice. 'It isn't that'" (15). The response suggests that Gumersindo may find the national character represented by the names Venustiano and Anacleto to be neither reprehensible nor ignoble. Rather the "It isn't that" suggests that Gumersindo, unlike his seditionist brother-in-law, recognizes the deadly consequences of retaining Mexican character for his son, and the "soft voice" registers his quiet acceptance of its necessary loss. As evidence of the deadly consequence of the inevitable failure to fully give up Mexican character, Gumersindo is later killed by Texas Rangers for being the brother-in-law of the seditionist Lupe García. However, the psychic consequences of *not* identifying with a revolutionary character are equally deadly: in order to assume U.S. character, one is required to disavow, to kill, that which savagely resists one's own racial subjection as abjection in the U.S. racial geography of the Southwest. It is a double death, as killing the resistance simultaneously kills any possibility for an integrated racial self, for recuperating the rich history of Mexican racial geography.

The grandmother continues the naming scene by insisting that the child should be named after his father because "that's the way you tell families apart. When he grows up people will say, 'Oh, you're Gumersindo Gómez, the son of Gumersindo Gómez and María García, and old Gumersindo Gómez, he was your grandfather.' That's the way to keep track of people and no need to put it down in writing" (15). The grandmother attempts to interpellate the

146 CHAPTER THREE

boy-child into the primary site of subject formation in the Southwest, the patriarchal tradition that grants social recognition to Mexican males without any "need to put it down in writing." Importantly, this patriarchal semiotics recognizes the child's mother as well, even though María García is folded into the generations of Gumersindos. But again, Gumersindo rejects this primary interpellative scene, with its folkloric, oral nuances, in another attempt to differentiate his child from inherited Mexican character: "I said I didn't want him to have my name" (15).

Once the three cultural cornerstones of "Mexican character" have been rejected—Catholic tradition, revolutionary nationalism, and folkloric patriarchy—as appropriate ideological scenes for the child's appointment as a subject, María offers her opinion: "I would like him to have a great man's name. Because he is going to grow up to be a great man who will help his people." Just as quickly as María's last name gets folded into the generations of Gumersindos in patriarchal interpellation, Maria's words get folded into Gumersindo's narrative for his son's interpellation into U.S. character. Though she has made no mention of Anglos, Gumersindo responds, "My son . . . He's going to be a great man among the Gringos. A Gringo name he shall have! Is he not as fair as any of them? Feliciano, what great men have the Gringos had?" (16). Gumersindo completely misinterprets María's words. He not only confuses the "a great man who will help his people" for "a great man among the Gringos" but further misinterprets her words by equating the moral characteristic of greatness with the physical characteristic of having fair skin, "Is he not as fair as any of them?" Gumersindo's words establish greatness and fair skin as the purview of U.S. character with the questions he directs toward Feliciano.

Feliciano tries to disrupt this assimilative appointment to subjection for his nephew by disrupting the racialized equation of U.S. character, fair skin, and greatness. He answers Gumersindo, "They are all great. . . . Great thieves, great liars, great sons-of-bitches." Gumersindo ignores his brother-in-law, however, and continues, "I was thinking of the great North American, he who was a general and fought the soldiers of the king." Once again the grandmother tries to intervene and return the boy's destiny to a Mexican narrative of interpellation, "That was Hidalgo, but he was a Mexican." Gumersindo will not be deterred in his quest for his son's assimilation of U.S. character. " 'I remember,' said Gumersindo, 'Wachinton. Jorge Wachinton. . . . Once he crossed a river while it was freezing. He drove out the English and freed the slaves' " (16). Gumersindo insists on the boy's assimilation into an idealized white racial character with his desire to interpellate his light-skinned son into a legacy of liberty (driving out the English) and of equality (emancipating the slaves). And yet Gumersindo exemplifies the difficulty, if not impossibility, of such an assimilative appointment as subject for Mexicans. Gumersindo himself disrupts the successful interpellation of the boy by confusing the slave owner with the emancipator of the slaves, and naming him after the former. And indeed, the impossibility of proper assimilation for Mexican character is underscored in the next chapter in which Gumersindo is killed by the four marauding *rinches*. Although the four Texas rangers had already met him— and Doc Berry had already vouched for his character—the rangers nevertheless mistake Gumersindo for a seditionist indio bárbaro, regardless of skin color, reinforcing the ambiguous racial character of all annexed Mexicans in the Southwest.

The final result of the naming scene recognizes the structure of identification and disavowal of a psychic formation, one that positions the boy's racial character in dangerous proximity to indios bárbaros but requires his renunciation of his indigenous ancestry. George Washington Gómez's grandmother defiantly mispronounces the phonetically hispanicized name "Wachinton" as "Guálinto," regardless of Feliciano's repeated attempts to correct her. The nickname Guálinto sticks with the protagonist through four-fifths of his narrative life. It thoroughly displaces his proper name. Although Gumersindo tries to disavow the identification with Indian difference by naming his boy after Anglo "greatness," it is the barbarous Indian identification that sticks. When Feliciano enrolls the boy in primary school and the teacher asks his name, Feliciano reflexively answers "Guálinto Gómez." Miss Cornelia, the teacher, comments, "'Strange name isn't it? Is it an Indian name?' 'Yes,' said Feliciano, 'It's an Indian name.' He looked at Guálinto and then he looked away" (110). It is significant that Miss Cornelia misreads Guálinto's ambiguous racial character as Indian although he is light skinned. While it is her job as a member of the educational state apparatus to properly interpellate the child into U.S. character, she insists on misreading his racial character as Indian, as inassimilable. As the other explicit example of an annexed Mexican in the text who strives toward assimilation into U.S. character, Miss Cornelia sees herself in competition with Guálinto for enfranchisement into full citizenship. Understanding that many are called to U.S. character, but few may enter, Miss Cornelia takes it on herself to *mis*-educate the annexed Mexican children in her charge, or rather to properly educate them on their distance from acceptable, civilized character. Of neither Mexican character nor U.S. character, Guálinto is consigned to the margins of social recognition as an approximate Indian.

Why does Feliciano agree with Miss Cornelia's reading of the name of his beloved nephew? It is certainly not because he wants to consign Guálinto

148   CHAPTER THREE

outside the racial geography of the U.S. nation. Rather I would argue that this is Feliciano's taciturn bid at prescribing a livable psychic life for his nephew; thus he looks at him and then looks away. Feliciano knows that the psychic life appointed to Guálinto by his proper name—founding-father first names, racially ambiguous last name—is simply an unlivable subject position. Indeed, Guálinto is tormented from the beginning of the novel until its end by the consequences of his proper name. Feliciano hopes that the (mis)identification of Guálinto with Indian difference might offer his nephew a viable alternative, a psychic life lived in savage resistance to the interpellative call for the disavowal of Mexican mixed racial character. For Guálinto can neither relinquish his Mexican character nor fully embrace his U.S. character without becoming undone psychically.

Relinquishing his Mexican character would not only require his relinquishing of his indigenous ancestry, it would require the loss of the Mexican abstract ideal of racial inclusion. The loss of indigenous ancestry and of an abstract Mexican equality are cathected onto the figure of the indio bárbaro who must be expunged from both nations. In order for Guálinto to become properly assimilated into U.S. character, he must relinquish as lost the indio bárbaro. Accordingly, on a drunken evening at the end of his senior year in high school, Guálinto shoots and kills his uncle, the seditionist Lupe García. It is important that Guálinto does not know it was his uncle he killed, or that García was a seditionist, for he is metaphorically killing a Mexican heritage he never fully comprehended. Indeed, the structure of identification and disavowal makes it impossible to comprehend his Mexican heritage. In order to enjoy "all the rights of the citizens of the United States," the boy must not only relinquish his rich Mexican heritage but denounce it at great psychic cost. Guálinto foreshadows his own psychic unraveling by literalizing the melancholic process of violent loss, of "unbecoming" Mexican in order to become (Mexican) American. This killing metonymically stands in as a rite of passage for Guálinto's own deadly assimilation into U.S. character. It is immediately after this event that Guálinto leaves the Texas valley for college, after which he enlists in the army.

When the novel continues in part 5, Guálinto has returned to the valley as a counterintelligence spy. He is posing as a Washington lawyer working for an unnamed real estate company interested in buying land in Texas, though he has actually been sent by the government to spy on his Mexican American cohort of former friends. The government believes that these friends may be involved in seditious activity and treason. Instead, they have organized a multiracial political party to challenge the racist and classist Democratic machine in the next election, echoing the principles of the Plan de San Diego in their electoral alternative to violence. His friends hope that Guálinto has returned to be their leader; however Guálinto has no interest in joining the party they have formed. Indeed, Guálinto no longer exists, as the protagonist has changed his name to George G. Gómez in a literalization of his assimilative efforts. Not only does our adult protagonist shed his childhood nickname in part 5, but by the time George returns to the Rio Grande Valley as a lawyer/spy, he has legally dropped "Washington" from his name as well. Although one may be tempted to read this second name change as a clandestine disavowal of his apparent patriotic allegiance to the United States, such a reading would be mistaken. In a literary flashback, the reader is informed that George decided to change his name legally only after meeting his future father-in-law. While George greets Ellen's father with a polite "Very pleased to meet you," his fiancé's father replies with racist alacrity, "George Washington Gomaize. . . . They sure screwed you up, didn't they, boy? . . . You look white but you're a goddam Meskin. And what does your mother do but give you a nigger name. George Washington Go-maize" (284). The narrator informs us that "it was then that he decided to legally change his name to George G. Gómez, the middle G for García, his mother's maiden name" (284). Ellen's father insists on doubly racializing this white-*looking* imposter. First, the father emphasizes George's continued dangerous proximity to Indian character by stressing the second syllable of George's last name as *maize*. However, it is his name's association with blackness that appears to be the most damning for George. Ellen's father refuses to acknowledge the name's association with the first U.S. president except by proxy, calling it a "nigger name" because of its historic use by blacks. This prompts George to drop "Washington" in a bid to disassociate himself further from any racial association with blacks (or afromestizos). In other words, although George *looks* white, his future father-in-law reminds George of the impossibility of his assimilating white character, insisting instead on George's denigrated, miscegenated Mexican "character." Indeed, the phonetic pronunciation of the word *Meskin* implies that his skin is as "messed up" as his naming. Although the narrator indicates that George chooses the "G" as a tribute to his mother, the G stands for Guálinto as well, as it is the resistant Indian character of his youth who haunts the adult George, not the patriot of the Potomac.

The expense of disavowing his Mexican character, however, is such that Guálinto's bid for assimilative subjection must be undone every evening. George G. Gómez is haunted in his dream life by Guálinto, by the Indian difference in Mexican character that he cannot fully relinquish without relinquishing his melancholic psyche itself. Every night he reenacts a childhood fantasy of Guálinto's by dreaming he is a participant in the battle of San Jacinto on the Mexican side of the U.S.–Mexico war, only this time the Mexican army, reinforced by Texas rancheros, wins the war and "Texas and the Southwest remain forever Mexican":

> He woke with a start, stared at the unfamiliar ceiling of the bedroom and cursed softly to himself. Again, the same mother-loving dream. The third time this past week. Goddam ridiculous, having daydreams of his boyhood come back to him in his sleep. . . .
>
> He would imagine he was living in his great-grandfather's time, when the Americans first began to encroach on the northern provinces of the New Republic of Mexico. Reacting against the central government's inefficiency and corruption, he would organize *rancheros* into a fighting militia and train them by using them to exterminate the Comanches. Then, with the aid of generals like Urrea, he would extend his influence to the Mexican army. He would discover the revolver before Samuel Colt, as well as the hand grenade and a modern style of portable mortar. In his daydreams he built a modern arms factory at Laredo, doing it all in great detail, until he had an enormous, well trained army that included Irishmen and escaped American Negro slaves. Finally, he would defeat not only the army of the United States but its navy as well. He would reconquer all the territory west of the Mississippi River and recover Florida as well.
>
> At that point he would end up with a feeling of emptiness, of futility. Somehow, he was not comfortable with the way things ended. There was something missing that made any kind of ending fail to satisfy. (281–282)

The protagonist's ambiguous identification with Indian difference is initially foisted on him by the combined logics of articles 9 and 11 of the Treaty of Guadalupe Hidalgo. Rather than simply allow his ambiguous identification to debilitate, this dream suggests that every night George becomes Guálinto once again as an unconscious strategy of resistance to the racism encountered by a little boy growing up in the segregated Southwest. The lost Indian object represented by Guálinto must be melancholically incorporated into this unconscious return to his boyhood dream life for his psyche to hold together. Publicly George must renounce the identification in the hopes of enjoying all the rights of U.S. citizenship, but privately he is left with a melancholic "feeling of emptiness," his "futility" indexing the withdrawal of his libidinal investment from the southwestern racial geography of the United States.

Importantly, his daydreams of reestablishing the Mexican racial character of the Southwest are historically in keeping with its liberal nineteenth-century meaning, for in his dreams he practices winning the war against the United States by exterminating the Comanche. Thus Guálinto Gómez's utopic dream life still maintains the liberal Mexican distinction demonstrated by multiracial scalping parties capable of including "Irishmen" and "American Negro slaves" and even pacified Indians, from those savage Indians who hover on/ as the border of Mexican national character, just as the peaceful Indians of Chihuahua protected the Chihuahuenses from the tribus salvajes in absence of the federal military in the nineteenth century. Good Indians like Guálinto, however, are not only part of Mexican national character in his dreams but redeem it from "the central government's inefficiency and corruption." There are no such fine distinctions made by the U.S. government, though, between "good" Indians and "bad." And so every day, George G. Gómez, assimilated and light-skinned, wakes from his dream identity to live a life of quiet desperation as a first lieutenant of counterintelligence who must disavow his seditious and savage "Indian" friends in order to save himself. The literary protagonist enacts for us the psychic consequences of the enactment of article 9 by the Mexican American inhabitants of the Southwest, required by the treaty to renounce their Mexican character—their indigenous difference. George's unconscious clings to this Indian difference for him, allowing it expression in his nightly dreams of reunification, not only of the Mexican nation, but of greater New Spain; not only of a physical geography but of the racial one fractured by scalping programs, raids, wars, and treaties.

Concluding Remarks

The character of George G./Guálinto Gómez embodies in literary form the psychic split enacted by the Treaty of Guadalupe Hidalgo in its racial construction of Chicana/os. From the Mexican colonists' perspective in the Southwest, the treaty granted all gente de razón the right of full enfranchisement into U.S. national citizenship. Though excluding "savage Indian tribes," Mexican character nevertheless encompassed mestizos, afromestizos, and pacified indios from the perspective of Mexico. However, from the perspective of a conquering U.S. imperial power, the treaty prescribed the whitening of only a small light-skinned minority of Mexican population, as the rest of those annexed were redefined as racially ineligible of citizenship. Enfranchisement for Mexicans required the disavowal of a rich, racial logic of inclusion. It required the abandonment of the very terms of sovereign Mexican character:

its combined mestizo, afromestizo, and Indian heritage. The legacy of the U.S. government's interpretation of the treaty can be found not only on the Indian reservations that riddle the U.S. Southwest but in the insistence of use of the term *Hispanic* in describing people of Latin American descent, for the very etymology of the term—of Spain—whitens its subject. However, the terms of this enfranchisement are not only about loss but also about an accretion of power to those who could accept these terms, for the treaty required the enfranchisement of whitened annexed Mexicans into a logic of domination of racial others. Thus, in the loss of Mexican character, what is gained is the privilege of conquest. Hence George G. Gómez returns to the Rio Grande Valley as an agent of neocolonial power to spy on his former friends.

Paredes's novel richly documents the psychic effect of this legacy for Chicana/o subjection. When Chicana/os embrace an Indian past categorically denied them by the U.S. interpretation of the treaty, they embrace an Indian identity that remains at the margins of social recognition. Not only at the margins of a normative, racist social recognition of imperial America, but at the margins of Mexican American social recognition as well. For generations of Mexican Americans, to recognize this savage Indian in oneself was to willfully embrace one's own disenfranchisement, as George G. Gómez attests. Nevertheless, as we shall see in the next chapter, the "Mexican American generation" of the 1940s and 1950s came up with creative ways of maintaining their racially mixed character, while circumventing the potential effect of psychic undoing evidenced in Guálinto.

In the embrace of Indian identity by Chicano nationalism, it is the treaty's history of stark racial division between colonized mestizos and Indians that is disavowed. To reclaim Indian heritage without recognition of the differences 150 years of U.S. racialization have wrought among southwestern indigenous peoples confined to reservations, African Americans, and southwestern mestizos is to reclaim an innocent history that is not so innocent after all, as I hope I have demonstrated. The psychic split registered by George G. Gómez should caution twenty-first-century readers on the difficult and ambivalent place of Indian identity in Chicana/o subject formation. Chicana/os continue to struggle with the place of an Indian identification foisted on a population by a racist state's interpretation of the treaty, and yet one also denied them, as any knowledge of the full import of the Indian contribution to mestizo history is methodically erased from the register of social recognition.

4

ADJUDICATING EXCEPTION
The Fate of the *Indio Bárbaro* in the U.S. Courts (1869–1954)

In chapter 3 we witnessed the brutal intercalation of Mexican and U.S. racial geographies of the nineteenth century. The nineteenth century ushered in a Mexican liberal nationalism premised on a mestizo model of abstract political emancipation that was broadly inclusive in terms of race. The exception to this racial inclusion was the indio bárbaro who in fact enabled the Mexican demos to come together in racial unity through the practices of scalping and beheading. Over the course of the liberal nineteenth century, the iteration of the indio bárbaro lost its colonial fluidity, ceased to be the potential economic and political ally, and instead became all that must be pushed out of the nation's borders. Mexico and the United States colluded in producing this iteration of the indio bárbaro through the transnational scalping posses and through the Treaty of Guadalupe Hidalgo (TGH), which brokered peace at the expense of the tribus salvajes. In this revised indio bárbaro we palimpsestically trace Sepúlveda's *indios nefastos* but gone is all possibility of remediation from its liberal enunciation.

Meanwhile, the racial geography of the United States was expanded and solidified through the Comanche and Apache Indians who not only held their territories, but expanded them into northern Mexico. The imagined Indian who holds ground and then cedes it to the United States was an operative and enabling force in U.S. expansion, however the Apache and Comanche refused to cede ground in the second half of the nineteenth century. Indeed they insisted on maintaining their territories rather than submit to reservation status. Thus the newly configured indio bárbaro once again was deployed.

Former allies against Mexico were placed beyond the pale of U.S. racial geography and became the targeted focus of military attacks between the U.S. and Mexican military. The production of this new iteration of the indio bárbaro in the liberal period is the singular point of complicity between two racial geographies that were otherwise quite different.

If the emergent nations of the United States and Mexico colluded in their production of the indio bárbaro in the mid-nineteenth century, to solidify their own boundaries and establish peace between the two nations, the racial geographies of the two countries collided spectacularly in the annexed territories along the border in the late nineteenth and early twentieth centuries. Mexico could not control the interpretation of the TGH in the annexed territories, nor could it have anticipated the violent dispossession a U.S. racial geography based on segregation and reservation would have imposed on annexed Mexicans. A multiracial Mexican male constituency enjoyed a panoply of rights after independence: the right to vote, to hold land privately or in common, to education, and to run for public office. White, mestizo, afromestizo, and indios, all enjoyed these and other rights formally bestowed on them by political emancipation, regardless of how their economic, social, and gendered conditions may have continued to curtail the full execution of some of these rights.

For U.S. federal, state, and territorial authorities, however, such a racial geography was incommensurate with its own, and state legislatures, courts, and the U.S. Congress repeatedly disenfranchised large swaths of Mexican indios, mestizos, and afromestizos who were formally enfranchised by Mexico. Despite their bodily presence in the annexed territories, they were placed outside the bounds of the racial geography of the United States, outside the political and democratic demos. It was again the trace of the indio bárbaro that enabled this, ever present in Mexicans' indeterminate racial embodiment (from an Anglo-American perspective). United States jurisprudence excised most Mexicans from the scene/seen of a conquered landscape envisioned in the terms of white citizenship. Even before the U.S. war against Mexico, it was Mexicans' "half-bred" status, their barbarous core, that required U.S. conquest for the proper administration of the frontier. Frederick Jackson Turner's frontier, horribly mismanaged by the lazy, half-breed Mexicans, had beckoned the Anglo-American settler to come and recue it; to release its democratic potential and develop its indigenous resources. Thus, after annexation, it is unsurprising that U.S. jurisprudence used Mexicans' racially indeterminate character to adjudicate a series of exclusions "democratically" and through the law. It is also unsurprising that it required the continued alienation of Mexicans from their indigenous origins in the process, to better parse its racially segregated landscape and dispossess barbarous peoples from their resources. This chapter examines a series of court cases in which we witness Mexican Americans attempting to claim rights for their racially mixed communities in the face of a U.S. jurisprudence that instead manipulated a Mexican racial indeterminacy to practice racial exclusion "democratically," to graph a neatly segregated racial geography in the Southwest.

Who's Your Mother?

The Spanish conquest of the Southwest, therefore, actually consisted in a Spanish-led Mexican northward movement; and one of the most significant, ultimate effects of the conquest was not the spread of the Spanish Empire but the diffusion of *Mexicanismo* far to the north (. . . while the Spaniards were attempting to hispanicize northern natives the cult of Moctezuma was actually spreading among the conquered. By the 1860's the Apaches were fighting for the cause of Moctezuma [from their viewpoint] and the Yaquis Revolt of 1825 was raised in the name of Moctezuma).

When we speak, therefore, of the Spanish intrusion into the Southwest we must actually correct ourselves by referring to its "Hispano-Mexican" rather than Spanish character.
—**Jack Forbes**, ca. 1961–1962

As to the *strictly proper* classification of the descendant of an aboriginal inhabitant of Mexico, whose ancestors had been, politically and religiously, incorporated for over 300 years with one of the proudest, finest, and purest scions of the *true Caucasian race*,—the Spaniards and their fellow countrymen, the Basques,—during which time even their very language has been lost, and their blood so freely intermingled with the pure stock of either that the fair, blue-eyed Castilian, or tawny, low-browed, straight coarse haired Aztec, is seldom met with. . . . All history points with unerring fingers to the inevitable fading away of every lesser and ruder form of civilization when brought in contact with the great dominant Latin race, whether Caesar, Charlemagne, Columbus, Cortez, Pizarro, or Napoleon marched at the head of their conquering legions, as it points with equal unerring certainty to the fact that the Anglo-Saxon has carried his language, his laws, his customs, his progress, and his institutions to every quarter of the globe where floats his flag. —Brief of **T. M. Paschal**, *In re Rodriguez,* 1897 (emphasis added)

These two quotations, separated by over sixty years of Mexican American, Chicana/o, and Native American civil rights and nationalist activism, represent distinct visions of mestizaje.

T. J. Paschal's quotation comes from his amicus curiae brief, submitted to the Texas Appellate Supreme Court on behalf of Ricardo Rodriguez. Rodriguez, originally from Guanajuato, Mexico, had lived in San Antonio, Texas, for ten years before deciding to apply for U.S. citizenship. The Bexar County

Court denied his application for U.S. citizenship in 1893 on racial grounds, as Rodriguez was neither white nor black, but of self-evident Indian ancestry. Rodriguez, classed as Indian in the lower court, was ineligible for citizenship under the Naturalization Act of 1870, which exclusively extended this right— previously reserved for alien whites—to "aliens of African nativity and persons of African descent." American Indians had already been excluded from the right to naturalization by the time of Rodriguez's application in two landmark cases, *In re Camille* (1880) and *Elk v. Wilkins* (1884).

Paschal's brief explains the ethnological reasons behind Rodriguez's qualification for citizenship, but his endorsement of Rodriguez's right to citizenship was necessarily predicated on several racist precepts of the day. Like the Bexar County Court, Paschal perceived Rodriguez to be visibly indigenous, hence the need to review the historical trajectory of the "coarse haired Aztec" race. His brief distinguished the trajectory of the Aztecs—more properly the Nahaus—from that of the North American Indians excluded by the courts in 1880 and 1884. Paschal sought to convince the judge that the Castilians and Basques in Mexico (New Spain), those "purest scions of the true Caucasian race," had "so freely intermingled" with the "low-browed" indigenous race, that they had become "incorporated"—physically made one— indistinguishable from each other over the course of three hundred years of miscegenation. And though it would be impossible to distinguish the progeny of the "fair" Spaniard and the "tawny" Nahua, it is nevertheless the "lesser and ruder" indigenous culture that must inevitably "fade away" in the face of the superior Latin race with their "conquering legions." In turn, the "unerring fingers" of history pointed the court toward the decision that this racial and cultural incorporation of the Latin and the Nahua races must inevitably give way, presumably, to a new amalgamation with the superior Anglo-Saxon race that now "floats [its] flag" in the formerly Mexican Southwest.

An implicit pyramid of races undergirds Paschal's argument. While the Anglo-Saxon race was clearly at its pinnacle, it is Paschal's task to convince the court that Mexicans like Rodriguez had traveled far enough from the pyramid's lowly base of indigeneity by virtue of their intermingling with the conquering "Latins" to qualify as racially "white," or at least as no longer Indian. While he fails to persuade the District Judge Thomas S. Maxey of this racial and cultural migration by the Nahuas, Judge Maxey rules in Rodriguez's favor on entirely different grounds, on the basis of several treaties passed by the U.S. Congress that granted Mexicans a singular exception to the 1870 Naturalization Act. Like the proverbial fig leaf, the unique path to citizenship for Mexicans covered over the unintended racial consequences of U.S. imperial conquest, as it would in the twentieth century for Puertoriqueños and Filipinos.

In contrast to Paschal's brief, the distinguished Native American scholar and activist Jack Forbes implies that Nahua culture triumphed over Spanish in the course of their incorporation. In his essay, "The Mexican Heritage of Aztlán (The Southwest), to 1821" Forbes offered the reader his own ethnological account of the presumably self-evident term *Mexican*. The term *Mexicano* initially applied only to the descendants of the Nahuas. As Forbes puts it, "In the sixteenth century and for many decades thereafter, one had to be Náhuatl-speaking to be Mexican, and, to be more precise, one had to be Aztec or Aztec-related" (1). In Forbes's "precise" vision, the descendants of the Nahuas—those authentic *Mexicanos*—were the actual colonizers of the northern territory presumably conquered by the Spanish. *Mexicanos* traveled north with the Spaniards, usurping the colonial mission for their own ends. Rather than hispanicizing northern Indians, these true *Mexicanos* finally accomplished a goal that had eluded their ancestors for the duration of the Aztec Empire: they conquered the *bárbaros del norte,* the Chichimecas, with aid of Spanish swords perhaps, but moreover with their own superior culture. The Nahuas' progeny surreptitiously appropriated the Spanish colonial mission to spread not only their language and customs, but also their anticolonial resistance. This anticolonialism was at the heart of Mexicanismo, and thus the Yaqui and Apache resisted both Mexican and U.S. liberal nationalism under Moctezuma's mantle.

Paschal and Forbes offer us two interpretations of the process and result of the biological and cultural amalgamation under Spain's colonial purview. Both claim a certain classificatory authority in describing Mexicans. Paschal invokes the eugenics of his day to classify the races as he carefully attempts to place Rodriguez on one side of the racial divide between whites and other inferior races, while Forbes invokes the precision of anthropology (language, kinship) to trace the genealogy of *Mexicanos* to their *Nahua* origins. Importantly, neither Forbes nor Paschal reduces culture to biology, but rather each sees culture as acting through biological amalgamation. For Paschal the crude cultural proclivities of the indigenous Nahuas were redeemed through miscegenation, as the Indian character dissolved—"has been lost"—into the superior white character of the Latin race. For Forbes, the stamp of indigenous resistance indefatigably persists in the anticolonialism of contemporary Mexicans who remain in the U.S. Southwest, especially in their misidentified "Spanish character" ("we must actually correct ourselves"). Forbes expressed the zeal of the Native American and Chicano nationalism of his day. His essay

158 CHAPTER FOUR

after all is about the *indigenous* sovereignty of the Chicana/o inheritors of *Aztlán*. Paschal, on the other hand, mobilized the racist eugenics of his day in the interest of Mexican incorporation into the franchise of U.S. citizenship. Forbes and Paschal articulate two distinct visions of Mexican racial character, but these two visions do not merely stand in for the Mexican and U.S. racial geographies of the twentieth century. Rather together they articulate the collision of these two racial geographies along the border, the impossibility of displacing one racial order with another.

Even as the United States and Mexico solidified their postcolonial racial requirements for citizenship in the post–Civil War and postrevolutionary eras respectively, the Mexican inhabitants of the border insistently challenged these requirements by their very racial embodiment, on the one hand, and by their geographical emplotment, on the other. The persistent recourse to classificatory language in both Paschal and Forbes is symptomatic of the unique challenge posed by Mexican racial character to the adjudication of the permissible categories of naturalized U.S. citizenship in the aftermath of the Civil War and before the civil rights era. Mexican Americans were but one of the many racialized minorities subject to de facto and de jure discrimination in the United States between 1870 and 1964, but they offer a unique window into U.S. jurisprudence during a period when the U.S. Congress and courts brutally attempted to turn a multiracial U.S. constituency into a biracial national geography. Mexican Americans embodied a racial multiplicity that challenged juridical means of accounting for political democracy: who within this motley racial crew of Mexicans would count for the purposes of citizenship? For rights, apportionment, and democratic representation? How to account for the racial diversity of Mexican citizenship within a U.S. racial geography committed to a reductive, bipolar mode of racial recognition?

Meanwhile, Mexicans' and Mexican Americans' testimony on behalf of their own racial character in U.S. courts revealed the banal brutality of mestizaje as a multiracial model of inclusion. The insistently *Mexican* racial character claimed by the inhabitants of the borderland attests to the success of liberal and revolutionary Mexican governments in wedding a national geography to a racial one. The Mexicans and Mexican Americans who applied for U.S. citizenship, who fought school segregation, and who challenged jury discrimination in U.S. courts reveal to us the racially restricted nature of political enfranchisement in the United States, while also enacting mestizaje as the racial embodiment of a Mexican political citizenship that occluded indigenous specificity in its own way. These cases attest to a U.S. racial geography that encompassed the daily cartographies of segregation and assimilation created in the Southwest, but they also trouble the triumphalist temporality of racial redemption presumed by a segregation-to-integration timeline. Moreover, these plaintiffs and witnesses offer us insight into their persistent embodiment of a mestizo racial and temporal geography in the territory of the U.S. nation. No matter how adamantly U.S. jurisprudence was in its attempt to adjudicate a bipolar racial geography in the Southwest, Mexican American legal activists were just as adamant in their recoding of "whiteness" into an iteration of revolutionary mestizaje.

Indian Given has thus far foregrounded the colonial space making of settlement as practiced by the Spanish and the Anglo-American, as well as the postcolonial space making of nation as practiced by Mexico and the United States in the nineteenth century. In the creation of the colonial and postcolonial geographies of race, the placement of the Indians in landscape—their spatial emplotment in the creation of frontiers—enabled the production of Spanish and British colonial spaces, and subsequently the emergence of early Mexican and U.S. nations. Spanish and British colonial elites imputed humanity to indigenous peoples in the terms given by Catholic unity and Anglo-Saxon sovereignty respectively. In turn, Mexican and U.S. elites reworked these colonial imputations of indigenous humanity to suit their rather distinct purposes of national enfranchisement. As evidenced by the last chapter, indigenous peoples like the Comanche and the Apache interrupted the postcolonial imposition of national boundaries on their territories, at times challenging the terms of their racial inscription in Mexico and the United States, at times avidly participating in the production of these terms. As an effect of these indigenous interventions, the racial geographies of Mexico and the United States colluded in the production of the indio bárbaro of the border region, exiled from the scene of both nations.

In this chapter, I follow the heterotemporal trace of the indio bárbaro into the making of the segregated twentieth-century landscape of the Southwest and the bipolar racial geography of the post–Civil War United States. Between 1896 and 1954, Mexicans and Mexican Americans fought a series of legal cases for naturalization, for ending segregation in schools, and for challenging discrimination in the empanelment of juries. In examining these cases, I focus neither on the history of political disenfranchisement they record, nor on the production of segregated space they encode. Cultural geographers have published many excellent volumes on the racially segregated spaces produced in the United States during and after the Jim Crow era. Similarly, Latina/o criti-

160   CHAPTER FOUR

cal legal theory (LatCrit) has exhaustively considered the role these specific cases played in the civil rights history of the United States. Instead, I consider how these cases produced space in the Lefebvreian sense: the litigation and resolution of these cases facilitated the *representation* of U.S. national space as emptied of indigeneity, while also encoding "America" as a representational space of democracy.

Two of the cases considered in this chapter—*Mendez v. Westminster* (1946), *Hernandez v. Texas* (1954)—have been richly studied. Many Chicano historians and LatCrit scholars have argued that Mexican American civil rights activists made a "Faustian pact with whiteness" in these cases by pursuing a legal strategy of Mexican American inclusion as part of the white race (Foley 2005a, 2005b, 1997; Haney López 2005, 2003b, 2001, 1998, 1996; Lovell Banks 2006; Trucios-Haynes 2000–2001). This legal strategy, these scholars suggest, not only expressed a regrettable aspirational whiteness, it also presumably distanced Mexican Americans from allies like African American civil rights activists. Other Chicana/o scholars like Martha Menchaca (1993), Christopher Arriola (1995), Thomas A. Guglielmo (2006), and Laura Gómez (2007) place this "other white" strategy within a longer trajectory of Mexican American legal activism dating back to the 1850s, but attribute its twentieth-century evolution to court decisions in the 1930s and 1940s that repeatedly classified Mexicans as white to circumvent charges of discrimination. Mexican American activists subsequently took up the "other white" category as part of a broader antisegregation strategy, in tandem with other minority legal advocacy organizations such as the NAACP, the ACLU, the American Jewish Congress, and the Japanese American Citizens League (Arriola 1995, 194; Sheridan 2003a, 113).[1] In this vein, dissenting critical legal theory scholars have found this "Faustian pact" interpretation of the "other white" strategy wanting not only because of the exigencies of particular trials, but also because of the difficulty of ascertaining racial consciousness from legal proceedings.[2] As Ariela Gross puts it, "Parties on both sides used arguments about racial identity strategically and instrumentally, and we cannot take their legal strategies as a simple reflection of their actual thoughts and feelings about racial or national identity" (2007, 342).[3] Scholars should not deduce from this "other white" strategy either a self-loathing or aspirational whiteness on the part of the legal activists who sponsored and prosecuted these cases, in other words.

Elsewhere I have argued that a careful reading of the archive attests not only to the nationwide alliances forged by this generation of legal activists with the NAACP and the ACLU, among others, but also to the deeply ironized and polemical claim to whiteness made by Mexican American activists. These activists wielded their Mexican "whiteness" as a wedge that at once pried open the door for other minority groups to share in the "equal protection" of their ambiguous racial hue and exposed the limits of an ambivalent white justice. Moreover, activists stretched the meaning of their whiteness to include every shade in the *casta* system (Saldaña-Portillo 2008). The debate over Mexican American aspirational whiteness is itself a red herring, as it was not Mexicans' alleged whiteness that at once enabled the further alienation of indigenous claims to territoriality *and* excluded indigenous peoples from the representational space of nation. Rather it was precisely Mexican mestizaje that the courts seized on to construct a bipolar racial geography in the United States, to distance Mexican Americans from any claim to their own indigenous belonging and from other minorities. The porosity of Mexicans' racial character in mestizaje enabled the courts to repeatedly rehearse former judicial precedents of *legal* racial exclusion and discrimination, reiterating the racial multiplicity of the nation *through* Mexican racial character only to reduce this multiplicity to a bifurcated notion of the national racial demos.

"A Pure-Blooded Mexican": In re Rodriguez

The founding and justifying moment that institutes law implies a performative force, which is always an interpretative force. —**Jacques Derrida**, "Force of Law"

To be just, the decision of a judge, for example, must not only follow a rule of law or a general law but must also assume it, approve it, confirm its value, *by a reinstituting act of interpretation, as if ultimately nothing previously existed of the law, as if the judge himself invented the law in every case....* This "fresh judgment" can very well—must very well—conform to a preexisting law, but the reinstituting, reinventive and freely decisive interpretation, the responsible interpretation of the judge requires that his "justice" not just consist in conformity, in the conservative and reproductive activity of judgment... *it must conserve the law and also destroy it or suspend it enough to have to reinvent it in each case,* rejustify it, at least reinvent it in the reaffirmation and the new and free confirmation of its principle. —**Jacques Derrida**, "Force of Law," emphasis added

In "Force of Law" Jacques Derrida (1989–1990) elucidates the gap between the infinite possibility of justice and its finite instantiation as law. The instantiation of justice as law requires the violence of interpretation, "an interpretative force" inevitably reductive of the idea of justice—brutal yet necessary. Whereas justice is free, responsible to the other, specific, undecidable, and urgent, the law is encumbered by general principles of universal application, bounded by convention, hesitant, and sluggish. Justice is an aporia that never-theless requires action, requires a path chosen. The enactment of the law, the in-terpretation of the case, necessarily entails *injustice*, either in the application of a "universal" rule to a specific case, or its suspension in the name of specificity.

Derrida's elucidation is most helpful in analyzing the cases brought by Mexicans and Mexican Americans seeking justice in U.S. courts, as well as the rulings made by superior court judges attempting to render justice for the plaintiffs but also for the U.S. polity they represented. As the cases consid-ered here were won on appeal, following Derrida we may surmise that these lower courts failed to approximate justice, "to be just," because they hewed too closely to the rule of law, simply applying it rather than "reinvent[ing] it in each case." In overturning the lower courts' verdicts, the superior court judges may be seen as "rejustifying" the law "by a reinstituting act of interpre-tation." In the briefs for these cases we see the advocates, counsels, and judges engaged in precisely such reinstituting acts of interpretation.

In these reinterpretations of precedent—in the reinvention of the law in the name of justice—we glimpse the violence of the previous rule of law with regard to naturalization, segregation, and discrimination. At the same time, as Derrida's own deconstruction makes evident, each "reaffirmation" of the law, each "new and free confirmation of its principle," enacts violence anew: "For in the founding of the law or in its institution, the same problem of justice will have been posed and violently resolved, that is to say buried, dissimulated, repressed" (963). Justice is "decided" in the law and with each such decision something is excluded or repressed. The resolution of justice on behalf of the plaintiffs in the cases considered here was predicated on the dissimulation, repression, burying of a fresh violence, of a fresh injustice against others, and each injustice is a space-making practice.

For T. M. Paschal, friend of the court in the case of *In re Rodriguez*, the chief impediment to Rodriguez's naturalization was the "ethnological fea-ture," the fact that he was "not a 'white' man, and apparently belong[ed] to the Indian or red race" (*In re Rodriguez*, 340). Rather than argue Rodriguez was *not* an Indian (as Rodriguez himself did in testimony), Paschal argued that the law never intended to exclude Native Americans in the first place. Paschal revisited *In re Ah Yup* and *In re Camille* in order to reinvent the law by considering which groups the Naturalization Act of 1870 specifically intended to *exclude* rather than *include*. He admitted these two cases seemed to provide "support for the proposition that the white, or Caucasian, and Negro, or African, race alone are eligible to citizenship" (340).[4] But instead, Paschal argued, the *Ah Yup* case proved the words *white* and *African* in the Naturalization Act inversely indicated only the intended *excluded* race: "The [*Ah Yup*] decision is clear and emphatic that the Chinese or Mongolian was intended *expressly* to be excluded by congress when the whole question was under discussion, in 1869–70" (340, emphasis added).

Paschal returns to the record of the congressional debate to "leave no shadow of doubt touching the [Mongolian] race that was intended to be denied the boon of American citizenship." While Congress in 1869–70 debated the possibility of simply removing the word "white" from the 1790 Naturalization Act, the senators decided against this "most natural mode" of expanding the franchise. Instead, they "decided, by separate provision, that the naturalization laws should apply to Africans and persons of African descent" (340). For Paschal, the Senate's refusal to remove the word *white* was evidence of its *singular* intention to exclude Asians.[5] Paschal inverts legislative intent with the force of his interpretation. The 1870 Naturalization Act did not affirmatively grant the right of naturalization only to whites and blacks. Rather, the language used "by separate provision" to extend the right to Africans was intended specifically to withhold this right from Mongolians, but not necessarily from any other races:

> The fear of Mongolian citizenship arose from considerations of the highest national policy. That race was not only alien in color, but was, in all things that render possible a sound citizenship, the very antipodes of the Anglo-Saxon or even native American races [*sic*]. His total inability to assimilate with our people in their laws, customs, institutions, or religion, or even to suffer his acquisitions to go into the general store of natural prosperity; his idol worship; his mode of living; his very vices; and, lastly, the countless myriads who stood hovering on the shores of Chinese waters, ready and anxious to swarm upon us . . . would have been unpatriotic and unwise in the extreme to have disregarded; and yet, when the word "white" was first inserted [in the 1790 Naturalization Act], no such danger confronted us, nor was anticipated, and it was solely intended to meet the then solely existing danger or evil of African citizenship, possibly of the numerous tribes of Indians in their wild or tribal state. (340)

Significantly, justice is exigent in the face of "ready and anxious" swarms: it could not wait. It would have been unjust ("unpatriotic," "unwise") to have opened the gates to the "hovering" Chinese, whose subpar character made "sound citizenship" impossible. Justice in Paschal's interpretation of the 1870

164   CHAPTER FOUR

law was as politically contingent as justice in the 1790 Naturalization Act. When the word *white* was inserted as a qualification for citizenship in that original act, he insisted, it was similarly inserted not so much to include whites as to exclude Africans. The "evil" posed by African citizenship is the "fear of interference with the unrestricted operation of slavery" (340). As that "evil" passed (an evil Paschal grammatically attributed to the Africans themselves), justice dictated extending the franchise to Africans but not to the Chinese, whose threat still lingered. Justice was enacted in 1870 in favor of African Americans, but this instantiation of justice was predicated on the violent, unstated (repressed) resolution to exclude the Chinese race. In this reinvention of the law in favor of justice for Rodriguez, Paschal surreptitiously aligned the character of Native Americans with proper citizenship twice. Anglo-Saxon and Native American races were aligned as "antipodes" of the degenerate Chinese race. More important, Native Americans were aligned with Africans as no longer posing any "existing danger" to the polity, acknowledging the possibility of the franchise for them.

If Paschal revisited *In re Ah Yup* to demonstrate that justice had been served, both in terms of congressional intent and political contingency, he revisited *In re Camille* to demonstrate that justice was travestied. Paschal admitted that the decision "point[ed] adversely to the eligibility of an Indian" to citizenship, but asserted "the case bears not the slightest evidence of having been well considered, and abounds in inaccuracies" (341). The greatest error committed in *Camille* was the court's *mis*interpretation of the meaning of "white person": "it [the Camille court] avers that the court, in Ah Yup's Case . . . declared that 'the words "white person," as used in the naturalization laws means a person of the Caucasian race.'" Instead of this mistaken interpretation, Paschal insists, "That case . . . simply decides that a Mongolian is ineligible" (341). Once again, for justice to be correctly served, it is most urgent that "white person" in the Naturalization Act be interpreted to mean the exclusion of the Mongolian race rather than the general inclusion of *only* Caucasians. Borrowing from Derrida, the force of Paschal's interpretations "conserve the law and also destroy or suspend it enough to have to reinvent it in each case." His reinterpretation "destroys" precedent in order to open the door to justice for Rodriguez specifically, for Indian inclusion more generally. To pry open the door of the law to justice for Native Americans, Paschal necessarily conserved it in the reaffirmation of the *ineligibility* of the Chinese. Naturalization *law* is predicated on exclusions that *justice* might not conscience.

ADJUDICATING EXCEPTION   165

Paschal proceeded to reinvent the law in *Elk v. Wilkins* as well. In that case the court found that although Elk had lived among white people and given up his tribal affiliations, his individual "surrender" of culture had not been formally recognized by the United States, and thus he was ineligible for citizenship.[6] This case was consistently interpreted as denying Native Americans the right to naturalization. Nevertheless Paschal interpreted *Elk* as hinging on the sole condition of U. S. recognition of indigenous surrender: "The question of eligibility of an Indian *depends not on his color*, but (1) whether there are treaty stipulations that make him a citizen . . . or (2) whether he has abandoned his tribal relations, and become subject to the jurisdiction of the United States, *and been recognized and accepted by the state or United States as such*, and makes application under our law to be naturalized" (342, emphasis added).[7] Paschal's selective interpretation focuses the impetus of the law on two conditions ameliorated in Rodriguez's petition. According to his own testimony and Paschal's history of Mexican miscegenation, Rodriguez had long since abandoned tribal affiliation or indigenous culture, and in the Treaty of Guadalupe Hidalgo, the United States recognized his surrender. Native American eligibility depended on the recognition of surrender rather than race. Paschal's bid for justice on behalf of Rodriguez and other Native Americans is exuberant in its unmooring of whiteness in the Naturalization Acts from the Caucasian race in favor of greater inclusion. Moreover, he reads the convention of "white" as unfixed, as alive to the contingency of justice. Nevertheless, his reinvention was predicated on the "buried, dissimulated, repressed" past of legal violence against the "negro" and on the reinstitution of legal violence against the Chinese.[8]

Floyd McGown and A. J. Evans submitted briefs on behalf of Bexar County's denial of Rodriguez's petition for citizenship. In stark contrast to Paschal's joyous encounter with justice, McGown and Evans revisited the law narrowly, finding no room for interpretation or contingency. McGown cited chapter and verse of the Naturalization Act, "Section 2169, Id., declares: 'The provisions of this title shall apply to aliens (being free white persons, and to aliens) of African nativity, and to persons of African descent'" (*Rodriguez*, 345). As Rodriguez was neither white nor black, he was ineligible, "He stated he was pure-blooded Mexican, having neither Spanish nor African blood in him." McGown also revisits *In re Ah Yup* and *In re Camille*, but only to affirm that the word "white" in the Naturalization Act referred specifically to the Caucasian race, and that Indians had never been considered white.[9] In short, "the applicant is not a white person" and was therefore ineligible for citizenship.

Evans continued where McGown left off: "Admitted and proven facts: Applicant is a native-born person of Mexico . . . and of pure Aztec or Indian race, of the races found in Mexico when conquered by Cortez, in 1519. . . . If an Indian, he cannot be naturalized" (346). Evans then also invoked *In re Camille* and *Elk v. Wilkins*, but again, only to underscore that Indians were ineligible for citizenship. He feared these precedents and Rodriguez's indigenous features were insufficient to ensure exclusion, for Evans then took an odd detour through the ethnological origins of Native Americans: "The most probable account of the origin of the aborigines of Mexico is that they are of Asiatic or Mongolian descent, and 'crossed from Asia to America by a chain of islands, which in the remote ages stretched at the north from the shores of the eastern to those of the western continent.' 11 Dana, Am. Enc. art. Mexico'" (347). By this point in his brief Evans has already argued that the Naturalization Acts of 1790 and 1870 explicitly excluded Indians, as per *Elk* and *Camille*. Furthermore, Evans has contended that the Naturalization Act of 1870 superseded any and all treaties that came before it, thereby voiding rights to citizenship granted by the TGH.[10] Thus Evans's appeal to the *American Encyclopedia*'s "Mexico" article to prove Indians are but descendants of Asians is gratuitous: a coup de grâce, an infelicitous reference to *Ah Yup* meant to establish that Native Americans were doubly excluded from the right of naturalization by a circuitous route travelled from "the shores of the eastern to those of the western continent."

For McGown and Evans, justice was best achieved by mechanically applying already established rules of law in each new case. There was no aporia to justice, no contingency, no "ghost of the undecidable" (Derrida 1989–1990, 963). To the contrary, for McGown and Evans the task of the court "simply consists of applying a rule, of enacting a program or effecting a calculation," and with Derrida, "we might say that [this] is legal, that it conforms to law . . . but we would be wrong to say that [such a] decision was just" (961). McGown and Evans adhered to the law, and in so doing they concentrically reproduced its violence. Justice, like Rodriguez's race, was calculable and finite. Rodriguez was calculably Indian; he was calculably Asian; he was calculably excluded.

Although the advocates for the plaintiff and Bexar County disagreed on Rodriguez's and Native Americans' eligibility for naturalization, it is noteworthy that all three agreed that Asians were irrevocably ineligible, their character irreconcilable with citizenship. Any resolution of Rodriguez's case was predicated on their shared view of denying "Mongolians" the right to active inclusion in the American polity. It is in this sense that the case produced a political geography of race. The case acknowledged the presence of Asians as permanent immigrants within the geography of the United States, for like *Ah Yup* there were dozens of cases decided all over the country in which naturalization was denied for East Asians, South Asians, and Middle Easterners.[11] These cases produced and reproduced the nation as a material geography inhabited by Asians, but politically free of their influence, as these immigrants would never be granted the rights of citizenship. Asian immigrants would toil, generate profit with their labor, invest capital in businesses, but they would never be counted as citizens.

With each legal argument, U.S. racial geography is reiterated: Asian immigrants shall be taxed, tithed, and even expropriated, but they shall not be accounted for with regard to apportionment and representation. This is a raced national space at once filled with Asians and politically free of them. Of course, they were not alone in this absent presence in the nation. Middle Easterners and South Asians were repeatedly denied the rights to naturalize by the courts during this period. More relevantly for our purposes, Native Americans, despite Paschal's best efforts at legal reinvention in this case, remained within the territorial boundaries of nation but outside any imagined American polity until 1924. It was precisely Rodriguez's miscegenation, his ambiguous and capacious racial standing, that enabled the advocates on both sides of the case to reiterate the racial geography of an American landscape abundant with Indians and Asians, but officially occupied by only whites and blacks. Rodriguez's racial miscegenation—read as racial ambiguity—facilitated, indeed required, a historical revision of the law and an ethnological revision of history, in order reinstitute a U.S. racial geography that vacated the landscape of a lived racial multiplicity. And so "the same problem of justice will have been posed and violently resolved, that is to say buried, dissimulated, repressed," but it is buried, dissimulated, repressed through mestizaje, not in spite of it. Rodriguez's racial mixture is put to work, paradoxically, to reinstitute the American polity as black and white.

District Judge Maxey ruled in favor of Rodriguez's appeal, but in granting him the right to naturalize, he sidestepped making a legal determination as to Rodriguez's race.[12] Maxey reviewed the decisions of *Ah Yup, Camille,* and *Elk* in some detail, only to find they did not apply to Mexicans. While Maxey agreed these precedents established the ineligibility of Asians and North American Indians, they had no legal bearing on the case because several U.S. and Texas treaties with the governments of Spain and Mexico had extended Mexicans the franchise "without discrimination as to color": "When all the foregoing laws, treaties, and constitutional provisions are considered, which either affirmatively confer the rights of citizenship upon Mexicans, or tacitly

168 CHAPTER FOUR

recognize in them the right of individual naturalization, the conclusion forces itself upon the mind that citizens of Mexico are eligible to American citizenship, and may be individually naturalized" (354). The language in the opinion is telling: justice "forces itself" upon a presumably unwilling mind. The mind, in this case Maxey's, resists the conclusion of Rodriguez's eligibility because of Mexicans' indeterminate racial status. For "[Rodriguez] is not an Indian," the Judge avers, as "he knows nothing of the Aztecs or Toltecs" (338). And yet, "If the strict scientific classification of the anthropologist should be adopted, [Rodriguez] would probably not be classed as white. It is certain he is not an African, nor a person of African descent" (349). Rodriguez's race resists his own knowledge ("he knows nothing of the Aztecs"), scientific knowledge (anthropological classification), and Maxey's common-sense knowledge. The court knows only what Rodriguez *is not*: he is not Indian; he is not white; he is not black. It cannot adjudicate affirmatively what he *is*, at least not by the hypodescent biometrics of the American polity. The contingency of Rodriguez's mestizaje, his resistance to simple racial categorization, defies understanding.

Rodriguez's mestizaje confounds visceral classification from the geographic perspective of the United States' bifurcated, white/black accounting of political rights in Maxey's view. International justice, however, is fortuitously blind, as "whatever may be the status of [Rodriguez] viewed solely from the standpoint of the ethnologist, he is embraced within the spirit and intent of our laws upon naturalization" (355). Maxey further privileges international law over domestic racial geography in noting that the United States, a signatory to conventions recognizing expatriation as "a natural and inherent right of all people" (354), was further obligated to grant Rodriguez citizenship. Regardless of his indecipherable race, Rodriguez is eligible for naturalization.

By deciding the case on these international grounds (treaties, conventions), rather than through domestic precedent (*Ah Yup, Camille, Elk*), Maxey was able to reinvent the law in the name of justice for Rodriguez and all Mexicans. Moreover, Maxey reinstituted the United States as a paradigmatically democratic space—performed it as a "just place" globally, alive to the contingency of justice—with his acknowledgment of international law, even as he reiterated racial exclusions.[13] His opinion freed the U.S. polity of Asians and Native Americans, even as, or especially because, he expanded the parameters of inclusion. The incalculability of Mexican mestizaje required Maxey to review precedent regarding race and naturalization, though he was "force[d]" to forgo precedent in favor of international law. In keeping with the "dialectic of enlightenment," the courtroom produces the United States as a democratic space with its performance of justly reasoned exclusion and exceptions to exclusion (Horkheimer and Adorno 2002). This is a spatial production analogous to the performance of the treaty between the U.S. government and the indigenous peoples in the eighteenth and nineteenth centuries discussed in chapter 1, in that the court formally recognized Native Americans' cumbersome presence within the territorial boundaries of the country, only to make them disappear from the political landscape.

Even though Judge Maxey did not ultimately decide the case on the basis of Rodriguez's race, Rodriguez's physical appearance nevertheless required an exegesis:

> As to color, he may be classed with the copper-colored or red men. He has dark eyes, straight black hair, and high cheek bones. He knows nothing of the Aztecs or Toltecs. He is not an Indian, and his parents informed him that he was a Mexican, and he claims to be "a pure-blooded Mexican." To extract from the applicant what knowledge he possessed concerning himself, counsel propounded, among others, the following questions: "Q. Do you not believe that you belong to the original Aztec race in Mexico? A. No, sir. Q. Do you belong to the aborigines or original races of Mexico? A. No, sir. Q. Where did your race come from? Spain? A. No, sir. Q. Where did your race come from? A. I do not know where they came from. Q. Does your family claim any religion? What religion do they profess? A. Catholic religion." (*In re Rodriguez*, 338)

With this description of Rodriguez's features and the transcript of his testimony, we witness the untranslatability of U.S. and Mexican racial geographies along the frontier. From the U.S. perspective, expressed in Maxey's interpretation of his face, Rodriguez is a "red man." Although Rodriguez professes no knowledge of his indigenous ancestry, he is still viscerally marked as Indian. In the description of Rodriguez's straight hair, dark eyes, and high cheekbones, it is the intractable "Indian" traits—the proof of the "Mexican character" he was required to shed by the TGH discussed in chapter 3—that cling to him even as he becomes citizen.[14] His racial difference is marshaled in the denial of the political emancipation of others. Although Maxey appears to take Rodriguez at his word ("He is not an Indian"), the account of his face, hair, and skin suggest the taint of the indio bárbaro lingers. With the right to naturalize, Rodriguez presumably gained the abstract right of the equality rendered by U.S. citizenship. Nevertheless, his racial ambiguity hounded his entrance into the public sphere, differentiating his ostensibly undifferentiated same-

170   CHAPTER FOUR

ness. Like all Mexican Americans before and after him, Rodriguez became a citizen, but his racial difference resisted privatization as he entered the arena of political emancipation. He continued to wear it on his face, and as such, his political rights continued to be limited in practice if not in law.

Rodriguez's indigenous stain conditioned the political emancipation he was granted through citizenship, just as it conditioned the conditional whiteness the courts bestowed on Mexican Americans in the first half of the twentieth century. Like a specter, this repressed indio bárbaro returns to haunt the white citizens' possession of the southwestern cartography as well. One haunting facilitates the other. On the one hand, *In re Rodriguez* makes evident the contingency of whiteness. In the visiting and revisiting of precedent, in the reinterpretations by the advocates, counsels, and judges, it is precisely the *un-fixity* of whiteness that becomes evident. The legacy of hypodescent in the United States conditions us to think of racial categories as fixed and fixing. Race locks one into one's body; one *is* black or one *is* white. Despite the United States' own rich history of miscegenation, this is how race is represented in the United States. *In re Rodriguez* demonstrates vividly how whiteness is not fixed but must be constantly readjudicated. It is shifting and shifty from the perspective of the courts. Whiteness must be made anew each time: it is contingent and reinstituted with each case, its parameters tested and blurred with each enactment of law. In *Mendez v. Westminster* and *Hernandez v. Texas*, Mexican American activists seize on the contingency of whiteness to transform it into another shade of mestizaje.

Judge Maxey's decision, like the TGH he cites, also alienates Mexicans from their indigenous ancestry.[15] Despite the indelibility of the indigenous racial stain, the judge inexplicably accepts Rodriguez's claim that he is not an Indian because his parents told him so, entering the testimony into the court record: "His parents informed him that he was a Mexican, and he claims to be 'a pure-blooded Mexican.'" Maxey's decision, a reiteration of the TGH articles discussed in chapter 3, also produced the geography of the Southwest through the space-making practice of dispossession. His opinion dispossessed Rodriguez, and subsequently all Mexicans, from their ancestral claims to indigeneity *by law*. As "pure-blooded Mexican[s]," they were no longer Indian. Maxey's recognition of "Mexican" as something othered from indigenous ancestry dispossesses Mexico and Mexicans of any original proprietary claim to the territory of the Southwest. Representationally, it vacates the Southwest landscape of indigenous Mexicans, rendering the term oxymoronic. Henceforth, all Mexicans shall be *immigrants* to the Southwest, regardless of their indigenous ancestors. In contrast, Rodriguez's own words suggested another racial geography, for he answered that he was Catholic, signaling the legacy of colonial unity that would have subsequently emplotted him within the liberal geography of the Mexican nation, within the gran familia mejicana.

The nineteenth-century racial geography of mestizaje conjoined indigeneity with what it meant to be Mexican precisely through miscegenation and the Catholic Enlightenment that had required it. Hence there can be no Mexican who is not indigenous to the Americas, not even an ethnologically white European. Mestizaje also produced a contingent whiteness, but it did so by transforming the dominant racial formation in New Spain (white Spaniards) into a dominant racial formation in Mexico (light-skinned Mexicans), rendered indigenous through the universal process of mestizaje. Hence, if we take Rodriguez at his naïve word, he is a "pure blooded Mexican" precisely because he refused to differentiate between "indigenous" blood and "white" blood, as any good liberal Mexican citizen would have done. In contrast, Maxey's reading of Rodriguez's claim to be "pure-blooded Mexican" effectively vacates the Southwest landscape of its previous inhabitants *for* U.S. white settlers by purposefully reading Mexicans as not indigenous to it, but rather as immigrants.[16] There is a subtle but important difference operating here, even as racial hierarchies persist on both sides of the Mexico–U.S. border. For Mexicans, national belonging was specifically contingent on the indigenous presence that preceded colonization: Indians make Mexicans Mexican. In contrast, belonging in the United States— the proper possession of formerly indigenous territory—is contingent on vacating the landscape of its indigenous inhabitants: Native Americans and Mexicans alike.

Furthermore, if Maxey's decision effectively produced southwestern space by representing it as devoid of Mexicans with any historical proprietary claims, it inversely alienated indigenous peoples from any historical proprietary claim to Mexicanness. Maxey's reading of "pure-blooded Mexican" as a racial formation that is other-than-Indian dispossessed southwestern indigenous peoples of their previous political affiliations with Mexican citizenship, producing space by enabling the dispossession of indigenous territories legally recognized by Mexico before 1848. By separating Mexicans and Indians, the Maxey opinion voids the property protections offered by the TGH to *all* Mexican citizens, including Southwest Indians formerly recognized as equal members of the Mexican nation and as holding property rights accordingly. This is not a historical argument for causality: Maxey's decision did not unilaterally sunder Mexican Americans from their indigenous heritage and vice versa. His decision does not "make it so." Rather, it is symptomatic of a larger

172   CHAPTER FOUR

historical process of indigenous dispossession transpiring in the Southwest, and it had the material effect of further facilitating this dispossession. His decision is the legal iteration of a process that was transpiring socially, culturally, and politically across the Southwest, furthering the material effect of Mexican and indigenous dispossession in the law. It produced a southwestern geography made *legally* available to white people for possession through statements like "Mexicans are not Indians," "Indians are not Mexicans," and "Mexicans are immigrants to the United States."

The U.S. government signed the TGH with congressional approval; nevertheless, from 1848 to the Civil Rights Act of 1866 individual states determined the requirements and rights of citizenship. States took the lead in disenfranchising Mexican Indians from their citizenship rights of voting, holding public office, and owning property, with the U.S. Congress colluding in this project when necessary. In this near-universal disenfranchisement of indigenous Mexicans we witness the incommensurability of the Mexican and U.S. racial geographies. Most Anglo-American legislators at the state and federal level found it simply incomprehensible that Mexico could have conferred full citizenship rights to Native Americans. Yet, even before Mexican independence, New Spain had extended full equality to indigenous peoples in 1812 during the Cortes de Cádiz. Mexican state and federal constitutions from 1824 through 1857 explicitly reiterated the formal extension of full citizenship rights to Indians and afromestizos. As discussed in the last chapter, an ethos of mestizaje required the incorporation of *all* ethnicities and races—with the notable exception of the reified indios bárbaros—into la gran familia mejicana. In contrast, during this period in the United States, the practice of citizenship rights was not only restricted to "free white males" but recursively *created* whiteness. As Ariela Gross has insightfully pointed out, for the antebellum South the very performance of civic duty conferred white racial citizenship on Anglo-Americans regardless of class difference: "The law—the public sphere—was involved not merely in reorganizing race but in creating it; the state itself—through its legal and military institutions—helped make people white. In allowing men of low social status to create their whiteness by voting, serving on juries and mustering in the militia, the state welcomed every white man into symbolic equality with the wealthy" (2008, 53–54). If the performance of the rights of citizenship recursively bestowed whiteness on poor southerners, creating an antebellum white demos, as Gross contends, then Anglo-American legislators in this newly annexed territory similarly restricted these civic enactments to Anglo-American settlers, at most extending these privileges to the few visually "white" Mexican elite.

Anglo-American legislators in the annexed territories of California, New Mexico, Arizona, and Texas went to great rhetorical lengths to circumvent the TGH and to deny all but "white" Mexicans the rights of citizenship. Legislatures with Euro-American majorities were the first to deny Mexican Indians, mestizos, and afromestizos their rights. The second article of California's 1849 state constitution explicitly restricted suffrage to "every white male citizen of the United States, and every white male citizen of Mexico, who shall have elected to become a citizen of the United States."[17] California legislators argued that the TGH required the state to confer citizenship on all Mexicans, including Indians, mestizos, and afromestizos, but it did not require the state to grant these citizens the right to vote or to stand for elected office (Menchaca 1993, 588). Upon separating from New Mexico in 1863, Arizona emulated California, its territorial legislature prohibiting all but a few white Mexican males from voting, holding public office, or even practicing law.

Texas and New Mexico were less discriminatory because Mexican elites maintained a numerical significance in the legislatures, courts, and public office. Texas extended full citizenship rights to male whites, Mexican mestizos, and detribalized Mexican Indians (mostly mission Apache) with statehood in 1845, with the telling caveat that any Mexicans entering the state after 1845 would have to prove they were white to become citizens (Menchaca 1993, 589). Mexicans dominated territorial government in New Mexico, and initially incorporated indigenous peoples fully.[18] At the 1850 constitutional convention, eleven of the twenty delegates were Mexicans, and consequently whites and *all* former Mexican citizens were granted the full rights of U.S. citizenship, in compliance with the TGH. The U.S. Congress intervened, exercising its veto power over territorial legislatures, and rescinded the right of Indians to vote in New Mexico in 1853. The territorial legislature circumvented the veto to some degree in 1854 by adhering to the long genealogy of their mestizo racial geography. The legislature permitted Pueblo Indians to vote in local elections and for town councils, as long as they could demonstrate that "they practiced a Mexican lifestyle" (Menchaca, 1993, 590). Non-Pueblo Indians were consequently denied any voting rights (Gómez 2007, 92). The New Mexican legislature's positions reiterated the "gente de razón"/indio division of late Spanish colonialism discussed in chapter 2. A majority of the sheriffs, bailiffs, and jurors in New Mexico were Mexican and Spanish speaking during this transitional period (Gómez 2007, 87–89). Hence it is not surprising that New Mexican courts during this period prohibited the placing of Pueblo Indians under reservation status, just as they ruled Pueblo communal lands were not subject to the Trade and Intercourse Act of 1834 that would have

174 CHAPTER FOUR

placed Pueblo lands under federal receivership and prohibited the private sale of Indian lands (Menchaca 1993, 591; Gómez 2007, 94–95).

"Passing Strange": United States v. Lucero, United States v. Joseph, *and* United States v. Sandoval

The legal trajectory from enfranchisement to disenfranchisement traveled by the Pueblo from 1850 to 1913 is illustrative of the discursive collusion and rupture between racial geographies. In the span of sixty years, legal decisions regarding the Pueblo rehearsed eighteenth-century U.S. tactics of imputing humanity-as-sovereignty, as discussed in chapter 1; nineteenth-century classifications of Mexican racial character from the TGH, as discussed in chapter 3; and twentieth-century tropes of the vanishing, infantile, reservation Indian. The Pueblo Indians morphed in the courts from "a peaceful, quiet, and industrious people, residing in villages" with the full rights of citizenship to childlike savages incapable of administrating their own property.

The spectrum of these discursive terms were on display in the first New Mexico Supreme Court decision regarding the Pueblo Indians' proprietary rights, *United States v. Lucero* (1869). In this case, the Supreme Court upheld a lower court decision in favor of the plantiff, Juan Jose Lucero, a Mexican American who had illegally settled on Cochiti Pueblo lands. He was fined for trespassing by the U.S. attorney under the 1834 Indian Trade and Intercourse Act, prohibiting the "settlement on any lands belonging, secured, or granted by treaty with the United States, to any Indian tribe" (*Lucero,* 423). Lucero's attorney argued that he could not be fined by the federal government for trespassing as the Pueblo Indians owned their lands and were not subject to the 1834 Intercourse Act. At stake was the status of the Pueblo Indians. Were they dependents of the U.S. government, like other indigenous peoples, their lands subject to the administration and "protection" of federal agents? Or were they full citizens of the United States by virtue of the TGH, their lands privately owned, even if held in common?[19]

In upholding the lower court decision revoking the fine, the New Mexico Supreme Court effectively decided that the Pueblo Indians were full citizens capable of holding and managing their own properties, not only because of the TGH but also because of their uniquely *civilized* character:

> The term pueblo Indian is a term used to separate and distinguish them from the general class of Indians, such as existed within the United States in 1834 . . . and the law then passed [Intercourse Act] could not

have been intended to operate upon or effect *a class of Indians differing widely from the Indians of the United States* in their habits, manners, and customs. Who and what are the Indians for whom said laws were passed, and upon whom they were intended to operate? They were wandering savages, given to murder, robbery, and theft, living on the game of the mountains, the forest, and the plains, unaccustomed to the cultivation of the soil, and unwilling to follow the pursuits of civilized man. Providence made this world for the use of the man who had the energy and industry to pull off his coat, and roll up his sleeves, and go to work on the land, cut down the trees, grub up the brush and briers, and stay there on it and work it for the support of himself and family, and a kind and thoughtful Providence did not charge man a single cent for the whole world made for mankind and intended for their benefit. Did the Indians ever purchase the land, or pay any one a single cent for it? Have they any deed or patent for it? (*Lucero*, 425, emphasis added)

What should have been a limited decision about Cochiti lands became instead a strategic occasion for the court to rehearse a universal justification of U.S. imperial history at a moment when the expansion by white settlers onto western indigenous territories was at its peak. "Providence" alone bestowed ownership of the continent through industrious labor, implicitly exemplified by Anglo-American settlers out cultivating southwestern soils. Even so, "savage Indians" never bothered to pay "a single cent" for the proper "patent" that would have guaranteed their ownership, making these territories doubly available for expropriation. Mere habitation of the land was insufficient claim, as the court continued:

The idea that a handful of wild, half-naked, thieving, plundering, murdering savages should be dignified with the *sovereign* attributes of nations, enter into *solemn treaties,* and claim a country five hundred miles wide by one thousand miles long as theirs in *fee simple,* because they hunted buffalo and antelope over it, might do for beautiful reading in Cooper's novels or Longfellow's Hiawatha, but is unsuited to the intelligence and justice of this age, or the natural rights of mankind. (426, emphasis added)

The possibility that indigenous peoples were the sovereign owners of their lands was dismissed as "beautiful reading," as a romantic fiction of another age that must give way to (Protestant) Enlightenment notions of social contract (solemn treaties) and property (fee simple).[20] It is not so much the

176   CHAPTER FOUR

racist participles that render the Indian a "savage" (thieving, plundering, murdering)—after all, these participles would have equally applied to the white settlers. Rather, it is their failure to properly access and possess their land that makes them so. The decision argued that the very fact that putatively sovereign indigenous nations had in the past sold lands to the U.S. government through treaties for pennies on the dollar value of the land proved their *lack* of sovereignty. If they were truly the owners of these lands, they would have realized its actual worth (426). In the court's decision we see the eighteenth-century tactic of imputing humanity through the recognition of sovereignty give way to the late-nineteenth century tactic of imputing savagery through the absence of indigenous sovereignty (*terra nullius*) for North American tribes, with the Pueblo peoples made the exception that proves the rule.

This digression on the status of the "general class" of North American Indians in the Southwest discursively justified the dispossession of several indigenous peoples that were in fact recognized by Mexico as full citizens (i.e., Navajo, Opate, Shoshone, specific Apache and Comanche bands, etc.), even as the court acknowledged the Pueblos as previous citizens of Mexico. The court attributed this singular case of proper indigenous sovereignty to Pueblo exceptionalism within the Spanish colonial record, dating back to Cabeza de Vaca in 1534 (427). Any contention that the Pueblo peoples were of the "wild, savage, and barbarous race" was "contradicted by the uniform history of the Spanish adventurers for over two hundred years" (427). When the Spanish arrived in force to colonize New Mexico in the early 1600s, "They found the pueblo Indians . . . a peaceful, quiet, and industrious people, residing in villages for their protection against the wild Indians, and living by the cultivation of the soil. Their villages are *described*, their locality *mentioned*, their habits and pursuits *delineated*" (427, emphasis added). Even Pueblo rebellion becomes a sign of civility, as they were "victims of [Spanish] cupidity and despotic rule" (427). Upon their return to New Mexico in 1689, and as if in reward for the Pueblos' valiant defense of territory against tyranny, "the Spaniards acknowledged their title to the land on which they were residing, and had resided time whereof the memory of man runneth not to the contrary, and a *written agreement* was executed and delivered to them; and so long as the Spanish rule was continued in America, these titles were respected" (428, emphasis added). The Spanish colonial archive established the Pueblos' humanity by documenting properly executed sovereignty (cultivation, defense, titles). In certain respects it echoes the early documentation of eastern seaboard indigenous cultures by British settlers discussed in chapter 1. The early Anglo-American archive established indigenous humanity in the seventeenth and eighteenth centuries through the imputation of indigenous sovereignty, but by the late nineteenth century the recognition of properly executed indigenous sovereignty was to be exclusively reserved for the Pueblo.

This convoluted decision is at once archive and apologia of U.S. imperialism against Mexican and indigenous territory in the second half of the nineteenth century.[21] Nevertheless, it is extraordinary that the court recognized and recorded the history of two distinct and competing racial geographies for mapping indigenous identity in the Southwest, taking on itself the task of meshing the two for the legal purposes of statecraft. With sweeping historical detail, the decision rehearsed indigenous incorporation from the arrival of the Spaniards to Mexican independence through the TGH, inaccurately concluding that Spanish law in New Spain reserved the word *Indian* exclusively for "that civilized race of people who live in towns and cultivate the soil" (430). In distinct contrast (though with similar historical inaccuracy) the court opines, "When the term Indian is used in our acts of [U.S.] congress, it means that savage and roaming race of red men given to war and the chase for a living, and wholly ignorant of the pursuits of civilized man, for the simple reason that when those laws had been enacted, no such class of Indians as the pueblo Indians of New Mexico existed within the existing limits of the United States" (431). The problem was not one of semantics or translation. The problem for the court was ontological. The Spanish *did* incorporate Indians into colonial society and jurisprudence, but *their* Indians were of an entirely different "class" than *ours.* The court acknowledged that a different racial order existed in New Spain, and subsequently in Mexico, but it refused to consider that it was premised on a different epistemology of indigenous character.

Instead, the court created an ontological bifurcation, concluding, "Neither the Spanish crown, its viceroys in the new world, nor the Mexican republic ever legislated for the savage class of Indians. They would as soon have thought of legislating upon what time the wolf should be admitted into their sheep-fold, the bear into their cornfields, the fox into their hen-roosts, or the skunk into their parlors" (431).[22] Of course, New Spain repeatedly established regulations specifically aimed at incorporating the indios bárbaros of the northern frontier, precisely in terms of "what time" they should be admitted into the "sheep-fold" of Christian unity. Nevertheless, the metaphors in the passage established differences in kind between domesticated Indians (sheep, chickens) brought under the mantle of the Spanish and Mexican law (like the Pueblo), and those wild Indians (wolves, bears, foxes, and skunks) never contemplated within such law (all northern tribes). Such categorical

178   CHAPTER FOUR

differences were not a tactic of Spanish colonialism or even Mexican liberalism. Even as northern Mexican states established the indio bárbaro as a categorical other in the interest of unifying the majority of Indians within the gran familia mejicana, they parsed the northern equestrian tribes according to behavior, not genus. Thus many equestrian tribes, and even some Apache and Comanche bands, were accorded full rights of citizenship after Mexican independence. Nevertheless, as the U.S. court reconciled distinct racial geographies at the height of westward expansion, it was essential that all *civilized* Indians remain on the southern side of the Mexican-U.S. border (with the notable exception of the Pueblo), and that only savage Indians remain in the north. Otherwise, how was the court to exclude the richly documented enfranchisement of indigenous peoples after Mexican independence? Only by creating such an ontological bifurcation could the interpretation of Mexican citizenship in the TGH remain limited: "It must be evident that at the date of the treaty of Guadalupe Hidalgo the Indian race, *in the Spanish sense of the term*, were as much and fully citizens of the republic of Mexico as Europeans or Africans" (432, emphasis added).

At this point in the decision, the court rehearsed in singularly accurate detail the history of Mexican independence and the incorporation of indigenous people as equal citizens of the republic, citing chapter and verse from the Plan de Iguala, from the Treaty of Cordova, and from the acts passed by the first "sovereign congress" after independence (432). There was no denying the equality of indigenous peoples before the law in Mexico, so it was necessary to parse the meaning of the Indian "in the Spanish sense of the term." Stunningly, this decision recognizes the differences between U.S. and Mexican racial geographies with respect to indigenous people, particularly as registered in law, but it does so in order to occlude these differences. The figure of the indio bárbaro enabled this occlusion at this key imperial moment of U.S. jurisprudence in the region. Despite the radical differences between the racial geographies of the United States and Mexico, the indio bárbaro proliferated and blurred all indigenous people together in the annexed territories, repeatedly making an appearance in the decision to justify the dispossession of all but the Pueblo. The decision cited the eighth and ninth articles of the TGH as guaranteeing the Pueblo (and only the Pueblo) a right to citizenship and property, but the eleventh article was decisive in establishing for the court that even the liberal and inclusive Mexican state drew the line at "tribus salvajes" (431). By virtue of this indio bárbaro, U.S. and Mexican racial geographies colluded to enable not only the dispossession of indigenous territory, but a discursive shift in the U.S. tactics for imputing humanity.

Gone from the annexed territories was the continuum of indigenous humanity embodied in the principles of inclusion of Catholic unity and of the gran familia mejicana, with their possibilities of assimilation and collaboration, of filial ties. All that remained were nomadic savages who vanished onto reservations, with state agents legislated for their care. Only the Pueblo were independent, law-abiding, property-owning quasi-citizens. Their exceptionalism before the law opportunistically enabled the project of making savage all other natives. The decision also differentiated Mexicans from Indians, for although the decision made clear that the Mexican nation had fully enfranchised the Pueblo as equals, Mexicans and Indians were not one in the same in the court ruling. The court found it "passing strange" that the U.S. government should attempt to apply the Intercourse Act to the Pueblo, thereby reducing "these citizens to a state of vassalage" (442). Stranger yet, I suggest, was the exceptional status accorded the Pueblo in the court's interpretation of Spanish/Mexican racial geography, and the discursive uses of this interpretation.

In *United States v. Joseph* (1876), a case that resembled *Lucero,* the U.S. Supreme Court reaffirmed the exceptional status of the Pueblo Indians. Anthony Joseph, a New Mexican land speculator, built ten houses with adjoining fields on Taos Pueblo lands in 1874. As in *Lucero*, federal agents fined Joseph for trespassing under the 1834 Intercourse Act. Joseph challenged the fine. Unsurprisingly, the New Mexico Supreme Court ruled in favor of Joseph. The U.S. attorney (the same as in the *Lucero* case) appealed the decision to the U.S. Supreme Court, but the Supreme Court followed the line of reasoning in *Lucero*, averring that at the time of the passage of the Intercourse Act, "there were no such Indians as these in the United States." With the "acquisition" of Mexican territory, it *was* necessary to apply the Intercourse Act, but only "among the nomadic Apaches, Comanches, Navajoes [*sic*], and other tribes whose incapacity for self-government required both for themselves and for the citizens of the country this guardian care of the general government" (*United States v. Joseph*, 617). The naming of these indigenous groups surely referenced the U.S. wars against them in the annexed territories. That Pueblo Indians like the Zunis acted as scouts and soldiers in these wars for the United States was perhaps indicated in the court's opinion that "the pueblo Indians, *if, indeed, they can be called Indians,* had nothing in common with this class" (617, emphasis added). The Taos "hold their lands by a right superior to that of the United States." If Joseph was trespassing on Taos land, they had the right to eject him and pursue a civil suit for trespass, but "we [the court] know of no injury which the United States suffers by his presence" (617). The

180 CHAPTER FOUR

Pueblo could take care of themselves, in other words, unlike the warring/ childish Navajo, Apache, or Comanche who required protection. As with certain Mexicans, the Pueblo were strangely passing into whiteness before the courts.

These cases were space-making practices in at least two ways. The courts' decisions overlaid a U.S. racial geography of permanent indigenous exclusion onto a Mexican one of liberal inclusion. Even before *Elk* and *Camille,* these decisions rendered the annexed territory a political space with no place for indigenous rights as citizens. This was made possible by the vicissitudes of the indio bárbaro in Spanish colonialism, but especially in the Mexican statecraft discussed in the last chapter. Moreover, these decisions were symptomatic of the discursive ascendance in U.S. racial geography of the vanished/vanquished Indian trope in the *visuality* of landscape. The space of indigeneity was reduced to extraterritorial places, reservations with rules and rights of their own that did not in any way impinge on the rights of white settlers.

The other space-making effect of these decisions was more tangible. They rendered *all* indigenous lands in the annexed territory available for usurpation, even if techniques varied. On the one hand, *savage* Indians had no right to territories that they could claim under the TGH, even if they held Spanish or Mexican land title. This enabled the reduction of these equestrian peoples to reservations after military campaigns ended their resistance, with the remainder of their vast territories going into national trusts for distribution to white settlers or as reserves. On the other hand, in the case of the Pueblo— proper citizens protected by the TGH—they had the right to sell their lands to white settlers (Gómez 2007, 98). Between the 1876 *Joseph* decision and the 1913 *United States v. Sandoval* Supreme Court decision that reduced the Pueblo to reservation status, individual Pueblo Indians had sold an estimated 30 percent of their lands.[23] In the case of the Pueblo, we witness the resuscitation of the late eighteenth-century trope of the Indians who hold land only to cede it willingly to U.S. settlers.

By the time New Mexico achieved statehood in 1912, it had transformed demographically into a majority white settler population, and the terms of Pueblo recognition and enfranchisement transformed as well. The 1910 state constitution ended the exceptional status of the Pueblo in New Mexico. Article 21 addressed the state's "compact with the United States." While the state constitution recognized that the Pueblo land titles were acquired under a "prior sovereignty," it declared Pueblo lands "subject to the disposition and under the absolute jurisdiction and control of the Congress of the United States."[24] The U.S. Supreme Court finalized this status in a 1913 decision *United*

ADJUDICATING EXCEPTION   181

States v. Sandoval. Indicted for selling liquor to the Santa Clara Pueblo on their lands, Sandoval fought the indictment on the grounds that the Pueblo were U.S. citizens who owned their lands in fee simple. Counsel for Sandoval reiterated the same arguments used in *Lucero* and *Johnson,* and despite the fact that Article 21 ceded Pueblo jurisdiction to the federal government, the U.S. District Court of New Mexico found for Sandoval. Upon appeal, however, the Supreme Court reversed the lower court decision, and *Johnson* in the process. Though the Pueblo were "sedentary rather than nomadic," and "disposed to peace and industry," the Supreme Court nevertheless overturned previous laudatory appraisals of them, finding them savage after all: "Adhering to primitive modes of life, largely influenced by superstition and fetishism . . . governed according to the crude customs . . . they are essentially a simple, uninformed and inferior people" (*Sandoval,* 39). Though Mexico had "enlarged" the Pueblo's political rights after independence, the Supreme Court doubted they had been embraced as full citizens; and it certainly "remains an open question whether they have become citizens of the United States" (*Sandoval,* 39). It was not necessary to resolve these questions, however, because Pueblo citizenship did not relieve the United States "as a superior and civilized nation [of] the power and the duty of exercising a fostering care and protection over all dependent Indian communities within its borders" (*Sandoval,* 46). The court cited numerous reports by Pueblo superintendents, all of which portrayed the Pueblo as variously incapable of properly administering their economic affairs, their lands, their morality, or their political rights (*Sandoval,* 41–44). That the Pueblo owned their lands in fee simple did not alter their reservation status either, as Article 21 of the New Mexico Constitution transferred control of Pueblo lands to the U.S. Congress, which had required the article as a condition of statehood (*Sandoval,* 36–35).

At the end of its decision, the Supreme Court acknowledged that their observations of the Pueblo were "not in accord" with those in the *Joseph* decision. The court attributed this discrepancy to the *Joseph* court's reliance on the territorial court's observations of the Pueblo, which "are at variance" with new "recognized sources of information, now available," presumably the superintendents' reports. In truth, the *Lucero* and *Joseph* decisions laid essential groundwork for the *Sandoval* decision by establishing the discursive terms of a racial geography in which indigenous savagery was the general condition of Indians, from which the Pueblo were (temporarily) spared. Historical anthropologist Martha Menchaca attributes this transformation in Pueblo status not only to the phenomenal growth in the Anglo-American population in New Mexico, but also to the rise to political power of recent white settlers unfamiliar with the Pueblo people or Mexico's racial order. Legal scholar Laura Gómez argues instead that it was the New Mexican elites that enabled the transformation in racial order by severing their ties with the indigenous population in favor of white identification and privilege. Both explanations are accurate, as together they register the U.S. racial geography supplanting Mexican racial geography. However, Menchaca and Gómez ascribe too much agency to elites (either Mexican or white), as it was the TGH that set the discursive terms of requiring the severance of mestizo and Indian relations. The usurpation of one racial geography by another was reiterated repeatedly by a U.S. jurisprudence that required whiteness as a condition for full citizenship. As a consequence, alliances were shattered, kinships sundered, new collaborations forged, all premised on a bifurcated U.S. racial geography that voided the demos of racial multiplicity and mestizaje. Once again, before the courts, Mexicans could not be Indians. Indians could not be Mexicans. Heterotemporally, though, mestizaje continues to speak in translation.

"Yet, God Bless the Law, He Is 'White'!":
Mendez v. Westminster *and* Hernandez v. Texas

> I speak in a language that is not my own because that will be more just, in another sense of the word *juste*, in the sense of justice . . . we can call juridico-ethico-political: it is more just to speak the language of the majority, especially when, through hospitality, it grants a foreigner the right to speak. It's hard to say if the law we're referring to here is that of decorum, the law of the strongest, or the equitable law of democracy. —**Jacques Derrida**, *Force of Law*

In October 1989, while delivering the keynote lecture at Cardozo Law School's colloquium on "Deconstruction and the Possibility of Justice," Derrida ruminated on the significance of the request that he address the colloquium in English: "*Je dois* speak English (how does one translate this 'dois,' this devoir? I must? I should, I ought to, I have to?)" (1989–1990, 923). It is *just* for him to speak the language of the majority not simply because they are the majority, but because the hospitality extended to the foreigner in granting him the right to address them requires it. It is significant that he qualifies this juridico-ethico-political *dois* as undecidable: is it "more just" that the foreigner speak the language of the host because of decorum (custom), strength (hegemony), or democratic equality (justice)? Or is it that all three aspects of the law bear down with equal force on the foreigner in his requirement to speak the language of the other?

Derrida's formulation can help us understand the juridical context for the "other white" strategy pursued by Mexican American legal activists during mid-twentieth-century desegregation and antidiscrimination struggles. In claiming whiteness, these activists spoke as foreigners in the majority language of the host country that granted them the right to address the government in the courts so long as they spoke the language of U.S. law. In the aftermath of the *In re Rodriguez* decision discussed above, Mexican American citizens were always already speaking as immigrants, never as proprietors in their own territory. They were required to speak the language of the very law that had dispossessed them of their indigenous heritage and proprietary claims to the Southwest. Even as *Rodriguez* affirmed their political emancipation, Mexican American legal activists bore the visceral mark of indigenous difference. Indeed, the necessity to bring these cases in the first place attests to Mexican Americans' residual (Indian) foreignness.[25] Nevertheless, it is "just" that these activists speak the legal language of the majority that entertains their motions. Thus they translate the racial coordinates of mestizaje into the bifurcated coordinates legible to the U.S. courts. Mexican Americans were white before the law. Though they spoke the language of the law inside the courtroom, they resignified the meaning of that whiteness in their daily lives.

In *Mendez v. Westminster* (1946) five migrant fathers won a landmark class-action suit against the school districts of Westminster, Garden Grove, Santa Ana, and El Modena, California, on behalf of their children who were forced to travel miles by bus to attend "Mexican" schools outside their districts (Arriola 1995, 185).[26] The decision benefited thousands of Mexican American and Mexican students alike and was the culmination of more than two years of activism across the four districts by parents for access to the closer and better neighborhood schools reserved for whites.[27] All the plaintiffs and defendants stipulated that Mexicans were considered legally white; all also agreed that Mexicans *were* in fact segregated into separate schools. The point of contention was the purpose of the segregation (Arriola 1995, 185). Were these children segregated for legitimate educational purposes? Or were state authorities abusing their power with arbitrary segregation, violating Mexican American rights under the Fourteenth Amendment?

While the case had multiple plaintiffs, the facts concerning the Mendez family were particularly poignant, again revealing the incongruity and hetero-temporality of racial geographies. In early 1945, Gonzalo and Felícitas Mendez asked Gonzalo's sister, Soledad Vidaurri, to enroll their three children in the nearby Seventeenth Street School where she was enrolling her own two children. When she tried to do so, Mrs. Vidaurri was informed that while she

184   CHAPTER FOUR

could enroll her own light-skinned children whose last name did not "sound" Mexican, she could not enroll their dark-skinned cousins of Mexican descent (Aguirre 2005, 323). The school administrator employed a fine, visceral calculus of racial geography when he knowingly divided first cousins based on what he could see (a visible racial difference) and what he could hear (discrete national origins in a last name). He rigorously maintained the racial space of segregation, reiterating the bifurcated geography of the racial demos in the public sphere of education.

Once again, the capaciousness of mestizaje within a single family required strict adjudication. Gonzalo and Soledad were themselves Mexican immigrants who had become naturalized U.S. citizens. Felícitas Mendez was Puertoriqueña and a U.S. citizen by virtue of the 1917 Jones-Shafroth Act.[28] One and another, then, had achieved whiteness as an effect of U.S. imperial adventure in Latin America. Felícitas was afromestiza, further complicating the matter of their children's racial character. Nevertheless, as litigants in a case premised on the whiteness of their children, how did Gonzalo and Felícitas understand the quality of such whiteness? It is insufficient to ascribe to them a naïve aspirational whiteness. In Mexico, their mixed racial status was the privileged term of citizenship, but in the United States their racial mixture hounded their political emancipation. As they insisted on the fullness of their political emancipation *through* whiteness, they destabilized the ontological presumptions of whiteness that underscored its iterative rather than essential life.

Gonzalo and Felícitas were tenant farmers, and two of the principal organizers of this civil rights effort. They were political agents in this challenge, and the school registration event was carefully orchestrated to set in stark relief the arbitrary and ridiculous division of "biological" divisions of race. The Westminster school district even offered to move the Mendez children to the neighborhood school in an effort to buy them off and quash the movement, but Gonzalo and Felícitas declined the offer, filing suit with other parents in May 1946. The League of United Latin American Citizens (LULAC)—the southwestern equivalent of the NAACP for Mexican Americans—organized fundraising for the case.[29]

Attorneys for school districts in previous antisegregation cases had argued successfully that Mexican children were segregated not because they were Mexican, but because of their poor language skills and because as migrant children, returning from the fields in mid-fall, their entry into white classrooms would be too disruptive. In anticipation of this defense, David C. Marcus, the attorney for the plaintiffs in *Mendez*, put nine-year-old Sylvia Mendez on the stand, where she testified in unaccented English that she was ready to go to the Seventeenth Street School with her cousins (Aguirre 2005, 325). Marcus also put a UCLA anthropologist on the stand who testified that such segregation created inferiority and superiority complexes in Mexican and white children respectively, and likened the practice to those of Nazi Germany. Meanwhile, the witnesses for the defense did not help their case. One school superintendent testified that he considered Mexicans inferior in hygiene, economic skills, and intelligence, and that he would never allow Mexicans in his all-white schools, even if they met all the qualifications (Aguirre 2005, 4).

The appellate court judge, Paul J. McCormick, sided with the plaintiffs, finding that the Mexican American children were being treated as an "other class" of whites and could not be legally segregated without proper and fair testing of each child to determine his/her language proficiency. Although Judge McCormick stopped short of saying that segregation was unconstitutional, he did state, in an eloquent opinion, that he feared segregation caused a sense of inferiority in the subordinate group and that it violated the spirit of democracy. The California Ninth Circuit Court of Appeals upheld the decision, adding that although California state law provided for the segregation of "Indians and certain Asiatics," it did not provide for segregation of those with "Mexican blood." Further complicating the case, the circuit court noted that "nowhere in any California law is there a suggestion that any segregation can be made of children *within* one of the great races" (*Mendez*, 781, emphasis added). Segregation *among* whites, in other words, was not contemplated within California law (or presumably among blacks, the other "great race" contemplated in the law). Consequently, the Ninth Circuit Court found the defendants in violation of "federal law as provided in the Fourteenth Amendment to the Federal Constitution by depriving them of liberty and property without due process of law and by denying to them the equal protection of the laws" (*Mendez*, 781).

Almost fifty years after *In re Rodriguez*, justice for Mexicans was *still* accomplished by reiterating the legal segregation/exclusion of Asian Americans and Indians in the law.[30] Once again, the parameters of the political demos were drawn through the mediation of Mexican American racial indeterminacy. This racial indeterminacy enabled Mexican American de facto discrimination in the classroom and de jure whiteness in the courtroom. Although all parties stipulated that Mexicans were white before the case began, their whiteness is an infelicitous performance. Mexican Americans' performance of whiteness "misfires," as they were not deemed "appropriate for the invocation of the par-

186   CHAPTER FOUR

ticular procedure" that is whiteness (Austin 1975, 15–16). The ruling affirms the misfire. McCormick and the Ninth Circuit Court concluded Mexicans existed as an "other class" of whites. Despite Silvia Mendez's unaccented English, her accomplishment of whiteness was tenuous at best. And once again, the ruling transpired on the international stage, as segregation was described as a fascist ideology. By deciding on the *full* inclusion of Mexican Americans within the bifurcated political demos, McCormick restored the United States to justice globally. Nevertheless, the misfired performance of whiteness destabilized the category of whiteness just as Rodriguez did fifty years prior: can whiteness ever be properly performed?

Several civil rights cases in the 1940s utilized this "other class of white" strategy, but *Hernandez v. Texas* (1954) was the only one to reach the U.S. Supreme Court. As Haney López avers, "[As] the first Supreme Court case to extend the protections of the Fourteenth Amendment to Latino/as, it is among the great early triumphs of the struggle for civil rights" (1998, 1145). This singular recognition also makes it the most notorious among Chicana/o historians and legal scholars critical of this strategy as a Faustian pact with aspirational whiteness.[31] In *Hernandez,* James DeAnda and John Herrera, civil rights lawyers with the American GI Forum (AGIF), appealed the 1951 murder conviction of Pete Hernandez to the Texas Court of Criminal Appeals (Appellate Court), arguing his due process rights were violated because Mexican Americans were systematically kept off Jackson County juries. The Appellate Court ruled against Hernandez. LULAC joined in the appeal to the U.S. Supreme Court, adding attorneys Gustavo C. Garcia and Carlos C. Cadena to the case.

To understand the *Hernandez* strategy, it is important to view it in context. In the 1930s and 1940s, civil rights attorneys initially appealed convictions on the basis of discrimination against the "Mexican race" in jury selection (*Ramirez v. Texas* 1931, *Carrasco v. Texas* 1936, *Lugo v. Texas* 1939, *Sanchez v. Texas* 1944, *Bustillos v. Texas* 1948) (Haney López 1998, 1166; Sheridan 2003a, 119). In these cases, the Texas Appellate Court did not question the category of the "Mexican race." Rather, they consistently ruled in favor of state's attorneys, who argued that Mexican Americans were not discriminated against on the basis of their race but because they were not qualified for jury duty. They lacked English, were of dubious character, or "were otherwise ignorant" (*Ramirez* 139, cited in Haney López 1998, 1167). Such discrimination, based on qualification rather than race, was deemed constitutionally acceptable. The unremarkableness of the "Mexican race" in these cases is a testament to the heterotemporal, layered racial geographies of Texas. We may assume the appellants and their attorneys did not hold the same estimation of the "otherwise ignorant" character of the Mexican race as did the Texas state's attorneys, but all did agree this Mexican race existed in the southwestern landscape, alongside and in agonistic relation to the white and black political demos.[32]

Indeed, these litigations, conducted in coordination with Texas civil rights organizations, were arguably an effort to bring U.S. political emancipation into line with Mexican political emancipation—to translate one racial geography into another in an effort to approximate justice. To the appellants, especially in the immediate aftermath of the 1910 Mexican Revolution, the "Mexican race" necessarily resounded with the success of the revolutionary project. After all, the revolution had conjoined nationality with mestizaje in the public sphere by conjoining citizenship rights with the political enfranchisement of all Mexicans regardless of race in the newly constituted demos. Revolutionary mestizaje reverberated with the inclusive nineteenth-century Mexican liberalism expressed in Rodriguez's "pure blooded Mexican" as well. Meanwhile, to the state's attorneys, at the height of Jim Crow, "Mexican race" could not but connote a congenital incivility. It reverberated with the sonic trace of the uncouth indio bárbaro, banished from both racial geographies. These Appellate Court decisions affirmed this connotation.

In *Salazar v. Texas* (1946) and *Sanchez v. Texas* (1951), the Appellate Court changed tack, due to the incredulity of the "unqualified Mexicans" defense and in an effort to quash equal protection arguments on the basis of a "Mexican race" (Haney López 1998, 1169–70). In these cases, the Appellate Court rejected discrimination claims by insisting that Mexican Americans were indeed white. The court ruled that no discrimination had occurred since white Mexican American litigants in these cases were judged by white jurors. Furthermore, the Appellate Court averred that "Mexican" was a nationality, not a race, and as such, the equal protection clause of the Fourteenth Amendment did not apply:

> The [Appellate] court dismissed the defendants' [Salazar, Sanchez] Fourteenth Amendment challenges, dispensing not only with the question of whether there had been discrimination, but also with its previous reformulation of that same question, whether there were qualified Mexican Americans. These were questions the Texas court no longer felt compelled to answer . . . it relied solely on the assertion that Mexican Americans were White in order to reject contentions of impermissible discrimination in jury selection. (Haney López 1998, 1170)

Herrera and DeAnda were the attorneys representing Sanchez in the 1951 decision. As a consequence, they devised a different strategy in *Hernandez*, arguing that Mexican Americans, though white, were discriminated against as a distinct class within whiteness. The Appellate Court applied the same reasoning to *Hernandez* as they did to *Salazar* and *Sanchez*, concluding that the "appellant seeks to have this court recognize and classify Mexicans as a *special* class within the white race and to recognize that *special* class as entitled to *special* privileges in the organization of grand and petit juries in this state. To so hold would constitute a violation of equal protection, because it would be extending to members of a class *special* privileges not accorded to all others of that class similarly situated" (*Hernandez* 535, cited in Sheridan 2003a, 121, emphasis added). It is in the language of this opportunistic decision aimed at avoiding the administration of justice against discrimination that we find the seeds of rhetoric used by conservative judicial activists today against the reparative justice represented by the 1964 Civil Rights Act and affirmative action: minorities seeking redress from institutionalized discrimination are instead seeking *special* privileges from the law that in turn take justice out of the hands of "all [white] others." On the eve of these civil rights victories, Garcia, Cadena, Herrera, and DeAnda, successfully appealed this decision to the U.S. Supreme Court, convincing the court that Mexican Americans were subject to discrimination. Though all parties involved stipulated that Mexican Americans were considered white, the Supreme Court, in a unanimous decision written by Chief Justice Warren, found that the petitioner's attorneys had demonstrated that Mexican Americans were treated as a "distinct class . . . single[d] out . . . for different treatment not based on some reasonable classification." Moreover, the court ruled the Fourteenth Amendment was not solely directed toward discrimination "based upon differences between 'whites' and blacks" (*Hernandez*, 478). Discrimination on the basis of nationality and ancestry was also addressed by the amendment.

It is by a circuitous route, then, that whiteness is bestowed and claimed in *Hernandez*. The Texas Appellate Court conceded Mexican whiteness in the law in order to defer justice for Mexican Americans. Meanwhile, Garcia, Cadena, Herrera, and DeAnda claimed whiteness to circumvent the law in an effort to attain justice. The Supreme Court confers a "distinct class" of whiteness on Mexican Americans, revising the law, presumably to arrive, finally, at a justice deferred. So what was the quality of this whiteness given so grudgingly by the law to Mexican Americans? Was it the same as the whiteness demanded, in turn, by this generation of Mexican American civil rights activists in the courts, even as they recognized that they could not properly possess it?

How did Mexican American activists challenge, even as they sought to fully occupy, their misbegotten whiteness?

To answer these questions, it is once again necessary to take a literary turn, to seek out the translation of this whiteness in the rhetoric of the letters, speeches, and codes written by the activist leaders of LULAC. The language of the law is itself full of metaphor, analogy, and poignant anecdote, like Sylvia Mendez's testimony. But the procedural staccato of the law cannot elucidate the psychic life of this distinct class of whiteness, nor discern the trace of the indio bárbaro that haunts it. It is in the private correspondence of these Mexican American activists, in the advice they give their sons and daughters, in the ethico-political codes they vowed to live by, that we can deduce the psychic life of this tenuous whiteness they claimed in translation. These were space-making practices as well, transforming with irony and allusion unlivable psychic and material spaces into livable ones.

George I. Sánchez, a University of Texas professor of education, was at the forefront of LULAC's mid-twentieth-century civil rights struggles. The author of several books on education in Mexico and in the United States, he was also a civic leader active in LULAC. In this capacity, he was a tireless consultant to lawyers involved in segregation and discrimination cases for over thirty years. In 1958, he penned a letter in response to Roger Baldwin's queries about the possibilities of setting up a legal defense fund comparable to the NAACP's. Baldwin, a representative of the ACLU, wrote to Sánchez informing him of their interest in assisting LULAC in establishing a national office. While expressing doubts that Latinos could ever be as homogenous in their interests as blacks, Japanese, or Jews, Sánchez nevertheless responded enthusiastically to Baldwin's query:

> If we [LULAC] could subsidize a national office for ten staff [members] . . . we would have made a major contribution—not only for the several million persons of Spanish-Mexican . . . or Puerto Rican . . . descent, but for the Negro, the Indian, the Jew and so on. Let us keep in mind that the Mexican-American can easily become *the front-line of defense* of the civil liberties of ethnic minorities. The racial, cultural, and historical involvements in his case embrace those of *all the other minority groups*. Yet, God bless the law, he is "white"! So, the Mexican-American can be the wedge for the broadening of civil liberties for others (who are not so fortunate as to be "white" and "Christian"!) . . . the procedures we have used in the segregation cases involving Mexican-Americans are guides for what the Negroes

190 CHAPTER FOUR

will have to do. I am sorry that Thurgood Marshall and the NAACP have not seen fit to consult us in these matters.[33]

Sánchez's claiming of white Christianity in this letter is ironic in the de Manian sense, as the "systematic undoing of understanding."[34] His ironic claim to whiteness, signaled by grammar (exclamation points, quotation marks) and by the implied double meaning of the blessing, makes clear that he not only understood the narrowness of the ground offered by whiteness to Mexicans, but also that he was already anxious to plan the next assault with other minorities from this narrow "wedge" provided by law.

Sánchez suggests Mexican Americans can be "the wedge" for broadening the civil liberties of other minorities, not because Mexican Americans have more experience in the courts, or because he naïvely believes as "whites" they can hold open the doors for others. Rather, on the heels of the *Hernandez* decision, Sánchez recognized that having presumably already arrived at the good fortune of white Christianity, Mexican American whiteness was always already distinct. Sánchez signaled, through irony, that Mexican American "whiteness" was pregnant with a difference that belied political emancipation and, in a Marxian sense, filled it with discrimination rather than liberation. Sánchez was also translating between the U.S. and Mexican racial geographies he simultaneously occupied, for the difference that made Mexican American whiteness distinct was precisely Mexican Americans' despicable racial ambiguity and dangerous proximity to indigeneity. Nevertheless, he filled this distinction, this ambiguity, with the radical potentiality of mestizaje: Mexican American whiteness "embrace[s]" the "racial, cultural and historical involvements" of "all the other minority groups." Here again is Sánchez's ironic undoing of whiteness: by letting Mexican Americans into "whiteness," the law unwittingly let in the entire motley crew of racial and ethnic others embraced in their mestizaje. Historian Neil Foley has specifically cited this passage as an example of LULAC's aspirational whiteness and retreat from coalitional politics. However, far from signaling a retreat from efforts at racial coalition—or a flight from racial identification with other minorities—Sánchez's letter bases Mexican American identification with other minorities in a racial geography of mestizaje. It has already happened. They have been embraced since the beginning of the Spanish colonial project and its racial geography of miscegenation.[35]

The letter is an ironic undoing of whiteness in another way as well. Though legally white, Mexican Americans who experienced de facto segregation daily revealed for minorities to come the *failure* of political emancipation to successfully emancipate groups from their racialized difference before the law, to successfully privatize their (racial) difference on behalf of their public equality. It is not only that the "blessed law" that accords Mexican Americans whiteness has yet to arrive at freedom, that there is a chronological gap between the law and justice that will be bridged eventually. Rather, *the law is the gap* between the contingency of the present and justice. The law will always require the violence of reinterpretation. Hence, the Texas Appellate Court found it incumbent to protect the general class of whites from the special interests of Mexican Americans. Given the fate of affirmative action in the courts, this is the interpretation of the law that has triumphed, regardless of the ongoing conditions of racial discrimination. Sánchez, then, is "undoing" the liberal idealist myth of abstract citizenship as the grounds for equality, forewarning those minorities who have yet to arrive at white freedom of an arrival perennially deferred.

Even those Chicano historians sympathetic to LULAC and this generation of Mexican American activists, like Mario Garcia or Richard A. Garcia, do not stop to read *how* its leaders defined their "distinct" whiteness. They assume that Mexican American civil rights activists passively accepted a given fact of whiteness prescribed/proscribed to them by law. Yet, when one parses the words LULAC used in its calls for Mexican Americans to assimilate to the United States, one sees that these calls are rife with the contradiction of overlapping racial geographies, a contradiction they did not feel particularly compelled to resolve.

The first article of LULAC's foundational 1929 Code of Conduct calls on Mexican Americans to "honor your country"—the United States—and to "embody yourself into its culture and civilization" (Yarsinke 2004, 18–19). The imperative to embodiment in this first article could certainly be read as an aspirational desire to disappear into whiteness. Yet such a reading is immediately troubled by the second article, which calls on LULAC members to "love the men of your race, take pride in your origin and maintain it immaculate, respect your glorious past, and help to vindicate your own people" (Yarsinke 2004, 18–19, translation my own). This article is a homopatriarchal and patriotic call to the love, respect, and vindication of a "race" and "people," harkening back to the coordinates of a Mexican racial geography. Here again we hear the echo of Christian unity, of nineteenth-century Mexican liberal inclusion, and of twentieth-century revolutionary mestizaje, one that forces a rereading of the previous call to white embodiment. These first two articles convolute the coordinates of Mexican and U.S. racial geographies that emplot Mexican American citizenship, but they also map the new coordinates of political demos LULAC hoped to materialize through their efforts. The code summons Mexican Americans at once to political integration in the United States and to political identifications of their "immaculate" Mexican "origin," conjuring that quintessential symbol of mestizo embodiment, the Virgin of Guadalupe. The code graphs the "glorious past" of mestizaje onto the "culture and civilization" of whiteness, proposing a livable embodiment, a new mode of mestizaje if you will. Well aware of the treacherous mapping of their daily lives charted by violence, denigration, and discrimination, LULAC members charted a new geography of racial translation, without any concern for the apparent contradictions in the coordinates of this "third space."

For another example of this effort to make (white) citizenship in the U.S. commensurate with mestizaje, let us turn to LULAC president Manuel C. Gonzalez's commencement speech before a graduating class of seniors in San Antonio in 1942. He opened by alluding to the World War II effort, telling the graduates that while previous Mexican American graduates thought only of the economic battles that lay ahead, this class "face[s] a world engulfed in struggle to determine whether we are to be ruled by the forces of tyranny and oppression, or whether democracy and the American way of life" will prevail (cited in R. Garcia 1991, 298). He summons them to action thusly: "You have for inspiration the patriotism, self-sacrifice and valor of Washington, Lincoln, Roosevelt, Simón Bolívar, Miguel Hidalgo and Benito Juarez" (R. Garcia 1991, 298). Gonzalez makes American patriotism into a transcontinental affair, with his list of past liberators of *América*. However, he goes further when he tells these seniors that when they fight for the United States in World War II they should seek courage in "Miguel Hidalgo, who, using the image of the Virgin of Guadalupe for a flag, led people in revolt against the yoke of Spain," and from "Cuauhtémoc, who endured the pains of hell as his feet were burned" by the Spaniards (R. Garcia 1991, 298).

Importantly, in choosing these two examples he is choosing not the coordinates of whiteness represented by Spaniards, but the privileged coordinates central to a *Mexican* racial geography of independence and revolution: mestizaje (represented by Hidalgo and the Virgin of Guadalupe) and indigeneity (represented by Cuauhtémoc). When Gonzalez hails these young men into (white) U.S. citizenship by way of (1) a mestizaje represented by the fidelity of the Virgin of Guadalupe and the patriotism of Miguel Hidalgo, and (2) indigenous resistance represented by Cuauhtémoc, he is the Mexican foreigner (always immigrant before the law) translating racial coordinates for the graduating students according to the law of "decorum," of "the strongest," of the "equitable law of democracy." In Derrida's terms, Gonzalez responds to the "dois"

ADJUDICATING EXCEPTION   193

of translating a Mexican racial code into the coerced racial code of his/their host country. In 1942, the U.S. military would enlist young men to fight and die on behalf of a country still segregating students and troops according to color. Gonzalez attempts to make the unlivable spaces of segregation—even in death—into a livable one by invoking the terms of a political enfranchisement they would comprehend. In so doing, he too is creating a third racial geography, the nascent geography of Aztlán. United States racial governmentality required that these young men go to war in segregated regiments, yet these same soldiers returned to the Southwest after World War II to challenge and permanently transform the racist terms of their own enfranchisement through the G.I. Forum and the civil rights movement. Gonzalez does not ask the young men to aspire to whiteness. Rather Gonzalez transformed the convolution of both Mexican and U.S. racial geographies into a translated space in which the graduating seniors were agents, not in spite of their racial origin, but because of it: a transnational geography of anticolonialism, of resistance, of independence, of revolution, of freedom that transcended a bifurcated logic of racial segregation. The racial geography imagined by this generation of Mexican American civil rights activists—masculinist, unrepentant, nostalgic, and politicized—was generated from the *loss* of Mexican character, the *loss* of indigenous ancestry, the *loss* of proper belonging: from the legal rending asunder of indigenous and white being. It is a space engendered by psychic loss, but also occupied surreptitiously by those inveterate lost objects of a political future. It is *this* generation, so chastised by the subsequent generation of Chicana/o activists for their aspirations, who laid the psychic groundwork of the racial geography of Aztlán by sublimating the legally foreclosed but psychically alive indigenous objects into their refashioned legal status as "white!"—into a future perfect of political belonging.

5

LOSING IT!
Melancholic Incorporations in Aztlán

Freudian melancholia designates a chain of loss, denial, and incorporation through which the ego is born. As other readers of Freud have pointed out, it is unclear in Freud's essay whether there could have been an ego prior to melancholia, since the ego comes into being as a psychical object, as a perceptual object, only after the "shadow of the object" has fallen upon it. By taking in the other-made-ghostly, the melancholic subject fortifies him- or herself and grows rich in impoverishment. The history of the ego is thus the history of its losses. More accurately, melancholia alludes not to loss per se but to the entangled relationship with loss. We might then say that melancholia does not simply denote a *condition* of grief, but is, rather, a *legislation* of grief. —**Anne Anlin Cheng**, *The Melancholy of Race*

Ladies and gentleman [*sic*] . . . my name is Oscar Acosta. My father is an Indian from the mountains of Durango. Although I cannot speak his language . . . you see, Spanish is the language of our conquerors. English is the language of our conquerors. . . . No one ever asked me or my brother if we wanted to be American citizens. We are all citizens by default. They stole our land and made us half-slaves. They destroyed our gods and made us bow down to a dead man who's been strung up for 2000 years. . . . Now what we need is, first to give ourselves a new name. We need a new identity. A name and a language all our own. . . . So I propose that we call ourselves . . . I propose we call ourselves the Brown Buffalo people. . . . No, it's not an Indian name, for Christ sake . . . don't you get it? The buffalo, see? Yes, the animal that everyone slaughtered. Sure, both cowboys and Indians are out to get him . . . and, because we do have roots in our Mexican past, our Aztec ancestry, that's where we get the *brown* from. —**Oscar Zeta Acosta**, *Autobiography of a Brown Buffalo* (ellipses in the original)

This mock introduction by the protagonist/author to the reader comes at the end of *The Autobiography of a Brown Buffalo* (*Buffalo*), after a journey of self-discovery has taken Oscar Zeta Acosta from his legal aid office in San Francisco, California, north to Ketchum, Idaho, then south through Colorado, New Mexico, and Texas to Ciudad Juárez, Chihuahua, and back again across the border to El Paso. Acosta's arrival at the truth about himself and about Mexican Americans in the aftermath of this manic journey is staged as an epiphanic moment of self-revelation and collective rebirth. Yet the shadows of many lost objects nevertheless fall over the "Brown Buffalo people," as this baptismal scene is also the scene of psychic becoming described by Anne Anlin Cheng. In the narrative chronology of the autobiography, the protagonist is on the brink of a (utopic) future predicated on these losses, on this personal and collective past cluttered with lost objects. Cheng's melancholic legislation of grief suggests the protagonist's ego has already taken shape in the shadow of these losses he only belatedly perceives: of indigenous culture (language, religion), of property (land), of sovereignty (half-slaves), of territory (imposed citizenship). In Acosta's litany we see that "the history of [his] ego is thus the history of its losses." So too the future of the narrator and his people is the history of their collective loss, the recognition of loss requiring immediate action: "Now what we need is . . . a new name." Loss constitutes the collective unconscious of the Brown Buffalo people who are yet to be. Underscoring the ego's melancholic incorporation of these losses, even the eponymous name Acosta chooses for himself and his people is that of an animal threatened with extinction that "everyone slaughtered." *Buffalo* provides a rich literary record of the Chicana/o generation's political consciousness and racial unconscious.

If *Buffalo* is a testament to Chicana/o racial melancholia writ large (à la Cheng), then who or what is the "other-made-ghostly" in Aztlán, mythical homeland of the Chicana/o people? *Buffalo* allows us to discern how Aztlán is also Indian given. The miscegenated indigenous ancestry of Mexican Americans lost to them during a century of treaties, legislation, and litigation casts a long formative shadow over this geography. Multifarious references to Indians in Acosta's autobiography are textually oblique yet hermeneutically central, inviting the reader to discern a geography of racial loss that is uniquely Chicana/o and contingent on the loss of indigeneity. The heterotemporal indios of the colonial and postcolonial archive provide Acosta with the coordinates for Aztlán as the incorporation and embodiment of a historical loss, at once the effect of a legislation of grief and a livable psychic space negotiated within the racial strictures of Mexico and the United States. The

Chicana/o movement produced physical space as well, reclaimed in thousands of cities and towns of the Southwest from the geography of discrimination and segregation.[1]

As a mythos, an imaginary nation, and a political program, Aztlán is copiously produced from the grief suffered at the legislated loss of indigeneity discussed in chapter 4, yet its ambition ironically impinged on the territory and identity of Native Americans. Its boundaries correspond simultaneously to those of the Provincias Internas of New Spain and to the boundaries of the Mexican territory annexed by the United States after 1848, demonstrating that the production of indigenous Aztlán draws directly from colonial and postcolonial racial geographies.[2]

This chapter investigates *why* the boundaries of Aztlán correspond so consistently with this doubly colonized space (figs. 5.1 and 5.2). Why does the southern border of Aztlán always end at the U.S.–Mexico border? Why must it appropriate the territory of thousands of Native Americans in its mapping? I unravel how Chicana/os arrived at this particular mapping of Aztlán, as the predictability of its borders is the surest symptom of its legislation by grief. If indigenous peoples were foreclosed to Mexican Americans through imperial annexation and racial legislation, the Chicana/o racial psyche grew rich through this impoverishment. Aztlán was produced not only through the melancholic and manic representational incorporation of lost indigeneity but also through the figurative incorporation of indigenous territoriality.

Oscar Zeta Acosta played a foundational role in the political history of the Chicana/o movement as an author, activist, and lawyer, producing with other activists and artists the problematic racial coordinates of Aztlán. Representing Chicanos simultaneously in the courtroom, in the press, and in his memoirs, Acosta not only transformed *the representation of space* in his creative writing, he also transformed *representational space* in his law practice. In the courtroom, Acosta was one of the first legal activists of his generation to un-map the legally segregated landscape of southern California. By so doing, Acosta also helped to clear the ground in order to transform the segregated and discriminatory racial geography of the Southwest into the geography of Aztlán. Acosta represented Chicano activists, popularly known as the East L.A. Thirteen and the Biltmore Six, in two of the most important cases of the post–civil rights era. Rather than insist on his clients' innocence, Acosta's defense strategy put the law itself on trial, exposing the racial contingency of justice in the California landscape, transforming the representational space of the political demos in the process. I begin with the transcripts of these trials, as well as Acosta's journalism about his cases, because of his defense strategy's

LOSING IT!   197

FIG. 5.1. One of several maps of Aztlán found online.

FIG. 5.2. Aztlán flag, with boundaries corresponding to 1848 annexed territory, ending discretely at the Mexico–U.S. border.

central function in producing space in the Lefebvrian sense discussed in the introduction, as a set of social relations lived through space and not merely in it.

Indigenous imagery abounds in Chicana/o literature and other canonical texts might also provide an analysis of Chicana/o consciousness during *el movimiento*. I focus on *The Autobiography of a Brown Buffalo* in the second half of this chapter, however, because it is a postcolonial travel narrative through the figural geography of Aztlán, one that stages an intertextual dialogue with Jack Kerouac's *On the Road* (*OTR*), urtext of countercultural travel writing. Acosta parodies Kerouac's narrative of American-freedom-as-travel as he mimes its melancholic imperialism.[3] As a postcolonial literary revision in the vein of Jean Rhys's *Wide Sargasso Sea* and J. M. Coetzee's *Foe, Buffalo* rescripts the transparent and idealized racial others of *OTR* by offering the reader an alternative mapping of the same American landscape. Beat aesthetics reiterated Fredrick Jackson Turner's frontier thesis of exceptional U.S. freedom, as writers like Kerouac rendered the Southwest a horizon for play, progress, and re-invention. *Buffalo* exposes the Beats' expansionist aesthetics by re-presenting the Southwest as the landscape of discrimination, segregation, and genocidal conquest. Acosta's parody transforms this violent landscape into one of collectivity and racial belonging, claiming this Beat territory for Aztlán, the physical and psychic landscape of liberation. Thus I also focus on *Buffalo* because it is the literary complement to Acosta's legal space-making project. It unmaps the segregated Southwest through representation, claiming it as *representational space* for the Aztlán nation of Brown Buffalo people.

Whiteness on Trial

Four years before publishing *The Autobiography of a Brown Buffalo,* Oscar Zeta Acosta worked in Los Angeles as a lawyer, an activist, and a gonzo journalist, penning missives from the front lines of el movimiento.[4] In true gonzo style, he wrote articles for Chicano newspapers and magazines on the police brutality he witnessed, on the political protests he helped organize, and on the defense strategy he devised. Tinged with the sexist bravado he was famous for, these articles were part legal analysis, part staccato historiography, part nationalist manifesto. In 1968 thousands of students staged walkouts from five predominantly Mexican American East Los Angeles high schools in protest of the schools' dilapidated condition. Acosta described them in cinematic detail:

> The myth of the passive Mexican blew up again in this anxious city's poisonous air. Waves of mini-skirted, brown-skinned and black-haired girls were echoing the angry, clenched fist cry of the new machos in the barrios: Viva La Raza! Chicano Power! Education—not Eradication! The young Chicano radicals (brown berets and khaki field jackets) were exhorting their poverty ridden camaradas to yell these gritos at the gabacho-gringo as they marched to the school board with their demands. The demands had been hammered out at countless community meetings over a preceding six month period. (Acosta 1970, 13)

Reiterating the Chicano family romance (Fregoso 2003), the objectified "girls" provide a colorful, leggy backdrop for the ferocious Chicano "radicals" whose "field jackets" signal, by contrast to the "mini-skirts," their military readiness. Moreover, the girls merely echo the political message crafted by the "new machos in the barrio" who we envision leading the "countless community meetings." While this passage bristles with the misogyny for which Acosta has been roundly and fairly criticized, it also documents the historic unmapping of the geography of segregation in California by the Chicana/o movement in real time, describing women and men in the very process of simultaneously drawing the new map of Aztlán.[5] As Acosta's description of the "waves" of marchers through the poisonous air of Los Angeles attests, the walkouts themselves recoded the segregated space of Los Angeles. Such a recoding of space led to the arrest and indictment of thirteen organizers on various misdemeanors and one conspiracy charge that carried a forty-five-year maximum sentence.

Acosta described his defense strategy to the Chicano community in the sardonically titled "The East L.A. 13 vs. L.A. Superior Court" for the quarterly journal *El Grito*, explaining that he had "challenged the jurisdictional power of the indicting body (the Grand Jury) on the grounds of discrimination in its very selection by the Superior Court judges" (1970, 14).[6] Acosta effectively turned the tables in the courtroom, requiring California Superior Court judges to take the stand and attest to their racial prejudices in the empanelment of grand jurors. In the East L.A. Thirteen and Biltmore Six cases combined, Acosta questioned more than one hundred Superior Court judges on their criteria for nominating candidates (Haney López 1999–2000, 1722). With rare exceptions, most of the judges had never nominated a Mexican.

Acosta's defense strategy was not solely or even principally interested in impugning the judges. Rather, as he informed the community in the article, he was determined "to legally establish [the defendants'] identity as a people separate and distinct from the majority" with "statistical evidence" and "expert witnesses" (1970, 14). Coming fourteen years after *Hernandez v. Texas*, Acosta's approach marked a sea change. In *Hernandez*, all the lawyers and judges involved with the case, from the lower to the Supreme Court, stipulated that Mexican Americans were white. In sharp contrast, Acosta insisted Mexican Americans were *not* white, but deserving of their own "classification":

> An expert urban sociologist lectured to a silent court and counsel *that the defendants did indeed belong to a separate and distinct group of persons* despite their governmental classification as Caucasians and their legal recognition as citizens. *As a heterogeneous group, Mexican Americans still meet all accepted criteria for ethnic classification. . . .* They retain, for example, *a communality of values and behavior patterns* even more amply than the Anglo-Caucasian majority and the unquestioned "Negro" minority. Furthermore . . . increasingly more and more members of other Hispanic-Indio cultures link themselves with the general "Spanish surnamed" identity because they, too, have been victimized in education, employment and housing . . . in the judicial process. All of these people, together, call themselves La Raza, connoting a sense of peoplehood—much as the Jews identify themselves as The Chosen People—binding together the meanest with the most virtuous, the richest with the most humble. (1970, 14–15, emphasis added)

Acosta sought this classification to qualify Mexican Americans for the protections gained by African Americans under *Brown v. Board of Education*, "a precondition" as he put it, for demanding "representation for their group on the Grand Jury" (1970, 14).[7] Acosta, however, was not strictly focused on the U.S. courts. Rather, he was taking his case before the court of Mexican American public opinion, seeking to convince this admittedly "heterogeneous group" into "self-identifying" with their "Hispanic-Indio cultural link" instead of "their governmental classification as Caucasians." Writing in the first *national* publication of this era for Mexican Americans, curating "evidence" in the trial culled from "experts," Acosta was summoning his Brown Buffalo people into becoming *before the law,* as he would later do in his eponymous memoir.

Acosta's article captures the very moment of the transformation of Mexican Americans into Chicana/os, the birth of a consciousness. Indeed, the article presages the transformation, capturing the fluidity of the moment but also the precariousness of *all* racial categorization. For the language Acosta uses in describing the distinctiveness of *La Raza*—"the race"—as a classification is genuinely the language of speculation, equivocation, improvisation, and aspiration. What begins as a stated plea for a separate and distinct *ethnic* classification on the basis of a "communality of values and behaviors" comparable to an "Anglo" ethnicity immediately slips into an appeal for *racial* classification ("Anglo-Caucasian"), for Acosta's true bid is for an unambiguous racial category comparable to the "unquestioned 'Negro' minority." There is a tinge of sarcasm in the use of the term "unquestioned," but also a tinge of longing for a similarly unambiguous position. The certainty of race that Acosta craves, however, is undone by the historical convolution of race and culture he is immediately mired in: is it values or skin color that constitutes a classification of people? With the "Hispanic-Indio *cultural* link" among "Spanish surnamed" people, Acosta would appear to shift the ground back to ethnicity, yet he relies on the biological tie implied by the hyphen, foregrounding a foundational miscegenation that unites *all* Latin American descendants under "La Raza." Acosta shifts the ground once more by insisting that Spanish-surnamed peoples share instead an *experience* of political and economic discrimination, undoing the very division from African Americans that he seeks in his bid for classification, as African Americans share cheek by jowl in this discrimination. His racial calculus is especially problematic given that many Spanish-surnamed people are afromestizo, further binding Latinos with, rather than separating them from, African Americans. The racial calculus of American jurisprudence, from which Acosta wishes to garner the benefits of *Brown,* requires stark racial division even after *Brown,* as U.S. racial geography continues to render the experience of race as discrete and absolute, and seeks to apportion justice according to rigid classification.

Acosta finally appeals to religion: "La Raza" is fused together by "a sense of peoplehood" like "the Jews," they too a chosen people. Like other Chicana/o nationalists of his day, Acosta uses "La Raza" in the hopes of naming a certainty, of christening a people, of calling forth a destiny. And yet the term indexed the very ambiguity and ambivalence that plague his attempt at a definitive racial identity. The Chicana/o movement derived "La Raza" from José Vasconcelos's *La Raza Cósmica,* a short essay published in 1925 on the merging of all races into one "cosmic" messianic race. According to Vasconcelos, the four "great races"—red, yellow, black, and white—brought together by the Spanish colonial project were conjoined by miscegenation into one superior race.[8] The problems of racial division so evident in the Mexico of his day would resolve themselves when all the races were made one, as all the good cultural qualities of the separate races would prevail, subsuming all the negative ones in the process.[9] Vasconcelos identified many positive (though predictable) cultural traits with Africans, Indians, and Asians, but true to the

Darwinist positivism of his day (and to New Spain's racial geography), Vasconcelos also identified laziness, barbarity, and infidelity with these races as well. And most intellection was ascribed to the white race.

Vasconcelos's project was at once utopian and racist, democraticizing and hierarchical. Most significantly, as I have argued elsewhere, with the subsuming of the "negative qualities" of some races to the "superior" ones of others, la raza cósmica implied the eventual erasure of indigenous specificity, especially as the Indian was at once identified as folkloric foundation and stroppy obstacle to Mexican modernity.[10] For our purposes, however, it is significant that Vasconcelos struggled mightily to define the very thing he was naming. He had a difficult time dividing the races, determining where indigenous qualities ended and black ones began, where black qualities ended and white ones began. La Raza Cósmica remains a muddled, ambivalent, and tenuous speculation on the definition of races in Mexico and their conjoined mestizo destiny. Indeed, at several points in the essay Vasconcelos was by turns enthralled and appalled by his own vision. When Chicana/o activists and writers adopted the term La Raza from Vasconcelos, they adopted this utopic hierarchy. Their appropriation of the term, like Acosta's, remains haunted by Vasconcelos's ambivalences, erasures, and elisions. In the process of becoming one ideal of cultural citizenship, La Raza obfuscated the multiple, rich racial histories brought together by European colonialisms in the Americas writ large, in Mexico, and in the figural geography of Aztlán.

In Acosta's formulation of the "Hispanic-Indio," the indigenous ancestry of Mexican Americans was once again relegated to a tangential role, called forth in the classically binominal form, as one half of a too simplistic dyad: Spaniards and Indians. The presence of the Indian was important to be sure, but only insofar as it secured the classification Acosta so desperately sought as *other than white*.[11] As in Vasconcelos, the Indian's presence becomes valuable to the extent that it ushers in a superior category.[12] Acosta's reductive reading of Mexico's racial geography erased not only the contributing history of afromestizos and Asian immigrants (acknowledged in Vasconcelos), but the indigenous plurality in the colonial and postcolonial history of Mexico (also acknowledged by Vasconcelos) and of the Southwest, as discussed in previous chapters.

For Mexican Americans to emerge as a *proper* minority apportioned the rights due them under new civil rights legislation, they needed to achieve the status of a unique racial classification distinguishable from that of African Americans and Native Americans. Paradoxically, to achieve this separate status Chicano nationalism chose a theory of mestizaje that negated such racial calculus. Nevertheless, Acosta rehearsed the racial division of U.S. jurisprudence, separating Chicana/os once again from contemporary indigenous identity. I am not suggesting that Chicanos eschewed indigeneity. To the contrary, Chicana/o consciousness embraced indigenous *ancestry* as the site of colonial violation, instrumentalizing it as a means for establishing a political identity and imaginative control of the Southwest. However, Acosta's speculations into the nature of La Raza reiterated the disaggregating logic of U.S. imperialism, dispossessing Mexican Americans of their indigenous identity and vice versa, even if his speculations improvised ways of imagining and disrupting other complex totalities.

Acosta defended both the East L.A. Thirteen and the Biltmore Six from 1968 to 1972. Although the Los Angeles Unified School District school board had granted a general amnesty to all those who had participated in the walkouts, nevertheless the defendants in the East L.A. Thirteen case were charged with conspiracy to disrupt public schools, in addition to various misdemeanors. The LAPD clearly targeted the leadership of Chicana/o youth and community organizations with the intent of deterring any further civil rights protests.[13] Instead these arrests escalated the protests. The California Department of Education dedicated its 1969 annual conference to examining the educational problems facing Mexican Americans in a desultory effort to respond to the walkouts. Held in April at the luxurious Biltmore Hotel, the conference had Governor Ronald Reagan deliver the keynote address, during which Chicana/o activists shouted and clapped in protest of the continuing inequity in school facilities and ongoing trial of the East L.A. Thirteen. The police quickly removed the protestors from the ballroom, but during the ruckus fires broke out on four floors of the hotel. Six protestors were eventually indicted on felony charges of arson, burglary, and malicious destruction, along with conspiracy charges in relation to the commitment of these felonies. Three members of the Biltmore Six were also defendants in the East L.A. Thirteen case. On trial in two cases for conspiracy, these three defendants now faced the possibility of life sentences.

As Acosta's article in *El Grito* makes clear, the defendants' guilt or innocence was irrelevant. His aim was to establish the defendants as members of a separate racial group denied equal protection under the Fourteenth Amendment. The indicting grand juries were unconstitutional because they were not representative of the defendants' racial category:

> From the testimony of thirty-three judges subpoenaed to testify [in the East L.A. Thirteen case], at times vague if not downright hostile, a reasonable composite of the 1959–1969 "grand juror" was constructed:

204   CHAPTER FIVE

(1) He is comparatively advanced in years. 2) He is wealthy, *of indepen-dent financial means.* 3) He is, or was, a *business owner, executive, or profes-sional*—or married to one. 4) He is a close personal friend, occasionally once removed, of a Superior Court Judge. 5) He is White. . . . In a word, as characterized by an appellate Judge: WASP. (1970, 15, emphasis added)

Acosta collapsed all these separate characteristics into the signifying term *WASP*, capturing the conjoined nature of race and class in the United States. Racialized ethnicity stands in for class. This analysis of the conjuncture of race and class was an essential aspect of early Chicana/o nationalism, an as-pect easily forgotten once the movement's demand for economic justice gave way to the reformist demand of symbolic representation within multicultur-alism. WASP signified the problem was not simply the empanelment of white male jurors but of people of considerable economic and political power. The division between these jurors as the capitalist class—"independent means," "owner, executive, professional"—and Chicana/os as the working class was vast. Chicana/os were subordinated in a racialized class hierarchy. Acosta's questioning exposed a relationship between ethnoracial specificity, own-ership of the means of production, and political power—revealing the jury room as a space of privileged access to justice. Indeed, the continued repro-duction of propertied social relation depended on this privileged access to justice. And Acosta's defense strategy, reprised in a community newspaper, was an attempt to transform this relation through community activism.

Prepared with ten years of jury rolls, Acosta questioned each judge in turn regarding how he chose his nominees.[14] Whether they had nominated hundreds or dozens of candidates, all were remarkably consistent. Eighty-seven percent of those nominated were friends, acquaintances, or family of the Superior Court judges, making it virtually impossible to serve on a grand jury without a personal connection to the judge. My focus here, however, is not this degree of relation but rather *where* the judges had met their nomi-nees. From the testimony of Judge Joseph Call:

Q. Do you know a Dora Rombeau, R-o-m-b-e-a-u?
A. Very well.
Q. How long have you known Mrs. Rombeau?
A. Well, it would go back to approximately the very early, early 1950s. . . . She is the wife of Dr. Rombeau, an outstanding physician, I believe, in Burbank. I know Dr. Rombeau and Mrs. Rombeau because they have been members of the Los Angeles Tennis Club since the early '50s. . . .

I see them twice a week on the courts at the Los Angeles Tennis Club, and have since 1950.

. . .

Q. Thank you. Do you know a Mr. George Goman?
A. Very well.
Q. Is Mr. Goman a member of the tennis club, too?
A. Yes.

(Motion to Quash Indictment, *People v. Castro*, cited in Haney López 1999–2000, 1732)[15]

From the testimony of Judge Bayard Rhone:

Q. How long have you known Mr. Dryden?
A. About eight or nine years.
Q. In what capacity do you know Mr. Dryden?
A. I met him through various Camellia societies that he belongs to and that I belong to.

. . .

Q. [Do you know a] Mr. William Coberly?
A. I do.
Q. How long and in what capacity did you know Mr. Coberly?
A. Let's see. I have known him about six or seven years. He is a member of the board of trustees of my church.
Q. What church is this, Your Honor?
A. First Congregational Church of Los Angeles.

(Trial transcript, 660–666, cited in Haney López 1999–2000, 1734–1735)

The testimony of nearly every judge demonstrated this spatial pattern of elite belonging and connection. George A. Dockweiler said of one nominee, "[He] lived just around the corner, and I knew him for some—well, we lived in Los Feliz for about 20 years, and he was a neighbor," and of another, "He was also a neighbor of mine. He was connected with the Security First National Bank, in the real estate department." Chambers of commerce, councils, and boards were a common denominator. Eugene H. Breitenbach met nominee Harland J. Nissen "when we were both on the recreation facilities committee of the Los Angeles Junior Chamber of Commerce in the early 1930s," and nominee Anthony Fogo "as a fellow member and later fellow board member of the Los Angeles Junior Chamber of Commerce." Breitenbach met nominee Eleanor Hiller when they were "both on the Los

206 CHAPTER FIVE

Angeles Community Council," and nominee Lindley Bryant once they had served on "the board of trustees of the Emanuel Presbyterian Church." Judges frequently mixed business and pleasure, thus James G. Whyte knew nominee Stanley E. Barnes as "a member of a bridge club where I played . . . and I have known him as a member of the Chamber of Commerce, and generally in the business world in the community." Meanwhile, Lt. Col. R. R. Bacon was Whyte's "commanding officer when I was in the R.O.T.C. at Pomona College. . . . He also is a member of the same bridge club I mentioned Mr. Barnes was a member of." Kenneth Chantry knew his nominees in several capacities, but most were also members of the Wilshire Country Club.[16]

Church, club, chamber of commerce; bank, law office, lodge. These spatial coordinates exceeded the segregated communities from which these judges hailed, as they crisscrossed the entire city in their daily social, economic, religious, and political life. Nevertheless, this circuit of places constituted a geography of power and privilege that was quite material, not only because nominating practices could be mapped according to the judges' everyday social activities, but because they were subsequently made manifest in indictments all over southern California. This made it impossible for Chicana/os—or any other racial minority or working-class white—to be tried by a grand jury of their peers. The performance of justice had an unacknowledged spatial organization then, as becoming a nominee was not simply a matter of personal intimacy or even neighborly proximity, but was contingent on a spatially diffuse grid of association and connection, a map of wealth, property, privilege, leisure, and religious practice.

This spatial grid was *not* exclusively white. Indeed, it could not be segregated and still function. Rather, the very minorities who never made it onto the jury rolls enabled this geography of power. When asked by Acosta if they knew any Mexicans, judges answered without irony that they knew their gardeners, their domestics, the custodial staff at the court, the gasoline attendant at the corner. From Acosta's examination of Judge Samuel Greenfield:

Q. Do you know any Spanish-surnamed persons in Los Angeles County?
A. One or two.
Q. Are these persons friends of yours?
A. No, they are domestics.
Q. Do they work as domestics for you, or for other people?
A. For us.

Q. Do you know any other Spanish-surnamed persons other than these two?
A. That is, I personally know them, is that what you are asking?
Q. Well, yes, your Honor.
A. The answer is no.

("Motion," 722, cited in Haney López 1999–2000, 1739)

Judge Harold W. Schweitzer seems to purposely misconstrue Acosta's question:

Q. I would like to ask you whether or not during the past 10 years you have known any persons of Spanish surname?
A. Yes, I have known many.
Q. Approximately how many, Your Honor?
A. I'd say hundreds . . . [d]own in Mazatlan, Mexico.
Q. Not here in the United States, then?
A. No.
Q. Okay. I'm referring to persons here in the United States, Your Honor, specifically in the California area. Do you know any persons of Spanish surname within the area here, the general area?
A. Yes, I know some.
Q. Approximately how many do you know?
A. Oh, when you say "know them," I know them only on a speaking basis, just to say hello, and maybe call them by their name, and they maybe know me by name; I'd say *several dozen*, I'd say, around the Civic Center. . . . Oh, some of them were working inside the Courthouse building, men that I would *see almost daily*, and others would be working around as gardeners, around the Civic Center.
Q. Then are the persons that you said that you know with Spanish surnames, are these persons that worked around and inside the Courthouse?
A. Both in and around the Courthouse area.

("Motion," 310–311, cited in Haney López 1999–2000, 1738–1739, emphasis added)

Once again from Judge Call:

Q. Do you know any Mexican-Americans, Judge?
A. Well, the gentleman that is a gardener at my house is a Mexican-American. I just signed his citizenship papers. I guess now he is a double-fledged citizen, if that's what you mean.

Q. Do you know any persons of Mexican descent who were born here in this country?

A. Mexican descent? If I do, I can't recall them. I probably do. Over the period of my life I have met *thousands, hundreds*. I have met *many, many*, but I can't recall it from memory. Undoubtedly, undoubtedly I know many of them.

("Motion," 386–387, cited in Haney López 1999–2000, 1738, emphasis added)

What if we took the candid Greenfield and the somewhat more clipped Schweitzer and Call at their word, interpreting what they said as an accurate representation of their racial geography? In their daily travels throughout Los Angeles County, "undoubtedly" these judges encountered "many, many" Mexican Americans serving them breakfast, trimming their lawns, pumping gas into their cars, taking their coats, helping them on with their robes, handing them a cup of coffee, a cocktail, a towel, as they specified in their testimony. They *did* know, or at least visually encountered, hundreds of Mexican Americans in their kitchens, at the bank, at the courthouse, in the public bathrooms, at the club, on the streets, as they made their predictable way from home to work to leisure and back again. Gardener, domestic, custodial worker, security guard, all of these brown people populated the geography of power within which these judges traveled. The number of times judges attested to knowing Mexican Americans in these *specific* capacities suggests that Mexican Americans were visualized as "guardians" of the land (gardener/guard) from whose polity they were excluded precisely because of the raced and classed *way* they occupied space, as if these antiquated professions (caretakers) barred their capacity in other more modern ones (justice makers).[17]

The judges' testimonies are travel narratives in their own right, constructing space through representation. Indeed, the judges represent themselves as the "mobile" occupants of Los Angeles County, zipping from one locale to the next, intersecting regularly with Mexican Americans who are represented as "immobile," as the custodians of *particular* locales. Mexican Americans were highly visible (and useful) in the multiracial landscape of Los Angeles, but through their working-class professions they were also reified as part of the (racial) landscape. Precisely because of Mexican Americans' seemingly fixed modes of spatial occupation, they were not seen as qualified in the universal capacity of justice except peripherally, as Judge Schweitzer notes, "both in and around the Courthouse area." Mexican Americans' visual emplotment in/as landscape precluded their service to the scene/seen of racialized justice.

Paradoxically, while the judges viewed Mexican Americans as marginal to justice, their testimony of knowing "hundreds, thousands" recentered Mexican Americans in the racial geography of the Southwest.[18]

This brings us to Acosta's second line of questioning. Since 1962 the presiding court justice had been sending the superior court judges administrative directives instructing them to ensure grand juries were "representative of a cross-section of the community . . . from the various geographical locations . . . and different racial groups, and all economic levels" ("Motion," 289, 299, cited in Haney López 1999–2000, 1792–1793). Acosta asked the judges if they adhered to these memos, and they fell back on the question of qualification when pressed. Robert Finerman bluntly explained his reasons for not complying: "What I was interested in was getting qualified people to serve on the Grand Jury, regardless of their ethnic and racial background, because I don't believe in quota systems, per se." Similarly, Leonard A. Diether insisted, "I think it is the duty of each Judge to pick a nominee who he feels is qualified for the position, regardless of what race, nationality, or religion he may be. It doesn't make any difference." By this reasoning, Mexican Americans were not qualified to serve. At least the judges did not know any who were. For instance, Bernard S. Jefferson answered, "Had I known . . . of anyone of a minority group who might have been qualified, and who would have accepted, I would have gone out of my way to have appointed him, if I could have." To meet qualified Mexican Americans Jefferson would have had to go "out of [his] way," outside his grid of spatial relation, or to have visualized the grid differently, as he admittedly crossed paths with Mexicans daily. Emmett E. Doherty did visualize these laborers differently—"I asked some of the colored men in the court if they could recommend some persons that were well-qualified"—but to no avail.

It is finally Judge Fildew who plainly speaks the racial unconscious, rearticulating the Mexican with the Indian in the court of law, reiterating the absolute boundaries of the demos and the cartography of imperial domination. Thrice Acosta asks Fildew if he agrees with the directives, and thrice Fildew answers no, not if it "impairs the quality" of the jury. Acosta presses Fildew: "What do you mean by 'impair the quality' by certain people?" A flustered Fildew responds, "Well if you are going to get somebody who isn't qualified just because he is an American-Indian or an Eskimo, because you have to have an Eskimo on the Grand Jury, but this fellow isn't qualified, I am against that. I don't think the Grand Jury should be composed of people like that" ("Motion," 653–654, cited in Haney López 1999–2000, 1817). The referent in "people like

210   CHAPTER FIVE

that" is purposefully ambiguous, as "that" refers simultaneously to unqualified people and to American Indians and Eskimos.

Once again, *American* Indians may be within the nation's geographical boundaries (though peripherally, as implied by the snide reference to Alaska), but they are not within the nation's *temporal* boundaries. Labor, after all, determines if and how one appears in the U.S. racial geography, and Native Americans cannot appear in the racial landscape as such. Rather African slaves and subsequent racial others must be imported to replace them as labor for whites. "American Indians" and "Eskimos" represent a time before the landscape was subjected to capital and its political institutions, and thus they cannot be imagined as part of the laboring classes. As Jean O'Brien explains, "The master narrative of [nineteenth-century] New England . . . involved the replacement of 'uncivilized' peoples whose histories and cultures they interpreted as illogically rooted in nature, tradition, and superstition, whereas New Englanders symbolized the 'civilized' order of culture, science, and reason" (2010, 3). Even when Native Americans labored for or alongside Anglo-American settlers—as fishermen, soldiers, indentured servants, farmers and wage laborers—settlers rendered indigenous labor invisible, often by legally designating them as "Negro" or "black" rather than "authentically" Indian (O'Brien 2010, 34, xvi). If Indians are "before labor," premodern within this colonially inherited economy of representation, they must also be "before law," categorically incapable of laboring *for* the law. By referring to American Indians and Eskimos as "people like that," Judge Fildew deftly placed them outside the *time* of political economy and liberal democracy. They demarcate the boundary of temporal possibility for Fildew, as the mere suggestion of an "Eskimo" participating in grand jury duty—an important performance of citizenship—is self-evidently far away and anachronistically absurd.[19]

Almost accidentally, "Eskimo" connects the racial geography of southern California to the imperial cartography of U.S. colonialism writ large. In summoning the Eskimo into the courtroom, Judge Fildew also summons the twinned history of the incorporation of Hawai'i and Alaska into the United States. The forty-ninth and fiftieth states were admitted into the union in 1959, each deeply signified by their indigenous populations and by the presumably "peaceful" incorporation thereof. The forty-seventh and -eighth states incorporated into the United States were Arizona and New Mexico in 1912. Thus this mention of the Eskimo reveals the racial unconscious of the nation by recalling the United States' long history of imperial conquest of indigenous peoples. "Eskimo" links these two seemingly discrete "eras" of neocolonial expansion—the forced annexation of Mexico and the "peaceful" incorporation of the two overseas sovereignties—into one imperial history: beyond manifest destiny, beyond the continental United States, the history of the United States *is* the history of imperial conquest of indigenous territories well into the twentieth century.

Although Mexicans and Eskimos occupy distinct temporal logics in U.S. racial geography, signifying distinct modes of production (Mexicans/wage labor, Eskimos/pastoral subsistence), they are linked by this imperial history of white settler colonialism and forced incorporation. And so "American-Indian" and "Eskimo" erupt into the transcript as the sign of a foundational repression that returns to link early and late colonialism. The Native American and Eskimo erupt into the courtroom, moreover, linking *themselves* with the repressed indio bárbaro in the racial unconscious of the judge, as all three are inside the nation but expunged from the demos. Fildew uncannily summons these twin figures into the courtroom as a way of disqualifying Mexican Americans through their association with indigeneity. Acosta was asking the judge specifically about the exclusions of Mexican Americans, after all, but in the judge's mind American Indians, Eskimos, and Mexicans converge, revealing the heterotemporal trace of the haunting indio bárbaro who, at a distance of over a hundred years, still refuses to disappear and threatens once again to impair the quality of the U.S. nation. Like the nineteenth-century Comanche or Apache peoples annexed within the Mexican territory, these lingering indios bárbaros should play no part in the finer aspects of democracy. In Fildew's racial imaginary, Mexican Americans are rightly excluded from the grand jury because of their ambiguous racial ancestry with its trace of savage unreason. At times Mexican Americans may be confused with whites, but they bear the trace of the indio bárbaro, ultimate sign of *proper* exclusion from American justice. "American-Indian" and "Eskimo" bear witness to repressed imperial dispossession: territorial dispossession of the indigenous peoples and Mexicans throughout U.S. imperial history, and the ancestral dispossession of Mexicans and Indians *from each other*.

With the East L.A. Thirteen and the Biltmore Six cases, Chicana/os attempted to take back possession of this lost territory and ancestry.[20] Acosta's defense strategy was an ontological experiment at defining a people as a classification deserving of legal rights. At its most creative, the defense strategy also rends asunder the apparent unity between *capital* and *labor*. When Acosta slips between identifying Mexican Americans as a race and a structurally oppressed group, when he conflates WASPs with the ownership of the means of production, when he reveals a spatial grid of capitalist class association utterly reliant on the exploited labor of others, he and the defendants are not only interested in making evident this subordinating hierarchy in the law, but in producing subjectivities capable of transforming this hierarchy in the streets.

In *Marx beyond Marx: Lessons on the* Grundrisse, Antonio Negri (1991) reinterprets the *Grundrisse* as the primary text of Marxist revolutionary theory. Writing in response to the scientific orthodoxy of a generation of Stalinist Marxists, Negri argues dialectical materialism was not a method for predicting the future, but a methodology for producing politicized subjectivities. As the production of revolutionary subjects emerged from antagonism, for Marx a "crisis" was only a crisis for capital. In the *Grundrisse* Marx binds dialectics to materialism as a dynamic method for transforming the subjectivities of exploited peoples into agents of change at a moment of crisis:

> Materialism and dialectics have given us totality and difference, as well as the structural link which subjectively unites them. . . . It remains insufficient as long as this structure, this totality is *not internally split*, as long as we do not succeed in grasping *not* the structural (capitalist) subjectivity *but* the subjectivities which dialectically constitute the structure (the two classes in struggle). . . . *The category of production . . . can only be constituted as a category of difference,* as a totality of subjects, of differences, of antagonism. (Negri 1991, 44)

Acosta and the Chicana/o movement sought to unleash this *antagonism* between the classes by grasping the structural subjectivities in struggle, and not simply by explicating capitalist structures. While awaiting trial, defendant David Sánchez presaged Negri in "Birth of a Symbol," a prison manifesto in which he instructed members of the Brown Berets: "a problem is not a problem, it is a situation to be dealt with."[21] From the perspective of the judges— and arguably the majority of Mexican Americans at the time—California's spatial grid of social relations of production was a transparent, benign totality. With their marches, protests, bombings, and trials, Acosta and the defendants sought to disrupt the placid surface unity of the racial geography, to "internally split" "this structure" of production. Acosta's clumsy efforts at establishing Mexican Americans as a "category of difference"—part structure, part biology, part culture—were also an attempt to bring minority labor to consciousness as category of production. His defense strategy was dialectical materialism in practice: an attempt at grasping *two* classes in struggle, of articulating the totality of *subjectivities* cleaved by difference, and moreover, making of this constitutive antagonism a revolutionary method for the community.

Herein lies the substantive difference between the Mexican American generation of activists and the Chicana/o generation. It is simply not the case that the Mexican American generation aspired to whiteness, while the Chicano generation aspired to mestizaje. It is the aims of the two movements that were different. The Mexican American generation did not seek to transform the totality of the relations of production, but to end discrimination within this totality. The interests of Acosta, the defendants, and the Chicana/o movement, however, were *operative*, showing a revolutionary "will and intelligence" to transform the relations of production. In its richest imaginative sense, Aztlán was a "transformation of knowledge" for the purposes of "taking possession" of territory, identity, of the means of production and not just a nostalgic rehashing of northern New Spain's boundaries on a map. The *classification* Acosta approximated was less one of racial difference than one that demonstrated how race and class worked in tandem to subordinate Chicanos, blacks, Native Americans, and others. Acosta and the defendants were engaged in an early mapping of Aztlán as a geography of revolutionary modes of production and social relations, and at its most radical it was multiracial space, peopled by "Negros," "Eskimos," "Japs," "American Indians," "Jews," and sundry working-class whites. At its best, it was the "birth of a new symbol," a multiracial, dialectical possibility, even as it relied on an essentialist "classification" of *a* people. Aztlán was also, however, mired in the racial geographies of Mexico and the United States, of colonial Spain and Britain, reiterating the unconscious idiosyncrasies and complicities of both.

Sad, Crazy Indians in the Psychic Space of Aztlán

The trial transcripts of the East L.A. Thirteen and the Biltmore Six speak the racial unconscious of the legal apparatus in the immediate aftermath of the Civil Rights Act, while Acosta's defense strategy and his journalism capture the political consciousness-in-formation of the Chicano movement. However, if we want to gauge the racial unconscious of the Chicano psyche, we must turn to Acosta's autobiography. Influenced by the Beat Generation and New Journalism, Acosta borrowed liberally from the prose styles, drug-induced thematics, and travelogue narrative form of Jack Kerouac, Tom Wolfe, and Hunter S. Thompson. Acosta claimed OTR as the literary predecessor for *Buffalo* with an allusion to Sal Paradise. Naming the owner of his favorite bar "Sal," Acosta twice refers to him as "my father," though the reader has already been introduced to his biological father. Moreover, Sal finances Acosta's trip, as Kerouac provides the literary formula for *Buffalo* (66).[22]

OTR, *Electric Kool-Aid Acid Test,* and *Fear and Loathing in Las Vegas* are all postmodern, open-ended quest narratives documenting the search for (neo)enlightenment through experimentation with aesthetics, drugs, sexuality, and spirituality. Sal and Dean search constantly for a new Beat vision of "the Word," of "it," while Ken Kesey, Neal Cassady, and the Merry Pranksters travel "Further" on their acid quest for new paths to "intersubjectivity." Despite melancholic turns in both texts, *Road* and *Acid Test,* like *Fear and Loathing,* endure as odes of joyful experimentation and visionary possibility. Yet unsurprisingly, the enlightenment these travelers experience most often is accomplished through the cipher of the many racial characters encountered on the road in the United States and in Mexico. While Acosta mimes Kerouac, Thompson, Wolfe's frenetic voice and manic pace, his is *not* a joyful account of a spiritual quest, but a painful parody of these texts. Sexual antics and drug-fueled hallucinations punctuate *Buffalo,* and Acosta does in the end achieve an awakening to the possibilities of a new Chicano identity, but the bulk of his narrative is an account of the racial violence and trauma he suffered as a child in Riverbank, California.[23]

Acosta explicitly compares himself to Allen Ginsberg and Kerouac early on in *Buffalo,* disparaging them for their romanticized representations of a literary era that coincided with Jim Crow. In contrast, Acosta says of himself, "I speak as a historian, a recorder of events with a sour stomach. I have no love for memories of the past" (1989, 18). By the end of *Buffalo* it is evident *why* Acosta would refuse sentimentality over this past and insist instead on a "sour" historicity. Acosta's mise-en-scène remembrances of ritualized racial violence in his childhood, encased within the present-tense descriptions of travel, foreground the racial privilege that enabled the spiritual quests of Sal and Dean, of Jack, Ken, Neal, and the Merry Pranksters. Their travel and experimentation are enabled by a class and racial privilege Acosta may have aspired to but never attained, despite his legal classification as white. Instead, Acosta exposes the violent geography of the bloody road, undermining Kerouac and Wolfe's experimental rescripting of the American frontier. It is Acosta's postcolonial revision of Kerouac and Wolfe that ultimately provides us with the interpretative key to Acosta's racial unconscious.

The narrative chronology of *Buffalo* follows the six-month period Acosta spent traveling after quitting his job as a legal aid attorney in San Francisco and before becoming the lead defense attorney for Chicano activists in Los Angeles (July 1967 to January 1968). The first-person, present-tense voice figuratively places the reader in the passenger seat of Acosta's "trusty green Plymouth," with an unadorned view of his present-day misogyny, sexual

LOSING IT! 215

impotency, hallucinations, drunken brawls, and bouts of self-loathing (1989, 16). Acosta intercuts his frantic tale, however, with dejected snippets of his childhood experiences of lynching, castration, and racial humiliation. As soon as Acosta hits the road he signals to the reader the recursive turn his narrative will take: "With thundering hoofbeats hammering and kicking whirlwinds of dust to my rear, I eat up the burning sands and concentrate on the white line, my only guide ... I dig my claws into the gas pedal ... plunging over the mountains and into the desert in search of my past" (71). Rather than projecting him forward into an experimental future, the road compels him into a past hidden from his own consciousness.

The tropes Acosta uses to tell his recursive tale recall the heterotemporal racial geographies—both U.S. and Mexican—that inscribe the road he travels: "Thundering hoofbeats" alludes to the buffalo that roamed freely and by association recalls the indios bárbaros who would have hunted them. The tropes of the buffalo and the indio bárbaro function as psychic derivatives, drawing Acosta's attention away from the repressed traumas and lost objects that constitute these convoluted racial geographies and shape Acosta's racial unconscious. Derivatives of a repressed lost object appear to consciousness, thereby drawing libidinal attention away from the object itself: "It is not ... correct to suppose that repression withholds from consciousness all the derivatives of what was primally repressed. If these derivatives are sufficiently far removed from the repressed instinct-presentation, whether owing to the process of distortion or by reason of the number of intermediate associations, they have free access to consciousness" (Freud 1963, 107). As derivatives the "hoofbeats," "whirlwinds of dust," and digging "claws" partake of the "primally repressed" trauma that shapes the racial landscape, nevertheless they may enter consciousness freely. Moreover, as derivatives, they may also play a role in maintaining the health of Acosta's psychic repression by allowing the trauma or loss expression through distortion.

Born in El Paso, Texas, to an "*indio* [father] from the mountains of Durango," and a light-skinned mother from Ciudad Juárez, Acosta presents himself to the reader as the proper mestizo subject of Mexican racial geography, his Indian paternity tempered by white maternity. Acosta tells us his parents moved the family from this cosmopolitan bordertown to "the sticks" of Riverbank, California (71), thereby allegorizing the "settlement" of northern Mexico by central New Spain in the eighteenth century discussed in chapter 2. Acosta even maps the town by the racial coordinates of Christian unity when he recounts the repeated attacks launched by Riverbank *pochos* on himself and his two brothers: "We were outsiders because of geography and outcasts because we didn't speak English and wore short pants" (77). Coming from the metropolitan south, speaking proper Castilian Spanish, and dressed in the attire of the mestizo bourgeoisie, these young *vecinos* are preyed upon by a "bunch of Apaches who lived in the edge of the barrio . . . ten brothers and seven dogs. . . . They were always slaughtering pigs and goats and young bulls, getting drunk on tequila and drinking raw blood" (77). The Indian savagery of the brothers is resplendent: living as/with dogs, slaughtering animals, getting drunk on blood. Naturally they resist the civilizing "Spanish" outsiders invading Apache territory.

Again the trope of the "Apache" in the passage functions as a psychic derivative of Acosta's repressed trauma. With "free access to consciousness," the Apache is not so much the savage bárbaro of the Mexican and U.S. nineteenth-century racial geographies that must remain repressed. Rather the Apache derivative distorts the traumatic loss of an indigenous past that must remain repressed. Acosta compulsively stages hallucinatory sessions with his psychiatrist for the reader to underscore his poor psychic health, but the Apache derivative aids in the necessary repression of the historic traumatic loss of indigenous heritage by rendering them in entirely familiar representational terms. These "Apache" boys correspond to a Mexican racial geography in which northern hostile Indians are sometime foes to the Spaniards, but always allies against Anglo-American incursion. True to these filial racial coordinates, Acosta refers to the battles as "family squabbles" (78). Although the Apache boys never accepted the Acosta brothers as "part of their tribe," they fought side by side against the town's Okies (77). The subtleties of Mexican racial order—mestizo and indio, at once other and brother—are lost on the Okies who do not distinguish between the two groups: "If you lived on the West Side, across from the tracks, and had brown skin, you were a Mexican" (78).

For a corresponding reenactment of U.S. racial geography, we turn to Acosta's description of his experience in the Boy Scouts under the tutelage of a "big, red-headed German kid who taught me how to leave markings on trees and traffic arrows made of rocks when I studied for my merit badges. . . . Since Vernon was a First Class Scout and about three years older, the tenderfoot that I was leaned on his every word. So that night, under the pup tent . . . I asked him how to make the bugger grow" (82). We witness Acosta and Vernon assimilate as immigrants into a U.S. racial geography by "playing Indian" American style. By learning to track, to hunt, to hide, and to trade like "Indians" in the Boy Scouts, Acosta actively situates Native Americans in what Philip Deloria has called the "precontact 'ethnographic present' always temporally outside of modernity." Living Mexican Indians like the Apache might be your brothers in battle against Okies, but U.S. Indians existed in a "different temporal zone" from "modern white Americans" (Deloria 1998, 106). Masturbation symbolically represents Acosta's entrance into masculinity, and as this representation suggests, adult (white) masculinity is predicated on Indian erasure. The Scouts learn to eviscerate the Indians from modernity, as Deloria suggests, by appropriating their culture to authenticate their own fraternity. But once again the Indians in the passage are signs of successful repression: derivatives that channel Acosta's libidinal drive away from any traumatic loss through imitation and masturbation.

If the chapter containing these pastoral memories models successful repression of the traumatic foundation of U.S. and Mexican racial geographies by Acosta's psyche, the following chapter signals the vengeful return of the traumatic lost object of libidinal attachment. No longer the benign, familiar Indian of lore, Acosta's severed and lost indigenous ancestry returns as the traumatic expression of the uncanny, at once registering Acosta's ambivalent attachments to it. The chapter recounts a horrific experience of childhood lynching and symbolic castration, but the three strangest paragraphs in the entire book precede this scene, each building up to the eruption of the traumatic loss of indigenous ancestry to consciousness. These paragraphs give insight not only to Acosta's psyche, but to the racial unconscious of Chicana/os and of white Riverbank as well.

In the first of these paragraphs, Acosta explains to the reader that his Okie buddies regularly called him a "Jigaboo," assuring us "the name was not meant as an insult. It was simply a means of classification. Everyone in the Valley considers skin color to be of ultimate importance. The tone of one's pigmentation is the fastest and surest way of determining exactly who one is" (86). Presaging his future, Acosta justifies the slur as simply "a means of classification" for locating people's spatial location: "There are only three races of people" in Riverbank—Mexicans, Okies, and whites (85). Yet the children must summon blackness into the seen/scene by assigning this epithet to the darkest Mexicans, a blackness being necessary to make the racial geography intelligible. *The Oxford English Dictionary* suggests the term *jigaboo* was derived from conjoining "jig," meaning black person, with "bugaboo," meaning "fancied object of terror." This would seem to indicate that it is black people who are the terrifying uncanny, the repressed object of Riverbank's racial unconscious that erupts into consciousness painfully. And yet, it is precisely the ubiquitous use of this term in Riverbank that again suggests it functions as a psychic derivative rather than as traumatic loss. Blacks function as the familiar "terrifying objects" allowing the Okies to continue to repress their own racial incompleteness, as we see below. The Okies' racial unconscious remains undisturbed through the use of terrifyingly familiar racial slurs, in other words.

Thus Acosta assures us that to his ears *jigaboo* was a term of endearment, even as it inextricably classified him as the recognizable racial mascot. As blackness is familiar, the slur forces Acosta's ambiguous race to reiterate the black/ white binary of Jim Crow. If only those once familiar things that have been made unfamiliar by a repressed trauma resurface as the uncanny, as Freud contends, then the reverse has happened in the use of this slur. The once terrifying "bugaboo" associated with blackness has been rendered entirely familiar, deflecting instead the traumatic loss of indigenous ancestry from consciousness. Freud explains this process by which an object becomes imbued with terrifying content: "The uncanny is in reality nothing new or foreign, but something familiar and old-established in the mind that *has been estranged* only by the process of repression. This reference to the factor of repression enables us, furthermore, to understand . . . the uncanny as something which ought to have been kept concealed but which has nevertheless come to light" (1958, 148). Unlike the derivative, the uncanny terrifies precisely because it is the expression of a repressed trauma that should not have come to light. The uncanny distresses the psyche greatly. Moreover, the uncanny becomes terrifying through a very specific process of *estrangement:* the transformation of the familiar into the *unfamiliar* through a traumatic repression.

In the second of the three paragraphs that precede his account of the lynching, Acosta explains that his mother immediately summoned the bugaboo of "acting just like Indians" anytime her children, her husband, or the neighbors misbehaved, got drunk, played loud music, gained weight, or most tellingly, refused to salute the flag. Meant to terrify her husband and children into behaving, her utterance actually bespeaks the mother's repressed terror erupting into consciousness and Acosta's autobiography. The familiar faces of her family are rendered suddenly unfamiliar by their resemblance to the barbaric indio, and this terrifies her, in part because it threatens the family's assimilation into the nation. After all, her son's refusal to salute the flag recalls the Apache and Comanche's refusal to surrender to Mexican *and* U.S. authorities in the nineteenth century. The son's lack of patriotism, in other words, makes him an indio bárbaro. But also, her once familiar indigenous heritage has been suddenly rendered "unfamiliar" in the faces of her children. *Familial* Indians were once *heimisch* after all, once "belonging to the home," before war, legislation, and separation made them *unheimlich*, bereft of familiarity by

LOSING IT! 219

their symbolic death and necessary repression under the onus of U.S. citizenship requiring Mexicans to be white by law (Freud 1958, 124). What terrifies the mother is the eruption of this repressed loss into her consciousness, a loss recalled, if only for an instant, in the uncanny faces and behaviors of her all-too-familiar children and husband. Her earthly children are suddenly made ghostly to her in their uncanny everyday practices.

In the following, third paragraph, Acosta recounts a dream he had, presumably before his lynching, given this paragraph's placement in the sequence of recalled events:

> In my first recorded dream I suddenly find myself crawling snake-like through the bushes toward the top of a hill. . . . I am on a scouting mission for the Texas Rangers. Our fort has been under siege for days. We are without food and water. All through the night we have heard their savage yells and tom-toms. Coyotes and rattlers lurk in the underbrush. I crawl carefully, my eyes in a squint just like I learned from Tom Mix. I place my ear to the ground and listen. There are at least 100 of them on horses, just due west over the ridge. I wiggle and writhe through the wild wheat. Now I'm at the crest of the small, golden hill. I ever so quietly hang my brown, narrow eyes just an inch above the grass. . . . I am looking directly at the black and white eagle feathers, I cannot see the faces of the wild Indians. With grace and guts only a Boy Scout who was specially trained by Tom Mix and Vernon Knecht can muster, I gently but rapidly pluck their feathers. . . . or symbols of bestiality, as Dr. Serbin said to me when I first reported this ancient dream to him. (1989, 86)

Boy Acosta identifies scopically with the victors of U.S. conquest, the notorious Texas Rangers who indiscriminately killed Mexicans and Indians in the nineteenth and twentieth centuries. Tom Mix, the Hollywood legend who played Texas Rangers in films, has taught Acosta the art of stalking Indians. Importantly, though boy Acosta sees *as* and *for* the Rangers, he is not *of* them. This is underscored by the mention of his "brown, narrow eyes" which trouble his identification with whiteness, standing out in contrast with the "golden" hill. Acosta writhes and wiggles through the underbrush like a snake or coyote, brought into dangerous proximity by these actions to the bestial Indians he spies. Perhaps again, the scout is merely playing Indian to catch an Indian, but the fact that this all occurs in a dream suggests more.

In *The Interpretation of Dreams,* Freud explains that in the content of dreams, "*a transference and displacement of psychical intensities occurs in the*

220   CHAPTER FIVE

process of dream-formation. . . . The consequence of the displacement is that the dream-content no longer resembles the core of the dream-thoughts and that the dream gives no more than a distortion of the dream-wish which exists in the unconscious" (342). The repressed content of the unconscious that enters the dream as dream thoughts does not "escape" the censor, rather the censor shapes this repressed content into dream-content through displacement, overdetermination, and condensation. These mechanisms in turn function as an "endopsychic defence," much like a psychic derivative in waking life (343). In light of this "distortion," the censored ideational content of Acosta's "dream-wish" becomes more apparent. The yells, tom-toms, and eagle feathers are condensations of the repressed ideational associations with "wild Indians" in Acosta's unconscious, but also of his lost indigenous heritage. Condensation ameliorates the repressed psychic terror of "wild Indians," especially as they never actually appear in his dream but are displaced onto these caricatured representations. But condensation also diverts attention away from the true cause of terror. If Acosta were to see "the faces of the wild Indians" in his dream, the true source of his repressed terror might be revealed. Like his mother, Acosta might recognize his face reflected in theirs. He would see the uncanny Indian staring back at him as Acosta's double, his severed twin denied by the racial geography of the U.S. Southwest.

Overdetermination is also at work in the eagle feathers that he "gently but rapidly plucks." He gently but rapidly pulls at the feathers as he has gently but rapidly pulled at his penis in the previous chapter. But as he successfully plucks the bestial members from the heads of the hidden Indians, a masturbation dream-wish gives way to a (racial) castration phantasy. As David L. Eng instructs in coining the term, racial castration has a double valence. First, the term captures the racialized dimensions of the castration complex, as for Freud "white European man represents civilized man, or what he suggests to be primitive man's unrealized psychic potential" (7). Castration anxiety—the anxiety over one's incompleteness—is projected by Freud onto the figure of this "primitive man" with a diminished psyche. Historically, castration anxiety is ameliorated for white masculinity by projecting (sexual) lack/perversion onto the racialized other, most evident in the prevalent representations of invaginated Asian American masculinity in dominant U.S. culture. As Eng explains, "Alongside the argument that the primitive lacks mental complexity and an adequate moral framework is the more pernicious, yet fundamental, conflation of sexual perversions with racial difference" (9). Primitive perversion and moral incompleteness are conflated "precisely

LOSING IT! 221

by the absence of unconscious regulation" (9). The primitive racial other lacks a properly functioning censor in Freud's view, and as such, Eng contends, Freud "embed[s] this racial narrative into his theory of the unconscious" (10). Second, racial castration denotes a profound anxiety over *racial* incompleteness, over a lack in one's idealized racial identification. This anxiety is expressed earlier in Acosta by "[e]veryone in the Valley" who "considers skin color to be of ultimate importance" in "determining *exactly who one is.*" To fall short of one's idealized identification is anxiously perceived as a racial castration.

Boy Acosta's plucking of the feathers from the unseen heads of the "wild Indians," then, expresses his anxiety over his racial incompleteness. He is not properly white, though his scopic identification with the Rangers reveals this idealized racial dream-wish. Desiring completion, he himself plucks out the condensed, bestial signs of his primitive lack and sexual perversion. In their overdetermined meaning, the feathers represent both the "wild Indians" that threaten the fort of white masculinity, and his own half-breed status that threatens his idealized white wholeness by signaling the return of the repressed indio bárbaro. Reading this scene of racial castration against the grain, however, the plucked feathers emblemize a prior scene of racial incompleteness: the fearsome loss of indigenous ancestry that has left Acosta bereft of a racial home to accommodate both the white and the red in a culturally intelligible way. The plucking of the feathers in this reading represents the displaced racial castration that Acosta's unconscious unsuccessfully tries to repress: the splitting of Mexican racial *and cultural* identity required by U.S. neocolonial law, the brutal severing of the red from the white, miasmic loss and incompletion. Emblemized by the "black and white eagle feathers" he spies on the horizon, boy Acosta identifies at first with whiteness, while his friends insist on identifying him with blackness, but this monochromatic vision of racial completion effaces the redness of those who wear the feathers, of the Indians who haunt Acosta's dream of racial wholeness, just as they haunt the racial lynching the dream portends.

In the lynching episode that is the heart of this chapter and of the book, Riverbank Okies project their own terror of racial and sexual incompletion onto the body of the boy Acosta, whom they figuratively castrate. Literary critics regularly interpret it as Acosta's moment of racial awakening, and yet analyzing the scene through the paradigm of racial castration complicates this redemptive reading. A prepubescent Acosta and his girlfriend Senaida are walking home late one Hallow's Eve from a birthday party:

Before I could answer they were upon us. A regular ambush with whoops and shrieks and screams of blood and rape. . . .

Ralph Watson, a red-faced Okie five years my senior, grabbed me by the hair and knocked me to the ground. He stood over me with his shoe on my chest. He put a flashlight to my face and screamed. "Hey Junior, look what I got me here," he called to his partner, who had Senaida by the neck with one hand over her gorgeous cans. . . .

Ralph kicked my balls. "Lookee here . . . I got me a fucking nigger." (1989, 87–88)

Together Junior and Ralph "beat the shit" out of young Acosta when he tries to defend himself and Senaida. Pulling down Acosta's pants, they shine the flashlight on his crotch, and Junior responds, "Whooee! Look at that. This nigger ain't even a man. . . . This pussy Jigaboo ain't even got hair on his prick." Finally, "With Ralph standing on each of my outstretched hands . . . both of them spit on my hairless crotch before they ran screaming into the night with the rest of the savages" (88). Unlike his "Okie buddies," when Ralph and Junior call Acosta a "Jigaboo" and a "nigger," they mean to injure and subordinate the boy, as the shoe on the chest immediately underscores. These "red-faced" Okies are making sure Acosta knows "exactly who [he] is" racially.

For two months following the incident, Acosta informs the reader, he endured the repeated humiliation of this racial castration, as Junior and Ralph inform the entire school that Acosta "didn't have any pubic hair" (92). When he finally exacts revenge on Junior Ellis in a schoolyard fight, he does so as much to even the score as to impress a new character in his life. A blond, blue-eyed girl has joined his class in the interceding months, and Acosta has immediately fallen in love with her, throwing over the Mexican Senaida in the process. Acosta defeats Ellis, but his blue-eyed "Miss It" rejects him, complaining to the teacher in the class following the fight that Oscar stinks. The conclusion Acosta draws from these related events—the lynching, his triumph over Ellis, Miss It's rejection—is this: "I *am* a nigger after all. My mother was right. I am nothing but an Indian with sweating body and faltering tits that sag at the sight of a young girl's blue eyes" (94). By inspecting, crushing, and spitting upon Acosta's genitals, the Okies projected their castration complex onto the racial other. The "*pussy* Jigaboo" is the one whose sexual inadequacy is exposed, his prick deficient, lacking; his masculinity invaginated, perverse, with no hair. By the end of the chapter, young Acosta has been racially castrated twice over, becoming not only woman, but also an abhorrent Indian woman, with sweaty, sagging, faltering tits, before the mirror of the beautiful "young girl's blue eyes."

Literary critics like Fredrick Aldama (2000, 207), Héctor Calderón (2004, 109), Michael Hames-Garcia (2000, 476), María Herrera-Sobek (2009, 83), and Ramón Saldívar (1990, 93) read this three-part lynching scene as the moment in which boy Acosta learns not only his true place in the United States—that he will never be able to assimilate into white society—but also learns where his true racial solidarity will lie: with the racial others reified by the racial epithets. However, all these critics fail to mention that at the time of the incident, boy Acosta is in blackface for Halloween, having smudged his face with coal, painted his lips with his mother's red lipstick, and borrowed a pair of his father's white work gloves. [24] It is a stunning bit of context to leave out of an analysis, especially since it helps to explain the racial epithets hurled at Acosta. His blackface is excised by these critics, because including it would disrupt their postcolonial "Romantic mode of emplotment," as discussed in chapter 2 (Scott 2004). Acosta's blackface makes impossible any anticolonial reading of the lynching as a racial awakening and expression of solidarity, for minstrelsy is always the preserve of the racially privileged.

Kerouac's *On the Road* helps to decipher this scene of racial violence and racial minstrelsy. Sal Paradise repeatedly appropriates the identities of the racial others he encounters. When Okies beat up the Mexicans in a work camp Sal shares with his Mexican girlfriend, Terry, for example, he avers, "They thought I was a Mexican, and in a way I am" (97). The midsentence switch in tense is noteworthy. Though the Okies confused him for a Mexican at the time of the attack, Sal continues to *be* Mexican in the present tense of narration. Later Sal observes a group of multiracial youth playing baseball in a field in Denver. Sal watches them, "wishing I were a Negro, feeling that the best the white world had offered was not enough ecstasy for me, not enough life, joy, kicks, darkness, music, not enough night . . . I wished I were a Denver Mexican, or even a poor overworked Jap, *anything but what I was so drearily, a 'white man' disillusioned*" (180). Though he cannot *be* them, this dreary, disillusioned white man nonetheless assumes the subject positions of all these racial others; capable of knowing, in an instant, their ambitions (or lack thereof), their "joys, kicks, darkness" (their illusion-free desires), from his vantage point of worldly, universal "white man." This is its own instance of racial castration, as Sal projects his anxiety of incompletion onto the underdeveloped, primitive youth to which he stands in fully developed contrast. In these scenes and countless others, Sal performs a racial minstrelsy familiar to the critic, appropriating for his own Beat literary vision the experiences of all racial others.

On the one hand, we could interpret Acosta's childhood act of black minstrelsy as an example of Acosta mimicking Kerouac. In putting on blackface

224   CHAPTER FIVE

as a boy, Acosta is inversely putting on the universal white racial privilege he wishes to embody. Acosta's minstrelsy would then be yet another form of claiming the white identity that was conferred on Mexican Americans by the Treaty of Guadalupe Hidalgo and by *In re Rodriguez*. Acosta puts on blackface because his idealized racial identification is with whiteness. The privilege of mocking black people, after all, is one reserved for white people. Ralph and Junior do not get the joke. To them, boy Acosta in blackface makes his otherwise ambiguous racial status finally legible as an object-suitable-for-lynching.

Acosta's blackface expresses a racial castration complex, to be sure. Boy Acosta puts on blackface because he desires, *avant la lettre*, an unambiguous racial identification. The phantasy of racial "completeness" is limited in U.S. racial geography to the categories of white and black. Acosta may be legally white, but he is never treated as such, as his Okie buddies make painfully clear even before the lynching. Indeed, neither Mexicans nor Okies "fit" within the idealized binomial racial logic of the Jim Crow era. It is the Okies who oddly constitute a "third race" in Riverbank, their own white racial incompleteness made evident by their poverty and history of forced migration. This migration is its own travel narrative, a flight from their traumatic loss of origin through migration and racialization. As Okies, Junior and Ralph enact their racial castration by subjecting Acosta to sexual violence, taking possession of a white privilege usually denied them. In other words, they strive to attain racial completeness by attacking Oscar sexually. Acosta puts on blackface as an expression of his own desire for the unambiguous racial status of blackness. It expresses his longing to be legible in the racial geography of the United States, to be like the "unquestioned . . . Negro minority" of his legal argument years later. But it also registers his own racial incompletion as the ambiguous racial other severed from his indigenous heritage. This may be an overly optimistic reading, verging on its own Romantic emplotment of anticolonialism. However, while his minstrelsy is an expression of his desire for white racial privilege, it is also an effect of a racial loss so deep that he must feign blackness.

What of the representations of Indians that haunt the scene of lynching? Though explicitly invoked only once, at the end, when Oscar affirms that he is an Indian after all, figures of indigeneity actually appear many times in the margins of this scene. The Okies are "red-faced" with their "whoops and shrieks and screams of blood and rape." Accordingly, after they have raped Acosta, stolen his property (Senaida), and generally pillaged the scene, they run "screaming into the night with the rest of the savages." The Okies are uncannily "playing Indian" in a transformative sense. In Acosta's manner of representing the attacking Okies, they have become for him the terrifying indio bárbaro of nineteenth-century Mexican and U.S. historiography. Acosta reiterates the representation of the "savage" Apache and Comanche in the Treaty of Guadalupe Hidalgo discussed in chapter 3, those who refused colonization by either nation and thus became the enemy of both, causing millions of dollars in losses on ranches and haciendas across Mexico's northern states and the U.S. Southwest. As Juliana Barr, Ned Blackhawk, Brian Delay, Nicole Guidotti-Hernández, Lisbeth Haas, Pekka Hämäläinen, and Karl Jacoby, among others, have made clear in their revisionist histories of the borderlands, indigenous people of the Great Plains and the Southwest had their own political ambitions for the contested territory and enacted these ambitions with the same brutality shown against them by the emergent national militaries of Mexico and the United States. Once again in Acosta's autobiography, the uncanny Indian returns from repression, in other words, this time in white face.

These white-faced Indians help us to interpret Acosta's declension from "I am a nigger after all" to "I am nothing but an Indian." "Nothing but an Indian" is clearly an abject, denigrated, and castrated category. After all, who would want to identify with the body-sweating, tit-faltering Indian? Years later, when the lawyer Acosta calls on the "Hispanic-Indio" link that makes Chicanos a "Chosen people," he is not drawing from his melancholic attachment to this faltering Indian, although Acosta never lets go of this loathsome abjection in his lifetime. Rather, he is drawing from the virile, rapacious agency of the indio bárbaro, appropriated by the Okies, and finally expressed in the warriors of Aztlán, the Brown Buffalo people he christens at the end of his autobiography. Once again the Brown Buffalo people, in his view, are not the "cowboys and Indians" caricature of Indians, but of "Aztec ancestry, that's where we get the *brown* from" (198). The ancestry of the Chicana/o nation, however, does not derive from the Aztecs, but from the "history of its losses" suggested by Cheng: the chain of loss of *Southwest* indigenous ancestry, which may have included the Aztec, but more likely included the Apache, the Comanche, the Pueblo, the Caddo, the Arapaho, the Navajo, and all the other indigenous peoples of the Southwest who mixed their lives and livelihoods with generations of mestizos. In other words, the phantasy of Chicana/o racial completion is derived from the productive uses to which the Chicana/o movement puts the uncanny Indian. Chicana/o identity is the uncanny incorporation of a lost indigenous heritage. This terribly productive loss renders the cultural identity of Chicana/os unfamiliar to any living Indians in Mexico or in the United States, for this loss appears to them as mere appropriation or affectation. Chicano identity is the effect of the racial geography of Mexico, but it is even more so the effect of the racial geography of the United States, as it was

226   CHAPTER FIVE

the jurisprudence and interests of the imperial United States that required the severing of Mexicans' ties from their own racial past.

So what to make, ultimately, of Acosta's blackface? Rather than read it as simply racist or simply an act of solidarity, it is a dream-wish deferred. A secondary haunting of the scene/seen by Indians is the fleeting presence of the red in the black and in the white, in his very embodiment of minstrelsy. For after all, let us recall that Acosta uses his mother's *red* lipstick and his father's *white* gloves to perform his blackface. What if Acosta is drawing from Paz's *hijos de la chingada*? The red and the white encode his own spatial production as at once the chingada and the chingón. It is a recuperative gesture at the heart of his minstrelsy, as mestizo miscegenation is invoked: the sensuality of the red kiss and the white touch performed in blackness. The trace of the Indian in this scene/seen of lynching marks the deferred confrontation of the United States with its racial geography. It is right on the lips, but cannot cross into consciousness. The racial geography of the United States is based on repression after all, the repression from consciousness not only of its violent and dispossessing foundation, but of its indigenous past and present, of its miscegenation across racial categories. Acosta's minstrelsy is an uncanny manifestation of this deferral, performing repressed loss in the racial unconscious of U.S. history.

Acosta's representation of the Okies in red face is particularly ironic as the Okies are Indian given in a profoundly imperial sense, deriving their geographic racial slur from indigenous dispossession. Today's Oklahoma was designated "Indian Territory" by the 1834 Organic Intercourse Act, set aside by American expansionism for those indigenous nations forcibly removed from the eastern seaboard by the 1830 Indian Removal Act. The territory was already the home of several indigenous nations, including the Caddo, Wichita, Kiowa, Apache, Comanche, and Osage, for whom this resettlement had far-reaching consequences. Bordered by Texas, Arkansas, and Kansas, Indian Territory became Oklahoma in 1907, its state borders commemorating the continued dislocation and dispossession.

Indian removal affected dozens of indigenous nations who were reduced to one small territory. Even so, unbridled settlement by Euro-Americans during the late nineteenth century led to further rounds of indigenous dispossession and reduction before and after statehood. Through Indian allotment policies, Indians were given private plots of individual property, thereby massively reducing indigenous communal landholdings. The name ' "Okie" then memorializes this process of settler colonialism and dispossession. Thus indigenous dispossession necessarily haunts Okie embodiment in Acosta's autobiography. Like a series of nesting dolls, these histories of migration, violence, and dispossession are embedded in Acosta's narrative and register the racial unconscious of a nation. Acosta's travel narrative emplots migration, creating space through indigenous expropriation and placement. The Okies migrate to California, but their migration necessarily recalls and entails the forced migration of the "Five Civilized Tribes," along the Trail of Tears to Indian Territory. As discussed in chapter 3, the placement of the Five Tribes in Indian Territory in turn set in motion other dispersals: of the Comanche, the Apache, and the Kiowa, who raided neighboring nations as an expression of territorial defense and expansion, but also of the Caddo, the Wichita, the Arapaho, the Cheyenne, who migrated to other states as their own territory and resources were reduced. The landscape itself incorporates—makes corporeal—this "lost" history of migrations, including indigenous migrations.[25] Acosta's road trip is less a splendid account of the pleasures and artistic freedom than a series of tales of the bloody road, an archive of space making by violent racial design.

In the present tense of Acosta's travel narrative, he moves from California through Idaho, Oklahoma, Colorado, New Mexico, and Texas and across the Mexican border to Juárez, impersonating Samoans, Sicilians, Hollywood tycoons, and Indian chiefs, and it is precisely his ambiguous racial identity that enables minstrelsy as well. And yet he is "free" to impersonate these multiple subject positions in an entirely different way than Sal. The racial ambiguity of Acosta's features curtails him as much as it enables him. After telling us about his childhood lynching on his way north to Ketchum, Acosta continues recounting his experiences with humiliation, prejudice, police brutality, discrimination, and physical harm all the way south to the border, transposing the microgeographies of his experience with racial power onto the Southwest landscape he traverses. The racial geography of the United States, in other words, is exposed precisely for the violent, discriminatory, dispossessing, exploitative space that Acosta showed it to be through the trial transcripts. Acosta decodes the sweeping landscapes of pristine American beauty as he transits through them, recoding them as saturated in the blood of the "frontier thesis." For him this has never been the landscape of American invention and democratic egalitarianism, but that of racial domination and exclusion. He traverses the landscape as liminal space by virtue of his indeterminate skin color. His is a painful purchase on this geography, at the expense of his racial ambiguity and loss of indigenous ancestry. Liminality reaches its limit, however, at the border of Mexico.

At the end of his journey across the Southwest, Acosta crosses into Ciudad Juárez from El Paso. At first he believes he has arrived home, as everywhere he sees "women of brown face, black, long hair and eyes. . . . And they all are speaking in the language of my youth . . . a language for moonlit nights under tropical storms, for starry nights in brown deserts . . . I hadn't heard the Spanish language spoken in public with such gusto since I'd left El Paso as a boy" (186). Brown skin, brown language, and brown landscape together signal home for Acosta. He is enveloped in the sound of brownness, a sound he has never heard in public in California. And yet, though the Spanish language feels like home to Acosta, it immediately betrays him. Though he looks Mexican, he cannot speak Spanish properly and this leads to repeated confusion over his identity.

For example, when Acosta enters a bordello in search of sex (not terribly unlike Sal and Dean when they enter Nuevo Laredo), the prostitutes cannot understand what he is saying. When he speaks to them in English, one asks the other, "Oye, que dice este indio? . . . no me digas que no es Mexicano?" (Hey, what is this Indian saying? Don't tell me he's not Mexican?) Not only are the prostitutes baffled by Acosta's inability to speak Spanish, they immediately impugn what they read as his arrogance in racial terms. "Indio" is meant as a slur, but it also locates him in the racial geography of northern Mexico. He looks like an Indian, so he must be a Mexican, but he refuses to speak Spanish. The two prostitutes are light skinned with blond and red hair, and Acosta in turn disbelieves that they are Mexican. He thinks the owner of the bordello is running a scam with gringa prostitutes. Misidentification ensues because Acosta has been alienated from his own heritage. Acosta cannot properly read the racial geography of northern Mexico. He has no idea of the history of alliances, intimacies, and betrayals that produced the mestizaje embodied by the light-skinned prostitutes.

In an entirely predictable fashion, Mexican sexualized femininity redeems his racialized masculinity: "Millions of women with black hair. Graceful asses for strong children; full breasts for sucking life. . . . Whatever Alice Joy or Jane Addison meant to me as a kid, now they were only grade school memories of a time gone by" (1989, 188). Acosta is miraculously cured of his attraction to white women, recuperating his misplaced masculinity by bedding the two Mexican prostitutes at once: "And they both took me into the bedrooms behind the *Cantina de la Revolucion* where I learned how to be a serious Mexican for the first time in my life. If you want an exact date, you can say that I became a true son of the *indio* from the mountains of Durango on January 9,

1968" (190). His recuperation of a "serious Mexican" identity full of sexual potency must happen by way of the indio, for this confirms his authenticity as much as the Mexican women confirm his manhood. In terms that Paz would certainly understand, Acosta becomes a chingón by *chingando*. He claims his rightful Mexican indio masculinity by subordinating women and Indians in a Juárez bordello by way of Durango. Acosta's phantasy of racial and sexual completion in the Mexican landscape is as short lived as it is fraudulent, as his inability to read the code of behavior or to speak Spanish fatally betrays him just one week and one page later.

On a cold day at the bordello where he is now living, Acosta demands heat from the bellhop in a manner even Acosta recognizes as filled with U.S. arrogance and privilege. After not getting the immediate service he believes he rightly deserves he says: " 'Well, fuck you too, you sonofabitch!' I shouted in my finest English" (191). He ends up in prison for the brawl with the attendant. When he appears before the judge he again tries to impress and intimidate with his command of English and his passport: " 'I am a citizen of the United States and an attorney at law, your honor,' I said in English" (193). The judge answers him in perfect English as well. Appalled equally by his *gringo* arrogance and his lack of knowledge of his Mexican culture and language, she passes judgment. She finds him guilty of his crime, but also finds him guilty of racial incompletion: "She looked at me directly in the face and said to me, 'Why don't you go home and learn to speak your father's language?' My father's language? What does she mean?" (194). Acosta is so alienated from this racial geography that he cannot even properly understand the question. Indeed, his positionality in the U.S. racial geography of the Southwest is what makes it difficult for him to understand the question, for his father pushed Acosta to forget his Spanish and master English.

The autobiography's denouement gives us the reason for the imaginary borders of Aztlán. Aztlán must end at the U.S. border with Mexico because the Chicana/o psychic structure of loss has no counterpart in Mexico. During his travels across the United States, the indecipherability of Acosta's skin is underscored repeatedly as it allows him to "pass" for whatever ethnicity or race is called for to get himself out of a jam. To white America, Mexican racial identity is always necessarily ambiguous. In Mexico, however, Acosta's brown skin is anything but indecipherable. It is quite legible; he is indigenous therefore he is Mexican. His skin color is banal, but his inability to speak Spanish is what confuses everyone he meets. Furthermore, his inability to *behave like an indio*, when he looks so much like one confuses the Mexicans he meets. And thus, they pass judgment. In their eyes, his brown skin does not make him any less gringo than all the white tourists. Juarenses see Acosta treating Mexico like a prostitute, buying into all of the stereotypes about Mexicans, and reproducing them as well. There is no phantasy of racial completion achieved through the melancholic incorporation of the lost Indian in Mexico. Acosta is neither a proper Indian nor Mexican, just one of thousands of tourists (like Sal and Dean) who cross into Juárez daily looking for drugs, sex, and spiritual redemption.

Immediately upon reentering El Paso after this incident with the judge, Acosta abruptly decides to end his road trip and to move to Los Angeles to join the Chicana/o movement. Acosta then utters the passage with which I began this chapter. During his short jaunt in Mexico, he is made aware of all he has lost growing up in the United States, but he also becomes aware of the fact that he is not Mexican. One more loss for him to add to the list of lost objects. Out of this sudden, traumatic awareness, he summons forth his Brown Buffalo people. But these people would be incomprehensible to the Mexicans across the border in Juárez, who opened his eyes precisely because they are not bereft of their own connection to their indigenous heritage. They have no use for imaginary Aztláns.

Acosta's narrative cuts across the very heart of the imaginary geography of Aztlán. Traveling through California, Utah, Colorado, New Mexico, Oklahoma, and Texas, Acosta's trip encompasses the Provincias Internas of eighteenth-century New Spain as well as the annexed territories of nineteenth-century U.S. expansionism. As he does so, the repressed contours of his racial unconscious reveal themselves to the reader. By conjoining the geography of Aztlán with the contours of his racial unconscious, Acosta maps for us the coordinates of Chicana/o identity. He demonstrates for the reader the intimate connection between these geographies of the border and the vexed psychic structure of Chicana/o consciousness. Once again we see that space and identity have been coproduced. The landscape of the border and the Southwest records centuries of violent becoming, of spatial practices centered on the domination, incorporation, exclusion, and control of the indigenous peoples, including indigenous Mexicans. To a distressing degree, Aztlán's cartography replicates this process, if only in the imaginary. But this landscape also witnesses the presence of indigenous inhabitants who through it all refuse to cede ground even when they have presumably been banished from sight. And in the case of Chicana/o identity, indigeneity refused to cede ground by becoming the incorporated lost object of a melancholic psychic structure that prolifically produced affect and embodiment. It is not a psychic structure with purely psychological effects. Rather this incorporation of the lost object of indigeneity into the psychic structure of Chicana/o identity actively produced the *embodiment* of the Brown Buffalo people as a community and the *embodiment* of Aztlán as the imaginative geography of this community. The lost racial object once incorporated into the psyche proliferates cultural identity. It is a *melancholic* structure to be sure, given the ambivalent attachment of Mexican Americans to their indigenous heritage. How could this attachment to their indigenous heritage be anything *but* ambivalent, when both the Mexican and U.S. racial geographies conspired to produce their indigenous identity along the Mexico–U.S. border as the indio bárbaro? Especially in the case of annexed Mexican Americans, the indio came to symbolize their exclusion from U.S. citizenship and nation. Until the Chicano movement, "behaving like an Indian" was to willfully inhabit a form of social death within these racial geographies. The racial unconscious of Chicana/o identity is located at the juncture of Mexican and U.S. racial geographies, indeed it is coproduced by these vexed and overlapping geographies, and in turn Chicana/o identity produces a geography of its own. As powerful and productive as this geography has been—evident in the political and cultural transformation of the Southwest in its aftermath—it was produced through an engagement with lost indigenous identity rather than through an engagement with contemporary indigenous peoples. That path was foreclosed to Mexican Americans by U.S. colonialism.

CONCLUSION

THE AFTERLIVES OF THE *INDIO BÁRBARO*

On May 2, 2011, U.S. Navy Seal Team 6 killed Osama bin Laden during a raid on his family compound in Abbottabad, Pakistan. The Seal Team leader informed President Obama about the success of the mission with the phrase "For God and Country, Geronimo, Geronimo, Geronimo." After a moment's pause, he clarified "Geronimo EKIA," meaning "Geronimo, Enemy Killed in Action." Despite military claims to the contrary, it remains unclear whether "Geronimo" was shorthand for the mission (official code name "Operation Neptune Spear"), for bin Laden (official codename "Jackpot"), or for the act of killing bin Laden. What remains clear is that the name linked Osama bin Laden's evasion of the U.S. military and intelligence communities for ten years at the beginning of the twenty-first century with the Apache leader's evasion of the U.S. and Mexican militaries for ten years at the end of the nineteenth. Though separated by more than a century of U.S. global warfare, Geronimo and bin Laden were linked as terrorists in this communication, which also linked the Christian God and the nation. Bin Laden and Geronimo were savvy and resourceful, perhaps even brave, but ultimately they were beaten (and conjoined) as "terrorists" in the nation's military memory and popular imagination.

One week later, on May 9, 2011, tens of thousands of demonstrators filled Mexico City's Zócalo to welcome the "March for Peace with Justice and Dignity," arriving after a five-day journey on foot from Cuernavaca, Morelos. Those marching were the families and friends of the victims claimed by Mexico's drug war. The demonstrators demanded an end to impunity and justice for their dead, but their chief demand was for then President Felipe Calderón to end his misbegotten policy of war against the drug cartels and instead enter into peace negotiations with their leaders as the only viable means of reestablishing national security. Calderón responded by insisting that while he was happy to dialogue with the good people of the peace movement, he would never enter into negotiations with "esos bárbaros en el norte." Though separated by more than a century, the twenty-first-century narco and the nineteenth-century Apache and Comanche were linked in Calderón's speech, again through historical allusion to the equestrian peoples, the original "bárbaros del norte."

The march from Cuernavaca to Mexico City was led by Javier Sicilia, a poet and a journalist whose twenty-four-year-old son Juan Francisco was killed, along with six friends, by a group of *sicarios*, or hit men, on March 28 of the same year. These young men were killed because they had unwittingly gotten into a bar fight with the nephews of a sicario who worked for the Pacifico Sur cartel. The sicario was an ex-military officer, allegedly drummed out of the military for drug-related corruption, who turned into a private security worker for the cartel. The nephews appealed to their uncle for revenge and he obliged. The torture and murder of these upper-crust university students and businessmen—one of whom was the son of the renowned poet Sicilia—brought into cruel relief the truth about Calderón's declared war on the drug cartels. Of the tens of thousands dead as a consequence of the war, a significant number, if not the majority, were innocent bystanders caught in the crossfire or swept up in the escalating violence of its perpetrators.[1] Five years into his presidential term, Calderón's administration had repeatedly portrayed all those killed as members of the cartels or as delinquents whose choice of lifestyle had inevitably led to their drug-related deaths. The participants in the March for Peace, carrying placards of their dead, made it all too evident that this was not the case. Instead of hardened drug dealers or strung-out junkies, the marchers told of students killed on the way to school, working-class women and men killed on the way to their jobs, and indigenous peasants killed for protecting their fields.

The speech acts of the Navy Seal to Obama and of Calderón to the national media remind us as well of the transnational complicity between the two nations, foregrounding the histories of war against the Apache and the Comanche that link U.S. and Mexican statecraft. They reiterate the colonial and national representations of the indio bárbaro that form the subject of *Indian Given*. These speech acts triangulate the globe, a triangulation through the Middle East enabled by the racial geographies of the borderland that are at once historically and cartographically specific yet heuristically and discursively diffuse, disentailed from the actual Mexico–U.S. border through the explanatory power of the heterotemporal and multispatial indio bárbaro. In this narrow sense, I suggest both of these wars are again *Indian given*. The indio bárbaro, a key figure in establishing the imperial boundaries of the United States and Mexico, now animates both of these contemporary wars and carries on with its racializing mission by demarcating in religious terms the boundary between the "good people" of a nation worth defending and the barbarous inhumanity of those who must be excluded, excised, eliminated at all costs.

The invocation of the indio bárbaro in the name of Geronimo and in the allusion to "pueblos bárbaros" signals the transposition of the racial geographies of the border onto other places and other times. In this coda I consider the afterlives of the indio bárbaro in the twenty-first-century drug war against the "pueblos bárbaros del norte" and in the global war on terror. As a metaphorical concept for a paradoxically *indigenous* foreign agent threatening "God and country," it has traveled far afield from its original home to present-day Pakistan, Iraq, Syria, central Mexico, Honduras, and beyond, signaling again and again a threat to the very form of the nation-state and presaging a need for ever-greater militarization and joint actions across the globe. Specifically, these speech acts conjoin the Muslim terrorist and the narco terrorist in the national imaginations of both countries as dangers that once again require the joint action of the U.S. and Mexican militaries to keep the borders of these nations "safe" from both. These wars are spatial practices in their own right, of course, reiterating the racial coordinates of the border but also materially remaking these specific geographies in the process.

As *Indian Given* demonstrates, the figure of the indio bárbaro is not representative of any historical actors. He does not reflect the fabled Chichimecas of the Aztec Empire nor the mobile traders of New Spain's northern frontier; he does not reference the equestrian peoples of the Great Plains nor even the Apache or Comanche warriors who militarily staved off British and Spanish colonialism and fought wars of expansion against the United States and Mexico. Rather it is precisely the catachrestic nature of the indio bárbaro that accounts for its long afterlives. Untethered from *any* historical referent yet encompassing all of these, the indio bárbaro floats across time and space, conditioning our repetitive futures. I am not suggesting a *causal* relationship between the indio bárbaro discussed in chapters 2 and 3 and the Muslim or narco terrorist of the present. Instead, repressed but always present in the manner suggested in chapters 4 and 5, the indio bárbaro conditions national responses to contemporary phenomena, functioning as an unconscious racial hermeneutic in the business of statecraft for Mexico and the United States. Thus free trade and the drug trade together produce the latest iteration of the indio bárbaro in the undocumented immigrant and the *narco-killer-terrorist*, threatening the borderlands, providing anxious national populations with facile explanations for the profound restructuring of the U.S. and Mexican economies over the last twenty years under the North American Free Trade Agreement (NAFTA).

Meanwhile beheadings and scalpings in Mexico and in the Middle East reiterate the violence of nineteenth-century liberal statecraft as practiced by the United States and Mexico against the equestrian nations. This is a reiteration with a difference, of course, as this contemporary violence-as-statecraft is expressive of an alternative sovereignty to that of the centralized nation-state, one that combines feudal territoriality with extra-economic compulsion in capitalist production for a global and integrated market. Taken as proof-positive of the barbarity of the drug cartels and of Mexico as ungovernable, instead these spectacular forms of violence are a new mode of governmentality that must be theorized rather than dismissed as merely the latest expression of brazen Mexican savagery. The figure of the indio bárbaro haunting the scenes of beheading performs two functions at once. It naturalizes the violence for national audiences that insist on reading scalping and beheading as anachronistic acts of indigenous barbarity, necessarily foreign to the modern practice of statecraft. The indio bárbaro at the same time functions as a psychic derivative enabling citizens of both countries to repress their own liberal complicity in such practices.

NAFTA *and Narcos*

Narcos and Muslim jihadists are brought together most often by U.S. government officials to justify defense budgets on the basis of their joint threat, but it is the figure of the indio bárbaro that ultimately enables this threat to cohere. State Department and Pentagon officials testify before Congress that drug trafficking threatens U.S. national security because profits could potentially fund jihadi terrorist organizations.[2] This facile connection would strike some observers as improbable given that Latin American drug lords are often explicit in their Christian devotion and notorious for their neoconservative politics. Cocaine profits have been siphoned off by leftist guerrilla movements and right-wing paramilitary forces in countries like Peru and Colombia, but the armed protagonists in these long-standing civil wars over economic inequity and political repression are not jihadists targeting the United States. The deadly irony of the Iran-Contra cocaine scandal uncovered by journalists like Gary Webb and Robert Parry in the 1980s bears remembering whenever U.S.

236 CONCLUSION

government officials insist on connecting Latin American drug smuggling with terrorist activity. The Reagan administration falsely and often accused the Sandinista government of funding its "terrorist" regime in Nicaragua by smuggling cocaine into the United States and poisoning urban youth. Instead, his CIA was all the while assisting the counterrevolutionaries (the Contra) with the shipment of cocaine from Colombia via Panama to the streets of Los Angeles in order to fund their criminal activities to overthrow the legitimately elected Sandinista government.[3] As this example illustrates, the U.S. government's arguments joining Latin American drug smuggling, terrorist activities, and the dangers to U.S. youth for political advantage predates 9/11. Indeed, both the Reagan and Clinton administrations signed executive orders that strengthened joint antidrug and antiterrorist enforcement. After 9/11, however, the terrorist in this equation took on a decidedly jihadist profile.

The United States has spent over $1 trillion in taxpayers' money persecuting its "war on drugs" in Latin America since the 1970s.[4] Since fiscal year 2000, the United States has spent over $12.5 billion on Plan Colombia alone "to stop drugs at the 'source'" (Isacson et al. 2013, 2).[5] Colombia remains the top recipient of U.S. military and police aid to fight the drug war; however Mexico is a close second, as Plan Merida (2008–present) is modeled on Plan Colombia. In 2010 military and police aid to Latin America peaked at a total of $1.6 billion in a single year. Mexico was the top recipient that year, capturing over $500 million—or one third—of the total dispensed (Isacson et al. 2013, al. 20). While military and police aid to Latin America has declined under the Obama administration due to budget cuts and sequestration, this does not necessarily signal a decrease in U.S. involvement with Latin American military and police. Rather, Obama's military strategy in Latin America mimics his "leaner and meaner" strategy in the Middle East, entailing the increased use of Special Operations teams; of cybersecurity and increased CIA surveillance; of drone and robotic targeting of suspected "terrorists"; and the training of armies by proxy (Isacson et al. 2013, 21–23).[6] As these tasks are dispersed across a greater number of U.S. government departments, militarized agencies and offices proliferate, as do budget allocations. Moreover, by collapsing antidrug and antiterrorist activities, the shift in strategy renders many of the budget allocations "classified" in the interest of national security and difficult if not impossible to trace.[7]

As a consequence of this mission creep, today Latin America receives more yearly military and police aid to combat drugs than it received in any given year during the Cold War to combat communism. As military security expert Adam Isacson compellingly argues in "The U.S. Military in the War on

Drugs," the militarization of the drug war under Reagan and Bush (1989–93) was a strategic response to the end of the Cold War by State Department and the Pentagon officials:

> The collapse of the Soviet block left few compelling missions or pretexts to justify either the large militaries in the region or large military aid programs in Washington. The U.S. government, which had spent the better part of a century cultivating close and costly military-to-military relationships, was faced with a stark choice: Southcom, and other U.S. bureaucracies responsible for security in Latin America, would have to adapt by finding new justifications for current budget levels—or undergo a deep reduction in size and influence. (2005, 22)

The appearance of crack in U.S. cities provided the Reagan administration with an easy alibi for pursuing the first option by reviving the "war on drugs" rhetoric of Nixon to great effect for military and police budgets. The "radical mission switch quickly acquired a firm legal basis" as Congress shifted central authority for drug interdiction and eradication from the Treasury Department to the Department of Defense and the Pentagon in the late 1980s (Isacson 2005, 28). Today we maintain more than four thousand U.S. military personnel on the ground in Latin America at all times, as well as additional agents from ten other law enforcement agencies. The U.S. Navy and Air Force maintain constant surveillance of Latin America's sea and sky.[8]

Arguing for escalating budgets in order to protect the United States from "terrorists" who might mix themselves among the immigrants (documented and undocumented) crossing U.S. borders, especially the southern border, Homeland Security has gotten into the game since its creation in the aftermath of 9/11.[9] For this reason Homeland Security absorbed the Border Patrol Agency, militarizing it in the process. Homeland Security has more than doubled the number of border patrol agents along the southern border with Mexico, from 9,100 in 2001 to more than 18,500 today.[10] Moreover, Homeland Security has also militarized the border with advanced weaponry and surveillance technology. This increase in technological sophistication in weaponry and surveillance is in part due to the U.S. war in the Middle East, as surplus military equipment, developed for surveillance and intelligence gathering in Iraq and Afghanistan, finds its way to the U.S.–Mexico border. An "Unmanned Aircraft System" (drones), for example, now patrols the entire two-thousand-mile southern U.S. border at all times.[11] By way of contrast, the Border Patrol has only 2,200 agents patrolling the more than 5,500 miles of Canadian border, and drones survey less than a thousand of those miles,

238 CONCLUSION

although this is the border that 9/11 terrorists used to cross into the United States.[12] The Border Patrol has yet to capture a single alleged Islamic terrorist crossing into the United States from Mexico, though agents have killed several Mexican citizens since 2010—in the double digits—including some who were clearly on the Mexican side of the border with no intention of crossing it.[13]

Night-vision goggles, drones, and M16s are all trained on undocumented Mexican immigrants crossing the border in search of work, and it is the figure of the indio bárbaro that enables this racialized distribution of military force and reterritorializes our "defense of the nation" along the Mexican border rather than the Canadian one. Indeed a comparison of the distribution of force along the two borders underscores how this racialized hermeneutic conditions the nation's response to the perceived violation of U.S. sovereignty by Mexican drugs and immigrants. While accounting for only 2 percent of U.S. marijuana seizures at the borders, Canada nevertheless supplies the U.S. market with over 1 million pounds of marijuana per year.[14] Canada is the leading foreign supplier of ecstasy, often laced with highly addictive methamphetamines, a drug of choice among high school and college-age students.[15] On the other hand, El Paso, Texas, just across the bridge from Ciudad Juárez, is consistently ranked the safest city in the United States. Yet there is a 3.7:1 ratio per border mile in the distribution of border patrol agents along the Mexican and Canadian borders. The racial hermeneutic of the indio bárbaro may also help to explain why U.S. drug interdiction and eradication policies are myopically focused on the "unholy trinity" of marijuana, cocaine, and heroin produced in Latin America when cocaine and heroin are not among the top-five drugs used by underage youth in junior high or high school. Indeed, they are last on the list of top-ten drugs used by U.S. citizens. In order, the drugs most used are alcohol, cigarettes, marijuana, ecstasy, tranquilizers, prescription drugs, methamphetamines, inhalants, cocaine, and heroin (Mares 2006, 40). The majority of these drugs are legally manufactured in the United States and Canada by powerful industries (pharmaceutical, tobacco, alcohol) that benefit handsomely from the illicit use of their inebriants. And yet, the southern hemisphere and the Mexico–U.S. border continue to draw the military heat because of the myopic focus on marijuana, heroin, and cocaine.

It is not just an irrational U.S. drug policy or even the generic fear of a brown planet that leads to the militarization of the southern border, but the specific if unconscious fear of the Mexican as the indio bárbaro, of the indio bárbaro as indigenous foreign terrorist. Behind every Mexican immigrant is not just a violator of borders, a usurper of jobs, or a pusher of drugs but also the uncomfortable reminder of an indigenous people who refused to cede ground to U.S. nationalism, who refused to willingly disappear into a narrative of the vanishing Indian, a reminder that must be repressed behind the figure of the indio bárbaro. The indigenous faces of Mexican migrants recall the terrorizing truth of a racial geography made through violent dispossession and repression: the Indians did not die, they did not willingly cede their sovereignty to more capable white sovereignty. They remain in the presence of Mexican mestizos and indigenas who refuse to acknowledge the fastidiousness of nation-state borders. It is in this sense that Mexicans, like the indios bárbaros, are indigenous people made foreign: like the indios bárbaros they must be alienated from the "American" landscape in order to preserve the myth of a U.S. racial geography founded on legal principles by scrupulous settlers who purchased the territory from sovereign if foolish Indians. The undocumented immigrants remind U.S. citizens of their own original undocumentation. They also recall the living Native Americans who continue to assert their own territorial sovereignty within a white settler nation-state. Thus, in addition to filling the coffers of the military industrial complex, the militarization of the border protects the racial unconscious of a U.S. citizenry: it protects their mythic origin story by naturalizing all Mexicans as barbarous, lawless people.

The irony is that many of the Mexicans crossing the border do so because they have lost their own jobs as a consequence of NAFTA or are fleeing the violence of an ever-intensifying drug war waged by the U.S. and Mexican militaries against the cartels. 2014 marked the twentieth anniversary of NAFTA, a trilateral agreement that required the elimination of all subsidies to small Mexican farmers, the privatization of Mexican communal lands, and the elimination of Mexican tariffs on imported U.S. and Canadian basic grains.[16] An estimated 2 million Mexican farmers have been displaced from their lands since the passage of NAFTA.[17] Of course, when a Mexican farmer abandons his farm it has a multiplying effect as a farm owned by the head of the household invariably employs family labor and seasonal itinerant labor.

Thus it should have come as no great surprise when by 2004, within the first ten years of NAFTA, a conservatively estimated 8 million Mexicans had migrated to the United States in search of work, many of them indigenous farmers and laborers displaced off their communal farms because they could not compete with foodstuffs produced by U.S. agroindustry. By the year 2000, 96.2 percent of Mexican municipalities had experienced international outmigration (Delgado Wise and Cypher 2007, 37).[18] Thus farms in New York's Hudson valley today employ increasing numbers of indigenous Mexican farmers, including entire villages of indigenous peoples who have abandoned the Mexican countryside (Grey 2007, 38, 41–51). But peasants are not alone in

240 CONCLUSION

their migration to the United States. Mexicans are also abandoning the urban centers because Mexico is deindustrializing as an effect of NAFTA.

NAFTA has created more than half a million jobs in the *maquiladora* industry (Polaski 2004, 15).[19] Mexican exports to the United States have grown accordingly. The value of trade between Mexico and the United States has more than tripled. Exports from the United States to Mexico increased from $41 billion in 1993 to $226 billion in 2013, an increase of 444 percent (Villarreal and Fergusson 2011, 14).[20] Mexican exports to the United States, meanwhile, increased from $40 billion in 1993 to $280 billion in 2013, an increase of more than 600 percent (Villarreal and Ferguson 2011, 14). Consequently, the United States is currently running an import-export deficit with Mexico, causing U.S. labor unions quite a bit of stress in the process (Villarreal and Ferguson 2011, 10).[21] This trade deficit should bode well for Mexico, but when one looks more carefully at these statistics a different picture emerges. While it is true that Mexico is exporting more value-added goods to the United States in 2014 than in 1993, this does not imply an intensification or extension of industrial manufacture in Mexico. Rather it is disarticulating the Mexican economy with profoundly negative effects on employment by transferring "Mexico's economic surplus away from its potential domestic usage" (Delgado Wise and Cypher 2007, 121).

Maquiladoras are a highly parasitical form of industrial manufacture. The trade agreement relaxed environmental and labor regulations for maquiladoras, but it also eliminated tariffs on imports needed in export production within the *maquila* sector, as it is popularly called. Transnationally owned factories located along the border assemble goods that are then exported, primarily to the United States, for consumption. However, the majority of the inputs used in the assembly of these consumer goods—and the technology embodied in those inputs—are imported into Mexico.[22] In 2013, 75 percent of Mexican exports were composed of imported inputs, representing an *increase* of 2 percent over the twenty years of NAFTA, as imported inputs made up 73 percent of Mexican exports in 1994 (Castañeda 2014, 138).[23] Even though export production has exploded over the last twenty years, the percentage of imported inputs in Mexico's export manufacture has remained stubbornly the same, leading Mexico's foreign minister Jorge Castañeda (2000–2003) to conclude that as a result "employment in the manufacturing sector has stayed unchanged, and so have salaries" (138). Paradoxically, most of the value added in Mexico's exports is not added within the country of Mexico, in other words. As the final step in the production process, assembling inputs produced in other countries into the final product to be consumed in other countries,

Mexican maquilas add but a tiny percentage of the value added to the commodity in the form of cheap labor rather than technically skilled labor.

This macroeconomic structure in maquiladora manufacturing, coupled with the increase in imported consumer durables and goods for the Mexican market, has created a downward pressure on wages. Consequently, "real incomes in the manufacturing sector and the rest of the formal economy have remained stagnant, even if the fall in the price of some goods [due to imports] has softened the blow for workers" (Castañeda 2014, 138). Nevertheless, the maquila sector acts as an important tax shield for transnational corporations whose tax load is reduced as inputs enter the country and as exports exit the country. Thus the figures accounting for Mexico's increase in value-added exports disguise the fact that the majority of the overall value added to exports is accrued outside of Mexico and leaves very little profits or taxes in the country. Furthermore, as corporations relocated factories to Mexico to take advantage of cheaper labor costs and exemptions from tariffs on inputs, their profit margins have dramatically increased, as the repatriation of profits without taxation is another benefit of the trade agreement (Ruiz Durán 2013, 55–56). Thus the export deficit that the United States is currently running with Mexico does not indicate a negative impact on profits under NAFTA but its reverse. The costs of these relocations and trade deficit are instead born by workers on both sides of the border.

Maquiladoras leave almost no technological footprint in the country because they do not produce any backward or forward linkages. They do not invest in the production of inputs and components; they do not invest in research and development within the country; they invest but minimally in the up-skilling of their workforce. They do not create domestic industries that would multiply economic growth through the development of technology and the production of inputs at home. While it is true that maquilas pay much more than Mexico's minimum wage, it is also true that they pay *less* than nonmaquiladora manufacturing that is subject to Mexican labor laws and unionized labor (Delgado Wise and Cypher 2007, 126; 128). Also the increase in overall wages due to the maquiladora manufacturing is offset by the decline in wages due to the closing of domestic factories that have not been able to compete with low-cost imports, or what Castañeda calls the "Walmart effect" (135).[24]

Compounding the negative effects on Mexican manufacturing is the reorientation of nonmaquiladora factories to export production, a reorientation that has come with the extension of NAFTA provisions to this sector. Nonmaquiladora and maquiladora export production together account for 85 percent of Mexican exports, with maquiladora manufacturing responsible for

242 CONCLUSION

55 percent. Historically, nonmaquila manufacture, such as the auto industry, has invested in the domestic production of inputs and components, in research and development, and in the training of their unionized workforce (backward linkages), as well as in the marketing and distribution of their products to Mexican consumers (forward linkages). But more nonmaquiladora industries are now taking advantage of "temporary import programs" that allow corporations to incorporate maquiladora-produced components or temporarily imported inputs into their finished manufactured export products without having to pay tariffs or taxes (Delgado Wise and Cypher 2007, 127, 125).

The dramatic increase of temporary import programs within the nonmaquiladora manufacturing sector has led Delgado Wise and Cypher to label the growing number of firms involved in these programs as a "disguised maquila sector":

> In the disguised maquila sector, nationally produced inputs/components have fallen from 32 percent in 1993 to 22.6 percent in 2004. In essence, export firms outside of the maquila sector are progressively *de-industrializing,* leaving only the value of Mexican labor as the determining component of value-added as 77 percent of the inputs into the production process are imported. Once again . . . in the final analysis for Mexico the net result of this sector is almost completely reducible to the disembodied export of the Mexican labor force as embodied in the exported products. Furthermore, when Mexican-made inputs are reduced the impact is not limited to destroying supplier firms and jobs but also the complex set of socioeconomic relationships and skills that have accumulated over decades. (2007, 129)

The export model of economic development that replaced the import substitution model instituted in the postwar period (1940–80) is dramatically deskilling Mexican labor and cheapening it in the process with devastating consequences for laborers in all three signatory countries. Thus foreign direct investment (FDI), which has skyrocketed under NAFTA, can at once increase gross manufacture (as it has done) and decrease the level of technological development of the country. This deskilling of the labor force in part explains why it is that the educational level of Mexican immigrants (documented and undocumented) in the United States is steadily rising, as these migrants cannot use their skills at home. In 2000, 27.8 percent of Mexican migrants over fifteen had a high school education or postgraduate degree, whereas by 2003, that figure had jumped to 34.9 (Delgado Wise and Cypher 2007, 37). Moreover, while 36.2 percent of the U.S. workforce in manufacturing is made up of Mexican workers, only 27.8 percent of the Mexican workforce in Mexico is in manufacturing, all of which suggests that U.S. businesses are indirectly benefitting from this brain drain in Mexican skilled workers (Delgado Wise and Cypher 2007, 38). Mexican immigrants are but an effect of this export model of neoliberal development, yet they are read as the cause of the downward pressure on wages they represent.

NAFTA was sold to the U.S. and Mexican audiences as a vehicle for job creation in Mexico that would significantly decrease immigration to the United States. As Mexican president Carlos Salinas de Gotari famously quipped during the lead-up to NAFTA: "We want to export goods, not people" (Castañeda 2014, 139). Instead, the increase in imports under NAFTA displaced millions of Mexican workers in agriculture *and* in industry and was unable to generate the jobs in export production to absorb these displaced workers, much less the new labor entrants. At the very least, NAFTA failed to create enough jobs in manufacture and industrial agriculture to absorb all those displaced by its development model. At the very worst, it has negatively affected domestic industrial manufacturing with devastating long-term consequences.

The one industry that NAFTA has indisputably helped is the drug industry, for two simple reasons. The exponential increase in trade over the Mexico–U.S. border that came with the more than tripling of exports and imports means that it is ever easier to conceal shipments of drugs into the United States and illegal arms into Mexico. For all the unmanned drones patrolling the border, a very small percentage of trucks crossing the ports of entry across the two-thousand-mile border are inspected. At some ports of entry as few as seven out of a hundred trucks crossing into the United States have their cargo inspected. To inspect a higher percentage of the cargo crossing into the United States would cause huge bottlenecks, slow down production times, and lead to spoilage, as has happened in the two instances when the United States attempted more rigorous inspections in the last fifty years (Andreas 2000, 41, 47). While the surveillance techniques get more sophisticated at the points of entry, so does the technology developed by drug smugglers to evade these techniques (Dermota 1999–2000, 17). Ironically, this is the one area of research and development in Mexico still thriving.

The second way in which free trade facilitates the drug trade is that it has also made it significantly easier to launder money. Foreign direct investment (FDI) by U.S. firms in Mexico increased from $15.2 billion in 1993 to $101 billion in 2012, an increase of 564 percent (Villarreal and Fergusson, 19). Meanwhile, Mexican FDI in the United States increased from $1.2 billion in 1993 to $14.9

billion in 2012, an increase of over 1,000 percent (Villarreal and Fergusson 19). The estimated profits from the global trafficking of the "unholy trinity"—cannabis, cocaine, and heroin—are estimated to be between $300 billion to $500 billion a year, or the equivalent of 8 to 10 percent of world trade (Gibler 2011, 34).[25] The Mexican share of that profit is considerably smaller. In 2010, the U.S. State Department estimated Mexico's share of the profit at $25 billion (Gibler 2011, 30). It is exceedingly easy for drug organizations to launder their money through the foreign direct investment traveling back and forth between the United States and Mexico, with banks in the United States and Mexico receiving mere slaps on the wrists for their key involvement in this process (Dermota 1999–2000, 21–22; Mares 2006, 104). It is also exceedingly difficult to keep drug capital and all other capital apart. Every year the Mexican banking system finds itself with an "extra" $10 billion in its coffers that "cannot be explained within the proper dynamics of the country's economic activity," according to the Mexican treasury secretary (cited in Gibler 2011, 33). Thus "legitimate" businesses in the United States and Mexico have become addicted to the money generated by the drug trade. Indeed, the global market is addicted to the drug market, as Rajeev Syal of the *Observer* suggests, "Drug money worth billions of dollars kept the financial system afloat at the height of the [2008] global crisis" (cited in Gibler 2011, 33).

Both the illegal drug economy and immigration from Mexico to the United States precede NAFTA; however the processes described above have considerably accelerated and intensified the trafficking in drugs and immigrants. NAFTA set millions of Mexicans in motion looking for work, from the countryside to the city, from the cities to the maquiladoras on the border, from the Mexican border to the United States. This is the new geography of NAFTA, a geography of motion that has emptied the Mexican countryside and filled up the urbanized spaces in Mexico and the United States. It is a racial geography of neoliberalism that is displacing indigenous peoples on a scale not seen since the conquest, and that is transforming the demographic makeup of the United States with the many shades of Mexican brown. NAFTA created a precarious life for the vast majority of Mexicans, and thus it should surprise no one that a portion of this vulnerable population would choose to migrate north, to take up low-wage agricultural, manufacturing, and service jobs that proliferate in the United States as an effect of NAFTA as well. Undocumented Mexican workers in the United States sort our chickens according to sex, harvest our fruits and vegetables by hand, build our condominiums, deliver our pizza, pick up our dry cleaning, console our young and our elderly. However, it should surprise us even less that a portion of this vulnerable and young population chooses to take up lucrative careers in the drug economy that thrives in the shadow of NAFTA. After all, a great reserve of displaced Mexican labor accumulates along the Mexico–U.S. border in the hopes of some sort of employment. With weekly salaries of three to four hundred dollars for low-level street dealers in cities like Nuevo Laredo and Ciudad Juárez, employment in this industry is lucrative even by U.S. standards. Arguably, like the Apache and Comanche before them, these drug dealers facilitate trade in illicit goods sought after by a gluttonous U.S. citizenry. In the nineteenth century the Apache and Comanche raided Mexican ranches for the horses, cattle, and captives that fetched a dear price from European settlers and dislocated eastern Indians pouring into the Great Plains. Today, these *narcotraficantes* bring us cocaine, heroin, and marijuana from the factories in Colombia and the fields in Mexico that fetch a dear price from the casual users and junkies proliferating in U.S. suburbs, cities, and countryside.

Rather than being recognized as model entrepreneurs responding to the laws of supply and demand—U.S. demand to be specific—these narcos and immigrants are instead vilified using the same language and tropes that were used against the equestrian nations in the nineteenth century. Narcos and immigrants are portrayed as aberrations of humanity, engaging in improper trade with improper methods, who should be excised from the borderlands at all costs, requiring the joint efforts of the Mexican and U.S. military to do so. Narcos, the twenty-first century tribus salvajes, trade drugs made more desirable and profitable because they are outlawed. Meanwhile migrants trade themselves, smuggling their cheapened labor across the border at great cost to their personal safety to sell to the highest bidder in the United States. And, of course, every Mexican immigrant looking for work is potentially a narco looking for his or her next victim, and thus the border wall grows longer each day, at seven hundred miles it covers one-third of the highly militarized border between the United States and Mexico. And thus the old racial geography of the borderlands informs the new, with the indio bárbaro as a simplistic explanation for the economic restructuring brought on both countries by NAFTA and the drug economy it enables. But the racial geography of neoliberal reform is remaking the space of the nation-state in significant ways as well.

Heads and Scalps

If one enters "narco beheadings" into any search engine, tens of thousands of images of defiled corpses fill one's screen: beheaded corpses, scalped corpses, dismembered corpses, corpses with their eyes gouged out or with the "Z" of the Zeta cartel carved in torsos or backs. Many of the corpses come with notes, pinned to the chest with a knife or written on the body with a marker, explaining the offense that led to such a terrible death. One might imagine that corpses are beheaded to prevent identification. One would be wrong, as the head is not removed from the scene, but rather cleverly arranged to punctuate it. In one photo, two skulls are cradled by severed forearms with hands, their corresponding scalps delicately placed above the scene on the railing of what appears to be one of the international bridges spanning the Rio Grande. To ensure identification, the accompanying sign informs us that these two are "el Chino" and "el Fantasma" and lists their crimes against the cartel. I remember that we too had a Chino and a Fantasma at our high school in Laredo, Texas. Doesn't every high school along the border have a Chino and a Fantasma?

In another photo, four heads are arranged in a row along the windshield of a car that reads, "ultima letra captura y ejecuta a asesinos debastadores" (the last letter [i.e., "Z" for the Zetas] has captured and executed devastating assassins). The hood of the car, directly in front of the skulls, reads "zzzzzz," a pun on the name of the executioners that suggest these four men, all with their eyes closed, are just sleeping. In another photograph, two corpses lean up against each other on a street corner, the heads of each completely flayed. They have been arranged to look like two drunks, sleeping it off, with cigarettes hanging from their lipless teeth and with ridiculous sombreros atop their bald skulls, the cartels parodying a parody of the lazy Mexican. Perhaps their crime was not working hard enough to secure the expected rate of return, or perhaps they used too much of the product themselves. There is no helpful caption explaining their deaths.

What is made clear by these photographs is that these executions are public events. They are not the private adjudications of crime syndicates but the public policing of a population. Indeed, in several of the photos there are crowds surrounding the scene of execution. The narcos upload real-time photographs of their crimes themselves from their cell phones, making it mercifully impossible to reproduce the images for you here in print. These staged scenes of performative violence/justice are not only directed at local communities intimidated into submission, but at the entire world that has access to the internet. They connote a spectacular and absolute form of territorial justice, established precisely because it "pursues the body beyond all possible pain" (Foucault 1979, 34). These narrative scenes set the parameters, in script, in blood, and in body parts, of what happens should you violate narco law. Thus this kind of death is not limited to cartel cadre but illustrative of a general if unwritten code of behavior that must be followed by everyone within cartel territory. For example, in one photograph seven men are arranged in a semicircle on a main rotary in Uruapan, Michoacán. They sit on plastic chairs, their eyes covered by bandanas, their bodies showing no visible signs of torture, a merciful death. Attached to several of the corpses' chests with knifes are posters that read: "¡Advertencia! Esto les va pasar a todos los asaltantes rateros de coches, casa[,] habitacion transeúntes[,] asi como sequestadores[,] violadores y extorcionistas" (Warning! This will happen to all of those assailant petty thieves of cars, houses, and temporary housing, as well as to kidnappers, rapists and extortionists). The cartels claim exclusive power to inflict violence as punishment in their system of criminal justice, prohibiting others from the actions that are their sole purview.

Another set of photographs establishes the parameters of permissible speech within the realm. In September 2011 a group of three social media activists were killed in Nuevo Laredo, Tamaulipas, for reporting on Zeta violence in the city. With more than eighty journalists killed or disappeared in Mexico during the Calderón presidency, Nuevo Laredo journalists had understandably stopped reporting on cartel activities. Filling the void were three young bloggers including "La Nena de Laredo," María Elizabeth Macías, who informed the public on where shoot-outs were transpiring, who was targeted and why, and how to evade checkpoints. Two were strung up from a pedestrian bridge in Nuevo Laredo, one disemboweled and hogtied, the other's arm almost severed and hung from his feet. The most spectacular assassination was reserved for Macías, who was suspected of providing information to the attorney general and the Mexican military, passed on to her by her Internet fans. La Nena's decapitated body was found in Nuevo Laredo's *zócalo*, or main plaza, partially undressed to show that the skin on her back and been flayed and to suggest that she had been raped. Her head was mounted on a large spherical sculpture in the plaza. Her keyboard was arranged to hang around what would have been her neck and her mouse was in her mouth. The poster accompanying her body conveyed the following:

> Ok. Nuevo Laredo en Vivo y Redes Sociales[,] yo soy la nena de Laredo y aqui estoy por mis reportes y los suyos . . . para los que no quieren creer esto me paso Por mis acciones por *Confiar* en SEDENA [Secretaría de Defensa Nacional] y MARINA [Procudadora General]. . . . Gracias por su Atención Atte: La "nena" de Laredo . . . zzzzz. (Okay Nuevo Laredo live and on the social networks, I am the Laredo Girl and I am here because of my posts and yours . . . for those of you who did not want to

believe, this happened to me because of my actions because I trusted SEDENA [Department of National Defense] and Mariana [Attorney General] . . . thank you for your attention. Attentively yours: Laredo Girl . . . zzzz.)

María Elizabeth Macías's courageous voice was silenced when the Zetas assassinated her, as is emblemized by her mouse shoved in her mouth. Yet the Zetas usurp her speech when they write the attached note in the first person, ventriloquizing her voice to articulate their law, their punishment pursuing her body beyond the point of death, she speaks in blood and print on their behalf to silence the future political speech of others.

After seeing these images of narco violence that pursues the body beyond death, it is easy to see the perpetrators as barbarians. It is easy to say *¡Qué bárbaros!* It is even easier to avert our eyes, to turn away, to refuse to see. And yet these scenes of violence are staged in zócalos and plazas, on rotaries and bridges, demanding that bystanders look and absorb the power the scenes convey. These spectacular public displays are a modern form of statecraft reminiscent of the nineteenth century parades for returning scalping parties; they are a mode of taking possession of state sovereignty in a Foucaultian sense. The perpetrators make it clear to the Mexican public that the *capos* decide who dies and how they die, but also who lives and how they should live. These scenes are a population-management technique, setting the parameters of media representation (as in the case of the bloggers in Nuevo Laredo killed for daring to reveal too much about the narco activities in their town), of proper law enforcement (as in the case of the thieves in Uruapan, Michoacán, killed presumably to protect the citizens), or to determine the terms of trade (as in the beheaded cartel members on the bridge or on top of a car with the letter Z). These beheadings, scalpings, hangings, and other forms of torture and defilement denote a territorial control of one's market, a policing of the plaza; alternately they are deployed to gain control of someone else's market share or plaza.[26] Most important, they make it clear that the cartel's control is exclusive, as no official state police, army, or judicial system may deter them or save you. They are the law.

Just in case we are tempted to say that this kind of violence is proof positive that Mexico has become ungovernable, let us remember the event of September 26, 2014. On that day forty-three male students of the Raúl Isidro Rural Teachers College of Ayotzinapa, Guerrero, were killed because they dared to question the macroeconomics of neoliberal reform. Ayotzinapa is a teachers college reserved for the children of peasant farmers. These colleges are iconic achievements of the Mexican Revolution, a key component in the nation-building project of educating the peasant and indigenous classes by the state. These forty-three men were training to be primary, secondary, and high school teachers who would return to teach in rural areas of agricultural production. They were on their way to Chilpancingo, Guerrero, the state capital, as part of a group of more than a hundred students to protest tuition hikes at the college. These kinds of protest have become a tradition for Mexican university students who are accustomed to free education provided by the state. The students were also demanding guaranteed posts after graduation, as budget cuts have severely cut back the number of positions available for teachers in rural schools. Given the devastation of small farming in Mexico, these teachers colleges and rural schools arguably provide one of the only remaining avenues to legal employment for the children of farmers. Federal and state police blocked the routes that led to the state capital, forcing the students to return to the municipal capital of Iguala, Guerrero, to hold their protest.

The students' new plan appeared to have been to interrupt a speech by the local head of the DIF, Mexico's office for the "Integral Development of the Family," a speech celebrating her achievements and launching her campaign for mayor of Iguala. She was the wife of the sitting mayor, and evidently the then-mayor and future-mayor did not like the fact that the students were flying in the face of neoliberal restructuring and demanding that the state provide employment and free education. Or perhaps they did not like the fact that rural colleges and schools provide an alternative avenue of employment for these capable young men, who should instead be swelling the pool of labor reserved for the drug economy from which the couple benefitted directly. Whatever the case may be, the mayor ordered the local police to stop the protests. Clashes ensued between the police and the protestors as the protestors were attempting to leave the city on buses. Several were killed on sight as the police opened fire, but most escaped unharmed. One student's corpse was found the following morning, with his eyes gouged out and his face scalped. The forty-three who did not escape were kidnapped by the police and handed over, this time by order of the police chief, to the local cartel, the Guerreros Unidos—United Warriors—a clever pun on the state's name that suggests at once a new mode of territorial control and a new form of political subjection. The leader of the Guerreros Unidos cartel then ordered the students killed, either because he mistook them for a rival gang or because he objected to their political speech, it remains unclear. I bring this case to our attention *not* to demonstrate the "lawlessness of Mexico" but rather to underscore its lawfulness. The collusion of the state, the party, and the cartel in the orchestration of this mass murder *is* a form of government, a new form of law. At every stage in this horrific event, decisions were made and actions coordinated between these three entities. The drug economy not only provides new modes of economic production, but also new sovereignties of power expressed through the extra-economic forms of compulsion emblemized by torture, killing, and defilement.

It is a feudalistic system of absolute sovereign power when the local lord (the mayor) genuflects before the king (the cartel capo) to ask his favor, and where it is the king (the capo) who ultimately distributes justice and decides the fate of his unruly subjects. The cartel leader is jury, judge, and executioner, the absolute power, while the police and sicarios are but lowly knaves and knights who carry out the orders of their superiors, pursuing the bodies of their victims beyond the point of death with the mark of the sovereign—the gouged eye, the flayed skin—lest they themselves fall out of favor and suffer the same fate. The deaths of these forty-three students make evident that political power and economic power are still one in Mexico, only now the primary source of this power is the drug economy with its ritualized forms of violence that are also a form of statecraft. The arbitrariness of the violence is part of the ritual. It is a pyramidal structure of power where everyone benefits economically from the extra-economic compulsion of the threat of death, but where almost everyone might also fall victim to it as well.

My use of the term *feudal* is not meant to signal an atavistic return to a precapitalist mode of power in Mexico, much less some return to some fanciful "barbarous Mexico." Rather it signals my return to an old debate regarding the coterminous development of the capitalist mode of production in Europe and Latin America. In his essay "Feudalism and Capitalism in Latin America," Ernesto Laclau took issue with Andre Gunder Frank's thesis of the development of underdevelopment.[27] Frank's argument, that because Latin America had been fully integrated into the world economy since the Spanish conquest it was fully capitalist, was pitched against the stage theories of capitalist development whose architects insisted that Latin American economies were trapped in feudal modes of development and must be led/guided/forced into capitalist modes of production in order to become fully modern. While Laclau agreed with Frank that Latin American economies were never "dualist" and were always fully integrated into a capitalist economic world system, he nevertheless insisted that much of Latin America's economy had indeed been trapped in a feudal-*like* mode of production that relied on extraeconomic compulsion in its labor arrangements. Moreover, Laclau argued that

THE AFTERLIVES OF THE *INDIO BÁRBARO*   251

Latin America's integration into the world capitalist system intensified rather than rectified its feudalist arrangements of labor.

Laclau's groundbreaking claim was his insistence that a global capitalist mode of production not only coexists with earlier modes of production but indeed relies on their extraeconomic labor compulsion to maintain an ever-increasing rate of profit. Far from being a closed system, feudal sectors of Latin American economies were fully integrated with capitalist modes of distribution and consumption, but their forms of *production* were "precapitalist." Laclau was making a historical argument in his article to account for Latin American plantation systems that had relied on both slavery and debt-peonage well into their liberal periods, but were nonetheless producing for a capitalist world economy. Following Laclau, I suggest that sectors of Latin America are today entering into a feudalistic future. The drug industry in Mexico, for example, employs a feudal-like mode of production when cartels compel peasant farmers all over Mexico to grow illicit crops on their ejidos and private lands on penalty of torture and death. These extraeconomic forms of compulsion are of course compounded by the fact that the agricultural products they would have previously produced cannot compete on the domestic market against agroindustrial imports. The cartels also rely on extraeconomic forms of labor compulsion for the distribution of their product, as evidenced by the seventy-two immigrants from Brazil, Ecuador, and other Latin American countries who were killed in San Fernando, Tamaulipas, in 2010 because they refused an offer by the Zetas to remain in Mexico as drug dealers for four hundred dollars a week. The innumerable mass graves that have been found in Guerrero, Durango, Michoacán, Sinaloa, and Tamaulipas are a testament to these extraeconomic forms of compulsion that are not exceptional but ordinary business practices. Beyond these feudal-like modes of production and distribution, however, I suggest this model of absolutist power is pluralizing territorial sovereignty within the nation-state, as capos use feudal-like modes of discipline and punishment to maintain control of their plazas and every level of their participation in a capitalist world system. In the spirit of Laclau's essay, these modes of production, distribution, and political power are not in aberration of capitalist relations, nor are they in any way "precapitalist," rather in all the ways discussed previously they are distinctly modern and capitalist, auxiliary to the liberalization of trade and articulated with capitalist modes of production. After all, the labor force for the drug economy is drawn from the unemployed and underemployed labor reserve created by neoliberal reform, and the cartels in turn help to maintain the discipline and control of those lucky few who have attained full employment in the maquiladora and nonmaquiladora sectors through the demonstrations of the violence of their law for all residing in the territory.

That this feudal-like, or feudal-light, mode of power is anything but "premodern" is underscored by the fact that it was the republican governments of Durango, Sonora, Coahuila, and Chihuahua that established beheadings and scalping as a form of modern statecraft, a mode of statecraft similarly employed by the U.S. military in its "Indian wars." Then and now these performative methods have been integral to the establishment of modern forms of sovereignty. As discussed in chapter 3, after establishing their bounty programs, all four states set up commissions to check the scalps and heads brought to their state treasuries for payment for the distinguishing tattoos and patterns of head shavings used by the equestrian nations, although of course there was no way to ascertain whether the dead were in fact participants in raiding parties. Similarly, sicarios sometimes miss their marks, killing indiscriminately as well as deliberately, although today there are no state commissions to validate their actions, in part because it is precisely such republican state agencies whose power the cartels contest and usurp. As suggested in chapter 3 with regard to the nineteenth century, scalping and beheading determined who was to be included in the new Mexican nation, and who was to be radically excluded, exacting unity through the practice of these ritualized forms of democratic violence. Today cartels display heads and scalps and tortured bodies with the same exuberance to establish who may be included within their territories and who must die. Unlike the killings in the nineteenth century, today's beheadings and scalpings are not the democratic enactment of violence but the ultimate expression of the cartel's monopolistic power over their plaza. The massive demonstrations and social movement begun by Mexicans all over the country in the aftermath of the killing of Ayotzinapa's forty-three students is a tribute to the truly democratic nature of Mexico's civil society, a civil society determined to wrest control of state-power away from the trilogy of the party, the state, and the cartel.

It would be easy to end here, implying that Mexico's history of war against northern indigenous peoples haunts these scenes of narco violence, and this wouldn't be entirely incorrect, as the narcos clearly borrow from a familiar lexicon of national state-making in their staged and spectacular displays of the dead. However, this would be an incorrect conclusion as it would wrongly trace the source of all this violence to the ever-present if repressed figure of the indio bárbaro del norte. Instead, as in all things, if one wants to get to the heart of the matter, one should follow the money. And what better way to follow the money than to follow the peace movement.

In 2012 Javier Sicilia and the Mexican peace movement that quickly sprang up around his deeply personal but broadly representative loss embarked on a six-thousand-mile journey across the United States to bring their grief to the attention of the U.S. public as it is our government that pays for the drug war and our citizens who consume the product supplied by the drug economy. The Caravan for Peace with Justice and Dignity was made up entirely of the families of the killed and disappeared, and they stopped at significant locations for the functioning of the drug economy and the execution of the drug war. They visited all the major border cities where Mexican imports, including drugs, cross into the United States: San Diego, Nogales, El Paso, Laredo. They visited Harlem and the south side of Chicago to meet with the families of those incarcerated in the United States for drug related crimes. They destroyed guns in a Houston parking lot outside a gun shop, to underscore the devastating effect of U.S. manufactured arms that are smuggled into Mexico by U.S. citizens, as Mexico manufactures no guns itself, not a one. They met with the congressional leaders who benefit politically from taking a hard stance on the war on drugs and Mexican immigrants.

The most moving stop they made however was at Fort Benning, the new home of the former School of the Americas. The Caravaners staged a die-in in front of the school, reminding the United States that the Mexican military who today carry out the drug war are trained and armed by the U.S. military (fig. C.1). It is not simply that the Mexican military accidently kills innocent bystanders in persecuting drug lords and their underlings, although there is an inordinate amount of "collateral damage" at their hands. It is that the Mexican military, trained by the United States in the most advanced killing and counterinsurgency techniques, often switch sides in the drug war, lured by the large sums of easy money. Indeed, the most notorious drug cartel of them all, los Zetas, were originally an army battalion of Mexican Special Forces trained by the United States at the School of the Americas in counterinsurgency tactics and drug interdiction. They initially defected to work for the Gulf Cartel in the 1990s. During Calderón's drug war, in response to a power vacuum created by the successful arrest and extradition of the leaders of the Gulf Cartel, the Zetas branched out on their own and diversified their economy with human smuggling and cattle rustling among other things. They are the largest cartel in terms of territory, and they employ the most brutal tactics in killing. Allegedly, they introduced the practices of beheading and scalping as a form of terror and intimidation. As the peace activists remind us, "Los asesinos no nacen, se hacen aquí" (Assassins are not born, they are made here) (fig. C.2). The peace activists write on their own bodies, literalizing the

FIG. C.1. Caravan for Peace with Justice and Dignity stages die-in at Fort Benning, Georgia, to underscore U.S. military's role in deaths of their relatives and friends in Mexico at the hands of drug cartel members, Mexican military, and local police forces, many of whom were trained at this base, Southcom, or the School of the Americas (as in the case of the Zetas).

FIG. C.2. Caravan for Peace die-in. "Assassins are not born, they are made here." Fort Benning, Georgia, September 12, 2012.

embodiment of their grief, but also emblemizing the chain of responsibility for their grief that ends, like the proverbial buck, at the gates of Fort Benning, Georgia, with the U.S. military. Similarly, narcos were made, not born, out of the economic and political conjunction of free trade and the drug trade, out of extraeconomic forms of coercion, out of U.S. military "schools" that train them for the violent production and transportation of the drugs consumed in the United States.

Narcos are not twenty-first-century indios bárbaros beyond the pale of humanity, but the end result of an explicit form of modern statecraft, that of the U.S. government's fifty-year war on drugs in Latin America for the protection of its "national security." The Caravan members and the peace movement they represent recognize this fact when thus they demand peace negotiations to end Mexico's civil war brought on by the drug war, and with these negotiations demand the reintegration of these cartel members with justice into the Mexican nation.

I will close by considering the relationship between the nineteenth-century indio bárbaro and today's Muslim terrorist emblemized in Osama bin Laden. The U.S. government was drawing such an analogy between Al Qaeda and the Apaches by giving bin Laden the codename Geronimo. Geronimo's own lifespan coincided with the fifty-year period of profound geographical transformation in the racial geography of the borderlands that is the subject of *Indian Given*. He was born in 1829 along the Gila River in what was then greater Nuevo Mexico, but is today Arizona. By the time Geronimo turned seventeen he had participated in four raiding parties into Sonora and Chihuahua, and lead his fifth to acquire the necessary horses for his wife's bride price.

There is dispute over the origins of his name. Named Goyahkla in Apache, he claimed Geronimo was a Latinization of his name given to him by Mexicans who cried out in fear of him, "Cuidado allí viene Geronimo!" I would suggest, however, that his name speaks to Apache accommodation with Spanish colonialism, as it is just as plausible that he was baptized under the name Geronimo after the saint on one of the many mission settlements in Nuevo Mexico. In 1851, while the men of his band were trading with Apaches from other bands at one such mission settlement in Janos, Chihuahua, four hundred Mexican soldiers attacked Geronimo's base camp, killing his mother, wife, and three children. Devastated by this loss, Geronimo became one of the most notorious Mexican raiders in history, and the principal buyers of his band's raided goods were U.S. military personnel, visiting the area to determine the new border between Mexico and the United States. By 1860, with its victory over Mexico, the U.S. military had lost its use for Apache and Comanche warriors, and they became the target of a series of massacres executed by U.S. miners who were flooding into the area with their families in order to dispossess the Apache of their mineral-rich territory. The Apache retaliated in kind, beginning a cycle of raids on U.S. soil and against Euro-American settlers. U.S. Army generals were dispatched to deal with the Apache, and most particularly Geronimo. He and his band of the Chiricahua Apache were the most effective in their battle against the U.S. military, and in resisting reservation status. Indeed, Geronimo's war with the U.S. government outlasted all the other indigenous wars in defense of territory. By 1881 to 1886, when Geronimo led his band in the last Indian war fought on U.S. soil, all other equestrian peoples—the Kiowa, the Comanche, the Cheyenne—had been forced onto reservations. Geronimo then famously led his small band of Chiricahua into the Mexican Sierra Madre, some voluntarily, some coerced, where they evaded five thousand U.S. soldiers and three thousand Mexican soldiers for five years. For this reason Geronimo earned the title of being the last Indian leader of the last Indian war against the United States.

Thus you can see how Geronimo and Apache history is *loosely* analogous to bin Laden and Al Qaeda history. Both men and their bands are famous for having taken aid from the United States to fight a foreign (Mexican/Soviet) threat in their own lands (Apache territory/Afghanistan). The U.S. military and intelligence communities then and now perceived both as biting the hand that had fed them once their bands were abandoned by the U.S. government. Both men and their bands evaded the long arm of the U.S. law for a significant period of time, even though they were vastly outnumbered. Both men and their bands produce absolute hysteria among a U.S. public that is entirely disproportionate to the threat actually posed to U.S. security. Finally, both men are considered terrorists because they are presumed to kill without mercy.

Analogies illuminate similar traits in phenomena presumed to have evolved separately. Instead I suggest a homologous relationship between Geronimo and bin Laden that led to the naming of the mission, as these men share traits as a result of a common ancestor, the indio bárbaro of the borderlands, who roams and raids and kills without mercy in the United States's imperialist imagination and who must be excised not simply from the geographical borders of nation, but from the very boundaries of humanity. The United States so successfully drew this homology between bin Laden and the Apache as indios bárbaros that no national or international body objected to his assassination, without any access to a trial or council, in front of his family, nor to the dumping of his body at sea. He had been so successfully

THE AFTERLIVES OF THE *INDIO BÁRBARO*   257

dehumanized that U.S. justice pursued the body beyond all possible pain, foreclosing bin Laden's body from the most holy of practices, mourning.

There is another compelling reason for naming the mission Geronimo however. By giving the leader of Al Qaeda the code name Geronimo, the United States renders Al Qaeda as anachronistic as the Apache. Actually, the naming gesture renders *both* the Apache and Al Qaeda anachronistic, turns them both into relics of a past. And as relics of a past long fought and forgotten, this naming gesture furthermore frees the imperial U.S. citizen equally from her responsibility in the U.S. genocidal past against indigenous peoples and from her responsibility over the U.S. genocidal present in the Middle East. Naming bin Laden Geronimo clears him and Al Qaeda out of the way of the United States' imperial, triumphal march toward instituting democracy everywhere, precisely as the indio bárbaro heterotemporally haunts the theater of war in the Middle East.

Narcos appear to be the modern day indios bárbaros as well, for all the reasons discussed above. The narcos, like the Apache, are after all facilitators of trade. They transport products illicitly from their producers in Mexico to their buyers in the United States. Once again, the U.S. government is completely complicit in this trade, even as it insists that Mexico execute a drug war against the cartels that has turned the borderland into a place of incomparable violence in the Americas. You have to work very hard to be the most dangerous geography in Latin America. *Qué bárbaros.* Again it is so easy to say, it slides off the tongue. But who are the bárbaros? For as the Mexican peace movement reminds us, and as I underscore again, narcos and terrorists are not born killers, rather they are made, by economic, political, and military conjuncture along the borderlands of two imperial nations. Meanwhile, the *figure* of the indio bárbaro is deployed over and over again, consciously and unconsciously, for imperial pursuits along the border and far beyond this region. One could say U.S. imperialism initiates and extends its life under the shadow of the indio bárbaro. Because the indio bárbaro can haunt two places at once.

258 CONCLUSION

NOTES

INTRODUCTION. **It Remains to Be Seen**

1 I have added the emphasis in the quotes from *On the Road* given in the chapter epigraph.

2 For a complete, comparative discussion of racial representations in Kerouac's *On the Road* and Ernesto "Che" Guevara's *Notas de viaje*, please see María Josefina Saldaña-Portillo, "On the Road with Che Guevara and Jack Kerouac: Melancholia and Colonial Geographies of Race in the Americas," *New Formations* 47 (summer) 2002: 87–108.

3 These maps always prominently feature the southwestern United States to remind the viewer of the contiguity of the two nations and the proximity of the danger. The cartel territories are always brightly colored (often in the green, white, and red of the Mexican flag) and always cover the entirety of Mexico, as if no space were free of drug violence. Starkly, these territories always stop at the border, although the United States is the main consumer of all the drug traffic and the main source of weapons used in the drug economy. It is *one economy* of production, distribution, and consumption, and it does not stop at the border, as I discuss in detail in this book's coda.

4 For a critique of comparative method, see Micol Seigel, "Beyond Compare: Comparative Method after the Transnational Turn" *Radical History Review* 91 (winter 2005): 62–90; and Ania Loomba, "Race and the Possibilities of Comparative Critique," *New Literary History* 40 (2009): 501–522.

5 See *Comparison: Theories, Approaches, Uses,* ed. Rita Felski and Susan Stanford Friedman (Baltimore: Johns Hopkins University Press, 2013), especially "Why Compare?" by R. Radhakrishnan (15–33) and "Why Not Compare?" by Stanford Friedman (34–45) therein.

6 For a discussion of transnationalism's own imbrication with neocolonial and Cold War interests, as well as a discussion of comparativism and transnationalism as methods, see David Kazanjian and María Josefina Saldaña-Portillo, "The Traffic in History," *Social Text* 25(3.92) (2007): 1–7. For an example of a transnational history of race, see James H. Sweet, "The Iberian Roots of American Racist Thought," *William and Mary Quarterly* 54(1) (January 1997): 143–166.

7 I am borrowing the term *flashpoint* from David Kazanjian's elaboration in *The Colonizing Trick: National Culture and Imperial Citizenship in Early America* (Minneapolis: University of Minnesota Press, 2003).

8 Jodi Byrd, in her groundbreaking *The Transit of Empire: Indigenous Critiques of Colonialism* (Minneapolis: University of Minnesota Press, 2011), defines

"Indianness" as a critical paradigm in the foundation of the United States and its empire: "Indianness has served as the field through which structures have always already been produced . . . Indianness moves not through absence but through reiteration, through meme . . . as ethnographic evidence and example, lamentable and tragic loss" (xviii). I am borrowing the term with its saturated meaning from Byrd. I engage more robustly with Byrd in the following chapter.

9 See Edmundo O'Gorman, *An Inquiry into the Historical Nature of the New World and the Meaning of Its History* (Bloomington: Indiana University Press, 1961); Roger Bartra, *Wild Men in the Looking Glass: The Mythic Origins of European Otherness* (Ann Arbor: University of Michigan, 1994); and Bartra's *La jaula de la melancholia: Identidad y metamorfosis del mejicano* (Mexico: Grijalbo, 2000). For the United States, see John F. Moffitt and Santiago Sebastian, *O Brave New People: The European Invention of the American Indian* (Albuquerque: University of New Mexico, 1998).

10 For a detailed history and critique of Mexican *indigenismo*, see María Josefina Saldaña-Portillo, *The Revolutionary Imagination in the Americas and the Age of Development* (Durham, NC: Duke University Press, 2003), chapter 6.

11 For contemporary scholarship on the United States pursuing a similar line of investigation and inspiring my own work, please see Philip Deloria, *Playing Indian* (New Haven: Yale University Press, 1999); Ned Blackhawk, *Violence Over the Land: Indians and Empires in the Early American West* (Cambridge, MA: Harvard University Press, 2008); Jean O'Brien, *Firsting and Lasting: Writing Indians Out of Existence in New England* (Minneapolis: University of Minnesota, 2010); Byrd, *Transit of Empire*.

12 For a discussion of Immanuel Kant's pivotal role in the foundation of imperial geographic theory and racial determinism based on climate, see Audrey Kobayashi, "The Construction of Geographical Knowledge: Racialization, Spatialization," in *Handbook of Cultural Geography*, ed. Kay Anderson, Mona Domosh, Steve Pile, and Nigel Thrift (London: Sage, 2014), 544–557.

13 Turner published his foundational essay, "The Significance of the Frontier in American History," in 1893, but his language, imagery, and argument are remarkably similar to José Martí's lauded essay "Nuestra América," first published in 1891. In "Nuestra América," Martí similarly called for an Americanization of the European descendants in Latin America through Indian embodiment. Martí's *criollos* dress in effete and inappropriate European jackets and jewelry, and like Turner's Anglo-American colonists, must exchange their garb and technology for indigenous ones. And like Turner's colonists in a "too strong" physical environment, Martí's Latin American *criollos* are similarly too effeminate in the face of the environment of the "New World" and are advised to mimic the more physically powerful indios and afromestizos if they wish to succeed in their American enterprise. Of course, in contrast to Turner's disappearance of the Indian, Martí calls for the biological miscegenation of all races to assure everyone's shared cultural continuity. Nevertheless, in both Martí and Turner, physical environment and the physicality of the Indian are aligned. Proper colonial masculinity can only be achieved *through* the location and appropriation of masculine Indians in landscape.

14 With their travels back and forth across the United States, Sal and Dean are reiterating Turner's frontier thesis and its masculinity, especially having reached the "end

260   NOTES FOR INTRODUCTION

of America" at the Mexican border. Their adventures through the West reiterate the "ingenuity" derived from conquering landscape as the source of their new Beat aesthetics, and they perform the closing of the "American frontier" so bemoaned by Turner when they arrive in Laredo having exhausted the possibilities therein and looking for equivalent frontiers in their Mexican adventure.

15 By contrast, when Webb discusses the "Spanish Approach" to the Plains (Walter Prescott Webb, *The Great Plains* [Boston, MA: Ginn and Company, 1931]), the conquistadors fail to apprehend the environment properly in part because they fail to conquer the Apache and Comanche. Though Webb recognizes and grudgingly admires early incursions onto the Plains, the Spaniards are "constantly getting lost" not for want of a compass, but because of their hunt for gold and meek indigenous labor (105). While the Spaniards note "the excellences of the soil and its products," they opt against settlement, according to Webb, because their lust for gold distracts them from appreciating the full agricultural potential of the Plains (107). Embodying a clichéd racist reading of the frontier thesis, the Spaniards, in other words, are improperly suited to the landscape and incapable of conquering Indians who are not already docile and willing to accept the impractical rule of the Spanish.

16 For a feminist critique of Paz's theorization of the historical and rhetorical figure of the Malinche in Mexican culture, see Norma Alarcón, "Traddutora, Traditora: A Paradigmatic Figure of Chicana Feminism," in *Dangerous Liaisons: Gender, Nation, and Postcolonial Perspectives*, ed. Anne McClintock, Aamir Mufti, and Ella Shohat (Minneapolis: University of Minnesota Press, 1997): 278–297.

17 For a feminist analysis of contemporary indigenous women's movements in the face of the latest attempts at territorial dispossession, see *Des/posesión: Género, territorio, y luchas por la autodeterminación*, ed. Marisa Belausteguigoitia Rius and María Josefina Saldaña-Portillo (México, D.F.: PUEG-UNAM, 2015).

18 In those sections of the book that explicitly take up indigenous protagonism, indigenous peoples are called by their proper names: Apache, Comanche, Navajo, Pueblo, etc.

19 I have added the emphasis in the Mbembe quote in the epigraph above.

20 For a critique of the relationship among the discipline of modern geography, racial formation, and the Enlightenment, see Audrey Kobayashi, "The Construction of Geographical Knowledge" in *Handbook of Cultural Geography*, ed. Kay Anderson, Mona Domash, Steve Pile, and Nigel Thrift (London: Sage, 2003) and Linda Peake, "Gender, Race, Sexuality," in *The SAGE Handbook of Social Geographies*, ed. Susan J. Smith, Rachel Pain, Sallie A. Marston, and John Paul Jones III (London: Sage, 2010), 54–78. See also Charles W. J. Withers and David N. Livingstone, *Geography and the Enlightenment* (Chicago: University of Chicago Press, 1999). Withers and Livingstone argue for the recognition of the multiple geographical origins of the Enlightenment, encompassing not only Europe but also the Pacific and the Americas as sites of exploration and production of heterogeneous Enlightenments. Moreover they argue for the recognition of Enlightenment knowledges as locally produced, negotiated, and debated (4). Nevertheless, when they cite Captain James Cook's 1769 entry into the Pacific as the commonly agreed-on "birth" of modern geography, they betray an unwitting Anglo-American bias by forgetting or ignoring more

than two hundred and fifty years of Spanish and Portuguese mapping, classification, and comparison in the Americas and the Pacific. It is precisely this kind of bias that I hope to address in this book by exploring the ways in which Spanish geographic practice produced its own set of Enlightenment ideals of humanity, racial differentiation, sovereignty, and subsequently, national identity.

21 Withers and Livingstone cite Edmund Burke's 1791 "Letter to a Member of the National Assembly" as an example of this metaphoric appropriation of geographical terms: "But now the Great Map of Mankind is unroll'd at once; and there is no state or Gradation of barbarism, and no mode of refinement which we have not at the same instant under our View. The very different Civility of Europe and of China; the barbarism of Persia and Abysinia. The erratick manners of Tartary, and of Arabia. The Savage State of North America, and of New Zealand." See the discussion in Peter Marshal and Glyndwyr Williams, *The Great Map of Mankind: British Perceptions of the World in the Age of Enlightenment.* (London: J. M. Dent 1982), 14.

22 For an analysis of racial geography as not simply a subdiscipline of geography, but rather a central feature of "both its physical and human branches," see Alastair Bonnett, "Constructions of 'Race,' Place and Discipline: Geographies of 'Racial' Identity and Racism," *Ethnic and Racial Studies* (19:4, 1996). As his article argues, "The political and intellectual axis of this dominance revolved around the imputed influence of the physical environment upon the social and intellectual characteristics of different races" (865).

23 For an intellectual history of colonial geography, see Daniel Clayton "Critical Imperial and Colonial Geographies," In *Handbook of Cultural Geography*, 354–369.

24 Furthermore, vision in both these guises refers us back to the Christian origins of colonialisms, and to the Enlightenment era that is ushered in by the "discovery" of America. Cosgrove offers a genealogy of the term that greatly influenced the Enlightenment and imperial origins of geography as a discipline, and that ties directly to my use of vision, indeed enabling its conditional form: "In treating mind and body as distinct aspects of being, vision becomes the principal channel through which intellectual reason and the 'reason' or order of the sensible world can be mapped onto one another: the eye is rendered the window to a rational soul" (Denis Cosgrove, "Landscape and the European Sense of Sight: Eyeing Nature," in *Handbook of Cultural Geography*, 249–250).

25 For a discussion of the palimpsest of race in Latin America, see Florencia E. Mallon, "A Postcolonial Palimpsest: The Work Race Does," in *Histories of Race and Racism*, edited by Laura Gotkowitz (Durham, NC: Duke University Press, 2011): 321–336. I engage more fully with Mallon's formulation in chapter 1.

26 As Kobayashi explains, geography as a discipline has participated in the racializing construction of "ethnohistorical categories" and their placement in spatially specific landscapes: "The construction of the human body is a historical form of geographical knowledge that reflects geography's ocularcentric past. Although they have seldom been explicit about doing so, geographers have usually followed dominant social norms and intellectual trends, placing human bodies in particular landscapes, setting spatial limits upon the activities of those bodies, and linking the characteristics of those bodies (their gender, 'race' or ability, for example) to specific places. In other

262 NOTES FOR INTRODUCTION

words, much of the history of cultural geography is about how bodies are—and should be—*seen*" ("Construction of Geographical Knowledge," 544).

27 In *The Production of Space* Lefebvre offers a formulaic but nevertheless useful method for deciphering the "logico-epistemological space, the space of social practice, the space occupied by sensory pheonomena, including products of the imagination such as projects and projections, symbols and utopias" (Henri Lefebvre, *The Production of Space,* trans. Donald Nicholson-Smith [Malden, MA: Blackwell, 1991], 11–12). Lefebvre outlines a triad of mechanisms that work together to produce social space as we occupy it, our perception of social space, and our social relations within these spaces. Without priority assigned to any one of these three mechanisms, they are spatial practices, representations of space, and representational spaces. My own methodological approach corresponds to this triad.

28 My use of heterotemporality as a theory of history is borrowed from Dipesh Chakrabarty's extended discussion of the term, and as such, in *Indian Given,* I hope to provincialize the racial paradigms within the United States. A fuller account of Chakrabarty's critique of historicist anachronism and its effect on the representation of indigenous life worlds in the present follows in chapter 2.

29 For a detailed history of the formation of mestizaje as the privileged form of revolutionary citizenship in twentieth-century Mexico, please see the sixth chapter of Saldaña-Portillo, *The Revolutionary Imagination.*

30 By limiting my study of racial geographies in the region to the mestizo and biracial orders that correspond roughly to Mexican and U.S. nationalism, I do not mean to foreclose Native American and Mexican Indian mappings of racial relations that would add other layers to the heterotemporality of the region.

31 Heterotemporality is an effect of the lived reality of multiple racial geographies unfolding in one place, but it is not exclusive to the contemporary moment. Thus Spanish colonialism on the northern frontier of New Spain was itself heterotemporal, as the time of Spanish conquest encountered, negotiated, and cohabited with the time of indigenous nations therein. The same is true, of course, for Anglo-American racial geographies.

32 For an extended discussion of the Anglo-American settlers' successful efforts to exclude indigenous peoples from the franchise of U.S. citizenship and to delegitimate their Spanish titles to territory, see Laura Gómez, *Manifest Destinies: The Making of the Mexican American Race* (New York: New York University Press, 2007); and Martha Menchaca's *Recovering History, Reconstructing Race: the Indian, Black and White Roots of Mexican Americans* (Austin: University of Texas Press, 2001). This topic will also be considered at length in the second chapter of this book.

33 For example, Article 15 of the Sentimientos de la Nación reads, "Que la esclavitud se proscriba para siempre, y lo mismo la distinción de castas, quedando todos iguales y sólo distinguirá á un americano de otro, él vicio y la virtúd" (Slavery is permanently prohibited, as are distinctions of caste, so that all are equal, and only virtue or vice will distinguish one American from another). The Plan de Iguala, issued by Agustín de Iturbide and Vicente Guerrero on February 24, 1821, reiterated the equal rights of all citizens in similar terms as the Sentimientos: "Todos los habitants de la Nueva España, sin distinción alguna de europeos, africanos, ni Indios, son ciudadanos de

esta Monarquía con opcion á todo empleo, segun su merito y virtudes" (All the inhabitants of New Spain, without any distinction between Europeans, Africans, or
Indians, are citizens of this monarchy with the option of any employment, depending on their merits and virtues).

34 I am indebted to Ian F. Haney López for my use of the phrase "white by law," which
I borrow from his book of the same title, *White by Law: The Legal Construction of
Race* (New York: New York University Press, 1996). Haney López's book provides
a history of the construction of racial categories through legislation and perquisite
cases in the United States, but the phrase "white by law" specifically refers to the
only two minoritized groups designated white through perquisite cases, Mexican
Americans and Armenians.

CHAPTER 1. **Savages Welcomed**

1 For a complete historical analysis, see Lewis Hanke, *All Mankind Is One: A Study of
the Disputation between Bartolomé de las Casas and Juan Ginés de Sepúlveda in 1550
on the Intellectual and Religious Capacity of the American Indians* (DeKalb: Northern
Illinois University Press, 1974), and *Aristotle and the American Indians: A Study in
Race Prejudice in the Modern World* (Don Mills, Ontario: Fitzhenry & Whiteside,
1959); Rolena Adorno, *The Polemics of Possession in Spanish American Narrative* (New
Haven: Yale University Press, 2007); and Luis N. Rivera, *A Violent Evangelism: The
Political and Religious Conquest of the Americas* (Louisville, KY: Westminster/John
Knox Press, 1992). The title of this section comes from *Sublimis Deus* (1537).

2 The treatment of the Indians was always tied to their "nature," as made evident in a
letter from the Dominican theologian and jurist Francisco de Vitoria to his fellow
Dominicans in Peru, "I do not understand the justice of this war . . . if the Indians
were not men but monkeys, *non sunt capaces iniurias*. But if they are men and our
fellow-creatures . . . I see no way to excuse these conquistadores nor do I know how
they serve Your Majesty in such an important way by destroying your vassals" (cited
in Hanke, *All Mankind Is One*, 15–16). The "if/then" structure of Vitoria's statement
makes evident that treatment hinged on the status of indigenous humanity. In his
own treatises on the matter, published in the late 1530s, Vitoria equivocated on
the Spaniards' grounds for just war and for dominion over the indigenous, in the
estimation of colonial historian Rolena Adorno (*Polemics of Possession*, 109–113).
Vitoria followed Aristotle in believing that a prince had the right to rule over
those foreigners who might by nature require governing, and he accordingly
concluded, "Truly, if there be peoples of such a nature, these barbarians are it above
all others for they are completely incapable of governing" (*Relatio*, 13–14; cited in
Adorno, *Polemics of Possession*, 110). However, Vitoria insisted that the indigenous
had held proper dominion over their lands before the arrival of the Spanish, and
that their limited intellect did not in itself deny them the right to self-government.
Adorno attributes the vexed nature of Vitoria's late writings to the pressure brought
to bear by the emperor and the advocates of Spanish dominion, "This might explain
the ambiguity and self-contradiction of his position, accepting the principle [of just

war] guardedly, approving its application only if for the good of the Indians, not the gain of the Spaniards" (*Polemics of Possession*, 112).

3 According to Adorno (*Polemics of Possession,* 2007), Las Casas's role in the promulgation of the New Laws was paramount. Over the course of several days in 1542 and at the behest of the emperor, Las Casas presented before the Council of the Indies a set of legislative proposals and a version of his *Bevisíma relación de la destrucción de las Indias.* His goal, according to Adorno, was to remove indigenous peoples from the private control of the conquistadors. "The outcome—which all his enemies recognized as being attributable to him—was the promulgation of the New Laws on November 20, 1542" (75).

4 For a history of the encomienda see Héctor Días Polanco, *Indigenous Peoples in Latin America: The Quest for Self-Determination* (Boulder: Westview Press, 1997). The encomienda is one of the earliest spatial practices by European colonizers to effectively remap the geography of America in racial terms. The encomienda required the resettlement of entire indigenous communities onto the haciendas of the conquistadors, altering the indigenous geopolitical landscape permanently. The encomienda also established a hierarchy of social space and of social relation within the domestic sphere of the hacienda, with the "amos" living within the central house and the "servidumbre" living around the estate.

5 In 1543, Las Casas went further, pressuring the king to revoke the licenses of conquistadors and to provide indigenous peoples with proper instruction before baptism (Hanke, *All Mankind Is One,* 61).

6 For a detailed history of the relationship between perceived Islamic threats and their influence on Sepúlveda's participation in the debate, see George Mariscal, "Bartolomé de Las Casas on Imperial Ethnics and the Use of Force," in *Reason and Its Others: Italy, Spain, and the New World,* ed. David R. Castillo and Massimo Lollini (Nashville: Vanderbilt University Press, 2006), 259–278; and Hanke, *All Mankind Is One:* 61–62.

7 Luther believed the Turkish invasion to be a divine punishment for the vices of Christianity, while Erasmus, in his 1530 "On War against the Turks," stated, "My message is that war must never be undertaken unless, as a last resort, it cannot be avoided; war is by its nature such a plague to man that even if it is undertaken by a just prince in a totally just cause, the wickedness of captains and soldiers results in almost more evil than good" (318, cited in Mariscal, "Bartolomé de Las Casas," 261). Mariscal notes that Las Casas's own position on just war, as that of other "erasmistas," would build on Erasmus's position.

8 According to legal scholar Robert A. Williams in *The American Indian in Western Legal Thought: The Discourses of Conquest* (Oxford: Oxford University Press, 1990), "At the dawn of Europe's age of expansion beyond the Mediterranean world, Western legal thought had legitimated a discursive foundation for Europe's will to empire. Conquest of infidel peoples and their lands could proceed according to a rule of law that recognized the right of non-Christian people either to act according to the European's totalizing normative vision of the world or to risk conquest and subjugation for violations of this Eurocentrically understood natural law" (67). Medieval law had a great influence on the conquest of the New World; however,

NOTES FOR CHAPTER ONE 265

what transpired there was not simply an application of medieval law. Rather, the very basis for the law governing conquest was thrown into crisis by the encounter with peoples who did not fit the category of religious *infidel*. Their status required a recalibration of the Christian laws of conquest and spurred the modernization and universalization of the law, as we shall see in the discussion of Vitoria.

9 To underscore the ubiquity of the belief in the propriety of enslaving the "enemies of Christianity," Las Casas was horrified when he discovered that African slaves brought to the New World had *not* been captured in just religious wars and believed he would burn in hell for his role in bringing this unjust enslavement to the Americas. He publically recanted his support for African slavery in his *Historia de las Indias*: "This advice with regard to providing licenses to bring black slaves to these lands was first given by the cleric Casas, not aware of the injustice of the Portuguese then taking and enslaving them; that advice, after he realized the situation, he would not give again for anything in the world, for he always considered that they [the blacks] were unjustly and tyrannically made slaves, the same as the Indians" (3.3.102:177, cited in Rivera, *A Violent Evangelism*, 189). Adorno underscores that at the time of the Valladolid controversy, Las Casas was neither a pacifist nor an opponent of all manner of slavery. Nevertheless, she states, "In Las Casas's view, peoples who had neither invaded nor attacked a Christian principality gave no just cause to make war against them. He applied this principle to the Indians of the New World, and when he learned about the origins of the international slave trade, to Africans as well" (*Polemics of Possession*, 66). For a complete analysis of Las Casas's initial support for introducing Africans as slaves to the Americas, as well as of his subsequent reversal of this position, see Rivera, *Violent Evangelism*, 183–195; Adorno, *Polemics of Possession*, 61–68.

10 All translations of Sepúlveda's *Demócrates II* to English are my own, and based on Marcelino Menéndez y Pelayo's translation from the original Latin into Spanish *Demócrates segundo o De las justas causas de la guerra contra los indios*, ed. and trans. Marcelino Menéndez y Pelayo (Alicante: Biblioteca Virtual Miguel de Cervantes, [1892] 2006). The pagination refers to this edition.

11 Sepúlveda uses the Latin term *tarditas insita*, which Menéndez y Pelayo translates as the Spanish "torpeza de entendimiento," an inherent or implanted clumsiness or slowness of understanding.

12 Sepúlveda recognizes individual Spaniards are also guilty of "torpeza" but they do not "impugn the fame of a race, which should be judged by its cultivated and noble men and by its customs and public institutions, and not by the depraved men who are like slaves, which this nation more than any other hates and detests" (*Demócrates II*, 307). Demócrates does not show the same generosity of spirit in his assessment of indigenous people, insisting that their institutions are corrupt for not punishing those guilty of sins and crimes.

13 See Juan Stam, "La Biblia en la teologia colonialista de Juan Ginés de Sepúlveda," *Revista de Historia* (25) (1992): 157–164, for a full discussion of the use of biblical analogies in *Demócrates II*.

14 Sepúlveda's use of the term *nefando* as a description of indigenous intellectual capacity underscores the close proximity he sees between inferior reason and *el pecado nefando*, sodomy.

15 The Requerimiento was a standard document that justified the conquest and functioned as a technique of Spanish colonialism. Written in Spanish, all conquistadors were required to read this document to indigenous populations before waging war against them. It stated that the Indians had the right to submit to Christ and his representative, the Spanish king, in which case they would enjoy all the rights and privileges of other vassals and the king's protection. They also had the right to refuse subjection and fight the Spanish, in which case the Crown would wage a war of destruction against them and their subsequent generations.

16 Las Casas discusses a fourth type of barbarism in chapter 5 of *Defense*, "which includes all those who do not acknowledge Christ" (Bartolomé de Las Casas, *In Defense of the Indians*, trans. Stafford Poole [DeKalb: Northern Illinois University Press, 1992], 49). In this category are all nonbelievers, though they are not "true" barbarians. Rather they are barbarians in that they live in vice, but may well have rational and ordered governments, like the Greeks or Romans before Christ's birth, or the Turks and Moors in Las Casas's time (52). These barbarians must be enticed by persuasion to the Christian faith as it "brings the Grace of the Holy Spirit, which wipes away all wickedness, filth, and foolishness from human hearts" (50).

17 As Adorno explains "Las Casas maintained the right to sovereignty of the American peoples, both before and after their acceptance of the Christian religion" (*Polemics of Possession*, 83). At this stage in his intellectual development, Las Casas believed that the Spanish monarchy exercised just dominion over the New World and that it was the duty of the Spaniards to convert the Indians to the Christian faith through peaceful persuasion. Toward the end of his life, however, due to the abuse he witnessed, Las Casas vehemently argued before the Crown that it would be best for the souls of both the Spanish and the indigenous if Spain renounced its dominion and efforts at Christian conversion in the New World and left the Indians to their own dominion (Hanke, *Aristotle and the American Indians*, 111).

18 The emphasis in this quote is mine. Las Casas echoes the argument for Indian rationality offered by Vitoria, who is generally considered the father of modern international law: "The true state of the case is that they [the Indians] are not of unsound mind, but have, according to their kind, the use of reason. This is clear because there is a certain method in their affairs, for they have polities which are orderly arranged and they have definite marriage and magistrates, overlords, laws and workshops, and a system of exchange, all of which call for the use of reason; they also have a kind of religion." Vitoria is cited in Antony Anghie, "Francisco de Vitoria and the Colonial Origins of International Law," in *Laws of the Postcolonial*, ed. Eve Darian-Smith and Peter Fitzpatrick (Ann Arbor: University of Michigan Press, 1999), 93–94. Vitoria delivered two lectures in 1532, "On the Indians Lately Discovered" and "On the Law of War Made by the Spaniards on the Barbarians," with which Las Casas would have been familiar as a Dominican friar from and student at the same School of Salamanca where Vitoria taught.

19 According to Hanke, there is a record indicating thirteen of the fourteen judges rendered their written opinions, but all but one of these opinions also remain lost (*All Mankind Is One*, 114).

NOTES FOR CHAPTER ONE   267

20 Las Casas certainly won the rhetorical battle with his success in persuading the Council of the Indies and the Council of Castile to censor Sepúlveda's treatise. Between 1553 and 1558 Las Casas published nine treatises in Sevilla, including the *Very Brief Account of the Destruction of the Indies,* while publication of *Demócrates II* in Spain and in the Americas was strictly prohibited (Hanke, *All Mankind Is One,* 114–115). According to Menéndez y Pelayo's preface to his edition, only two extant copies of *Demócrates II* existed by the end of the nineteenth century (259).

21 In 1571, before drafting the new laws, the president of the Council of the Indies, Juan Manzano y Manzano, requested that all of Las Casas's manuscripts from the Valladolid debate be sent to Madrid so that the council might study them (Hanke, *Aristotle and the American Indians,* 86–87).

22 Had Vitoria not died in 1546, he would most likely have participated as a jurist at the Junta de Valladolid, given his renown as a theologian, jurist, and philosopher.

23 These early iterations of modern international law resonate, heterotemporally, in the international requirement that all nations recognize the right of international free trade.

24 Vitoria, from *De Indies et de Ivra Belli Reflectiones*: "So long as the Spaniards do no harm to the Indians, neither may the native princes hinder their subjects from carrying on trade with the Spanish. . . . Also, the sovereign of the Indians is bound by the law of nature to love the Spaniards" (E. Nys, ed., J. Bates, trans., 1917, cited in Robert A. Williams, *The American Indian in Western Legal Thought: The Discourses of Conquest* [Oxford: Oxford University Press, 1990]).

25 See María Elena Martínez, *Genealogical Fictions: Limpieza de Sangre, Religion, and Gender in Colonial Mexico* (Stanford: Stanford University Press, 2011), for a discussion of the religious and biological meaning of the word *raza* in the early colonial period of New Spain. She provides an insightful analysis of the transition of the meaning of *raza* once the concept of *limieza de sangre* is carried to the Americas by Spanish nobility.

26 Achivo General de Indias (AGI): Mexico, 690, *Expediente sobre la población del Seno Mexicano (1736–1750)* Documento No. 5 and 5ª. I discuss this petition for settlement in greater detail in chapter 2.

27 The subtitle above comes from Levi Frisbie, *Discourse before the Society for Propagating the Gospel among the Indians, and Others, in North America* (Charlestown, MA: Samuel Ethridge, 1804).

28 For further critique of these two tropes in U.S. discourse and history of dispossession, see Brian W. Dippie's *The Vanishing American: White Attitudes and U.S. Indian Policy* (Lawrence: University Press of Kansas, 1991); and Eric Olund's "From Savage Space to Governable Space: The Extension of US Judicial Sovereignty over Indian Country in the Nineteenth Century," *Cultural Geographies* 9(2) (2002): 129–157. As examples of the continuing force of the myth of the vanishing Indian in the twentieth and twenty-first century, please see Zane Grey, *The Vanishing Indian* (London: Hodder and Stoughton, 1936); and Florence C. Greybill and Victor Boesen, *Edward Sheriff Curtis: Visions of a Vanishing Race* (New York: Crowell, 1976). Between 1904 and 1930, Edward Sheriff Curtis took portraits of Indians from nations he believed would soon be extinct: the Apache, Sioux, Nez Pierce, Cheyenne, Wichita, among

others. His choice to develop the photos in sepia tones added to the sense of nostalgia over the passing away of these great nations. Despite the fact that all of the nations he documented persist to this day, the publication and republication of his collection of photos still insists on their vanishing away. Whatever their intentions, Grey and Curtis's representations were not innocent. Indian reformers in the late nineteenth century used the threat of the extinction of Indian nations to successfully lobby Congress for allotment of private parcels to reservation Indians as the means for their salvation. The allotment policies that were eventually adopted by the U.S. Congress are principally responsible for the reduction of Indian territory in the United States to less than 3 percent of the national territory (Olund, "Savage Space," 134–135).

29 I am indebted to Saidiya V. Hartman in my use of the term *imputation of humanity*, which I borrow from her suggestive theorization of the same in the introduction to her *Scenes of Subjection: Terror, Slavery and Self-making in Nineteenth Century America* (New York: Oxford University Press, 1997).

30 For examples of arguments about the rights of Christians over heathens and on the right of discovery, see the writings of Minister William Symonds (Virginia Company), William Strachey (Virginia Company), and Robert Gray (Virginia Company); on the notion of just conquest, see John Smith (1616) and William Loddington; on the notion that the Indians lacked proper conceptions of property, see John Lederer (Maine colony) and John Winthrop (Massachusetts Bay Company); all cited in Stuart Banner, *How the Indians Lost Their Land* (Cambridge: Harvard University Press, 2005), 16–19. In making these arguments, these colonial writers borrowed surreptitiously from both Sepúlveda's and Vitoria's legal rationales, based as they were in natural and religious legal cannons. Given the antipapist arguments against the Bulls of Donation offered by those in favor of British colonization of America, however, the Protestant and Puritan colonists could not openly cite these Spanish theologians and jurists, though their influence is evident.

31 There is a vast body of scholarship on the treaty as the primary mode of early colonial encounter. For a nuanced discussion of tactics such as negotiation and mediation during the early colonial period, see Daniel K. Richter, *The Ordeal of the Longhouse: The People of the Iroquois League in the Era of European Colonization* (Durham, NC: University of North Carolina Press, 1992).

32 The investors in these speculative land companies acquiring Indian lands for future sales were often also same public officials charged with approving the sales: "Among them were Richard Henry Lee, a shareholder in the Mississippi Company and a member of the Virginia House of Burgesses; William Franklin, who had 10 percent of the Illinois company while governor of New Jersey; Franklin's more famous father Benjamin, another Illinois Company shareholder while representing Pennsylvania's interests in England; Indian Superintendent William Johnson and his deputy George Croghan, who owned shares in the Illinois Company and the Indiana Company; Jonathan Trumbull, governor of Connecticut and shareholder in the Susquehannah Company; and Thomas Jefferson and Patrick Henry, both of whom invested in several western land ventures while they were members of the Virginia House of Burgesses" (Banner, *How the Indians Lost Their Land*, 106).

NOTES FOR CHAPTER ONE   269

33 In contradistinction, the Spanish Crown monopolized all access to land among the colonists, and as such the Spanish colonial administration was more successful in protecting indigenous lands. Ironically, indigenous peoples also received land grants from the kings of Spain to protect their territories from incursions.

34 These differences in power are summarized by Banner: "In the end, the acquisition of land in North America is a story of power, of the displacement of the weak by the strong; but it was a more subtle and complex kind of power than would have been necessary to seize land by force. It was the power to supplant Indian legal systems with the English legal system, the power to have land disputes decided by English officials using English law rather than Indian officials using Indian law. The threat of physical force was always present, but most of the time it could be kept out of view, because most of the time it was not needed" (*How the Indians Lost Their Land*, 82).

35 For an extended analysis of the racialized development of property as a liberal legal concept, see Harris's full article, "Whiteness as Property," *Harvard Law Review* 106(8) (1993): 1710–1791. See also Margaret Radin, "The Liberal Conception of Property: Cross Currents in the Jurisprudence of Takings," *Columbia Law Review* 88 (8) (1988): 1667–1696.

36 Text of Proclamation available at http://indigenousfoundations.arts.ubc.ca/home /government-policy/royal-proclamation-1763.html.

37 This is in line with Immanuel Wallerstein's interpretation of the American Revolution in his *Modern World System III: The Second Era of Great Expansion of the Capitalist World Economy, 1730–1840s* (Berkeley: University of California Press, 2011). Wallerstein argues the American Revolution was not a revolution but a realignment of power among British elites.

38 For detailed analyses of the treaty form as it developed in the colonial period with regard to indigenous peoples and its significance for indigenous sovereignty, see Bruce Johansen, ed., *Enduring Legacies: Native American Treaties and Contemporary Controversies* (Westport, CT: Praeger, 2004); Curtis Mahoney, "Treaties as Contracts: Textualism, Contract Theory and the Interpretation of Treaties," *The Yale Law Journal* 116(4) (2007): 824–857; Robert J. Miller, "Indian Treaties as Sovereign Contracts," *Flash Point* 9 (2007); Francis P. Prucha, *American Indian Treaties: The History of a Political Anomaly* (Berkeley: University of California Press, 1994).

39 All citations from *Johnson v. McIntosh*, 21 U.S. (8 Wheat.) 543 (1823) full trial brief available at http://supreme.justia.com/cases/federal/us/21/543/case.html. For a full analysis of the Marshall Court's decision in *McIntosh* from a legal perspective, see Eric Kades, "The Dark Side of Efficiency: Johnson v. McIntosh and the Expropriation of Amerindian Lands," *University of Pennsylvania Law Review* 148 (1999–2000): 1065–1190; Philip P. Frickey, "(Native) American Exceptionalism in Federal Public Law," *Harvard Law Review* 119(2) (2005): 431–490, and "Marshalling Past and Present: Colonialism, Constitutionalism, and Interpretation in Federal Indian Law," *Harvard Law Review* 107(2) (1993): 381–440. For an analysis of the Marshall court's rulings in the equally determinant Cherokee cases, see Jill Norgren, *The Cherokee Cases: The Confrontation of Law and Politics* (New York: McGraw-Hill, 1996). For a settler colonial analysis of the Cherokee cases, see Patrick Wolfe, "Against the Intentional Fallacy: Logocentrism and Continuity in

the Rhetoric of Indian Dispossession," *American Indian Culture and Research Journal* 36(1) (2010): 3–45.

CHAPTER 2. Affect in the Archive

1 Archivo General de Indias (AGI) (Estado: Mexico, 690), *Expediente sobre la población y pacificación del Seno Mexicano*, henceforth "Testimonio 1736." A note at the side of the document indicates the "Testimonio" accompanied Document No. 3 from this same *Expediente*, titled "Carta de Don José Antonio Fernández de Jáuregui Urrutia, Gobernador del Nuevo Reino de León, a S.M. Informa de la situación, fortalezas y estado de aquellas tierras" (September 16, 1736) 4 folios. For a published version of this *testimonio* that reproduces the list of Indian nations at the margins of Jáuragui's text, see "Descripción del Nuevo Reino de León excrito por su gobernador Josseph Antonio Fernández de Jáuregui," in *El Nuevo Reino de León en voz de sus contemporáneos,* ed. Lydia Espinosa Morales and Isabel Ortega Ridaura Monterrey (Monterrey, Mexico: Fondo Editorial Nuevo León, 2006) 1–42. All aberrations in spelling and grammar in the transcriptions from this and future documents cited from this *Expediente,* and appearing in this chapter, are from the original colonial Spanish.

2 *Expediente sobre la población y pacificación del Seno Mexicano* (1738), AGI (Estado: Mexico, 690), Antonio Ladrón de Guevara, Document No. 5a, titled "Noticias sobre los indios bárbaros y sus costumbres," 12 folios, not paginated; henceforth "Ladrón de Guevara 1738." The annotation reads "Resolucion de Su Magestad. Como parece, y ha Mandado que Por la Thesoreria General se le dén A este sugeto La ayuda de costa Que se propone. Listas Publicada en 13 de Abril 1739. Baxó puesto de la [illegible] Reservada: Firma: Don Francisco Campo de Arbe" and appears in the left-hand margin of petition.

3 Literally meaning neighbor, *vecino* is the most common term used in the archive of this area to describe the Spanish subjects who "poblar" the Spanish settlements. Guevara and Escandón both use the term to describe those who will be joining them to populate the territory between Nuevo León and Texas. Jiménez Núñez explains the political significance of vecino in the specific arena of the northern frontier: "En este escenario tan distinto a otras regiones de la América española o inglesa, hay que contemplar y tartar de entender a quienes no eran *colonies, settlers, pioneers o frontiersmen.* Tampoco aquellos españoles eran ciudadanos sino vasallos del rey. La ciudadanía es un concepto y fenónomeno social nacidos de la Revolución Francesa. La mejor designación para los que no eran miliatres ni eclesiásticos es la de vecinos o cabezas de familia que constituidos en cabildos o ayuntamientos defendían sus intereses y se relacionaban como grupo con las autoridades" (In this scenario, so different from other regions of Spanish or British America, one has to contemplate and try to understand that these people were not organized into colonies, nor were they settlers, pioneers, or frontiersmen. Nor were these Spaniards citizens but vassals of the king. Citizenship is a concept and phenomena of the French Revolution. The best designation for those who were not members of the military or clergy is that of the neighbor, or head of house, who organized in towns

and municipalities and defended their interests and related with the authorities as groups.) (42). In terms of trades and professions, the vecinos were principally miners, ranchers, merchants, artisans, scribes, and notaries (*letrados*), doctors, domestic servants and field hands (*peones*). Vecino was a political category, indicating a set of rights, privileges and also obligations bestowed on them as Spanish *vasals*, ultimately answering to the Crown for their endeavor. See Alfredo Jiménez Núñez, "Los *vecinos* Españoles ante los indios de frontera: El gran norte de Nueva España," *Brocar* 30 (2006): 37–63.

4 Ladrón de Guevara is perhaps best known today for his "Noticias de los Poblados de que se Componen el Nuevo Reino de León, Provincia de Coahuila, Nueva-Extremadura y La de Texas," published in 1739. This pamphlet provided detailed descriptions of the Indians in these already established colonies, though he decried the governing strategies of the colonial administrators of all four provinces. Together, these provinces encircled the territory he petitioned to *poblar*. Guevara's 1739 published document also glorified his own deeds in the service of the Crown, and perhaps his critique of the established provinces was meant to throw his petition for settlement of the new territory into positive relief, so that the king would grant his permission to his venture.

5 All transcriptions from the archive and translations from Spanish are my own. I thank Edith Norma Betancourt for her assistance on some of the more difficult colonial paleography. I use the verb form "to populate" (a literal translation of "poblar") because it more accurately conveys the Spanish intent to fill the geography with Spanish and Indian towns, for evangelization and for the harnessing of indigenous labor. The "settlement," used to describe Anglo-American western expansion, carries the mythical sense of "rugged individualism" taming an unruly wilderness devoid of human civilization. In contrast, the Spanish envisioned the territory already filled with Indians, who needed to be arranged into more orderly towns. Mexican historian Alfredo Jiménez Núñez ("Los *vecinos* Españoles") describes Spanish colonization as an "empresa indiana," an "Indian enterprise": "Tras la conquista—a veces antes de lograrse una verdadera pacificación, como en el caso de tantas fronteras—el objetivo era poblar la tierra con españoles y evangelizar al indio. Este doble principio suponía fundar villas y ciudades y crear pueblos de indios." While it is necessary to differentiate between the implications of populating a territory and settling it, I at times use "Spanish settlement" for simplicity's sake, with the caveat that it implies filling an area with Spanish *and* Indian towns.

6 I use the term *appropriation* rather than *theft*, following from frontier historian Sara Ortelli. In her article, "Crisis en subsistencia y robo de Ganado en el septentrión novohispano" she explains that the Apache and other *nonreduced* indigenous groups of the northern frontier did not understand the act of taking Spanish livestock, often unbranded and free ranging, as stealing: "La práctica de apropiación de animales por parte de los groupos indígenas no reducidos, no tenía la misma significación que para lo españoles. . . . Incluso, la percepción acerca de lo que se entendía por robo de Ganado fue transformado según las épocas" (The practice of animal appropriation by some of these indigenous groups who had not been placed into towns or missions did not have the same meaning [for them] as it did for the Spanish . . .

Indeed, the perception they have of livestock theft changed according to the times). ("Crisis de subsistencia y robo de ganado en el septentrión novohispano: San José del Parral (1770–1790)," *Relaciones (Zamora)* 31(121): 23–24).

7 See Salvador Álvarez, "Manuel San Juan de Santa Cruz: Governador, Latifundista y Capitán de Guerra de la Frontera Norte," *Revista de Indias* 70 (248) (2010): 101–126, for the provocative effects of Spanish expansion in Nueva Viscaya on "nonsedentary" indigenous groups. See also Cecilia Sheridan Prieto, "Reflexiones en torno a las identidades nativas en el noreste colonial," *Relaciones* 92 (23) (2002): 76–106. In "Reflexiones" Sheridan Prieto critiques the Spanish descriptive categories for indigenous peoples, particularly their distinction between "nomadic" and "sedentary" peoples in the northern frontier. This distinction, she argues, was the effect of Spanish political interests and their "mesoamerican centricism." The Nahuas, Incas, and Mayas, with their hierarchical structure and analogous institutions, emblemized "civilized" and sedentary nations for the Spanish colonizers. The indigenous people on the northern frontier who did not approximate this type of spatial organization were necessarily considered "bárbaros" and "salvajes." Rather than corresponding to any objective characteristics or practices, Sheridan Prieto argues that the Spanish labeled Indians inclined to alliance "civilized" and those that refused such political overtures "savages"; hence, the fluid nature of these designations along the northern frontier (85–88).

8 For a discussion of the multiplying effects of cattle ranching in Texas on indigenous peoples' hunting practices, see Jesús F. de la Teja, "Sobreviviencia económica en la frontera de Texas: Los ranchos ganaderos del siglo XVIII en San Antonio de Béxar," *Historia Mexicana* 42(4) (1993): 837–865.

9 See also Mexican frontier historian Martín González, "¿Amigos, Enemigos o Socios? El comercio con los 'Indios Bárbaros' en Nuevo México," *Relaciones* 92(23) (2002): 108–134.

10 The Province of Nueva Viscaya was comprised of today's Chihuahua and Durango, eastern parts of Sonora and Sinaloa, southwestern parts of Coahuila, Arizona, and parts of New Mexico, Colorado, and Texas.

11 For more on the creation of markets in Spanish livestock among Europeans and pueblo communities alike, and the corresponding growth in livestock appropriation, see Alfredo Jiménez Nuñez, "Los vecinos españoles ante los indios de la frontera: El Gran Norte de Nueva España," *Brocar* 30 (2006): 37–63 and 62–61. See also Ortelli, "Crisis en Substancia," 32, and "Enemigos internos y súbditos desleales: La infidencia en Nueva Vizcaya en tiempos de los Borbones," *Relaciones (Zamora)* 31(121) (2004): 488–489; and Edward K. Flager, "La Politica Española para pacificar a los indios Apaches a finales del siglo XVIII," *Revista Española de Antropología Americana* 30 (2000): 221–234 and 223–224. On the continuing centrality of these trade patterns after Mexican independence and the trouble this caused between the Mexican state and the Apache, see Edwin R. Sweeney, "Mangas Coloradas and Apache Diplomacy: Treaty-Making with Chihuahua and Sonora, 1842–43," *Journal of Arizona History* 39(1) (1998): 1–22.

12 Just as the Apache and Comanche incorporated Spanish livestock into their stock of goods to trade, so too did they incorporate the Spanish into the market for Indian

slaves. Historically, the Apache and the Comanche were purveyors of slaves for the agricultural communities of this northern territory. They sold Indians captured in their raids against each other, or against other indigenous communities, as agricultural and domestic labor. Upon arrival, the Spanish became purchasers of Indian slaves from the Apache and Comanche as well. Though the Spanish Crown prohibited the Indian enslavement in the early sixteenth century, the settlers justified their purchases as "liberating" the captives from the barbarous nations. Although these captives *were* technically free, they could nevertheless be exploited as domestic labor in exchange for "evangelization," especially if the captives were children (David J. Weber, *Bárbaros: Spaniards and Their Savages in the Age of Enlightenment* [New Haven, CT: Yale University Press, 2005], 238–40). Indeed, the association of the Spanish word "criado" with household labor stems from this period, when Spaniards would purchase Indian children to *crear* (literally, to rear) in their homes under the Christian faith and Spanish customs.

13 Indeed, Guevara publicly criticized Jáuregui and Montecuesta for their poor administration of the neighboring provinces, arguing this was the root cause of problems with Indians in the region (see footnote 4).

14 Montecuesta's petition is also located in AGI (Estado: Mexico, 690), *Expediente sobre la población y pacificación del Seno Mexicano*, Document No. 1, titled "Memorial de Don Narciso Barquín Monte-Cuesta, proponiendo el descubrimiento de las tierras comprendidas entre la Huasteca y el Nuevo Reino de León y la reducción de los indios bárbaros que las habitan" (April 2, 1736).

15 There is debate as to whether Jáuregui, Montecuesta, and Guevara were rivals or allies in their efforts to acquire a license for the territory that would eventually become the Province of Nuevo Santander. This confusion may be due to the fact that all three requests went forward in the same "*expediente*," or docket, first to New Spain's viceroy, then to King Felipe V, and eventually to an Audience of the Consul of the Indies. According to Gabriela Vázquez García, "José de Escandón y las nuevas poblaciones del Nuevo Santander," *Scripta Nova* 10(218): 85 (2006), Guevara *had* supported previous petitions for settlement by Jáuregui: "En 1726, el gobernador del Nuevo Reino de León, don José Jáuregui, secundado por el propio Ladrón de Guevara y don Narciso Marquín de Montecuesta, alcalde mayor de la villa de Santiago de los Valles, presentaron un memorial a Felipe V, en que solicitaban la autorización para la conquista y poblamiento de la Costa del Seno Mexicano, y la reducción y conversión de sus naturales, cuyas hostilidades inhibían la colonización de la región y la explotación de sus recursos." Nevertheless, by 1738, the year of Guevara's own petition, he clearly understood himself as a rival in these efforts with these two men. In the second section of Guevara's published account of his travels throughout the provinces of the northern frontier, *Noticias de los poblados de que se compone el Nuevo Reino de León, Provincia de Coahuila, Nueva Extremadura y la de Texas*, Guevara vociferously condemns Jáuregui for his corruption and for the harsh and harmful methods used by his captains and sergeants against the indigenous populations of the region (Espinosa and Ortega, *El Nuevo Reino de León en voz de sus contemporaneous*, xvii–xviii). The ultimate evidence of the rivalry, however, is the king's initial decision to grant Guevara's petition because his methods are the most

"suaves" and to fund the endeavor with five hundred pesetas. Once granted the license, however, Guevara proceeded to petition the Crown for additional funds for soldiers and presidios. The Crown rescinded Guevara's license and granted it to José de Escandón in 1748.

16 This is a common trope in the literature of conquest. In both Hernán Cortés's *Letters from Mexico* and Bernal Díaz Del Castillo's *The True History of the Conquest of New Spain,* the indigenous groups they encounter are by turns fierce warriors and cowardly lions.

17 The Spanish from "Noticias" 1738: "Con algún modo particular y experimentado de lo que para ello se requiere como así tengo experimentado de unos y otras, en las entradas que hice a sus dichas habitaciones."

18 From the Spanish: "Y este es el motivo por que nunca son castigados los indios agresores quedando estos avilantados menos preciando el gobierno de la Nación española, pues para constigar [*sic*] a los que tales invaciones causan más se requiere prontitud para seguirlos que no cuantos número de soldados mal equipados procurando alcansarlos antes de que se tripulen y confundan con las otras naciones que se allan inocentes las que muchas veces y aun de continuo pagan por las agresiones a manos de los españoles con lastima de quitarles las vidas A sus hijos y mujeres de lo que no pocos extremos hacen no siendo de menos considerazion que lo que redunda de ello es, que agraviados solicitan la venganza, como tan lastimados y valiéndose los perversos que han causado el Daño de esta occasion los solicitan y convocan para ejecutar mayors invaciones, engañadolos para animarlos de que también a ellos los han estropeado y de Rocado en la misma manera, Y este es el motive de tantas inquietudes e inconsecuencias experimentadas entre Indias y españoles, procediendo todo, de los malos Naturales de los unos, agravios, experimentados por los otros." (Ladrón de Guevara 1738).

19 Even the Spanish geographical nomenclature in the region is an example of process of reinscription *and* adaptation. For if the indigenous peoples the Spaniards encountered were frequently ascribed the names of the geographical places in which they lived, the names of many local places were often ascribed a Latinized version of their indigenous designations. If Spaniards imposed dominion along the northern frontier by naming provinces after regions in Spain—Nuevo *León*, Nueva *Vizcaya*, Nueva *Extremadura*—they also ascribed provinces a Latinized name corresponding to dominant indigenous populations—*Tejas, Coahuila, Tamaulipas.*

20 As Ortelli explains, "Entre las decadas de 1770 y 1780 las incursiones alcanzaron niveles sin precidentes por dos factores: la gran cantidad de personas que dependían del robo de Ganado para sobrevivir y el incremento de la demanda de caballos entre indios y europeos en regiones ubicadas más al norte" (During the 1770s and the 1780s the incursions reached unprecedented levels for two reasons: the great number of people who depended on livestock theft to survive and the increase of demand for horses among the Indians and Europeans who moved into regions farther north.) ("Crisis en Substancia," 32).

21 De la Torre illustrates this point with several cases. One example is taken from a letter by Fray Ángel Antonio Núñez regarding "Juan," a cook from a community in Sonora: "En 1776 el presidio de Janos fue atacado por una banda de 'apaches'

encabezada por un español [Juan] que había sido aprehendido por los apaches en tiempos recientes. Durante el ataque de referencia, el cabecilla de la banda se encontró frente a un miembro de su propia familia: un tío que imploraba por su vida en virtud del parentesco que le unía con el atacante. En respuesta el líder de la partida rebelde dijo 'que no tenía más tío ni padre que el cerro' y acto seguido mató a su pariente" (In 1776 the Janos presidio was attacked by a band of "Apaches" headed by a Spaniard [Juan] who had been recently captured by the Apache. During the referenced attack, the head of the band came upon a member of his own family: an uncle who begged for his life on the basis of this family tie with the attacker. In response, the leader of the rebel band said that "he no longer had any other uncle or father than the mountain" and he immediately proceeded to kill his relative.) (Núñez; cited in José R. de la Torre Curiel, "Con la sierra a cuestas: Apaches y españoles en la frontera sonorense en el siglo XVIII," *Nuevo Mundo, Mundos Nuevos* [January 31, 2011], 4).

22 A *legua* is a Spanish form of measurement that equals roughly three and a half miles. From the Spanish: "El modo que tienen para mantenerse las naciones de dichos gentiles es el que cada una de ellos reconoce sus terminus. Dentro de los cuales forman sus viviendas que son chozas o barracas de forma que para poderse mantener sin tanto afán se reparten en tres o cuartro escuadras y retiradas unos de otros ocho o diez leguas forman sus dichas viviendas y los Indios Grandes salen al campos a la caza de venados, pavos, conejos, tortugas y jabalíes que de todo lo referido teine mucha abundancia en los campos y por la tarde van viniendo cada uno con lo que a podido Matar y para comerlo cocido hacen en la tierra un poso en el cual echan mucha leña hasta que lo ponen como un horno de caliente y dentro de el meten aun que sea un venado entero al cual le dejan piel para que sirva de resguardad a la carne para que no coje tierra . . . y dentro de dos o tres horas lo sacan tan cocido que sale desasiéndose sin quemarse ni otro defecto y de muy buen gusto" (Ladrón de Guevara 1738).

23 From the Spanish: "La seña general que observan para avisarse de una o otra parte es pegar fuego al pasto seco que ay en el campo y como el humo sube tan alto aun que estén lejos lo devisan y se corresponden con otro humaso o quemazón y asi se entienden y sabe por el rumbo que andan unos y otros."

24 From the Spanish: "La docilidad de dichos Gentiles es mucha y mientras más remotos son más dociles y sencillos" and "la honestidad que gastan es natural que se observa sin Malicia ni otra compostura en tal mente campestre."

25 From the Spanish: "Y si se les muere lo entierran y dentro de la sepultura le meten el arco, las flechas y lo demás que ha sido uso de dicho Difunto y del paraje donde se le ha muerto no paran un instante sin mudarse para otro y al año por el tiempo de las frutas vuelven a paraje donde lo enterraron y le hacen una fiesta que dura todo un día y la fiesta se reduce a bailar y cantar en el modo que ellos lo acostumbran y dicen que baja de lo alto el dicho difunto y que les dice que allá arriba hay mjores venados y frutas que comer . . . el luto que se guarde el padre por el hijo o el hijo por el padre es quitarse todo el cabello, y por hermanos la mitad y si son tíos o primos amasan una poca de ceniza con el sumo de las tunas y se embarran cara y cuerpo y esto lo ejectuan cada que se acuerdan del dicho difunto."

26 AGI (Estado: Mexico, 1933A&B), *Las Invaciones de los Apaches en el territorio de Tejas, 1763: Testimonios de autos sobre ataques de indios comanches y apaches, su reducción, erección de presidios en los ríos San Javier y San Sabá, visitas a presidios, fundación de misiones, deserción de soldados y descubrimiento de minas.* Henceforth *Invaciones.* English translation: *The Invasions of the Apache in the Territory of Texas: Testimonials of Apache and Comanche Attacks, Their Resettlement, the Bulding of Presidios on the San Saba and San Javier Rivers, Visits to Presidios, the Foundation of Missions, the Dessertion of Soldiers and the Discovery of Mines.* Aberrations in spelling and grammar from the original.

27 The Spanish provided the requested presidio and mission, but their placement of it in the isolated valley, 135 miles away from San Antonio and at the edge of the Comanche range, was dangerously miscalculated. Most of the Apache tribes who requested the mission refused to move onto it as initially agreed, because of its proximity to the Comanche territory. Pekka Hämäläinen, in *The Comanche Empire* (New Haven, CT: Yale University Press, 2008), suggests the Lipan Apache themselves understood it to be a provocation to the Comanche. As a consequence, no Apache lives were lost in the initial Comanche attack on the presidio (see endnote 31 below for more information on the attack) (Hämäläinen 2008, 55–62).

28 The Comanche attacks against the Lipan Apache villages and Spanish settlements in the San Saba and San Antonio valleys continued until 1766, when the Spanish abandoned their alliance with the Apache, with rippling consequences for the colonists of the northern frontier and their Indian allies: "Comanche colonization, moreover, had dislocated thousands of Apaches from the Great Plains [to] south and west of the Río Grande, where they joined other Apache groups in raiding Spanish villages, haciendas, and ranches. By mid-century the Apaches had forged an immense war zone that stretched 750 miles from northern Sonora through Nueva Vizcaya to Coahuila, posing a severe threat to Northern Spain's mining districts" (Hämäläinen, 64).

29 David Scott, *Conscripts of Modernity.* (Durham, NC: Duke University Press, 2004).

30 This counteroffensive failed and forced the Spanish Empire into retreat.

31 AGI (Estado: Mexico, 1933A), *Invaciones,* Document No. 1.1, titled "Testimonio de los autos sobre el asalto y ataque que los indios comanches hicieron en el presidio de San Luis de las Amarillas, que está a cargo del coronel Diego Orttiz Parrilla" (1763) Folios 1–111, Fojas 1–228. The Spanish original reads: "Don Diego Orttiz Parrilla Coronel de los Reales Exercittos de S.M. y Commandante En este Real Pressido y Rio de Sansava, A Vuestro exelicismo el Sr. Don Angel de Marttos y Navarrette, Governador y Capitan General de la Provencia de Tejas; Hago saver como poco despues de haver salido el Sol, el Dia de oy, cargaron sobre la esquadra de la Caballade de este Pressido y sobre el Rancho del Ganado mayor un cressido num.o de Indios Enemigos, Armados todos de fuzileria, y con la mayor intrepidez, y exfuerzo de Suertte, que aun havido hecho la mayor resistenzia nuestra gentte, hasta mas de las deiz del Dia quedaron muerttos el Sargento y dies y nueve Soldados en el mismo terreno de donde Sacaron toda la Caballada, y mulada a poderandose de ella enteramente pues quando llegó el resfuerzo, que con un ofizial despache a el primer avisso, ya se havian rettirado con ella, y solo encontraron a los cadabers despojados

NOTES FOR CHAPTER TWO   277

de sus Aramas, Vestiduras, y Menages de Caballos y aunque al rettirarse este ofical alcansó a ver, muchedumbre de enemigos, y oyo que lloraban, como acostumbran la perdida de gente que tubieron en el combatte, no se dettermino á atacarlos por la superioridad que reconocio en ellos; pues aseguran los soldados que pudieron desprenderse de la furia que les fué Imperceptible el numero de Indios Armados" (8V–8R). Henceforth "Carta Orttiz Parrilla."

32 AGI (Estado: Mexico, 1933A), *Invaciones,* Document No. 1, Ibid. From the Spanish: "Y tambien porque solo la nacion Cumanche es muy numerosa, que no es capaz un dia para trancittarse su Poblazion y que aunque esta Nacion no concurrio en las primeras desgracias de Sansaba, se hallaron en las segundas por causa de que . . . ellos se ofrecieron siempre contra los Españoles" (91V).

33 AGI (Estado: Mexico, 1933A), *Invaciones,* Document No. 1, Ibid. From the Spanish: "Que los Españoles no heran Buenos, porque no les dan lo que los Franzeses, por lo que les dixeron los Taguacanas en que acabando el Pressidio de Sansaba acabarian las dos Missiones de Nacadoches y Ais, para que biniessen los Franceses a Poblarlas, y de essa fuentte estatrian mas promptamente socorridas otras Naciones" (Foja 91R–91V).

34 AGI (Estado: Mexico, 1933A), *Invaciones,* Document No. 1, Ibid. From the Spanish: "Que el Indio Sanchez le aseguro que hallandose Juntas todas las Naciones del Norte en el Nacimiento de los rios de los Brazos de Dios con el motibo de Salir á cazar en otro Paraje se hallaba un franzes con ellos, comerciando bolbosa, Balas, fusiles, y demas Armas, y cosas de su [undicipherable]: les dijo que si encontraser los Apaches, procuraran tomarles los Hijos, que el se los compraría; a lo que le comentaron otros Indios que si se hallban con los Españoles y estos los oculttaban, o defendian, que debian hazer, a lo que les respondio que para esso heran muchos, y llebaban bastanttes municiones que quand no los quiziessen entregar los Españoles, o los defendiessen rompiessan tambiem Guerra con ellos" (The Indio Sanchez assures us that, finding themselves all together at the mouth of the Brazos de Dios rivers, all the nations of the north with the intent of hunting in that place, there was a French man among them, selling gunpowder, bullets, guns and other arms, and things from his [indecipherable]: he told them that should they come across Apaches to be sure to take their children because he would buy them[.] When the Indians asked what they should do if they came across Spaniards who were protecting the Apache, he answered that they [the Indians] were many and had plenty of munitions so if the Spaniards refused to turn them [the Apache] over or defended them, they should start a war with them also.) (Foja 93R–94V).

35 The French, the British, and the "Americanos" are all designated "estranjeros." Only the indigenous peoples are referred to as nations.

36 For examples of contemporary historians working against this Romantic model of indigenous subjection, see María Elena Martínez, *Genealogical Fictions: Limpieza de Sangre, Religion, and Gender in Colonial Mexico* (Stanford: Stanford University Press, 2011); and Juliana Barr, *Peace Came in the Form of a Woman: Indians and Spaniards in the Texas Borderlands* (Chapel Hill: University of North Carolina Press, 2007).

37 I use the term *postcolonial* guardedly as it is a contested term from the perspective of the indigenous nations within the United States, for whom the situation remains very much colonial. Postcolonial scholarship nevertheless helps us to discern the layered modalities of colonialisms past and present, and even to recognize the paradoxical function ascribed to the figure of the Indian within the context of the elite anticolonialism of the United States.

CHAPTER 3. Mapping Economies of Death

1 The aberrations in Spanish spelling and grammar in the epigraphs at the beginning of the paragraph are from the original archive, cited in G. Emlen Hall, "Mexican Liberals and Pueblo Indians, 1821–1829," *New Mexico Historical Review* 59(1).

2 This is not meant to suggest that the administrators during the Bourbon era were somehow more altruistic or conciliatory toward the equestrian tribes on the northern frontier than administrators of previous eras. Rather, according to Weber, the Bourbon reforms elevated trade to the place of religion in their policies toward these Indians, and Bernardo de Gálvez was particularly skilled in this regard. His policy was to apply military pressure to the Apache in order to force them into peaceful trade relations. This would simultaneously make them "realize the advantages of rational life" and make them dependent on the Spanish. See David. J. Weber, *Bárbaros: Spaniards and Their Savages in the Age of Enlightenment* (New Haven, CT: Yale University Press, 2005), 184. Gálvez also promoted the sale of arms and alcohol to the indios bárbaros both to increase dependence and to increase wars among the equestrian tribes.

3 The republica de los indios was a legal concept rather than a spatial mode of organization, denoting the rights and obligations of indigenous peoples in relation to the rights and obligations of the Spaniards and the *castas*. Spatially, Spanish and indigenous populations and towns were superimposed and intermingled.

4 Spanish authority appeared to have effortlessly grafted itself onto indigenous governmental structures, but as historian James Lockhart has established, this replacement of indigenous structures with Spanish ones was superficial rather than substantive. In *Nahuas and Spaniards: Postconquest Central Mexican History and Philology* (Stanford, CA: Stanford University Press, 1991), Lockhart interprets the minutes of communal assemblies held under the guise of Spanish town councils. Lockhart demonstrates how the Nahuas pueblos in central Mexico continued to conduct their affairs according to indigenous mandates and forms. Nahuas communities maintained their punctual modes of regionally based governments under the guise of the colonial *alcaldias mayores* system of New Spain.

5 In 1823, the Mexican Constitutional Congress decreed the eagle in profile perched atop a cactus with a snake in its beak the official insignia of the Mexican flag. Early versions of the flag had alternately brandished an image of the Virgin of Guadalupe or an eagle donning a crown.

6 Ralph Smith suggests the pressure applied by ex–Texas Rangers was not merely rhetorical: "The prospects for reviving a bounty program anywhere in Mexico still looked unpromising when a party of *well-armed, well-mounted* 'forty-niners' rode

NOTES FOR CHAPTER THREE 279

into Ciudad Chihuahua. They were mostly ex-Texas Rangers, seasoned in Indian warfare and in special duty against Mexican guerrillas during the campaigns of Generals Zachary Taylor and Winfield Scott. Learning of the legislative impasse, these Americans influenced the Chihuahuan Congress to pass the controversial bill over the governor's veto. Thus former enemies of Mexico induced Chihuahua to reinaugurate bounty hunting as a state policy which continued three and a half decades." See Smith, "Scalp Hunting: A Mexican Experiment in Warfare," *Great Plains Journal* 23 (1984): 43, emphasis added.

7 The Spanish term *pieza* shared the same range of meaning as the nineteenth-century English term "piece." In addition to indicating, as in English, an article that is part of a set (chess piece), an input in the manufacture of another commodity (cloth for textile, or a part for an engine), a performance (theatrical or musical), or a head of livestock, the term in Spanish is also used to indicate the carcass of an animal that has been hunted. It is from this last, linguistically specific sense that use of the term in the bounty programs derives its macabre meaning. However, the presenting of the *piezas* to the commissions also takes on a distinctly performative and theatrical function, as discussed below. Real Academia Española website: http://lema.rae.es/drae/?val=pieza.

8 Raids persisted for more than fifty years, as these bounty hunters failed to curtail their intensity or frequency, instead inflaming the conflict. During the Spanish period raiding parties focused on the theft of horse herds; beginning in the 1840s, raiders began killing all adult males, capturing women and children as slaves by the hundreds, burning crops, and destroying all domestic livestock that could not be carried away. See Brian Delay, *War of a Thousand Deserts: Indian Raids and the U.S.–Mexican War* (New Haven, CT: Yale University Press, 2008), 114–138.

9 While the changing central governments consistently repudiated these bounty laws, the capital's attitude toward the Apache, Comanche, and Kiowa tribes did change as a consequence of raiding. By 1852 the *national* Congress issued an opinion that nomadic northern tribes were *not* part of the Mexican nation (Durazo Herrmann). Mexican conservative and liberal leaders came together to disown these "native sons" even while the liberal philosophy of the independence movement required the assimilation of millions of other indigenous peoples into the nation.

10 Liberal ideals establishing the Mexican nation held that all Indians born within the national boundaries of Mexico were considered citizens of the new nation with full and equal rights. This was reiterated in all the early manifestos and state and federal constitutions. Independent indigenous peoples living within the territorial boundaries of Mexico (as well as those independent Indians north of its border) were "treated as separate political entities. State governments made war against Indians, exempted them from taxes, and signed treaties with them as if they were sovereign powers." David J. Weber, "American Westward Expansion and the Breakdown of Relations Between Pobladores and 'Indios Bárbaros' on Mexico's Far Northern Frontier, 1821–1846." *New Mexico Historical Review* 56(3) (1981): 103.

11 Historian Brian Delay describes central Mexico's reaction thusly: "Presidents and prominent ministers in the nation's capital thought the northern rhetoric excessive, and insisted not just that Apaches, Comanches, Navajos, and other raiders were

human, but that they were Mexican. This was consistent with the sweeping claim of the Constitution of 1824 that everyone born inside Mexico's territorial limits was *mexicano*, but it was also important because Mexican political elites contrasted their own enlightened, inclusive benevolence with the aggressive exclusionism of the United States, and especially with remembered Spanish cruelties." See Delay, "Independent Indians and the U.S.–Mexican War." *American Historical Review* 112(1) (2007): 54.

12 The Crown officially changed its position on intermarriage in 1575, prohibiting the upper echelons of Spanish colonizers from marrying Indian women, though there was no such prohibition on midlevel criollo administrators. Criollo was the term for presumably pureblooded Spaniards born in New Spain. The policy of rewarding intermarriage among military men through pecuniary incentives, however, continued. By 1575 Spain had succeeded in creating an elite criollo managerial class in New Spain. Menchaca argues the Spanish prohibited intermarriage among the elites to ensure its loyalties remained undivided: "It had become necessary to form a loyal class with limited social commitment to the inhabitants of Mexico." Martha Menchaca, *Recovering History, Constructing Race: The Indian, Black, and White Roots of Mexican Americans* (Austin: University of Texas Press, 2001), 56.

13 See Jonathan Goldberg, *Sodometries: Renaissance Texts, Modern Sexualities* (Stanford: Stanford University Press, 1992), for a deconstructive analysis of the role that sexuality played in the conquest of North America.

14 For an in-depth historical analysis of the difference between the colonial concept of casta and the modern concept of race, see María Elena Martínez, *Genealogical Fictions: Limpieza de Sangre, Religion and Gender in Colonial Mexico* (Stanford: Stanford University Press, 2011).

15 See Martínez (2011), chapters 4 and 5 for analysis of *limpieza de sangre* and the creation of *republicas*.

16 See Alicia J. Tjarks, "Comparative Demographic Analysis of Texas 1777–1793," *Southwestern Historical Quarterly* 77(3) (1974): 291–338, for a comprehensive analysis of the census and ecclesiastic records according to racial and gender breakdown. According to the 1780 census, afromestizos of all castas (mulattos, lobos, and coyotes) made up 24 percent of San Antonio de Bejar (San Antonio, TX) and 33.64 percent of La Bahía (Goliad, TX), while mestizos of all castas made up 3.5 and 4 percent respectively (324–325). These censuses underrepresented afromestizo and mestizos as a portion of the population, since all soldiers were listed simply as "Spaniard," although records of the Texas garrisons indicate many mestizo and mulatto soldiers in the ranks. Europeans from countries other than Spain were also counted as "Spaniards," with their country of origin indicated as well, though they were legally forbidden from settling in the Interior Provinces at the time (297–98, 327). The 1789 census of Nuevo Santander reflects a similar make up for the city of Laredo, with 22 percent afromestizo and 17 percent mestizo (Menchaca, *Recovering History*, 116–117).

17 Indigenous peoples native to Texas and Nuevo Santander, and indigenous immigrants as well, continued to enjoy an elevated racial ranking because of the special privileges indios continued to enjoy, as evidenced by the census. Mestizo and afromestizos regularly married neophyte Indian women on the missions—as male

neophytes frequently deserted the missions—thereby gaining access to status and land reserved for them (Tjarks, "Comparative Demographic Analysis," 323).

18 This major shift in the census categories of New Spain under the Bourbon reformers is indicative of the growing influence of European liberalism on Spain. Thus "reason" no longer retains its Aristotelian meaning or the meaning it had in the Valladolid debate. In that context, reason indicated a natural human capacity, and moreover indigenous modes of political organization were considered reasonable and legitimate. Reason in "gente de razón" indicates a shared recognition of the superiority of a particular mode of political organization, in this case Spanish. We can see the rise of the nation-state liberal hegemony in the Bourbon reforms.

19 Étienne Balibar, "Racism and Nationalism," in *Race, Nation and Class: Ambiguous Identities,* ed. Étienne Balibar and Immanuel Wallerstein (New York: Verso, 1993), 37–68.

20 The original Spanish text for the epigraphs above is, "Esta misma voz que resonó en el pueblo de los Dolores el año de 1810 . . . fijo tambien la opinion pública de que la union general entre europeos y americanos, indios é Indigenas es la única base solida en que puede descansar nuestra comun felicidad . . . 12. Todos los habitantes de la Nueva España, sin distinction alguna de europeos, africanos, ni Indios son ciudadanos de esta Monarquía con opcion á todo empleo, segun su mérito y virtudes." *Plan de la Independencia de Mexico proclamada y jurada en el Pueblo de Iguala en los dias 1 y 2 de marzo de 1821 por el Serenísimo Sr. D. Agustin de Iturbide, Generalísimo Almirante, y Presidente de la Regencia Gobernadora interina del Imperio.* http://www.mexicomaxico.org/zocalo/zocaloPlanIguala.htm.

21 English translation of the the Constitution of Coahuila and Texas, Texas A&M University web site. http://www.tamu.edu/faculty/ccbn/dewitt/constitcoatex.htm.

22 Though Indian slavery was illegal under Spanish rule as well, settlers on the northern frontier were free to purchase the captives of the equestrian tribes under the guise of "Christian rescue." These captives were technically not considered slaves if acquired in this fashion. Hence the name given to these indigenous captives when "rescued" by the settlers was "creados": those "reared" or "raised" in the home under the auspices of Christianity and Spanish civilization. For a full discussion of *creados* on the northern frontier, see Weber, *Bárbaros,* 238–40.

23 As Menchaca underscores, "The difference between the new republic's proclamation[s] and Spain's previous legislation was that the new racial policy was to be enforced with deliberate speed. This meant that Indians were to be assimilated and incorporated as practicing citizens, even if they refused" (*Recovering History,* 160).

24 For a full discussion of the role of indigeneity in the formation of liberal and revolutionary Mexican citizenship, see Alan Knight, "Racism, Revolution, and *Indigenismo*: Mexico, 1910–1940," *The Idea of Race in Latin America, 1870–1940,* ed. Richard Graham (Austin: University of Texas Press, 1990), 71–113.

25 See David Lloyd and David Kazanjian for a discussion of how the political process of political emancipation and abstraction *produces* racial difference. See Lloyd, "Race under Representation," *Oxford Literary Review* 13(1–2) (1991): 62–94, for the production of racial subjectivity in Kant's theory of aesthetic value. See Kazanjian, *The Colonizing Trick: National Culture and Imperial Citizenship in Early America*

(Minneapolis: University of Minnesota Press, 2003), for the production of racial character in the nationalist thought of Jefferson.

26 According to historian David B. Adams, the state of Nuevo León alone suffered 809 incursions by the "indios bárbaros" between 1848 and 1870. More than one thousand citizens of the state were abducted, and property damage was conservatively estimated at more than 4 million pesos. See Adams, "Embattled Borderland: Northern Nuevo León and the Indios Bárbaros, 1686–1870," *Southwestern Historical Quarterly* 95(2) (1991): 220. Delay estimates that in the twelve years prior to the U.S.–Mexico War, the Comanche killed more than two thousand Mexicans in their raids. Raids were made up of one hundred to five hundred warriors and would make off with up to ten thousand heads of livestock per raiding period. Delay, "Independent Indians and the U.S.–Mexican War," *American Historical Review* 112(1) (2007): 44–45.

27 According to Hall, the Pueblos were experts at getting around this stipulation. The Pecos Pueblo, for example, successfully argued before the commission in 1826 that their communal land holdings were *private* property, and as such, their rights as citizens to their property must be respected. G. Emlen Hall, "Mexican Liberals and the Pueblo Indians, 1821–1829," *New Mexico Historical Review* 59(1) (1984): 17–18. Translation of Land Commission decision is my own.

28 Adding insult to injury, the northern states were utterly unable to assist the Apache and the Comanche in the defense of territories. The Spanish Crown had allied with the Comanche and Apache to fend off Anglo-American incursion from mutually constituted geographies of defense. The crippled Mexican federal government, and the abandoned state governments, had certainly betrayed the Comanche and Apache in this regard as well.

29 As mentioned in the introduction, the seventeen Mexican families that decamped from Laredo, Texas, in 1848 to found Nuevo Laredo in Tamaulipas took advantage of this article in the treaty, though the property rights to their lands that remained on the U.S. side of the border were repeatedly violated or impeded.

30 *Oxford English Dictionary Online*, James McCraken, ed. (Oxford: Oxford University Press, 2012).

31 Article 10 stipulates that all titles issued by any and all Mexican authorities must be respected, including those existing in Texas before its independence in 1836. The article clarified the property rights of annexed Mexicans, although it is unlikely that its inclusion would have protected these rights.

32 In Spanish, the article reads, "En atención de que en una gran parte de los territorios que por el presente Tratado van a quedar para lo futuro dentro de los límites de los Estados Unidos, se haya actualmente ocupada por tribus salvajes que han de estar en adelante bajo la exclusiva autoridad de los Estados Unidos, y cuyas incursiones sobre los distritos mexicanos serían en extremos perjudiciales; está solemnemente convenido que el mismo Gobierno contendrá las indicadas incursiones por medio de la fuerza, siempre que así sea necesario; y cuando no pudiere prevenirlas castigará y escarmentará a los invasores, exigiéndoles además la debida reparación: todo del mismo modo y con la misma diligencia y energía con que obraría, si las incursiones se hubiesen meditado o ejecutado sobre territorios suyos o contra sus propios ciudadanos."

33 For an example of this perspective in history, see David Montejano, *Anglos and Mexicans in the Making of Texas, 1836–1986* (Austin: University of Texas Press, 1987); in popular culture, see Gloría Anzaldúa, *Borderlands/La Frontera: The New Mestiza* (San Francisco, CA: 1987), and Rodolfo "Corky" González, *I Am Joaquin* (New York: Bantam, 1972).

34 Early maps of the Republic of Mexico specified the "Apachería" and the "Comanchería" as part of the Mexican nation, as spaces on the map that were equivalent to the states and adjacent to them. The designation and naming of these areas as such suggests an early acceptance of layered sovereignties within the nation.

35 For a discussion of this shared history of struggle that refuses to collapse the differences in the social formation of Native Americans and Chicana/os, see Rodolfo O. De la Garza et al., *Chicanos and Native Americans: The Territorial Minorities* (Englewood Cliffs, NJ: Prentice-Hall, 1973).

36 Afromestizos were forced to move back to Mexico as the legislatures of the annexed territories, often still dominated by Mexicans, were nevertheless unable to protect their freedom from enslavement or their properties from dispossession by the Anglo-American settlers who flooded the annexed territories. See Laura Gómez, *Manifest Destinies: The Making of the Mexican American Race* (New York: New York University Press, 2007).

37 As Ramón Saldívar explains in his essay, "The Borderlands of Culture: Américo Paredes's *George Washington Gómez*," in *Mexican Americans in Texas History: Selected Essays,* ed. Emilio Zamora, Cynthia Orozco, and Rodolfo Rocha (Austin: Texas Historical Association, 2000), 175–186: "[The novel] takes especially as its moment the 1915 uprising in South Texas by Mexican Americans attempting to create a Spanish-speaking republic of the Southwest. Dismissed as 'Mexican Bandits' by Anglo historians, the *sediciosos* (seditionists) . . . were acting under a carefully considered revolutionary manifesto, the 'Plan de San Diego,' that called for the union of Texas Mexicans with the American Indians, African Americans and Asian Americans to create an independent border republic of the Southwest."

CHAPTER 4. **Adjudicating Exception**

1 Early in the twentieth century Mexican American civil rights activists did pursue redress under the equal protection clause of the Fourteenth Amendment as a "Mexican race" deserving of judicial protection from discrimination, similar to African Americans. The superior courts shut down this strategy by repeatedly finding the plaintiffs to be members of the white race, facilitating further discrimination, undoubtedly part of the courts' intent. See Stephen H. Wilson, "Brown Over 'Other White': Mexican Americans' Legal Arguments and Litigation Strategy in School Desegregation Lawsuits," *Law and History Review* 21(1) (2003): 145–194, and "Response: Tracking the Shifting Racial Identity of Mexican Americans," *Law and History Review* 21(1) (2003): 211–213; Claire Sheridan, " 'Another White Race': Mexican Americans and the Paradox of Whiteness in Jury Selection," *Law and History Review* 21(1) (2003): 109–144, and "Response: Cultural Racism and the Construction of

Identity," *Law and History Review* 21(1) (2003): 207–210; and Ariela Gross, "Texas Mexicans and the Politics of Whiteness," *Law and History Review* 21(1) (2003): 195–207.

2 See Ariela Gross, " 'The Caucasian Clock': Mexican Americans and the Politics of Whiteness in the Twentieth-Century Southwest," *Georgetown Law Journal* 95 (January 2007): 337–392, and "Texas Mexicans"; Kevin R. Johnson, "*Hernandez v. Texas*: Legacies of Justice and Injustice," *Chicano-Latino Law Review* 25(1) (2005): 153–231; Stephen H. Wilson, "Brown Over 'Other White,' " "Response," and "Some Are Born White, Some Achieve Whiteness, and Some Have Whiteness Thrust upon Them: Mexican Americans and the Politics of Racial Classification in the Federal Judicial Bureaucracy, Twenty-Five Years after *Hernandez v. Texas*," *Chicano-Latino Law Review* 25(1): 201–239; and Clare Sheridan, " 'Another White Race' " and "Response." For a transcript of the panel discussion including Neil Foley and Ian Haney López on the topic of the "other white group" strategy used in *Hernandez v. Texas*, see Marcos Guerra, ed., "Symposium: Hernandez v. Texas: A 50th Anniversary Celebration," in *Texas Hispanic Journal of Law and Policy* 11 (fall 2005): 10–42.

3 Gross, " 'The Caucasian Clock,' " summarizes the debate thusly, "Some scholars portray whiteness claims as primarily strategic, while others see them as a deeper impulse towards assimilation and rejection of other people of color . . . the critics have . . . adopted the perspective of the 1970s Chicano movement, taking the previous generation to task for its lack of racial pride and refusal to join coalitions with African Americans" (343–344). This perspective blinds Chicana/o scholars from recognizing the creative strategies for preserving mestizaje or racial inclusion by this previous generation of activists.

4 In *Ah Yup* the court ruled against the right of a Chinese man to naturalize; in *Camille* against a Canadian man of white and Indian descent. Paschal found *Ah Yup* "the ablest and best considered case." T. M. Paschal, Brief, *In re Rodriguez* (1897), 340.

5 In this interpretation of the *Ah Yup* decision, Paschal is closely following the opinion of Judge Lorenzo Sawyer against Ah Yup. From that opinion: "Many other senators spoke pro and con on the question, this being the point of the contest, and these extracts being fair examples of the opposing opinions. . . . It was finally defeated (the amendment to strike the word 'white' from the naturalization laws); and the amendment cited, extending the right of naturalization to the African only, was adopted. It is clear from these proceedings that congress retained the word 'white' in the naturalization laws for the sole purpose of excluding the Chinese from the right of naturalization. . . . Thus, whatever latitudinarian construction might otherwise have been given to the term 'white person,' it is entirely clear that congress intended by this legislation to exclude Mongolians from the right of naturalization" (cited in *Rodriguez*, 349). Though Paschal followed Sawyer's interpretation of the legislative debate, he nevertheless reinvented Sawyer's opinion when he interpreted it as consequently permitting the naturalization of Native Americans.

6 From Justice Gray's 1884 opinion: "Though the plaintiff alleges that he 'had fully and completely surrendered himself to the jurisdiction of the United States,' he does not allege that the United States accepted his surrender, or that he has ever been naturalized, or taxed, or in any way recognized or treated as a citizen, by the

State or by the United States. Nor is it contended by his counsel that there is any statute or treaty that makes him a citizen." *Elk v. Wilkins* 112 U.S. 94 (1884).

7   Elk performed the trope of the quintessential Indian who has ceded ground, but to no avail. He had surrendered himself to U.S. culture. Importantly, even his ceding of ground needed to conform to U.S. interests. Elk had no actual ground left to concede to the U.S. government except his self-possession. However, his racial embodiment excluded him from the ground of (white) racial geography. In short, the United States was happy to incorporate his land but not his Indian difference into its racial geography.

8   Should this interpretation of an Indian's right to naturalize fail to convince the superior court judge, Paschal went on to argue that Rodriguez could scarcely be considered an Indian anymore given Mexico's history of intermingling, as cited in the epigraph. Paschal was clearly playing all the legal angles on behalf of Rodriguez, but this should not lead us to discount his impassioned plea for justice on behalf of Native Americans, nor his equally impassioned screed against the "Mongolian hordes" in the name of justice.

9   From McGown's brief: "On April 29, 1878, in the case of In re Ah Yup, 1 Fed. Cas.223, Mr. Justice Sawyer said: 'As ordinarily used in the United States, one would scarcely fail to understand that the party employing the words 'white person' would intend a person of the Caucasian race.' On November 2, 1880, in the case of In re Camille, Mr. Justice Deady, 6 Fed 256, after quoting from the opinion in the Ah Yup Case, used this language: 'In all classification of mankind hitherto color has been a controlling circumstance, and for the reason Indians have never, ethnologically, been considered white persons, nor included in any such designation. From the first our naturalization laws only applied to the people who had settled the country, the European or white race.'" (*Rodriguez*, 345).

10 From Evans's brief, "If such a treaty did exist before that date, it is wiped out by the act of 1870, which covers the whole ground" (*Rodriguez*, 347).

11 As Ian Haney López has cogently argued in *White by Law: The Legal Construction of Race* (New York: New York University Press, 1996), legal rulings in prerequisite cases not only sanctioned racial restrictions regarding citizenship, these rulings give racial categories new lives: "The courts that ruled on the race of 'Mongolians,' 'whites,' and 'Hindues' validated those racial categories, giving them prestige of law and rendering them that much more credible as categories of difference.... The prerequisite statute required that each person seeking citizenship be assigned a race. The declaration that Ah Yup was a 'Mongolian' made it impossible to imagine him in different racial terms, much less completely nonracial ones" (124).

12 In his 1998 article, "Race, Ethnicity, Erasure: The Salience of Race to LatCrit Theory," *La Raza Law Journal* 10: 1143–1211, Haney López contends that the Texas court in this case "recognized persons of Mexican descent as 'white persons' . . . in the context of federal naturalization law, under which Whiteness was a prerequisite for citizenship." While white for the purposes of law, Judge Maxey explicitly says that Rodriguez is *not* white on ethnological grounds (1170). This is an important distinction made by the Maxey court that conditions Mexican whiteness as always bearing the trace of the indio bárbaro. Haney López's interpretation of Maxey's decision is

286   NOTES FOR CHAPTER FOUR

symptomatic of this "Faustian pact," LatCrit mode of determining all Mexican legal activism before the Chicano period as anachronistically contaminated by aspirational whiteness.

13 Though Maxey agrees that these decisions exclude Asians and Indians from naturalization, the tone of Maxey's evaluations of these decisions, especially in light of the Fourteenth Amendment, suggest he disagrees with the barring of Asians and American Indians from naturalization.

14 Challenging Marx's analysis of the privatization of the inequity of difference in the achievement of liberal freedom, *In re Rodriguez* shows us how the Mexican carries his racial difference with him into the *public* sphere in the very process of becoming citizen, of attaining political emancipation. See Karl Marx, "On the Jewish Question," in *The Marx-Engels Reader*, ed. Robert C. Tucker (New York: W. W. Norton, 1978), 26–52.

15 In LatCrit studies, *In re Rodriguez* is read as the inauguration of Mexicans' white racial status in the United States. If Mexicans are granted the right to naturalize, and only whites and blacks had this right under the 1870 Naturalization Act, then Mexicans are ipso facto white according to the court, regardless of the fact that the decision did not hinge on race. See, for example, the special issue, "Forum: Whiteness and Others: Mexican Americans and American Law," *Law and History Review* 21(1) (spring 2003). Rather, by parsing the language in the Maxey opinion, we see that Maxey never offers a determination of Rodriguez's race, but instead evades the question. Rodriguez's racial character remains enigmatic to Maxey. If Maxey accepts any racial categorization of Rodriguez, it is his own, seeming to take Rodriguez at his word that he is a "full-blooded Mexican." Ironically self-evident to Maxey and LatCrit scholars alike is the "fact" that Rodriguez could not possibly have any African ancestry: "It is certain he is not an African," Maxey exclaims. Why is this certain? Twenty to 30 percent of the settlers on the northern frontier were afromestizo after all. What would it have signified to have opened up the door to naturalization for Mexicans through their afromestizo lineage? Perhaps for Maxey to have contemplated the possibility of Rodriguez having African ancestry would have made it impossible for him to recognize the "Indian" in Rodriguez's appearance.

16 Though opposed to Forbes in sentiment and implication, Maxey's reading of Rodriguez's racial proclamations shares certain historical preconceptions with Forbes's "The Mexican Heritage of Aztlán (The Southwest), to 1821," unpublished essay. As per the court's questions, Rodriguez's only option for acknowledging his indigenous heritage was acknowledging the Nahuas as his ancestors, given that the Toltec culture had disappeared centuries before the Aztec empire. *If Nahuas, then indigenous*, was the deductive reasoning of the court. Perhaps Rodriguez's answer would have been different if the court representatives had asked if his ancestors were Opate or Pima, as there is no reason to assume the term "aborigines" would have made any sense to Rodriguez.

17 The full text of the 1849 California State Constitution is available at the website http://www.sos.ca.gov/archives/collections/1849/full-text.htm.

18 As Menchaca explains, "Between 1850 and 1913 the citizenship laws extended to the Indians in New Mexico were ambiguous, and . . . vacillated between liberal and racist positions. The differing attitudes toward the Indians appear to have been strongly

NOTES FOR CHAPTER FOUR   287

associated with the shifts of political power from the Mexican mestizos to the Anglo Americans. Martha Menchaca, "Chicano Indianism: A Historical Account of Racial Repression in the United States," *American Ethnologist* 20(3) (1993): 589.

19 The New Mexico Supreme Court appended a lower court decision, *United States v. Ortiz*, to their own because of the similarity between the cases. In that case, the judge made explicit the task of determining the proper character of the Pueblo Indians, especially in comparison with "wild" North American Indians: "Now let us inquire as to the character of the pueblo Indians" (452). This court determined, after a detailed review of Pueblo religious, economic, and political practices, that "they are Indians only in features, complexion and a few of their habits; in all other respects superior to all but a few of the civilized Indian tribes of the country, and equal to the most civilized thereof" (454). This case appears to have established the parameters of judgment for the Supreme Court and also serves as discursive precursor to Judge Maxey's decision, where features and complexion persist, even as indigenous character is presumably surpassed.

20 Fee simple indicates that the property holder owns all rights over an estate, including the right to sell or transfer the property to another.

21 Despite Spain's superior documentary skill, the court decision in *Lucero* actually invalidated Spanish colonial rule in Mexico: "The Spanish rule in Mexico was partial and unjust" (*United States v. Lucero*, 430). Without any practical or evidentiary reason, the court decision rehearsed the entire history of Spanish colonialism in Mexico as Black Legend, exercised with all the cruelties and "privileges of royalty" (430). This history stands in stark contrast to the industrious settlement of the Anglo-Europeans in the north whose settlement was blessed by providence, referenced at the beginning of the decision. Whereas the Anglo-Americans clear brush and cultivate the soil to support themselves, the Spanish and their "favorites" live off of "the great body of the Mexican people, equally honest and more industrious than themselves" (430). The decision suggests it was only proper for Spanish despotism to give way to U.S. white settler colonialism—the proper expression of sovereignty as possession bestowed by providence on the United States.

22 Laura Gómez in *Manifest Destinies: The Making of the Mexican American Race* (New York: New York University Press, 2007), writes about this case, "The more dominant strand of this [court] reasoning, was the drawing of a bright line between Pueblos as 'civilized' and other Indians as 'savage'" (95). I am indebted to Gómez for this line of argument, though we draw rather different analyses of the period.

23 From the New Mexico Museum of Art website, "The result of this [1876] decision was that individual Indians sold 30% or more of Pueblo lands to non-Indians during ensuing decades." http://online.nmartmuseum.org/nmhistory/people-places-and -politics/statehood/history-statehood.html.

24 New Mexico's Statehood: One Hundred Years of Enchantment website. Commission of Public Record-State Records Center and Archive. http://www .newmexicohistory.org/centennial/documents/NMConstitution.pdf.

25 Illustrative of the ongoing linguistic foreignness of Latina/os within the confines of the law, we have the decision reached by the Supreme Court in *Hernandez v. New York*. In this 1991 case, the Supreme Court "approved a prosecutor's use of peremptory

challenges to strike Latinos from the jury, based on the 'race-neutral' explanation that Spanish speakers would not accept the translator's version of the trial testimony" (Gross, "'The Caucasian Clock,'" 339). Gross explains that this decision is, from one perspective, entirely consistent with the equal protection guaranteed by the Fourteenth Amendment, as it protects against discrimination on the basis of race and national origin, but "allows discrimination on other rational bases, such as language or culture" (339). Instead, she argues, seemingly neutral cultural characteristics such as language are used to "cloak" racism. This is particularly true with regard to Mexican Americans and Latina/os, Gross contends, because they were rendered legally white by the TGH: "This unique legal status [white by treaty] meant that the far-reaching exclusion of Mexican Americans from full social and political citizenship had to be justified on cultural, rather than racial grounds" (341). This displacement of race onto culture also works to render Mexican Americans persistently foreign. In *Hernandez v. New York*, for example, rather than potentially augmenting justice, the knowledge of Spanish was seen as subverting the language of justice, which the court decided must transpire in officially sanctioned English. Cultural differences, here telescoped onto linguistic difference, are interpreted as, most benignly, hindering assimilation into the political demos, or at worst, as a sinister impeachment of civic life, as the court decided in *Hernandez v. New York*.

26 The case was neither the first case brought on behalf of segregated Mexican American children in the Southwest, nor the first legal victory of this type. Nevertheless, it is considered the most significant because it was precedent setting and provoked the rescinding of state segregation laws by the California legislature. This case is also important as a sign of early legislative cooperation between blacks and Mexican Americans, as Thurgood Marshall, Robert L. Carter, and Loren Miller authored an amicus brief filed on behalf of the NAACP. In legal scholarship, this amicus brief is considered Marshall's "test case" for the NAACP's attempt to overturn *Plessy v. Ferguson* (Fredrick P. Aguirre, "*Mendez v. Westminster School District*: How It Affected *Brown v. Board of Education*," *Journal of Hispanic Higher Education* 4: 5). The first NAACP brief filed in *Brown V. Board of Education* borrowed heavily from the brief filed in *Mendez*. Marshall borrowed language from Judge McCormick's decision when he argued *Brown* before the Supreme Court as well. See Christopher Hilger, "A Local Desegregation Case—Eight Years before *Brown v. Board of Education*," *Orange County Lawyer* (June 2001): 2–3.

27 It is important to underscore that children of Mexican nationals also benefited from the victories in such legal actions, as the school administrations did not differentiate between Mexican Americans and Mexican nationals in their segregation, and subsequently, desegregation efforts.

28 After almost twenty years of nebulous status, the act finally granted citizenship to Puerto Ricans who were annexed after the 1898 Spanish-American war; although the act also established Puerto Rico as a (separate but equal) territory of the United States, with its own bill of rights and branches of government.

29 In 1929, a number of clubs composed of both Mexicans and Mexican Americans came together to form LULAC. At its founding conference in Corpus Christi, TX,

Mexican American leaders voted to limit membership in the organization to U.S. citizens. Reportedly half of their audience left the conference in protest. Despite this rocky and divisive start, LULAC succeeded in organizing Mexican Americans. At the pinnacle of its organizing success in the 1940s and 1950s LULAC had tens of thousands of members in eighty dues-paying chapters from California to Louisiana. These chapters were instrumental in waging the civil rights struggle in the courts, funding efforts and hiring lawyers across the Southwest.

30 The *Mendez* decision led the California legislature to repeal segregation laws against Asians and Indians. Thus we witness an agreeable flux in the mediating function of Mexican American mestizaje before the law, mediating for inclusion rather than exclusion. Once again, the decision and its aftermath underscore the pivot that is Mexican enfranchisement in the accomplishment of the political demos.

31 See the 2005 special issue of the *Chicano-Latino Law Review* on the case, "Commemorating the 50th Anniversary of *Hernandez v. Texas*" volume 25, in particular articles by Foley, Haney López, and Olivas. Also see "Forum: Whiteness and Others: Mexican Americans and American Law," "Comment," and "Response" in *Law and History Review* 21.1 (spring 2003): 109–211. Also see María Josefina Saldaña-Portillo, "'How Many Mexicans Is a Horse Worth?' The League of United Latin American Citizens, Desegregation Cases, and Chicano Historiography," *South Atlantic Quarterly* 107(4) (2008): 809–831, for a counterargument to the "aspirational whiteness" or "Faustian pact with whiteness" critique.

32 As argued by Claire Sheridan, the enactment of civic duty itself conferred equality. Hence the focus on the right to serve as jurors as a way of conferring political emancipation: "Jury service was viewed by Mexican American civic leaders as vital to securing their political and civil rights. The connection between civil and political rights and social equality was made explicit, and they encouraged Mexican American citizens to exercise their rights in order to influence the political process" (Sheridan, "'Another White Race,'" 116).

33 Letter from George I. Sánchez, to Roger N. Baldwin (August 27. 1958) in George I. Sánchez Papers, Box 31, Folder 8 (Benson Latin American Collection, General Libraries, University of Texas at Austin) (emphasis in the original).

34 Paul de Man, *Allegories of Reading: Figural Language in Rousseau, Nietzsche, Rilke, and Proust* (New Haven: Yale University Press, 1979), 301.

35 In a special issue of the *Chicano-Latino Law Review* commemorating the 50th anniversary of *Hernandez v. Texas*, Neil Foley chastises Sánchez: "Perhaps Marshall had good reason not to [consult with LULAC on desegregation cases]. Marshall, after all, did not bless the law that granted white privilege to Mexican Americans but denied it to blacks, nor could he bless a strategy that opposed segregation on the narrow ground that Mexicans could not be segregated from whites." Foley, "Over the Rainbow: *Hernandez v. Texas, Brown v. Board of Education,* and Black v. Brown," *Chicano-Latino Law Review* 25(1) (spring 2005): 151. As a historian necessarily adjudicating the success or failure of civil rights coalitions, distributing blame as the historical scorekeeper must, Foley cannot read the record for its ironic specificity. Instead, he mistakenly reads this passage from the letter as more evidence of the Mexican Americans' racial treason.

CHAPTER 5. **Losing It!**

1 Chicano Park, in the heart of Logan Heights, San Diego, is an example of the reclamation of space by the Chicana/o movement. Logan Heights is one of the oldest predominantly Mexican American neighborhoods in California, dating back to the nineteenth century. After Interstate 5 and the Coronado Bay Bridge on-ramp bifurcated the neighborhood in 1963 and 1969 respectively, the residents took over the space beneath the pylons with the assistance of Chicana/o artists, transforming it into a neighborhood park in June, 1969. The residents accomplished this primarily through the painting of murals on the pylons under direction of the artists. Applying almost exclusively "Aztec" iconography and generic Mexican representations of Indians, residents remade the space through the representation of themselves as part of Chicana/o Aztlán, turning the park into a gathering space for both political and recreational purposes. The park even includes a gazebo in the shape and style of a pyramid. A second recuperation of space through indigenous iconography took place with La Raza Unida Party's victories in Crystal City and Cotulla, Texas, in the early 1970s. The party, predicated on the representation of Mexican Americans as united through their indigenous heritage, successfully took over the city councils and mayors' offices, transforming the nature of politics in Texas in a way that litigation alone had never succeeded in doing.

2 See John R. Chávez, "Aztlán, Cibola, and Frontier New Spain" and Ramón A. Guitiérrez, "Aztlán, Montezuma, and New Mexico: The Political Uses of American Indian Mythology" for an analysis of Aztlán as a concept developed out of the previous indigenous histories of the border area. Both are in *Aztlán: Essays on the Chicano Homeland*, ed. Rudolfo A. Anaya and Francisco Lomeli (Albuquerque: University of New Mexico Press, 1989), 49–71, 172–190.

3 Elsewhere I have argued that *On the Road* provided the reader with a literary mapping of the segregated and discriminatory geography of the United States in the forties and fifties through Sal Paradise's narration of his travels in the Southwest and Mexico. Kerouac demonstrated the melancholic, expansionist nature of Sal's (white) American freedom, incorporating the racial other into his own melancholic (Beat) ego, precisely because this other was lost to him as loved object through segregation and discrimination. Sal is thus recentered in the novel as a consequence of his ruthless incorporation of the "Beat" experience of racial others, even when this identification was performed from a sympathetic or empathetic position. Sal's appropriation of the experience of the racial other was itself a form of literary dispossession as lost racial others were reduced to the abstract ideals of U.S. colonialism. Saldaña-Portillo, " 'On the Road' with Che and Jack: Melancholia and the Legacy of Colonial Racial Geographies in the Americas," *New Formations: A Journal of Culture/Theory/Politics* 47: 87–108.

4 Acosta insisted he coinvented gonzo journalism with Hunter S. Thompson. Certainly from the style of his articles, he was a masterful practitioner of the form. When *Playboy* first attributed "gonzo journalism" to Thompson in 1973, Acosta sent an angry letter to the Forum: "Your November issue . . . on Mr. Hunter S. Thompson as the creator of Gonzo Journalism, which you say he both created and

named. . . . Well, sir, I beg to take issue with you. . . . In point of fact, Doctor Duke and I—the world famous Doctor Gonzo—together we both, hand in hand, sought out the teachings and curative powers of the world famous Savage Henry, the Scag Baron of Las Vegas, and in point of fact the term *and* methodology of reporting crucial events under fire and drugs, which are of course essential to any good writing in this age of confusion—all this I say came from out of the mouth of our teacher who is also known by the name of Owl." *Oscar Zeta Acosta: The Uncollected Works*, ed. Ilan Stavans (Houston: Arte Público Press, 1996), 109. The character of Gonzo in *Fear and Loathing in Las Vegas* is modeled after Acosta, who accompanied Thompson on the trip.

5 Acosta's heterosexist documentation of events offers the reader an unadorned view of the *indigenismo* of the Chicano nationalist movement as rendered by one of its principal architects—himself. For this reason this egregious offender of feminist principles remains a focus of Chicana/o criticism, providing crucial insight into the geography of Aztlán. For a feminist critique of the heteronormativity and misogyny of the Chicano nationalist era and its cultural production (like that of Acosta), see Cherríe Moraga, Gloria Anzaldúa, Sonia Saldívar-Hull, Chela Sandoval, Norma Cantú, Rosalinda Fregoso, and Norma Alarcón, among other Chicana feminists.

6 Founded in 1967, *El Grito: A Journal of Contemporary Mexican American Thought* was the "first national Chicano literary magazine. Behind its appearance lay . . . [a] desire to create a magazine through which 'la gente humilde', or the common folk could express themselves" (Carlos Muñoz, *Youth, Identity, Power: The Chicano Movement* [London: Verso, 1989], 144). Acosta's explanatory prose style suggests that he well understood his role as educator and rabble-rouser.

7 Acosta was among the first two Mexican American attorneys to finally abandon the precedent set by *Hernandez* in favor of that set by *Brown*, that is, abandoning the "other white" legal rationale in favor of the rationale that Mexican Americans were a group akin to blacks. The other lawyer was none other than James DeAnda, a lead attorney in *Hernandez*. In 1968 DeAnda began litigation in a class-action suit against the Corpus Christi Independent School District (CCISD). In *Cisneros v. CCISD* DeAnda argued "the *Brown* rationale should apply to—and condemn as a clear denial of equal protection—the widespread segregation of Mexican Americans" (cited in Wilson 2003a, 181). DeAnda argued Mexican Americans constituted a de jure minority under *Brown*, but hedged his bets in his closing argument, suggesting a line of reasoning for deciding the case under the *Hernandez* precedent as well. As Wilson puts it, DeAnda "resorted to the lawyer's ancient practice of arguing in the alternative" (185). DeAnda won his case, permanently transforming Mexican American civil rights litigation. The Fifth Circuit Court of Appeals upheld the lower court's decision in *Cisneros*, affirming that Mexican Americans constituted a minority equivalent to African Americans.

8 See Guillermo Lux and Maurilio E. Vigil, "Return to Aztlán: The Chicano Recovers His Indian Past," in *Aztlán*, ed. Anaya and Lomeli, 93–110, for a full discussion of Vasconcelos's influence.

9 Rather than envisioning the actual biological amalgamation into one super race, Vasconcelos used the term as a concept-metaphor. The merging of the best cultural

292 NOTES FOR CHAPTER FIVE

characteristics associated with the different "races" into a cultural mestizaje would produce an idealized form of political citizenship in Mexico.

10 This erasure never came to pass, clearly, because of the concerted efforts of indigenous peoples. Agrarian reform, however, also enabled the reproduction of indigenous peoples and life ways. Though aimed at the peasant classes with developmentalist ends, revolutionary agrarian reform secured indigenous classes economic autonomy and security at the level of the community. For a full discussion of Vasconcelos's essay, see Saldaña-Portillo, *The Revolutionary Imagination in the Americas and the Age of Development* (Durham, NC: Duke University Press, 2003), chapter 6.

11 Forty years later, the success of Acosta and el movimiento's transformation of racial consciousness is evident, but so too is the heterotemporality of racial geographies. In the 2010 U.S. Census, members of the "Hispanic" population were asked to identify themselves both by national origin and by race. Under the options for race chosen by Latinos were "White," "Black or African American," "American Indian or Alaska Native," "Asian," "Native Hawaiian and Other Pacific Islander," and "Some other race." Fifty-three percent of the Latino population opted for "white," reflecting a profound understanding of the Machiavellian terms of assimilation into the U.S. geography of race. Nevertheless, 37 percent opted for "some other race." This figure, combined with the remaining 6 percent of those who chose two or more races, suggests that nearly half of all Latinos refused to conform with the schematic nature of U.S. racial categories, opting for Latin American racial logics, these now encroaching on the census. Latinos identified as multiply raced at a ratio of 3:1, as only 2 percent of non-Hispanics reported more than one race. See Humes et al., "Overview of Race and Hispanic Origin: 2010," (Washington, DC: U.S. Census Bureau, 2010), 6. This self-identification as "some other race" or as multiracial by almost half the U.S. Latino population would be unimaginable today without the influence of the Chicana/o movement, but it is just as unimaginable without the influence of Mexico's racial geography of mestizaje.

12 For an analysis of the racial dynamics of the Mexican revolutionary period, see Alan Knight, "Racism, Revolution, and *Indigenismo*: Mexico, 1910–1940," in *The Idea of Race in Latin America, 1870–1940*, ed. Richard Graham (Austin: University of Texas Press, 1990), 71–113; see also Saldaña-Portillo, "The Politics of Silence: Development and Difference in Zapatismo" in *The Revolutionary Imagination*, 191–258.

13 The defendants in the East L.A. Thirteen case included David Sánchez, at nineteen the prime minister of the Brown Berets; Eliezer Risco, at thirty-one the founder of the community paper, *La Raza*; Joe Razo, at twenty-nine Risco's coeditor at the paper; Moctezuma Esparza, at nineteen a leader of the United Mexican American Students (UMAS); Gilbert Cruz Olmeda, at twenty-three Brown Berets chairman and decorated Vietnam veteran; Sal Castro, a thirty-three-year-old teacher at Lincoln High School, one of the principal schools involved in the walkouts.

14 All the judges were men, hence my use of the masculine pronoun. For a full analysis of Acosta's motion to quash the indictment, see Haney López's *Racism on Trial: The Chicano Fight for Justice* (Cambridge, MA: Harvard University Press, 2003), and "Institutional Racism: Judicial Conduct and a New Theory of Racial Discrimination," *Yale Law Journal* 109 (1999–2000): 1717–1884.

NOTES FOR CHAPTER FIVE   293

15 Hereafter "Motion." The full citation from Haney López (1999–2000): Motion to Quash Indictment, *People v. Castro*, No. A-232902 (Cal. Super. Ct. 1968) (on file with the Oscar Zeta Acosta Papers, California Ethnic and Multicultural Archives, Department of Special Collections, University of California, Santa Barbara).

16 All quotations from "Motion," cited from Haney López's "Appendix A: Excerpts from the *East L.A. 13* Transcript Regarding Grand Jury Nominees," (1999/2000, 1845–1875).

17 I would like to thank the American Studies Working Group at Haverford College who workshopped an early draft of this chapter. In particular I would like to thank Andrew Freidman, Gustavus Stadler, and Jennifer Harford Vargas for their generous sharing of their ideas on this section of the argument.

18 All quotations in this paragraph and the following are from the transcript for the "Motion," cited here from Haney López's "Appendix C: The Cross-Section Requirement" (1999–2000, 1877–1883).

19 Thanks to Gus Stadler for drawing my attention to the function of laboring in making one visible in landscape, and to the specific ways in which Native Americans cannot represent labor in the American context, in contradistinction to Mexico, where they are the epitome of the laboring body. Thanks also to Andrew Freidman for pointing out how the figure of the Eskimo in the testimony linked two eras of U.S. colonial expansion discussed in the next paragraph.

20 As Haney López affirms in *Racism on Trial*, "Acosta and the defendants conceived of these cases as vehicles to promote the Chicano movement . . . to use the courts as a stage upon which to unmask judicial bias against Mexicans. Even more basic than this, however, the defendants, first and foremost, would seek to prove through their trials that Mexicans existed as a subordinate group in the American Southwest. In the end, whether they convinced the judges who sat over them mattered less than whether they convinced the Mexican community as a whole, and themselves in particular" (40).

21 Mimeographed copy provided to me from the private archive of historian Ernesto Chávez.

22 For discussion of Acosta's literary relationship to this previous generation of experimental writers, see Rachel Adams, "Hipsters and *jipitecas*: Literary Countercultures on Both Sides of the Border," *American Literary History* 16(1) (2004): 58–84; and Michael Hames-García, "Dr. Gonzo's Carnival: The Testimonial Satires of Oscar Zeta Acosta," *American Literature* 72(3) (2000): 463–493.

23 True to the allusion in the title, his autobiography strives toward *The Autobiography of Malcolm X* rather than *On the Road* or *Electric Kool-Aid Acid Test*.

24 Reading only the third scene of this literary triptych—the fight with Junior before the blue-eyed Miss It—critic Genaro M. Padilla suggests that it is only when Junior and the other Okies hail Acosta as a "fucking black nigger" that young Oscar's "attention is drawn to a blue-eyed girl who is watching." The Okies' racist epithets and the girl's eyes are reflections that alert boy Acosta to a racially "divided world" in which Oscar is required to identify as white or black, despite the complexity of his heritage (1984, 247–48). Despite the inadequate nature of these reflections, Acosta

is not allowed to identify with the white girl who sees him only as smelly and dirty. Thus Acosta must align his identification with the denigrated term. While Padilla fails to mention Acosta's minstrelsy as well, unlike these other critics he reads boy Acosta's affirmation "I *am* a nigger, after all" not as a moment of racial solidarity but as Oscar's awakening to a racially dichotomous interpellation that is more powerful than any aspirations or dreams the boy may have about his future.

25 The very meaning of the contemporary term *indigenous* suggests a rootedness in the land, but indigenous identities in the Americas are also mobile and adroit in their migrations, both those that colonialism forced on them and those that derived from other motivations. This sense of indigenous peoples being of one place is terribly important for political purposes, but what might come of recognizing the uprootedness of indigenous experience in the Americas that is itself a consequence of colonialism, nationalisms, but also migration patterns that today are largely motivated by economic reasons. Does the migration of an indigenous person from southern Mexico to northern New York make them any less indigenous to the Americas?

CONCLUSION. The Afterlives of the *Indio Bárbaro*

1 A joint publication by the Center for International Policy, the Latin American Working Group Education Fund, and the Washington Office on Latin America estimates seventy thousand Mexicans killed as a consequence of Calderón's policy over the course of his six-year term (2006–2012). See Isacson et. al., *A Time to Listen: Trends in U.S. Security Assistance to Latin America and the Caribbean* (Washington, DC: Center for International Policy, Latin America Working Group Education Fund, and Washington Office on Latin America, 2013), 4.

2 See Dario Lopez et al., "U.S. Military Expands Its Drug War in Latin America," *USA Today*, February 3, 2013. http://www.usatoday.com/story/news/world/2013/02/03/us-expands-drug-war-latin-america/1887481/.

3 No evidence was ever produced by the Reagan administration of Sandinista smuggling activity, and today Nicaragua remains the one country in Central America relatively free of drug trafficking and gang violence due to the effectiveness of the Sandinista reforms of the military and the police during the party's ten years in power (1979–1989). In fact, while the United States is the primary destination for families evading drug violence in Honduras, El Salvador, and Guatemala, Nicaragua is the second destination of choice. See Robert Parry, "The Warning in Gary Webb's Death" for a discussion of the connections between the Contra, the CIA, and cocaine shipments through Noriega's Panama. *Consortium News*, December 9, 2011. http://consortiumnews.com/2011/12/09/the-warning-in-gary-webbs-death/.

4 David Huey, "The U.S. War on Drugs in Latin America and Its Legacy," *The Guardian*, February 3, 2014. http://www.theguardian.com/global-development-professionals-network/2014/feb/03/us-war-on-drugs-impact-in-latin-american.

5 For an analysis of the diversion of U.S. monies from Plan Colombia to counterinsurgency in Colombia's civil war, and the proven connections between U.S. military

NOTES FOR CONCLUSION   295

aid and the human rights abuses and assassinations of civilians, see Douglas Stokes, "Better Lead than Bread? A Critical Analysis of the US's Plan Colombia," *Civil Wars* 4(2) (summer 2001): 59–78. See also Ellen O'Grady, "Petraeus Statement on Plan Colombia at Odds with Reality," Center for Economic and Policy Research, October 3, 2013. http://www.cepr.net/index.php/blogs/the-americas-blog/petraeus-statement-on-plan-colombia-at-odds-with-reality.

6 Currently the Colombian military trains the Central American militaries in counterinsurgency and drug interdiction, transferring the technologies of war learned from the U.S. military through Plan Colombia.

7 See Isacson et al., *A Time to Listen,* for a full discussion of this shift in strategy and its consequences for budgetary transparency and citizen oversight.

8 Lopez et al., "U.S. Military Expands Its Drug War."

9 The first sentence of the Border Patrol's Mission Statement, posted on the official web site of the Department of Homeland Security, states, "The priority mission of the Border Patrol is preventing terrorists and terrorists' weapons, including weapons of mass destruction, from entering the United States. Undaunted by scorching desert heat or freezing northern winters, they work tirelessly as vigilant protectors of our Nation's borders." http://www.cbp.gov/border-security/along-us-borders/overview.

10 Department of Homeland Security, "Border Security Results," official web site, November 1, 2013. http://www.dhs.gov/border-security-results.

11 Department of Homeland Security, "Border Security Results," official web site, November 1, 2013. http://www.dhs.gov/border-security-results.

12 Department of Homeland Security, "Border Security Results," official web site, November 1, 2013. http://www.dhs.gov/border-security-results.

13 John Carlos Frey, "Over the Line," *Washington Monthly,* May–June 2013. http://www.washingtonmonthly.com/magazine/may_june_2013/features/over_the_line044512.php?page=all. See also American Civil Liberties Union Press Release, "Mother of Slain Mexican Teen Sues U.S. Border Patrol Agents, Seeks Trial in Shooting Death of Her Son," July 29, 2014, ACLU official website. https://www.aclu.org/immigrants-rights/mother-slain-mexican-teen-sues-us-border-patrol-agents-seeks-trial-shooting-death.

14 "Archive Canada–U.S. Border Drug Threat Assessment," Public Safety Canada, Government of Canada official web site, October 2004. http://www.publicsafety.gc.ca/cnt/rsrcs/pblctns/archive-us-cnd-brdr-drg-2004/index-eng.aspx.

15 On Canada as primary foreign source of ecstasy, see Bureau of International Narcotics and Law Enforcement Affairs, "2013 International Narcotics Control Strategy Report (INCSR): Country Reports—Afghanistan through Costa Rica," March 1, 2013, U.S. Department of State web site. http://www.state.gov/j/inl/rls/nrcrpt/2013/vol1/204048.htm. On lacing of ecstasy with methamphetamines, see "Canada Border is Drug War's Second Front," *Washington Times,* July, 26, 2009. http://www.washingtontimes.com/news/2009/jul/26/canada-border-is-drug-wars-2nd-front/?page=all. On use of ecstasy in relation to other drugs among U.S. population, see David R. Mares, *Drug Wars and Coffeehouses: The Political Economy of International Drug Trade* (Washington, DC: CQ Press, 2006), 41.

16 As Patricia Fernández Kelley and Douglass Massey explain, "The reduction of public spending in Mexico, the removal of subsidies to subsistence agriculture, the opening of feed and seed markets, and the commercialization of communal lands have had a displacing effect, leading peasants to seek economic opportunities in the neighboring country" ("Borders for Whom? The Role of NAFTA in Mexico-U.S. Migration," *Annals of the American Academy of Political and Social Science* 610 [March 2007], 116).

17 Laura Carlsen, "NAFTA is Starving Mexico," October 20, 2011. In *Foreign Policy in Focus*. http://fpif.org/nafta_is_starving_mexico/. As of 2002, the last year for firm figures, 1.3 million jobs had been lost in agricultural employment, combining farm owners and workers. See Sandra Polaski, "Jobs, Wages, and Household Income," in NAFTA's *Promise and Reality: Lessons from Mexico for the Hemisphere*, ed. John Audley, Demetrios G. Papdemetriou, Sandra Polaski, and Scott Vaughan (Washington, DC: Carnegie Endowment for International Peace, 2004), 20.

18 It would be disingenuous to blame NAFTA for the majority of immigration to the United States since its implementation. Mexico's economy would have needed to produce 1.2 million net *new* jobs just to keep up with the influx of new entrants into the job market; see Raúl Delgado Wise and James M. Cypher, "The Strategic Role of Mexican Labor under NAFTA: Critical Perspectives on Current Economic Integration," *Annals of the American Academy of Political and Social Science* 5(610) (March 2007), 123. Nevertheless, NAFTA was (and is) repeatedly represented to the U.S. and Mexican population as creating jobs that curb emigration. In this regard, NAFTA has not only failed to curtail emigration, but has stimulated job loss, as will be discussed below. Emigration to the United States is so pronounced that 31 percent of the municipalities in Mexico are experiencing depopulation (Delgado Wise and Cypher, "Strategic Role of Mexican Labor," 123).

19 According to a 2009 Carnegie Endowment for International Peace Policy Outlook paper, NAFTA had created 660,000 jobs in the maquiladora sector by 2006, the last year of available figures on job growth in this sector of Mexican industry. See Eduardo Zepeda, Timothy A. Wise, and Kevin P. Gallagher, *Rethinking Trade Policy for Development: Lessons from Mexico Under NAFTA*, December 2009, Carnegie Endowment for International Peace Policy Outlook, 10–11. However, employment in the nonmaquila industrial sector was lower in 2008 than it had been in 1994, leading the authors to estimate a net gain of between 500,000 to 600,000 in manufacturing attributable to NAFTA (10–11).

20 With more than three thousand factories clustered along the border, employing 1.2 million workers, the *maquila* sector accounted for 55 percent of Mexico's export production (Delgado Wise and Cypher, "Strategic Role of Mexican Labor," 125).

21 For a discussion of the concern of U.S. unions with the impact of the trade deficit on U.S. workers, see AFL-CIO, NAFTA *at 20: Overview and Trade Effects*, AFL-CIO official web site. http://www.aflcio.org/Issues/Trade/NAFTA/NAFTA-at-20.

22 As Delgado Wise and Cypher explain, "For the most part, maquiladoras import inputs—components, parts, design, engineering, and so on overwhelmingly from the United States, combine those various inputs with cheap assembly (pay per day in 2005 ranged from $4 to $10) and a slight element of technical labor, assemble

NOTES FOR CONCLUSION   297

the finished products and reexport the finished products back to the United States" ("Strategic Role of Mexican Labor," 125).

23 When one disaggregates, separating inputs used in maquiladora export production and nonmaquiladora export production, the figure is even more startling. Figures for 2004, marking the tenth anniversary of NAFTA, indicated that 97 percent of the components used in maquiladora production were imported, with only 3 percent produced in Mexico (Polaski, "Jobs, Wages, and Household Income," 16).

24 It is difficult to isolate for other factors when estimating the closing of domestic manufacturing plants due to NAFTA. Nevertheless, according to Public Citizen's Global Trade Watch's research team, "An estimated 28,000 small- and medium-sized Mexican businesses were destroyed in NAFTA's first four years, including many retail, food processing and light manufacturing firms that were displaced by NAFTA's new opening for U.S. big box retailers that sold goods imported from Asia." See Ben Beachy, *NAFTA's 20-Year Legacy and the Fate of the Trans-Pacific Partnership* (Washington, DC: Public Citizen's Global Trade Watch, 2014), 22. At the tenth anniversary of NAFTA, employment in the nonmaquiladora sector had shrunk by 100,000 jobs, from 1.4 million to 1.3 million (Polaski, "Jobs, Wages, and Household Income," 16). Again, it is difficult to isolate how much of that job loss was attributable to NAFTA, but as manufacture in the nonmaquiladora industry has also been reoriented toward production for export, at least some of that loss in jobs is attributable to a combination of a shrinking U.S. demand due to recessionary cycles and the shrinking of domestic demand due to the Walmart effect (Polaski, "Jobs, Wages, and Household Income," 16).

25 Peter Andreas's estimates are significantly lower, between $180 and $300 million in global retail sales. Andreas also points out that the United States may be the largest target for illegal drug entries, but it is also the largest purveyor of illegally smuggled goods to the world when one considers smuggled American cigarettes, pornography, money, weapons, and stolen cars. As Mexico does not manufacture any guns or arms, the smuggling of arms to Mexico over the last two decades is a boon to the U.S. arms industry. See Andreas, *Border Games: Policing the U.S.–Mexico Divide* (Ithaca, NY: Cornell University Press, 2000), 16.

26 *Plaza* is the term cartels use to designate their territory. While these plazas—or territories—are vast, often spanning several Mexican states, the use of the term connotes the quaint and intimate center of a town, as well as the use of public space as the scene of democratic enactment.

27 Ernesto Laclau, "Feudalism and Capitalism in Latin America," *New Left Review* 67 (1971): 19–38; Andre Gunder Frank, *Monthly Review* (September 1966): 17–31.

BIBLIOGRAPHY

Archival Manuscripts

SEVILLE, SPAIN

Archivo General de Indias (AGI)
Estado: Mexico, 690: *Expediente sobre la población y pacificación del Seno Mexicano.*
—Josseph Antonio Fernández de Jáuregui
—Antonio Ladrón De Guevara
—Narciso Barquín Monte-Cuesta
Estado: Mexico, 1933A&B: *Las Invaciones de los Apaches en el territorio de Tejas, 1763: Testimonios de autos sobre ataques de indios comanches y apaches, su reducción, erección de presidios en los ríos San Javier y San Sabá, visitas a presidios, fundación de misiones, deserción de soldados y descubrimiento de minas.*
—Diego Orttiz Parrilla
Estado: Guadalajara, 406
—Felipe Arispe De Neve

AUSTIN, TEXAS

Benson Latin American Collection, University of Texas
George I. Sánchez Papers, Box 31, Folder 8
—George I. Sánchez

Works Cited

Aboites Aguilar, Luis. 1991. "Poder politico y 'bárbaris' en Chihuahua hacia 1845." *Secuencia* 19: 17–32.
Acosta, Oscar Zeta. 1970. "The East LA 13 vs. the LA Superior Court." *El Grito: A Journal of Contemporary Mexican American Thought* 3(2): 12–18.
———. 1989. *Autobiography of a Brown Buffalo.* New York: Vintage.
———. (1973) 1996. "Letter to *Playboy.*" In *Oscar Zeta Acosta: The Uncollected Works,* ed. Ilan Stavans, 109. Houston: Arte Público Press.
Acuña, Rodolfo. 1972. *Occupied America: The Chicano's Struggle Toward Liberation.* San Francisco: Canfield Press.
Adams, David B. 1991. "Embattled Borderland: Northern Nuevo León and the Indios Bárbaros, 1686–1870." *Southwestern Historical Quarterly* 95(2): 205–220.

Adams, Rachel. 2004. "Hipsters and *jipitecas*: Literary Countercultures on Both Sides of the Border." *American Literary History* 16(1): 58–84.

Adorno, Rolena. 2007. *The Polemics of Possession in Spanish American Narrative.* New Haven, CT: Yale University Press.

Aguirre, Hon. Fredrick P. 2005. "*Mendez v. Westminster School District*: How It Affected *Brown v. Board of Education.*" *Journal of Hispanic Higher Education* 4: 321–332.

Aitken, S. C. 2001. "School Yard Shootings: Racism, Sexism, and Moral Panic over Teen Violence." *Antipode* 33(4): 593–600.

Alarcón, Norma. 1997. "Traddutora, Traditora: A Paradigmatic Figure of Chicana Feminism." In *Dangerous Liaisons: Gender, Nation, and Postcolonial Perspectives,* ed. Anne McClintock, Aamir Mufti, and Ella Shohat, 78–297. Minneapolis: University of Minnesota Press.

Aldama, Frederick L. 2000. "Oscar 'Zeta' Acosta: Magicorealism and Chicano Auto-bio-graphé." *LIT: Literature Interpretation Theory* 11(2): 199–218.

Álvarez, Salvador. 2010. "Manuel San Juan de Santa Cruz: Gobernador, latifundista, y capitán de guerra de la frontera norte." *Revista de Indias* 70(248): 101–126.

Anaya, Rudolfo A., and Francisco Lomeli, eds. 1989. *Aztlán: Essays on the Chicano Homeland.* Albuquerque: University of New Mexico Press.

Anderson, Kay. 1991. *Vancouver's Chinatown: Racial Ideology in Canada, 1875–1980.* Montreal: McGill-Queen's University Press.

Anderson, Kay, and Mona Domosh. 2002. "North American Spaces/Postcolonial Stories." *Cultural Geographies* 9(2): 125–128.

Anderson, Kay, Mona Domosh, Steve Pile, and Nigel Thrift, eds. 2003a. *Handbook of Cultural Geography.* London: Sage.

———. 2003b. "A Rough Guide." In *Handbook of Cultural Geography,* ed. Kay Anderson, Mona Domosh, Steve Pile, and Nigel Thrift, 1–37. London: Sage.

Andreas, Peter. 2000. *Border Games: Policing the U.S.–Mexico Divide.* Ithaca, NY: Cornell University Press.

Anghie, Antony. 1999. "Francisco de Vitoria and the Colonial Origins of International Law." In *Laws of the Postcolonial,* ed. Eve Darian-Smith and Peter Fitzpatrick, 89–104. Ann Arbor: University of Michigan Press.

Anzaldúa, Gloria. 1983. "La Prieta." In *This Bridge Called My Back: Writings by Radical Women of Color,* ed. Cherríe Moraga and Gloria Anzaldúa, 198–209. New York: Kitchen Table: Women of Color Press.

———. 1987. *Borderlands/La Frontera: The New Mestiza.* San Francisco, CA: Aunt Lute Books.

Arriola, Christopher. 1995. "Knocking on the Schoolhouse Door: *Mendez v. Westminster,* Equal Protection, Public Education, and Mexican Americans in the 1940s." *La Raza Law Journal* 8: 166–207.

Austin, John L. 1975. *How to Do Things with Words.* Ed. J. O. Ormson and Marina Sbisá. Cambridge, MA: Harvard University Press.

Babcock, Matthew. 2009. "Rethinking the Establecimientos: Why Apaches Settled on Spanish-Run Reservations." *New Mexico Historical Review* 84(3): 363–397.

Balibar, Étienne. 1993. "Racism and Nationalism." In *Race, Nation, and Class: Ambiguous Identities*, ed. Étienne Balibar and Immanuel Wallerstein, 37–68. New York: Verso.

Banner, Stuart. 2005. *How the Indians Lost Their Land*. Cambridge, MA: Harvard University Press.

Barbosa de Vasconcelos, Eduardo H. 2012. "Porfirio Díaz under the Foreign Eye: The Representation of the President and His Government Years by American and British Writers (1901–1911)." *Delaware Review of Latin American Studies* 13(2). http://www.udel.edu/LAS/Vol13-2Vasconcelos.html.

Barquín Monte-Cuesta, Don Narciso. 1736. "Memorial de Don Narciso Barquín Monte-Cuesta, proponiendo el descubrimiento de las tierras comprendidas entre la Huasteca y el Nuevo Reino de León y la reducción de los indios bárbaros que las habitan" (April 2). Documento No. 1. In AGI, *Expediente sobre la población y pacificación del Seno Mexicano*.

Barr, Juliana. 2007. *Peace Came in the Form of a Woman: Indians and Spaniards in the Texas Borderlands*. Chapel Hill: University of North Carolina Press.

———. 2011. "Mapping Indian Borders in the 'Borderlands' of the Early Southwest." *William and Mary Quarterly* 68(1): 5–46.

Bartra, Roger. 1994. *Wild Men in the Looking Glass: The Mythic Origins of European Otherness*. Ann Arbor: University of Michigan.

———. 2000. *La jaula de la melancholia: Identidad y metamorfosis del mejicano*. Mexico: Grijalbo.

Beachy, Ben. 2014. *NAFTA's 20-Year Legacy and the Fate of the Trans-Pacific Partnership*. Washington, DC: Public Citizen's Global Trade Watch.

Belausteguigoitia Rius, Marisa, and María Josefina Saldaña-Portillo, eds. 2015. *Des/posesión: Género, territorio y luchas por la autodeterminación*. México, D.F.: PUEG-UNAM.

Bennett, Herman. 2003. *Africans in Colonial Mexico: Absolutism, Christianity, and Afro-Creole Consciousness, 1570–1640*. Bloomington: University of Indiana Press.

Berger, John. 1972. *Ways of Seeing*. London: Penguin.

Blackhawk, Ned. 2006. *Violence over the Land: Indians and Empires in the Early American West*. Cambridge, MA: Harvard University Press.

———. 2007. "The Displacement of Violence: Ute Diplomacy and the Making of New Mexico's Eighteenth-Century Northern Borderlands." *Ethnohistory* 54(4): 723–755.

Blunt, Alison, and Gillian Rose. 1994. "Introduction: Women's Colonial and Postcolonial Geographies." In *Writing Women and Space: Colonial and Postcolonial Geographies*, ed. Alison Blunt and Gillian Rose, 1–25. New York: The Guilford Press.

Bonnett, Alastair. 1996. "Constructions of 'Race,' Place, and Discipline: Geographies of 'Racial' Identity and Racism." *Ethnic and Racial Studies* 19(4): 864–883.

———. 1997. "Geography, 'Race,' and Whiteness: Invisible Traditions and Current Challenges." *Area* 29(3): 193–199.

————. 2000. *White Identities: Historical and International Perspectives*. London: Prentice Hall.

Bonnett, Alastair, and Anoop Nayak. 2003. "Cultural Geographies of Racialization: The Territory of Race." In *Handbook of Cultural Geography*, ed. Kay Anderson, Mona Domosh, Steve Pile, and Nigel Thrift, 300–313. London: Sage.

Bradford, William. 2009. *Bradford's History "Of Plymoth Plantation": From the Original Manuscript*. New York: Heritage Books.

Brown, Wendy. 1995. *States of Injury: Power and Freedom in Late Modernity*. Princeton: Princeton University Press.

Byrd, Jodi A. 2011. *The Transit of Empire: Indigenous Critiques of Colonialism*. Minneapolis: University of Minnesota Press.

Calderón, Héctor. 2004. " 'A Recorder of Events with a Sour Stomach': Oscar Zeta Acosta and *The Autobiography of a Brown Buffalo*." In *Narratives of Greater Mexico: Essays on Chicano Literary History, Genre, and Borders*, 85–110. Austin: University of Texas Press.

Campbell, T. N. 1983. "Coahuiltecans and Their Neighbors." *Handbook of North American Indians* 10: 343–358.

Carlsen, Laura. 2011. "NAFTA Is Starving Mexico," October 20. In *Foreign Policy in Focus*. http://fpif.org/nafta_is_starving_mexico/.

Carrigan, William D. 2003. "The Lynching of Persons of Mexican Origin or Descent in the United States, 1848 to 1928." *Journal of Social History* 37(2): 411–438.

Castañeda, Jorge G. 2014. "Nafta's Mixed Record: The View From Mexico." *Foreign Affairs* 93.1 (January/February): 134–141.

Castillo, David R., and Massimo Lollini. 2006. *Reason and Its Others: Italy, Spain, and the New World*. Nashville: Vanderbilt University Press.

Chakrabarty, Dipesh. 2000. *Provincializing Europe: Postcolonial Thought and Historical Difference*. Princeton: Princeton University Press.

Chávez, John R. 1989. "Aztlán, Cíbola, and Frontier New Spain." In *Aztlán: Essays on the Chicano Homeland*, ed. Rudolfo A. Anaya and Francisco Lomeli, 49–71. Albuquerque: University of New Mexico Press.

Cheng, Anne A. 2001. *The Melancholy of Race: Psychoanalysis, Assimilation, and Hidden Grief*. Oxford: Oxford University Press.

Cisneros v. Corpus Christi ISD. 1970. 324 F. Supp. 599 (S.D. Texas).

Clayton, Daniel. 2003. "Critical Imperial and Colonial Geographies." In *Handbook of Cultural Geography*, ed. Kay Anderson, Mona Domosh, Steve Pile, and Nigel Thrift, 354–369. London: Sage.

Coen, Joel, and Ethan Coen (directors). 2007. *No Country for Old Men*. (DVD). Miramax Films.

Commager, H. S., ed. 1968. *Documents of American History*. New York: Appleton.

Condé, Maryse. 1999. *Hérémakhonon*. Boulder, CO: Lynne Rienner.

Coombes, Annie, ed. 2006. *Rethinking Settler Colonialism: History and Memory in Australia, Canada, Aotearoa New Zealand, and South Africa*. Manchester, NY: Manchester University Press.

Cooper, Fredrick. 2005. *Colonialism in Question: Theory, Knowledge, History*. Berkeley: University of California Press.

Cosgrove, Denis. 2003. "Landscape and the European Sense of Sight: Eyeing Nature." In *Handbook of Cultural Geography*, ed. Kay Anderson, Mona Domosh, Steve Pile, and Nigel Thrift, 249–269. London: Sage.

Crashaw, William. 1610. *A Sermon Preached in London.* London: William Welby.

Cross, Malcolm, and Michael Cross, eds. 1993. *Racism, the City, and the State.* London: Routledge.

Curtis Graybill, Florence, and Victor Boesen, eds. 2000. *Edward Sheriff Curtis: Visions of a Vanishing Race.* Albuquerque: University of New Mexico Press.

de la Flor, Fernando R. 2006. "Sacrificial Politics in the Spanish Colonies." Translated by Rose Seifert. In *Reason and Its Others: Italy, Spain, and the New World,* ed. David R. Castillo and Massimo Lollini, 243–258, Nashville: Vanderbilt University Press.

de la Garza, Rodolfo O., Anthony Kruszewski, and Tomás A. Arciniega. 1973. *Chicanos and Native Americans: The Territorial Minorities.* Englewood Cliffs, NJ: Prentice-Hall.

Delaney, David. 1998. *Race, Place, and the Law: 1836–1948.* Austin: University of Texas Press.

———. 2005. *Territory: A Short Introduction.* Malden, MA: Blackwell Publishing.

de Las Casas, Bartolomé. 1992. *In Defense of the Indians.* Translated and ed. Stafford Poole. DeKalb: Northern Illinois University Press.

de la Teja, Jesús. 1993. "Sobrevivencia económica en la frontera de Texas: Los ranchos ganaderos del siglo XVIII en San Antonio de Béxar." *Historia Mexicana* 42(4): 837–865.

de la Torre Curiel, José R. 2008. " 'Enemigos encubiertos': Bandas pluriétnicas y estado de alerta en la frontera sonorense a finales de siglo XVIII." *Takwá* 14 (otoño): 11–31.

———. 2011. "Con la sierra a cuestas. Apaches y españoles en la frontera sonorense en el siglo XVIII." *Nuevo Mundo, Mundos Nuevos.* January 31. http://nuevomundo.revues.org/60707.

de Man, Paul. 1979. *Allegories of Reading: Figural Language in Rousseau, Nietzsche, Rilke, and Proust.* New Haven, CT: Yale University Press.

Delay, Brian. 2007a. "Independent Indians and the U.S.–Mexican War." *American Historical Review* 112(1): 35–68.

———. 2007b. "The Wider World of the Handsome Man: Southern Plains Indians Invade Mexico, 1830–1849." *Journal of the Early Republic* 27(1): 83–113.

———. 2008. *War of a Thousand Deserts: Indian Raids and the U.S.–Mexican War.* New Haven, CT: Yale University Press.

Delgado, Richard, and Jean Stefanic. 2001. *Critical Race Theory: An Introduction.* New York: New York University Press.

Delgado Wise, Raúl, and James M. Cypher. 2007. "The Strategic Role of Mexican Labor under NAFTA: Critical Perspectives on Current Economic Integration." *Annals of the American Academy of Political and Social Science,* 5(610) (March) 120–142.

Delgado Wise, Raúl, and Mariana Ortega Breña. 2006. "Migration and Imperialism: The Mexican Workforce in the Context of NAFTA." *Latin American Perspectives,* 33.2 (March) 33–45.

Deloria, Philip J. 1998. *Playing Indian*. New Haven, CT: Yale University Press.

de Neve, Felipe Arispe. 1783. "Bando prohibiendo que los indios salgan de sus pueblos sin certificaciones de sus justicias o párrocos" (10 de diciembre). AGI (Estado: Guadalajara, 406).

Dermota, Ken. 1999–2000. "Snow Business: Drugs and the Spirit of Capitalism." *World Policy Journal* 16(4) (winter): 15–24.

Derrida, Jacques. 1989–1990. "Force of Law: The 'Mystical Foundation of Authority.'" *Cardozo Law Review* 11: 920–1045.

Díaz Polanco, Héctor. 1997. *Indigenous Peoples in Latin America: The Quest for Self-Determination*. Boulder, CO: Westview Press.

Dippie, Brian W. 1991. *The Vanishing American: White Attitudes and U.S. Indian Policy*. Lawrence: University Press of Kansas.

Durazo Herrmann, Francisco Julián. 2001. "México y la Apachería." *Estudios Fronterizos* 2(3): 91–105.

Dwyer, Claire, and Caroline Bressey, eds. 2008. *New Geographies of Race and Racism*. Hampshire, UK: Ashgate.

Dwyer, Owen J., and John Paul Jones III. 2000. "White Socio-Spatial Epistemology." *Social and Cultural Geography* 1(2): 209–222.

Elkins, Caroline, and Susan Pedersen, eds. 2005. *Settler Colonialism in the Twentieth Century: Projects, Practices, Legacies*. New York: Routledge.

Emmanuel, Arghiri. 1972. "White-Settler Colonialism and the Myth of Investment Imperialism." *New Left Review* 1(73) (May–June): 35–57.

Eng, David L. 2001. *Racial Castration: Managing Masculinity in Asian America*. Durham, NC: Duke University Press.

Espinosa Morales, Lydia, and Isabel Ortega Ridaura, eds. 2006. *El Nuevo Reino de León en voz de sus contemporaneos*. Monterrey, Mexico: Fondo Editorial Nuevo León.

Farhi, Paul. 2008. "The Iraq War in Hollywood's Theater; Despite the Drama, Films about the Conflict Fizzled at the Box Office." *Washington Post*, March 25. http://articles.washingtonpost.com/2008-03-25/news/36829101_1_war-big -budgets-big-stars.

Felski, Rita, and Susan Stanford Friedman, eds. 2013. *Comparison: Theories, Approaches, Uses*. Baltimore: Johns Hopkins University Press.

Fernández de Jáuregui, Josseph Antonio. (1735) 2006. "Descripción del Nuevo Reino de León Escrita por su Gobernador." In *El Nuevo Reino de León en voz de sus contemporaneos*, ed. Lydia Espinosa Morales and Isabel Ortega Ridaura, 5–19. Monterrey, Mexico: Fondo Editorial Nuevo León.

———. 1736. "Carta de Don José Antonio Fernández de Jáuregui Urrutia, Gobernador del Nuevo Reino de León, a S.M. Informa de la situación, fortalezas y estado de aquellas tierras." Documento No. 3, 4 folios. In AGI (Estado: Mexico, 690), *Expediente sobre la población y pacificación del Seno Mexicano*.

———. 1736. "Testimonio." Documento No. 3b, 24 folios. In AGI (Estado: Mexico, 690), *Expediente sobre la población y pacificación del Seno Mexicano*.

Fernández-Kelley, Patricia, and Douglas S. Massey. 2007. "Borders for Whom? The Role of NAFTA in Mexico-U.S. Migration." *Annals of the American Academy of Political and Social Science* 610 (March): 98–118.

Flagler, Edward K. 2000. "La politica Española para pacificar a los indios Apaches a finales del siglo XVIII." *Revista Española de Antropología Americana* 30: 221–234.

Flores, Dan. 2008. "Bringing Home All the Pretty Horses: The Horse Trade and the Early American West, 1775–1825." *Montana: The Magazine of Western History* 58(2): 3–21.

Foley, Neil. 1997. *The White Scourge: Mexicans, Blacks, and Poor Whites in Texas Cotton Culture*. Berkeley: University of California Press.

———. 1998. "Becoming Hispanic: Mexican Americans and the Faustian Pact with Whiteness." In *Reflexiones 1997: New Directions in Mexican American Studies*, ed. Neil Foley, 53–70. Austin: University of Texas, Center for Mexican American Studies.

———. 2005a. "Over the Rainbow: *Hernandez v. Texas, Brown v. Board of Education*, and Black v. Brown." *Chicano-Latino Law Review* 25 (spring): 139–152.

———. 2005b. "Statement by Dr. Neil Foley." In "Symposium: *Hernandez v. Texas*: A Fiftieth Anniversary Celebration," ed. Marcos Guerra. *Texas Hispanic Journal of Law and Policy* 11 (fall): 13–18.

Forbes, Jack. ca. 1961–62. "The Mexican Heritage of Aztlán (The Southwest), to 1821." Unpublished essay.

Foucault, Michel. 1972. *The Archaeology of Knowledge and the Discourse on Language*. New York: Pantheon Books.

———. 1979. *Discipline and Punish*. New York: Random House.

Frank, Andre Gunder. 1966. *Monthly Review* (September): 17–31.

Fregoso, Rosalinda. 2003. "The Chicano Familia Romance." In *meXicana encounters: The Making of Social Identities on the Borderlands*, 71–90. Berkeley: University of California Press.

Freud, Sigmund. 1958. "The Uncanny" (1919). In *On Creativity and the Unconscious*, 122–162. New York: Harper & Row.

———. 1963. "Repression" (1915). In *General Psychological Theory: Papers on Metapsychology*, 104–115. New York: Collier Books.

———. 1965. *The Interpretation of Dreams* (1899). New York: Avon Books.

Freud, Sigmund, and Joseph Breuer. 1974. "On the Physical Mechanism of Hysterical Phenomena: Preliminary Communication." In *Studies on Hysteria*. Vol. 13. London: Pelican Books.

Frey, John Carlos. 2013. "Over the Line," *Washington Monthly*, May–June. http://www.washingtonmonthly.com/magazine/may_june_2013/features/over_the_line044512.php?page=all.

Frickey, Philip P. 1993. "Marshalling Past and Present: Colonialism, Constitutionalism, and Interpretation in Federal Indian Law." *Harvard Law Review* 107(2): 381–440.

———. 2005. "(Native) American Exceptionalism in Federal Public Law." *Harvard Law Review* 119(2): 431–490.

Frisbie, Levi. 1804. *Discourse before the Society for Propagating the Gospel among the Indians, and Others, in North America*. Charlestown, MA: Samuel Ethridge.

Gaido, Daniel. 2006. *The Formative Period of American Capitalism: A Materialist Interpretation*. London: Routledge.

García, Mario T. 1991. *Mexican Americans: Leadership, Ideology, and Identity, 1930–1960*. New Haven, CT: Yale University Press.

Garcia, Richard A. 1991. *Rise of the Mexican American Middle Class: San Antonio, 1929–1941*. College Station: Texas A&M University Press.

Gibler, John. 2011. *To Die in Mexico: Dispatches from Inside the Drug War*. San Francisco, CA: City Lights Books.

Ginés de Sepúlveda, Juan. [1892] 2006. *Demócrates segundo o De las justas causas de la guerra contra los indio*. Edited and translated by Marcelino Menéndez y Pelayo. http://www.cervantesvirtual.com/obra/j-genesii-sepulvedae-cordubensis -democrates-alter-sive-de-justis-belli-causis-apud-indos—democrates -segundo-o-de-las-justas-causas-de-la-guerra-contra-los-indios-o/.

Goldberg, Jonathan. 1992. *Sodometries: Renaissance Texts, Modern Sexualities*. Stanford, CA: Stanford University Press.

Gómez, Laura. 2007. *Manifest Destinies: The Making of the Mexican American Race*. New York: New York University Press.

Gonzales, Manuel G. 1999. *Mexicanos: A History of Mexicans in the United States*. Bloomington: Indiana University Press.

González, Martín. 2002. "¿Amigos, enemigos o socios? El comercio con los 'indios bárbaros' en Nuevo México, siglo XVIII." *Relaciones* 92(23): 108–134.

González, Rodolfo "Corky." 1972. *I Am Joaquin*. New York: Bantam Press.

Gray, Robert. 1609. *A Good Speed to Virginia*. London: William Welbie.

Gregory, Derek. 1994. *Geographical Imaginations*. Oxford: Blackwell.

Grey, Maggie, with Emma Kreyche. 2007. *The Hudson Valley Farmerworker Report*. Annandale-on-Hudson: Bard College Migrant Labor Project.

Grey, Zane. 1934. *The Vanishing Race*. London: Hodder and Stoughton.

———. 1936. *The Vanishing Indian*. London: Hodder and Stoughton.

Greybill, Florence C., and Victor Boesen. 1976. *Edward Sheriff Curtis: Visions of a Vanishing Race*. New York: Crowell.

Griffen, William. 1985. "Problems in the Study of Apaches and Other Indians in Chihuahua and Southern New Mexico during the Spanish and Mexican Periods." *Kiva* 50(2–3): 139–151.

Gross, Ariela. 2003. Texas Mexicans and the Politics of Whiteness." *Law and History Review* 21(1): 195–207.

———. 2007. " 'The Caucasian Clock': Mexican Americans and the Politics of Whiteness in the Twentieth-Century Southwest." *Georgetown Law Journal* 95 (January): 337–392.

———. 2008. *What Blood Won't Tell: A History of Race on Trial in America*. Cambridge, MA: Harvard University Press.

Guerra, Marcos, ed. 2005. "Symposium: *Hernandez v. Texas*: A Fiftieth Anniversary Celebration." *Texas Hispanic Journal of Law and Policy* 11 (fall): 10–42.

Guevara, Ernesto "Che." 1993. *Notas de viaje*. La Habana, Cuba: Editorial Abril.

Guglielmo, Thomas A. 2006. "Fighting for Caucasian Rights: Mexicans, Mexican Americans, and the Transnational Struggle for Civil Rights in World War II Texas." *Journal of American History* 92 (March): 1212–1237.

Guha, Ranajit. 1988a. "On Some Aspects of the Historiography of Colonial India." In *Selected Subaltern Studies*, ed. Ranajit Guha and Gayatri Chakravorty Spivak, 7–44. London: Oxford University Press.

———. 1988b. "The Prose of Counterinsurgency." In *Selected Subaltern Studies,* ed. Ranajit Guha and Gayatri Chakravorty Spivak, 45–89. London: Oxford University Press.

Guidotti-Hernández, Nicole. 2011. *Unspeakable Violence: Remapping U.S. and Mexican National Imaginaries.* Durham, NC: Duke University Press.

Gutiérrez, David G. 1995. *Walls and Mirrors: Mexican Americans, Mexican Immigrants, and the Politics of Ethnicity.* Berkeley: University of California Press.

Gutiérrez, Ramón A. 1989. "Aztlán, Moctezuma, and New Mexico: The Political Uses of American Indian Mythology." In *Aztlán: Essays on the Chicano Homeland,* ed. Rudolfo A. Anaya and Francisco Lomeli, 172–190. Albuquerque: University of New Mexico Press.

Haas, Lisbeth. 2011. *Pablo Tac, Indigenous Scholar: Writing on Luiseño and Colonial History, c. 1840.* Berkeley: University of California Press.

———. 2013. *Saints and Citizens: Indigenous Histories of Colonial Missions and Mexican California.* Berkeley: University of California Press.

Haitt, Burritt. 1958. "James M. Haworth, Quaker Indian Agent." *Bulletin of Friends Historical Association* 47(2): 80–93.

Hall, G. Emlen. 1984. "Mexican Liberals and the Pueblo Indians, 1821–1829." *New Mexico Historical Review* 59(1): 5–32.

Hämäläinen, Pekka. 2008. *The Comanche Empire.* New Haven, CT: Yale University Press.

Hames-Garcia, Michael. 2000. "Dr. Gonzo's Carnival: The Testimonial Satires of Oscar Zeta Acosta," *American Literature* 72(3): 463–493.

Haney López, Ian. 1996. *White by Law: The Legal Construction of Race.* New York: New York University Press.

———. 1998. "Race, Ethnicity, Erasure: The Salience of Race to LatCrit Theory." *La Raza Law Journal* 10: 1143–1211.

———. 1999–2000. "Institutional Racism: Judicial Conduct and a New Theory of Racial Discrimination." *Yale Law Journal* 109: 1717–1884.

———. 2001. "Protest, Repression, and Race: Legal Violence and the Chicano Movement." *University of Pennsylvania Law Review* 150(1): 205–244.

———. 2003a. *Racism on Trial: The Chicano Fight for Justice.* Cambridge, MA: Harvard University Press.

———. 2003b. "White Latinos." *Harvard Latino Law Review* 6(1): 1–7.

———. 2005. "Statement of Professor Ian F. Haney López." In "Symposium: *Hernandez v. Texas*: A Fiftieth Anniversary Celebration," ed. Marcos Guerra. *Texas Hispanic Journal of Law and Policy* 11 (fall): 18–26.

Hanke, Lewis. 1959. *Aristotle and the American Indians: A Study in Race Prejudice in the Modern World.* Don Mills, Ontario: Fitzhenry & Whiteside.

———. 1974. *All Mankind Is One: A Study of the Disputation between Bartolomé de Las Casas and Juan Ginés de Sepúlveda in 1550 on the Intellectual and Religious Capacity of the American Indians.* DeKalb: Northern Illinois University Press.

Harris, Cheryl I. 1993. "Whiteness as Property." *Harvard Law Review* 106(8): 1710–1791.

Hartman, Saidiya V. 1997. *Scenes of Subjection: Terror, Slavery, and Self-making in Nineteenth Century America.* New York: Oxford University Press.

Harvey, David. 1989. *The Condition of Postmodernity: An Enquiry into the Origins of Cultural Change*. Oxford: Blackwell.

Haylett, C. 2001. "Illegitimate Subjects? Abject Whites, Neoliberal Modernization, and Middle-class Multiculturalism." *Environment and Planning D: Society and Space* 19(3): 351–370.

Herrera-Sobek, Maria. 2009. "Constructing Masculinities: Mapping the Male Body in Oscar Zeta Acosta's *The Autobiography of a Brown Buffalo*." *Revista Canaria de Estudios Ingleses* 58: 77–87.

Hilger, Christopher. 2001. "A Local Desegregation Case—Eight Years before *Brown v. Board of Education*." *Orange County Lawyer* (June): 30–33.

Holdich, T. 1916. *Political Frontiers and Boundary Making*. London: Macmillan.

Horkheimer, Max, and Theodor W. Adorno. 2002. *Dialectic of Enlightenment: Philosophical Fragments*. Stanford, CA: Stanford University Press.

Hudson, B. 1977. "The New Geography and the New Imperialism: 1870–1918." *Antipode* 9: 12–19.

Huey, David. 2014. "The U.S. War on Drugs in Latin America and Its Legacy," *The Guardian*, February 3. http://www.theguardian.com/global-development-professionals-network/2014/feb/03/us-war-on-drugs-impact-in-latin-american.

Humes, Karen R., Nicholas A. Jones, and Roberto R. Ramirez. 2010. "Overview of Race and Hispanic Origin: 2010." Washington, DC: U.S. Census Bureau.

Huntington, E. 1924. *The Character of Races as Influenced by Physical Environment, Natural Selection, and Historical Development*. New Haven, CT: Yale University Press.

Isacson, Adam. 2005. "The U.S. Military in the War on Drugs." In *Drugs and Democracy in Latin America*, ed. Coletta A. Youngers and Eileen Rosin, 15–60. Boulder, CO: Lynne Rienner.

Isacson, Adam, Lisa Haugaard, Abigail Poe, Sara Kinosian, and George Withers. 2013. *A Time to Listen: Trends in U.S. Security Assistance to Latin America and the Caribbean*. Washington, DC: Center for International Policy, Latin America Working Group Education Fund, and Washington Office on Latin America.

Jackson, Peter, ed. 1987. *Race and Racism: Essays in Social Geography*. London: Allen & Unwin.

———. 1988. "Street Life: The Politics of Carnival." *Environment and Planning D: Society and Space* 6: 231–237.

———. 1989. "Geography, Race and Racism." In *New Models in Geography*. Vol. 2, ed. Richard Peet and Nigel Thrift, 176–195. London: Unwin Hyman.

———. 1992. "The Racialization of Labour in Post-War Bradford." *Journal of Historical Geography* 18(2): 190–209.

———. 1998. "Constructions of 'Whiteness' in the Geographical Imagination." *Area* 30(2): 99–106.

Jackson, Peter, and Jan Penrose, eds. 1993. *Constructions of Race, Place, and Nation*. London: UCL Press.

Jacoby, Karl. 2008. *Shadows at Dawn: A Borderlands Massacre and the Violence of History*. New York: Penguin Press.

Jiménez Núñez, Alfredo. 2006. "Los *vecinos* Españoles ante los indios de frontera: El gran norte de Nueva España." *Brocar* 30: 37–63.

Johansen, Bruce E., ed. 2004. *Enduring Legacies: Native American Treaties and Contemporary Controversies*. Westport, CT: Praeger.

John, Elizabeth A. H. 1985. "La situación y visión de los indios de la frontera norte de Nueva España (Siglos XVI–XVIII)." *América Indígena* 45(3): 465–483.

Johnson, Kevin R. 2005. "*Hernandez v. Texas*: Legacies of Justice an Injustice." *Chicano-Latino Law Review* 25(1): 153–231.

Joseph, Gilbert, Catherine C. LeGrand, and Ricardo D. Salvatore, eds. 1998. *Close Encounters of Empire: Writing the Cultural History of U.S.-Latin American Relations*. Durham, NC: Duke University Press.

Kades, Eric. 1999–2000. "The Dark Side of Efficiency: *Johnson v. McIntosh* and the Expropriation of Amerindian Lands." *University of Pennsylvania Law Review* 148: 1065–1190.

Kaplan, Amy, and Donald E. Pease, eds. 1993. *Cultures of United States Imperialism*. Durham, NC: Duke University Press.

Kazanjian, David. 2003. *The Colonizing Trick: National Culture and Imperial Citizenship in Early America*. Minneapolis: University of Minnesota Press.

Kazanjian, David, and María Josefina Saldaña-Portillo. 2007. "Introduction: Traffic in History." *Social Text* 25 (3.92): 1–7.

Keith, M., and S. Pile. 1993. *Place and the Politics of Identity*. London: Routledge.

Kerouac, Jack. 1957. *On the Road*. New York: Viking Press.

Keyes v. School District Number One. 1973. Denver, 413 U.S. 189.

King, C. Richard, ed. 2000. *Postcolonial America*. Chicago: University of Illinois Press.

Knight, Alan. 1986. *The Mexican Revolution*. Vol. 2. *Counterrevolution and Reconstruction*. Lincoln, Nebraska: University of Nebraska Press.

———. 1990. "Racism, Revolution, and *Indigenismo*: Mexico, 1910–1940." In *The Idea of Race in Latin America, 1870–1940*, ed. Richard Graham, 71–113. Austin: University of Texas Press.

Kobayashi, Audrey. 2003. "The Construction of Geographical Knowledge: Racialization, Spatialization." In *Handbook of Cultural Geography*, ed. Kay Anderson, Mona Domosh, Steve Pile, and Nigel Thrift, 544–557. London: Sage.

Kobayashi, Audrey, and Sarah de Leeuw. 2010. "Colonialism and the Tensioned Landscapes of Indigeneity." In *The SAGE Handbook of Social Geographies*, ed. Susan J. Smith, Rachel Pain, Sallie A. Marston, and John Paul Jones III, 118–139. London: Sage.

Laclau, Ernesto. 1971. "Feudalism and Capitalism in Latin America." *New Left Review* 67: 19–38.

Ladrón de Guevara, Antonio. 1738. Document No. 5a, titled "Noticias sobre los indios bárbaros y sus costumbres," 12 folios, not paginated. In AGI (Estado: Mexico, 690), *Expediente sobre la población y pacificación del Seno Mexicano*.

———. (1739) 2006. "Noticias de los poblados de que se componen el Nuevo Reino de León, Provincia de Coahuila, Nueva Extremadura y la de Texas." In *El Nuevo Reino de León en voz de sus contemporaneos*, ed. Lydia Espinosa Morales and Isabel Ortega Ridaura, 47–74. Monterrey, Mexico: Fondo Editorial Nuevo León.

Lederer, John. 1958. *The Discoveries of John Lederer*, ed. William P. Cumming. Charlottesville: University of Virginia Press.

Lefebvre, Henri. 1991. *The Production of Space*. Translated by Donald Nicholson-Smith. Malden, MA: Blackwell.

Livingstone, David N., and Charles W. J. Withers. 1992. *The Geographical Tradition*. Oxford: Blackwell.

———. 1999. *Geography and Enlightenment*. Chicago: University of Chicago Press.

Lloyd, David. 1991. "Race under Representation." *Oxford Literary Review* 13(1–2): 62–94.

Lockhart, James. 1991. *Nahuas and Spaniards: Postconquest Central Mexican History and Philology*. Stanford, CA: Stanford University Press.

Loddington, William. 1682. *Plantation Work, the Work of This Generation*. London: Benjamin Clark.

Loomba, Ania. 2009. "Race and the Possibilities of Comparative Critique." *New Literary History* 40: 501–522.

Lopez, Dario et al. 2013. "U.S. Military Expands Its Drug War in Latin America," *USA Today*, February 3. http://www.usatoday.com/story/news/world/2013/02/03/us-expands-drug-war-latin-america/1887481/.

Lovell Banks, Taunya. 2006. "Mestizaje and the Mexican Mestizo Self: No Hay Sangre Negra, So There is no Blackness." *Southern California Interdisciplinary Law Journal* 15(2): 199–234.

Lux, Guillermo, and Maurilio E. Vigil. 1989. "Return to Aztlán: The Chicano Rediscovers His Indian Past." In *Aztlán: Essays on the Chicano Homeland,* ed. Rudolfo A. Anaya and Francisco Lomeli, 93–110. Albuquerque: University of New Mexico Press.

Mahoney, Curtis J. 2007. "Treaties as Contracts: Textualism, Contract Theory, and the Interpretation of Treaties." *Yale Law Journal* 116(4): 824–857.

Mallon, Florencia E. 1995. *Peasant and Nation: The Making of Postcolonial Mexico and Peru*. Berkeley: University of California Press.

———. 2011. "A Postcolonial Palimpsest: The Work Race Does." In *Histories of Race and Racism*, ed. Laura Gotkowitz, 321–336. Durham, NC: Duke University Press.

Mamdani, Mahmood. 2001. "Beyond Settler and Native as Political Identities: Overcoming the Political Legacy of Colonialism." *Comparative Studies of Society and History* 43.2 (October): 651–664.

Mares, David R. 2006. *Drug Wars and Coffeehouses: The Political Economy of International Drug Trade*. Washington, DC: CQ Press.

Mariscal, George. 2006. "Bartolomé de las Casas on Imperial Ethics and the Use of Force." In *Reason and Its Others: Italy, Spain, and the New World*, ed. David R. Castillo and Massimo Lollini, 259–278. Nashville: Vanderbilt University Press.

Marshall, Peter, and Glyndwyr Williams. 1982. *The Great Map of Mankind: British Perceptions of the World in the Age of Enlightenment*. London: J. M. Dent.

Martínez, María Elena. 2011. *Genealogical Fictions: Limpieza de Sangre, Religion, and Gender in Colonial Mexico*. Stanford: Stanford University Press.

Marx, Karl. (1843) 1978. "On the Jewish Question." In *The Marx-Engels Reader,* ed. Robert C. Tucker, 26–52. New York: W. W. Norton.

Mateos, Cuenya. 1991. "La población de México (1810–1880), elementos para su estudío." *Temas de Población* 1(3): 10–14.

Mather, Cotton. 1691. *The Life and Death of the Renown'd Mr. John Eliot*, 2nd ed. London: John Dunton.

Mbembe, Achille. 2003. "Necropolitics." Translated by Libby Meintjes, *Public Culture* 15(1): 11–40.

McCarthy, Cormac. 2005. *No Country for Old Men*. New York: Knopf.

McGuinness, M. 2000. "Geography Matters? Whiteness and Contemporary Geography." *Area* 32(2): 225–30.

Medina, Luis. 2009. "La Comanchería." *CIDE* 62: 1–19.

Menchaca, Martha. 1993. "Chicano Indianism: A Historical Account of Racial Repression in the United States." *American Ethnologist* 20(3): 583–603.

———. 2001. *Recovering History, Constructing Race: The Indian, Black, and White Roots of Mexican Americans*. Austin: University of Texas Press.

Mikesell, Marvin W. 1960. "Comparative Studies in Frontier History." *Annals of the Association of American Geographers* 50(1): 62–74.

Mill, H. 1905. "The Present Problems of Geography." *Geographical Journal* 25(1): 1–17.

Miller, Robert J. 2007. "Indian Treaties as Sovereign Contracts." *Flash Point* 9. http://www.flashpointmag.com/indtreat.htm.

Moffitt, John F., and Santiago Sebastian. 1998. *O Brave New People: The European Invention of the American Indian*. Albuquerque: University of New Mexico Press.

Montejano, David. 1987. *Anglos and Mexicans in the Making of Texas, 1836–1986*. Austin: University of Texas Press.

Moraga, Cherríe. 1983. "From a Long Line of Vendidas." *Loving in the War Years*, 90–144. Boston: South End Press.

Morin, Karen M. 2002. "Postcolonialism and Native American Geographies: The Letters of Rosalie La Flesche Farley 1896–1899." *Cultural Geographies* 9(2): 158–180.

Muñoz, Carlos. 1989. *Youth, Identity, Power: The Chicano Movement*. London: Verso.

Nash, Catherine. 2003. "Cultural Geography: Anti-racist Geographies." *Progress in Human Geography* 27(5): 637–648.

Nast, Heidi J. 2000. "Mapping the 'Unconscious': Racism and the Oedipal Family." *Annals of the Association of American Geographers* 90: 215–255.

Negri, Antonio. 1991. *Marx beyond Marx: Lessons on the* Grundrisse. Brooklyn, NY: Autonomedia.

Norgren, Jill. 1996. *The Cherokee Cases: The Confrontation of Law and Politics*. New York: McGraw-Hill.

Núñez, Fray Ángel Antonio. 1777. "Carta edificante histórico-curiosa, escrita desde la misión de Sta Maria de Baserac . . ." Santa María de Basarac, 31 de marzo. Tucson: University of Arizona Library, Special Collections, MS 193, 127.

O'Brien, Jean M. 2010. *Firsting and Lasting: Writing Indians Out of Existence in New England*. Minneapolis: University of Minnesota Press.

O'Gorman, Edmundo. 1961. *An Inquiry into the Historical Nature of the New World and the Meaning of Its History*. Bloomington: Indiana University Press.

O'Grady, Ellen. 2013. "Petraeus Statement on Plan Colombia at Odds with Reality," Center for Economic and Policy Research, October 3. http://www.cepr.net/index.php/blogs/the-americas-blog/petraeus-statement-on-plan-colombia-at-odds-with-reality.

Olund, Eric N. 2002. "From Savage Space to Governable Space: The Extension of U.S. Judicial Sovereignty over Indian Country in the Nineteenth Century." *Cultural Geographies* 9(2): 129–157.

Ortelli, Sara. 2004. "Enemigos internos y súbditos desleales. La infidencia en Nueva Vizcaya en tiempos de los Borbones." *Anuario de Estudios Americanos* 61(2): 467–489.

———. 2006. "Apaches hostiles, apóstatas rebeldes o súbditos infidentes? Estado borbónico y clasificaciones etnopolíticas en la Nueva Vizcaya de la segunda mitad del siglo XVIII." *Anuario IEHS: Instituto de Estudios histórico sociales* 21: 79–94.

———. 2010. "Crisis de subsistencia y robo de ganado en el septentrión novohispano: San José del Parral (1770–1790)." *Relaciones (Zamora)* 31(121): 21–56.

Orttiz Parrilla, Diego. 1763. "Testimonio de los autos sobre el asalto y ataque que los indios comanches hicieron en el presidio de San Luis de las Amarillas, que está a cargo del coronel Diego Orttiz Parrilla." Folios 1–111, Fojas 1–228. In AGI (Estado: Mexico 1933A&B) *Las Invaciones de los Apaches en el territorio de Tejas, 1763.*

Padilla, Fernando V. 1980. "Early Chicano Legal Recognition: 1846–1897." *Journal of Popular Culture* 13(3): 564–574.

Padilla, Genaro M. 1984. "The Self as Cultural Metaphor in Acosta's *Autobiography of a Brown Buffalo." Journal of General Education* 35(4): 242–258.

Paredes, Américo. 1990. *George Washington Gómez: A Mexicotexan Novel.* Houston: Arte Público.

Parry, Robert. 2011. "The Warning in Gary Webb's Death" *Consortium News,* December 9. http://consortiumnews.com/2011/12/09/the-warning-in-gary-webbs-death/.

Paz, Octavio. (1950) 1994. "Hijos de la Malinche." In *El laberinto de la soledad,* 27–36. Mexico: Fondo de Cultura Económica.

Peach, Ceri. 2000. "Discovering White Ethnicity and Parachuted Pluralism." *Progress in Human Geography* 23(2): 282–288.

———. 2002. "Social Geography: New Religions and Ethno-burbs—Contrasts with Cultural Geography." *Progress in Human Geography* 26: 252–260.

Peake, Linda. 2010. "Gender, Race, Sexuality." In *The SAGE Handbook of Social Geographies,* ed. Susan J. Smith, Rachel Pain, Sallie A. Marston, and John Paul Jones III, 54–78. London: Sage.

Peake, Linda, and Richard H. Schein. 2000. "Racing Geography into the New Millennium: Studies of Race and North American Geographies." *Social and Cultural Geography* 1(2): 133–142.

Peña, Roberto I. 1989. "La teoría teocrática de Fray Bartolomé De Las Casas O.P. y el regnum Indiarum." *Anales de la Universidad de Chile* 20: 401–424.

Pierson, Ruth Roach, and Nupur Chaudhuri, eds. 1998. *Nation, Empire, Colony: Historicizing Gender and Race.* Bloomington: Indiana University Press.

Polaski, Sandra. 2004. "Jobs, Wages, and Household Income." In *NAFTA's Promise and Reality: Lessons from Mexico for the Hemisphere*, ed. John J. Audley, Demetrios G. Papademetriou, Sandra Polaski, and Scott Vaughan, 11–38. Washington, DC: Carnegie Endowment for International Peace.

Prakash, Gyan. 1994. "Subaltern Studies as Postcolonial Criticism." *American Historical Review* 99(5): 1474–1490.

———. 1996. "Who's Afraid of Postcoloniality?" *Social Text* 49: 187–203.

Pratt, Mary Louise. 1992. *Imperial Eyes: Travel Writing and Transculturation*. New York: Routledge.

Prucha, Francis P. 1994. *American Indian Treaties: The History of a Political Anomaly*. Berkeley: University of California Press.

Pulido, Laura. 1996. *Environmentalism and Economic Justice: Two Chicano Struggles in the Southwest*. Tucson: University of Arizona Press.

Radhakrishnan, R. 2013. "Why Compare?" In *Comparison: Theories, Approaches, Uses*, ed. Rita Felski and Susan Stanford Friedman, 15–33. Baltimore: Johns Hopkins University Press.

Radin, Margaret. 1988. "The Liberal Conception of Property: Cross Currents in the Jurisprudence of Takings." *Columbia Law Review* 88(8): 1667–1696.

Rama, Angel. 1996. *The Lettered City*. Translated by John Charles Chasteen. Durham, NC: Duke University Press.

Ramirez v. Texas. 1931. 40 S.W. 2d 138 (Tex. Crim. App.).

Richter, Daniel K. 1992. *The Ordeal of the Longhouse: The People of the Iroquois League in the Era of European Colonization*. Durham, NC: University of North Carolina Press.

Rifkin, Mark. 2009. *Manifesting America: The Imperial Construction of U.S. National Space*. New York: Oxford University Press.

Rivera, Luis N. 1992. *A Violent Evangelism: The Political and Religious Conquest of the Americas*. Louisville, KY: Westminster/John Knox Press.

Roediger, David. 1999. *The Wages of Whiteness: Race and the Making of the American Working Class*. London: Verso.

Romero de Terreros, Juan M. 2004. "The Destruction of the San Sabá Apache Mission: A Discussion of the Casualties." *Americas* 60(4): 617–627.

Rose, Gillian. 1995. "Tradition and Paternity: Same Difference?" *Transactions of the Institute of British Geographers* n.s. 20(4): 414–416.

Ruiz Cameron, Christopher David. 2000. "One Hundred Fifty Years of Solitude: Reflections on the End of the History Academy's Dominance of Scholarship on the Treaty of Guadalupe Hidalgo." In *The Legacy of the Mexican and Spanish-American Wars: Legal, Literary, and Historical Perspectives*, ed. Gary D. Keller and Cordelia Candelaria, 1–24. Temple, AZ: Bilingual Review Press.

Ruiz Durán, Clemente. 2003. NAFTA: Lessons from an Uneven Integration." *International Journal of Political Economy* 33.3 (fall): 50–71.

Saldaña-Portillo, María Josefina. 2002. "'On the Road' with Che and Jack: Melancholia and the Legacy of Colonial Racial Geographies in the Americas." *New Formations: A Journal of Culture/Theory/Politics* 47: 87–108.

———. 2003. *The Revolutionary Imagination in the Americas and the Age of Development*. Durham, NC: Duke University Press.

———. 2004. " 'Wavering on the Horizon of Social Being': The Treaty of Guadalupe-Hidalgo and Its Racial Character in Américo Paredes's *George Washington Gómez.*" *Radical History Review* 89 (winter): 135–161.

———. 2008. " 'How Many Mexicans Is a Horse Worth?' The League of United Latin American Citizens, Desegregation Cases, and Chicano Historiography." *South Atlantic Quarterly* 107(4): 809–831.

———. 2011. " 'No Country for Old Mexicans': The Collision of Empires on the Texas Frontier." *Interventions* 13(1): 67–84.

Saldívar, Ramón. 1990. *Chicano Narrative.* Madison: University of Wisconsin Press.

———. 2000. "The Borderlands of Culture: Américo Paredes's *George Washington Gómez.*" In *Mexican Americans in Texas History: Selected Essays,* ed. Emilio Zamora, Cynthia Orozco, and Rodolfo Rocha, 175–186. Austin: Texas Historical Association.

Santleben, August. (1874) 1910. *A Texas Pioneer: Early Staging and the Overland Freighting Days on the Frontiers of Texas and Mexico,* ed. I. D. Affleck. New York: Neale.

Schein, Richard H. 2006. "Race and Landscape in the United States." In *Landscape and Race in the United States,* ed. Richard H. Schein, 1–22. New York: Routledge.

Scott, David. 2004. *Conscripts of Modernity.* Durham, NC: Duke University Press.

Seed, Patricia. 2001. *American Pentimento: The Invention of Indians and the Pursuit of Riches.* Minneapolis: University of Minnesota Press.

Seigel, Micol. 2005. "Beyond Compare: Comparative Method after the Transnational Turn." *Radical History Review* 11: 62–90.

Sheridan, Claire. 2003a. " 'Another White Race': Mexican Americans and the Paradox of Whiteness in Jury Selection." *Law and History Review* 21(1): 109–144.

———. 2003b. "Response: Cultural Racism and the Construction of Identity." *Law and History Review* 21(1): 207–210.

Sheridan Prieto, Maria Cecilia. 2001. " 'Indios Madrineros': Colonizadores Tlaxcaltecas en el Noreste Novohispano." *Estudios de Historia Novohispana* 24: 15–51.

———. 2002. "Reflexiones en torno a las identidades nativas en el noreste colonial." *Relaciones* 92(23): 76–1067.

———. 2007. "Cambio y continuidades en la territorialidad nativa: El espacio noroeste Novohispano, siglos XVI–XVIII." *Anuario* IEHS: *Instituto de Estudios histórico sociales* 22: 131–160.

Silva Prada, Natalia. 1999. "Contribución de la población indígena Novohispana al erario real: El donativo gracioso y voluntario o 'rigorosa pensión' de 1781 y su impacto en recaudaciones posteriores." *Signos Históricos* 1(1): 28–58.

Slater, David. 2003. "Beyond Euro-Americanism: Democracy and Post-Colonialism." In *Handbook of Cultural Geography,* ed. Kay Anderson, Mona Domosh, Steve Pile, and Nigel Thrift, 420–433. London: Sage. http://dx.doi.org/10.4135/9781848608252.n30.

Slavin, David Henry. 2001. *Colonial Cinema and Imperial France: White Blind Spots, Male Fantasies, and Settler Myths.* Baltimore: Johns Hopkins University Press.

Smith, John. 1612. *A Map of Virginia: With a Description of the Countrey, the Commodities, People, Government and Religion.* London: Joseph Barnes. http://mith.umd.edu/eada/html/display.php?docs=smith_map.xml.

Smith, Ralph A. 1963. "Indians in American-Mexican Relations before the War of 1846." *Hispanic American Historical Review* 43(1): 34–64.

———. 1984. "Scalp Hunting: A Mexican Experiment in Warfare." *Great Plains Journal* 23: 41–81.

———. 1985–1986. "The Comanches' Foreign War: Fighting Head Hunters in the Tropics." *Great Plains Journal* 24/25: 21–44.

———. 1991–1992. "The Bounty Wars of the West and Mexico." *Great Plains Journal* 30/31: 107–126.

Sparke, Matthew. 2005. *In the Space of Theory: Postfoundational Geographies of the Nation-State.* Minneapolis: University of Minnesota Press.

Spivak, Gayatri Chakravorty. 2003. *Death of a Discipline.* New York: Columbia University Press.

Stam, Juan. 1992. "La Biblia en la teologia colonialista de Juan Ginés de Sepúlveda." *Revista de Historia* (25): 157–164.

Stanford Friedman, Susan. 2013. "Why Not Compare?" In *Comparison: Theories, Approaches, Uses,* ed. Rita Felski and Susan Stanford Friedman, 34–45. Baltimore: Johns Hopkins University Press.

Stanley, Amy D. 1998. *From Bondage to Contract: Wage Labor, Marriage, and the Market in the Age of Slave Emancipation.* New York: Cambridge University Press.

Stavans, Ilan, ed. 1996. *Oscar Zeta Acosta: The Uncollected Works.* Houston: Arte Público Press.

Stokes, Douglas. 2001. "Better Lead than Bread? A Critical Analysis of the US's Plan Colombia," *Civil Wars* 4(2) (summer): 59–78.

Strachey, William. 1849. *The History of Travaile into Virginia Britannica.* London: Hakluyt Society (probably written between 1612 and 1616).

Sweeney, Edwin R. 1998. "Mangas Coloradas and Apache Diplomacy: Treaty-Making with Chihuahua and Sonora, 1842–1843." *Journal of Arizona History* 39(1): 1–22.

Sweet, James H. 1997. "The Iberian Roots of American Racist Thought." *William and Mary Quarterly* 54(1): 143–166.

Symonds, William. 1609. *Virginia: A Sermon Preached at White-Chappel.* London: Eleazer Edgar and William Welby.

Takaki, Ronald. 1990. *Strangers from a Different Shore: A History of Asian Americans.* New York: Penguin Books.

Thompson, Hunter S. (1977) 2011. "Fear and Loathing in the Graveyard of the Weird: The Banshee Screams for Buffalo Meat." In *Fear and Loathing at Rolling Stone: The Essential Writing of Hunter S. Thompson,* ed. Jann Wenner, 384–405. New York: Simon & Schuster.

Thomson, David. 2008. "America's Pain Inside: U.S. Audiences May Have Rejected Films About the War, but a Thirst for Blood Reveals the Nation's Mood." *The Guardian* (UK), January 16.

Tjarks, Alicia. 1974. "Comparative Demographic Analysis of Texas, 1777–1793." *Southwestern Historical Quarterly* 77(3): 291–338.

Treaty of Guadalupe Hidalgo. 1848. Washington, DC: Library of Congress. http://www.loc.gov/rr/program/bib/ourdocs/Guadalupe.html.

Trucios-Haynes, Enid. 2000–2001. "Why 'Race Matters': LatCrit Theory and Latina/o Racial Identity," *La Raza Law Journal* 12(1): 1–42.

Turner, Fredrick Jackson. [1893] 1921. "The Significance of the Frontier in American History." In Fredrick Jackson Turner, *The Frontier in American History*. New York, NY: Henry Holt and Company.

Turner, John K. 1910. *Barbarous Mexico*. Chicago: Charles H. Kerr.

United States v. Joseph. 1876. 94 U.S. 614; 24 L. Ed. 295; 1876 U.S. LEXIS 1918. October Term.

United States v. Lucero. 1869. 1 N.M. 422, 1869 WL 2423 (N.M. Terr.).

Vasconcelos, José. (1925) 1997. *The Cosmic Race/La Raza Cósmica: A Bilingual Edition*. Translated and annotated by Didier T. Jaén. Baltimore: Johns Hopkins University Press.

Vázquez García, Gabriela. 2006. "José de Escandón y las nuevas poblaciones del Nuevo Santander." *Scripta Nova* 10(218): 85. http://www.ub.edu/geocrit/sn/sn-218 -85.htm.

Velázquez Estrada, Rosalía. 2000. "John Kenneth Turner Autor del México Bárbaro: Su Horizonte de Enunciación." *Revista Fuentes Humanísticas* 10(20): 77–89.

Villarreal, M. Angeles, and Ian F. Fergusson. 2011. NAFTA *at 20: Overview and Trade Effects*. Washington, DC: Congressional Research Service, Prepared for Members and Committees of Congress. http://fas.org/sgp/crs/row/R42965.

Wallerstein, Immanuel. 2011. *Modern World System III: The Second Era of Great Expansion of the Capitalist World Economy, 1730–1840s*. Berkeley: University of California Press.

Warrior, Robert A. 1996. "Canaanites, Cowboys, and Indians: Deliverance, Conquest, and Liberation Theology Today." In *Native and Christian: Indigenous Voices on Religious Identity in the United States and Canada*, ed. James Treat, 93–104. New York: Routledge.

Webb, Walter Prescott. 1931. *The Great Plains*. Boston, MA: Ginn and Company.

———. [1935] 1965. *The Texas Rangers: A Century of Frontier Defense*. Austin: University of Texas Press.

Weber, David J. 1981. "American Westward Expansion and the Breakdown of Relations Between Pobladores and 'Indios Bárbaros' on Mexico's Far Northern Frontier, 1821–1846." *New Mexico Historical Review* 56(3): 221–238.

———. 2005. *Bárbaros: Spaniards and Their Savages in the Age of Enlightenment*. New Haven, CT: Yale University Press.

Weiner, Mark S. 2006. *Americans without Law: The Racial Boundaries of Citizenship*. New York: New York University Press.

Williams, Robert A. 1990. *The American Indian in Western Legal Thought: The Discourses of Conquest*. Oxford: Oxford University Press.

Wilson, Steven H. 2003a. "Brown over 'Other White': Mexican Americans' Legal Arguments and Litigation Strategy in School Desegregation Lawsuits." *Law and History Review* 21(1): 145–194.

———. 2003b. "Response: Tracking the Shifting Racial Identity of Mexican Americans." *Law and History Review* 21(1): 211–213.

———. 2005. "Some Are Born White, Some Achieve Whiteness, and Some Have Whiteness Thrust upon Them: Mexican Americans and the Politics of Racial

Classification in the Federal Judicial Bureaucracy, Twenty-Five Years after *Hernandez v. Texas.*" *Chicano-Latino Law Review* 25(1): 201–239.

Wilton, R. D. 2001. "Critically Understanding Race-connected Practices: A Reading of W.E.B. DuBois and Richard Wright." *Professional Geographer* 54(1): 31–41.

Winders, J. 2003. "White in All the Wrong Places: White Rural Poverty in the Postbellum U.S. South. *Cultural Geography* 3(3): 303–21.

Withers, Charles W. J., and David N. Livingstone. 1999. *Geography and Enlightenment.* Chicago: University of Chicago Press.

Wolfe, Patrick. 1994. " 'White Man's Flour': Doctrines of Virgin Birth in Evolutionist Ethnogenetics and Australian State-Formation." *History and Anthropology* 8(1–4): 165–205.

———. 1999. *Settler Colonialism and the Transformation of Anthropology: The Politics and Poetics of an Ethnographic Event.* London: Cassell.

———. 2012. "Against the Intentional Fallacy: Logocentricism and Continuity in the Rhetoric of Indian Dispossession." *American Indian Culture and Research Journal* 36(1): 3–45.

Wolfe, Tom. 1969. *The Electric Kool-Aid Acid Test.* New York: Bantam.

Woods, Clyde. 1998. *Development Arrested: The Blues and Plantation Power in the Mississippi Delta.* New York: Verso.

Yarsinke, Amy W. 2004. *All for One and One for All: A Celebration of 75 Years of the League of the United Latin American Citizens (LULAC).* Virginia Beach, VA: Donning.

Zepeda, Eduardo, Timothy A. Wise, and Kevin P. Gallagher. 2009. *Rethinking Trade Policy for Development: Lessons from Mexico under NAFTA.* December. Carnegie Endowment for International Peace Policy Outlook. http://carnegieendowment.org/files/nafta_trade_development.pdf.

Zinn, Howard, and Anthony Arnove. 2004. *Voices of a People's History of the United States.* New York: Seven Stories Press.

INDEX

Bold numbers refer to images

abjection, 36, 85–86, 94, 143, 146, 226
Abraham, 56
Abysinia, 262n21
Acosta, Oscar Zeta, 197, 199–205, 207–208, 210, 212, 291n4, 292n5, 292n7, 293n11, 294n20; *The Autobiography of a Brown Buffalo*, 31, 195–196, 214–232, 294n24
activism: Chicana/o activism, 156, 194, 197, 199–215; indigenous activism, 14–15, 23, 156, 158; Mexican American activism, 30–31, 135, 156–194, 214, 284n1, 285n3, 286n12, 290n32; peace activism, 233–234, 254, **255**; social media activism, 248
Adams, David B., 283n26
Adorno, Rolena, 264n2, 265n3, 266n9, 267n17
Afghanistan, 22, 100–102, 106, 238, 257
African Americans, 114, 116, 130, 142, 153, 186, 188–190, 203, 214, 224–225, 284n37, 285n3, 287n15, 289n26, 292n7; civil rights and, 161, 190; enslavement of, 150–152; racial classification of, 157, 163–166, 169, 201–202, 211, 285n5, 293n11
Africans, 117, 121, 161, 164–165, 179, 202, 211, 263n33, 266n9
afromestizos, 27, 141, 143, 155, 185, 202–203, 260n13, 287n15; in bounty programs, 114, 130; in Mexico, 116–117, 152–153, 173; in New Spain, 71, 78–79, 92, 118–119, 128, 281n16, 281n17; treatment by U.S., 134, 140–142, 155, 174, 284n36

Alaska, 211
Alaska Natives, 293n11. *See also* Eskimos
Aldama, Fredrick L., 224
Alfonso, 39
Al Qaeda, 98, 256–258
Álvarez, Salvador, 74
American Civil Liberties Union (ACLU), 161–162, 190
American GI Forum (AGIF), 187
American Indians, 63, 130, 157, 168, 210–211, 211–212, 214, 284n37, 287n13, 288n19, 293n11. *See also* Amerindians; indigeneity; Native Americans; *individual indigenous peoples or nations*
American Jewish Congress, 161
American Revolution, 270n38
Americas, 31, 35, 172, 258, 268n20, 295n25; Christianity in, 49–50; conquest of, 39, 203, 266n9; humanism and, 33, 261n20; racial geographies of, 6, 8, 35–36, 268n26. *See also individual countries*
Amerindians, 39. *See also* American Indians; Indians; Native Americans
Amiyayas, 68
Anderson, Kay, 20
Andrada, Friar Rodrigo de, 38
Andreas, Peter, 298n25
Anghie, Antony, 50
Anglo-American colonialism and, 24
Anglo Americans, 6, 23, 64, 66, 113, 133, 142, 144, 147–148, 173, 217, 261n20, 284n37,

Anglo Americans (*continued*)
287n18; Anglo-American colonialism, 8–9, 15, 18–19, 24–25, 28, 57, 70, 160, 176–177, 211, 260n13, 272n5, 283n28, 284n36, 288n21; race and, 69, 133, 155, 173–174, 182, 201–202, 263n31; treatment of Indians, 109, 113, 115

Anglo-Saxons, 61, 157, 164–165

animality, 42–44, 46, 196. *See also* bestiality

anthropology, 8, 16, 74, 85, 158, 169, 182, 186

anticolonialism, 28, 62, 83, 85–86, 91, 107, 158–159, 194, 224–225, 279n37. *See also* postcolonialism

Apache, 11, 121, 137, 156, 217–218, 226, 261n18, 268n29, 280n11, 284n34; Chiricahua Apache, 257; food production by, 74, 78–79, 272n6, 273n12; Lipan Apaches, 83–84, 109, 277n27, 277n28; Mescalero Apache, 109; Mexico-Apache relations, 113, 115, 122, 138–140, 146, 158, 160, 177, 179, 219, 233–235, 280n9, 283n28, 284n34; in *No Country for Old Men*, 95, 105; raids by, 124–133, 228, 246; Spanish-Apache relations, 77, 82–92, 109–113, 119–120, 235, 261n15, 275n21, 277n27, 278n34, 279n2, 283n28; spatial practices of, 30, 108; U.S.-Apache relations, 114, 138, 143–144, 154, 158, 160, 174, 180–181, 212, 219, 227, 235; war on terror and, 22, 256–258. *See also* Geronimo

apostates, 25, 78, 89, 92, 94, 127

Arabia, 262n21

Aranames, 89

Arapaho, 226, 228

Archivo General de Indias (AGI), 68–69, 83

Aristotle, 33, 38–39, 41–43, 45–46, 48, 51, 282n18; *Ethics,* 45; *Politics,* 45

Arizona, 7, 174, 211, 256, 273n10; Nogales, 254

Arizona SB1070 (Support Our Law Enforcement and Safe Neighborhoods Act), 7

Arkansas, 227

Armenians, 264n34

Arriola, Christopher, 161

Asian Americans, 186, 221, 284n37

Asians, 167–168, 203, 293n11

Atayeyes, 89

Austria: Vienna, 38

authenticity, 2, 15, 158, 211, 218, 230

The Autobiography of a Brown Buffalo, 31, 195–196, 214–232, 294n24

The Autobiography of Malcolm X, 294n23

autonomy, 14–15, 54, 117–118, 120, 122, 124, 128, 293n10

aztecas del norte, 140–141

Aztecs, 109, 140, 156–158, 167, 169–170, 195, 226, 235, 287n16, 291n1

Aztlán, 64, 158–159, 292n5; as Chicano homeland, 7, 22, 140–141, 196–203, **198,** 214, 226, 230–232, 291n1; racial geographies of, 29, 31, 194, 197, 232. *See also* nationalism: Chicano nationalism

Bacon, Lt. Col. R.R., 207

Baldwin, Roger, 190

Balibar, Etienne, 120

Banner, Stuart, 57–58, 270n35

barbarian, figure of, 39, 42, 44–46, 48, 70, 249, 264n2, 267n16. *See also* indios bárbaros

Bardem, Javier, 96–97, **99**

Barnes, Judge Stanley E, 207

Barr, Juliana, 226

Basques, 156–157

Beat Generation, 199, 214–215, 260n14, 291n3

beheading, 121, 126, 129–130, 132, 137, 154, 236, 246–247, 249, 253–254

Bennett, Herman, 116–117

Berger, John, 2

bestiality, 43, 48, 220–222. *See also* animality

Betancourt, Edith Norma, 272n5

Bexar County Court, 157, 167

Bible, 44, 48

Biltmore Hotel, 204

Biltmore Six, 197, 200, 204, 212, 214

Bin Laden, Osama, 233, 256–258

"Birth of a Symbol," 213

blackface, 224–225, 227

Blackhawk, Ned, 110, 226

Black Legend, 20, 86, 288n21

blackness, 150, 202–203, 211, 214, 219, 222, 293n11, 294n24; mestizaje and, 25, 27; in Treaty of Guadalupe Hidalgo, 134, 141;

in U.S. law, 144, 157, 164, 166, 168–169, 171, 186, 188–190, 292n7; uncanniness and, 218
Blunt, Allison, 20
Bocas Prietas, 68, 73
Bolívar, Simón, 193
Borrados, 68
bounty programs, 113–115, 126, 128–132, 253, 279–280
Bourbon, House of, 110, 119–120, 123, 127, 279n2, 282n18
Boy Scouts, 217, 220
Brazil, 252
Breitenbach, Judge Eugene H., 206
Breuer, Joseph, 95, 106
Brolin, Josh, 95
Brown Berets, 213, 293n13
Brown v. Board of Education, 201–202, 289n26, 292n7
Bryant, Judge Lindley, 207
Bulls of Donation, 269n31
Burke, Edmund, 262n21
Bush, George H.W., 238
Bustillo v. Texas, 187
Byrd, Jodi, 35, 259n8

Cabeza de Vaca, Álvar Núñez, 177
Caddo, 226–228
Cadena, Carlos C., 187, 189
Cadimas, 68
Caesar, Julius, 156
Calderón, President Felipe, 31, 233–234, 248, 254, 295n1
Calderón, Héctor, 224
California, 31, 197, 208, 211, 228–229, 231, 289n29; Alta California, 34; Burbank, 205; El Modena, 184; Garden Grove, 184; Logan Heights, 291n1; Los Angeles, 199–200, 204–209, 215, 231, 237; Los Feliz, 206; racial segregation in, 186, 200, 213, 289n26, 290n30; Riverbank, 215–216, 218, 222, 225; San Diego, 254; San Francisco, 196, 215; Santa Ana, 184; Westminster, 184–185. *See also* Mendez v. Westminster
California Constitution, 174
California Department of Education, 204
California gold rush, 113

California Superior Court, 200, 205, 210, 286n8
Call, Judge Joseph, 205, 209
Calvo, José J., 112–113
Canadian Americans, 285n4
Canadian-U.S. border, 19, 238–240
Caodachos, 90
Caravan for Peace with Justice and Dignity, 254–256, **255**
Cardozo Law School, 183
Carlos I, King. *See* Carlos V, Holy Roman Emperor
Carlos V, Holy Roman Emperor, 34, 37–38, 50, 117
Carnegie Endowment for International Peace, 297n19
Carranza, Venustiano, 145
Carrasco v. Texas, 187
Carter, Robert L., 289n26
Cassady, Neal, 215
Castañeda, Jorge, 241–242
caste system, 26, 79, 116–123, 132, 140, 162, 263n33, 279n3, 281n16. *See also* miscegenation
Castile and Aragon Monarchy, 41
Castilians, 156–157
Castro, Sal, 293n13
Catholicism, 81, 112, 116, 120, 127, 145, 147, 170; Catholic Enlightenment, 17, 44, 51, 172; Catholic unity, 128, 160, 180; treatment of Indians, 36–53, 76, 109, 122
Caucasians, 156–157, 163, 165–166, 201–202, 286n9. *See also* whiteness
Center for International Policy, 295n1
Central America. *See individual countries*
Central Intelligence Agency (CIA), 237
Chakrabarty, Dipesh, 24, 70, 104, 263n28
Chantry, Judge Kenneth, 207
Chapulines, 68
Charlemagne, 156
Cheng, Anne Anlin, 195–196, 226
Cherokee, 10, 113, 139
Cheyenne, 228, 257, 268n29
Chicano-Latino Law Review, 290n35
Chicano Park, 291n1
Chicanos, 7, 27–28, 65, 141–142, 152, 156, 286n12, 292n5, 292n6; Chicano nationalism, 22,

INDEX   321

Chicanos (*continued*)
31, 153, 159, 195–232, 285n3, 292n5, 293n11, 294n20; Chicano scholarship, 135, 140, 161, 187, 192, 285n3. *See also* Aztlán

Chichimecas, 109, 158, 235

Chickasaw, 139

China, 262n21

Chinese Americans, 164–166, 285n4, 285n5

la Chingada, 13–14, 227. *See also* Malinche

chingón, 13, 227, 230

Choctaw, 139

Christiancentrism, 40

Christianity, 36–58, 61, 75, 91–93, 98, 116–119, 128, 145, 190–191, 233, 236, 262n24, 265n7, 266n9, 267n16, 267n17, 273n12, 282n22; Christian unity, 41, 47–53, 77, 81–84, 89, 94, 109–112, 138, 178, 192, 216. *See also* Moriscos; Petrine responsibility; *individual denominations*

Cisneros v. CCISD, 292n7

citizenship, 14, 123, 127–128, 236, 271n3; British citizenship, 61; cultural citizenship, 203; indigeneity and, 52, 110; Mexican citizenship, 114–117, 122, 124, 130–132, 145–146, 177, 239, 280n10, 282n23, 283n26, 292n9; racial citizenship, 13, 25–29, 174, 286n11, 286n12; Spanish citizenship, 121, 263n33; under Treaty of Guadalupe Hidalgo, 22, 108, 133–141, 172–175, 179–181, 195–196, 288n25; U.S. citizenship, 63–65, 87, 106, 148–149, 151–152, 155, 157–160, 164–171, 182–185, 188, 192–193, 201, 208, 211, 220, 230, 232, 240, 246, 254, 258, 285n6, 287n14, 287n18, 289n28, 289n29, 290n32

Civil Rights Act (1866), 173

Civil Rights Act (1964), 189, 214

civil rights movements, 197, 204; indigenous civil rights movement, 23, 156; Mexican American civil rights movement, 22, 30–31, 156, 159, 161, 185, 187–194, 289n29, 290n32, 290n35, 292n7

Clement VII, Pope, 39

Clinton, Bill, 237

Coberly, William, 206

Coetzee, J.M.: *Foe*, 199

Cohen brothers: *No Country for Old Men*, 30, 69–70, 94–107, **97, 99, 103**

Cold War, 6, 237–238

Colegio de Nuestra Señora de Guadalupe, 89

Colombia, 236–237, 246, 296n6

colonialism, 26, 29, 33, 102, 108, 172, 196–197, 262n24, 269n32; Anglo-American colonialism, 8–9, 15, 18–19, 24–25, 28, 57, 70, 160, 176–177, 211, 260n13, 272n5, 283n28, 284n36, 288n21; British colonialism, 6–7, 17–18, 20, 22, 34–36, 54–55, 57–61, 57–62, 64–65, 83, 160, 177, 214, 235, 269n31, 271n3; colonial masculinity, 10–11, 13, 218, 221–223, 260n13, 260n14; colonial paleography, 272n5; European colonialism, 6, 8, 21, 34–35, 48, 51, 54–55, 60–64, 83–85, 137, 203, 246, 265n4, 265n8, 288n21; French colonialism, 70, 83–84, 89–91, 94; gender and, 11; indigeneity and, 15–16, 21–24, 57, 154, 234, 295n25; Portuguese colonialism, 261n20, 266n9; Spanish colonialism, 3, 6–8, 12–14, 16–20, 22, 24–28, 30, 34, 36–56, 64–95, 98, 104–105, 109–111, 116–129, 132, 136–141, 145, 156, 158–160, 174, 177–181, 191, 193, 202–204, 214, 235, 251, 256, 261n15, 261n20, 263n31, 267n15, 267n17, 269n31, 270n34, 271n3, 272n4, 272n5, 275n19, 279n2, 279n4, 280n8, 281n12, 288n21; U.S. colonialism, 3, 6, 9, 31, 35, 62–63, 65, 105, 211–212, 232, 288n21, 294n19. *See also* anticolonialism; imperialism; Manifest Destiny; neocolonialism; settler colonialism

Colorado, 196, 228, 231, 273n10; Denver, 224

Colt, Samuel, 151

Columbus, Christopher, 15, 34, 156

Comanche, 11, 30, 69, 83–86, 91, 115, 120, 130, 132, 137–138, 143, 151, 152, 160, 226, 234, 235, 256–257, 261n18, 277n28, 284n34; Mexico-Comanche relations, 108–110, 112–113, 121–122, 124–127, 133, 139, 146, 177, 179, 219, 234, 246, 280n9, 280n11, 283n26, 283n28; in *No Country for Old Men*, 95, 102, 104–105; Spanish-Comanche relations, 74, 78–79, 82–91, 110–112, 119, 127–129, 261n15, 273n12, 277n27; U.S.-Comanche relations, 108–110, 114, 124–125, 124–126, 133, 138–140, 144, 154, 180–181, 212, 227–228; war on terror and, 22

322 INDEX

Comanchería, 125

comparison, 6–7, 13, 17–18, 22, 36, 239, 261n20, 288n19

Connecticut, 269n33

conquistadors, 12, 36–37, 47, 52, 112–113, 261n15, 264n2, 265n3, 265n4, 265n5, 267n15

Constitución Política, 26

Constitution of the State of Coahuila and Texas, 121

Cook, Captain James, 261n20

Cooper, James Fenimore, 176

Corpus Christi Independent School District, 292n7

Cortes de Cádiz, 173

Cortéz, Hernán, **12**, 156, 167, 275n16

Cosgrove, Denis, 16, 18–19, 262n24

Council of Castile, 38, 40, 268n20

Council of the Indies, 36–37, 39–40, 265n3, 268n20, 268n21

counterinsurgency, 83, 254, 295n5

coyotes, 118–119, 281n16

Crashaw, William, 56

Creek, 139

criollos, 64, 71, 79, 116–117, 119–121, 260n13, 281n12

critical legal theory, 161. *See also* Latina/o critical legal theory

critical race studies, 25–26

Croghan, George, 269n33

Crusades, 40

Cruz Olmeda, Gilbert, 293n13

Cuauhtémoc, **12**, 193

Curtis, Edward Sheriff, 268n29

Cypher, James M., 243, 297n22

DeAnda, James, 187, 189, 292n7

deconstruction, 18, 31, 35, 95, 163, 183

De la Torre Curiel, José R., 77–78, 275n21

Delay, Brian, 124–128, 226, 280n11, 283n26

Delgado Wise, Raúl, 243, 297n22

Deloria, Philip, 217–218

de Las Casas, Bartolomé, 30, 34–35, 37–38, 40–41, 67, 75, 111, 265n3, 265n5, 265n7, 266n9, 268n20, 268n21; *In Defense of the Indians,* 45–53, 81, 267n16, 267n17, 267n18

de Man, Paul, 191

Demócrates Primero, 39

Demócrates Segundo, 39, 41–43, 45, 266n12, 268n20

Derrida, Jacques: "Force of Law," 162–163, 165, 167, 183–184, 193

dialectical materialism, 213

Díaz Del Castillo, Bernal, 275n16

Diether, Leonard A., 210

disavowal, 138, 142, 146, 148–150, 152–153

Dockweiler, Judge George A., 206

Doherty, Emmett E., 210

domestic workers, 207–209, 245, 271n3, 273n12

Dominican missionaries, 37–38, 264n2, 267n18

DREAM Act, 130

drones, 237–239, 244

drug cartels, 6, 233–234, 236, 240, 247–258, 259n3, 298n26. *See also* narco-terrorism; *individual cartels*

drug war, 6–7, 22, 24, 233–240, 244–246, 250–256, 258, 259n3, 295n3, 296n6, 298n25; in *No Country for Old Men,* 70, 95–99, 102. *See also* Iran-Contra cocaine scandal; narco-terrorism

Dryden, Mr., 206

East L.A. Thirteen, 197, 200, 204, 212, 214, 293n13

Ecuador, 252

Elementos Constitucionales, 26

Elk, John, 166, 286n7

Elk v. Wilkins, 157, 166–169, 181, 285n6, 286n7

El Salvador, 295n3

Emanuel Presbyterian Church, 207

empiricism, 6

emplotment, 9, 19, 22, 54, 68–72, 85–86, 89–93, 159–160, 172, 209, 224–225, 228

encomiendas, 22, 37–38, 44, 49, 116, 122, 265n4

Eng, David L., 221–222

England, 55, 57, 60–61, 91, 147, 269n33, 270n35. *See also* Great Britain

Enlightenment, 17, 33, 44, 47, 50–51, 62, 94, 120, 170–172, 176, 261n20, 262n24

Erasmus, 39, 265n7

Escandón, José de, 67–68, 271n3, 274n15

Eskimos, 210–212, 214, 294n19. *See also* Alaska Natives

Esparza, Moctezuma, 293n13

establecimientos, 113

ethnic studies, 26, 31

Eurocentrism, 40, 47, 265n8

Europe, 10, 45, 90–91, 121, 123, 125, 172, 179, 221, 251, 260n13, 262n21, 263n33, 275n20, 281n16, 286n9; Enlightenment in, 17, 33, 94, 261n20, 282n18; European colonialism, 6, 8, 21, 34–35, 48, 51, 54–55, 60–64, 83–85, 137, 203, 246, 265n4, 265n8, 288n21; fears of Ottoman Empire, 36, 38–39, 50; slavery in, 40–41. *See also individual countries*

Evans, A.J., 166–167, 286n10

Expediente sobre la población y pacificación del Seno Mexicano, 53, 67–69, 75

Fear and Loathing in Las Vegas, 215, 291n4

Felipe II, King, 38, 50

Felipe V, King, 274n15

femininity, 10, 101, 132, 229, 260n13

feminism, 18, 292n5

Ferdinand, King, 37

feudalism, 60–62, 123, 130, 236, 251–253

Fifth Circuit Court of Appeals, 292n7

Fildew, Judge, 210–212

Filipinos, 158

Finerman, Robert, 210

First Congregational Church of Los Angeles, 206

Five Civilized Tribes, 228. *See also* Cherokee; Chickasaw; Choctaw; Creek; Seminole

Florida, 115, 151

Foe, 199

Fogo, Anthony, 206

Foley, Neil, 191

Forbes, Jack, 156, 158–159, 287n16

foreign direct investment (FDI), 243–245

Fort Benning, 254–256, **255**

Foucault, Michel, 93, 129, 249

Fourteenth Amendment, 184, 186–189, 204, 284n1, 287n13, 288n25

France, 278n34, 278n35; French colonialism, 70, 83–84, 89–91, 94. *See also* French and Indian War; French Revolution

Franciscans, 83–84, 89, 92

Francisco, Juan, 234

Frank, Andre Gunder, 251

Franklin, Benjamin, 34, 61, 269n33

Franklin, William, 269n33

Free Society of Traders, 55

free trade, 24, 235–236, 244, 256, 268n24. *See also* North American Free Trade Agreement

Freidman, Andrew, 294n17

French and Indian War, 59–60

French Revolution, 271n3

Freud, Sigmund, 95, 106, 195, 216, 219–222

Frisbie, Minister, 54, 95

frontier thesis, 9–10, 199, 228, 260–261

Gálvez, Bernardo de, 110–111, 279n2

Garcia, Gustavo C., 187, 189

Garcia, Mario, 192

Garcia, Richard A., 192

gender, 118, 155, 174, 229–230, 262n26; colonialism and, 10–11, 13–14; geography and, 20, 56. *See also* femininity; feminism; masculinity; patriarchy; sexism

genocide, 20, 25, 31, 77–78, 86, 105, 141, 151–152, 199, 258

geo-graphing, 19, 23, 88, 91, 107, 110, 111, 137, 142. *See also* mapping; maps; racial geographies

geography. *See* mapping; maps; racial geographies

George III, King, 60, 62

George Washington Gómez, 30, 142–153, 284n37

Georgia. *See* Fort Benning

Germany, 16, 186

Geronimo, 131, 233, 235, 256–258

Gila River, 256

Ginés de Sepúlveda, Juan, 30, 34–35, 38–53, 67, 75, 154, 266n11, 266n14, 269n31; *Demócrates, Primero*, 39; *Demócrates Segundo*, 39, 41–43, 45, 266n12, 268n2

Ginsberg, Allen, 215

God: Indian policy and, 37, 43, 45–47, 49–50, 190, 233, 235

Goman, George, 206

Gómez, Laura, 161, 183, 288n22

Gonzalez, Manuel C., 193–194

Good Samaritan, 44, 67, 73, 75

governmentality, 6, 14, 51, 78, 111, 116, 249–250

Goyahkla. *See* Geronimo

grand juries, 200–201, 204–205, 207, 210–212
la gran familia mejicana, 110, 112, 115, 124, 127, 132–133, 137, 146, 172–173, 179–180
Gray, Horace, 285n6
Great Britain, 63, 270n38, 278n35; British citizenship, 30, 61; British colonialism, 6–7, 17–18, 20, 22, 34–36, 54–55, 57–62, 64–65, 83, 160, 177, 214, 235, 269n31, 271n3; London, 55; Whitehall, 60. *See also* England
Greece, 47–48, 267n16
Greenfield, Judge Samuel, 207–209
Grey, Zane, 268n29
gringos, 147, 200, 230–231
El Grito: A Journal of Contemporary Mexican American Thought, 200, 204, 292n6
Gross, Ariela, 161, 173, 285n3, 288n25
Guatemala, 295n3
Guerrero, Vicente, 121, 263n33
Guerreros Unidos cartel, 250
Guevara, Don Antonio Ladrón de, 53, 274n13; *Expediente sobre la población y pacificación del Seno Mexicano,* 53, 67–69, 75; *Noticias de los Poblados,* 272n4, 274n15; *Noticias sobre los indios barbarous y sus costumbres,* 67–69, 71–82, 73, 88–89, 102, 271n3
Guglielmo, Thomas A., 161
Guha, Ranajit, 83
Guidotti-Hernández, Nicole, 226
Gulf cartel, 6, 254
Gulf Coast, 69, 71–72
Gulf of Mexico, 71

Haas, Lisbeth, 226
Hall, G. Emlen, 283n27
Hämäläinen, Pekka, 82–85, 226, 277n27
Hames-García, Michael, 224
Haney López, Ian F., 187–188, 264n34, 286n11, 286n12, 294n20
Hanke, Lewis, 33–34, 37–41, 50, 267n19
Harper, Tess, 100
Harris, Cheryl, 23, 59
Hartman, Saidiya V., 269n30
Haverford College: American Studies Working Group, 294n17
Hawai'i, 211
hegemony, 16, 69, 128, 183, 282n18

Henry, Patrick, 269n33
Hernandez, Pete, 187
Hernandez v. New York, 288n25
Hernandez v. Texas, 161, 171, 187–189, 191, 201, 290n35, 292n7
Herrera, John, 187, 189
Herrera-Sobek, María, 224
heterosexism, 292n5
heterotemporality, 22, 24–25, 27–28, 70, 85–86, 88, 95, 98, 105, 184, 263n28, 263n30, 263n31, 293n11
Hiawatha, 176
Hichitas, 89
Hidalgo, Miguel, 147, 193
Hiller, Judge Eleanor, 206
Hispanic (term), 153, 293n11
Hispanic-Indios (term), 201–203
hispanicization, 122, 148, 156, 158
historiography, 9, 11–12, 18, 23, 27, 36, 83–86, 89, 100, 104–106, 125–126, 199, 226
Hollywood, 228
Holy Land, 40
Honduras, 235, 295n3
Hoyoso, 112
humanism, 33–34, 44, 47, 64, 115
humanity, global theory of, 50, 94
Hungary, 38
hysteria, 95, 257

Idaho: Ketchum, 196, 228
Illinois: Chicago, 254
Illinois Company, 269n33
imperialism, 31; European imperialism, 6
Incas (Indians of Peru), 38, 273n7
In Defense of the Indians, 45–49, 81, 267n16, 267n17, 267n18
Indiana, 125
Indiana Company, 269n33
Indian giver, 12, 14
Indian Intercourse Act (U.S.), 62–63
Indianness, 8, 35–36, 259n8
Indian removal, 54, 59, 64, 110, 124–126, 139, 141, 227–228. *See also* Trail of Tears
Indian Removal Act, 108, 125, 227
Indians, 1–3, 33, 110, 114, 143, 195, 246, 260n13, 279n37; British colonialism and, 35, 54–62, 270n35; Chicano national identity

INDEX   325

Indians (*continued*)

and, 31, 153, 196–199, 202–203, 217–223, 225–232, 291n1; imagined Indians, 16, 61, 93–94, 102, 105, 154; Mexican national identity and, 13, 15, 27, 115–116, 121–132, 280n10, 282n23; racial geographies and, 7–13, 17–23, 148–152, 160, 263n30; Spanish colonialism and, 24, 27–28, 30, 35–53, 66–94, 102, 104, 109, 117, 119–121, 261n15, 263n33, 264n2, 266n9, 267n15, 267n17, 267n18, 268n25, 272n4, 272n5, 273n7, 273n12, 274n13, 277n27, 277n28, 278n34, 279n2, 281n12, 281n17, 282n22; in the Treaty of Guadalupe Hidalgo, 133–142; U.S. colonialism and, 62–65, 99, 102, 253, 257, 269n33, 279n6; U.S. national identity and, 28, 94–107, 157–158, 163–184, 186, 190, 210–212, 214, 285n4, 286n7, 286n8, 286n9, 287n13, 287n15, 287n18, 290n30; vanishing Indians, 54, 64, 94, 107, 109, 175, 240, 268n29. *See also* Amerindians; Native Americans; wandering savage, figure of; *individual indigenous peoples or nations*

Indian Territory, 108, 113, 125, 139, 227–228, 268n29

indigeneity, 18, 31, 56, 142–143, 148–149, 175–178, 193–194, 196–197, 257, 261n18, 263n28, 267n15, 272n6, 278n35, 279n37, 282n18, 282n22, 293n10, 295n25; in Chicano nationalism, 198–199, 202–204, 218–222, 226, 291n1; citizenship and, 52, 59, 110; colonialism and, 15–16, 20–24, 47, 57, 59–65, 154, 234, 295n25; in Mexico, 6–9, 11–14, 24–29, 110, 112–115, 128–130, 134, 152–156, 179–180, 217, 234–235, 250, 253, 279n4, 280n9, 280n10, 280n11, 284n34, 294n19, 295n25; in Mexico-U.S. borderlands, 2–3, 18–19; in New Spain, 12–13, 17, 25, 34–54, 66–94, 109–112, 115–121, 123, 173, 178, 261n15, 263n31, 264n2, 265n3, 265n4, 266n12, 266n14, 267n17, 270n34, 272n5, 272n12, 273n7, 275n16, 275n19, 279n3, 279n4, 281n17; racialization of, 30, 36, 84, 133–134, 138, 153, 156–162, 165–174, 183–184, 191–193, 210–212, 287n16, 288n19; in the Treaty of

Guadalupe Hidalgo, 133–141; in the U.S., 10, 15, 94–109, 181–182, 211–212, 224–232, 235–236, 239–240, 245, 258

indigenous rights movements, 14

indigenismo, 292n5

indigenous studies, 15, 16

indios, 35, 66, 152, 196, 217, 260n13; Mexican national identity and, 11, 116, 229–230; racial geographies and, 8–9, 15, 17–21, 29; Spanish colonialism and, 35–53, 68–74, 77–82, 89–94, 111, 116, 118–123, 174, 281n17. *See also individual indigenous peoples or nations*

indios bárbaros, 16, 22, 24, 55, 158, 173, 232, 273n7; in *Autography of a Brown Buffalo*, 216–217, 219, 222, 226; construction by Mexico, 128–130, 134, 179, 234; construction by Spain, 42–45, 53, 73, 79, 84, 89, 92–94, 98, 108–110, 112, 114–115, 137, 177–178, 181, 279n2, 283n26; construction by Treaty of Guadalupe Hidalgo, 138, 140–141; construction by U.S., 154–155, 160, 170–171, 188, 190, 212, 234–236, 239–240, 246, 249, 253, 256–258, 286n12; in *George Washington Gómez*, 143–144, 148–149

Indios Grandes, 72–73, 79–82

indios nefastos, 154

innumerable places, 66, 70, 107

In re Ah Yup, 163–169, 285n4, 285n5, 286n9, 286n11

In re Camille, 157, 163, 165–169, 181, 285n4, 286n9

In re Rodriguez, 156–159, 163–172, 184, 186–188, 225, 286n8, 286n9, 286n10, 286n12, 286n15, 286n16, 287n14

Integral Development of the Family (DIF), 250

Las Invaciones de los Apaches en el territorio de Tejas (Invasions of the Apaches in the Territory of Texas), 83, 86–94, 104

Iowa, 125

Iran-Contra cocaine scandal, 236–237

Iraq, 22, 100–103, 106, 235, 238

Irish Americans, 151–152

Iroquois, 10

Isabel, Queen, 34

Isacson, Adam, 237–238
Iscanses, 89
Islam, 38–41, 50, 87, 104; Islamic jihad figure, 7, 22, 31, 98, 100–102, 105, 235–237, 239, 256. *See also* Moors; Moriscos; Saracens
Italy: Bologna, 38–39; Rome, 40, 50
Iturbide, Agustín de (order), 121, 263n63. *See also* Plan de Iguala

Jacoby, Karl, 226
Jamestown colony, 55
Janambres, 68
Japanese American Citizens League, 161
Japanese Americans, 190, 214, 224
Jáuregui, Josseph Antonio Fernández de, 67–68, 72, 75, 274n13, 274n15
Jefferson, Judge Bernard S., 210
Jefferson, Thomas, 34, 61, 269n33
jihad: Islamic jihad figure, 7, 22, 31, 98, 100–102, 105, 235–237, 239, 256
Jim Crow laws, 142, 161, 188, 215, 219, 225
Jiménez Núñez, Alfredo, 271n3, 272n5
Johnson, William, 269n33
Johnson v. McIntosh, 63, 182
Jones, Tommy Lee, 96, **99,** 100
Jones-Shafroth Act, 185
Joseph, Anthony, 180–182
journalism, 197, 234, 236, 248; gonzo journalism, 199, 291n4; New Journalism, 214
Juarez, Benito, 193
Judaism, 40, 41, 43, 61, 190, 201–202, 214
Junta de Valladolid, 34, 36, 38–40, 45–52, 60, 67, 92, 109, 266n9, 268n2, 282n18

Kansas, 227
Kant, Immanuel, 9
Kazanjian, David, 135
Kelley, Patricia Fernández, 297n16
Kerouac, Jack: *On the Road,* 1–3, 19–20, 199, 214–215, 224, 228–229, 231, 260n14, 291n3, 294n23
Kesey, Ken, 215
Kickapoo, 113
Kiowa, 108, 112–115, 121, 137, 227–228, 257, 280n9
Kobayashi, Audrey, 23, 262n26

Laclau, Ernesto, 251–252
La Raza Cósmica, 202–203, 292n9
Laredo, San Agustín de, 3
LareDos: A Journal of the Borderlands, **5**
Las Casas, Bartolomé de, 30, 34–35, 37–38, 40–41, 67, 75, 111, 265n3, 265n5, 265n7, 266n9, 268n20, 268n21; *In Defense of the Indians,* 45–53, 81, 267n16, 267n17, 267n18
Las Invaciones de los Apaches en el territorio de Tejas (Invasions of the Apaches in the Territory of Texas), 83, 86–94, 104
Latin America, 8, 36, 52, 185, 237–239, 251–252, 256–258, 260n13, 293n11. *See also individual countries*
Latin American studies, 31
Latin American Working Group Education Fund, 295n1
Latina/o critical legal theory (LatCrit), 161, 286n12, 287n15
Latinos, 187, 190, 202, 288n25, 293n11. *See also* Spanish surnamed people
Lawson, John, 55
League of United Latin American Citizens (LULAC), 185, 187, 190–193, 289n29
Lee, Richard Henry, 269n33
Leeuw, Sarah de, 23
Lefebvre, Henry, 19, 22–23, 66–67, 70, 108, 133, 161, 199, 263n27
Leopoldo, 39
liberalism, 127, 252, 282n18, 287n14; colonialism and, 27, 55, 61–62; mestizo liberalism, 116, 140; Mexican liberalism, 108, 110–124, 129–132, 136, 143, 146, 152, 154–155, 158–159, 172, 179, 181, 188, 236, 280n9, 280n10; in Treaty of Guadalupe Hidalgo, 137–138; U.S. liberalism, 100, 106, 108, 158, 192, 211, 236, 287n18
Liberating Army for Races and Peoples, 142
Lincoln, Abraham, 193
Lincoln High School, 293n13
Livingstone, David N., 261n20, 262n21
Loaysa, García Jofre de, 38
lobos, 119, 281n16
Locke, John, 9
Lockhart, James, 279n4
Longfellow, Henry Wadsworth, 176
Los Angeles Chamber of Commerce, 207

Los Angeles Community Council, 206–207
Los Angeles Junior Chamber of Commerce, 206
Los Angeles Police Department (LAPD), 204
Los Angeles Tennis Club, 205–206
Los Angeles Unified School District, 204
Los Dos Laredos, 2–3, **4, 5**
Louisiana, 289n29; Natchitoches, 89–90
Lucero, Juan Jose, 175–180
Lugo v. Texas, 187
Luther, Martin, 38–39, 265n7
Lutherans, 38
lynching, 216, 218–225, 220, 227–228

Macías, María Elizabeth (La Nena de Laredo), 248–249
Magón, Ricardo Flores, 145
Malinche, 12–13. *See also* la Chingada
Malincheños, 68
Manifest Destiny, 20, 22, 212
Manzano y Manzano, Juan, 268n21
mapping, 21, 23–31, 48, 114, 137, 139, 216, 231; colonialism and, 8, 33, 35, 41, 53, 69, 75, 81, 92, 108, 111, 124, 261n20; legal mapping, 27, 58, 64, 178; race and, 17–18, 140–141, 193, 197, 207, 263n30, 291n3; unmapping, 199–200. *See also* geo-graphing
maps, 19, 70, 125, 284n34; of Aztlán, 197–199, **198,** 200, 214; of drug cartels, 6, 259n3; Map of Mankind, 262n21
maquiladoras, 241–243, 245, 253, 297n19, 297n20, 297n22, 298n23, 298n24. *See also* temporary import programs
March for Peace with Justice and Dignity, 233–234
Marcus, David C., 185–186
Mariscal, George, 39, 47, 265n7
marriage, 79, 82, 267n18; intermarriage, 26, 116–117, 281n12. *See also* miscegenation
Marshall, John, 63–64
Marshall, Thurgood, 191, 289n26, 290n35
Martí, José, 260n13
Martínez, María Elena, 268n26
Marx, Karl: *Grundrisse,* 213; "On the Jewish Question," 123, 287n14
Marxism, 31, 93, 191

masculinity, 28, 194, 229–230; colonial masculinity, 10–11, 13, 218, 221–223, 260n13, 260n14; masculine melancholia, 95–97, 100–101. *See also* patriarchy
Massachusetts: Boston, 61
Massey, Douglass, 297n16
Mather, Cotton, 55
Maxey, Judge Thomas, 158, 168–172, 286n12, 287n13, 287n15, 287n16, 288n19
Mayas, 273n7
Mbembe, Achille, 16, 18
McCarthy, Cormac, 69
McCormick, Judge Paul J., 186–187, 289n26
McGown, Floyd, 166–167
medieval philosophy, 40–47, 50, 265n8
melancholia, 2, 31, 215; Chicano nationalism and, 195–199, 226, 231–232, 291n3; racialized masculinity and, 95–97, 100–102, 104–107, 151
Menchaca, Martha, 161, 182–183, 281n12, 282n23, 287n18
Mendez, Felícitas, 184–187
Mendez, Gonzalo, 184–187
Mendez, Sylvia, 185–186, 190
Mendez v. Westminster, 161, 171, 184–187, 289n26
Menéndez y Pelayo, Marcelino, 266n10, 266n11
Merry Pranksters, 215
mestizaje, 13, 25–30, 115–117, 133, 156, 160–162, 168–173, 183–185, 188, 191–193, 203, 214, 229, 285n3, 290n30, 292n9
mestizos, 3, 71, 102, 130, 193, 203, 226–227, 287n18; Mexican nationalism and, 9, 12, 115–117, 152–155, 173; racial geography and, 20–28, 216–217, 240, 263n30; Spanish colonialism and, 78–79, 92, 118–119, 128, 281n16, 281n17; Treaty of Guadalupe Hidalgo and, 133–134, 137–143, 183; U.S. nationalism and, 114, 155, 160, 174. *See also* afromestizos
Mexican Americans, 145, 152–153, 199, 214, 284n1, 285n3, 286n12, 289n29, 291n1; Mexican American activism, 30–31, 135, 290n32; racialization of, 23, 28, 31, 134, 144, 156–194, 201–214, 284n1, 290n30, 290n35, 292n7

328 INDEX

Mexican Army, 151, 254. *See also* Mexican Special Forces

Mexican Constitution, 26, 121–122, 124, 173, 280n10, 280n11

Mexican Constitutional Congress, 279n5

Mexicanismo, 156, 158

Mexicanos, 158

Mexican peace movement, 233–234, 253–254, 258

Mexican Revolution, 27–28, 145–146, 186, 250

Mexican Special Forces, 254

Mexican Wars of Independence, 27, 112, 119, 122

Mexico, 151, 167–169, 190, 212, 259n3, 279n6, 291n3, 298n25; Ayotzinapa, 249, 253; Chiapas, 38, 54; Chihuahua, 109, 113, 129–131, 152, 196, 253, 256, 273n10; Chihuahua City, 112, 130, 279n6; Chilpancingo, 250; Coahuila, 113, 121, 129, 253, 273n10, 275n19, 277n28; Cuernavaca, 233–234; Cuidad Juárez, 196, 216, 228–231, 239, 246; Dolores, 121; Durango, 113, 129, 195, 216, 229–230, 252–253, 273n10; Guanajuato, 157; Guerrero, 54, 113, 249–250, 252; Iguala, 250; indigeneity in, 6–9, 11–14, 110, 128–130, 134, 152, 154–156, 179, 234–235, 279n4, 280n11, 284n34, 294n19, 295n25; Jalisco, 125; Janos, 113, 131, 256, 275n21; Mazatlán, 208; Mexican citizenship, 114–117, 122, 124, 130–132, 145–146, 159, 177, 239, 280n10, 282n23, 283n26, 292n9; Mexican liberalism, 108, 110–124, 129–132, 136, 143, 146, 152, 154–155, 158–159, 172, 179, 181, 188, 236, 280n9, 280n10; Mexican nationalism, 9, 12, 27, 115–117, 122–124, 145–147, 152–155, 158, 173, 263n30; Mexico-Apache relations, 113, 115, 122, 138–140, 146, 158, 160, 177, 179, 219, 233–235, 280n9, 283n28, 284n34; Mexico City, 12, 112–113, 233–234; Mexico-Comanche relations, 108–110, 112–113, 121–122, 124–127, 133, 139, 146, 177, 179, 219, 234, 246, 280n9, 280n11, 283n26, 283n28; Michoacán, 248–249, 252; Morelos, 233; NAFTA and, 235–256, 297n16, 297n18, 297n19, 297n20, 298n23, 298n24; National Palace, 12; Nuevo

Laredo, 1–3, **4, 5, 12,** 229, 246, 248–249, 283n29; Nuevo León, 283n26; Oaxaca, 38, 54, 121; racial geographies of, 7–8, 11, 14, 18–31, 33, 35–36, 64, 102, 108–110, 116–117, 121, 128, 132, 146, 152–153, 152–155, 170–185, 173–179, 182, 183, 185, 192–194, 196, 202–203, 214–218, 226, 229–232, 263n30, 284n36, 286n8, 293n11; San Fernando, 252; Santa Fe, 112; Sinaloa, 252, 273n10; Sonora, 78, 83, 91, 113, 129, 253, 256, 273n10, 275n21, 277n28; Spanish colonialism in, 3, 6–8, 13–14, 17–20, 22, 25, 28, 30, 34, 36–56, 64–95, 98, 104, 109–111, 116–129, 132, 136–141, 158, 160, 174, 177–181, 191, 202–204, 214, 235, 256, 263n31, 269n31, 270n34, 272n4, 281n12, 288n21; Tamaulipas, 3, **4,** 53, 68, 248, 252, 275n19, 283n29; Tampico, 70–71; Tlatelolco, **12;** Uruapan, 248; Zacatecas, 89, 125. *See also* Los Dos Laredos; Mexico-U.S. border; Treaty of Guadalupe-Hidalgo; U.S.-Mexico War

Mexico-U.S. border, 1–3, 6–7, 14, 18, 20, 22–25, 28–29, 125–126, 142, 145, 155, 172, 179, 197, **197,** 228, 230–232, 231–232, 234, 260n14; Aztlán and, 197, **198,** 230; formation of, 66–67, 128, 159–160; remapping of, 127–138, 234–246, 254, 256–258. *See also* Treaty of Guadalupe-Hidalgo

Middle East, 43, 70, 95, 101–102, 168, 234, 236–238, 258. *See also individual countries*

migration, 6, 79–84, 118–119, 125, 158, 225, 228, 240, 244–245, 295n25, 297n18

militarization, 24, 235, 237–240, 246

Miller, Loren, 289n26

miscegenation, 26, 143, 150, 157, 166, 168, 171–172, 191, 196, 202, 227, 260n13, 281n12; in Spanish caste system, 115–121, 140–141. *See also* la Chingada; chingón

missionaries, 37, 41, 92–93, 110–111. *See also individual denominations and individuals*

missions, 22, 68, 69, 71, 77–78, 83–84, 87, 89–90, 92, 111–112, 122, 128, 256, 272n6, 277n27

Mississippi Company, 269n33

Mississippi River, 108–109, 151

Missouri, 125

INDEX   329

Mix, Tom, 220
Moctezuma, 156, 158
modernity, 52, 86, 94, 104, 203, 218
Montecuesta, Narciso Barquín y, 67, 75, 274n13, 274n14, 274n15
Moors, 43, 267n16
morality, 2, 9, 40, 56, 61, 85, 113, 136, 143–145, 147, 182, 221
Moriarty, Dean, 1–2, 215, 229, 231, 260n14
Moriscos, 38–39

NAACP, 161–162, 185, 190–191, 289n26
Nadotes, 90
Nahuas, 12, 109, 116, 158, 273n7, 279n4, 287n16
Náhuatl (language), 109, 158
Napoleon Bonaparte, 156
narco-terrorism, 7, 22, 24, 31, 99, 101, 234–236, 246–258. *See also* drug cartels
nationalism, 21, 28, 33, 52–53, 109, 127, 134, 136, 140, 156, 295n25; Chicano nationalism, 22, 31, 153, 159, 195–232, 285n3, 292n5, 293n11, 294n20; Mexican nationalism, 9, 12, 27, 115–117, 122–124, 145–147, 152–155, 158, 173, 263n30; Native American nationalism, 159; U.S. nationalism, 114, 155, 158, 160, 174, 240, 263n30. *See also* Aztlán; postnationalism; transnationalism
Native American historiography, 125
Native Americans, 11, 63, 197, 211–212, 214, 217–218; citizenship and, 163–170, 172–173, 240, 285n5; Native American civil rights movement, 156; Native American nationalism, 159; racialization of, 27, 203, 211, 263n30. *See also* American Indians; Amerindians; Indians; indigeneity; *individual indigenous peoples or nations*
Native American studies, 16, 140, 158
naturalization, 30; of African Americans, 157, 164–165, 285n5, 287n15; of indigenous people, 157, 163, 166–169, 285n4, 285n5, 285n6, 286n8, 287n13; of Mexicans, 158–160, 185, 286n12, 287n15; of white people, 164–166, 286n9, 286n12
Naturalization Acts, 157–158, 164–167, 285n5, 287n15

Navajo, 119, 177, 180–181, 226, 261n18, 280n11
Nazis, 186
Negri, Antonio, 213
La Nena de Laredo. *See* Macias, María Elizabeth
neocolonialism, 3, 6, 20, 30, 106, 139, 153, 211–212, 222
neoliberalism, 21, 28, 240–246, 249–250, 252. *See also* foreign direct investment; maquiladoras; North American Free Trade Agreement; temporary import programs
New Jersey colony, 57, 269n33
New Laws for Governing the Indies and for the Good Treatment and Preservation of the Indians, 37–38, 265n3
New Mexico, 34, 74, 83, 109, 111, 120, 174–182, 196, 211, 228, 231, 273n10, 287n18; Land Commission, 110
New Mexico Constitution, 181–182
New Mexico Land Commission, 110, 128
New Mexico Supreme Court, 175, 180, 288n19
New Philippines, 70–71
Noticias sobre los indios barbarous y sus costumbres, 67–69, 71–82, 73, 88–89, 102, 271n3
New Spain, 3, 127–128, 145, 152, 157, 197, 214, 216, 231, 235, 263n33, 274n15, 279n4, 282n18; Adaes, 84, 89–90; afromestizos in, 71, 78–79, 92, 118–119, 128, 281n16, 281n17; La Bahía, 118, 281n16; caste system, 26, 281n12; Goliad, 71, 118, 281n16; making of, 9; Nueva Extremadura, 275n19; Nueva Viscaya, 74, 273n7; Nuevo León, 67–68, 74–75, 83, 271n3; Nuevo Santander, 16, 68, 86, 89, 93–94, 118, 274n15, 281n16, 281n17; Provincia de Tejas, 16, 22, 34, 53, 67, 69–71, 74, 83, 83–86, 89–90, 95–96; Provincias Internas, 110, 126, 197, 231; race in, 116–121, 172, 203, 268n26; San Antonio de Béxar, 71, 84, 118, 281n16; San Luis Potosí, 75
New Spain census, 117–120, 281n16, 281n17, 282n18

330 INDEX

New World, 18, 22, 34, 37, 39–42, 46–53, 60, 178, 265n8, 266n9, 267n17
New York, 288n25, 295n25; Harlem, 254; Hudson valley, 240. *See also* Hernandez v. New York
New Zealand, 262n21
Nez Pierce, 268n29
Nicaragua, 237, 295n3
9/11, 98, 106–107, 237, 239
Ninth Circuit Court of Appeals, 186–187
Nissen, Judge Harland J., 206
Nixon, Richard, 238
No Country for Old Men, 30, 69–70, 94–107, **97, 99, 103**
Normans, 61–62
North America, 7, 54, 57, 108, 114, 137, 147, 157, 177, 263n21, 270n35, 288n19. *See also* *individual countries*
North American Free Trade Agreement (NAFTA), 19, 137, 236, 240–246, 297n17, 297n18, 297n19, 298n23, 298n24. *See also* maquiladoras
North Carolina, 55
Noticias de los Poblados, 272n4, 274n15
Nuñez Vela, Blasco, 37

Obama, President Barack, 31, 233–234, 237
O'Brien, Jean, 211
Observer, 245
Okies, 217–219, 222–228, 294n24
Oklahoma, 227–228, 231. *See also* Okies
On the Road, 1–3, 19–20, 199, 214–215, 224, 228–229, 231, 260n14, 291n3, 294n23
Opate, 177, 287n16
Operation Neptune Spear, 233
Organic Intercourse Act, 227
Orientalism, 1–2
Ortelli, Sara, 78, 272n6, 275n20
Orttiz Parrilla, Don Diego, 87–88, 90
Osage, 227
Otis, James, 61
Ottoman Empire, 36, 38, 265n7, 267n16

Pacific Islanders, 293n11
Pacifico Sur cartel, 234
Padilla, Genaro M., 294n24
Pakistan, 235; Abbottabad, 233

Pamoranos, 68
Pampospas, 89
Panama, 237
Pápagos, 113
Paradise, Sal, 1–3, 214–215, 224, 228–229, 231, 291n3
parajes, 70–72, 79, 82
paramilitary forces, 236
Paredes, Américo: *George Washington Gómez,* 30, 142–153, 284n37
Parry, Robert, 236
Paschal, T.J., 157–159, 163–166, 168, 285n4, 285n5, 286n8
Pastias, 89
patriarchy, 20, 147, 192. *See also* masculinity; sexism
Paul III, Pope: *Sublimis Deus* papal bull, 37, 40, 43
Paz, Octavio, 12–13, 20, 227, 230
Peake, Linda, 21, 49, 52
peninsulares, 116–117, 119
Penn, William, 55
Pennsylvania, 55, 269n33
Pentagon, 236, 238
Persia, 262n21
Peru, 37–38, 236, 264n2
Petrine responsibility, 40–41, 47, 50, 52, 111
philosophy, 18, 38–42, 41, 45–48, 52, 61–62, 116, 121, 268n22, 280n9. *See also* Enlightenment; liberalism
Pima, 287n16
Pizaña, Aniceto, 142–143
Pizarro, Francisco, 37, 156
Pizarro, Gonzalo, 37–38
Plains Indians, 11, 102. *See also individual indigenous peoples or nations*
Plan Colombia, 237, 296n6
Plan de Iguala, 26, 121, 124, 128, 179, 263n33
Plan de San Diego, 150, 284n37
Plan Merida, 237
Playboy, 291n4
Plessy v. Ferguson, 289n26
Plymouth colony, 57
poblar, 67, 70–71, 77, 119, 271n3, 272n4, 272n5
Pomona College, 207

INDEX   331

Portugal: Portuguese colonialism, 261n20, 266n9

postcolonialism, 25–26, 28, 31, 59, 65, 70, 128, 159–160, 196–199, 203, 215; limitations of, 279n37; Romantic employment and, 85–86, 91, 93–94, 224. *See also* anticolonialism

postcolonial studies, 6, 31, 85

postnationalism, 28

presidios, 22, 69, 84, 87, 90, 119, 274n15, 275n21, 277n27

Proclamation of 1763, 34–35, 60–63

profligates, 92, 94

Protestant Reformation, 39

Protestants, 17, 41, 176, 269n31

psychoanalysis, 29, 93, 102. *See also* abjection; disavowal; hysteria; melancholia; racial castration; trauma; uncanny; unconscious

Public Citizen's Global Trade Watch, 298n24

Pueblo Indians, 110–111, 120, 127–128, 141, 174–183, 226, 261n18, 288n19, 288n22, 288n23; Cochiti Pueblo, 175–176; Pecos Pueblo, 283n27; Santa Clara Pueblo, 182; Taos Pueblo, 180

pueblos (communities), 68; Indian pueblos, 69, 74–75, 77, 111–112, 279n4; Spanish pueblos, 68–69, 71–72, 74–75, 77–79, 83–84, 121

Puertoriqueños, 158, 185, 190, 289n28

race, 73, 94, 129, 154, 202–203, 239, 262n26, 263n28, 284n1, 287n14; in *Autobiography of a Brown Buffalo*, 214–232, 294n24; caste and, 116–123, 281n16; census categories, 293n11; in Chicano nationalism, 195–199, 201–204, 285n3; citizenship and, 13, 18, 25–29, 53, 64, 114, 122, 128, 152, 156–194, 199–201, 205–212, 264n34, 286n9, 286n11, 286n12, 287n15, 287n16, 288n25; class and, 205, 214; colonialism and, 6, 9, 33–34, 136, 281n17; in *George Washington Gómez*, 142–152; property and, 23, 59; psychoanalysis and, 29–30; in *On the Road*, 1–3, 291n3; visuality and, 20, 144; white/black binary, 25, 27, 169, 219. *See also* mestizaje; miscegenation; La Raza; whiteness

racial castration, 221–226

racial geographies, 15–17, 262n26, 265n4; of Aztlán, 29, 31, 194, 197, 232; of Mexico, 6–8, 11, 14, 18–31, 33, 35–36, 64, 102, 108–110, 114–117, 121, 128–133, 146, 152–155, 170–185, 192–194, 196, 202–203, 214–218, 226, 229–232, 263n30, 284n36, 286n8, 293n11; of Mexico-U.S. border, 2–3, 28–29, 67, 159–160, 234, 245–246, 256; of Spanish colonialism, 34–36, 39, 48–50, 52–54, 58, 66–70, 75–79, 82, 84–89, 91–94, 102, 110, 120–121, 128–129, 145, 180, 191, 203, 261n20, 263n31; of the Treaty of Guadalupe Hidalgo, 133, 137–142; of the U.S., 6–11, 14, 27, 30, 33, 35, 54, 64, 70, 95–110, 115, 131, 134–136, 141, 143–144, 149, 151, 154–155, 159–162, 168–170, 173, 178–185, 188, 192–194, 209–213, 216–218, 221, 225–232, 240, 263n30, 286n7

racialization, 27, 30, 50, 70, 79, 86, 102, 150, 229, 235, 239; of indigeneity, 30, 36, 84, 133–134, 138, 153; of Mexican Americans, 154–194, 200–214; of space, 2, 7–8, 18, 22, 24–26, 54, 88, 94, 262n26; of U.S. citizenship, 147

racial melancholia, 195–196

racism, 97, 114, 149–151, 153, 176, 203, 227, 261n15, 294n24; citizenship and, 157–159, 194, 288n25. *See also* blackface

Ramirez v. Texas, 187

Ranitas, 89

Raúl Isidro Rural Teachers College, 249–250

La Raza, 200–204, 268n26

La Raza (publication), 293n13

La Raza Cósmica, 202–203

La Raza Unida Party, 291n1

Razo, Joe, 293n13

Reagan, Ronald, 204, 237–238, 295n3

Reconquista, 36

Renaissance, 38, 41

representation, 17

republica de los indios, 111, 118, 279n3

Requerimiento, 45, 49, 267n15

Rhone, Judge Bayard, 206

Rhys, Jean: *Wide Sargasso Sea*, 199

Rio Bravo, 3

Rio Brazos, 90

332   INDEX

Rio Grande, 2, 72, 80, 112, 125–126, 142, 145, 150, 153, 247

Risco, Eliezer, 293n13

Rivera, Diego, 12

Rivera, Luis N., 47

Rodriguez, Ricardo, 157–159

Roman Empire, 34, 47, 267n16; Holy Roman Empire, 34, 50, 117; Roman philosophy, 47

Romanticism, 85–86, 91–93, 225, 234

Rombeau, Dora, 205

Romero de Terreros, Juan M., 84

Roosevelt, Theodore, 193

Rosa, Luis de la, 142–143

Rose, Gillian, 20

Ruiz Cameron, Christopher David, 134–135

Saint Joseph Bay, 71

Salazar v. Texas, 188–189

Saldivar, Ramon, 224, 284n37

Salinas de Gotari, President Carlos, 244

Salineros, 68

Samoans, 228

Sánchez, David, 213, 293n13

Sanchez, el Indio, 89–91, 142, 278n34

Sánchez, George I., 190–192, 290n35

Sánchez de Barrera y Gallardo, Don Tomás, 3

Sanchez v. Texas, 187–189

San Clemente de Los Españoles College, 38

Sandinistas, 237, 295n3

San Saba River, 83

Santleben, August, 130–132

Saracens, 43

Sarnosos, 68, 73

savage tribes (term), 130, 136–139. *See also* tribus salvajes (term)

Sawyer, Judge Lorenzo, 285n5, 286n9

scalping, 10, 22, 30, 113–115, 121, 126–133, 137, 152, 154; in drug war, 236, 246–247, 249, 250, 253–254. *See also* bounty programs

Schein, Richard H., 20

School of Salamanca, 37, 267n18

School of the Americas (Southcom), 238, 254, **255**

Schweitzer, Judge Harold W., 208–209

Scott, David, 85–86, 91–93

Scott, Winfield, 279n6

Security First National Bank, 206

sedition, 142–146, 145, 148–149, 152, 284n37

Seed, Patricia, 36

Seminole, 113, 139

Seno Mexicano, 69

Sentimientos de la Nación, 26, 263n33

Sepúlveda, Juan Ginés de, 30, 34–35, 38–53, 67, 75, 154, 266n11, 266n14, 269n31; *Demócrates, Primero,* 39; *Demócrates Segundo,* 39, 41–43, 45, 266n12, 268n20

Seri, 108, 112–115, 121, 137

Serranos, 68

settler colonialism, 9, 23, 56, 86, 95, 227, 246, 287n15; Anglo-American settler colonialism, 155, 173, 176, 211, 284n36; British settler colonialism, 17, 36, 55, 59–60, 65, 83, 176–177; French settler colonialism, 83; Spanish settler colonialism, 17, 36, 53, 65, 82–83, 93, 119, 139, 271n3, 273n12, 282n22; U.S. settler colonialism, 35, 61, 63, 83, 126, 140, 172, 181, 240, 257; white settler colonialism, 31, 64, 67, 93, 172, 176, 181, 212, 288n21

sexism, 199–200, 215. *See also* patriarchy

sexuality, 41, 42, 116, 218; in *Autobiography of a Brown Buffalo,* 215, 221–223, 229–231. *See also* heterosexism; miscegenation

sexual violence, 13, 223, 225, 248

sex workers, 13, 229, 231

shame, 106–107

Sheridan, Claire, 290n32

Sheridan Prieto, Cecilia, 74, 273n7

Shoshone, 177

sicarios, 234, 251, 253

Sicilia, Javier, 234, 254

Sicilians, 228

Sinaloa cartel, 6

Sioux, 268n29

slavery, 33, 136, 147–148, 195, 252, 266n12; abolition of, 26, 263n33; enslaved blacks, 115, 117, 266n9; enslaved indigenous people and mestizos, 74, 111, 137–138, 273n12, 280n8, 282n22; in Mexico, 121–122; in New Spain, 36–37, 40–47, 74, 111, 116–118, 266n9, 273n12, 280n8, 282n22; in the U.S., 113, 115, 125–126, 141, 151–152, 165, 211, 284n36

Smith, John, 55

Smith, Ralph, 279n6
Socrates, 39
sodomy, 41, 43, 266n14
Soviet Union, 238, 257
Spain, 102, 153, 166, 168, 170, 190, 268n20, 268n26; caste system, 116–121, 281n16; indigeneity and, 33–53, 56, 64–79, 82–95, 109–113, 122–132, 177–181, 264n2, 267n16, 267n18, 268n25, 272n6, 273n7, 273n12, 277n27, 277n28, 279n3, 282n22, 282n23, 283n28; Madrid, 268n21; Reconquista, 36, 151; Seville, 68, 268n20; Spanish-Apache relations, 77, 82–92, 109–113, 119–120, 235, 261n15, 275n21, 277n27, 278n34, 279n2, 283n28; Spanish citizenship, 121, 263n33; Spanish colonialism, 3, 6–8, 12–13, 16–20, 22, 24–28, 30, 34, 98, 104–105, 109–111, 116–129, 132, 136–141, 145, 156, 158–160, 174, 177–181, 191, 193, 202–204, 214, 235, 251, 256, 261n15, 261n20, 263n31, 267n15, 267n17, 269n31, 270n34, 271n3, 272n4, 272n5, 275n19, 279n2, 279n4, 280n8, 281n12, 288n21; Spanish-Comanche relations, 74, 78–79, 82–91, 110–112, 119, 127–129, 261n15, 273n12, 277n27. *See also* Bourbon, House of; New Spain
Spanish-American War, 289n28
Spanish-Indian wars, 70
Spanish Royal Army, 87
Spanish surnamed people, 201–202, 207–208
Sparke, Matthew, 19, 21
Special Operations teams, 237
Stadler, Gustavus, 294n17
Stalinism, 213
subaltern, 68, 79, 83–86, 88, 91–92, 94
subaltern studies, 85, 94
subjection, 28, 55, 77, 145–147, 150, 153, 250, 267n15
Sublimis Deus papal bull, 37, 40, 43
Suleiman I, 38
Susquehannah Company, 269n33
Syal, Rajeev, 245
Syria, 235

Taguacanes, 89–90
Tamaces, 89
Tarahumaras, 113

Tartary, 262n21
Taylor, Zachary, 279n6
Tecoltes de Los Dos Laredos, **4**
temporary import programs, 243. *See also* maquiladoras
terra nullius, 9, 80, 177
Texas, 119, 121, 130, 142–143, 149, 168, 187–189, 227–228, 231, 271n3, 273n10, 281n16, 283n31, 284n37; Brownsville, 142; Corpus Christi, 289n29; Cotula, 291n1; El Paso, 196, 216, 229, 231, 239, 254; Houston, 254; indigeneity in, 22, 30, 53, 69–71, 83–86, 89–105, 109, 111–113, 115, 126, 174, 281n17; Jackson County, 187; Laredo, 1–4, **5**, 118, 151, 247, 254, 260n14, 281n16, 283n29; San Antonio, 84, 89, 157, 193, 277n27, 277n28; San Jacinto, 151; San Saba, 69, 83–84, 86–87, 89–90, 95–96, 102, 104, 277n28. See also New Spain: Provincia de Tejas
Texas Court of Criminal Appeals, 157, 187–189, 192
Texas Rangers, 99, 113, 143, 145–146, 148, 220, 279n6
Thompson, Hunter S., 214; *Fear and Loathing in Las Vegas*, 215, 291n4
Tjarks, Alicia V., 118–119
Toltecs, 169–170, 287n16
Trade and Intercourse Act (1834), 174–175, 180, 227
Trail of Tears, 228
transit of empire, 35
transnational economy of death, 114, 136
transnationalism, 6–7, 27, 69, 114–115, 129, 137, 154, 194, 234, 241–242
trauma, 28, 65, 106–107, 215–219, 225, 231. *See also* melancholia; uncanny
Treaty of Cordova, 179
Treaty of Guadalupe-Hidalgo (TGH), 22, 30, 115, 142, 166–167; indigeneity in, 129, 154, 170–175, 181, 183, 226; racial geographies of, 108, 133–141, 151–152, 155, 178–179, 225, 288n25
Trías, Angel, 113
tribus salvajes (term), 130, 136–139, 141, 152, 154, 179, 246. *See also* savage tribes
Trinity River, 90
Trumbull, Jonathan, 269n33

334 INDEX

Turner, Fredrick Jackson, 9–11, 13, 20, 96, 99, 155, 199, 260n13, 260n14

uncanny, 21, 24, 219–221, 226; blackness and, 218

unconscious, 102, 151, 152, 221–222, 239, 240, 258; racial unconscious, 29–30, 97, 196, 210–219, 227–228, 231–232, 235

United Mexican American Students (UMAS), 293n13

United States, 1–2, 17–18, 35, 67, 150, 215, 260n14, 280n11, 291n3, 296n9; Allegany mountains, 34, 59–60; Apache-U.S. relations, 114, 138, 143–144, 154, 158, 160, 174, 180–181, 212, 219, 227, 235; Appalachian mountains, 34, 59; Atlantic seaboard, 10, 34, 55, 57–59; Comanche--U.S. relations, 108–110, 114, 124–125, 124–126, 133, 138–140, 144, 154, 180–181, 212, 227–228; drug war and, 234–240, 254–256, 259n3, 295n3, 298n25; Great Plains, 9–10, 82, 96, 115, 125, 140, 235, 246, 277n28; indigeneity in, 10, 14–16, 36, 54, 59, 61–65, 70, 94–109, 124, 129, 154–155, 175–183, 181–182, 210–212, 211–212, 224–232, 235–236, 239–240, 245, 257–258, 259n8, 268n29, 285n6, 286n7; NAFTA and, 240–246, 297n18, 297n22; New England, 34, 211; racial geographies of, 2–3, 7–11, 14, 18, 19–31, 33, 35, 54, 64, 70, 95–110, 114–115, 131, 133–143, 149, 151, 154–155, 159–162, 168–170, 173, 178–194, 196, 205, 209–214, 216–218, 221, 225–232, 263n28, 263n30, 264n34, 286n7, 286n9, 287n15; slavery in, 113, 115, 122, 125–126, 141, 151–152, 165, 211, 284n36; Southwest, 9, 23, 30–31, 35, 69–70, 82, 85, 108, 133–134, 139–144, 146–148, 151–153, 156–160, 171–173, 177–178, 184, 194, 197–199, 203–204, 221, 226–232, 289n26, 289n29, 291n3; U.S. citizenship, 63–65, 87, 106, 148–149, 151–152, 155, 157–161, 164–174, 182–185, 188, 192–193, 201, 208, 211, 220, 230, 232, 240, 246, 254, 258, 285n6, 287n14, 287n18, 289n28, 289n29, 290n32; U.S. colonialism, 3, 6, 9, 31, 35, 59, 62–63, 65, 86–87, 105, 211–212, 232, 279n37, 288n21, 289n28, 291n3, 294n19; U.S. nationalism, 114, 155, 158, 160, 174, 240, 263n30. *See also* Canadian-U.S. border; Mexico-U.S. border; Treaty of Guadalupe-Hidalgo; *individual colonies and states*

United States v. Joseph, 180–182

United States v. Lucero, 175–182, 288n21

United States v. Ortiz, 288n19

United States v. Sandoval, 181–183

University of California, Los Angeles (UCLA), 186

University of Texas, 190

Urrea, General José de, 151

U.S. Air Force, 238

U.S. Army, 125, 142, 151, 257

U.S. Border Patrol Agency, 238–239, 296n9

U.S. Census, 293n11

U.S. Civil War, 159–160

U.S. Congress, 62–63, 135, 155, 158–159, 164–165, 173–174, 181–182, 236, 238, 254, 268n29, 285n5

U.S. Constitution, 35, 135, 187, 204. *See also* Fourteenth Amendment

U.S. Continental Congress, 61

U.S. Department of Defense, 239

U.S. Department of Homeland Security, 238, 296n9

U.S. Department of State, 236, 238, 245

U.S. Department of the Treasury, 239

U.S. District Court of New Mexico, 182

U.S.-Mexico War, 3, 108, 110, 114, 129–130, 133, 140, 151, 155, 234–235, 283n26; San Jacinto battle, 151. *See also* Treaty of Guadalupe-Hidalgo

U.S. Navy, 151, 238; Seal Team 6, 233–234

U.S. Supreme Court, 63, 180–182, 187, 189, 201, 288n25, 289n26

Utah, 231

Uto-Aztecan languages, 140

Vargas, Jennifer Harford, 294n17

Vasconcelos, José: *La Raza Cósmica*, 202–203, 292n9

vecinos, 23, 68, 76, 91–92, 109, 118, 127, 140, 217, 271n3

Victoria, Francisco de, 50, 264n2

Victoria, President Guadalupe, 112

INDEX   335

Vidaurri, Soledad, 184–187
Vietnam War, 95, 101, 106, 293n13
Virginia, 57; Crystal City, 291n1. *See also* Jamestown colony
Virginia Company, 56
Virginia House of Burgesses, 269n33
Virgin of Guadalupe, 193, 279n5
Vitoria, Francisco de, 50–52, 264n2, 265n8, 267n18, 268n22, 268n25, 269n31

Wallerstein, Immanuel, 270n38
Walmart effect, 242, 298n24
wandering savage, figure of, 54, 95
war on terror, 30, 70, 87, 98–102, 233–239, 256–258, 296n9. *See also* narco-terrorism
Warren, Earl, 189
Washington, George, 61, 193
Washington Office on Latin America, 295n1
WASPS (white Anglo-Saxon Protestants), 205, 212
Webb, Gary, 236
Webb, Walter Prescott, 10–11, 20, 96, 99, 145, 261n15
Weber, David J., 128, 279n2
Wharton, Samuel: *Plain Facts,* 61–62
whiteness, 2, 20–22, 134, 138, 202–203, 211, 221, 231, 291n3, 293n11; caste system and, 119; citizenship and, 23, 26, 28, 59, 155, 157–177, 183–194, 220, 264n34, 285n4, 285n5, 286n9, 286n11, 286n12, 287n15; colonialism and, 9, 11; fictive nature of,

28–30; indigeneity and, 25, 137, 181, 218, 285n4, 286n7; Mexican Americans and, 23, 140–141, 144–145, 147, 150, 152–153, 162–175, 184–194, 201, 205–209, 212, 214–215, 220, 222, 224–227, 229, 230, 264n34, 284n1, 285n3, 286n12, 287n15, 288n25, 290n35, 292n7, 294n24; white/black binary, 25, 27, 169, 219; white masculine melancholia, 94–107; white settler colonialism, 31, 64, 67, 93, 172, 176, 181, 212, 288n21; white vigilantism, 7. *See also* Caucasians
Whyte, Judge James G., 207
Wichita, 89, 228, 268n29
Williams, Robert, 40, 58, 60–62, 265n8
Wilshire Country Club, 207
Wilson, Stephen H., 292n7
Withers, Charles W.J., 261n20, 262n21
Wolfe, Tom, 214; *Electric Kool-Aid Acid Test,* 215, 294n23
World War II, 142, 193–194; postwar period, 243

Yaqui, 158
Yaquis Revolt, 156
Yattasi, 90
youth, 31, 150, 193–194, 200, 204, 217, 224, 229, 237, 239, 245, 246, 248. *See also* Biltmore Hotel; East L.A. Thirteen

Zavayas, 89
Zetas cartel, 6, 247–249, 252, 254–255

Printed and bound by CPI Group (UK) Ltd, Croydon, CR0 4YY

26/08/2025

14724581-0001

DE FAIT, LES MACHINES N'ÉTAIENT PAS INHUMAINES, ET NE POUVAIENT LE DEVENIR, SEULS LES HUMAINS POUVAIENT ÊTRE INHUMAINS.

MÉMOIRE D'ENCRIER

1260, RUE BÉLANGER — BUREAU 201
MONTRÉAL, QUÉBEC   H2S 1H9
INFO@MEMOIREDENCRIER.COM
MEMOIREDENCRIER.COM

DISSIDENT

DU MÊME AUTEUR

Tireur embusqué (roman)
Montréal, Mémoire d'encrier, 2020

Rescapé (roman)
Montréal, VLB Éditeur, 2015

Montréal, 2033. Adel est un jeune informaticien brillant, tourmenté par des idées révolutionnaires. Incapable de réconcilier ses aspirations utopistes avec le poste qu'il occupe chez Eagle Eyes Systems, une firme en cybersécurité, il rejoint un groupe anarchiste qui le bannit à la suite d'une querelle. Un acte de sabotage aux conséquences terribles le confronte à ses paradoxes, dans une société où rien n'échappe à l'œil de l'intelligence artificielle.

Né à Montréal en 1986, JEAN-PIERRE GORKYNIAN est l'auteur de trois romans. À travers ses œuvres, il tisse des liens entre le Québec et le Moyen-Orient, terre de ses ancêtres. Son roman *Tireur embusqué* (Mémoire d'encrier, 2020) a été finaliste au Prix littéraire des collégien.ne.s et au Prix du livre Lorientales.

JEAN-PIERRE GORKYNIAN

DISSIDENT

À Em,
et cette prison que je n'aurais jamais construite,
grâce à toi.

Que signifie le mot crime ?

Dostoïevski
Crime et châtiment

MONTRÉAL, 15 NOVEMBRE 2033

L'itinérant somnolait encore, sur le quai du métro Champ-de-Mars. L'agent Youri Akoulov achevait de lui dresser son constat d'infraction. L'assistant personnel Colombus, opéré depuis ses lunettes intelligentes, avait rempli tous les champs pour lui. Ne manquait plus qu'à les réviser.

NOM : Yasine El-Bachir
DATE DE NAISSANCE : 28 avril 2004
INFRACTION : Désobéissance civile

Akoulov, qui patrouillait seul ce matin-là, demanda au jeune homme de confirmer son adresse ; il n'en avait pas. Ou plutôt, n'en avait plus. Il logeait au refuge, mais sa fiche signalétique précisait qu'il avait déjà résidé dans le quartier Saint-Michel. Le policier mira le clochard. Un Arabe. Un peu plus vieux que lui. Traits foncés. Pouilleux. Se dégageait de lui une odeur nauséabonde, un mélange de jus d'ordure et de merde. Ses vêtements au complet étaient infestés de grillons aux longues antennes. D'où pouvaient provenir ses bestioles ? Akoulov réprima une grimace de dégoût et maintint l'adresse du refuge au dossier. Puis, le ticket imprimé, il le remit au contrevenant, lui indiquant par la même occasion le pictogramme à côté du banc : interdiction à toute personne d'y dormir ou de s'y étendre.

Akoulov pesta intérieurement. C'était la cinquième contravention du genre qu'il donnait aujourd'hui. Les gens n'avaient plus nulle part où aller. Le pays était englué dans la récession. La crise n'épargnait personne. L'inflation ne montrait aucun signe de ralentissement. La vague de privatisation avait pris trop d'ampleur, outrepassait les limites de la bienséance. Tout – jusqu'à l'eau potable – coûtait plus cher. Trop cher pour un pouvoir d'achat qui stagnait depuis un demi-siècle. Les faillites personnelles se multipliaient. Les évictions de locataires se comptaient par milliers. Les ressources d'hébergement et les refuges débordaient. Des familles entières jetées à la rue, privées d'eau courante et de nourriture, abandonnées à elles-mêmes. Ce phénomène s'observait d'un bout à l'autre du pays.

Akoulov reprit sa ronde. Son regard se perdit sur l'écran mural qui annonçait l'arrivée du prochain métro dans trois minutes. Il faisait 24 °C sur le Grand Montréal. Le Bitcoin franchissait le seuil historique des 1,2 million de dollars US. Une Lavalloise remportait la 21e saison de *Canada's Got Talent*. Les Canadiens avaient perdu 3-2 contre les Bruins de Boston.

Soudain, Akoulov sursauta à la vue du visage familier qui emplit l'écran. La sentence venait de tomber. Adel Salem, 22 ans, premier Canadien à se voir accusé d'activité terroriste par une intelligence artificielle, écopait d'une peine d'emprisonnement à perpétuité, sans libération conditionnelle avant vingt-cinq ans. Un jeune finissant de l'école Polytechnique. Au nombre de ses victimes alléguées figurait Daryl Thomassen, PDG de la firme en cybersécurité Eagle Eyes System, qui survécut après avoir été atteint de deux projectiles d'armes à feu, tirés par Adel Salem lui-même.

L'opération policière s'était soldée par une autre victime qui, elle, succomba à ses blessures. C'était Akoulov qui avait tiré par mégarde, mais Akoulov avait été acquitté. Certes, il avait écopé d'un transfert ; il considérait sa mutation à l'unité du métro comme une rétrogradation. L'enquêteur responsable de son dossier avait conclu que la force utilisée par le policier était légitime, étant donné qu'il craignait réellement pour sa vie.

Akoulov avait suivi attentivement le procès Salem, tout au long duquel il bénéficia d'un soutien psychologique. Heureusement pour lui, l'affaire n'avait pas traîné en longueur.

Les images firent place au plus récent sondage électoral qui plaçait les conservateurs en tête. Akoulov eut un soupir de soulagement. Justice avait été rendue. Quant à lui, il ne tarderait pas à réintégrer ses fonctions.

ACTE TERRORISTE :

Action ou omission, commise au Canada ou à l'étranger :
    (A) Au nom d'un but, d'une cause de nature politique, religieuse ou idéologique.
    (B) En vue d'intimider la population quant à sa sécurité, entre autres sur le plan économique, ou de contraindre une personne, un gouvernement ou une organisation nationale ou internationale à accomplir un acte ou à s'en abstenir, que la personne, la population, le gouvernement ou l'organisation soit ou non au Canada.

— Code criminel du Canada

LE 7 JUIN 2032
(17 MOIS PLUS TÔT)

Les doigts gantés d'Audrey étaient pleins de sang, à force de remuer la pointe du bijou dans l'oreille charnue d'Adel. Une épaisse tignasse de cheveux bouclés lui gênait la vue. Faute d'espace, elle avait fait asseoir Adel sur le rebord de son matelas, posé à même le sol. À lui seul, le lit accaparait la moitié de la chambre. La position était inconfortable. Déjà près d'une vingtaine de minutes qu'elle essayait, mais l'aiguille ne voulait tout simplement pas percer le lobe. Pourtant, un peu plus tôt, le poinçon qu'elle avait chauffé à blanc à l'aide d'une bougie avait pénétré sans problème. C'est que, le bijou – une petite étoile anarchocommuniste en argent – n'était tout simplement pas adéquat pour un premier piercing. Il aurait fallu choisir un clou ou une tige de diamètre moyen, qui aurait permis un meilleur guidage. Mais, Adel ne s'y connaissait pas. Il ne lui avait pas demandé conseil. Il était passé à la bijouterie après le boulot et l'avait retrouvée sitôt après. Or, tous deux avaient prévu se rejoindre au QG un peu plus tard. Le commando chargé de mettre en branle le « méchoui La Grange » les attendait. Le moment était mal choisi, c'était peu dire...

Mis à part ces considérations logistiques, sa demande l'avait d'abord surprise. Combien de fois, pendant qu'ils sortaient ensemble, avait-elle offert de percer son oreille et essuyé un refus net ? Il prétextait toujours des raisons quelconques, souvent familiales et professionnelles. Elle lui proposait pourtant des boucles d'oreille anodines, toutes petites et discrètes. Contrairement aux tatouages, qu'elle jugeait trop conformistes, les trous pouvaient se cicatriser et disparaître avec le temps. Elle-même en avait exactement six : cinq au niveau des oreilles et un sur le nez – tous faits maison. Rien n'avait pu convaincre Adel. Ce soir-là, sans qu'elle puisse se l'expliquer, il voulait son piercing à tout prix. Une étoile anarchocommuniste, en plus ! Elle n'y était pas préparée. Le « méchoui » accaparait toute son attention. L'entreprise était périlleuse et nécessitait qu'elle s'y attelle au plus vite. Adel aussi, d'ailleurs, mais il refusait de remettre sa coquetterie à un autre jour. Elle avait fini par se plier à ses caprices. Sa coloc Juju avait consenti à lui prêter du matériel. Du reste, il fallait faire avec les moyens du bord. Elle lui remonta la crinière à l'aide d'une pince à cheveux trouvée dans sa commode, puis força une fois de plus la petite aiguille dans la chair molle. Un petit bruit sec se fit entendre. Adel grimaça. Victoire ! La boucle était finalement passée.

Audrey retira ses gants chirurgicaux, puis tendit un miroir à Adel.

— Pas mal, non ? s'exclama-t-elle avec enthousiasme. Elle pouffa de rire. En tous cas, j'espère qu'ils diront rien à ta job !

— Penserais pas, rétorqua Adel, médusé par son reflet.
Il se contemplait de biais pour faire ressortir son nouvel
ornement. Son oreille était rouge comme une tomate. Du
sang en dégoulinait. Le chatoiement de l'étoile le fit sourire. Rien de très ostentatoire, songea-t-il. C'était limite.
De toute façon, il s'en foutait.

— T'avais pas fait une croix sur ce stage ? s'enquit-elle.

— Non... j'ai jamais dit ça.

— Donc, t'es content ?

— Ça va... laissa-t-il tomber. C'est juste un stage, rec-
tifia-t-il en tentant d'y mettre un peu plus de conviction.

Adel mentait. Il détestait son boulot plus que tout au
monde. Mais c'était un passage obligé pour l'obtention de
son baccalauréat en génie informatique. Le programme
requérait deux stages en entreprise. Il avait eu la chance, l'an
dernier, d'être recruté à un poste extrêmement contingenté
dans une firme de renom. Il avait obtenu « A+ » à sa première évaluation. On lui avait proposé un nouveau stage,
cet été ; il n'avait pas pu dire non. L'expérience lui appor-
terait des privilèges et une belle notoriété. Audrey n'insista
pas davantage. Après tout, ce n'était plus son affaire. Elle
commença à ranger le matériel de Juju.

Adel fixait son reflet dans la glace. Son oreille chauf-
fait, mais il s'abstint de la toucher, pour ne pas l'infecter.
Sa douleur était rédemptrice. Il pensait à la réaction de son
père, Mohamed Salem. C'était un descendant kurde d'une
longue lignée de propriétaires terriens dans le Rojava.
Ancien cultivateur de blé et russophile, il était demeuré
résolument communiste, comme en faisait foi la carte du

parti qu'il avait conservée jusqu'à ce jour. C'était un homme austère, peu enclin aux épanchements sentimentaux, même nationalistes. Étrange pour un Kurde, avait toujours pensé Adel, lui qui était très attaché à ses racines et à l'héritage de ses ancêtres. Il aurait aimé pouvoir s'en réclamer plus ouvertement – après tout, il était né au Kurdistan et y avait passé les premières années de sa vie avant que la guerre l'en expulse. Son père, toutefois, avait tout fait pour l'en empêcher. C'était un universaliste pur et dur, conviction renforcée par quelques études en mathématiques faites à Moscou. Les identités plurielles, autant que les nombres, faisaient toutes partie – en importance égale – du patrimoine universel de l'humanité. Pour lui, l'identité kurde n'était ni supérieure ni inférieure à une autre. En véritable communiste, il souscrivait à cet idéal que toutes les cultures se valent entre elles, et que tous les citoyens sont égaux devant la loi. Il réprouvait le culte de l'individualisme et cette manie de promouvoir les diversités en tous genres. Il ne se considérait pas comme différent des autres et avait en horreur toutes les manifestations de pitié qu'il pouvait bien susciter. Rien, pas même le chagrin de l'exil, le passage des saisons, la douceur du sirop d'érable ou même l'élégance des caribous traversant les surfaces glacées des lacs canadiens, n'étaient parvenus à l'attendrir. Un véritable spartiate. La vue d'un bijou fantaisiste à l'oreille de son fils ne pouvait lui inspirer que dégoût et aversion. Adel le savait. Il en tirait d'ailleurs une certaine fierté, lui qui d'ordinaire, n'osait défier l'autorité du père. Il savait qu'Audrey comprenait, et espérait d'elle un peu plus d'égard.

Un signe d'approbation, à tout le moins. Tandis qu'elle lui nettoyait l'oreille à l'aide d'une compresse d'eau oxygénée, les yeux d'Audrey trahirent un émoi. La chose le troubla. Elle s'était assise près de lui. L'odeur de sa transpiration avait réveillé de tendres souvenirs. La vue de sa nuque, mise en évidence par sa nouvelle coupe de cheveux à la garçonne style cyberpunk, avait attisé en lui un ardent désir de la prendre. C'était comme s'il découvrait, pour la toute première fois, la beauté de cette partie du corps. Il posa une main maladroite contre ses cuisses mises à nu par ses shorts troués. Leurs regards se croisèrent. Peut-être n'était-ce pas le bon moment, le geste tomba à plat. Audrey lut le désarroi dans les yeux de celui qu'elle avait jadis considéré, sans ambages, comme son seul et unique amoureux. Les temps avaient changé. Plus rien de tout ça n'était clair. Le passé n'était plus garant du présent. Encore moins de l'avenir. Ses sentiments avaient bifurqué au gré d'une rencontre inattendue, bouleversante. Son désir violent d'assouvir une passion charnelle avec un autre avait laissé au passage des émotions inexpliquées, inexplicables, et un cœur tourmenté que rien ne pouvait apaiser. Une dispute avait éclaté entre eux. S'en était conclu qu'ils devaient, pour un temps, prendre leurs distances pour repenser la relation.

Pourquoi Adel était-il venu la retrouver chez elle ? se demandait Audrey. L'excuse du piercing était boiteuse. Jusque-là, elle s'était gardée de tout commentaire. Une impression d'étrangeté l'envahit, et elle se leva d'un bond. La chambre étant minuscule, elle ne put aller bien loin. Et de n'importe où qu'elle ait pu se trouver, il était impossible de briser la troublante intimité qui s'était installée entre eux. Adel était demeuré assis. Elle s'adossa contre le mur du fond, croisa bras et jambes, et un silence malaisant s'installa. Son regard fuyait vers la fenêtre. S'y élevait un vieux chêne aux longs bras clairsemés que des chenilles spongieuses, à sa grande tristesse, avaient lentement pris d'assaut.

— Je croyais que c'était fini entre nous...

— Fini ? s'enquit Adel avec effroi.

— Ben... Tu me l'as bien fait comprendre, l'autre jour. Je me sens plus à l'aise de...

— Je comprends, trancha l'autre avec regret, baissant les yeux, comme si le simple fait de la regarder le fit trop souffrir. Cet amour platonique qui les unissait désormais, ce pacte d'amitié, ce respect réciproque qu'ils se vouaient l'un l'autre, rien de tout cela ne pouvait apaiser cette violente douleur sur laquelle il ne se reconnaissait aucun droit, et qui pourtant s'arrogeait tant de droits sur lui. Après tout, Audrey pouvait coucher avec qui elle voulait.

Il se leva pour partir, mais Audrey fit un mouvement pour le retenir.

— Désolé, je voulais pas te...

— C'est correct.

Il semblait hésiter entre partir ou rester.

— Es-tu stressé pour ce soir ? lui demanda Audrey, comme pour l'inviter à se vider le cœur.

Adel n'était pas du genre très bavard et bien qu'elle excellât dans l'art de le faire parler, il parvenait toujours à s'esquiver.

— Ce soir ?

— Oui, La Grange... le « méchoui »... précisa-t-elle, sur un ton agacé.

— Pas vraiment. Peut-être un peu.

— Tu t'en mets pas un peu trop sur les épaules ?

Adel reçut le reproche sans sourciller.

— Tu sais, t'es pas obligé... osa-t-elle prudemment.

Elle n'avait pas bougé de sa place.

— Pas obligé de quoi ?

— On peut toujours annuler, si tu veux.

— Et pourquoi est-ce qu'on annulerait ?

— J'sais pas... Peut-être à cause de Maximilien et moi ? avança-t-elle en haussant les épaules.

— Aucun rapport ! mugit Adel. Il détestait Maximilien Caron et tout ce qu'il représentait. C'était le genre d'individu qui se targuait d'être activiste, mais qui en réalité n'était qu'un *douchebag* dont l'unique souci était de se faire valoir, à grands coups de bluff. Adel ne croyait guère aux causes politiques de son rival. Elles tenaient du mirage. Le mec filmait ses actions dans l'unique but de se vanter sur les réseaux sociaux, avec toujours sa figure en gros plan. Un vrai frimeur. Il connaissait un certain succès, c'était indéniable. Mais aux yeux d'Adel, Caron n'était qu'un misérable fanfaron. Il aurait voulu qu'Audrey ait assez de discernement pour voir la même chose. Bien au contraire ! Elle s'était vite entichée de lui. Adel n'avait jamais osé lui dire le fond de sa pensée. Il était trop orgueilleux pour admettre qu'Audrey puisse s'éprendre d'un autre que lui. À présent, le ton de sa voix trahissait sa blessure.

— Aucun rapport, répéta Adel en fixant le sol. J'me fous de ce que vous faites ensemble. Ça me regarde pas. Je fais ça pour la cause, uniquement pour la cause, maugréa-t-il.

Il leva les yeux, constata avec effarement qu'Audrey était bouche bée.

— Je m'excuse, balbutia-t-il, désemparé. Je voulais pas... Je m'excuse.

Il se leva maladroitement et faute d'espace, fit quelques pas autour de lui. Puis, il ouvrit enfin la porte. Jetant un dernier coup d'œil vers Audrey (elle n'avait pas bougé d'un poil), il dit : « À tout à l'heure. » Puis, il referma la porte derrière lui.

Il commençait à être tard. Une longue, très longue nuit l'attendait.

La boutique La Grange, spécialisée dans la vente de mobilier haut de gamme en bois rustique, avait pignon sur la rue Jean-Talon, dans le quartier Saint-Michel. Au rez-de-chaussée, la salle d'exposition abritait une impressionnante collection internationale de meubles luxueux en tous genres : tables, buffets, bars, comptoirs, garde-robes, armoires en bois massif aux essences les plus nobles, provenant de forêts exploitées aux quatre coins du globe.

Établi depuis 2026, le commerce prospérait à la faveur d'un embourgeoisement du quartier qui avait vu un nombre grandissant de nouveaux ensembles résidentiels. Des tours à condos flanquées de certifications environnementales avaient colonisé toutes les rues de cet arrondissement, autrefois parmi les plus pauvres de Montréal.

Pour répondre à la croissance des ventes, le groupe Prestige, propriétaire de la boutique La Grange, avait décidé d'annexer au magasin le local d'à côté, une gargote où avaient l'habitude de se réunir les habitués du coin. Un cabinet d'architecture ainsi qu'une firme de design intérieur avaient investi l'étage du dessus, et offraient leurs services aux promoteurs locaux.

Groupes citoyens et militants associatifs avaient organisé nombre d'évènements anticapitalistes aux abords de ces commerces, dans l'espoir de démobiliser clients et propriétaires. De la distribution de tracts aux manifestations virant en parade de foire, en passant par les barbecues solidaires, ils avaient tout tenté pour déloger ces malvenus. L'enracinement de ces commerces était devenu d'autant plus durable qu'ils incarnaient désormais le symbole d'une nouvelle ère de prospérité pour le quartier, en dépit de la crise qui affectait les pauvres.

Dernièrement, plusieurs attaques avaient ciblé les vitrines de ces établissements, à la faveur du mouvement populaire EAU SECOURS visant à contrer le projet de loi sur la privatisation de l'eau potable. Les employés avaient été menacés, des voitures vandalisées. Pour sécuriser les lieux et dissuader les casseurs, on avait installé un système de caméras intelligentes aux abords du terrain, le tout couplé à un dispositif de marquage ADN anti-cambriolage à l'intérieur. En cas de braquage, des brumisateurs cachés diffusaient un traceur à la fluorescéine indélébile, uniquement visible à la lumière d'une lampe UV. Le produit imprégnait la peau, les cheveux et les vêtements pour des semaines, voire des mois, permettant de retracer les coupables et les objets volés. Deux casseurs – un homme et une femme – avaient d'ailleurs été interpellés, appréhendés, déclarés coupables, puis incarcérés grâce à cet équipement sophistiqué qui allait bientôt devenir la norme en matière de protection antivol. La sentence qui les condamnait chacun à deux ans de prison ferme était tombée le mois dernier.

En ce soir du 7 juin 2032, un groupe se faisant passer pour le Resco – les compagnons de la résistance – préparait une contre-attaque. Avec la ferme intention de venger leurs confrères et consœurs emprisonnés, de descendre en flammes le bâtiment, avec ses meubles, ses bureaux et toute sa paperasse.

Ce soir-là, huit compagnons membres du Resco s'étaient réunis dans le sous-sol d'un atelier de réparation de vélos, pour repasser en détail toutes les étapes de l'offensive baptisée « opération méchoui ». Fidèle à son habitude et à son tempérament fougueux, celui aux cheveux longs qu'on surnommait affectueusement Maximus (au lieu de Maximilien) sautait toujours les étapes, outrepassait ses fonctions pour enjoindre chacun et chacune à répéter son rôle. La chose ne manquait pas de faire grincer des dents la plus féministe du groupe ; Manon « Sœur » Bouchard l'interrompit subitement.

— *Time out, time out,* le jeune, s'exclama-t-elle à son intention, agitant ses mains en croix. Maximus lui céda la parole, à contrecœur.

— Est-ce que tout le monde comprend pourquoi on est ici ? Est-ce qu'on est à l'aise avec ce qu'on s'apprête à faire ? s'enquit l'activiste d'expérience en prenant soin de dévisager ses interlocuteurs.

Une femme qui peinait à soutenir le regard de ses compères se leva et prit la parole. C'était une mère monoparentale.

— J-j-je dois me retirer... P-pour mes filles, vous comprenez ? J-je sais à quel point c'est important pour nous, et, et, rendu là, c-croyez-moi, je n'avais pas l'intention de vous faire ça... commença-t-elle, d'une voix chevrotante. Mais j'peux juste pas risquer la prison.

Yeux larmoyants, elle guettait la réaction de ses camarades. Manon « Sœur » Bouchard se leva pour la serrer dans ses bras. Elle caressa ses cheveux.

— Tu peux y aller, ma chouette. On fera sans toi.

— Sûrs ? demanda-t-elle en s'adressant aux autres. Les compagnons approuvèrent d'un hochement de tête.

« Sœur » Bouchard l'accompagna jusqu'à la sortie, et vint se rasseoir avec les autres. Les regards se tournèrent vers Adel Salem.

— Pis toé, es-tu toujours partant ? demanda « Sœur » Bouchard.

La fébrilité était palpable. La tension, à son paroxysme. Jamais de leur vie, ces activistes ne s'étaient attelés à une tâche aussi complexe. Quoiqu'accoutumés aux incendies (c'était d'ailleurs leur image de marque), ceux-ci avaient l'habitude de viser des cibles moins audacieuses. Du mobilier urbain, par exemple, ou la voiture d'un riche notable. Ou encore, à la rigueur, une roulotte de chantier. L'embrasement d'un bâtiment complet avec ses bureaux et son entrepôt représentait une première. Jamais, toutefois, ses membres n'avaient été aussi motivés, les préparatifs peaufinés à ce point. Préparation des armes incendiaires, acquisition de masques à gaz, sélection de vêtements de rechange, ils avaient pensé à tout. Jusqu'à la disposition de vélos géoréférencés aux abords du théâtre d'opérations, pour assurer le repli. Tout avait été planifié, oui, jusque dans les moindres détails, pour préserver la sécurité des camarades.

Ce soir-là était spécial, à n'en pas douter. En plus de venger leurs amis emprisonnés – tous deux demeurés fidèles au serment du silence –, le Resco accueillait un nouveau compagnon dans ses rangs : Adel Salem. Fait plus notoire encore, Adel avait lui-même proposé la mission du jour, comme le voulait la tradition qui enjoignait le novice à choisir son « baptême du feu ». La cible désignée, la recrue était ensuite conviée à mettre le feu aux poudres. Le projet qu'Adel avait choisi impressionnait par son envergure. Qu'il incendiât une poubelle aurait suffi pour faire acte d'allégeance. La proposition de brûler La Grange avait d'abord entraîné une levée de boucliers. Certains avaient crié à la folie. Les risques étaient démesurés. La Grange était une véritable forteresse, en comparaison de leurs cibles antérieures. C'était *big* ! Le Resco avait déjà perdu deux compagnons pour s'être lancé à l'assaut de ses murailles. Adel était toutefois parvenu à les convaincre en se portant garant du succès de l'entreprise. Son plan ? Désarmer le bastion ennemi en piratant le système domotique. Simple comme bonjour, avait-il assuré. Maximilien et Audrey avaient cautionné l'initiative ; ils ne laissaient planer aucun doute sur ses capacités. Adel avait déjà fait ses preuves. L'informatique n'avait aucun secret pour lui. Il était capable de mettre à sa merci n'importe quels ordinateur, puce ou robot connectés à un réseau. Il n'aurait aucun mal à pirater le système de sécurité de la boutique La Grange. L'idée avait fait sourciller, mais elle avait fini par faire son chemin. Le désir de venger les frères et sœurs tombés au combat l'avait emporté sur la raison. Le projet s'était donc mis en branle.

Il était pourtant très difficile d'intégrer le Resco. N'entrait pas qui voulait. Il fallait, pour ce faire, avoir un contact direct de l'intérieur – de préférence un membre actif. À l'époque, Adel sortait avec Audrey, qui, elle, commençait à fréquenter Maximus. Le triangle amoureux avait suscité une certaine méfiance. Leur relation était-elle saine ou pas ? Aucun révolutionnaire ne veut risquer sa tête, nul n'entend s'exposer à x années de prison à cause d'une opération qui aurait « foiré » pour une simple « histoire de cul ». Interrogés à ce sujet, les trois avaient juré partager, entre eux, une relation harmonieuse, basée sur le respect. En outre, tous les trois se considéraient comme non monogames. Ces arguments avaient rassuré la compagnie. Quoi de plus révolutionnaire que de considérer ses amants, et les amants de ses amants, comme des alliés ? Que vaudrait une organisation anarchiste, si elle ne valorisait pas la libre rencontre des désirs individuels ? Il n'y a pas de révolution sans désir. C'est la jalousie et la compétitivité qui isolent les individus et qu'il faut combattre par la lutte anticapitaliste, l'abolition du patriarcat et la décolonisation des corps. Là-dessus, il y avait consensus. Mais jusqu'ici, les récents déboires du trouple étaient demeurés inconnus de la cellule. À vrai dire, Maximus même ignorait encore à quel point le fiel corrompait le cœur de celui qu'il considérait comme son métamour. Adel n'avait jamais osé s'exprimer sur sa détresse, tant elle lui semblait humiliante, inavouable à lui-même.

Manon « Sœur » Bouchard répéta sa question. Adel restait absent. Audrey et Maximus accaparaient toute son attention. Ils avaient choisi de s'asseoir ensemble et s'étaient enlacés spontanément. Le geste attisa sa jalousie et lui fit l'effet d'une gifle. Des pensées tourbillonnaient dans sa tête. Pourquoi était-il là ? Que faisait-il ici ? Était-il là pour les bonnes raisons ?

— Adel ? Adel, es-tu toujours avec nous ? claironnait « Sœur » Bouchard en claquant des doigts.

Adel sortit de sa léthargie. Ses yeux parcoururent l'assemblée. On le fixait du regard, il lui sembla qu'Audrey évitait le sien. Ou avait-elle simplement la mèche à l'œil ? Il n'aurait pas su dire.

— Es-tu toujours partant pour l'action, répéta « Sœur » Bouchard.

— Oui, oui, parvint-il à articuler.

En réalité, il n'en était plus sûr du tout. Et son oreille tout juste percée lui faisait atrocement mal.

À l'heure convenue, six compagnons de la résistance avaient quadrillé les alentours de la boutique La Grange et attendaient le signal d'Adel. Deux d'entre eux sirotaient un café, à la table d'un McDonald's. Deux autres patientaient à un arrêt d'autobus. Les deux derniers, munis d'un *scanner* de police, faisaient les cent pas dans un appartement voisin.

Non loin de là, caché derrière une benne à ordures, au coin d'une ruelle, Adel faisait courir ses doigts sur le clavier d'un micro-ordinateur piraté pour l'occasion. Le but : se connecter à la centrale domotique du bâtiment ennemi – centrale qui contrôlait non seulement la température et l'éclairage des locaux, mais aussi tout le dispositif anti-cambriolage, incluant les caméras de surveillance. Un seul courriel frauduleux avait suffi pour enjoindre la réceptionniste du Groupe Prestige à télécharger le catalogue 2032-2033 de la compagnie fictive « Ameublement Deschênes & Fils Laval ». L'hameçonnage réussi, un cheval de Troie désactiva le pare-feu des serveurs, livrant ainsi les clés de la boutique La Grange. Une technologie 7G entièrement chiffrée préserva l'anonymat de la cyberattaque.

L'opération complétée, Adel ramena son capuchon sur son visage, enfila son sac à dos et sortit de sa cachette pour se diriger d'un pas naturel vers le magasin. L'entrepôt donnait sur la ruelle. Se souvenant qu'il n'y avait pas de caméra le long de cette allée, il s'efforça de maintenir une allure décontractée. Arrivé devant la porte de l'arrière-boutique, il tira sur la poignée qui (comme le lui avait assuré un employé de la place, allié du Resco) n'offrit aucune résistance. Il pénétra à l'intérieur du bâtiment. La porte se referma derrière lui.

Son cœur battait la chamade. Il s'adossa contre le mur de parpaing et se laissa glisser vers le sol pour reprendre son souffle. Il consulta sa montre à écran tactile, vint pour pianoter un message, mais dut y renoncer tant sa main tremblait. Il ferma les yeux, prit trois grandes inspirations. « Jusqu'ici, tout va bien. Jusqu'ici, tout va bien », se répéta-t-il. Aucune alarme n'avait sonné. Aucune lumière ne s'était allumée. Tout se passait exactement comme prévu. Retrouvant son sang-froid, il essaya une deuxième fois. « L'oiseau est dans le nid », parvint-il à écrire. Puis il attendit.

Dix minutes. C'est le décompte généralement admis pour, au besoin, avorter la mission ou sonner la retraite. Le message délivré, les compagnons de la résistance attendirent comme des faucons aux aguets, prêts à abandonner l'un des leurs au moindre pépin, au moindre signe suspect. Le sacrifice d'un membre valait toujours mieux que le démantèlement de la cellule au grand complet. À mesure que les minutes s'écoulaient sans qu'aucune auto-patrouille ne vienne troubler leur quiétude, sans qu'aucun drone ne vienne miner leur confiance, les cœurs se galvanisaient. Ainsi, Adel Salem avait réussi l'impossible. Il avait gagné son pari. « Sœur » Bouchard, Maximus, Audrey et les autres empoignèrent leurs affaires. Telle une armée resserrant son étau autour de l'ennemi, ils convergèrent progressivement vers la boutique.

Trois petits coups discrets à la porte. Adel ouvrit pour accueillir ses complices dans le ventre de la baleine. Il faisait noir à l'intérieur. La vision, pratiquement nulle à travers les cagoules ; rien toutefois pour freiner l'ardeur des révolutionnaires. Ils avaient mémorisé les plans par cœur et connaissaient l'édifice jusque dans ses moindres recoins. Quelques marchandises traînaient ici et là, mais ils reconnurent très vite, à la lueur d'une lumière bleutée, le monte-charge, à gauche, qui permettait d'accéder au sous-sol. En haut, à droite, le petit escalier débouchait sur les bureaux. Derrière, sur le mur du fond, ils trouvèrent le câble de fibre optique à côté de l'entrée d'eau et du panneau électrique. Un compagnon s'empressa de le sectionner à l'aide d'un sécateur. Tout droit, ils repérèrent la porte ouvrant sur la salle d'exposition. Ils vérifièrent : comme toutes les autres, elle était bien déverrouillée. Ne restait plus qu'à tirer les rideaux de la vitrine, puis à se mettre au travail. Sans perdre un instant.

Dans la salle d'exposition, ils disposèrent les meubles en une sorte de construction en tipi, pour favoriser la combustion. À la base, ils empilèrent le mobilier en cèdre blanc et en cèdre espagnol, puis le bois de grange vieilli naturellement, au fini tendre, idéal pour l'allumage. Vinrent ensuite les bois un peu plus durs, meubles en acajou, chêne et noyer, excellents pour entretenir la combustion et dégager de la chaleur. Tout au sommet et en périphérie, ils disposèrent les bibliothèques d'amarante, le dressoir en frêne, le vaisselier en cerisier et le secrétaire en bois d'ébène pour conférer au brasier un fumet digne des méchouis les plus grandioses.

Le matériel empilé, ils se rassemblèrent autour de la construction, qu'ils estimèrent à une centaine de milliers de dollars, tout au plus, en se fiant aux étiquettes de prix. Un compagnon alla couper l'entrée d'eau. Un autre ouvrit une bouteille de whisky pour la partager avec ses confrères et consœurs. L'une d'entre elles, après avoir contemplé l'œuvre, baissa ses culottes, s'accroupit et urina sur le tas. On disposa au centre une immense boule de papier et de carton provenant des bureaux, à l'étage supérieur. Pour agrémenter le système d'allumage, on dénicha dans l'entrepôt, de la paille sèche. Enfin, pour couronner le tout, on plaça au sommet du bûcher un immense bidon rempli d'huile, d'essence et de copeaux en styromousse qui, en fondant, allait engendrer la « mère de tous les brasiers ».

Les préparatifs terminés, une bouteille incendiaire se mit à circuler de mains en mains jusqu'à Adel. Deux ou trois têtes s'inclinèrent vers lui, avec déférence. Briquet dans une main, cocktail Molotov dans l'autre, Adel resta figé devant l'étrange édification, comme saisi d'un doute. Il chercha le regard d'Audrey, mais celle-ci s'obstinait à fixer, sourire aux lèvres, le monticule de bois. Les secondes s'égrainèrent, solennellement, pendant que les autres attendirent. Et pourtant, Adel restait immobile, comme si l'espace de quelques instants, un profond abîme s'était creusé entre lui et les êtres.

Maximus, qui se tenait tout juste à côté de lui, ricana : « Allo allo, la Terre appelle la Lune ». Sans doute espérait-il faire débloquer les choses. Adel demeura de marbre. Une minute s'écoula ainsi avant que Maximus perde patience et lui arrache la bouteille des mains. Allumant le torchon lui-même, il balança la boule de feu contre les meubles. Un millier d'étincelles et de flammes fusèrent aussitôt au ras du sol, embrasant le chaume, le papier et le carton. Des cris de joie jaillirent. Quelques compagnons se livrèrent à une danse folâtre autour du feu. La fille qui avait uriné devant tout le monde prit une dernière rasade de whisky avant de balancer la bouteille contre les meubles, attisant les flammes qui s'élancèrent jusqu'au plafond.

À l'écart, Adel observait la scène sans dire un mot. Maximilien échangea quelques paroles avec Audrey. Il avait levé sa cagoule pour l'embrasser sur la bouche ; elle s'était laissé faire. La scène le fit trembler d'une rage idiote. La cérémonie terminée, Manon « Sœur » Bouchard lui donna une tape sur l'épaule. Il était déjà temps de décamper.

La fibre optique ayant été coupée et les rideaux tirés, le service d'incendie ne fut pas prévenu avant une bonne heure. Ce sont des passants qui, alertés par la forte odeur de fumée et la lueur des flammes à l'intérieur de la bâtisse, auraient pris l'initiative d'appeler les pompiers.

Entre-temps, le feu avait déjà ravagé la salle d'exposition et s'était propagé vers les locaux du deuxième, consumant une partie de la toiture. Bien avant, donc, que l'incendie ne soit maîtrisé, les compagnons de la résistance avaient rejoint leur quartier général, prenant bien soin de brouiller les pistes, empruntant des chemins différents, coupant par les ruelles et les arrière-cours, où certains en profitèrent pour se changer.

Adel s'accroupit derrière un cabanon, n'osant sortir de sa cachette tant il était perturbé. Que s'était-il passé ? Pourquoi avait-il figé ? Il renifla ses doigts, sentit une odeur d'essence et d'huile, pourtant il ne se rappelait pas en avoir manipulé. La nausée lui monta à la gorge, et il vomit sur la pelouse fraîche. Un grillon, ému par la scène, stridula.

Était-ce parce qu'il était jaloux de Maximus ? « Non ! », se surprit-il à clamer haut et fort. Évidemment non ! Enfin, peut-être un peu... Il n'en était plus certain. Il n'était plus sûr de rien. S'en voulait-il d'avoir pris ses distances avec Audrey ? Il s'efforça d'observer ces questions avec tout le détachement dont il était capable. Vrai, il aimait encore Audrey. De tout son cœur, même. Comme amie, s'empressa-t-il de se préciser à lui-même – il n'était plus amoureux d'elle. Plus du tout. Et donc, logiquement, il ne pouvait être jaloux, conclut-il. Il avait laissé Audrey, en toute connaissance de cause. Les sentiments qu'elle éprouvait pour Maximus ne le regardaient pas, ne le concernaient plus, essayait-il de se convaincre.

La curieuse stridulation retentit encore et encore. Adel prêta l'oreille et se laissa transporter par l'étrange résonance. Il se pencha pour mieux en saisir la provenance. Comme de fait, un grillon bien gras se tenait là, tout près du cabanon. La chose piqua sa curiosité. Il tendit la main vers la mystérieuse créature qui ne fit qu'un bond pour venir à sa rencontre. Adel ramena son bras pour contempler l'insecte. Il remarqua sa tête aux longues antennes et ses yeux exorbités. Des ailes nervurées palpitaient sur son thorax, s'y frottant à la manière d'un archet sur une caisse de résonance. Quel fascinant phénomène. Un musicien célébrant ses amours passés et sa vie de célibataire, songea Adel avec humeur et bienveillance, lui qui estimait avoir eu son lot de malheurs et de sensations fortes pour la soirée. Il vint pour redéposer l'animal au sol, quand celui-ci l'apostropha. Il clama d'une voix forte et vibrante que dans les jeux de l'amour, nous devions tous renoncer à une part de nous-mêmes.

— Encore faut-il ne pas y perdre la tête, gazouilla-t-il pour rectifier ses propos. Comme mon regretté pote, mante religieuse, ce grand romantique qui mourut dévoré par son amoureuse, après s'être accouplé avec elle, poursuivit-il avec mélancolie.

Adel Salem sursauta. Le ventru grillon remarqua sa réaction et cessa de chanter. Il s'approcha de l'être humain, remonta ses phalanges et, après s'être éclairci la gorge, s'adressa à lui en des termes plus familiers.

— Tu es perdu, mon gars ? Ta vie n'a plus aucun sens, je sais, je sais... Ne le vois-tu donc pas ? Ou préfères-tu te complaire dans le mensonge ?

— C'est pas vrai, rétorqua Adel, piqué au vif. Je sais très bien où j'en suis, et ce que je fais ! avança-t-il encore, confus par ses propres paroles.

— Tu parles ! Tu rumines ta peine d'amour. Tu aimes encore Audrey. Avoue-le donc que tu l'aimes encore et que tu regrettes d'avoir rompu avec elle ! Mais, par-dessus tout, tu hais Maximus... Tout ce que tu souhaites, secrètement,

43

c'est qu'Audrey plaque ce vantard et retombe amoureuse de toi ! Seulement, tu n'as pas le courage de lui en parler, stridula le grillon. Tu as peur du ridicule. Oh, mais quelle vanité, ces humains !

Adel tressaillit à ces mots sortis tout droit de la bouche d'un grillon. Était-il en train de devenir fou ? Les vapeurs toxiques lui avaient-elles monté à la tête ? Le stress et l'adrénaline ne provoquaient-ils pas en lui ces étranges hallucinations ? Le sensible orthoptère, qui n'en était pas à ses premières déclarations fracassantes adressées aux êtres humains, nota le trouble d'Adel Salem et reprit sur un ton plus amical et plus doux.

— Allons, allons l'ami, ressaisis-toi. Tu n'as pas à avoir honte de ton chagrin. Tu as perdu confiance en toi ? C'est normal. Il nous arrive à tous de vivre des moments difficiles. Qui crois-tu être pour te croire invincible ? Regarde-moi, misérable bête. Ô combien dois-je faire preuve d'humilité pour vivre en ce bas monde ! Nous autres, insectes, connaissons bien notre valeur, malgré tout le mépris que vous nous affichez. Tu ne me crois pas ? Je parle par expérience : nous sommes sur Terre depuis la nuit des temps. Tu veux un bon conseil ? Laisse-moi te dire. Tu as toujours voulu plaire aux autres ; apprends un peu à te foutre de ce que les gens pensent ! Le Resco ? Mais qu'est-ce que tu fous là ? Tu n'as jamais voulu en faire partie. Tu t'es prêté au jeu parce que tu aimes Audrey. Tu veux la vérité ? Tu n'arrives pas à lui dire simplement. Tu souhaites la reconquérir en te mesurant à son amant. Tu vas te casser la gueule, mon pote.

Adel vint pour lui donner une chiquenaude quand l'impudent insecte bondit de sa main pour disparaître dans la pelouse.

Des sirènes de pompiers retentirent au loin. Adel vérifia sa montre et se rendit compte qu'on avait tenté de communiquer avec lui. On l'attendait pour commencer le débreffage. Avisant ses compagnons qu'il serait en retard, il se leva d'un bond, sortit de sa cachette et sauta par-dessus une clôture.

— Ah, si jeunesse savait, si vieillesse pouvait, reprit le grillon de sa voix mielleuse qui vibra dans la nuit.

Il était environ 4 h du matin lorsque Adel Salem revint à l'atelier de vélo. Une odeur de graisse, d'essence et d'alcool régnait dans l'air. Des éclats de rire retentirent du sous-sol. Il y avait de la musique. Empruntant l'escalier pour descendre à la cave, Adel croisa un camarade aviné qui lui sauta au cou.

— Hey, t'étais où, man ? On t'a cherché partout !

Adel se dégagea de son étreinte, laissant la question sans réponse.

Le débreffage avait été écourté. Audrey portait la touche finale au communiqué de presse. On s'adonnait déjà à la boisson. Des pilules avaient circulé. L'ambiance était à la fête. Visage austère, Adel arriva au beau milieu de ce joyeux monde comme un cheveu sur la soupe.

— Hé, regardez qui arrive ! hurla un autre compagnon, à la vue d'Adel Salem. Bouteille à la main, il tituba vers lui pour le prendre dans ses bras avant de trébucher sur le coin d'un établi. La bière décrivit un arc parabolique et vint éclabousser les vêtements du survenant. Les regards se braquèrent sur lui. Le gaffeur se confondit en excuses.

— Mais qu'est-ce que vous avez à le regarder comme ça ? s'écria Maximus qui s'approchait de la scène en faisant tournoyer entre ses doigts une bouteille de whisky. N'est-ce pas un champion ? Notre champion ? Un peu étourdi... mais un champion quand même ! s'exclama-t-il encore en flanquant une claque retentissante sur l'épaule d'Adel. Il l'étreignit vigoureusement ; Adel le repoussa.

«Sœur» Bouchard qui, d'un coin, observait silencieusement la scène se leva. Audrey fit de même. Les deux hommes se dévisageaient.

— Qu'est-ce qu'il y a, mon beau Adel ? Tu t'esquives encore ? Ça nous arrive à tous de *choker,* tu sais. Bon, je te l'accorde : ton piratage nous a permis de faire le coup du siècle. Et ça... ça mérite qu'on boive à ta santé !

Il leva sa bouteille bien haut, enjoignant les autres à en faire autant. Une ou deux personnes l'imitèrent. Il prit une longue rasade.

Maximus tendit la bouteille à Adel.

— Tiens, bois si t'es bien des nôtres, lui intima-t-il, comme s'il s'agissait d'un nouveau test. Adel écarta le bras de Maximus. Le geste parut le contrarier. Il revint à la charge.

— Bois ! lui commanda-t-il en lui flanquant la bouteille contre le torse. Son regard lançait maintenant des éclairs. Un frisson parcourut l'échine d'Adel. Son œil cligna, comme sous l'effet d'un tic.

— Non, pas ça ! cria « Sœur » Bouchard qui présageant le pire, avait bousculé deux personnes pour se frayer un chemin jusqu'à eux. Trop tard.

Adel poussa l'autre si fort qu'il en perdit l'équilibre. La bouteille de whisky se fracassa au sol. Des clameurs retentirent. Maximus parut un instant ébahi. Puis, tel un taureau, il fonça tête première sur son rival. Et tandis que les coups de poing s'échangèrent de part et d'autre, sous le regard incrédule d'Audrey, une petite voix résonnait dans la tête d'Adel : « Le grillon... il avait raison, pensait-il. Il avait raison. »

Le constable de classe 7, agent Youri Akoulov, matricule 274, était fraîchement promu de la 380e cohorte de l'École nationale de police, et avait rejoint les effectifs du SPVM au printemps 2032.

N'étant pas encore affecté à un local en particulier, comme bien des nouvelles recrues, il occupait différentes fonctions non permanentes au sein de la police : factionnaire, remplacements de congé maladie, garde de détenus, patrouille motorisée, etc. Les quarts de jour étant d'ordinaire attribués en fonction de l'ancienneté, comme le veut l'usage, il arrivait la plupart du temps qu'Akoulov travaille de nuit.

Ses instructeurs se souvenaient de lui comme d'un candidat dynamique, à fort potentiel. Dévoué, il s'était investi corps et âme dans sa formation, qu'il avait d'ailleurs terminée avec une mention « remarquable ». Ses évaluateurs avaient été impressionnés par la maîtrise de ses compétences, ses talents, son sens du devoir et sa capacité de supporter la pression.

Youri Akoulov était un passionné. Il rêvait de gravir les échelons du corps policier, de faire partie d'une unité spécialisée comme l'escouade antigang ou le groupe d'intervention tactique, selon les perspectives qui s'offriraient à lui. Motivé comme pas un, l'agent Akoulov avait accepté volontiers de faire partie d'un projet pilote initié par le SPVM dont l'ambition à terme était de doter ses effectifs d'un assistant numérique personnalisé. Le but : assurer une prestation de service optimale, selon les objectifs du dernier plan stratégique « Analyser, Comprendre, Agir ».

Baptisée Colombus, l'application était conçue comme une interface personne-machine dotée d'une intelligence artificielle, capable d'accompagner les forces de l'ordre dans leurs interventions. Parmi les mérites qu'on lui attribuait, le logiciel pouvait aider les policiers à mieux identifier les personnes et les véhicules, utiliser le degré de force approprié, respecter les règles de déontologie, communiquer avec la centrale, et bien d'autres fonctions encore reposant sur la réalité augmentée. Le SPVM comptait ainsi répondre à plusieurs besoins au sein de son service. D'abord, en actualisant en temps réel les connaissances et les compétences des policiers selon la situation en cours. Ensuite – et c'était peut-être la fonctionnalité la plus importante – en enrayant plusieurs phénomènes récurrents et non souhaitables au sein de son service, tels que le profilage racial et social. Les études parlaient d'elles-mêmes : la sixième génération d'IA propulsant cet appareil se révélait plus fiable que le cerveau humain pour contrer ces biais déplorables.

Intégré aux lunettes intelligentes du policier, Colombus était présent aussi bien dans son auto que dans son téléphone, et accessible à travers ses nombreux écrans. Peu importe où il se trouva, Colombus pouvait, par le biais de ses applications, aider le policier à prendre les meilleures décisions possibles, en plus de l'aviser des meilleures techniques à privilégier pour mieux intervenir, à tout moment.

En cette nuit du 7 juin 2032, l'agent Akoulov était de garde. Affecté cette semaine-là au poste de quartier 30 dans Saint-Michel, il patrouillait en véhicule avec un certain Sergio Gabriel Martinez, matricule 621.

Le PDQ 30 Saint-Michel était l'un des plus actifs de l'agglomération métropolitaine, et son profil de criminalité, des plus diversifiés. Si les problèmes liés aux gangs de rue et à la prolifération d'armes à feu dans le quartier s'étaient résorbés au cours des dernières années, les vols de véhicules et les entrées par effraction, eux, connaissaient une hausse significative en raison de l'embourgeoisement du secteur. Dernièrement, dans la foulée du mouvement EAU SECOURS, qui ne cessait de prendre l'ampleur, ce sont les méfaits et actes de vandalisme sur la propriété privée et le domaine public qui remportaient la palme.

Au *fall-in*, le sergent Baptiste Ténor avait lancé le mot d'ordre de la soirée : demeurer à l'affût des activités suspectes aux abords des commerces. Garder un œil sur le parc François-Perrault – où se déroulaient quelques soirs des attroupements illégaux de jeunes festoyeurs. Du reste, rien d'anormal à signaler. À la radio : le train-train habituel. La soirée s'annonçait comme les autres.

Youri Akoulov connaissait Saint-Michel comme le fond de sa poche : il y avait grandi, angle 19ᵉ avenue et rue Bélair. Les visages lui étaient familiers. Il connaissait les enjeux de sécurité du coin. C'était un gars de la place. N'en demeure, le paysage urbain avait changé depuis ses jeunes années et avec lui, les formes de criminalité. La construction de la ligne rose, qui reliait désormais Montréal-Nord au centre-ville en moins de vingt minutes – interruptions de service en sus – avait fait bondir le prix des terrains et repoussé vers la couronne nord les habitants natifs de ce quartier. Et le nouveau centre technologique de recherche sur le génome humain, construit à même le territoire de l'ancienne carrière Francon, attirait des étudiants et des professeurs du monde entier, venus pour travailler et s'établir dans le complexe à usage mixte annexé à l'institution. Au fil des ans, ces nouveaux arrivants avaient fini par constituer une nouvelle frange de la population, plus riche et huppée, friande de cafés, bistros et autres petits commerces.

Le mouvement EAU SECOURS n'avait pas épargné ces nouveaux venus. Les manifestations des derniers mois avaient laissé de profondes cicatrices sur le paysage urbain. Vitrines brisées, devantures de commerces défigurées, poubelles publiques carbonisées. Les grabuges et actes de vandalisme sur le domaine public et la propriété privée étaient devenus monnaie courante dans ce quartier populaire en proie à des débordements quotidiens.

Quelques jours plus tôt, l'agent Akoulov et son partenaire Martinez pouvaient se féliciter d'avoir procédé à une douzaine d'interpellations, incluant quatre arrestations. Grâce à Colombus, chacune des interventions avait été exécutée selon les règles de l'art. À preuve, aucune plainte, aucune allégation de profilage ou d'usage disproportionné de la force n'avait circulé à leur endroit. Ses confrères n'avaient pas manqué de lui faire des éloges. L'agent Akoulov s'était alors trouvé dans un état de grâce. C'était comme flotter sur un nuage, tellement il était fier de porter l'uniforme, de réaliser son rêve le plus cher : celui de contribuer à changer le monde par ses actions.

La nuit du 7 au 8 juin 2032, l'agent Akoulov se sentait d'attaque, prêt à intervenir au moindre signe suspect. Le quart s'annonçait tranquille, en ce lundi soir. Vers 1 h du matin, la patrouille n'avait répondu qu'à un seul appel 911, pour une femme à moitié nue et intoxiquée traînant sur la voie publique.

Vers 2 h 30 du matin, un appel radio rapporta que des témoins avaient aperçu de la fumée se dégageant d'un commerce sur la rue Jean-Talon, angle Molson. Les pompiers confirmèrent qu'ils étaient en route. Les agents Akoulov et Gabriel Martinez, qui se trouvaient à proximité, furent les premiers répondants. Or, à leur arrivée, les flammes étaient déjà hors de contrôle. Le spectacle du brasier, vu son intensité, saisit l'agent Akoulov de stupeur.

Tandis qu'il s'affairait à établir le périmètre de sécurité, son embarras était évident. Comment un tel incendie avait-il pu échapper à son regard ? Ne venait-il pas juste de passer par là, il y a vingt minutes à peine ? Pourquoi n'avait-il pas vu ni senti quoi que ce soit ? Les collègues qui vinrent en renfort ne manquèrent pas de le taquiner.

— Comme ça, Colombus, dernière innovation en matière de technique policière, pouvait bien aider un policier à intervenir auprès d'un Noir ou d'un Arabe, mais ne pouvait manifestement rien contre un flair exécrable ! gloussèrent-ils.

Ils trouvaient comique qu'un incendie puisse dégénérer de la sorte, en plein quartier achalandé, sans que personne n'ait remarqué quoi que ce soit de suspect. Ainsi allaient les commentaires à l'égard de l'agent Akoulov. Heureusement, l'incident n'avait fait aucune victime ; que des dégâts matériels.

L'agent Gabriel Martinez lui avait conseillé de ne pas trop s'en faire avec ces railleries. Surtout, « ne pas le prendre personnel ». Tous passaient par là. Et puis, la Section des incendies allait sans doute le confirmer : il y avait fort à parier que le feu fut d'origine criminelle. Autrement, il ne se serait pas propagé aussi vite, et tous deux s'en seraient aperçus bien avant que le bâtiment ne soit une perte totale. Vraiment, l'agent Akoulov n'avait rien à se reprocher.

Celui-ci opina de la tête. Il allait mettre du temps – beaucoup de temps – à digérer cette humiliation.

8 JUIN 2032

La fenêtre était restée fermée, malgré la chaleur étouffante de cette nuit-là. L'air était humide et chargé de poussière. De l'intérieur, on pouvait entendre la rumeur de la ville qui grondait, avec ses voitures, ses drones, ses embouteillages, ses chantiers, ses ivrognes que le matin avait rejetés sur les trottoirs. Un épais rideau filtrait la lumière qui éclairait la pièce d'une pâle lueur.

Dans sa chambre, Adel dormait d'un sommeil agité. Il portait encore les vêtements souillés de la veille. Dans son rêve, il vit une maison à plusieurs étages, plongée dans l'obscurité. Bien que l'endroit lui semblât familier, il ne sut dire exactement où il se situait. Il gravit un escalier aux marches vétustes, tentant d'échapper à des assaillants. Au dernier palier se déroulait une fête, une sorte de bal masqué. Il se faufila parmi les convives, comme pour échapper au regard de ses agresseurs. Dans un coin sombre, un petit singe et un homme au nez crochu jouaient sur un orgue de barbarie. Quelqu'un vint lui offrir un gin, précisant que l'alcool avait été distillé en Mauricie. Adel refusa d'un geste de la main, craignant d'être sur écoute. Derrière lui, une porte s'ouvrit, donnant sur une pièce où se déroulait une bacchanale. Le fugitif hésita, puis voulut faire demi-tour quand un valet s'avança vers lui pour lui souffler à l'oreille : « Trace ta propre voie ». Adel acquiesça et se laissa entraîner par la musique. Il fit un pas à l'intérieur. Un drone flottait au-dessus d'un culte orgiaque. Il s'approcha et crut reconnaître Audrey et sa coloc Juju copulant avec Maximus. Il se pencha pour mieux distinguer, parmi les corps enchevêtrés, s'il s'agissait bien d'eux. On lui tapota l'épaule. Il se retourna et vit un canon de fusil braqué sur son front. Puis soudain, la déflagration.

Son réveil sonna, crachant un air techno tonitruant.

Adel ouvrit les yeux, ne réalisant qu'au bout d'un moment qu'il était bel et bien dans sa chambre, au beau milieu de ses draps pêle-mêle. Il s'empara de sa montre à écran tactile pour en éteindre la déstabilisante mélodie. La luminosité de l'appareil contrastait avec la pâleur des lieux. Adel grogna, sa tête alourdie par les relents du haschich qu'il avait fumé en rentrant la veille, et tous les coups qu'il s'était pris sur la tronche. Ses doigts tâtèrent ses joues, elles lui faisaient mal. Un frisson de fatigue parcourut son corps, tandis qu'il enfilait son bracelet connecté. Il avait dormi trois heures, à peine. Les évènements de la veille lui revinrent confusément à l'esprit. Un cocktail Molotov. Quelques éclats de verre. Des jets de flammes. Des meubles en feu. La fuite. Le cliquetis métallique des chaînes de vélos. La bagarre. Son visage ensanglanté. Les poings rouges de Maximus. Les cris. Les coups. Les clameurs stridentes. Les injures. « Gros crisse d'épais ! », lui avait dit Audrey. « Gros crisse d'épais... », se répéta-t-il, dans son lit.

Massant le bout de son gland, il y recueillit le liquide pré-séminal sécrété pendant la nuit, puis renifla ses doigts, se surprit alors de l'odeur d'hydrocarbures. Son corps entier puait un mélange de sueur, d'ordures, d'alcool, d'huile et de solvant. Ce matin, la douche n'était pas optionnelle. Il arriverait en retard pour le boulot, tant pis. Adel esquissa un mouvement pour sortir du lit, et se laissa retomber sur le matelas, le corps rompu de courbatures. Quelques jurons sortirent d'entre ses dents. Décidément, Maximus ne l'avait pas manqué... Il se donna un nouvel élan. L'impulsion du mouvement provoqua un vertige qui lui fit perdre l'équilibre. S'appuyant contre le mur, il palpa ses membres endoloris, tachetés d'ecchymoses. Il n'avait rien de cassé.

Son appartement, un vieux deux et demi mal entretenu, infesté de vermines et hors de prix, était pratiquement vide. Mis à part le matelas poisseux et un bureau sur lequel trônaient trois moniteurs à écran, quelques boîtes empilées contre le mur jauni du fond agrémentaient ce pauvre espace. Déjà trois mois qu'Adel vivait là. Il y avait emménagé en catastrophe. C'était un plan temporaire.

Devant la glace éclairée par une petite ampoule nue, Adel inspecta son visage. « Merde! » pesta-t-il : un œil au beurre noir. Son oreille gauche avait enflé ! La plaie du piercing suintait. Il pressa le lobe pour en drainer le pus et grimaça de douleur. Il essuya l'excédent de liquide nauséabond avec un petit papier mouchoir. Son regard se perdit de nouveau dans le reflet du miroir. Comme il se détestait !

Comme il détestait sa vie ! Tout ce qu'il entreprenait se vouait à l'échec. Cette pensée l'obsédait. Jamais, de toute son existence, il ne s'était senti autant déphasé avec le reste du monde. Le boulot, la famille, les amis... Plus rien n'avait de sens pour lui. Et pourtant, il restait impuissant devant cette fatalité qui s'acharnait sur lui. Il avait l'impression d'être sur le pilote automatique, fonçant droit dans un mur de briques, à pleine vitesse. Il goba deux Tylenol.

Adel passa à la douche et tourna le robinet d'eau froide. Jaillissant sur son corps, le jet glacial produisit un choc brutal, perçant le brouillard mental qui l'enveloppait. Se collant contre la tuile, Adel s'abandonna à son sort, bouche béante. Ses nerfs se raidirent. Ses membres tressaillirent. Il prit de grandes inspirations et expira bruyamment. De l'échine, le sang porteur d'oxygène afflua de la tête aux pieds. La contraction libéra l'urine qui fusa en jet chaud à ses pieds, disparaissant en spirale dans le trou de la baignoire. Des frissons le traversèrent d'abord, puis au bout d'un moment, l'eau lui parut brûlante. Il se frotta avec du savon, lava son sexe. Fit mousser ses cheveux. Prit soin de bien savonner son oreille et son visage. Puis il se rinça. Lorsqu'il ferma le robinet et sortit du bain, il se sentait revigoré.

Ses chemises étaient éparpillées sur des boîtes. Il prit la plus propre et l'enfila. Même chose pour les pantalons, qu'il remonta en prenant bien soin d'ajuster sa ceinture. Un nuage de parfum et un coup de peigne rehaussèrent son image qu'une poche de glace agrémentait dans l'espoir de dissiper l'enflure au visage. Ne manquait plus que le sucre et la caféine pour sa résurrection. Dieu merci, à ce chapitre, il pouvait compter sur Maidong, une eau multivitaminée énergisante à saveur de fraises et de lychees. Livrées à sa porte en caisse de douze, les bouteilles occupaient, à elles seules, une tablette entière du frigo. À croire qu'Adel considérait cette boisson comme un groupe alimentaire à part entière... La première gorgée avalée, une pensée le foudroya : l'incendie de la boutique La Grange, le communiqué. L'incident devait faire les manchettes. D'un revers du poignet, Adel activa son bracelet et cliqua sur l'application de nouvelles. Une publicité de Gillette promouvant *La perfection au masculin* exhiba un homme au torse nu imberbe et bien musclé. La réclame fit bientôt place à la une, arborant la photo du magasin en flammes.

Des extrémistes revendiquent un incendie criminel qui a ravagé la boutique La Grange, un magasin de meubles dans l'arrondissement Saint-Michel, la nuit dernière. Un communiqué, publié sur le site de Montréal Contre-Attaque, indique que le groupe a mis le feu aux locaux et réduit en cendres toute la marchandise. « Nous ferons tout le nécessaire pour lutter contre l'embourgeoisement de notre quartier », assure le groupe, qui se fait connaître sous le nom de Resco : les Compagnons de la Résistance.

Cet incident n'est pas sans rappeler les six autres du genre survenus depuis le début de l'année, alors que des incendies criminels ont visé le mobilier urbain.

*Jusqu'à ce jour, aucun suspect n'a été identifié dans
cette affaire. Des évènements qui soulèvent plusieurs
inquiétudes chez les résidents du quartier et les propriétaires de commerces qui exhortent d'ailleurs le
ministre de la Sécurité publique à démasquer les
coupables au plus vite, et les traduire en justice [...]*

Adel fit défiler les images de l'incendie. Le groupe Prestige
avait refusé de répondre aux journalistes. Le SPVM invitait
le public à contacter Info-Crime pour toute information
pouvant mener à des arrestations. Adel repéra le communiqué et reconnut le phrasé d'Audrey Lavoie.

Une ombre passa sur son visage. La bagarre resurgit
dans sa mémoire. Spontanée. Foudroyante. C'était Adel qui
avait provoqué Maximus et qui lui avait infligé les premiers
coups. Mais l'autre, plus grand et plus fort, échauffé par
l'alcool, était parvenu à le plaquer au sol. Il l'avait saisi à
la gorge pour le tabasser. Adel avait tenté de se déprendre,
en vain.

Étrangement, il avait éprouvé une satisfaction jouis-
sive au contact des poings s'abattant sur son propre visage.
Combien de coups pouvait-il encaisser comme ça avant
de crever ? s'était-il demandé. Il avait aimé ce mélange
d'adrénaline et d'endorphine qui l'éveillait à la vie, et ce
goût d'hémoglobine dans la bouche. C'était comme si la
douleur physique avait atténué toutes les autres, moins
saisissables. Curieusement, cela lui avait procuré un sentiment de plénitude, qui semblait le remettre en harmonie
avec la nature même des choses. Il en aurait pris davantage.

Un combat à mort, aurait-on dit, si les deux n'avaient pas été séparés juste à temps par les autres membres du Resco.

Les petits accrochages étaient monnaie courante au sein de cette formation qui se targuait de s'attaquer aux structures de pouvoir. Les missions étaient stressantes, les enjeux grands et les risques considérables. La pression, parfois intenable. Les disputes étaient fréquentes. Rarement, toutefois, on en arrivait aux poings. Mais lorsqu'un évènement survenait, le provocateur était invité à répondre de ses actes. Un ou deux épisodes de violence pouvaient être ainsi tolérés. Au troisième, le trublion se faisait montrer la porte. Vrai, les Compagnons de la résistance *se crissaient* de la loi, mais la loi du groupe prévalait sur toutes les autres. Adel et Maximus en étaient à leur première escarmouche, mais celle-ci avait détonné par sa brutalité.

Les rivaux s'étaient dévisagés comme des chiens haletants. On fit deux cercles pour les isoler l'un de l'autre. On exigea d'Adel des explications. Tout compte fait, c'était lui qui avait commencé. Maximus avait agi en légitime défense. Tous avaient vu la même chose. « Qu'une personne insiste un peu trop pour vous faire boire un verre, ne constitue quand même pas une raison pour lui infliger une raclée » était l'avis partagé par la fraternité. Quelque chose de louche ne tournait pas rond dans cette triade, et on le leur avait caché. Déception et consternation se lisaient dans leurs yeux.

Adel vint pour répondre. Il baragouina quelques mots inintelligibles, puis se tut, le regard fuyant. Il était amoché. Pourquoi ? Pourquoi toute cette haine, toute cette violence avaient-elles surgi d'un coup ? La parole lui faisait défaut. On l'avait poussé vers la sortie. Il était parti sans dire un mot à personne.

D'un mouvement du poignet, Adel interrogea sa montre une seconde fois et réalisa qu'Audrey lui avait laissé un message. Elle s'excusait de l'avoir insulté. En repensant à la scène, Maximus était tout aussi blâmable. Elle espérait revoir Adel en « terrain neutre ». Seul à seul.

Adel relut trois fois le message, avant de le fermer.

Il agrippa son sac à bandoulière qu'il passa autour du cou, puis sortit de son appartement. Il était déjà très en retard.

Débouchant sur l'artère principale, Adel marchait d'un pas rapide, malgré la chaleur accablante de ce début du mois de juin. Son front couvert de sueur, la bouche quelque peu pâteuse, l'œil tuméfié, Adel était parti de chez lui sans avoir déjeuné ni pris le temps de mettre de l'ordre dans ses idées. Il courait vers la station de métro, ignorant les feux de signalisation, comme un fou, quand soudain il coupa une voiture qui fonçait tout droit. Les pneus crissèrent sous l'action des freins. Le véhicule s'arrêta net au contact du piéton, comme par magie, comme s'il eut percuté un mur imaginaire. L'impact projeta Adel au sol qui, à la surprise générale, se releva presque aussitôt, pressé de poursuivre son chemin. Des témoins hébétés insistèrent pour lui venir en aide. Il venait d'échapper à la mort, comme si de rien n'était.

De la station TOHU, angle Jarry et Pie IX, trois arrêts sur la ligne rose le séparaient de la station Masson, où siégeaient les bureaux de Eagle Eyes Systems, firme qui encadrait son stage d'été pour une deuxième année. S'y déroulait en ce jour du 8 juin 2032 un test d'intrusion sur leur nouveau système de sécurité baptisé « 2E2S ». Prononcé en anglais, le sigle *Two E-Two S* référait à EE-SS, acronyme correspondant lui-même à « Eagle Eyes Security System », un progiciel sur mesure, à l'état de prototype, dont le déploiement avait déjà coûté près de 2,5 millions de dollars à même les fonds de l'entreprise. Ce module devait remplacer son prédécesseur, une plateforme standard sous licence, configurée pour les besoins de l'entreprise. Un investissement rendu nécessaire vu la hausse, l'agressivité et surtout la complexité des cyberattaques observées au cours des dernières années. Conçu en grande partie dans les laboratoires de l'entreprise, 2E2S utilisait l'IA et l'apprentissage machine pour désamorcer les menaces émergentes sur leur réseau.

L'assaut était mené par SkyBox Security, une entreprise basée à Toronto. Un essai évalué à quelques centaines de milliers de dollars, qui avait mobilisé près du trois quarts des ressources du fournisseur. Chez EES, une équipe spéciale avait été mise en place pour l'occasion. L'objectif : évaluer la performance de 2E2S et en repérer les vulnérabilités. Un exercice requérant la plus grande rigueur, dans une entreprise qui avait fait de la sécurité informatique son image de marque.

Située en plein cœur d'une technopole, la tour EES se démarquait de son environnement par sa haute stature et le verre sérigraphié rouge qui caractérisait son enveloppe constituée de panneaux photovoltaïques. Véritable fleuron du développement durable, le bâtiment était carboneutre grâce à sa conception en boucle fermée. Construit sur trente-quatre étages, dont huit au sous-sol, l'immeuble abritait un centre de données, des bureaux, des laboratoires de recherche, un auditorium et des salles de cours. Un système domotique sophistiqué contrôlait la température et l'éclairage des locaux en fonction de leur taux d'occupation, tout en gérant les droits d'accès via une technologie de reconnaissance faciale.

Le bâtiment pouvait compter sur ses propres serveurs, situés entre les 5e et 6e étages du sous-sol. Une solution de stockage qui fut privilégiée à l'infonuagique étant donné le caractère hautement confidentiel des données d'entreprise, dont la clientèle se composait principalement de ministères provinciaux, fédéraux et de quelques gouvernements étrangers. À cet effet, les salles de serveurs constituaient une véritable forteresse, étanche à toute intrusion extérieure, conçue à l'épreuve du feu et des inondations. Abritant le cerveau numérique de l'entreprise, ces locaux étaient régis par des protocoles de sécurité rigoureux. La sauvegarde et l'archivage des données étaient assurés quotidiennement, par deux fibres optiques souterraines dédiées. Le cryptage s'effectuait à même les ordinateurs de EES, avant le transit des données vers les centres d'hébergement. Un nuage sur mesure fut conservé pour certaines équipes de projets afin de faciliter les échanges internes.

Au cœur du bâtiment, au rez-de-chaussée, était aménagé un lieu ouvert et convivial, communément appelé

« l'agora ». Inondé de lumière naturelle, il couvrait tout l'espace central et constituait le point focal où convergeaient tous les parcours. Un circuit muséal virtuel animait l'espace en proposant une sélection de thèmes inspirés de la nature en fonction de l'heure de la journée : *forêts boréales* le matin, *Surfing in Tofino* sur l'heure du lunch et *chutes Niagara* en fin d'après-midi. Trois robots humanoïdes assuraient l'accueil des visiteurs, leur fournissaient des indications, confirmaient les rendez-vous et les informaient au besoin des salles de cours, des conférences ou tout autre évènement programmé au calendrier. Suspendu au-dessus de cette esplanade, un immense panneau central de dix mètres arborant le logo de l'entreprise suivi de la devise : *Intelligence et sécurité à portée de la main.*

Compte tenu des contusions qu'il arborait au visage, et de son nouveau perçage en pentagramme qui gonflait disgracieusement son oreille gauche, le système de reconnaissance faciale mit une seconde de plus à identifier Adel Salem. Son profil validé, l'ascenseur le déposa au vingt-quatrième étage. En quittant la cabine, la voix non genrée du répartiteur intelligent retentit : « Adel Salem. Êtes attendus au local B-24.37.4. Êtes en retard d'une heure. Cinquante-six. Minutes. » La prise en défaut de même que sa nouvelle photo de profil furent automatiquement consignées à son dossier d'employé.

Le local B-24.37.4 était un laboratoire équipé d'une cinquantaine de postes informatiques. La salle était bondée, grouillante d'activité. Le test d'intrusion avait débuté à l'heure prévue et tirait déjà à sa fin. Il s'était avéré catastrophique. Deux heures avaient suffi à SkyBox pour pénétrer le réseau local et l'infester grâce à un ver autorépliquant. Heureusement, pour les besoins de la simulation, le script qu'il disséminait était inoffensif. Mais, à la vue des informations projetées sur les écrans moniteurs suspendus, on pouvait constater l'étendue de l'infection qui avait gagné plusieurs grappes de serveurs locaux. La situation était hors de contrôle. Le test avait visiblement échoué. Une telle circonstance aurait nécessité, en temps normal, la mise hors ligne de tous les serveurs et leur redémarrage dans une séquence bien précise, pour les en purger de tout élément viral. Une situation qui aurait entraîné un délestage des services pour un temps indéterminé. Résultat ? Des coûts exorbitants, une couverture médiatique désastreuse et un discrédit total : rien pour plaire aux actionnaires.

Outre une étudiante ontarienne et deux étudiants internationaux qui assistaient à l'évènement en téléprésence holographique, un groupe de dix jeunes stagiaires de première année, entassés dans un coin et munis de tablettes électroniques, observaient la situation. Saisis d'appréhensions, ils attendaient des commentaires de leur accompagnateur Victor Lacroix, responsable de cet essai, question qu'on veuille bien leur expliquer enfin ce qui se passait. Visiblement, Victor Lacroix ne les accompagnait plus, tant il était lui-même dépassé par les évènements, absorbé dans quelques pensées profondes, essayant à l'évidence d'articuler une excuse pour justifier l'échec lamentable de cet audit, qui avait coûté près de 350 000 dollars. Vêtu d'un veston-cravate bien cintré, qui semblait même le gêner dans ses mouvements, Lacroix glanait ici et là, virevoltant d'un poste à l'autre, interrogeant techniciens et ingénieurs qui s'affairaient devant leurs écrans, essayant de contrer, limiter, endiguer l'attaque lancée par SkyBox Security. C'était peine perdue. Propulsé par une armée de bots, le ver se répliquait à une vitesse fulgurante, se propageant dans les systèmes névralgiques de la compagnie, sans que 2E2S n'en détecte la virulence. Force était d'admettre que le logiciel, dans sa version actuelle, présentait un défaut technique... majeur.

— On s'en fait passer une grosse !

— Oui, toute une grosse !

— Elle fait mal, celle-là !

— Ça déchire !

Ainsi s'entendaient les programmeurs, toujours friands de métaphores phalliques.

Au moment où il entra dans la pièce, les regards se braquèrent sur Adel Salem. S'ensuivit un lourd silence. Quelques murmures s'échappèrent, puis le pianotage des claviers recommença. Adel hésita un instant avant de se diriger vers un poste libre, quand Lacroix lui fit signe d'attendre à la porte. Un étudiant osa lever la main, interpellant le responsable de l'essai en cours.

— Monsieur ?

Lacroix réfréna son impatience. L'étudiant, qui s'était retenu de tout commentaire depuis le début, poursuivit tout de même avec sa question.

— Que savons-nous exactement des « pirates » qui ont attaqué 2E2S ?

L'étudiant avait mimé des guillemets en prononçant le mot « pirates ».

Victor Lacroix mit quelques secondes à retrouver ses esprits. Il redressa son torse, força un sourire professionnel et se tourna vers les étudiants, heureux de pouvoir enfin noter quelque chose sur leurs tablettes.

— Ils sont surnommés YUX-40, et travaillent pour les services de renseignements chinois, selon le scénario de la simulation que nous avons reçu ce matin et que je rendrai disponible pour consultation avant ce soir, dit Victor en ouvrant ses mains pour tenter de cacher un embarras évident. Ils sont parvenus à pirater les serveurs locaux de notre compagnie, en cryptant à l'aide d'une clé connue d'eux seuls les données de quelques clients – il hésita un long moment – environ soixante mille membres, concéda-t-il en toussant.

— Ils demandent une rançon de huit millions de dollars pour libérer les données. Évidemment, tout ceci est fictif, s'empressa-t-il d'ajouter en pouffant d'un rire nerveux. L'attaque ne contenait aucune charge active...

Les réactions fusèrent. Les stagiaires firent courir leurs stylets sur leurs tablettes. L'étudiante ontarienne en téléprésence leva la main à son tour, au grand dam de Victor.

— Mais comment s'y sont-ils pris, exactement, pour y parvenir ? demanda l'étudiante sur un ton neutre.

Victor parut incommodé. Il dandina sa tête, avant de répondre.

— Le logiciel malveillant s'est installé dans nos systèmes via le service de la comptabilité, en se faisant passer pour une pièce jointe comptable. Une simple facture, précisa-t-il, avant de se taire à nouveau.

— Un cheval de Troie, vous voulez dire ? insista l'avatar holographique de l'étudiante.

Victor acquiesça d'un hochement de tête. Son malaise était évident. Stylets levés, les étudiants demeurèrent bouche bée, eux aussi, comme abasourdis devant la simplicité du subterfuge. Eux qui s'étaient attendus à une attaque plus sophistiquée, par force brute peut-être ou déni de service, en tout cas, clairement plus impressionnante.

À ce moment, Victor se tourna vers un jeune homme blond à côté de lui.

— Thomas, pouvez-vous me remplacer, j'ai à faire au bureau.

— Bien sûr, Victor.

Victor Lacroix sortit de la salle, et fit signe à Adel Salem de le suivre.

En 2032, Eagle Eyes Systems figurait parmi les cinquante sociétés les mieux gérées au Canada, selon le palmarès annuel publié par Deloitte. Fondée à Montréal en 2027 par un ancien policier de la Gendarmerie royale du Canada et un programmeur de la Banque Nationale, la firme a su se tailler une place importante dans l'univers de la cyber-sécurité, en offrant des solutions d'authentification et de gestion d'accès. Né en tant que *startup* sous l'appellation Solutions Mirador inc., le remaniement organisationnel opéré en 2029 permit l'adoption de la marque Eagle Eyes Systems, une tournure qui cadrait mieux avec la nouvelle image de marque de l'entreprise. Cette orientation straté-gique favorisa l'exportation de leurs produits et services, d'abord à l'extérieur de la province puis à l'international.

Spécialisée en conception et mise en service de logi-ciels, EES offrait une vaste gamme de produits allant des systèmes antivirus aux applications de messagerie, de traçage et de paiements sécurisés sur une variété de plate-formes et métaplateformes. Leur suite logicielle Harmony+ proposait un guichet unique pour gérer tous les aspects de la sécurité numérique d'un usager, peu importe qu'il se trouvât dans le monde réel, virtuel ou métavers. La com-pagnie devait surtout son succès à la commercialisation d'une solution d'authentification hors du commun : un implant numérique à radiofréquence, doté d'une puce SIM compatible avec les réseaux 5G et 6G. Baptisé « e-Claw », ce dispositif sous-cutané, généralement logé entre le pouce et l'index, avait été pensé pour remplacer à la fois les noms d'utilisateur, mots de passe, clés, portefeuilles, billets de transports, passeport vaccinal et autres badges. Que ce fût pour effectuer un paiement ou pour contrôler l'accès à un compte bancaire, l'entrée au bureau, au restaurant, à une salle de spectacle, pour déverrouiller les portes de la maison, d'une automobile, ou même d'une arme à feu enregistrée, la puce e-Claw permettait à un usager de s'authentifier rapidement, d'un simple geste de la main, sans avoir à mémoriser une légion de mots de passe.

Sa pose était assez simple. Commercialisée dans la plupart des boutiques d'électronique, la e-Claw pouvait être implantée soit en magasin, soit par un agent autorisé dans un point de service agréé. Un prototype de cabine de puçage automatique appelé e-Claw Booth (eCB) destiné aux centres commerciaux et gares de trains était en développement pour conquérir des parts de marché en Afrique et en Asie centrale.

Quoi qu'il en soit, en 2032-2033, la e-Claw commençait tout juste à sortir des salons technologiques où elle avait vu le jour. Elle connaissait un vif succès auprès des boîtes de nuit qui s'en servaient comme laissez-passer VIP. Les formules 5 à 7, où il fut possible d'acheter et de se faire implanter la puce sur place, gagnaient également en popularité. La pratique permettait aux tenanciers de tenir à jour le registre de leur clientèle. Les banques encouragèrent cette pratique, offrant aux détenteurs de la puce des rabais sur leurs services. La stratégie visait à combattre les fraudes dont le total des coûts mondiaux s'élevait à quelque 375 milliards de dollars pour la dernière décennie seulement.

Antérieurement réservée aux sciences vétérinaires pour l'identification des animaux, la technologie se répandit au commun des mortels, vu son immense potentiel. Les paiements en espèces, vecteurs de transmission virale, évoquaient un passé archaïque ; les cartes d'identité et les cartes bancaires devinrent trop encombrantes et vulnérables à la fraude. Leur utilisation engendrait des hausses de primes d'assurance. Plusieurs commerçants les refusèrent, tout simplement. À l'instar des téléphones intelligents, des médias sociaux et des bracelets connectés, le marché des micropuces sous-cutanées présenta un taux de pénétration stupéfiant. Au Canada, les institutions scolaires et universitaires commencèrent à offrir des programmes de puçage, à l'image des vastes campagnes de vaccination. Nombre d'établissements hospitaliers offrirent gratuitement leur implantation aux nouveau-nés. À ce mouvement s'opposa bientôt le contre-mouvement « *Fuck* ta puce », avec ses fervents adeptes du « dépucelage » et ses techniques artisanales vantées sur le web pour en faciliter l'extraction.

Ce qui contribua vraiment à populariser la e-Claw fut la possibilité de s'en servir comme solution d'authentification forte, grâce à sa clé de cryptage interne à 2048 bits. Un algorithme de chiffrement asymétrique opéré par le système d'exploitation EOS (Eagle Operating System) garantissait le renouvellement des différentes clés publiques, toutes les demi-heures, pour l'ensemble des usagers. Enfin, la clé maîtresse de 65 536 bits, servant à déchiffrer les centaines de milliers de clés en circulation, était elle-même régénérée tous les mois. De sorte que, si une entité organisationnelle ou gouvernementale parvint par miracle à briser le chiffrement presque impénétrable de cette clé – opération qui normalement prendrait au minimum quelques milliards d'années au moyen de l'informatique séquentielle, et pas moins de trente jours en faisant appel à l'informatique quantique, celle-ci ne soit déjà plus valide. La sécurité des opérations répondait donc aux devis les plus exigeants en matière de protection des données personnelles. La connexion 6G, établie grâce à un opérateur de téléphonie mobile, permettait l'authentification en une microseconde, délai cent fois plus court que celui des technologies Touch ID, Face ID et Windows Hello. Des micros-capteurs biométriques, sensibles au pouls, au groupe sanguin et à la température corporelle, furent intégrés dans le cryptage et rendirent le piratage de ces implants numériques quasi impossible. Combinant le trousseau d'accès des produits Apple, Microsoft, Google, Amazon, Meta et Mozilla, le protocole d'authentification EES déclassa rapidement les solutions classiques à deux facteurs, qui employaient généralement un nom d'utilisateur et un mot de passe, tous deux très vulnérables aux vols d'identités. En cas de panne réseau, chose rarissime, la composante radiofréquence agissait comme une clé sans contact normale, permettant ainsi de déverrouiller les portes ou de faire démarrer sa voiture. Fonctionnalité qui, là aussi, eut tôt fait de déclasser les technologies reposant uniquement sur les normes web.

En 2030, la campagne de promotion internationale « Prenez le plein contrôle de votre vie, grâce à e-Claw ! », permit à Eagles Eyes Systems de tabler sur une base de données client de 33 millions d'usagers, faisant de cette marque canadienne un leader mondial dans ce marché de niche. Leur volonté de mettre l'expérience client au

premier plan avait, sans nul doute, joué un rôle de cataly-
seur dans ce succès, et permit de déployer à vaste échelle
leur technologie clé en main.

Le bureau de Victor Lacroix était situé au vingt-sixième
étage. Il était bordé de larges baies vitrées, avec vue imprenable sur le pont Jacques-Cartier. Par beau temps, les monts
Saint-Hilaire et Saint-Bruno se profilaient à l'horizon,
comme deux masses découpées au scalpel. Par temps plu-
vieux, les amas de nuages se dressant au-dessus de la ville
offraient un spectacle époustouflant. Pour Victor Lacroix,
toutefois, aussi beaux et poétiques fussent ces paysages,
ils ne rivalisaient pas avec ce qui était visible les jours de
grands rassemblements. On pouvait y distinguer les longs
cortèges de manifestants défiler dans les rues de Montréal,
fonçant tout droit sur les barrages de boucliers en plexiglas
tenus par les forces de l'ordre. Le spectacle des marches
dégénérant en confrontation ouverte avec les policiers était
saisissant. De là-haut, on avait parfois l'impression que
certains quartiers se transformaient en véritables champs
de bataille quand, entre les hélicoptères, les colonnes de
fumée s'élevaient vers le ciel. Victor Lacroix aimait porter
son regard sur ces panoramas spectaculaires, tous aussi
distrayants les uns que les autres, en se disant qu'ici, derrière le triple vitrage de la fenestration thermos, dans le
confort de son bureau, il était à l'abri de tout ; l'isolation
acoustique était excellente, la température était contrôlée

au dixième de degré près, et la qualité de l'air se conformait aux plus hauts standards.

Victor Lacroix fit entrer Adel Salem en premier, puis referma la porte derrière lui. Il prit place sur son fauteuil ergonomique, derrière sa table de travail, une table à surface en verre, comme tout le reste du mobilier qu'il prenait soin de faire désinfecter par le personnel d'entretien deux fois par jour, avec une puissante solution antivirale.

Son visage était tendu. Les rebondissements des dernières heures avaient mis à mal sa nouvelle coiffure qui, en temps normal, avait l'apparence d'une garniture de cupcake. Il s'empressa de passer un coup de peigne dans ses cheveux, avant d'inviter Adel à s'asseoir à son tour, le toisant des pieds à la tête.

Victor Lacroix était un cadre dans la jeune trentaine, affecté à la cellule Eagle LAB, véritable fer de lance du département R&D chez EES. La division pouvait compter sur une soixantaine de professionnels. Elle jouissait d'un budget considérable pour mener à bien les projets d'innovation. Victor était le fils cadet du VP Finance, Paul-André Lacroix, dont les bureaux étaient situés deux étages plus haut. Comme son grand frère, Côme Lacroix, Victor avait amorcé des études en génie au MIT. Contrairement à son aîné, il les avait abandonnées. À Montréal, il avait fini par décrocher un baccalauréat aux HEC, mais ce fut de peine et de misère. Le jeune homme préférait de toute évidence la fréquentation des bars et des jeunes femmes aux classes et aux manuels scolaires.

Malgré ce tempérament frivole, son père avait réussi à le faire placer au sein de l'entreprise. Il avait vanté « sa personnalité charismatique et joviale ». Certes, il était un peu tête en l'air... Mais, à long terme, il laissait entrevoir un certain potentiel. Pour autant qu'il bénéficiât d'un encadrement approprié. Peut-être qu'en le plaçant au sein d'une équipe performante, telle que le LAB, Victor se découvrirait une nouvelle motivation ? Peut-être. Le jeu en valait la chandelle.

Une opportunité ne tarda pas à se présenter : Eagle LAB avait besoin d'un responsable qualité pour gérer son programme d'audits internes. Victor serait placé directement sous la supervision de Rohin Mahal, le directeur du LAB. Celui-ci gérait un portefeuille annuel d'une vingtaine de projets. En gros, la tâche pour Victor s'annonçait relativement simple. Il fallait suivre des processus ; ceux-ci étaient déjà rédigés. Ne manquait plus qu'à les planifier. Le reste – les batteries de tests et de validations – « la petite cuisine », comme on dit, les professionnels s'en chargeraient. D'ailleurs, ceux-ci étaient hautement qualifiés. La plupart détenaient des maîtrises et des doctorats dans leur domaine. À Victor, on n'exigeait aucun génie, aucune créativité, aucune aptitude intellectuelle particulière, mis à part le contrôle des coûts et des échéanciers. Mais depuis qu'il occupait son poste, Victor avait connu plusieurs ratages. Non pas tant de nature technique (Victor ne touchait pas à la technique), mais plutôt sur le plan de l'administration : mauvais rendements, mauvaise gestion des ressources, manque de disponibilité, personnalité toxique, désengagement et ainsi de suite. La liste des manquements était longue, sans parler de ce scandale sexuel qui fut évité de justesse, et qui passa pour un « problème de communication » ... Et pourtant, Victor demeurait en poste, bénéficiant d'une immunité totale au sein de l'entreprise, qu'aucune plainte, même celle de M. Mahal, ne pouvait ébranler. La situation était à ce point désespérée qu'on avait fini par en rire, faute d'en pleurer, et dans les coulisses du LAB, Victor faisait l'objet d'impitoyables moqueries, sans se douter de rien.

Hélas, Adel Salem ne riait pas. Depuis son embauche au LAB, l'été précédent, il avait eu le malheur de retenir l'attention de Victor Lacroix, bien qu'en théorie, le stagiaire relevait de M. Mahal. Brillant et talentueux, Adel Salem présentait aux yeux de Victor Lacroix une ressource stratégique, qu'il n'hésitait pas à réclamer pour l'affecter à sa planification, quel qu'eût été l'avis du principal intéressé. Du reste, un stagiaire peut-il seulement dire « non », ou est-il plutôt condamné, selon l'expression consacrée, à devenir une « pute de service » ? Adel n'avait pas tardé à comprendre que son talent l'avait voué ici à un destin tragique. Il se devait de l'affronter avec courage. Or aujourd'hui le courage lui faisait défaut.

Un silence s'était installé. Victor Lacroix jaugeait sa proie d'un œil attentif. Assise devant lui, comme trônant sur un socle au milieu de sa renardière, elle portait autour d'elle un regard fuyant, évitant de croiser les yeux de son prédateur. Victor Lacroix remarqua son souffle court, sa transpiration abondante, ses cheveux en bataille, mais surtout ce terrible œil au beurre noir. Il n'y avait pas à dire, le mec s'était fait rosser. Victor vint pour le confronter à ce sujet, mais se ravisa au tout dernier instant. Inutile de le malmener davantage. De toute évidence, il avait affaire à un cas typique de gueule de bois. *Been there, done that,* estima Victor, qui se félicitait intérieurement de son diagnostic. Lui aussi avait connu ses premières frasques, avait jeté sa gourme, avait fait les frais de ses conneries. Combien de fois avait-il passé près de se faire péter la gueule à la sortie des bars pour avoir tiré la queue du lion ? Sa réputation de « p'tit crisse » lui collait à la peau. Oui c'est vrai, il connaissait : alcool et cocaïne constituaient un mélange explosif. Il soupira avec nostalgie. Putain, on ne l'avait pas manqué, celui-là, songea-t-il avec compassion en toisant son interlocuteur. Aïe aïe aïe. Et il y avait, en plus, cette oreille massacrée. Le bijou, une étoile scindée en deux, était grotesque. Que cela pouvait-il signifier ? Ses doigts tambourinaient sur la vitre de son bureau. Tout de même, Adel était un brave gaillard. Motivé et ambitieux, lui semblait-il. Désireux, en tout cas, d'avoir une bonne note à l'issue de son stage, malgré ses dernières incartades. Une folie « passagère » spécula-t-il. On a tous nos mauvaises passes. D'ailleurs, Adel n'en était pas à sa première brosse. Il savait gérer. Il n'allait pas faire la fine bouche face à un employé (un stagiaire, de surcroît) un peu excentrique. Même laid, même ivre, même battu à mort, celui-là était capable de faire des miracles. L'informatique était son dada. Il pouvait se taper la pire des cuites et, en un rien de temps, vous localiser un bogue, rafistoler un algorithme ou même vous retaper un programme en entier. C'était une ressource stratégique. À ménager.

Victor Lacroix dévisagea Adel Salem un long moment, laissant planer un silence malaisant. Le téléphone fixe sonna. Victor Lacroix jeta un œil sur l'afficheur puis, ignorant l'appel, porta à nouveau son attention vers Adel Salem, et s'adressa à lui sur un ton grave.

— Alors comme ça on arrive en retard, un jour d'audit ?

Adel, qui – d'expérience – appréhendait déjà ce que lui réservait cette réunion, opta pour la posture du roseau, préférant le silence aux paroles inutiles. Aussi espérait-il, par son mutisme, exhorter son bourreau à en finir au plus vite. Moins long durerait sa détention, mieux ce serait pour lui. Victor Lacroix ne l'entendait pas ainsi et, tel un chat tenant une souris entre ces pattes, une souris immobile, figée de peur, il ne put se résoudre à un dénouement aussi ennuyeux. Il s'adossa sur sa chaise, emprunta un ton de reproche bien calibré.

— Il faut dire qu'on t'a déjà connu plus motivé, plus... (il frotta son pouce contre son index) assidu. Enfin, il me semble. Est-ce que tout va bien, Adel ? As-tu besoin d'aide ? Est-ce qu'on peut faire quelque chose pour toi ?

Son téléphone sonna à nouveau ; encore une fois, il ne lui prêta aucune attention. Il continuait de fixer son interlocuteur.

— Non non, tout va bien, hasarda Adel, l'œil enflé.

Son cerveau peinait à réagir. Il cherchait une excuse, mais sentait en même temps que l'exercice était futile. Victor força un sourire sympathique.

— Allons, allons, tu sais que tu peux te confier à moi comme un ami, insista-t-il davantage.

Trois petits coups discrets frappés à la vitre vinrent interrompre l'entretien. Les deux hommes se tournèrent en direction de la porte et virent l'adjointe administrative de Victor, une femme dans la jeune vingtaine. Elle était en poste depuis quelques semaines et succédait à quatre autres femmes, toutes ayant démissionné de leur propre chef. Victor Lacroix lui fit signe d'entrer.

Vêtue de leggings et de talons hauts, elle s'avança vers son patron avec élégance, l'air préoccupé. Elle se pencha ensuite vers lui pour lui souffler quelque chose à l'oreille. Elle pointait le téléphone qui avait sonné. Victor acquiesça de plusieurs hochements de tête, avant de s'exclamer :

— C'est noté !

L'adjointe parut déroutée par sa réponse, se pencha de nouveau pour ajouter quelque chose, mais il l'interrompit en frappant la table de son index.

— Plus tard, je le contacterai plus tard !

Arborant un sourire de façade, l'employée fit un pas en arrière et acquiesça poliment, avant de tourner les talons pour se diriger vers la porte. Victor dirigea sur elle un regard obscène, et desserra sa cravate. C'était Rohin Mahal qui tentait de le rejoindre. Il était furieux. L'essai de ce matin avait tourné au fiasco. Un plan de reprise s'avérait nécessaire dans les meilleurs délais. Sans quoi, tout un calendrier de mise en service risquait de décaler. Victor rumina. 2E2S présentait une bonne vingtaine de composantes logicielles à réviser. Or, le budget du projet avait été épuisé jusqu'au dernier sou, et sa réserve de contingence, déjà affectée à un autre projet. La créativité était de mise.

Le gestionnaire pouvait grignoter d'autres budgets ici et là ; il charcuterait les réserves de quatre ou cinq projets mineurs. Son subterfuge passerait inaperçu. Il faudrait compter sur des ressources rigoureuses, peu dispendieuses et surtout, qui ne rechignerait pas. De nouveau, il força un sourire cordial. Il avait devant lui le candidat parfait. Même amoché, un Adel Salem valait deux employés. Un stagiaire, en plus ! Victor consulta la grille salariale et confirma son taux horaire : deux fois moindre que celui d'un régulier. C'est ce qu'il pensait. Rien qu'en misant sur sa personne, Victor Lacroix quadruplait son rendement. Il pointa l'oreille purulente du stagiaire.

— Joli, dit-il. Moi aussi, plus jeune, j'ai fait la même chose... lui confia-t-il en esquissant, non sans peine, un sourire complice.

Le visage du stagiaire se plissa en une moue dépitée. Victor abandonna cette entrée en matière pour tenter une autre approche. Il força le dynamisme de sa voix.

— Tu sais, Adel, nous avons tous nos hauts et nos bas. Je peux en témoigner personnellement. Tu me diras peut-être que ça ne me regarde pas. Mais sache que si tu as besoin d'aide, tu peux compter sur moi, ou encore, sur le service d'aide aux employés. Nous sommes là pour toi... et n'oublie pas : chez EES, notre ressource la plus importante, notre âme : ce sont nos employés. D'accord ?

Adel Salem leva vers lui un regard piteux. Victor Lacroix joignit ses mains en prière.

— Très bien. En attendant, si tu acceptes, j'ai un petit service à te demander...

ÉLÉMENT DE PREUVE DÉPOSÉ EN COURS
DANS LE CADRE DU PROCÈS SALEM :

Apprends à te blâmer toi-même, plutôt qu'à imputer tes échecs aux autres.

Je vais te dire un secret, mon homme : tu es la somme de tes propres choix. Tu reflètes ce que tu attires. Le cynisme attire le cynisme. Le succès attire le succès. Et n'oublie pas : tu vaux beaucoup plus que ce que tu possèdes. Le succès ne tient ni à la marque de ta voiture, ni à la valeur de ta maison, ni même au montant que tu détiens en banque. Le succès, c'est d'œuvrer à déployer ton plein potentiel. Rappelle-toi : ne te soumets à aucun ordre, à aucune personne, à aucune volonté.

Vis ta vie comme tu l'entends et trace ta propre voie.

> — Extrait du balado *Forge ton mental*, répertorié 56 fois dans les archives électroniques de l'accusé, entre le 7 et 17 juin 2033

Plus jeune, Adel rêvait de faire carrière dans l'aérospatiale. Mais depuis la déroute de l'équipage Tesla-Google en route vers Mars, dont on perdit la trace, la plupart des missions dans l'espace furent suspendues et, avec elles, les contrats en robotique spatiale. Tout le contraire du marché de la cybersécurité qui, de son côté, se portait fort bien avec une valeur mondiale estimée à quelque mille milliards de dollars en 2028.

Au printemps 2031, Adel Salem posait sa candidature à un poste de stagiaire en sécurité informatique chez Eagle Eyes Systems. L'entreprise tenait alors un kiosque de recrutement, à même le campus de l'école Polytechnique. Elle promettait de loin de meilleures conditions que la concurrence. Les étudiants de premier cycle admissibles à ces emplois devaient faire preuve d'une excellence académique hors norme et passer des tests de connaissance.

Les recruteurs qui examinèrent la candidature de Salem furent séduits par la qualité du candidat : résultats scolaires remarquables ; intérêts personnels palpitants (jeux vidéo, actualités scientifiques et sports de ballon).

En outre, les résultats de ses tests d'aptitude démontrèrent de prodigieuses capacités de raisonnement et de détection des menaces. Qui plus est, le postulant prouva sa maîtrise parfaite des langages de programmation les plus communs, sans compter de prodigieuses habiletés dans les microlangages moins usuels et plus nichés. C'était parmi les candidats les plus prometteurs, pourvu qu'il satisfasse aux exigences de la cote fédérale de sécurité *secret*, niveau 3. Une enquête menée par la GRC devait le confirmer.

Ce rapport de 2031 démontra que les origines kurdo-syriennes d'Adel Salem intéressèrent un temps les enquêteurs. Certes, il était né en Syrie et avait séjourné dans un camp de réfugiés, quelque part au sud de la frontière syrienne, dans le nord-est du Liban. Mais à l'époque, il n'était qu'un nourrisson. Il était arrivé au Canada très jeune ; il avait à peine trois ans. Ses parents, qui avaient été sélectionnés selon des critères très stricts par des fonctionnaires fédéraux de l'immigration, avaient bénéficié d'un programme humanitaire spécial pour ressortissants syriens. Selon les recherches effectuées à l'époque, la famille s'était bien intégrée. Les parents avaient ouvert une petite épicerie dans le quartier Saint-Michel. Spécialisé dans les produits orientaux, le commerce avait prospéré à la faveur d'une clientèle fidèle et régulière. Quant aux enfants, Adel et sa sœur, Myriam Salem, ils avaient tous deux fréquenté des institutions privées et laïques, cotées parmi les meilleures du Québec, et ce, dès leur plus jeune âge. Se dessinait là le profil typique d'une famille bien assimilée et participant de façon constructive à la société canadienne. Sur ce point, le profil d'Adel Salem présentait, en apparence, un risque pratiquement nul.

Une chose toutefois avait retenu leur attention suite à l'examen de son historique de navigation. C'est que, outre son intérêt pour les jeux de rôle en ligne, Adel Salem semblait verser dans un militantisme de gauche, plutôt léger. Il faut dire qu'un profil neutre aurait suscité des questions, et même incité à des recherches plus approfondies. Mais ceux qui prirent en charge son dossier vinrent à l'évidence que, loin d'être un homme vertueux, comme en témoignaient sa consommation régulière de pornographie *hardcore* et son goût prononcé pour les jeux de tir à la première personne, Adel Salem présentait le profil typique de n'importe quel garçon intelligent de son âge : galopin, turbulent et quelque peu politisé. À ce titre, les résultats d'analyse biométrique avaient révélé, avec un taux de certitude au-delà des 98 %, selon le croisement de différentes sources, sa présence à quelques manifestations anticapitalistes, survenues entre 2026 et 2027. Or, encore une fois, rien de très anormal, avaient-ils conclu, pour un adolescent de seize, dix-sept ou dix-huit ans. Participer à une manifestation de ce genre était ce qu'il y avait de plus tendance chez les jeunes. Bien entendu, qu'il soit de gauche plutôt que de droite avait fait légèrement sourciller. Loin de le nier, le candidat à l'examen avait plutôt invoqué une lubie passagère. Il se considérait désormais plutôt centriste. Et, comme pour brouiller les pistes, ses dernières apparitions le montrèrent dans des manifs de droite. Aujourd'hui, bien sûr, on comprend que tout ceci était possiblement calculé, qu'Adel avait façonné un profil, que celui-ci était crédible et que les enquêteurs responsables de son dossier n'y virent que du feu. Et la cote *secret* lui fut accordée. Plus encore, celle-ci fut maintenue sans autre enquête, suite à sa réembauche en 2032. On confirma par la suite, chez EES, que ce manquement avait été causé par une situation exceptionnelle : crise de main-d'œuvre oblige. Et que, loin d'avoir été omise, l'enquête qui devait renouveler la cote de sécurité d'Adel Salem avait tout bonnement été reportée.

À cause de l'horaire d'été, le bureau s'était vidé de ses employés. Il était 19 h. Les robots ménages s'affairaient, dans un léger vrombissement, à passer l'aspirateur dans les allées.

Suivant son meeting avec Victor, Adel avait consulté le rapport de simulation transmis par SkyBox Security. Il s'était ensuite entretenu avec l'équipe responsable de l'essai, question de mieux comprendre ce qui avait mal tourné. Le test était voué à l'échec. « C'était écrit dans le ciel », s'accordèrent pour dire ses collègues. Le projet, qui était sur les rails depuis janvier, avait pris du retard. Dans la hâte, les prétests nécessaires à chaque composante logicielle avaient été bâclés ; en réalité, plusieurs n'avaient tout simplement pas eu lieu. Résultat ? Leur fameux 2E2S s'était avéré aussi utile qu'un parapluie dans un ouragan. Tous les scripts étaient à revoir ; les tests de validation à refaire. Un travail qui requérait non pas tant de grandes aptitudes, mais du temps, et un capital de concentration qu'Adel ne possédait plus à cette heure du jour, il va sans dire.

Adel s'affala sur sa table de travail et soupira. Une heure plus tôt, Audrey avait encore tenté de le joindre, mais il avait ignoré son message. Que lui dirait-il ? Il n'avait pas envie de s'excuser ni de s'expliquer. Et d'ailleurs, il ne se comprenait pas lui-même. Comment faisait-il pour se saboter systématiquement ? La colère et la honte le gagnèrent à cette pensée, à son incapacité de gérer sa vie. Il enfila son gros casque d'écoute, posa ses coudes sur le bureau et se massa les tempes.

Peu à peu, il se détendit. Il n'avait plus la force de lutter. Sa tête devint lourde. Il pressa le front contre son bureau. Inspira et expira profondément. Quelques souvenirs d'hier refirent surface, sans suite logique. Ils s'estompèrent dans les confins de sa mémoire. À un moment, il crut entendre Victor Lacroix, debout, tout près de lui, le sommer de répondre. Un bref regard au-dessus de son épaule lui confirma qu'il fabulait. Il s'assoupit de nouveau sur la table. Sa vision se troubla. Il vit des flammes, un morceau de verre brisé. Des colonnes de chiffres vacillèrent ; il crut entrapercevoir le dos courbé de son père. Puis tout se brouilla dans sa tête, et il sombra dans un profond sommeil.

Équipée de capteurs radar et de caméras disposées tout le tour de sa carrosserie, la Volvo édition 2032 est entièrement électrique et autonome. Grâce à la reconnaissance visuelle et à l'apprentissage machine, elle peut détecter les véhicules, cyclistes, piétons, animaux, panneaux de circulation, feux rouges et lignes de démarcation routières. Son « cerveau » est un logiciel doté d'une intelligence artificielle, propulsée par vingt-quatre processeurs et une bande passante de 3 Tbit/sec. Deux cartes graphiques et quatre unités de calcul centrales autorisent ce système neuronal à effectuer 196 milliards d'opérations par seconde. La machine collige les données via un système d'acquisition pour modéliser son environnement au millimètre près, et prendre les meilleures décisions en une fraction de seconde. Jamais un véhicule n'a été doté d'un meilleur système anticollision. Un GPS permet à l'appareil d'établir ses itinéraires à travers la trame urbaine.

L'habitacle est un véritable salon offrant une vue panoramique à 360°. Sa conception traduit une volonté de dialogue entre l'occupant et son environnement. Fait à noter : aucun volant n'agrémente cet espace. Pleinement modulable, la cabine peut servir de bureau comme de chambre à coucher pour les trajets nocturnes. Une application mobile permet à l'usager de calibrer la température du mini frigo tout en choisissant parmi une gamme d'ambiances sensorielles, celle qui convient le mieux à son humeur du moment. Il peut ainsi passer d'une expérience apaisante de type « Forêt suédoise » à un inspirant décor «Fabuleuses aurores boréales » ou même, se dynamiser au rythme de l'ambiance « Énergie vibrante ». Autant d'atmosphères que la voiture est capable de reproduire grâce à un gigantesque moniteur en ciel de toit et à un système audio haute fidélité. Toutes les fonctionnalités de son véhicule dernier cri ne semblaient pourtant pas apaiser l'humeur de Daryl Thomassen, en retard d'une bonne demi-heure à son rendez-vous chez Me Dorothée Morel, notaire, dont les bureaux se situaient dans le quartier Saint-Michel. Le secteur était en proie à plusieurs soulèvements et accrochages, en ce matin du 8 juin 2032. Or, Daryl Thomassen devait absolument se rendre sur place pour signer son entente de divorce. Il avait beau avoir insisté pour une rencontre en visioconférence, le divorce devait absolument se prononcer en présence de sa femme Ashley Jones – une Américaine. D'autres procédures étaient prévues à Atlanta, le mois prochain. Daryl consulta une fois de plus l'itinéraire pour connaître le temps estimé d'arrivée : il en avait encore pour une vingtaine de minutes. On allait lui reprocher son retard. Ce n'était pas ce qui le préoccupait le plus. Ni le divorce qu'il peinait toujours à digérer.

C'était plutôt ce qui, dans son agenda, venait juste après :
une rencontre avec la Défense nationale pour la signature
d'un contrat. Le plus important de sa carrière.

L'aventure entrepreneuriale de M. Daryl Thomassen débuta
dans un laboratoire de l'université McGill, alors qu'il ter-
minait ses études doctorales en informatique. Boursier
du fonds canadien de soutien à la recherche, Thomassen
s'appliquait à concevoir, pour Pêches et Océans Canada,
l'architecture d'un réseau de neurones artificiels capable
d'améliorer la vision-ordinateur des satellites à très basse
altitude pour la détection et le suivi des mammifères marins.
La population des cétacés connaissait une baisse préoccu-
pante dans le Saint-Laurent. Grâce à l'infrarouge et au sang
chaud de ces animaux aquatiques, le logiciel permettait de
suivre leur déplacement.

Les recherches de Thomassen et al., publiées dans la
revue *Nature* en octobre 2027, ne tardèrent pas à tomber
dans l'œil des ministères de la Sécurité publique et de
la Défense nationale. Son algorithme de reconnaissance
visuelle, baptisé Hélios, combiné à un système optronique
de lentilles UV et de capteurs thermiques, rendait possible, beau temps mauvais temps, le repérage d'un bébé
béluga nageant sous une couche de glace de 500 mm, à
partir d'une orbite de 300 km d'altitude. Mieux encore,
en milieu terrestre et à une altitude équivalente, l'organe
de vision numérique d'une résolution de 0,5 cm/pxl en

mode panchromatique, pouvait repérer une fourmi dans un désert de sel. Performances qui ouvraient la porte à toute une gamme d'applications en matière de défense.

La vente en 2029 d'une première licence d'exploitation d'Hélios (HiOS-1) au coût de 1,2 million de dollars permit le développement d'une version bêta, qui équipa les drones d'endurance de type Athéna. Équipée de moteurs rotatifs permettant le décollage vertical, et capable de voler à des altitudes allant jusqu'à 15 240 m, avec une autonomie de 50 heures, Athéna constituait une plateforme mature, performante, dont la capacité opérationnelle avait été démontrée lors de nombreuses missions. Conçu expressément pour répondre aux besoins du Canada, ce drone de moyenne altitude et de longue endurance (communément appelé MALE) était doté d'un large éventail de capteurs, et d'autres charges utiles pouvant atteindre 2500 kg. Il devait permettre au Canada de préserver sa sécurité nationale et d'assurer sa souveraineté territoriale, même dans les endroits les plus reculés.

Dès les premiers essais, le logiciel de vision Hélios se révéla d'une compatibilité parfaite avec le système de navigation d'Athéna. Son acuité visuelle et son adaptabilité remarquable aux impératifs de vol en firent un copilote idéal.

Ainsi naquit, sous la forme d'un partenariat public-privé, le projet Hélios-Athéna. L'initiative devait s'inscrire dans le cadre plus vaste du programme *Flyborg,* dont l'objectif à terme était de doter l'Aviation royale canadienne (ARC) d'une flottille d'aéronefs sans pilote, pour assister ses effectifs dans différentes missions de reconnaissance.

Skyline Solutions, la compagnie nouvellement fondée par Daryl Thomassen, devait y jouer un rôle de premier plan : concevoir et arrimer au système de pilotage autonome un organe de vision artificielle, capable de détecter des mouvements, analyser des scènes, suivre des objets au sol, sur mer, dans les airs et les identifier.

Les premiers prototypes opérationnels intégrant Hélios-Athéna furent d'abord affectés aux missions de patrouille à longue portée. La mise en service de ses appareils connut un succès. Tout au long de l'année 2030, le duo Hélios-Athéna effectua de façon autonome, sans télépilote, des patrouilles de souveraineté dans l'archipel Arctique et dans les zones maritimes. Le passage du Nord-Ouest rendu pleinement navigable 365 jours par année, plusieurs pays limitrophes multipliaient les tentatives de mainmise sur le pétrole, le poisson et les diamants. Comme aucun traité n'avait encore réussi à délimiter ce territoire par des frontières consensuelles, tous les efforts pour défendre la souveraineté du Canada sur ces terres isolées étaient *de facto* justifiés.

Pénurie de main-d'œuvre oblige, le succès des opérations menées par Hélios-Athéna conduisit l'ARC à délester ses pilotes des missions de surveillance nordiques pour les affecter à des mandats plus critiques. Les systèmes autonomes, quant à eux, devinrent la norme dans l'archipel arctique, et peu à peu, dans les maritimes, puis le long des frontières américaines. Autant de secteurs qu'on peinait autrement à surveiller de façon adéquate.

Bientôt, le programme *Flyborg* devait inclure dans sa portée la mise en service d'autres appareils. Daryl Thomassen qui, grâce à ses beaux-parents, entretenait d'excellentes relations avec le Department of Defense, en vint à nouer des partenariats avec la US Navy et les US Marine Corps. Ses affaires allaient prendre d'incroyables proportions. Fin 2031, Skyline Solutions comptait déjà un carnet de commandes internationales bien garni, si bien que son chiffre d'affaires totalisait près d'un demi-milliard, une augmentation de mille pour cent par rapport à la même période, en 2030.

Des mises à jour ne tardèrent pas à s'opérer sur la plateforme Hélios-Athéna pour l'adapter aux opérations de sauvetage et missions humanitaires. On exigea de ces appareils plus de capacités opérationnelles. Exécuter un tir de précision, par exemple, neutraliser une cible ennemie ou, tout simplement, protéger les pilotes amis en cours d'opération devenaient de criantes nécessités. Le tout, sans intervention humaine. Bref, un cahier de charges des plus denses et complexes.

Le Canada, comme ses alliés, n'en était pas à leurs premières armes dans le domaine de l'intelligence artificielle appliquée aux opérations militaires. Nombre de plateformes avaient déjà été testées par le passé. Mais les bavures en Afghanistan, où un centre culturel avait été frappé par erreur, puis en Irak et au Yémen, où des civils avaient été pris pour cible, avaient mis un frein au développement de cette technologie – du moins au Canada – de peur que son utilisation n'entraîne de graves violations du droit international. Le Haut-Commissariat des Nations Unies avait d'ailleurs appelé à un moratoire sur l'utilisation de ces armes. Plusieurs états avaient tenté de négocier un traité d'interdiction. Faute de consensus sur un texte contraignant, ceux-ci s'étaient contentés de simples déclarations de principe, vu les investissements majeurs réalisés par d'autres puissances dans ce domaine. Face à ces contraintes, il fallait envisager des situations où l'utilisation des systèmes robotiques serait éventuellement plus éthique : pour protéger ses propres combattants, par exemple. Mieux encore, il devenait irresponsable d'envoyer ses propres soldats affronter des unités autonomisées des autres armées sur un champ de bataille. Fort de ce raisonnement, plusieurs nations comme la France, l'Allemagne et l'Angleterre, qui s'étaient montrées, a priori, fortement opposées à la conception et à la fabrication des armes létales autonomes, en vinrent à revoir leur position. Ainsi avons-nous assisté pendant les années 20 à une course aux armes intelligentes.

Au Canada, l'élection d'un gouvernement conservateur avait remis ce débat épineux au goût du jour, et balayé du revers de la main toutes les tergiversations. Le retard encouru par le pays était préjudiciable. Il devenait évident qu'une machine dotée d'IA pouvait tuer et en avait le droit dans certains contextes. Aucune puissance mondiale digne de ce nom ne remettait en doute cette position. De fait, les machines n'étaient pas inhumaines, et ne pouvaient le devenir ; seuls les humains pouvaient être inhumains. Une machine ne pouvait violer ni agir par la haine, la peur ou le racisme. Une machine ne connaissait ni la fatigue, ni le froid, ni la tendance à s'enivrer d'alcool... Beaucoup d'hommes avaient violé le droit humanitaire international sous l'influence de l'alcool. Enfin, toutes ses images et ses commandes enregistrées, un robot ne pouvait prétendre n'avoir « rien vu » ou « rien fait ». De même, les paramètres généraux et spécifiques de la mission ayant concouru à son raisonnement pouvaient être extraits et analysés dans le cadre d'une enquête ultérieure. C'étaient là quelques-uns des nombreux arguments en faveur de l'IA, laquelle on supposait correctement programmée, dans un cadre prédéterminé – un lieu pacifique et réglementé, tel que les bureaux lumineux et climatisés de Skyline Solutions, par exemple. Cadre que l'on s'imaginait mieux approprié au respect du droit international que celui d'une ligne de front disputée, où périssaient des soldats sous le feu.

En sa qualité de membre de l'OTAN, le Canada se prononçait toujours en faveur du règlement pacifique des conflits. Or, nul ne pouvait le nier, le pays était un important exportateur de technologies militaires. L'objectif actuel n'était ni de réduire la production ni de limiter les exportations. Mais plutôt de changer d'argument de vente, en comparant les armes « traditionnelles » avec les nouvelles que le Canada s'engageait désormais à développer : des armes plus éthiques. Il y avait vraiment là une opportunité à saisir, un potentiel d'amélioration, une façon de faire la guerre de manière plus juste. Un positionnement sur les marchés qui placerait le Canada à l'avant-plan de l'armement éthique.

La plateforme Hélios-Athéna présentait la maturité nécessaire pour briguer ce mandat : faire disparaître l'humain du circuit décisionnel visant à reconnaître les cibles et les abattre de façon autonome. Son algorithme d'apprentissage et d'exécution conforme au droit international pouvait prévenir les erreurs humaines. Cette capacité de frappe « proprement canadienne » allait reposer essentiellement sur l'analyse des scènes et la compréhension des situations tout en répondant du droit des conflits armés, tels que le principe de précaution et de proportionnalité. Le premier prototype ayant passé tous les tests « à la satisfaction du Ministère de la Défense nationale », il devenait nécessaire d'adapter cette technologie à d'autres types d'aéronefs.

Tel fut l'objet de l'entente que Thomassen s'apprêtait à signer, en ce 8 juin 2032, contrats totalisant 75 millions de dollars canadiens. L'accord prévoyait l'achat de deux cents licences HiOS programmables sur mesure, devant être livrées à brève échéance. Conçue selon une architecture modulaire, cette version d'HiOS présenterait une composante principale à laquelle viendraient se greffer différentes extensions. Ainsi, de simples modules d'extensions, communément appelés *plugins,* suffiraient à adapter HiOS pour ses différentes missions en Afrique, en Asie ou en Amérique du Sud, sur des appareils de type Athéna ou tout autre aéronef compatible avec son programme.

Durant la dernière année et demie, Thomassen avait travaillé d'arrache-pied pour honorer ce contrat. Il lui avait fallu engager du personnel pour éviter la sous-traitance. Les exigences de sécurité de la Défense nationale étaient strictes. Tous les processus de l'entreprise avaient été révisés un à un. Ces opérations avaient nécessité de gros investissements. Les audits externes avaient risqué, à maintes reprises, de compromettre les livrables, mais Thomassen et son équipe étaient parvenus à respecter leurs engagements. Sa cote de crédit était excellente, malgré ses dettes colossales. Il était encore jeune et en parfaite santé, capable d'endurer le stress inhérent à son métier. HiOS était un produit prometteur, résultat d'un important investissement de l'Aviation royale et de la Défense nationale. Les Américains s'y impliquaient également. La technologie développée par Skyline Solutions offrait, sans nul doute, la meilleure garantie pour minimiser – voire éliminer – les bavures et autres erreurs de frappes meurtrières. Il mettait au monde la première arme intelligente politiquement et moralement défendable, se félicitait Thomassen. Il ressassait ses souvenirs quand la voiture freina brusquement après avoir percuté un objet, tout juste au moment où elle s'apprêtait à franchir une intersection. Les lumières de la cabine virèrent au rouge puis clignotèrent.

« Collision frontale. Collision frontale. Collision frontale » claironna l'assistant vocal.

Thomassen déboucla sa ceinture, et se précipita à l'avant du véhicule pour voir ce que la Volvo avait heurté. À sa grande surprise, il vit un jeune homme, étendu au sol, à quelques mètres de son véhicule. Thomassen ouvrit la portière en catastrophe, se précipita vers le jeune qui, déjà, se remettait sur pied. Il sursauta à la vue de son visage tuméfié.

— Ça va ? ! demanda Thomassen, confirmant d'un coup d'œil – et avec soulagement – que le feu pour piétons était bel et bien rouge.

L'individu considéra Thomassen d'un air hagard, puis épousseta ses pantalons. Des passants ahuris s'étaient arrêtés. L'accident aurait-il causé ces vilains hématomes au visage ? se demanda Thomassen paniqué. Impossible. Il ne l'avait quand même pas battu... Il attendit du blessé une réponse, un reproche, une réclamation. Mais non. Rien. Pas même une insulte. Pourquoi restait-il planté là, muet et immobile ? se demanda Thomassen. Était-il en état de choc, sous l'effet d'un quelconque psychotrope... avait-il toute sa tête ? Thomassen remarqua l'oreille suppurante de l'imprudent piéton.

— J'appelle les secours ! dit Thomassen.

Ce dernier mot arracha la victime à sa torpeur. Elle se leva à la hâte pour s'éloigner de la scène. Thomassen courut derrière elle pour obtenir ses coordonnées. Le piéton ne se serait d'ailleurs pas arrêté si son poursuivant n'était pas parvenu à lui mettre la main sur l'épaule, quelques mètres plus loin. L'individu se retourna vivement, prêt à se battre pour se dégager, quand Thomassen s'esquiva pour sortir de sa poche une carte qu'il lui tendit en main propre : « Voici mes informations de contact. N'hésitez pas à me joindre pour quoi que ce soit. » Le jeune homme nota son accent anglais et leva sur lui des yeux éberlués. Thomassen tourna les talons, puis regagna sa voiture. Il l'avait laissée en plein milieu de la chaussée. Elle bloquait toute la circulation. Il eut droit à un concert de klaxons.

Il prit place à l'intérieur de sa Volvo 360.

« Obstacle. Obstacle. Obstacle », répétait l'assistant vocal, entêté. D'un simple appui sur un bouton pressoir, Thomassen réinitialisa le système. Il confirma l'adresse de sa destination. L'ordinateur de bord recalcula l'itinéraire. Il serait chez Me Morel dans vingt-cinq minutes. Thomassen jeta un œil à l'horloge. Il allait être très en retard à son audience de divorce.

Adel entendit une voix familière à l'oreille : « Vis ta vie comme tu l'entends et trace ta propre voie. » C'était son podcast préféré qui jouait dans ses écouteurs. Il se réveilla en sursaut, dans la noirceur, et ôta son casque. Les capteurs réagirent à son mouvement. Les lumières s'allumèrent aussitôt, éblouissant sa vue. Elles s'étaient éteintes en passant au mode de nuit.

Adel jeta un œil sur sa montre : 22 h 18. Il bâilla. Bientôt trois heures qu'il dormait. Jetant des regards autour de lui, Adel se rendit compte qu'il était seul. Même les robots ménages avaient quitté le plancher : pas un bruit, pas un chat. Et pourtant, au-dessus de sa tête, les rangées de DEL brillaient de tous leurs feux. Devant lui, son écran avait quitté le mode veille. Il lui restait encore beaucoup à faire. Malheureusement, ce n'était pas encore le temps de partir. Il se leva pour aller aux toilettes, fit un détour par les machines distributrices pour s'acheter de quoi à boire. Retournant vers son bureau, il s'arrêta devant l'une des baies vitrées qui donnaient sur le centre-ville et s'y accouda, contemplant le vide. Les lumières en bas scintillaient, minuscules, multicolores, comme dans une immense salle de serveurs. Sur un gigantesque panneau publicitaire, au-dessus de la rue Rachel, une jeune femme aux cheveux bleus exhibait sa e-Claw. « Sors ta griffe ! », exhortait-elle. Adel resta songeur. Ainsi donc, de par ses origines kurdes, il avait hérité d'une tradition révolutionnaire. Il pouvait valablement se réclamer d'une descendance directe avec plusieurs générations de combattants qui – avait-il lu dans les livres de son père – avaient sacrifié leur vie pour la patrie, la liberté, le peuple, le féminisme et l'écologie... Enfin, toutes ces luttes aux grands et nobles principes... Pour que lui, petit stagiaire minable, soit condamné à cumuler les heures sup au bénéfice d'une poignée d'actionnaires. Était-ce là sa destinée ? Il ne pouvait s'y résoudre. Adel avait le sentiment que son identité kurde, pourtant peu affirmée, pouvait l'appeler à quelque quête grandiose, héroïque. Enfin, bien plus que n'importe quelle autre appartenance.

La posture universaliste de son père le décevait, car elle semblait le diluer dans une identité commune beaucoup trop vaste, exempte de repères culturels. Et pourtant, il avait l'impression de porter en lui la mémoire de son village natal, le saccage de sa maison et le massacre des siens... même s'il n'en avait pas le souvenir. Il assistait toutefois, impuissant, au spectacle désolant d'un Moyen-Orient à feu et à sang, terre écartelée de ses ancêtres qu'il fantasmait de délivrer du mal, tel un héros mythologique descendu du ciel. Sa kurdicité, pour autant qu'il en possédait une, était beaucoup plus porteuse de sens à ses yeux. Elle s'inscrivait dans un récit qui le dépassait et qui prenait racine dans une histoire qui ne disait pas son nom. Il aimait penser à ce Kurdistan mystérieux, ce pays imaginaire ou imaginé, au désert de sable et de silence dont il venait. Dans ses veines coulait un sang torréfié. Oui, il aimait penser à tout ça, beaucoup plus qu'au Québec de sloche et de givre dans lequel il avait grandi et qu'il trouvait atrocement pacifique. Il s'était tourné, pour un temps, vers des groupes et des associations de jeunes kurdes, espérant peut-être y assouvir un désir d'appartenance. Ceux-ci l'avaient rejeté. Ou, à tout le moins, avaient témoigné peu d'intérêt à son égard, tant il ne présentait, à vrai dire, rien de bien kurde. Quel dommage, pensait-il, que son riche héritage ne trouvât écho nulle part.

Toute son aventure humaine se résumerait-elle donc à passer sa vie enchaîné devant un ordinateur, dans l'unique but de faire fructifier le capital d'une société dont il n'a rien à foutre ? Autant en finir tout de suite alors, d'une balle dans la tête ou carrément, se défenestrer, s'offrant un saut de l'ange depuis le vingt-troisième étage. La mort, à dire vrai, ne l'effrayait pas. Au contraire, elle l'avait toujours fasciné. Il s'émerveillait à l'idée que sa chair, ses tissus, ses organes et ses os puissent, un jour, redevenir terre et poussière. Qu'ils puissent servir de nourriture aux mouches nécrophages, asticots et autres insectes du genre, capables de faire disparaître un squelette en deux ou trois ans. Quel sens revêtait la vie, vue de cette perspective ? Il aimait considérer le suicide d'un point de vue théorique et, bien que les raisons de quitter ce monde lui paraissaient nombreuses, il se trouvait encore trop jeune pour mourir. La vie devait certainement lui réserver quelques surprises, quelques belles occasions d'infléchir le cours de son existence. À condition de revoir son agenda, et surtout, travailler moins, s'avisa-t-il. Mais pouvait-il seulement se le permettre ? Il croulait sous les dettes, peinait à joindre les deux bouts. Son contrat arrivait à terme fin août. Après quoi, il devrait décrocher un nouveau boulot, et ainsi de suite. Sans doute serait-il plus heureux ailleurs, plus relaxe, mais à quel prix ? Il se laissait séduire par la perspective d'une carrière en *freelance*, mais celle-ci présentait trop de risques ; il n'en avait pas les moyens ni les compétences sociales. Il avait besoin de revenus stables. En même temps, Adel était dû pour de vraies vacances. Il aurait donné cher pour tout arrêter et reconsidérer sa vie. Le marché du travail était certes plus favorable aux employés qu'aux employeurs, mais cela ne l'empêchait pas de se sentir piégé dans un engrenage avec ses factures, son appartement et sa marge de crédit à payer ; dernièrement, la chute du Comet coin l'avait définitivement ruiné, le laissant dans un trou de trente mille dollars en moins d'une semaine. Le monde allait vite, beaucoup trop vite pour qu'il puisse se permettre d'*arrêter*. Qui, dans les années 2030, pouvait se permettre un arrêt total de travail à moins d'être assis sur une fortune ?

Un bâillement mélancolique le tira de ses réminiscences. De retour à son poste, il se remit à l'ouvrage. Une demi-heure ne s'était pas écoulée qu'un *pop-up* l'avisa de sauvegarder ses fichiers en cours. Une maintenance du système était planifiée dans cinq minutes. Surpris, il consulta le calendrier des mises à jour : l'opération concernait le serveur de sauvegarde. Une mise à jour spéciale nécessitait le redémarrage complet du serveur. Il en avait pour une bonne trentaine de minutes. Il consulta le journal du serveur : son entretien avait été repoussé plusieurs fois, en raison de mises à jour logicielles plus urgentes requises pour les tests de ce matin. La maintenance était désormais inévitable. L'opération avait été déclenchée par un algorithme probabiliste qui avait déterminé l'heure du début de la séquence, entre 21 h et 5 h. Le hasard ayant voulu que le téléchargement de la mise à jour débute à ce moment précis, Adel n'avait d'autre choix que de patienter...

Il abattit son poing sur la table. « Putain de *fuck* de merde ! » vociféra-t-il. Cette journée a-t-elle une fin ? Une petite fenêtre du moniteur affichait le compte à rebours. Dans quatre minutes, le moindre poste réseau serait inutilisable. Que faire ? Adel se leva d'un bond, fit les cent pas, considéra l'écran avec dédain. L'idée de le balancer à bout de bras lui traversa l'esprit. Ou, mieux encore, d'y vider un chargeur, asperger le local d'essence, et foutre le feu à la bâtisse. L'idée lui donna presque une érection.

Comme il se résignait à patienter lui vint l'idée de télécharger les fichiers sur son disque local, pour travailler hors réseau. « Bon, pensa-t-il, ce n'est pas très protocolaire – en fait, pas protocolaire du tout – mais qui se soucie du protocole, à onze heures moins quart ? » Il n'aura qu'à recopier les fichiers sur le serveur une fois le travail terminé, et leur sauvegarde se fera tout naturellement le lendemain : ni vu ni connu. Il parvint à effectuer l'opération et se débrancha du réseau. Juste à temps.

De ce geste spontané surgit à la mémoire trouble d'Adel le souvenir de son précédent stage. Ici même, à cet endroit, il y a un an précisément, alors qu'il travaillait avec ses collègues du LAB à optimiser cette séquence de redémarrage. Celle du serveur de sauvegarde, justement. Comme il était docile et méticuleux, à cette époque. Un jeune stagiaire pimpant, tout frais sorti de l'école, qui ne se serait permis aucune excentricité. Poli, ponctuel, présentable, chaussures neuves aux pieds, la chemise ne dépassant jamais du pantalon, la barbe rasée de près et la peau délicatement parfumée. Il avait tout à prouver. Il n'osait jamais dire non. Les qualités ne manquaient pas pour le décrire : consciencieux, ordonné, scrupuleux, etc. Il avait terminé son stage avec la mention « remarquable ». Lors de son évaluation, son responsable *Talent et culture* attitré lui avait posé quelques questions, dont une qui l'avait particulièrement marqué : à savoir si, dans dix ans, il se voyait toujours dans l'entreprise. Adel Salem avait répondu :

— Bien sûr.

— À quel poste ?

— Directeur, avait osé Salem, pour faire bonne impression.

Son interlocuteur avait sourcillé.

— Directeur ?

— Oui.

Dans une note au dossier, l'employé RH avait consigné l'enthousiasme de la nouvelle recrue, et spécifié : « Candidat prometteur. À surveiller. » Son équipe avait même organisé un 5 à 7 pour souligner son départ.

Adel soupira. Que restait-il, aujourd'hui, de ce stagiaire modèle ? Il se leva, se mit à arpenter la pièce. Autour de lui, quelques centaines d'écrans noirs disposés sur les rangées de tables se contentaient de retransmettre l'état d'avancement de la sauvegarde automatique, miroitant l'exécution inexorable des lignes de codes qu'il avait lui-même jadis programmées. L'opération était pilotée par un logiciel depuis les salles de serveurs, au sous-sol. Emporté par un élan de nostalgie, Adel eut envie de s'y rendre pour contempler les machines à l'œuvre.

L'ascenseur répondît à sa commande et le déposa à l'étage SS-05, signe qu'il avait conservé tous les accès de l'an dernier. Surpris, il s'engagea dans le long corridor blanc qui le menait aux portes à ouverture automatique, conscient des caméras biométriques qui analysaient sa démarche. Arrivé au seuil, une autre caméra authentifia son visage et autorisa son accès dans le sas. Là, une pèse enregistra son poids. Enfin, Adel apposa sa main droite sur la plaque de numérisation qui authentifia ses empreintes digitales et sa e-Claw.

Construits comme une véritable forteresse, les deux étages de serveurs étaient isolés du reste du bâtiment par une épaisse enceinte en béton armé, que seuls les ascenseurs, le filage du réseau local, deux fibres optiques souterraines dédiées et quelques puits de ventilation traversaient. En cas d'incendie, un système vacuum aspirerait l'oxygène vers l'extérieur. L'air des locaux était constamment refroidi à même l'eau d'une nappe phréatique par un système de climatisation indépendant.

Franchissant l'ultime portail donnant sur le local SS-05.1, un flot de souvenirs remonta à la mémoire d'Adel Salem. Ce lieu avait été son école, son terrain de stage, là où il avait, au fond, tout appris du métier. Là où, chaque jour, le stagiaire qu'il était vérifiait les machines, programmait les ordinateurs, inscrivait des commandes, mettait une section en arrêt, en redémarrait une autre, le tout dans un ordre spécifique, et dans le plus grand respect des procédures.

Sitôt entré, Adel reconnut l'odeur caractéristique de la salle. La température ambiante et l'humidité relative demeuraient deux constantes contrôlées en permanence. La configuration de la pièce lui était familière. La salle SS-05.1 hébergeait toutes les données des bureaux canadiens, avec leurs redondances, tandis que sa sœur jumelle, la salle SS-06.1, située tout juste en dessous, conservait celles des succursales internationales. Ensemble, ces deux pièces fortifiées constituaient un système robuste, fiable, qu'aucune défaillance ou presque ne pouvait compromettre. À moins d'être pénétrée par une attaque semblable à celle de ce matin.

Adel parcourut les allées où régnait un silence aseptisé. S'y cordaient d'immenses châssis dans lesquels s'empilaient les serveurs lames, formant des chapelets de soixante unités par colonne. Adel reconnut aisément les serveurs dédiés aux succursales de Vancouver, puis ceux de Toronto, d'Ottawa, de Québec et d'Halifax. À eux seuls, les serveurs de Montréal occupaient trois rangées. Des guirlandes de voyants bleus, blancs, verts clignotaient allègrement ; les ordinateurs communiquaient entre eux selon un langage codifié d'algorithmes et de commandes qui ne présentaient, pour Adel, aucun secret. Lorsque l'exécution d'un code est en faute, il est facile de se tourner vers son créateur. Celui-ci localise alors la panne, constate son erreur, corrige le problème, fait rouler le programme à nouveau. Et ainsi et de suite. Le succès de l'opération repose sur le talent du programmeur. Les mathématiques sont une science juste et exacte structurant le monde, aimait à se rassurer l'apprenti ingénieur capable de modéliser un univers entier par des opérations, des données et des circuits électroniques. Les mathématiques sont solides et ne pourraient être fautives. Contrairement au langage humain qui déforme les objets. Voilà pourquoi l'amour et les relations humaines avaient toujours semblé, pour Adel Salem, très compliqués. Déroutants et aléatoires.

Tout au fond de la salle, Adel reconnut le serveur de sauvegarde qui occupait un pan complet du mur. La sauvegarde automatique des données de Montréal, d'Ottawa et de Toronto s'achevait. Elle donnait l'aval à la réinitialisation des ordinateurs. Les témoins lumineux scintillèrent. Le vrombissement des machines lui fit penser à une chorale sur le point de livrer un opus. Adel parcourut le pan de mur le long duquel s'alignait une dizaine de châssis connectés les uns aux autres. Tous reliés par une même alimentation électrique et un même système de refroidissement, chacun disposant d'accès réseau indépendants et des particularités connectiques propres à leurs appareils pour en maximiser la redondance.

113

La remise sous tension d'un serveur est toujours un moment critique, Adel en était bien conscient. La réalimentation séquentielle des six cents disques du serveur de sauvegarde aboutirait à l'exécution parfaite d'un code pourvu de quelques milliers de commandes, toutes aussi cruciales les unes que les autres. Le système reprenait ainsi le contrôle de ses périphériques en rechargeant les couches applicatives nécessaires à son opération. Le moindre défaut dans cette séquence pouvait s'avérer fatal, entraîner la défaillance du serveur au grand complet et une facture grimpante des plus salées. Le cauchemar de tout ingénieur informatique.

Adel connaissait cette séquence par cœur, dans ses moindres détails, pour l'avoir révisée mille fois. Il avait travaillé à son optimisation, parfois des nuits entières. Tous ses temps libres de l'été dernier y avaient été engloutis. Il remâchait sa rancœur quand une petite extrusion sur le châssis de l'extrémité gauche capta son attention. C'était un petit interrupteur. Un bouton pressoir dont lui seul connaissait l'existence. Lui, et son ancien superviseur, Mahmoud Bennani. Mahmoud Bennani était analyste-programmeur et percussionniste professionnel en même temps. Il disait travailler pour payer ses *bills,* mais ce qui le faisait triper, c'était de fumer des « gros bats » et donner des « *shows* » au Balattou. En gros, ce n'était peut-être pas le plus protocolaire des informaticiens, mais certainement le plus créatif qu'Adel n'eût jamais rencontré. Ce bouton – mieux connu sous le sobriquet de « bidule » – ils l'avaient tous deux posé là, l'an dernier, alors qu'ils travaillaient sans relâche à ce qu'ils se plaisaient à appeler « ce foutu bordel ». À l'époque, la séquence de redémarrage présentait plusieurs bogues. Lorsqu'actionné au bon moment, ce « bidule » suspendait l'exécution du code pendant 300 secondes ; tout juste le temps de vérifier que chaque composante du noyau avait redémarré sans anicroche. Une kyrielle de commandes lançaient alors les systèmes applicatifs. Après quoi, il devenait impossible d'identifier l'origine du problème. C'était comme chercher une aiguille dans une botte de foin. Ce dispositif enclenché au bon moment permettait de restreindre la recherche du défaut à une poignée de commandes. Parmi les systèmes en attente se trouvait le module de surveillance et de contrôle d'accès. Mais surtout, le système de sauvegarde lui-même. Ainsi privé de son bouclier, par l'interruption volontaire de son déploiement, le système était à son plus vulnérable. En temps normal, cet interrupteur aurait dû être enlevé. Une fois leur travail terminé, Bennani et Salem avaient jugé bon de le laisser là, craignant que d'autres bogues ne surviennent. Depuis, personne n'avait pensé à le retirer. Ce qui devait constituer une solution temporaire s'était malencontreusement muté en un dispositif permanent qui, en cette seconde précise, ouvrait une brèche de sécurité ultime aux yeux d'Adel Salem.

Il reconnut d'instinct, au son des convertisseurs, le moment précis où ce commutateur devait être actionné. Faisant mine de s'appuyer contre le châssis pour tromper l'œil de la caméra de droite, Adel posa sa main dessus puis enfonça le bouton. La danse des lumières bleues cessa, les voyants devinrent fixes. Adel fit un pas en arrière. Il venait de suspendre l'exécution du code. La machine au grand complet retenait son souffle. Il resta là, immobile, fasciné devant ce mastodonte numérique, aux capacités computationnelles inconcevables pour le cerveau humain. Puissance mystérieuse à laquelle il se savait asservi. Dans ce système, Adel n'était rien d'autre qu'un misérable pion. Or, voilà que, par un concours de circonstances inattendu, le rapport de pouvoir venait de s'inverser. Voilà que maintenant, fort de son savoir, Adel avait le dessus sur ce système qu'il avait entraîné et qui lui avait siphonné tant d'énergie. Voilà que ce système était entièrement soumis à sa volonté. À sa merci.

Une lumière s'alluma sur le panneau de contrôle, signe que le circuit électronique principal était coupé. Adel fixa le voyant lumineux avec une fascination incrédule, comme si c'était le fruit défendu. Des gouttes de sueur commencèrent à perler sur son front. Sur l'échelle des conneries qu'il avait faites dans sa vie, celle qu'il s'apprêtait à commettre – s'il cédait à la tentation – méritait le trophée de la bêtise humaine, pensa-t-il. Le « méchoui » de la boutique La Grange lui semblait soudain un crime dérisoire, comparé à celui-ci. Une idée commença à l'obnubiler : et s'il LE faisait ?

Il tenta de donner un sens au hasard qui l'avait conduit jusqu'ici.

Était-il possible que cette circonstance soit le simple fruit du hasard ? Le hasard, existe-t-il vraiment ? Si oui, existerait-il toujours, si l'on pouvait calculer la probabilité inhérente à chaque évènement tributaire de ce moment décisif ? Adel rabouta dans sa tête les péripéties qui l'avaient conduit jusqu'ici, depuis hier. Et puis non, il se ravisa. Son cerveau surchauffait. Pourquoi pas depuis sa naissance – ou tant qu'à faire –, depuis la naissance même de l'univers, jusqu'à ce tournant capital où – fort de son expertise – il était parvenu à aveugler son ennemi ? Une fenêtre de 300 secondes venait de s'ouvrir à lui comme un signe du destin. Il hésita. Oui, c'était bel et bien un signe du destin, car que valaient 300 secondes à l'échelle de son existence ? Ou plutôt, à l'échelle cosmique ?

Une question plus importante encore vint interrompre le cours de ses pensées philosophiques : où en était le décompte ? Combien de temps restait-il avant que le système ne recouvre la vue ? Impossible de le savoir. Chose certaine, la fenêtre se rétrécissait, chaque seconde. Et pourtant, Adel restait figé. Son premier réflexe ? S'en retourner à son poste, au vingt-troisième étage : faire comme si de rien n'était. Une voix intérieure le retint. Il fixa le sol et son regard s'arrêta sur ses chaussures abîmées. Il les considéra un instant, avant de s'arrêter à ses pantalons froissés. La médiocrité de sa vie lui apparut soudain avec une éblouissante clarté. « J'ai été un mouton toute ma vie... », pensa-t-il, comme s'il venait de mettre le doigt sur une plaie aussi purulente que douloureuse. Et s'il bifurquait ? S'il perturbait le cours ennuyeux, aliénant et prévisible de sa vie, où cela pouvait-il le mener ? « Trace ta propre voie », murmura-t-il à lui-même.

Il s'approcha d'un terminal à écran et, à l'aide de sa e-Claw, s'authentifia d'un geste rapide de la main. Une interface de commande apparut aussitôt. Tel un braconnier dans l'antre d'un lion endormi, Adel accéda en quelques lignes de code au volume de la mémoire, puis à l'arborescence de la compagnie et, de là, au fichier *Administration* sans qu'aucune authentification ne lui fût demandée. Le protocole de redémarrage n'avait appliqué aucune consigne de sécurité. Le système était bel et bien aveugle.

Le monde sembla se dissoudre dans le silence bourdonnant des serveurs. Un abîme s'ouvrit dans l'âme du jeune homme. La tentation de soustraire du système des données était irrésistible. Assorties d'informations bancaires et biométriques, les données personnelles pouvaient valoir une petite fortune sur le marché noir. Un ou deux Bitcoins, à coup sûr. De quoi se remettre de la chute du Comet coin. Il garderait ce magot bien en sécurité dans un portefeuille numérique, à l'abri de l'impôt, et pourrait en tirer profit dans les années à venir.

D'un autre côté, les conséquences d'une fuite de ce type étaient énormes. Cela pouvait lui valoir deux-trois ans derrière les barreaux. Minimum. De quoi perdre son emploi, son diplôme, ruiner sa réputation, bref, de quoi *merder* sa vie. Le jeu en valait-il la chandelle ? Allait-il tout sacrifier pour une aventure incertaine ? N'était-il pas plus simple de tourner la page, de passer l'éponge, d'oublier la soirée d'hier, la bagarre, son amour pour Audrey et les revendications du Resco ? Ne gagnait-il pas plutôt à reprendre l'ascenseur, retrouver son poste, effectuer son travail, puis rentrer chez lui ? Pourquoi tout risquer ?

Revinrent à l'esprit d'Adel les cités de sable et de pierres qui l'ont vu naître sur les steppes sans fin du Rojava.

Il se rappela les récits héroïques de ses aïeux, et la fratrie de ses ancêtres révolutionnaires se mit à chanter dans sa mémoire l'éloge de leurs exploits, avec les voix courageuses de frères et sœurs qui l'enhardissaient. Un geste décisif restait à poser. Et il devenait lui-même comme un membre véritable de ce clan. D'ailleurs, n'avait-il pas assez souffert aux mains de ce conglomérat, pour ne pas se venger de lui ?

Il est de ces occasions qui ne se présentent qu'une seule fois dans la vie, songea Adel. Il aimait se les imaginer comme des trains s'arrêtant à une gare. Que lui réservait la destination ? Nul ne pouvait vraiment le prédire. N'en tient qu'au voyageur d'embarquer ou pas, sans savoir où le périple le conduira : vers le bonheur ou la catastrophe ? Peut-être quelque part entre ces deux extrêmes, philosopha-t-il. Impossible de le savoir, à moins de monter à bord et de quitter le quai.

Son front était couvert de sueur. Adel avala sa salive, et fit un pas vers le moniteur. De tout temps, l'aventure a été un passage du connu vers l'inconnu. On choisit d'y rentrer, mais nul ne peut prédire quand il en sortira ni où. Chose certaine, choisir l'aventure répond d'abord à un désir de mouvement. À l'impulsion de rompre le cours du destin pour qu'émerge de cette brèche une lueur d'espoir. Et c'est cette pensée qui traversa l'esprit d'Adel, au moment où, commandé par une main divine, il franchit le point de non-retour, et téléchargea vers la partition de stockage de sa e-Claw le fichier *ClientsQC* du répertoire \\EES2032\\R\ Admin\ClientsQC\2032\.

Les compagnies ont beau investir des millions
de dollars en sécurité, l'humain demeurera toujours
le maillon faible de tout système informatique.

— Un expert en cybersécurité
ayant témoigné au procès d'Adel Salem

Il était 23 h 30 lorsqu'Adel sortit enfin dehors. Le ciel était couvert ; la nuit sombre. Il s'arrêta net, comme indécis, sous la marquise de l'entrée principale, hésitant entre poursuivre sa route ou revenir sur ses pas. Le doute s'était emparé de lui. Pourtant, jusqu'ici, ses dernières actions s'étaient succédé avec une fluidité stupéfiante. Après avoir extrait son fichier de données, il avait fermé la session, remonté à l'étage pris ses affaires, puis s'était dirigé vers la sortie. Tout s'était enchaîné avec la plus grande simplicité, avec un désarmant naturel. Le délai de redémarrage du serveur n'avait pas dépassé sa plage de tolérance. Rien toutefois pour faire descendre l'adrénaline. Peut-être réalisait-il soudain la gravité du geste. Il restait cloué sur place.

Pendant ce temps, trois secondes avaient suffi au système de reconnaissance faciale pour réaliser une modélisation mathématique de sa physionomie. Opération qui, en dépit de son œil au beurre noir, avait non seulement permis de l'identifier, avec un taux de certitude au-delà des 99 %, mais aussi de lui prêter plusieurs comportements suspects. La cinétique rapide et aléatoire de ses mouvements traduisait une nervosité perceptible, confirmée d'ailleurs par une caméra thermique qui dénota une température corporelle supérieure à la moyenne. Détails suffisants pour que le système de surveillance s'intéressât de plus près à son comportement. Les traits de Salem révélaient une inquiétude manifeste, et l'analyse de sa démarche trahissait une apparente hésitation. Autant d'attributs convertis en autant de variables qui intégrèrent un modèle mathématique pour calculer son degré de risque global.

En vérité, Adel restait inconscient de l'activité numérique qu'il suscitait. Son cœur battait la chamade. « Qu'avait-il donc fait ? », se demandait-il en pétrissant convulsivement sa main gauche. S'y stockaient désormais près de 100 Mo de données volées. « Avait-il laissé des traces ? » L'idée de revenir sur ses pas pour en avoir le cœur net lui hantait l'esprit. Tentation qu'il devait combattre. Revenir en arrière était impossible, il ne le savait que trop bien. Tous les modules du serveur de sauvegarde étaient opérationnels. Dès lors, n'importe quelle requête ou commande exécutée serait enregistrée, redondances multiples à l'appui. Et puis, retourner au bureau ? Non, ce serait trop louche. Soudain, un déclic. Adel remarqua du coin de l'œil les caméras de surveillance braquées sur lui. Que faire ? Une défilade trop brusque éveillerait des soupçons. D'un autre côté, son inaction prolongée risquerait de déclencher une alerte. À court d'inspiration, il se tapa le front, comme s'il venait de se souvenir de quelque chose, puis s'éloigna aussitôt, dodelinant de la tête, livrant une performance digne d'un acteur hollywoodien. Le jeu fut suffisamment convaincant pour dissiper les soupçons des caméras intelligentes. Ayant parcouru une distance respectueuse en direction du métro, il dévia de sa route, s'engagea dans une ruelle, puis s'arrêta de nouveau, le temps de reprendre son souffle.

Allait-on le retracer ? Non. Impossible, se persuadait-il. L'opération avait été exécutée dans les règles de l'art. Bennani était en tournée avec un nouveau *band* et ne reviendrait jamais plus travailler chez EES. Sans doute. Ils étaient les seuls à connaître l'existence de cet interrupteur. Et puis, au point où il en était, que pouvait-il faire ? Absolument rien. Advenant le pire, il pourrait très bien prétexter un accident. Ou, mieux encore, un acte volontaire... Ne cherchait-il pas à *vérifier quelque chose*, le tout, bien sûr, par souci d'apprentissage académique ? Oui, oui. C'était bien, ça. Académique. Il avait mis au jour une vulnérabilité du système. Le fichier avait été téléchargé dans le but de prouver l'existence de ladite vulnérabilité. Au fond, il n'avait rien à se reprocher. Demain, à la première heure, il avouerait, et tout rentrerait dans l'ordre, pensait-il naïvement.

La ruelle était sombre et crasseuse. Un chien errant, fouillant du museau les détritus abandonnés, déguerpit à la vue de l'arrivant inopiné. Adel s'accroupit, le dos contre un mur. Il inspira et expira longuement. Une stridulation se fit entendre. Adel reconnut le chant du vieux grillon. Sa tête lui jouait-elle un tour ?

— Alors comme ça, on n'a pas fini de faire les quatre cents coups, mon jeune ami. Te voilà dans de beaux draps, se moqua le pansu grillon. Ah, la folie des hommes ! Elle concourra à votre perte. Et quand vous aurez anéanti le monde, par votre barbarie : nous les insectes, premiers animaux terrestres, régneront de nouveau en maîtres sur cette planète.

L'indulgent grillon modula sa voix sur un ton moins cynique.

— Mais toi, Adel Salem, pourquoi n'as-tu pas encore parlé à Audrey Lavoie, comme je t'ai suggéré de le faire ? Pourquoi lui fais-tu subir ces tourments ? Regarde où t'ont conduit ton hypocrisie et ta folie. Est-ce une façon de te venger d'elle ? Douterais-tu de son amour ? Les choses sont parfois beaucoup plus simples qu'elles n'y semblent. Suffit de voir avec le cœur, mon jeune ami, car l'essentiel est invisible pour les yeux.

Adel sourcilla.

—Je connais mes classiques, reprit l'insecte. Si vous lisiez un peu plus, vous les humains, au lieu d'être obnubilés par vos ego !

— Depuis quand lisent les grillons ? répondit Adel avec embarras, ne sachant s'il parlait véritablement à un grillon, ou s'il délirait.

— Ah ! pouffa le grillon. Depuis que le monde est monde, mon cher ami... Regarde mes antennes. Elles captent les vibrations de la terre et de ses vivants. Nous déchiffrons pour vous le mystère des origines. Nous vous instruisons dans les sciences humaines et naturelles. Nous avons porté, pour vous, l'âme de vos ancêtres et avons servi d'intermédiaires entre le royaume des humains et celui des esprits. Et qu'avons-nous reçu en retour ?

Adel resta muet d'étonnement.

— C'est ce que je croyais ! Mépris... que du mépris. Ah, pauvres hommes. Vous creusez votre propre tombe. Regarde-moi bien Adel, car je suis ton ami. Je n'ai rien à gagner, et tout à perdre, en m'adressant à toi. Tu as commis une grave erreur. Retourne d'où tu viens, pour la réparer. Il n'est pas trop tard pour battre sa coulpe.

— Fiche-moi la paix, rétorqua Adel, quelque peu confus.

Le grillon courba la tête d'un air désappointé. Il tint à rajouter quelques paroles, espérant peut-être consoler cette âme en peine, mais vit que son réconfort ne serait d'aucun secours. Il modula alors sa voix pour entonner cette triste cantilène.

> *Dans l'ombre de l'orgueil, te voilà*
> *Aveuglé par ton propre éclat*
> *Refusant de voir le miroir de ta vanité*
> *Ta fierté t'égare voilà la vérité*
> *Tissant les voiles de ton égarement*
> *Ton délire perdure, impénitent*

Lorsque le grillon eut fini de chanter les torts d'Adel Salem, celui-ci se leva et partit sans dire au revoir. Ce soir, il préféra emprunter les ruelles sombres au lieu de prendre le métro, où il risquait d'être capté une fois de plus par les caméras de surveillance organisées en réseau intelligent.

Quand Adel arriva chez lui, il était minuit passé. Il prit un grand verre d'eau, urina, puis se laissa tomber sur le lit, tout habillé. Il resta allongé là, les mains en croix sur son ventre, en proie à un tourbillon de pensées. La fatigue accumulée depuis la veille commençait à prendre le dessus sur lui, pesant sur sa tête comme une chape de plomb. Puis, juste comme il cédait au sommeil, il sentit la petite bosse formée par la micropuce sous-cutanée. Il sursauta. Il fit un bond hors du lit. Un frisson parcourut son corps, il ravala sa salive, puis s'avança vers les écrans d'ordinateur disposés en mur devant lui. Et les alluma un à un.

Il manœuvra la souris sans peine, vérifia dans le répertoire racine que sa e-Claw avait bel et bien été détectée, et double cliqua sur l'icône, puis sur le volume de stockage. Le fichier était là, avec ses données brutes, non cryptées, non compressées, non protégées. Comme un joyau étincelant dans un précieux coffret. Adel tressaillit. D'un mouvement de la souris, il importa le fichier et l'ouvrit à l'aide d'un logiciel *open source*. Puis, comme par enchantement, les données apparurent à l'écran, structurées en lignes et en colonnes. Des dizaines de milliers de noms jumelés à leurs identifiants e-Claw, assortis de leurs données personnelles, médicales et bancaires.

Il filtra, puis survola la clientèle de Montréal. Quelques noms retinrent son attention. Atillio Dandalero, vingt-trois ans, habitant au 7469 rue Saint-Denis, appartenant au groupe sanguin AB+, détenteur d'une carte Flexi Visa avec Desjardins. Il bénéficiait d'un tarif réduit sur sa e-Claw. Un étudiant, déduisit Adel. Il vérifia le registre : Dandalero possédait trois comptes bancaires. Adel se les imagina bien garnis. Dandalero devait être un fils de bourge, préjugea-t-il. Il lança une recherche anonyme à son sujet et les images qu'il vit confirmèrent ses intuitions. Dandalero publiait sans égard aux règles de confidentialité. Ses vidéos le montraient devant chez lui, devant son campus, devant sa bagnole. Il se mettait en scène dans diverses situations aussi superficielles qu'insignifiantes. Ici il faisait le coq. Là, il était ivre mort. Tout compte fait, Dandalero ne présentait rien d'intéressant.

Son regard s'arrêta sur un autre nom. Neela Bakshi, 49 ans. Elle était abonnée au forfait *Concierge* qui prenait en charge la plupart de ses authentifications courantes : comptes bancaires, cartes de crédit, factures de téléphone, Hydro, Internet, chaînes télévisuelles, paiements automobiles, abonnements au gym, polices d'assurance, etc. Le service *Concierge* administrait pour elle ses paiements mensuels. Quant aux réseaux sociaux, elle était plus discrète. Son profil LinkedIn la présenta comme titulaire et vice-directrice adjointe à la faculté de droit de McGill. Une femme à problèmes, donc : mieux valait s'en tenir éloigné, songea Adel, en passant à un autre numéro.

Il passa ainsi quelque temps, les yeux rivés sur ses écrans, choisissant des noms au hasard. Une pensée traversa son esprit. Il fouilla dans ses poches et en sortit la carte d'affaires, tendue ce matin même par le type qui avait failli l'expédier à l'hôpital. Il lut : « Daryl Thomassen. CEO. Skyline Solutions inc. » Il lança une recherche de caractères dans son document, et tomba pile-poil dessus.

Il est, dans la vie, des mystères que nul ne peut expliquer. Des questions insolubles à jamais. Adel se frotta les yeux, regarda à nouveau sur l'écran, puis sur la carte professionnelle obtenue. Oui, c'était bien le même nom, les mêmes coordonnées. Daryl Thomassen, lui, était abonné au service Harmony+. Qui était-il ? Adel Salem n'allait pas tarder à le découvrir.

Située rue Puccini, près de la 17e avenue, dans le quartier Saint-Michel, la minuscule chambre qu'Audrey louait à des circassiens au rez-de-chaussée d'un immeuble à deux étages possédait une géométrie tout à fait singulière. Le mur côté sud, percé d'une large fenêtre guillotine, coupait la pièce obliquement, de sorte qu'un angle anormalement aigu allait se perdre quelque part au fond. S'y entassaient une bibliothèque bien fournie et quelques livres posés à même le sol. Quant à l'autre angle, démesurément obtus, un matelas posé par terre faisait office de lit, ou de banc de perçage improvisé. De ce côté, une porte condamnée donnait sur la chambre de sa coloc Juju. Une autre donnait sur la cuisine. Mis à part une petite commode sur laquelle reposaient quelques objets hétéroclites, il n'y avait pas d'autres meubles dans la pièce.

La fenêtre donnait sur une petite cour, en plein centre de laquelle se dressait un immense chêne que les circassiens prenaient en affection en se balançant au bout de ses vieilles branches. Laissé tranquille, on pouvait entendre de l'intérieur, comme ce matin, le bruissement de son feuillage clairsemé qui faisait écran à la rumeur cacophonique de la ville, bondée de véhicules et de drones livreurs. La paix de cette pièce semblait alors imperméable. Paix désormais menacée, à la grande tristesse des locataires, par un printemps trop chaud qui avait favorisé, à même l'écorce de ce pauvre arbre, la prolifération de nids de chenilles spongieuses toutes aussi gourmandes qu'indolentes. Toutes les méthodes naturelles avaient échoué à le préserver de sa lente défoliation.

Dans cette modeste chambre que les premières lueurs matinales éclairaient, Audrey dormait d'un sommeil agité. Un brise-bise flottait dans l'espace. L'air était humide. Dans son rêve, Audrey parcourait un tunnel sombre. Une lumière en émanait, au bout. Au fur et à mesure qu'elle s'en approchait, la voie semblait se rétrécir et les parois de cet étrange canal, se refermer sur elle. Elle pressa le pas pour échapper au piège. Ses pieds devenaient de plus en plus lourds. Le souffle vint à lui manquer. Elle fit volte-face pour revenir sur ses pas. Un immense mur de brique barrait la voie. À l'autre extrémité, la lumière pâlit avant de s'éteindre, la plongeant dans l'obscurité totale. Elle voulut crier. Aucun son ne sortit de sa bouche. Une trappe s'ouvrit en dessous d'elle. Puis ce fut la chute libre. Infinie.

Audrey se réveilla en sursaut, haletante, le corps frissonnant, malgré la chaleur accablante. Réalisant qu'elle était bel et bien dans sa chambre, elle se laissa retomber sur le lit, soulagée. Les évènements d'hier lui revinrent à la mémoire en un crépitement de flash. Une oreille percée, un incendie, du sang, beaucoup de sang. Elle se secoua la tête, vérifia son téléphone. Adel ne lui avait pas répondu. Elle regrettait de l'avoir insulté.

Audrey Lavoie et Adel Salem s'étaient rencontrés au cégep Marie-Victorin, à l'automne 2026. C'est dans un cours de français que leur aventure amoureuse avait débuté, à cause du « A » de leur prénom respectif. Pour cette génération Z accoutumée aux *dating apps,* cette rencontre fortuite, fruit d'un hasard véritable (que certains imputent au destin), libre de tout algorithme déterministe, était source de fierté pour Audrey. La perspective d'une vie ordinaire et prévisible la rebutait au plus haut point.

Elle avait vécu une enfance heureuse. Millénariaux montréalais, ses parents – M. Patrick Parent, art-théra-peute, et Mme Sylvie Lavoie, comptable à son compte – lui avaient donné tout l'amour du monde. À l'exception des cours de piano qu'elle suivit religieusement dès l'âge de six ans, Audrey Lavoie ne fut contrainte d'aucune façon et jouit d'une liberté sans pareille. Au demeurant, M. Parent et Mme Lavoie s'étaient fait un point d'honneur de ne jamais intervenir dans ses choix. Si bien que son secondaire ter-miné, ses parents accueillirent avec enthousiasme son désir de prendre une année sabbatique en Oregon.

Ses pérégrinations la menèrent de ferme en ferme, au gré des récoltes, sous le soleil brûlant de la côte ouest. Pour y cueillir, dans les champs, fruits, légumes et cannabis, en échange de couverts et de gîtes. Elle fit l'expérience du surf et des vagues, consolida son lien profond avec la Terre-Mère et s'instruisit de plusieurs expériences sociales et communautaires, enrichies par quelques déceptions amou-reuses. Déceptions desquelles elle se remit rapidement, sans rancune ni amertume. À toute fin pratique, elle avait vécu là ce qu'elle avait à vivre, puis était passée à autre chose. Son voyage avait éveillé en elle la compassion, et malgré le charme bucolique des paysages de l'Oregon, son magnifique littoral, ses lacs aux eaux cristallines, ses montagnes, ses vignobles, ses forêts, ses rivières et ses champs de marijuana en fleurs, Audrey fut bouleversée par les évènements qui secouèrent le monde durant cette année-là. Elle ne manquait pas d'être informée par les réseaux sociaux et autres applications de nouvelles, des catastrophes naturelles qui affligeaient alors les populations des quatre coins du globe. Elle assista en direct au coup d'État qui renversa le gouvernement libyen. Au sauvetage d'ouvriers enfouis sous les décombres d'une fabrique de jouets effondrée au Sri Lanka. Elle fut avisée de la survie de cette militante chinoise qui échappa de justesse à une tentative d'assassinat sur *YouTube Live*. Depuis son téléphone, Audrey s'invitait en quelque sorte aux premières loges des atrocités de la guerre : elle visita, en réalité virtuelle, les décombres d'un village rasé par les bombes ; pénétra dans une mine d'uranium clandestine, où s'entassaient par dizaines des prisonniers travaillant nu-pieds, en plein désert d'Égypte. Elle fut témoin des premiers pas d'un éléphanteau, dernier de sa lignée, dans un zoo à l'autre bout du monde. Elle siégea aux premiers rangs d'une conférence à l'ONU, écouta en direct des déclarations menaçant les équilibres géopolitiques partout sur terre ou saluant la signature d'un récent accord de paix. Elle regarda les Chinois entreprendre de construire une base permanente sur la Lune. Des femmes labourer des champs de manioc en Amérique du Sud. Des enfants, mourir dans les bras de leurs mères au Soudan. Elle entendit le dernier souffle d'un chef de village amazonien, ultime descendant de sa tribu décimée par la surexploitation forestière. Elle se trouva nez à nez avec des *boat-people*, venant tout juste de traverser la Méditerranée. Elle assista à la répression sanglante de la troisième intifada, à l'invasion de Taïwan, au début de l'insurrection contre la maison des Saoud, à l'annexion de l'Ukraine par la Russie et fut au chevet du pape François, mourant dans sa luxueuse résidence du Vatican, des suites d'un cancer du côlon.

Ces évènements décisifs qui déboulèrent, un à un, durant son aventure ouest-américaine, l'éveillèrent aux injustices et aux violences du *système*. Loin de la désensibiliser, les images – souvent choquantes – dont elle s'abreuvait quotidiennement suscitaient en elle une profonde empathie pour les victimes d'abus et les peuples condamnés à l'inaction politique. Leurs souffrances, s'était-elle convaincue, ne pouvaient rester lettre morte. Son devoir était d'en être le porte-voix. Elle prêchait avec ardeur une sororité planétaire, n'hésitant pas à relayer l'information, partager et commenter les vidéos qui la bouleversaient. Une communauté de sympathisants prenait forme au bout de ses doigts. Tout autant, une légion de détracteurs pour l'accabler d'invectives. D'où provenait cette haine ? Pourquoi en avait-on après elle ? L'information était-elle la même pour tout le monde ? Comment distinguer le vrai du faux ? Telles étaient les questions qui, à dix-huit ans, accaparaient son esprit. C'est donc mû par ce besoin de trouver des réponses, de nommer des choses, de défendre des idées, qu'Audrey revint à Montréal, persuadée qu'une éducation supérieure lui serait nécessaire pour appréhender le monde et ses défis. Sa vie, anticipait-elle, elle la consacrerait à révéler des histoires, informer le public. À se battre pour la vérité, et donc, pour la justice. Le journalisme lui était alors apparu comme son métier de prédilection. Les tests d'orientation le lui avaient confirmé. Le programme en Sciences humaines, profil Monde, du cégep Marie-Victorin, allait lui ouvrir des portes au sein de la profession, et lui permettre de réaliser ses rêves. C'est ainsi qu'elle y fut admise à l'automne 2026, collège où elle allait rencontrer Adel, son premier véritable amour.

Comment, dans le continuum spatiotemporel, deux trajectoires aux origines si différentes pouvaient-elles se croiser ? Certains argueront que leur rencontre est le fruit des circonstances. Hasard qui apparaît comme un caractère fondamental de notre existence, et en vertu duquel, la vie est imprévisible. Dans cet esprit, il est fort probable qu'en *d'autres circonstances*, Audrey Lavoie et Adel Salem ne se seraient jamais rencontrés. D'autres croiront plutôt à une compatibilité chimique entre deux entités biologiques aux patrimoines génétiques distincts, attirance résultant d'une complexe mécanique entre circuits neuronaux et cocktails hormonaux. D'autres encore diront que leur amour n'était qu'un besoin réciproque, que leur complémentarité a permis de combler. Tous ces facteurs jouèrent probablement un rôle dans cette singulière union.

À l'instar des révolutions et les grands chamboulements qui marquèrent son époque, l'amour avait ouvert pour Audrey de nouveaux horizons, créé de nouvelles perspectives et suscité un regain d'espoir. Ce monde qu'elle voyait en ébullition, marqué par de profondes inégalités, elle entendait l'appréhender avec un compagnon qui partagerait sa quête de liberté. De fait, Adel allait se montrer un allié dévoué et loyal. Ce qui, en dépit de son expérience sexuelle limitée, allait faire changement du carrousel de prétendants qui inondaient ses *stories* de *likes* et de cœurs. Des beaux gosses, elle en avait connu à la pelletée, mais leurs intérêts étaient visiblement plus portés vers le cul, qu'à l'apaisement de ses troubles écoanxieux et son désir de changer le monde. Vraie, Adel manquait de confiance. C'était un *geek* timide, qui ne savait pas parler aux femmes. Qui préférait bidouiller ses petites machines, écrire des programmes en langage Python. Mais c'était un gars indépendant. Elle aimait sa maladresse, ses yeux troublés de chat. Dans ce corps d'homme battait un cœur d'enfant, né dans un camp de réfugiés. Cette vision ne cessait de la troubler. Adel était une victime, après tout. Il y avait dans son regard quelque chose d'inoffensif. Cet homme-là, s'était-elle convaincue, jamais il ne lui ferait mal.

Le mouvement EAU SECOURS (communément appelé EAU CRISSE) vit le jour au printemps 2030. Il réclamait l'abolition du projet de loi visant à privatiser l'eau potable.

Des quatre coins de la province, un vaste effort de mobilisation s'était mis en branle dans l'espoir de faire reculer le gouvernement. Audrey et Adel avaient rejoint les rangs du mouvement et pris part aux piquets de grève érigés devant leurs universités.

La grève de 2030 fut, pour Audrey, sa véritable école. Là où elle allait apprendre à écrire, là où elle allait se forger un style. Des tracts aux manifestes, en passant par les propositions d'AG, les amendements et sous-amendements, l'écriture était pour Audrey un acte collectif, pluriel. Certes, les générateurs de textes étaient puissants et permettaient de gagner beaucoup de temps, mais à la longue, ils recrachaient toujours la même bouillie. À trop s'y fier, on se prenait le doigt dans l'engrenage propagandiste des compagnies tech et leurs commanditaires. Ces machines n'étaient pas au service du bien commun ; plutôt de ceux et celles qui les avaient créés et entraînés. C'est de ces intelligences qu'il fallait se méfier comme la peste. À travers l'écriture, cet art ancien, Audrey se posait en gardienne de la mémoire humaine, rédigeant le soir, après les manifs, maniant une langue acérée et dérangeante qui embrassait le présent et qui faisait battre son cœur. Son cœur d'écrivaine. Émergeait sous sa plume sa propre vision du monde. À vingt ans, elle pouvait se vanter d'avoir adopté des résolutions, écrit des discours et fait face à l'antiémeute. D'avoir changé le cours de l'histoire, en somme.

C'est à l'été 2030 qu'Audrey Lavoie allait rencontrer Maximilien Caron, alias Maximus, lors d'un camp de formation militant tenu dans la région de Lanaudière. Loin d'être insensible à son charme, une aventure tumultueuse devait débuter avec lui. Le séduisant Maximus était connu pour grimper des infrastructures urbaines sans corde ni harnais pour y pendre des bannières. Il avait ainsi escaladé les colonnes de la mairie d'arrondissement de Villeray-Saint-Michel-Parc-Extension, la veille de la fête nationale, pour y poser une banderole proclamant : « *ASSEZ, LES CONDOS ! ON VEUT DES LOGEMENTS SOCIAUX !* ».

Audrey avait été conquise. D'autant plus que ce week-end-là, elle avait retrouvé Maximus dans un rassemblement anar tenu dans le fin fond d'un rang, dans la région de Québec. Il ne l'avait pas lâchée d'une semelle, lui offrant à même sa besace en macramé, drogue et alcool tout au long de la soirée. Adel n'était pas présent ce soir-là, ce qui facilita les rapprochements. Du reste, Audrey ne se sentait coupable de rien. Il était déjà entendu entre eux qu'ils avaient droit de céder au désir, si celui-ci devait se présenter. Et il se présentait. L'insurrection populaire avait créé de nouveaux chemins et brisé des digues. Réfréner l'Amour qui émergeait d'une telle intensité était ridicule – comme essayer d'éteindre un feu de forêt avec un verre d'eau. La question avait été posée, mais il semblait que la réponse allait de soi. Quatre ans qu'ils étaient ensemble. Le couple était assis sur du roc. Bien sûr qu'ils avaient le droit de céder au désir. Bien sûr que ça ne lui dérangeait pas, à Adel, d'ouvrir son couple (il avait répété « bien sûr » plusieurs fois, machinalement). Tout le monde le faisait. Refuser aurait relevé de l'anticonformisme. L'aurait conduit à une rupture. L'idée de perdre Audrey le hantait tellement qu'il avait préféré garder ses craintes pour lui. De toute façon, cela n'allait pas lui faire de mal, d'aller voir ailleurs. Il était beau garçon. Les occasions ne manquaient pas.

Adel n'était donc pas présent ce soir-là, ce qui facilita les rapprochements entre Audrey et Maximus. Elle s'était émue du fait qu'il lui ait confié, autour d'un feu de la Saint-Jean, ses questionnements sur son identité de genre. Chose qu'Adel n'aurait jamais osé faire, lui qui était cisgenre, malgré lui, en dépit de tous ses efforts pour ébranler, remettre en question son hétérocisnormativité. Maximus, lui, prétendait être de genre fluide. La chose avait intrigué Audrey, l'avait même séduite, si bien qu'elle s'était retrouvée avec lui, dans sa tente, avec une autre amie. Elle n'allait pas tarder à repérer le canular : Maximus faisait le coup à toutes les filles qu'il trouvait de son goût. Mais quelque chose en lui la subjuguait, malgré son côté niais. Quelque chose comme sa folâtrerie. Son je-m'en-foutisme charmant. Sa frivolité désarçonnante. Quelque chose qui lui rappela ses voyages dans l'Ouest. Ils s'étaient revus par la suite. Adel n'avait soulevé aucune objection. Peu à peu, une relation s'était construite – ouverte, il va sans dire. Maximus se définissait comme un anarchiste relationnel, entretenant plusieurs relations à la fois, sans privilège d'ancienneté. Il était clair (du moins, cela semblait clair) aux yeux d'Audrey que cette relation n'irait nulle part et qu'elle était de l'ordre d'une passion, aussi fougueuse que passagère. Du reste, Adel avait aussi des aventures et cette dynamique semblait leur convenir.

Loin de les désunir, ces liaisons les rapprochèrent, dans un premier temps. Mais le désir est un concept difficile à saisir, une force insondable, un magma issu de nos profondeurs. Tel Éros, issu de Chaos, il peut agir sur nous autant comme une puissance créatrice que destructrice, selon notre capacité à satisfaire ou non ses caprices. Il en va de même des révolutions qui, lorsque freinées par des structures oppressantes, peuvent échouer... voire tout simplement, mourir dans l'œuf.

Audrey restait pensive. Elle revit la bagarre et réprima une grimace de dépit à ce souvenir. Adel en avait mangé toute une.

Elle fit un bond pour se tirer du lit, ouvrit son ordinateur puis alla à la page des nouvelles. Le spectaculaire incendie de la boutique La Grange faisait la une. Elle cliqua pour visionner le contenu. Une publicité lui vanta le caractère écologique et non intrusif des culottes menstruelles Sœurs de la république. La capsule publicitaire fit place à l'information.

> *Des extrémistes revendiquent un incendie criminel qui a ravagé la boutique La Grange, un magasin de meubles dans l'arrondissement Saint-Michel, la nuit dernière. Un communiqué, publié sur le site de Montréal Contre-Attaque, indique que le groupe a mis le feu aux locaux et réduit en cendres toute la marchandise. « Nous ferons tout le nécessaire pour lutter contre l'embourgeoisement de notre quartier », assure le groupe, qui se fait connaître sous le nom de Resco : les Compagnons de la résistance.*

Cet incident n'est pas sans rappeler les six autres du genre, survenus depuis le début de l'année, au cours desquels des incendies criminels ont visé le mobilier urbain. Jusqu'à ce jour, aucun suspect n'a été identifié dans cette affaire. Des évènements qui soulèvent plusieurs inquiétudes chez les résidents du quartier et les propriétaires de commerces qui exhortent le ministre de la Sécurité publique à démasquer les coupables au plus vite, et les traduire en justice [...]

La nouvelle s'était répandue comme une traînée de poudre, suscitant plusieurs réactions et commentaires. Audrey contempla les images, fascinée. Elle ne put s'empêcher d'esquisser un sourire. Elle voyait là, la manifestation probante d'une œuvre collective. À laquelle elle avait pris part. Dont elle pouvait revendiquer sa part d'héroïsme. Audrey n'était pas un électron libre. Audrey appartenait à un groupe, d'individus réels, faits de chair et d'os. Elle partageait avec eux un idéal, un rêve collectif. Aucun gouvernement, aucune fortune, aucune police ne pouvait rivaliser en puissance à la force d'un tel groupe, soudé par des liens de cœur et d'esprit. Ça, c'était important pour elle. Ça avait du sens, malgré tout. *Ça valait la peine.*

Son visage s'obscurcit. Elle était déjà en retard pour le travail.

16 JUIN 2032
(UNE SEMAINE ET UN JOUR PLUS TARD)

Le ciel était chargé de nuages, la pluie tombait à flots, en ce mercredi soir. On dit que le temps arrange les choses. Pour Audrey, il ne semblait rien arranger. Elle était triste. Au boulot, la semaine avait été éprouvante. Au comité A.P.P.A.R.T (Alliance populaire pour un accès rapide au toit) où elle consacrait son été, la misère humaine était son pain quotidien. N'ayant crainte de plonger dans les affres de l'itinérance, elle était appréciée de ses collègues, et développait des relations significatives avec sa clientèle. Celle-ci était composée principalement d'adolescents et de jeunes adultes (surtout des femmes) en difficulté. Elle leur vouait un amour inconditionnel. Cela avait un coût. Audrey ne passait pratiquement pas une journée sans essuyer de revers funeste, sans que le deuil vienne frapper dans ses plus chères affections ; untel s'était enlevé la vie, telle autre était morte d'une overdose, une autre encore avait été arrêtée et croupissait en prison. Ces nouvelles la bouleversaient. D'aucuns argueraient qu'elle l'avait cherché : rien ne l'obligeait à opter pour un boulot mal payé dans le domaine du travail social. Après tout elle étudiait en journalisme.

Le domaine offrait de bons débouchés, pourvu qu'elle s'y investisse pleinement et qu'elle arrête de se laisser distraire. Sa mère, comptable professionnelle agréée, ne manquait pas de le lui rappeler. Leurs rapports en souffraient. Audrey lui en voulait d'être devenue, avec les années, cette femme à succès imbue de pouvoir et d'autorité qui jugeait ses choix et s'immisçait dans sa vie. Elle lui reprochait de faire la même chose avec son père et de le maintenir dans une relation toxique. Après tout, c'est elle qui produisait leurs déclarations de revenus. Audrey n'avait que faire de ses conseils financiers, de sa Liberté 45, de son plan d'investissement et de carrière. Audrey était gréviste. La grève n'était pas une distraction. Elle appelait à la solidarité. Le journalisme pouvait attendre, ses travaux aussi. Ses études, d'ailleurs, commençaient à lui casser les pieds. Elle méprisait ses professeurs, leur manière restrictive de parler de l'actualité, leur manie de hiérarchiser les sources d'informations, d'occulter la question des violences gouvernementales et policières au profit de « l'éclairage objectif sur les faits ». Le journalisme des grandes agences, avait-elle fini par conclure, était inféodé au pouvoir et répondait à des commandes. L'université n'en était pas assez critique. Le métier manquait d'ambition. Ses collègues, scotchés à leurs écrans, aussi. Audrey rêvait de changer le monde. Pas d'être l'impuissante témoin de sa déchéance.

Ce n'étaient pas ces tourments, toutefois, qui l'accablaient de tristesse, ce soir-là. Une profonde rancœur bouillait en ses veines. Voilà déjà une semaine qu'Adel ne lui avait donné aucun signe de vie. Une semaine, c'est beaucoup. L'absence est à l'amour ce que l'essence est au feu : elle ravive même les plus petites braises. Audrey n'avait pourtant pas manqué de solliciter Adel pour qu'ils « se parlent ». Bien qu'elle ne fût plus avec lui, elle le considérait toujours comme un ami, un compagnon. Comment allait-il ? Avait-il besoin de se confier ? Était-il fâché contre elle ? Son silence pesait lourd. Il n'avait répondu à aucun de ses textos. Devait-elle croire que tout était de sa faute ?

Il lui semblait qu'Adel traversait des moments difficiles, avec la fin de son bac et le début de son second stage. Difficultés qui se traduisaient par de profondes remises en question sur le sens de sa vie, et par une perte de confiance en ses moyens. Or, avait-il seulement le temps de s'arrêter ? On exigeait beaucoup de lui. La compétition était féroce. Il s'en mettait beaucoup sur les épaules, ne voyait plus personne, même plus ses fréquentations. Il méprisait les psychologues. Ses temps libres, il les passait à se défouler sur des jeux vidéo violents. Adel était un jeune homme talentueux, capable de faire face à la musique, mais était-ce sur ce pas qu'il voulait danser ? Audrey avait l'intime conviction qu'il s'était mis en mode « pilote automatique », pour éviter de s'attarder à ses blessures qu'elle soupçonnait de nature familiale. Adel avait toujours ressenti, de la part des siens, une grande pression de « réussir dans la vie ». Ses parents – son père surtout – avaient surmonté plusieurs difficultés – la pauvreté, la discrimination, la pénurie de logements, etc. Pour des réfugiés, ils s'en étaient bien sortis. Ce traumatisme les avait toutefois marqués au point de perturber psychologiquement leurs enfants, estimait-elle. Adel était hanté par la peur de ne pas trouver de travail, d'être sans le sou. Des peurs irrationnelles, mais qui semblaient tout de même influencer ses décisions. Audrey, aussi, avait plusieurs peurs, comme celle de passer à côté de sa vie, de ne pas être aimée ou même encore de voir les conservateurs reportés au pouvoir. Mais c'étaient des peurs qui, selon elle, l'emmenaient à s'ouvrir aux gens, et non pas à se refermer sur elle. Elle avait cru bon de le *challenger* sur les différents aspects de sa vie, mais (était-ce son approche ou le ton qu'elle avait employé ?) Adel avait adopté une position défensive. Et plutôt que de s'ouvrir, s'était refermé comme une huître, retranché dans un mutisme inquiétant. Quelque chose avait changé en lui, depuis quelques semaines. Cela avait commencé un peu avant la fin de session. La chose lui avait échappé, mais tout compte fait, elle ne le reconnaissait plus. Elle-même avait été happée dans le tourbillon des préparatifs pour le Jour de la Terre et la manif contre la brutalité policière. Avec le recul, pourtant, et depuis qu'Adel l'avait plaquée sans raison apparente (car à bien y penser, en dépit de tout ce qu'elle pouvait croire, Maximus n'était pas LA raison, du moins, pas l'UNIQUE raison), elle se rendait bien compte que tous les signes avant-coureurs de sa détresse s'étaient manifestés et qu'elle les avait ignorés. Ou du moins, qu'elle ne leur avait pas donné toute l'importance qu'ils méritaient.

D'un autre côté, jaugeait-elle, lui comme elle avaient ouvert leur couple en toute connaissance de cause, conscients des risques et des dangers qui les guettaient. Nul ne s'attaque aux organisations politiques, aux grandes institutions et au capitalisme, sans d'abord se mettre en danger soi-même. N'était-il pas naïf de croire qu'en une seule personne, ils puissent combler tous leurs besoins amoureux et affectifs ? Il sembla à Audrey qu'il y avait eu consensus là-dessus. N'était-ce pas pour sauver leur couple qu'ils avaient tenté de l'ouvrir ? Alors, pourquoi se sentir coupable d'avoir fait de leur propre chair un lieu de résistance ? Oui, c'est vrai, ça n'allait pas sans heurts. L'aventure avait connu quelques ratés. Elle les avait poussés l'un et l'autre à des excès qu'ils n'avaient jamais cru possibles.

« Non », trancha-t-elle avec conviction, elle ne méritait pas l'opprobre de cet accrochage. Adel et Maximus avaient été cons, mais Maximus l'avait été davantage, mesurait-elle avec le recul. Pourquoi avait-il cogné si fort ? D'ailleurs, ce dernier lui paraissait encore plus con depuis qu'il avait décidé de se réfugier chez son autre amante. C'était comme si, avec un peu de distance, tous ses défauts ressortaient d'un coup. Comme elle se sentait stupide de s'être amourachée de lui. Adel était peut-être trop sensible, mais Maximus avait outrepassé les limites de la décence. Elle ne pouvait en vouloir à Adel d'avoir pété les plombs. De toute évidence, elle était maintenant de son bord. Sans lui, le « méchoui » de La Grange serait resté une mission impossible. Un fantasme irréalisable. Elle tenait en estime Adel, avait de la considération pour lui. Pourquoi refusait-il de lui parler, à présent ? Se croyait-il dans le tort ? Ces questions harassaient son esprit.

Pendant ce temps, les circassiens, eux, se prélassaient au sous-sol. Ils avaient invité quelques amis. Une petite soirée copains et colocs se donnait en bas. On y buvait des boissons infusées au cannabis tout en pratiquant des figures au sol sur des tatamis. L'écho de leurs rigolades parvint jusqu'à sa chambre. Elle n'avait pas envie de se joindre à eux. Elle avait allumé des bougies, fermé ses écrans. Les haut-parleurs débitaient les morceaux d'une liste de lecture intitulée *DJ Conscious Mind*, savant concert de flûtes de bois et de tambours tribaux, sur fond de synthétiseurs électroniques.

Trois petits coups discrets retentirent à sa fenêtre. Audrey se redressa d'un bond. De qui pouvait-il s'agir ? Elle s'approcha de la glace, tentant de reconnaître le visage du visiteur dans la pénombre. Elle étouffa un cri de stupeur à la vue de l'intrus : c'était Adel. Que diable faisait-il ici ? Un sentiment de joie et d'effarement l'envahit. Enfin, elle ouvrit. Adel enjamba le rebord de la fenêtre avec un sans-gêne déconcertant et se trouva presque nez à nez avec Audrey. La chambre était minuscule. Les deux portes fermées – celle condamnée de la coloc Juju, et l'autre donnant sur la cuisine – conféraient à l'endroit un caractère intime. Audrey considéra Adel avec stupeur, indiciblement ébranlée par sa visite. L'autre évitait toujours de croiser son regard. Il embrassa la pièce exiguë d'un coup d'œil ; l'endroit lui rappela quelques souvenirs.

La lumière était tamisée par un abat-jour. Les chandelles créaient une ambiance chaleureuse. Réalisant qu'elle n'était vêtue que d'une veste de pyjama, Audrey se pressa d'enfiler des shorts. Le geste sembla bouleverser son visiteur qui, jusqu'ici, était demeuré étrangement silencieux.

Comme si, prenant conscience de son intrusion, il avait oublié la raison même de sa venue. Et ce qu'il voulait lui dire. Audrey lui paraissait plus belle que jamais. Elle ne portait pas de soutien-gorge. Il lui était facile de deviner le contour de ses seins à travers le tissu léger de sa chemise de nuit. Ses cheveux courts ébouriffés avec ses quelques mèches éparses tombant sur son visage et la petite gemme nichée dans la chair de son nez lui donnaient un charme irrésistible. Adel en était déstabilisé. Pas seulement par son physique – il est vrai toutefois qu'on est affecté par le physique et l'apparence des gens beaucoup plus qu'on aimerait l'admettre – mais aussi par tout ce que cette femme avait représenté pour lui. Jamais de sa vie une personne n'avait exercé autant de pouvoir sur lui. Audrey avait été sa première vraie blonde, celle qui l'avait initié aux premières fois, celle qui l'avait rendu ivre d'amour. C'était une personne libre qui contrastait avec l'univers rigide et patriarcal dans lequel il avait grandi, régi par toutes sortes de règles, de conventions et de responsabilités. Univers dominé, aussi, par une crainte constante de sortir des sentiers battus. Comme si toutes ses pensées avaient été, jusqu'alors, harnachées par la nécessité d'une vision rationnelle et intelligible du monde. Tel avait été le legs de son père, sceptique à toutes les fantaisies qui menaçaient la rationalité du jugement – en l'occurrence, toutes les formes d'art. Son approche par résultats, couplée à sa détermination, avait réussi à sortir la famille de la pauvreté. Adolescent, Adel avait été constamment rappelé à l'ordre pour le moindre écart de conduite, confiné à l'intérieur du commerce les soirs et les week-ends. Pour y apprendre, à la dure, que la vie est un combat et qu'elle se gagne à la sueur du front. Voilà pourquoi Audrey lui avait semblé si belle, si parfaite, si libre, au premier regard : comme si elle faisait ça sans effort.

Cette fille-là, dont il avait encore du mal à accepter tout l'amour, avait été sa lumière, sa bouffée d'oxygène. Elle avait réussi à tordre l'armature de sa raison jusqu'à faire exploser la chape de béton qui obstruait son esprit. Audrey avait apporté de la poésie dans sa vie. Il avait cette dette imprescriptible envers elle. Il l'aimait comme un fou, en dépit de tous leurs récents déboires. Ce qu'il n'osait s'admettre, tellement sa propre vulnérabilité lui était gênante.

Audrey remarqua son trouble ; la chose attendrit son cœur. Adel dégoulinait de partout, avait passé plus d'une demi-heure sous la pluie à se demander s'il devait frapper ou non à sa fenêtre. Et pourtant, maintenant qu'il était ici, maintenant qu'il avait atteint son objectif, il semblait perdu.

— Je suis venu... suis venu pour... bégaya-t-il.

Il fit un tour sur lui-même, comme pour trouver où s'asseoir. Là, juste derrière lui, il vit une chaise couverte de vêtements. Il tassa les habits d'un geste du bras, et s'affala sur le siège. Il était essoufflé ; son corps, recroquevillé vers l'avant. Leurs regards finirent par se croiser et quelque chose comme une magie s'opéra. La peur s'estompa. La colère s'évanouit. Le grand fossé qui les séparait se résorba d'un coup. Comme si leur amour n'avait souffert d'aucun manque, comme si aucun verni n'avait craqué, comme si leur unité était redevenue parfaite, indissociable.

Entraînée par un élan d'amour et de compassion, Audrey osa une main vers son homme insécure. Il avait maigri depuis la dernière fois. Ses ecchymoses avaient disparu, mais la fatigue avait creusé son visage. Son oreille commençait à se cicatriser. Elle caressa ses cheveux et s'agrippa à ses boucles. Soudain, il la saisit par le bras et l'attira jusqu'à lui. Audrey poussa un cri, se retrouva aussitôt assise sur ses genoux. Ils échangèrent un bref regard qui, sans crier gare, révéla la profondeur de leur déchirure, un abîme dont le fond n'est autre que l'âme de l'être aimé, s'offrant l'un l'autre un moment d'éternité. Leurs lèvres s'effleurèrent puis, comme si c'était mektoub, ils s'embrassèrent d'un baiser qui leur rappela les premiers temps de leur histoire d'amour.

Ils se donnèrent en partage ce qu'ils avaient de plus intime, leur douleur et leur manque. Leurs mains redécouvrirent une chair longtemps laissée pour compte. La lumière des chandelles dansa sur leur peau. Leurs corps ne firent plus qu'un avec l'univers entier. Et leurs bouches exhalèrent des soupirs de jouissance qui se mêlèrent au rythme des tambours battants de *DJ Conscious Mind*.

Adel se réveilla en sursaut, flambant nu. La musique s'était arrêtée. Une main caressait ses cheveux. Il s'était assoupi dans les bras d'Audrey. Réalisant l'heure qu'il était, il se leva pour enfiler ses vêtements.

— Qu'est-ce qu'il y a ? Tu pars déjà ? lui demanda Audrey, incrédule.

— Oui, je dois partir.

— Mais où ?

— Chez moi... dit-il en agrippant ses pantalons.

— Mais reste un peu !

— Peux pas... grosse journée demain, rétorqua-t-il avec un zèle excessif.

Audrey sourcilla.

— La job ?

Adel s'était rassis sur le bord du lit pour enfiler ses bas, son corps dans un angle pour éviter de croiser les yeux d'Audrey.

— Non... autre chose, répliqua-t-il à voix basse.

— Quoi ?

Audrey se redressa, prenant soin de dissimuler sa nudité sous les couvertures.

— Un grand coup, ajouta-t-il de la même voix.

— Quoi ? Mais parle plus fort, j'entends rien ! s'écria-t-elle en se hissant à sa hauteur. Adel se leva d'un bond comme pour esquiver la question, mais c'était peine perdue.

— Je suis sur un grand coup, j'ai dit.

Audrey écarquilla les yeux, sidérée. Un silence troublant plana dans la pièce, comme si l'un et l'autre craignaient la suite. Audrey ne comptait pas lâcher le morceau. Adel avait beau regretter de s'être échappé, il comprit pertinemment qu'il serait inutile de résister davantage. Il se mit à arpenter l'espace exigu, de long en large.

— Ce que je vais te dire est top confidentiel... Je peux te faire confiance ?

Audrey replaça une mèche derrière son oreille criblée de piercings et acquiesça d'un mouvement de tête.

— Je compte *me faire* la maison d'un développeur d'armes, souffla-t-il en plaçant une main en cône autour de sa bouche.

— Un développeur d'armes ?

— Chuuut... pas si fort ! siffla-t-il entre ses dents.

— Un fabricant d'armes, tu veux dire ?

— Il fait plutôt dans les robots tueurs, laissa-t-il tomber avec une étonnante désinvolture.

— De... quoi ?

Adel soupira.

— Il conçoit des programmes informatiques et des logiciels pour engager des cibles et les abattre, automatiquement. Comme ça, pouf ! Sans intervention humaine.

Audrey écarquilla les yeux.

— OK... et tu veux faire quoi avec sa maison, au juste ? Un méchoui ?

— Non, plutôt la cambrioler.

— La cambrio... ? M-mais pourquoi ?

Sa question demeura quelques secondes en suspens. Elle arborait un air interrogateur. Elle tendit une main douce vers lui.

— Attends-là, peux-tu tenir en place deux secondes ? On vient juste de faire La Grange ! Qu'est-ce qui te crinque de même ? Elle le scruta du regard comme pour percer sa carapace. La claque que tu t'es prise sur la gueule ? s'échappa-t-elle.

— Reviens pas là-dessus, rugit Adel, les yeux injectés de sang. J'ai pas envie d'en parler !

Un silence glacial s'ensuivit.

— OK OK, calme-toi. J'voulais pas te vexer.

— C'est rien... c'est juste que... j'ai pas envie d'en parler tout de suite, maugréa Adel.

Audrey enfila sa veste de pyjama.

— OK. Ben euh... C'est quoi l'affaire ? Tu veux cambrioler sa maison ? Tu penses qu'il garde ses logiciels chez eux ?

— Pas mal sûr que j'vais en trouver dans son ordi. J'ai juste besoin d'un accès physique à son matériel.

Les yeux d'Adel brillaient. Elle sentit un frisson la secouer. Était-il devenu fou?

— Et tu comptes faire quoi, après ?

— Les fuiter.

— Les... ? Mais fuiter quoi, au juste ?

— Leur code source... Sur le web, j'veux dire! Divulguer dans les moindres détails leur architecture, pour que le monde réalise enfin de quoi il retourne ! répondit Adel avec entrain.

Il s'arrêta un moment pour jauger ses paroles. Audrey était de glace. Il poursuivit, gesticulant avec ses mains.

— Et puis, au cas où t'aurais pas encore compris, avança-t-il prudemment, fuiter ces logiciels reviendrait à les détruire. Une fois leur code source révélé, ces programmes deviennent complètement inutilisables, fit-il en écartant les bras.

Audrey porta une main à son front. Elle ne comprenait pas où Adel voulait en venir.

— Et pourquoi est-ce qu'ils deviennent inutilisables, ces codes ? murmura-t-elle, comme prise de vertige.

— Secret militaire classifié, éventé, tout simplement, répondit Adel en haussant les épaules.

D'un geste du doigt, il déverrouilla l'écran tactile de son bracelet électronique, et se mit à clavioter dessus, tout en monologuant :

— Aucun pays au monde ne veut révéler l'architecture logicielle qu'il emploie pour traquer et tuer ses ennemis, tu vois? Et puis, quel développeur voudrait exposer à la critique des médias les cibles qu'il tient dans sa mire ? Regarde : c'est lui.

Il s'accroupit à la hauteur d'Audrey, tendit vers elle l'écran de son bracelet. Il fit défiler une à une les pages du navigateur, où apparaissait Daryl Thomassen. Tantôt derrière un lutrin, tantôt serrant la main d'un ministre, tantôt posant devant un drone militaire et un drapeau du Canada. Audrey zooma avec son pouce et son index. L'image montrait un grand gaillard, d'apparence plutôt jeune et flegmatique. Des articles détaillés accompagnaient les photographies de l'homme d'affaires. Une ombre passa sur son visage.

— Crois-moi, si ça marche, c'est vraiment le coup du siècle ! clama encore l'autre, avant d'échapper un rire sardonique.

Le visage d'Audrey s'était détourné pour ne pas avoir à affronter son regard. Au bout d'un moment, elle finit par demander sur un ton faussement détaché :

— Il habite où, ce Thomassen ?

— Ici, à Montréal, répondit prestement Adel, qui n'avait pas encore remarqué le trouble d'Audrey.

— Où ça, à Montréal ?

— Westmount, sur la montagne.

Audrey sursauta. Était-il tombé sur la tête pour imaginer un coup pareil ? L'homme était puissant. Le quartier, des plus cossus. Sa maison, une vraie forteresse ! Le risque de se faire prendre était majeur. Les conséquences à donner froid dans le dos.

— Et pourquoi lui, spécifiquement ? se hasarda-t-elle.

Adel s'était relevé, avait repris ses allers-retours nerveux dans la petite chambre.

— Le fédéral s'apprête à signer un gros contrat pour l'achat de ses armes... de ses logiciels, j'veux dire. Des modules programmables de vision artificielle pour drones de combat. *Ils* veulent s'en servir en Iran. La Turquie prévoit aussi en acheter une bonne vingtaine, selon ce que j'ai pu lire. Le pays n'a pas spécifié pourquoi, mais je parierais que c'est pour bombarder les populations kurdes, le long de la frontière syrienne, déclara-t-il avec aplomb.

— Les populations kurdes ?

— Oui, kurdes, confirma Adel en zieutant la bibliothèque au fond de la pièce.

— Mais comment sais-tu tout ça ? Qui t'a donné son adresse ? lui demanda-t-elle soucieuse.

— Je suis tombé dessus par pur hasard, résuma-t-il, évitant de s'aventurer dans les détails. Il avait le regard perdu dans un livre, pigé sur une étagère.

— Par pur hasard ?

— Oui... Le mec est un client de ma boîte... lâcha-t-il en étouffant un rire nerveux.

— Mais t'es malade, ou quoi ? s'exclama-t-elle. T'imagines si tu te fais pogner ? C'est toute ta vie qui prend le bord. Le réalises-tu, ça ?

— T'inquiète. Ils n'ont rien vu ; personne n'est au courant. Tout se passe comme si de rien n'était. J'en suis moi-même surpris. Ça doit être le destin... Et si tu veux vraiment savoir, ma vie n'a jamais eu autant de sens qu'aujourd'hui, répliqua Adel.

Il remit le livre à sa place. Ses yeux scintillaient. Sa riposte laissa Audrey pantoise. Il s'approcha de nouveau d'elle et, pointant d'un doigt accusateur l'écran de son bracelet connecté, il reprit avec fougue.

— Ces personnes sont responsables de tellement d'injustices et de destructions. Mais, regarde : leurs vies sont complètement banales ! Ils s'enrichissent sur le dos des contribuables. On coupe à répétition dans les services. Pourquoi, tu penses ? Pour financer l'armée. Enrichir les compagnies. Sécuriser des intérêts stratégiques dans le Moyen-Orient. Déposséder les peuples de leurs ressources naturelles. C'est dégueulasse ! Tu vois pas que ces gens sont la racine du mal ?

— Mais depuis quand tu t'intéresses à... commença Audrey, avant de se faire interrompre.

— Pendant longtemps, je me suis demandé d'où venait ma souffrance, enchaîna-t-il sur un ton plus songeur. Je voyais bien que j'avais des angoisses, des nœuds intérieurs qui m'empêchaient de vivre pleinement... Comme toi, comme tout le monde, tu vois ? Mais d'où venait ce mal ? C'est *en faisant mes recherches* que j'ai compris que ma souffrance venait d'un *autre temps*, déclara-t-il comme sur le point de vivre une épiphanie.

— Un autre temps ?

— Oui, mes ancêtres, victimes d'un génocide... nié jusqu'à ce jour ! avança-t-il hardiment en se rassoyant à côté d'Audrey.

— Un génocide ? Mais de quoi tu parles ? reprit-elle, ébahie.

— Le génocide kurde ! s'écria Adel. En Turquie, en Syrie, en Iran et en Irak ! tonna-t-il encore pour en souligner l'évidence.

Audrey fronçait les sourcils, désemparée.

— Je comprends, je comprends, Adel... fit-elle sur un ton conciliant, empreint de culpabilité blanche. C'est juste que... je veux pas mettre en doute ce que tu dis, mais tu m'en as jamais parlé, et je savais pas à quel point cette cause te tenait à cœur...

— Elle m'a toujours tenu à cœur, clama-t-il d'une voix forte, mais indulgente. Ce n'était pas un reproche dirigé contre Audrey, mais plutôt contre l'absurdité de son existence.

— Sauf que... j-je m'en étais jamais rendu compte, laissa-t-il tomber, tout en réalisant le ridicule de la chose. Il rougit.

Au fond, raisonna Audrey en son for intérieur, elle n'était qu'une blanche bien née qui ne pouvait pas comprendre *toutes ces choses* – combien de fois le lui avait-on répété ? Il est vrai que, contrairement à elle, Adel avait toujours souffert d'une profonde ambiguïté identitaire. Il s'était toujours senti perdu, exclu du monde. Ce mal le rongeait de l'intérieur. Comme si, d'après lui, il n'avait jamais été à la hauteur du passé dont il avait hérité. De là à vouloir se lancer dans une mission suicide, Adel avait certainement disjoncté, elle le sentait, le voyait.

— Écoute, si c'est à cause de ce qui s'est passé l'autre soir, sache que j'ai coupé les ponts avec Maximilien et que...

— Mais de quoi tu parles ? s'écria Adel d'une voix fêlée. De quoi tu parles ? Ça n'a aucun rapport... aucun rapport, répéta-t-il, comme un perroquet.

Son regard avait brusquement changé. Le sang martelait ses tempes. Audrey eut un mouvement de recul, tandis que l'autre crispa les poings. Un silence pesant, que seule la respiration d'Adel troublait, envahit la pièce.

— Veux-tu qu'on en parle ? insista Audrey, préférant crever l'abcès.

Adel répondit par la négative en levant sa main droite. Ses lèvres remuèrent. Il vint pour dire quelque chose, mais semblait avoir besoin de se ressaisir.

— Te rappelles-tu, quand on était plus jeunes ? Tu me disais tout le temps : « Trouve-toi une cause à laquelle tu tiens, défends là jusqu'au bout, et je serai là pour la défendre avec toi... », reprit-il, avec des trémolos dans la voix. Sa vue s'était embrouillée, une larme perla sur ses joues.

— Hé bien, j'ai trouvé ma cause ! trancha-t-il avec émotion.

— Ta cause ?

Adel s'agitait dans tous les sens.

— Regarde-moi deux secondes, lui intima-t-elle. Prends le temps de décanter La Grange ; c'est vrai qu'on y est parvenu grâce à toi — mais en équipe. Là, t'es seul, pis pas préparé. Tu vas te faire prendre comme un épais pis passer le reste de tes jours en prison !

— Je sais ce que je fais !

— Vas-y pas, j't'en prie ! supplia Audrey, à court d'arguments. Elle enlaça spontanément son cou. Regarde, je t'aime... lui dit-elle en l'embrassant. Adel n'offrit point de résistance. Leurs corps se fusionnèrent à nouveau. Ils échangèrent plusieurs baisers. Adel se dégagea de son emprise puis bondit hors du lit.

Déjà, il enfilait ses chaussures.

— Attends ! Où vas-tu ? s'exclama Audrey.

— Je dois partir, trancha-t-il catégoriquement.

— Reste un peu ! l'implora-t-elle.

— Je vais la faire seul, s'il le faut, cette mission !

— T'es con ou quoi ? Qu'est-ce tu veux prouver ? ! Tu veux la gloire, c'est ça ?

Adel demeura impassible. Il se dirigea vers la fenêtre par où il était entré, échangea un dernier regard avec Audrey, mais le courant ne passait plus.

— Désolé de t'avoir dérangée, laissa-t-il tomber.

— Attends, pars pas ! lui cria Audrey en se rhabillant pour se lancer à sa poursuite.

Trop tard. Adel avait bondi hors de la pièce, s'était évanoui dans la nuit.

Audrey referma la fenêtre derrière lui et soupira. Les bougies, entièrement consumées, s'étaient éteintes. Elle se laissa tomber sur le lit. Des éclats de rire fusèrent d'en bas. Ce devait être Bingo le trapéziste, qui faisait encore ses singeries. La soirée était encore jeune pour les circassiens. Elle éteignit les lumières, et tenta de dormir, mais n'y parvint pas.

Derrière la porte à droite, cette même porte qu'on croyait condamnée et qui donnait en réalité sur la chambre de Juju, funambule et tatoueuse de métier, se trouvait Juju en personne. Pendant tout ce temps, elle avait épié la conversation. Comment ? C'est qu'un peu plus tôt, elle était montée dans sa chambre, ne se sentant pas d'humeur, elle non plus, à partager une soirée en compagnie des circassiens. De sa chambre, qui donnait aussi sur l'extérieur, elle avait entraperçu Adel se faufilant dans la cour pour venir frapper à la fenêtre d'Audrey. La scène avait piqué sa curiosité, à un tel point qu'elle était parvenue, sans faire de bruit, à déplacer le meuble qui obstruait la porte condamnée pour tendre l'oreille. La conversation qu'elle avait entendue lui parut fort intéressante, d'autant plus qu'elle avait eu vent, plus tôt cette même semaine, de l'incident survenu entre Adel et Maximus. À plusieurs reprises, durant la soirée, elle voulut intervenir pour mettre en garde sa coloc contre son ex impulsif. Par souci de pudeur, elle n'avait osé s'immiscer dans leurs conversations. Juju s'était toutefois promis de revenir sur le sujet, dès que l'occasion s'en présenterait. Malheureusement, dans les heures et les jours qui suivirent cet incident, elle n'en eut pas la chance. Quels ne furent donc pas sa surprise et les regrets immenses qui tourmentèrent Juju, suite au drame qui allait s'accomplir.

Ce n'est que bien plus tard, dans le cadre du procès Salem, pendant lequel elle fut appelée à témoigner, qu'elle livra à la cour tous les détails de cette tumultueuse soirée, qui allaient précipiter les évènements tragiques que nous nous apprêtons à dévoiler.

La pluie s'était calmée. Adel décida de remonter la 20e avenue pour rentrer chez lui. Il marchait d'un pas régulier. D'Audrey, il ne songeait plus que comme à une chose abstraite. « Drôle », songea-t-il. Combien de fois avait-il quêté ses caresses, cherché son assentiment. Désormais, ça lui était égal. Il n'existait plus pour elle – ni pour personne, d'ailleurs. C'était, en quelque sorte, ce qu'il avait cherché à confirmer en allant la retrouver. Il était bel et bien aux commandes de sa vie, et plus personne – absolument personne – n'allait lui dire quoi faire ni quoi penser. « Trace ta propre voie », se plut-il à radoter, comme retournant un bonbon dans sa bouche.

Traversant la rue Villeray, il vit un petit parc à sa droite, et décida de s'y asseoir pour laisser décanter ses idées. Il palpa ses poches, réalisa qu'il avait un peu de haschich et du papier. Il sortit le tout et commença la préparation d'un joint, en égrainant la petite boule résineuse contre ses genoux.

— Ah ces êtres humains, toujours à vouloir fuir la réalité ! lui lança cavalièrement le gros grillon qui refit son apparition, sans crier gare.

— Encore toi ? Mais vas-tu bien finir par me laisser tranquille ! s'exclama Adel Salem, qui aurait bien voulu chasser l'insecte d'un coup de pied, mais qui demeura immobile de peur de faire tomber son précieux kif au sol.

— Vous n'avez pas le courage de voir la réalité en face. Vous vivez dans vos mondes d'illusions, créés sur mesure ! renchérit le grillon.

Adel essaya de se concentrer et fit aller ses pouces sur le papier pour compacter le mélange, ignorant les reproches de l'orthoptère. Or, Monsieur Grillon comptait bien se faire entendre, et se faire répondre ! Il s'approcha d'Adel Salem, tout en agitant ses antennes, puis entonna a cappella un air mélancolique.

> *Audrey, Audrey, ta bien-aimée,*
> *Il te faut l'écouter : abandonne ton idée*
> *Je t'en supplie, mon ami, je t'en conjure*
> *Un pressentiment de sinistre augure*
> *M'agite en cette nuit enchantée*
> *Où tout pourrait basculer*

— Ridicule, maugréa Adel. Tu sais même pas de quoi tu parles !

— Vraiment ? interrogea le grillon.

— Audrey et moi c'est fini. Je lui dois rien.

— Mais comment peux-tu dire une chose pareille ? Ne vient-elle pas de te dire qu'elle t'aime ? Et toi, Adel, serais-tu allé la retrouver si tu ne l'aimais pas ? Dis-moi la vérité.

— Je... je... bégaya le jeune homme.

— Écoute-moi bien, mon ami, car c'est un vieil insecte qui te parle, sorti du fin de fond de la terre, du plus profond de ses entrailles. Je viens de la nuit des temps pour annoncer aux Hommes les grands malheurs qui les guettent. Je te l'implore, mon ami. Ne sois pas entêté comme ce pharaon, que j'ai jadis connu. Ouvre ton cœur, embrasse ta vulnérabilité. Cours rejoindre Audrey pour lui dire que tu l'aimes. Elle t'attend !

Écœuré par les conseils du grillon, Adel Salem se leva brusquement pour écraser l'insolent insecte. Celui-ci parvint à s'échapper à temps, d'un bond spectaculaire. Il disparut dans la pelouse.

— T'avise plus de revenir me déranger ! s'écria Adel, au milieu de la nuit.

Le grillon rétorqua d'une stridulation dissonante.

Adel porta le joint à sa bouche. Il en alluma l'embout et tira quelques bouffées. Les cannabinoïdes entrèrent en action et lui procurèrent une douce ivresse. Ses tourments se dissipèrent. Il aimait cette méthode d'absorption du cannabis – par inoculation de la fumée – bien plus que toutes les autres, même si elle lui paraissait quelque peu archaïque. Il n'aimait pas les produits transformés vendus sous forme de pilules ou de gélules. Et l'absorption de la fumée lui donnait un *buzz* plus fort que celui des huiles et des atomiseurs oraux.

Adel se remit en marche. Arrivé à l'intersection de la vingtième avenue et du boulevard Crémazie, il s'arrêta. La route était peu achalandée. Les véhicules venant de l'ouest roulaient à grande vitesse. Leur débit était saccadé, régulé par les feux de circulation au coin du boulevard Saint-Michel. Lui vint en tête, à cet instant précis, le souvenir de l'incident de la semaine dernière, où la voiture dernier cri de Daryl Thomassen passa près de le faucher. Son salut in extremis, il le devait aux capteurs et à l'algorithme de pilotage automatique de la Volvo 360. Était-ce l'œuvre du destin ? Il interrogea le ciel, dans l'espoir d'en recevoir un quelconque signe, mais ne vit qu'un rideau noir tiré sur les mystères de l'univers. Il songea un bref instant à cet équipage d'astronautes égarés dans l'espace, entre la Terre et Mars, perdus à jamais dans un cosmos de silence et de roches. Allaient-ils rejoindre le cimetière des étoiles ? La décomposition de la chair était-elle possible dans l'univers ? La fraîcheur de la nuit ne lui apporta ni réponse ni réconfort. Son regard revint au trottoir, à la rue, aux voitures qui défilaient par moment à toute vitesse.

La vie avait-elle un but ? Était-elle plutôt soumise au hasard des choses ? Étions-nous comme des algorithmes, conçus et programmés dans un objectif bien précis ? Si oui, qui en était le programmeur en chef et quel était son dessein ? Toutes ses réflexions traversèrent le cerveau bouillonnant d'Adel, dont l'esprit altéré par le cannabis était chauffé à blanc. Une pensée lui vint en tête : si les algorithmes gouvernaient réellement nos vies, alors, le hasard n'y occuperait qu'une place minime, voire, inexistante. Tout serait, pour ainsi dire défini, préétabli d'avance. Ce qui expliquerait pourquoi Adel était ici, bien vivant, debout devant cette intersection, avec en tête le projet de défier l'ordre mondial. Depuis une semaine, les évènements lui semblaient se succéder avec une logique implacable. Cette séquence avait commencé par sa rencontre pour le moins insolite et inopinée avec Daryl Thomassen – un quidam travaillant dans l'industrie militaire, dont il n'avait jamais entendu parler jusqu'ici. Suivie, le soir même, par la subtilisation de ses données personnelles grâce à l'algorithme probabiliste qui détermina le début de la séquence de maintenance informatique du serveur de sauvegarde. Serveur qui – faut-il le rappeler – fut le centre d'intérêt de son stage l'été dernier ET sur lequel il avait, avec un collègue, bricolé un dispositif qui, actionné au bon moment, lui permettait d'ouvrir la caverne d'Ali Baba dans l'anonymat le plus total. Accédant ainsi aux fichiers administratifs de la compagnie Eagle Eyes Systems.

Pris séparément, tous ces évènements ne présentaient aucune signification particulière : ils semblaient même tout à fait banals. Mais mis bout à bout, dans un ordre précis, comme les axiomes d'un théorème, ils formaient une démonstration mathématique, signée CQFD. Un système d'équations complexes, posées et résolues par quelque singulier penseur. Dieu agirait-il à la manière d'un mathématicien ? Ou d'un programmeur ? Était-il l'Intelligence suprême régnant sur toutes les autres ? Pour Adel, cette perspective était envisageable et avait quelque chose de rassurant. Il était séduit par l'idée qu'il y ait une force le dépassant, une puissance bienveillante qui avait pu envisager, jusque dans les moindres détails, ce scénario sur mesure dont il serait peut-être le héros. Certes, le monde était sens dessus dessous. Le monde était chaos. Mais il n'était pas seul à l'affronter. Bien au contraire, cette force était là pour le guider. Il y avait un plan pour s'en sortir. Ce plan avait été élaboré pour lui, et nul autre que lui. Pour autant qu'il puisse en décoder les signes, s'aventurer à suivre le programme. Comme si Dieu lui-même lui avait donné accès au code source de son existence, pour qu'il puisse en exécuter les instructions. L'idée qu'il puisse être investi d'une sorte de mission divine trouvait progressivement son chemin dans son esprit troublé.

De fait, devant le boulevard Crémazie qui longeait l'autoroute métropolitaine, où les voitures filaient à vive allure, une idée macabre lui vint en tête : pourquoi ne pas mettre son hypothèse à l'épreuve, en traversant cette route à l'aveugle au milieu des voitures en trombe ? S'il parvenait à traverser sain et sauf, ne serait-ce pas preuve suffisante d'un ordre cosmique déterminé en sa faveur, un signe fort de prédestination ?

Il réfléchit. Cette aventure pouvait raisonnablement lui coûter la vie. Était-il prêt à mourir ce soir, là tout de suite ? Peut-être que non. Advenant son succès, toutefois, il en aurait le cœur net, quant à la validité de son destin, et au bien-fondé de son entreprise. Il pesa le pour et le contre ; les voitures devant lui filaient à vive allure, certaines en

170

pilotage automatique, d'autres conduites par des humains. Les chances de survivre à une telle folie étaient minimes. Seulement, le but n'était-il pas justement de confronter la théorie du hasard ? « Mektoub », souffla-t-il à lui-même, avant de fermer les yeux et de prendre une grande inspiration. Il fit un pas sur la chaussée. « Mektoub ! », cria-t-il, cette fois, en direction des voitures, tandis qu'il enchaînait les pas à l'aveugle. Trois voies le séparaient de l'autre extrémité. « Mektoub ! Mektoub ! », gueulait-il encore dans le vide, comme pour vaincre la tentation d'entrouvrir les yeux, ne serait-ce que pour marcher droit. Jamais n'avait-on vu détermination plus effrayante.

Arrivé en plein milieu du premier couloir, il sentit le déplacement d'air des voitures, à quelques mètres de lui. Il s'arrêta un instant, hésitant entre poursuivre et faire demi-tour. « Mektoub, mektoub, mektoub », murmurait-il frénétiquement. Dix secondes s'écoulèrent ainsi. Dix secondes de cécité et d'immobilité qui furent inconcevablement rompues par un nouveau pas en direction des deuxième et troisième corridors. Une nouvelle salve de bolides fonça devant lui. Un premier klaxon retentit, puis un deuxième. Des pneus crissèrent. Une voiture passa à un centimètre de le faucher. Adel s'arrêta une seconde fois, sous l'effet de la surprise et de la frayeur, écartant ses bras comme un funambule. Ses lèvres remuaient toujours : « Mektoub, mektoub, mektoub ». Les phares l'éblouissaient, malgré ses yeux fermés. Les coups de klaxon déferlaient à tue-tête. Adel huma l'air, comme un animal égaré, avant de reprendre sa marche avec un étrange et sinistre entêtement. Pariant sur sa vie à chaque pas, comme un joueur de roulette russe ferait tourner un barillet. Un automobiliste en colère ouvrit sa portière pour s'adresser à lui. « Mektoub ! Mektoub ! », reçut-il en guise de réponse. Le conducteur fit un pas dans sa direction avant de retourner à son véhicule en lâchant une bordée d'injures.

Parvenu enfin de l'autre côté de la rue, Adel trébucha sur la marche du trottoir, et ouvrit enfin les yeux, ses dents claquant comme des castagnettes. Son cœur battait la chamade. Ses mains grelottantes parcoururent son visage, palpèrent son corps secoué de spasmes. Et pourtant son esprit voltigeait comme un oiseau, évadé de sa prison de codes, libéré de toute contrainte, comme si les colonnes de chiffres avaient volé en éclats. Son cerveau avait créé de nouvelles perspectives, brisé des lignes de fuites, ouvert de nouveaux horizons et ranimé l'espoir. Adel Salem était devenu poète. Un vertige le saisit. Il fit demi-tour et contempla la distance parcourue, hébété par le lugubre miracle accompli. La circulation avait repris ses droits. Les automobilistes fonçaient dans la nuit. « Mekkktttouuub! », hurla à nouveau Adel, cette fois de toutes ses forces, comme un cri victorieux adressé aux djinns du désert. Il garda ses bras ouverts et le regard braqué vers le ciel.

Une notification retentit. Il jeta un coup d'œil à sa montre : c'était Audrey. « T'es con, mais je t'aime » lui écrivait-elle. Puis l'instant d'après : « Je viens avec toi ».

Adel fondit en larmes. Le code de sa vie était sans faille. Le programme avait été exécuté parfaitement. Sa vie avait donc un sens. Plus jamais il ne remettrait en doute sa destinée. Sa mission, il allait l'accomplir avec tout le soin et la diligence requise pour assurer son succès. Et Audrey l'accompagnerait ; elle lui devait bien cela pour tout ce qu'elle lui avait fait subir. De ça, il en était résolument convaincu, comme d'une certitude mathématique. Comme le pendule revient toujours à son point d'équilibre. Comme la masse et l'accélération décrivent le parcours d'un objet en chute libre. Aucune trajectoire n'est le fruit du hasard. Elles sont toutes soumises à des forces qui nous échappent. Voilà que les astres s'étaient alignés. Leurs trajectoires avaient décrit pour lui un univers des plus cohérents, songea-t-il en reprenant la route vers son domicile, où il s'adonna, hébété, à des jeux vidéo violents jusqu'au petit matin. Ce n'est qu'après une masturbation nerveuse et molle qu'il parvint à s'endormir, l'esprit agité par le haschich et la lumière bleue de ses écrans.

LE SOIR DU JEUDI 17 JUIN 2032
(20 H 15)

La luxueuse et coquette résidence de Daryl Thomassen était située dans Wesmount, au 13 rue Summit, en bordure d'un bois homonyme donnant sur le flanc sud-ouest du Mont-Royal. Il l'avait acheté en 2030, à un philanthrope, président d'une firme en gestion d'actifs et fonds d'investissement. Répartie sur deux étages et un sous-sol, cette maison unifamiliale à façade de briques rouges comprenait quatre chambres à coucher, trois salles de bain, une immense cuisine, un salon et un charmant boudoir. Le spacieux garage, muni de bornes de recharge, pouvait accueillir deux véhicules électriques, et la cour, cet élégant jardin, avait été aménagée par un architecte paysagiste. Le prix qu'elle lui avait coûté à l'époque – 7,8 millions de dollars, incluant les frais de commission – lui avait paru un peu élevé pour cette maison qu'il considérait, somme toute, comme plutôt modeste. Sa femme Ashley Jones, jeune maman d'un bambin de trois ans, Angus Thomassen, était « tombée amoureuse » de l'endroit. La fenestration abondante et la vue imprenable sur la ville l'avaient conquise. Le bois Summit, véritable sanctuaire d'oiseaux et de fleurs sauvages, allait leur offrir d'agréables marches et de précieux moments de répit.

Daryl Thomassen avait pesé le pour et le contre. C'était le quartier où il avait grandi ; ses parents habitaient tout près, et pouvaient être d'une grande aide durant ses absences. D'autre part, la construction de la maison était relativement récente (1975) ; la fondation en béton était intacte ; la toiture avait été récemment refaite ; la plomberie et l'électricité pratiquement remises à neuf, la maçonnerie était, elle aussi, en bon état. Côté finances, ses affaires allaient bien, le projet Helios-Athéna avait le vent dans les voiles ; Skyline Solutions était devenue une entreprise internationale, dotée d'une clientèle principalement institutionnelle ; son chiffre d'affaires connaissait une croissance exponentielle. Afin de sécuriser l'achat de la maison et éviter qu'elle tombe entre les mains d'un autre acheteur, il avait bonifié son offre de quinze pour cent. Cette maison-là, avait-il songé : il l'achetait pour sa femme, pour son enfant, pour leur garantir une collection de souvenirs impérissables. Pour bâtir une famille, à vrai dire.

Née dans la ville d'Atlanta, en Géorgie, Ashley Jones avait été élevée dans une famille au conservatisme emblématique de la droite américaine. Son père, riche héritier d'une compagnie de construction spécialisée en terrassement et infrastructures, était un généreux donateur du parti républicain. Sa mère, de descendance franco-acadienne, avait été femme au foyer toute sa vie. Fille cadette d'une famille de trois enfants, Ashley Jones avait grandi avec deux frères aînés, en qui avaient reposé beaucoup d'espoir et d'ambition. Tout le contraire dans son cas ; d'Ashley, on n'avait attendu pratiquement rien de spécial, comme ce fut d'ailleurs le cas pour sa mère, quand elle était plus jeune. Attelés dès leur jeune âge aux affaires familiales, les deux frères avaient ainsi privé leur sœur, bien malgré elle, de leur compagnie. Le terrassement, les tractopelles et les camions, ça n'était pas une affaire de gamine. Du moins, dans cette famille soucieuse de son image et des traditions. Les poupées et les livres constituaient des passe-temps beaucoup plus convenables pour une bourgeoise. Ashley allait vivre une enfance plutôt solitaire, recluse dans une grande maison de banlieue, livrée aux bons de soins de sa maman qui avait à cœur la transmission du français cajun, langue pourtant réputée morte. C'est ainsi que, faute d'amis, se développa prématurément chez elle un imaginaire foisonnant de personnages féériques sortis tout droit des contes merveilleux dont elle se fit faire la lecture, dans la langue de Molière.

Plus tard, à l'école, Ashley Jones allait devenir une étudiante très calme et sans histoire. Le genre d'étudiante qui s'efface, qui n'élève jamais le ton, ne provoque aucun remous, ne témoigne d'aucune excentricité. Bref, une étudiante à qui l'on ne put rien reprocher. Même pas une crise d'adolescence. Des amis, elle en avait très peu, probablement rebutés par le port, tout au long du *high school*, d'appareils orthodontiques encombrants, pour corriger une dentition irrégulière, qu'aucune chirurgie ne parvint à rectifier. Elle détestait prendre des *selfies* et avait en horreur les réseaux sociaux, avec raison : à 14 ans, un groupe virtuel avait établi un palmarès des filles les plus laides de l'école et lui avait décerné la palme. L'expérience lui valut un trauma, bien que les coupables se soient repentis. De petit copain, elle n'en avait jamais eu. Elle en avait souffert, en secret. Puis, elle avait fini par s'y faire. Se résigner. Se forger une carapace. Elle n'était pas du genre à se lamenter *ad vitam aeternam*. Ses frustrations, elle les canaliserait à travers la littérature, qu'elle découvrit à un très jeune âge, grâce à sa maman, à son souci de défense de leur langue. Elle ne fit qu'une bouchée des romans qui se trouvaient dans la bibliothèque familiale qui, faute d'intérêt et pour dégager le passage, auraient fini à la poubelle s'ils n'étaient pas tombés entre ses mains. Elle fit déménager la bibliothèque dans sa chambre, où elle avait l'habitude de s'enfermer pendant des heures, mue par une furieuse envie de lire. À quinze ans, elle lisait aussi bien en français qu'en anglais. Toute l'œuvre de Charles Dickens, Mark Twain, Jack London et John Steinbeck y était passée. La collection complète des voyages extraordinaires de Jules Verne, aussi. Plus tard, ses goûts allaient évoluer. Emily Dickinson et Anaïs Nin devinrent ses meilleures amies. Leurs lectures se révéleraient une expérience mystique. La littérature allait la préserver de sa propre souffrance. Son bovarysme précoce l'avait sauvée, en quelque sorte.

Elle courait le monde à travers les livres. Un jour, elle vivait avec des loups, un autre, parcourait à cheval des contrées lointaines ; sautait dans un train vers l'inconnu ; prenait un coup avec des étrangers ; tombait en amour avec des brigands. À tout prendre, elle aimait la compagnie des personnages de romans bien plus que celle des êtres humains, qu'elle trouvait lassante et ennuyeuse. Les écrans, elle s'en éloignait le plus possible, grand bien lui fit. Son insociabilité ne manqua pas d'inquiéter ses parents. D'un autre côté, pensèrent-ils, elle excellait à l'école. Elle ne fumait ni ne buvait, elle ne fréquentait pas les vilains garçons ni ne sortait avec les Noirs. Elle ne rentrait pas tard. Comparée aux ennuis que leur avaient coûtés les frasques des deux frères, la lecture boulimique de leur fille leur sembla représenter un moindre mal. Demeurait un seul problème à l'horizon : était-elle mariable ?

Qu'elle ne fût pas leur surprise lorsque Ashley Jones proposa d'aller faire des études à Montréal, au Canada. La nouvelle stupéfia. D'où pouvait provenir cette hardiesse. Aucune idée. Que voulait-elle étudier ? La littérature française. Soit. Une excentricité comme ça. Pourquoi pas ? Que pouvait leur importer ce qu'elle désirait étudier ? Que pouvait leur importer si c'était rentable ou non ? Tout le monde s'en foutait, de toute façon ; elle n'aurait pas besoin de travailler. La fortune familiale suffirait à l'entretenir toute sa vie. Même célibataire.

Les démarches administratives furent entreprises auprès de l'université McGill. Ashley Jones réussit haut la main les tests de compétences linguistiques. Papa Jones lui fit cadeau d'un luxueux condominium de trois pièces et demie dans Milton Park. En mai 2025, Ashley fut admise au programme de premier cycle en littérature, et s'installa à Montréal l'été de la même année.

La ville lui plut beaucoup avec sa canopée qui lui rappela celle de sa ville natale. Elle aima ses cafés, ses terrasses et ses nombreux restaurants aux offres alimentaires des plus variées. L'été, Montréal était une fête. La ville était pleine à craquer. Elle découvrit le Festival international de Jazz, les Francofolies et le Piknic Électronik. Pour la première fois, elle goûtait à la liberté. C'était grisant. Montréal n'était pas hautaine et froide, comme ces grandes villes américaines qu'elle avait jadis connues. Elle était plutôt souple et nerveuse, bourgeonnante de vie, invitante comme un fruit qui ne demande qu'à se cueillir.

Les cours commencèrent à l'automne et, avec eux, les lectures, les travaux et les examens. Ashley Jones découvrit une littérature québécoise foisonnante. On se délecta de son accent cajun, unique en son genre. La sympathie de ses collègues était sincère. Ses professeurs l'appréciaient pour la qualité de ses travaux et la pertinence de ses interventions. Ashley Jones vivait bien la distance avec sa famille. Elle prenait des nouvelles, une fois par semaine, échangeait régulièrement avec sa mère. De temps en temps, elles se faisaient un petit « *catch up* ». Pour une fois dans sa vie, Ashley Jones avait l'impression d'être appréciée à sa juste valeur. D'être aimée. Pour une fois dans sa vie, Ashley Jones avait le sentiment d'être au bon endroit, au bon moment.

C'est dans ces dispositions favorables qu'Ashley Jones fit la rencontre de Daryl Thomassen, l'automne de cette même année. Un vent frais commençait à balayer les rues de la ville. Le mont Royal arborait des couleurs flamboyantes. Dans les rues tombaient les feuilles rougissantes, tourbillonnant dans une valse mélancolique, plantant le décor parfait pour les âmes romantiques. Ashley Jones et Daryl Thomassen habitaient le même immeuble centenaire, ce dernier occupant un condominium légèrement plus modeste, à l'étage du dessous.

C'était un homme plus âgé qu'elle. Ashley avait dix-neuf ans ; Daryl en avait vingt-neuf. Grand, bien bâti et sportif, il sortait régulièrement dehors – beau temps, mauvais temps – en tenue de *spandex* pour faire son jogging. Lorsqu'ils se croisaient, ils échangeaient quelques brèves salutations. Ces face-à-face, presque quotidiens, ne laissaient ni l'un ni l'autre indifférent. Daryl Thomassen n'avait jamais vu sourire plus radieux que celui d'Ashley Jones, si bien qu'il ne put résister à l'envie de lui faire la cour. Ainsi, s'aventura-t-il à faire les premiers pas en invitant la jeune femme à une promenade sur le Mont-Royal.

Elle apprit de Thomassen qu'il était natif de Montréal. C'était donc un vrai Montréalais, mais un anglo, comme ceux qu'on trouve dans cette partie ouest de l'île. Son français était terrible. On pouvait raisonnablement défendre qu'elle le parlât mieux que lui. Daryl avait fréquenté le Bishop's College School, un collège privé anglophone, où il avait été pensionnaire. Il avait ensuite fait des études au MIT et y avait complété un master en intelligence artificielle. De belles perspectives d'avenir s'offraient à lui, mais il avait préféré revenir à Montréal pour y compléter un doctorat. Son directeur de recherche bostonnais l'avait référé à un professeur désireux d'encadrer sa thèse, à McGill. Daryl aimait Montréal. C'était sa ville natale – il n'y avait pas plus belle métropole en Amérique du Nord, selon lui. Il aimait les francophones, les trouvait sympathiques, même s'il ne parlait pas le « *French* ». En outre, Montréal était reconnue comme l'une des capitales mondiales de l'intelligence artificielle, son domaine d'étude. Son département était tout proche du sien, au coin des rues Milton et University.

Daryl Thomassen venait d'une famille très fortunée, mais pas comme elle. Médecins radiologues, ses deux parents avaient fait carrière au Jewish General tout en exerçant dans le privé. Ils habitaient « sur la montagne ». C'étaient donc des bourgeois tandis que ses parents, à elle, se réclamaient d'une certaine aristocratie. Au fil de leur promenade qui fut agrémentée d'un chocolat chaud au Pavillon du Lac-aux-Castors, Ashley Jones découvrit qu'elle partageait beaucoup de points en commun avec Daryl Thomassen. C'était en plus un homme brillant, ouvert d'esprit, avec beaucoup d'ambition, remarqua-t-elle.

De retour chez eux, Daryl Thomassen lui avait proposé de prendre un verre chez lui ; Ashley avait accepté. Daryl avait opté pour l'artillerie lourde ; il avait ouvert le Porto. Le tout avait débuté par une petite coupe puis, mine de rien (le vin était excellent), ils consommèrent la bouteille au complet. Enivrés d'alcool, fascinés l'un par l'autre, l'ambiance s'était réchauffée. Tous deux s'adressaient œillades complices et rictus coquins. Sentant sur elle le désir manifeste de Thomassen, sensation tout aussi excitante qu'effrayante, Ashley Jones ne put réfréner quelques gestes furtifs pour dissimuler ce sourire gingival qui lui faisait honte, innocente coquetterie qui acheva de conquérir le cœur de Thomassen. Émoustillé, il avait pris ses mains et, pour la rassurer, l'avait regardée tendrement. « Jamais de sa vie n'avait-il connu d'aussi belle, d'aussi désirable femme qu'elle. » Il était sérieux. Sincère. Ne « disait pas ça pour lui faire plaisir ni dans l'unique but de coucher avec elle », la rassurait-il vertueusement. À ce stade-ci, Ashley Jones se foutait royalement de ce que Thomassen voulut juste la baiser ou qu'il entretint à son égard des intentions plus nobles. Elle ne demandait que ça : se sentir désirée. Elle espérait qu'il la prenne, avait multiplié les signes révélant son appétit sexuel, en vain. Trop gêné peut-être ou pas encore assez saoul, Daryl n'osait faire le saut, préférant tourner autour du pot. Un vrai *geek*, projeta-t-elle. La tension érotique devint à ce point intenable, qu'à la dernière gorgée de Porto, Ashley Jones dégrafa d'un coup la chemise de Daryl Thomassen pour se jeter sur sa robuste poitrine.

Les débuts de la relation laissèrent présager un bel avenir. Sincère, charnel, tendre et exclusif, leur amour semblait jaillir d'une source intarissable. Il est vrai pourtant que leur différence d'âge attisa son lot de préjugés et de regards indiscrets. Rien, toutefois, pour ébranler la force de leurs sentiments réciproques.

Financièrement indépendants l'un de l'autre, bénéficiant chacun de généreux dons de leurs parents, ils vivaient sans autre souci que celui d'étudier, de s'aimer et de profiter de la vie. Comme seuls les fortunés de leur acabit peuvent le faire. Mangeant aux meilleures tables, s'offrant de petites escapades à New York et Paris, profitant plus souvent qu'à leur tour de petits chalets loués au bord d'un lac dans les Laurentides.

Ils emménagèrent ensemble à l'été 2026, dans un condominium plus spacieux, distribué sur deux étages et une mezzanine. Daryl vendit son condo pour lever le capital nécessaire à l'achat de cette nouvelle propriété, tandis qu'Ashley déserta le sien, tout simplement. Sa mise en vente au prix de 1,5 million de dollars étant une aventure administrative trop compliquée à gérer à distance pour M. Jones, le patriarche fournit, à même sa poche, le capital nécessaire pour accoter la mise de fonds de Thomassen. Afin que « ses deux enfants puissent concrétiser leur rêve de vivre ensemble. »

Monsieur et Madame Jones aimaient Daryl Thomassen de tout leur cœur. À dire vrai, la différence d'âge les avait d'abord troublés. Cela dit, Daryl Thomassen était de race blanche et de famille chrétienne ; c'était un parti tout à fait respectable, tout à fait présentable. Du reste, Thomassen était un homme sérieux et travaillant.

Ils avaient eu l'occasion de faire connaissance à quelques reprises. De disputer, même, une ou deux parties de golf au East Lake Golf Club d'Atlanta. M. Jones admirait le swing de Daryl Thomassen. Mais ce qui l'impressionna le plus, ce fut les recherches savantes que conduisait son gendre, à l'époque, sur l'amélioration des capacités de vision artificielle pour la détection et le suivi d'animaux aquatiques à partir de la thermosphère. « Votre système peut-il détecter les islamistes à partir de la même orbite ? »

lui avait-il demandé ingénument. Daryl Thomassen s'était esclaffé, se gardant d'afficher son trouble. Il était soucieux de conserver la sympathie de ses beaux-parents. Il avait répondu par l'affirmative, précisant au passage que les facteurs limitants n'étaient ni d'ordre focal ni liés à l'architecture du réseau de neurones, mais bien à la capacité de calcul des processeurs, devant établir avec un taux de certitude suffisamment grand – dans un laps de temps suffisamment court – si le sujet d'observation était bel et bien un islamiste ou pas. Lorsque Thomassen lui demanda de préciser l'usage d'une telle fonctionnalité – la reconnaissance d'islamistes à basse altitude – M. Jones avait pouffé de rire en guise de réponse, et avait frappé sa balle au loin.

Un an s'écoula. Les études doctorales de Daryl Thomassen progressaient superbement. La bourse qu'il avait obtenue, du Fonds canadien de soutien à la recherche, lui avait ouvert plusieurs portes. L'une d'entre elles, incontestablement la plus importante, lui permit d'obtenir accès à un satellite de la Défense nationale, doté de tout l'arsenal optique nécessaire à la bonne conduite de ses expérimentations. Son algorithme de vision artificielle et reconnaissance d'images, baptisé Hélios, produisait des résultats très prometteurs. Les marges d'erreur étaient minimes. Le logiciel parvenait à distinguer un rorqual à bosse d'un rorqual commun ; un globicéphale d'une baleine noire, à partir d'une orbite de 300 km. Le suivi en temps réel de ces populations marines devenait désormais chose possible. L'évaluation par les pairs s'avéra un succès retentissant, si bien que la prestigieuse revue *Nature* fit de ses recherches la une de son numéro d'octobre 2027, vantant le potentiel de cette technologie dans l'évaluation environnementale des projets miniers et d'infrastructures. Thomassen avait dès lors acquis une renommée mondiale. Ses voyages devinrent plus fréquents. Les occasions d'affaires n'allaient pas tarder à se présenter.

Pendant ce temps, Ashley Jones poursuivait ses études en littérature française, envisageant d'entamer une maîtrise. Le sujet ? Elle ne le savait pas encore, mais son mémoire tournerait autour de la quête d'identité des femmes dans la littérature franco-louisianaise. Pourquoi ? Rendue là, Ashley n'aurait su dire. C'était comme si ce fût la seule voie qui se présentait à elle, la seule avenue qu'il lui fût possible d'envisager. Elle n'avait jamais travaillé de sa vie. Poursuivre dans la voie académique lui semblait couler de source. L'avenue du mariage aussi. D'ailleurs, Daryl Thomassen n'allait pas tarder à lui demander sa main. Proposition qu'Ashley Jones accepterait. Non pas tant par conviction profonde que Daryl Thomassen était l'homme de sa vie, mais plutôt parce qu'elle n'avait jamais connu l'amour avec d'autres personnes que lui.

Ils se marièrent à l'église, à l'été 2028, année où Ashley Jones obtint son diplôme universitaire. Le couple célébra son union au Golf Club. Une idée de M. Jones, qui en avait profité pour inviter quelques amis du parti. Un imposant cortège de voitures luxueuses et claironnantes avaient défilé sur East Lake Road, sous une canopée d'arbres aux feuilles colorées. La robe d'Ashley traîna sur la pelouse en une longue écharpe d'un blanc bientôt taché de chlorophylle.

C'est sous une grande tente dressée derrière le *clubhouse* que se tint la réception. Au design épuré et moderne du chapiteau blanc, s'ajoutait une décoration florale en arches de roses, d'orchidées et d'anémones sauvages. Des tables dressées pour deux cents convives furent garnies de vaisselles étincelantes et de chandelles élégantes, merveilleusement assorties. Un traiteur de la région proposa une carte des plus exquises. En entrée, plusieurs hors-d'œuvre ; confits de canard croustillant à la sauce framboise, tartelettes de crabes royaux à la coriandre et aux échalotes, et sashimi de sériole chicard aux avocats et à la sauce ponzu. Le second service offrit un choix de trois plats de rôt : truite montagnaise aux champignons shiitake et vinaigrette à la truffe noire, tournedos façon Rossini et salade du ramasseur au simple foie gras truffé, filet mignon de bœuf Black Angus servi avec courge musquée et estouffade de pommes de terre aux truffes. Enfin, le dessert se composa d'une variété d'entremets et de fruits qui, avec les cafés et les liqueurs, occupaient à eux seuls une table entière. Le gâteau nuptial fut impressionnant avec ses six étages glacés au citron meringué, arborant colonnades et statuettes en sucre et pâte d'amande à l'effigie des mariés. Le champagne coula à flots. On avait invité un quintette de jazz qui joua jusqu'à minuit. Après quoi, un DJ assura l'ambiance pour le reste de la soirée. Vers une heure du matin, les derniers invités se transformèrent en festivaliers. On sortit des bouteilles de fort, et la fiesta prit une autre tournure.

Ashley Jones avait supplié ses frères de lui épargner leurs plaisanteries. Ceux-ci s'étaient donc tournés vers leur beau-frère pour lui bander les yeux, et lui demander de frapper des balles de golf à l'aveugle. Deux balles avaient atterri dans le stationnement, l'une avait fracassé le pare-brise d'une Porsche ; l'autre avait endommagé la carrosserie d'une Mercedes. On remorqua à l'aide d'une voiturette de golf un ancien collègue de Daryl Thomassen, venu exprès de Cambridge pour assister à la cérémonie, qui s'était écroulé ivre mort, près de l'étang. On fit un feu de camp sur un *green* et organisa une course de karts qui se termina en séance d'autos tamponneuses. Le mariage avait coûté en tout et pour tout trois quarts de millions de dollars, incluant les frais occasionnés par les dégâts au East Lake Golf Club. Facture qui fut partagée sans sourciller entre les Jones et les Thomassen.

Deux jours après la noce, les époux rentrèrent à Montréal. Leur lune de miel aux Bahamas avait été repoussée : Daryl Thomassen devant prendre l'avion pour préparer une conférence qu'il tenait le surlendemain, à Tel-Aviv, dans le cadre d'un symposium international consacré aux systèmes de défense intelligents. Les mois qui suivirent furent très occupés pour Thomassen, l'illustre chercheur planchant déjà sur une variété de projets qui – compte tenu de leur rentabilité et des opportunités sous-jacentes – l'éloignaient de plus en plus de sa passion première, les mammifères marins. De son côté, Ashley Jones qui avait vu son sujet de maîtrise accepté dut y renoncer quelques mois plus tard. Elle était tombée enceinte, à la grande joie de son mari. Elle abandonna ses études, faute d'encouragement à les poursuivre.

Comme la vie avait vite passé ! Ce constat avait frappé Ashley Jones dans la piscine municipale, en pleine séance d'étirements aquatiques prénataux. Tandis que ses jambes moulinaient dans l'eau, elle avait l'impression de surgir d'un long sommeil. Comme si elle prenait conscience de son existence. Comme si toute sa vie, elle avait été en dormance. Que se passait-il ? Le vertige s'empara d'elle.

Judeline Duval, qui nageait tout juste derrière, remarqua son trouble et vint à son secours. Dans les vestiaires, Ashley ne manqua pas de lui exprimer sa gratitude et, pour la remercier, l'invita à prendre un café. Judeline y consentit, sans trop d'insistance. Elles s'attablèrent au comptoir d'un torréfacteur artisanal, commandèrent pâtisseries et cafés gourmands. Les deux femmes connectèrent ensemble comme des amies de longue date, bien qu'elles aient été de parfaites inconnues. Sans pouvoir se l'expliquer, Ashley Jones en vint à se confier, à raconter une enfance solitaire parmi les siens, sans autres amis que les bouquins et les personnages de fiction. Elle avait souffert du regard des autres. L'école avait été un enfer sur terre. Comme elle fut plongée dans le désarroi ! se souvint-elle. Pour seul refuge, des murailles de livres. Elle culpabilisait à ce souvenir. Qu'est-ce qu'un visage atypique, contraire aux diktats de la beauté, face à la misère du monde ? Aujourd'hui, cette peine de jadis lui semblait futile. Preuve que rien dans la vie ne lui avait manqué. Rien ne semblait l'avoir exhorté à un courage plus admirable. L'abondance avait fini par l'avachir avec les années. Fille entretenue par sa famille, Ashley l'était désormais par son époux qui, comme les siens, n'avait jamais cru en son potentiel, présumait-elle. Une conviction croissante commençait à la tourmenter : elle n'était qu'un ventre. Un ventre pour son mari, un ventre pour sa famille. Des enfants, c'est tout ce qu'on attendait d'elle. Des larmes lui montèrent aux yeux. Elle regrettait sa jeunesse perdue. Elle était tombée enceinte trop vite. D'un garçon, en plus ! Elle aurait préféré une fille. Elle l'aurait encouragée à être hardie et indépendante. Elle l'aurait trouvée belle et n'aurait pas manqué de lui répéter. Elle aurait eu une carrière, d'innombrables aventures et beaucoup d'amis. Elle aurait *fait quelque chose de sa vie*. Elle l'aurait nommée Charlotte, comme Charlotte Gainsbourg. Elle aurait été la revanche sur ses propres impuissances, sa grande amie, son alliée, sa complice de tous les instants. Le destin avait voulu qu'elle mette au monde un garçon qui, sans doute, allait requérir toute sa présence et son amour. Comment en vouloir à ce petit homme de désirer vivre avec sa maman une relation fusionnelle ? Saurait-elle l'aimer suffisamment ? Saurait-elle, à nouveau, sacrifier sa vie pour un autre être ? Tantôt, dans la piscine, cette idée l'avait foudroyée, au point qu'elle faillit se noyer.

Judeline Duval, qui en était à sa troisième grossesse, l'avait écoutée attentivement, sans dire un mot, savourant avec délectation l'amandine au chocolat qu'elle s'était fait offrir. Elle ne tombait pas de la dernière pluie ; ce n'était pas la première Blanche à venir vers elle pour épancher son trop-plein d'anxiété. À croire qu'elle les attirait toutes. Elle secoua les miettes de viennoiseries collées à son chandail, prit la main d'Ashley Jones dans la sienne, et lui dit que le courage viendrait en son temps. Qu'il ne fallait rien forcer. Du reste, elle la rassura : elle n'avait pas à ressentir ni honte ni culpabilité. Elle-même était passée par là, « en quelque sorte ».

Née Lamothe, Judeline Duval venait d'une famille de quatre enfants. Le tremblement de terre qui fit trois cent mille morts en Haïti avait réduit sa maison à un amas de gravats. D'un coup, elle avait perdu la moitié de ses oncles, tantes, cousins et cousines. « Dieu merci », ses parents et ses deux frères étaient sortis indemnes. Après une année à vivre dans des camps, elle avait atterri au Québec en 2011, grâce à un programme de parrainage. Sa famille était du lot. Judeline avait dix ans quand elle vit le Canada pour la première fois. Les premières années ne furent pas de tout repos. Le pays, l'hiver, la langue ; il fallait s'adapter. Son papa faisait chauffeur de taxi ; sa maman, ménagère dans un immeuble à condos. Tous deux bossaient, jour et nuit. Quant à ses deux frères, l'un devint prêtre. L'autre, cimentier. Judeline, elle, travaillait comme préposée aux bénéficiaires. Elle était mariée à un épicier et portait fièrement son nom. Celui-ci tenait une échoppe sur le chemin de la Côte-des-Neiges. Ensemble, ils vivaient avec leurs deux enfants et leurs beaux-parents dans un petit appartement du quartier Notre-Dame-de-Grâce. La vie n'était pas facile, mais ils s'en sortaient, bon an mal an.

Émue par tant de misères et de malchances, mais surtout par tant de résilience, Ashley Jones demanda à sa nouvelle amie, en toute humilité, en quoi toutes deux étaient passées par les mêmes épreuves, comme le laissait entendre la jeune mère haïtienne, quelques instants plus tôt ? Ashley avait l'impression, à juste titre, de venir d'une planète différente. « Le doute est universel, lui répondit Judeline, comme possédant une vérité infuse qui semblait convenir à presque toutes les circonstances. Comme un démon, il peut nous ronger. D'où l'importance d'accepter la volonté de Dieu. »

Quelque chose dans le sourire rayonnant de Judeline Duval lui fit l'effet d'une formidable gifle, ce qui n'était pas pour lui déplaire.

Judeline et Ashley passèrent beaucoup de temps ensemble, à la faveur des sorties succédant à leurs activités prénatales : cafés, musées, restos, boutiques. Au détour, Ashley fit connaissance avec la famille Duval. Leurs enfants étaient adorables. Le père, avenant et généreux. C'étaient des gens très modestes et pieux. S'y organisaient dans leur humble demeure de grands repas caribéens, les dimanches après-midi, après la messe. On chantait et priait ensemble. L'ambiance était joviale. Le griot était excellent. Le riz djon-djon, succulent. C'était une famille pleine de vie qui contrastait fortement avec la sienne. Pour la première fois de son existence, Ashley Jones se sentait entourée d'amis, de vrais.

Angus Thomassen, fils de Ashley Jones et Daryl Thomassen, naquit en parfaite santé, le 8 mars 2028, au terme d'une grossesse normale. Après le bonheur des premiers jours vint l'enfer du quotidien. Le bébé se montra criard et turbulent. Ses coliques semblaient incurables. Sa constipation, des plus sévères. Ashley rivalisait de créativité pour soulager cet enfant qui drainait toute son énergie. À cette lourde responsabilité, s'ajoutèrent les conseils de maternité non sollicités, à la pelle. Mme Thomassen, qui habitait à deux coins de rue, avait le don de lui en faire. Elle ne se gênait pas pour interférer dans sa vie, la gratifiant de visites surprises, à n'importe quelle heure du jour. Après les salles de radiologie qui avaient fait l'essentiel de sa carrière, la maternité était définitivement son domaine d'excellence, là où elle se sentait supérieure, là où elle entendait réaffirmer son autorité. Parce qu'après tout, elle était médecin. Elle avait « déjà eu Daryl ».

Galvanisé par le succès d'Hélios-1, Thomassen planchait déjà dès 2029 sur le développement d'une nouvelle version bêta, destinée à équiper les drones d'endurance MALE de type Athéna. Récemment incorporée, Skyline Solutions avait le vent dans les voiles. Les absences de Daryl devinrent plus fréquentes. Entretenait-il des maîtresses ? La question traversait bien sûr l'esprit d'Ashley. Étrangement, elle ne lui faisait ni chaud ni froid. Les rapports extraconjugaux de son mari ne semblaient pas l'inquiéter outre mesure. Celui-ci, d'ailleurs, semblait tout à fait innocent, ses intérêts davantage portés vers le business plutôt que les plaisirs charnels. C'était un véritable bourreau de travail reconnu pour son sens du devoir. Il vouait, d'autre part, une admiration sans bornes pour son beau-père et mentor, M. Jones, à qui il devait nombre de ses juteux contrats auprès de la US Navy et des US Marine Corps. Depuis, ses ventes avaient atteint de nouveaux sommets, accaparant tout son temps et son énergie.

Faute d'un mari pour partager ses journées, ses soirées, voire le même fuseau horaire, l'amour d'Ashley pour Judeline grandit au fil des ans, à mesure qu'inversement, il décrut pour Daryl. Comme si le besoin d'aimer son époux fut moindre. L'attirance pour lui, tant sur le plan affectif que sexuel, avait diminué au point de disparaître. Déjà un an qu'ils n'avaient pas fait l'amour ; elle n'en éprouvait ni l'envie ni le besoin. Et pourtant, la chose ne semblait pas la préoccuper – son partenaire non plus d'ailleurs. Trop absorbé par ses gadgets peut-être, Daryl ne vit pas la progressive dérive qui, lentement mais sûrement, achevait de rompre ses liens avec Ashley. Ainsi croyait-il vraiment que son achat, rue Summit, fut une bonne affaire. Rien dans l'attitude de sa femme ne lui avait laissé croire le contraire. Cette maison, s'était-il convaincu tout seul comme d'une chose évidente, allait prodiguer le luxe et le confort que sa femme méritait. Du reste, ses parents résidaient tout près. Ils seraient d'une précieuse aide avec l'arrivée de leurs enfants. Sa femme s'était montrée enthousiaste. Mais derrière ces apparences de bonheur se dissimulait un sentiment d'étrangeté, de plus en plus envahissant. Comme si tout à coup, Ashley Jones était tombée dans une errance existentielle et affective – trajectoire qui, jusque-là, lui était inconnue. Ashley Jones débutait un voyage qui allait l'amener à la découverte d'elle-même. Malheureusement pour Daryl, il ne sut lire entre les lignes. Il n'avait pas réalisé que sa femme avait changé. Et que le luxe et l'abondance dans lesquels elle avait grandi... lui puaient désormais au nez.

C'était un soir de janvier 2032. Ashley Jones, Daryl Thomassen et leur petit Angus rentraient d'Atlanta, où ils avaient séjourné quelques jours pour célébrer les fêtes de Noël en famille. Le voyage s'était avéré ordinaire. Angus, qui allait bientôt fêter ses quatre ans, était devenu un garçon turbulent, attiré par le goût de l'aventure, la découverte et les sensations fortes. Il affectionnait les jeux de guerre, les sports de combat, et avait la manie de se battre contre des ennemis imaginaires. Ses coups dans le vide étaient accompagnés de *kiais* japonais, qui n'étaient pas sans exaspérer sa maman. De ses grands-parents et de ses oncles, le petit Angus avait reçu d'innombrables cadeaux, parmi lesquels – au grand dam de sa maman – tout un arsenal de jouets de guerre : fusils, grenades, hélicoptères et mitraillettes aux effets sonores désagréables. Quant à Ashley, elle avait obtenu de son mari, en témoignage de son amour, un somptueux collier de précieux diamants, orné d'un solitaire à un carat, le tout niché dans un magnifique écrin de velours. Le cadeau avait suscité une vive réaction et, après être passé entre les mains de tout le monde, avait obtenu une approbation unanime. « Chanceuse » était le mot qui circulait sur toutes les lèvres à propos d'Ashley Jones. Elle avait mimé une joie contenue pour ne pas décevoir la galerie. Dans son for intérieur, elle avait été déroutée, voire troublée par ce présent qui ne résonnait aucunement avec ses valeurs et qui, par surcroît, ne présentait aucune utilité. Qui plus est, l'admiration sans bornes que vouaient ses parents à son mari l'horripilait. Daryl était devenu à leur image. Et elle, qu'avait-elle accompli ? Elle songea alors à tous ces livres qu'elle avait lus, portés par de véritables héroïnes. Une armada de femmes courageuses qui avaient lutté contre les déterminismes sociaux, pour s'affranchir, s'émanciper et *accomplir* des choses formidables. Pourquoi n'y était-elle pas parvenue, elle qui avait tout ? L'opulence avait fini par l'abêtir. Son sort aurait été tout autre si elle avait été obligée de prendre sa vie en main, songea-t-elle. Cette prise de conscience la consterna. C'était comme se réveiller au beau milieu du cauchemar qu'était devenue, pour elle, sa vie. Que dirait Judeline pour la consoler ? Son amie lui manquait terriblement.

De retour à Montréal, Ashley laissa retomber la poussière. Quelques jours passèrent ainsi, à lire, à écrire, à réfléchir, à verbaliser ses émotions. Elle se confia auprès de Judeline, qui l'écouta attentivement et qui lui conseilla de voir dans son agitation l'appel du Seigneur. Un soir, donc, bien décidée, elle alla trouver Daryl pour lui annoncer de but en blanc qu'elle désirait se séparer. Ce n'était rien contre lui, ni contre Angus, mais parce qu'elle avait « besoin de se retrouver ».

Daryl crut d'abord à une blague, tant il ne s'attendait pas à semblable nouvelle. Ils venaient de passer de belles vacances en famille ; aucune dispute n'avait éclaté ; son cadeau à huit mille dollars US avait fait l'unanimité ; tout le monde était rentré à la maison heureux et satisfait, lui sembla-t-il. Mais, au fur et à mesure qu'il interrogea sa femme, il devenait de plus en plus clair qu'Ashley ne blaguait pas – qu'elle était même très sérieuse.

Où allait-elle habiter ? s'enquit-il.

Dans son ancien condo de Milton Park. Le logement était laissé vacant, depuis que les derniers locataires l'avaient déserté en septembre dernier.

Très bien. Qu'allait-elle donc y faire ?

Elle ne savait pas encore, mais sa première idée était de reprendre les études, pour se lancer en traduction.

En traduction ?

Oui, en traduction *littéraire*.

Qui allait donc s'occuper du petit Angus, pendant son absence ?

Ils allaient trouver un arrangement pour se partager la garde du petit et au besoin, engager le personnel adéquat ; ce n'était plus à elle d'assumer cette responsabilité seule.

Daryl prétexta une crise passagère, comme celles que vivent tous les bons ménages. Selon lui, les choses allaient se replacer d'elles-mêmes, avec le temps. Ashley avait besoin de plus d'espace. Elle était encore jeune. Il était donc normal – selon des amis et collègues qu'il avait consultés à ce sujet – qu'elle prenne un peu ses distances. Qu'elle s'éloigne momentanément. Ne serait-ce que « pour mieux revenir ». Il ne fit pas grand cas de cette conversation, et poursuivit ses activités, comme si de rien n'était.

Qu'elle ne fût pas sa surprise lorsque, peu après le quatrième anniversaire du petit Angus, comme il se trouvait à Berlin sur un panel d'experts, Ashley lui annonça, sur WhatsApp, son désir de divorcer. Daryl Thomassen en tomba de sa chaise. Ce n'était pas à cause de lui, avait-elle assuré. C'était autre chose. Elle ne savait pas quoi, au juste. Mais cela rimait avec la nécessité de « refaire sa vie ».

Daryl proposa d'entreprendre une thérapie de couple, à son retour. Il promit de prendre le premier avion pour Montréal. Cela ne servit à rien. Ashley Jones n'entendait pas revenir sur sa décision.

Le soir du 17 juin 2032, donc, aux environs de 19 h 30, Daryl Thomassen rentrait chez lui en voiture, après avoir déposé le petit Angus chez sa maman. Plus tôt, il était passé le chercher à l'école, lui avait préparé à souper, et l'avait aidé avec ses devoirs.

Sur le pas de la porte, il avait tenté une fois de plus de lui faire entendre raison, à sa douce moitié, en vain. Devant sa mine basse et désespérée, Ashley Jones avait même trouvé à rire. Il s'en remettrait, l'avait-elle assurée. Après tout, ils avaient eu un enfant ensemble. Ils allaient demeurer complices. Privilégier la bonne entente. « Rester amis », pour le restant de leurs jours.

« Amis... » avait répété Daryl Thomassen, hébété, avant qu'elle ne referme la porte.

Il était donc de retour chez lui vers 19 h 30, ruminant des pensées moroses. La journée au boulot avait été très mauvaise. Les TI avaient repoussé deux attaques. Il fit un peu le ménage. Le téléphone sonna, c'était son vieil ami Mike, qui appelait pour prendre de ses nouvelles. Il avait eu vent de leur séparation.

— Un divorce ? ! s'était-il exclamé.

— Oui, un divorce, avait confirmé Daryl.

— Ah, les femmes... avait compati Mike. L'essentiel, observa-t-il, était qu'il ne se laisse pas plumer dans cette affaire. Les pensions alimentaires, la séparation des biens... il s'y connaissait. Lui aussi était passé par là. Il pouvait lui recommander un bon avocat.

Ce n'était pas nécessaire, avait rétorqué Daryl Thomassen.

— Comment, « pas nécessaire » ? s'était enquis Mike.

Ashley ne demandait rien du tout, avait laissé tomber, penaud, Daryl Thomassen. « Pas de pension. Pas d'argent. Rien. » Ils s'étaient tous deux entendus à l'amiable pour la garde de l'enfant, et puis c'est tout. Il espérait encore qu'elle revienne sur sa décision. Un silence se fit entendre. Dérouté, Mike enchaîna sur un autre sujet. Ils parlèrent ensemble du boulot, de la pluie et du beau temps, des Bruins de Boston. Daryl ne vit pas le temps passer.

À 20 h 33, il se rendit compte qu'il était en train de manquer l'heure du bain libre. Il raccrocha rapidement, empoigna son sac de sport, et se précipita vers son véhicule, stationné dehors. La piscine Memorial de l'université McGill était située sur l'avenue des Pins à une bonne dizaine de minutes de sa demeure, en voiture.

À 20 h 48 précises, alors que la Volvo 360 naviguant de manière autonome sur le chemin de la Côte-Sainte-Catherine entamait son virage à droite sur l'avenue du Parc, Daryl Thomassen reçut un appel téléphonique. C'était Ashley. Elle avait beau chercher dans les affaires d'Angus, elle ne trouvait pas son kimono pour le cours de karaté du lendemain. Avait-il oublié de glisser le vêtement dans le bagage du petit bonhomme ?

— Fort possible, répondit promptement Daryl Thomassen. Seulement il n'était pas à la maison pour vérifier. Il était en route vers la piscine. De retour chez lui, il pourrait jeter un œil dans le placard du petit, vérifier si le kimono y était. Il reviendrait le lui laisser, vers 22 h 30. L'heure était trop tardive pour Ashley. Elle tempéra les ardeurs de son ex-mari. Il n'était pas indispensable de récupérer le kimono ce soir. Il pouvait très bien passer le lui porter demain, dans le courant de la journée. Daryl insista pour le lui rendre ce soir ; l'enjeu lui semblait capital. Il proposa de faire demi-tour pour le lui livrer de suite. Il promit d'être à sa porte, avec ledit uniforme, dans une vingtaine de minutes, tout au plus. Soit vers 21 h 15.

Il raccrocha et commanda à la Volvo un nouvel itinéraire.

Cachés dans les fourrés en pente du bois Summit, étendus sur le dos à même le sol humide, Adel et Audrey attendaient. Le flanc du mont Royal, sur lequel ils reposaient, s'inclinait doucement, sans accroc, jusqu'à rejoindre plus bas les sentiers pédestres qui le sillonnaient, fréquentés par les riches riverains du quartier Westmount.

La main d'Adel fouilla le petit sac à dos en étoffe de nylon légère qu'il avait posé sur son ventre pour mieux l'examiner. Dedans, il y avait rassemblé tout le matériel nécessaire au succès de son opération. Il en sortit un micro-ordinateur piraté pour l'occasion, le même genre d'appareil à usage unique qu'il avait employé pour désactiver le système anti-intrusion de la boutique La Grange, dix jours plus tôt.

Il se connecta au réseau 7G ; la couverture était bonne. Le signal était relayé par une caméra cachée. L'appareil avait été discrètement installé trois jours plus tôt, à l'orée du bois, de l'autre côté de la rue. À son tour, la caméra (munie d'une carte réseau spéciale), relayait le signal d'un autre appareil du voisinage, qui à son tour, relayait le signal d'un autre, et ainsi de suite, formant une chaîne anonyme, un réseau distinct des services mobiles traditionnels.

Les images transmises par la webcam apparurent à l'écran. La résolution était mauvaise, mais la lumière s'échappant des stores lui permit de distinguer la silhouette de Daryl Thomassen. L'homme était vêtu d'un jeans et d'un t-shirt. Il parlait seul, faisant les cent pas dans son salon. Adel déduisit qu'il était en communication. Il vérifia l'heure – il était 20 h 19 – puis tourna l'écran vers Audrey pour qu'elle puisse voir.

— Son emploi du temps est assez régulier, remarqua-t-il à voix basse, battant l'air pour chasser les moustiques. Au travail, j'ai pu vérifier le registre de déplacements de sa e-Claw. Une semaine sur deux, le mec se rend à la piscine Memorial, situé tout près d'ici, en bas de la côte. Les mardis et jeudis. Le bain libre commence à 21 h.

— Comment peux-tu en être sûr, lui demanda Audrey, tout en se grattant l'avant-bras.

— Sûr ? Je ne suis sûr de rien, déclara Adel, sans ambages. Il ramena vers lui le micro-ordinateur.

— Les chances sont bonnes, c'est tout. Autrement, on ajournera.

— En tous cas, il n'est pas près de sortir, murmura Audrey, soulagée à l'idée de remettre la mission à un autre soir.

L'air était chaud et humide, malgré la nuit tombée. Ils attendaient là, camouflés, depuis une heure, repoussant la horde de moustiques voraces qui bourdonnaient autour d'eux. La moiteur était étouffante. Ils transpiraient, se grattaient. Leurs vêtements laissaient passer les bibites. Leur patience s'épuisait à mesure que les minutes s'écoulaient, Daryl Thomassen sortant tantôt du cadrage, tantôt le réintégrant.

À 20 h 30, Daryl Thomassen était toujours au téléphone, et il sembla à Adel et Audrey qu'ils perdaient leur temps. Sans doute était-il préférable de laisser tomber ; mieux valait revenir un autre soir. Mardi ou jeudi dans deux semaines, peut-être. Adel se résignait à cette option quand il vit les lumières de la maison s'éteindre. Daryl embarqua dans sa voiture puis s'en alla. La voie était libre !

Adel pianota sur le clavier de son micro-ordinateur, parvint en moins de deux à se connecter via VPN aux serveurs locaux d'Eagle Eyes Systems. Il avait créé le matin même un profil fantôme pour lui permettre cet accès, planifiant l'effacer à la première heure, le lendemain. Il accéda au profil Harmony+ de Daryl Thomassen, puis au panneau de commande numérique du système d'alarme de sa résidence. Enfin, il désactiva d'un simple clic les notifications, puis d'un autre clic, activa le mode « maintenance » du système, coupant ainsi toute communication entre la maison et les appareils électroniques de Thomassen. Une fois les commandes exécutées, Adel rangea l'ordinateur dans son sac, enfila sa cagoule et ses gants. Il n'y avait pas une minute à perdre.

Audrey suivit Adel jusqu'à l'orée du bois, d'où ils retirèrent le petit caméscope qui, plus tôt, leur transmettait les images. Audrey assurerait le guet, et le préviendrait via téléphone, en cas de pépin. Elle lui demanda s'il était sûr de son coup. Adel lui confirma d'un hochement de tête. Plus question, pour lui, de revenir en arrière. Ils se séparèrent.

Audrey se cacha derrière un arbre. Adel traversa la rue, puis monta les marches menant au portail du 13 rue Summit. Il vérifia la poignée de porte ; elle était verrouillée, comme il l'avait prévu. Il passa un clone devant le lecteur, et entendit le déclic de la serrure. Le tour était joué. La porte se déverrouilla comme par enchantement, et Adel Salem disparut derrière.

Tout à ses pensées, Daryl Thomassen esquissait son plan d'attaque tandis que la Volvo 360 remontait la voie Camillien-Houde. Au fond, cet appel tombait à point : ce n'était pas lui qui avait cherché à communiquer avec Ashley, mais plutôt elle qui l'avait contacté. Il n'avait donc rien à se reprocher, s'il se pointait chez elle, ce soir même, avec en main le kimono de leur fils. De toute évidence, elle se sentirait émue par cet acte diligent, ouvrant la voie à un dialogue plus serein, plus constructif. Plus fécond, entre eux. À vrai dire, Daryl Thomassen espérait encore qu'Ashley Jones revienne vivre avec lui, et change d'attitude à son égard. Même divorcé, il lui était inconcevable que *sa femme* ne fût plus encore *sa femme*. Kimono en main, il lui prouverait son dévouement inconditionnel, lui ferait prendre conscience de sa nécessité dans sa vie, et susciterait en elle un désir de renouer leur relation. Peut-être le laisserait-elle entrer. Peut-être le laisserait-elle passer la nuit avec eux. Peut-être...

Habité par ces différents scénarios, Daryl Thomassen se laissa conduire jusque chez lui, le cœur plein d'anticipations. L'automobile se gara d'elle-même devant le 13 rue Summit. Daryl descendit de voiture et s'arrêta net devant le portail. Les lumières étaient allumées. Étrange, surtout qu'il était sûr de les avoir éteintes en sortant. Il consulta les réglages de son appareil mobile ; à sa grande surprise, il constata que le système d'alarme à domicile était désactivé, en mode « maintenance ». Aucune notification ne l'en avait avisé.

Daryl Thomassen décida quand même de rentrer chez lui, ignorant de fait les précautions de sécurité les plus élémentaires.

La première chose qui frappa Adel Salem, en entrant chez Thomassen, fut la configuration de l'espace. En commençant par le rez-de-chaussée, dont l'absence totale de cloisons lui fit perdre le sens de l'orientation, surtout qu'il se dirigeait à tâtons, dans le noir. Il alluma une lampe de poche et découvrit un aménagement intérieur épuré, minimaliste. La cuisine, la salle à manger et la salle de séjour constituaient une seule vaste pièce. Les murs étaient blancs. Hormis une table en verre, trois chaises, un sofa et, accroché au mur, un immense tableau abstrait, l'espace était pratiquement vide. Exempt de tout objet superflu, comme si on venait d'en faire le ménage. Ce qui frappa Adel fut l'absence totale d'appareils électroniques, à l'exception des électroménagers. Pas même pas un écran intelligent. Dans la salle de bain, le miroir était conventionnel, et ne semblait répondre à aucune commande. Guidé par son intuition, Salem prit l'escalier et descendit au sous-sol, dans l'espoir d'y trouver quelque chose. Là encore, l'endroit lui sembla singulièrement dépouillé : un sofa, un coin jeu pour enfants, une bibliothèque et, accroché au mur, un tableau peint au couteau. Adel déplaça quelques livres sur les étagères. Décrocha le tableau, espérant trouver derrière un coffre-fort, une trappe ou un dispositif caché, qui ferait basculer le mur vers une chambre secrète. Là encore, ses attentes le trompèrent. Il remonta au rez-de-chaussée. Cette fois, il ouvrit les lumières pour s'assurer qu'il n'avait rien manqué au premier passage. Il revit la table, les trois chaises, le sofa et l'œuvre abstraite géante, qu'il décrocha à son tour, pour en avoir le cœur net. Rien.

Refusant de céder au désespoir, Adel passa au deuxième étage : même constat. La chambre principale comportait seulement un lit, une pièce-penderie ainsi qu'une armoire remplie de chaussettes et de caleçons, cordés comme du bois de foyer. Sur le mur, une autre œuvre abstraite. Une porte donnait sur la salle de bain, l'autre donnait directement sur la chambre d'enfant, où il repéra plusieurs figurines de super héros, et un kimono de karaté pendouillant sur le dossier d'une chaise.

La panique commença à s'emparer de lui, et avec elle, la gratouille. Comment était-il possible qu'aucun ordinateur, disque dur ou support de stockage, pas même un écran ne puisse exister en la demeure d'un informaticien du calibre de Daryl Thomassen ? De grosses gouttes de sueur commencèrent à perler le long de son visage. La cagoule qu'il portait sur la tête l'étouffait et provoquait de vives démangeaisons. Il se gratta pour se soulager, mais le picotement ne fit qu'empirer. Tout son plan avait reposé sur cette unique certitude, celle de trouver chez Daryl Thomassen un ordinateur ou une partition de mémoire quelconque, pouvant contenir une propriété intellectuelle de Skyline Solutions : une version antérieure d'HiOS, par exemple, ou même, un des nombreux modules en développement. Thomassen venait de décrocher une commande auprès de la Défense nationale. Ne devait-il pas être en train de plancher dessus, actuellement ? N'était-il pas, en ce moment même, débordé par le boulot à abattre et les échéances à respecter ? Comment un individu de son acabit, un programmeur de surcroît, pouvait-il s'en tirer sans télétravail ? Sans même disposer d'un bureau, voire d'un ordinateur personnel à domicile ! Cela dépassait l'entendement d'Adel Salem.

Il alluma toutes les lumières de la maison, fouilla tous les recoins, les étagères et armoires – dans la cuisine, les chambres à coucher, le sous-sol – dans l'espoir d'y découvrir ne serait-ce qu'une petite clé USB, qui contiendrait l'objet de sa convoitise. Rien.

Dans le sous-sol – c'est là qu'il passa le plus de temps –, il fouilla la bibliothèque de fond en comble, en déplaça les livres, les jeta même par terre, exaspéré. Rien à voir avec l'informatique ou la programmation. C'était, pour la plupart, de vieux romans et des recueils de poèmes. Daryl passait-il ses soirées à lire des romans, de la poésie ? se demanda Adel, éberlué.

Soudain, horreur. Il entendit une porte s'ouvrir et se refermer. Puis des pas à l'étage. Quelqu'un venait d'entrer. Serait-ce Audrey venue le rejoindre ? Il déposa le livre en main, puis monta prudemment les marches. Daryl Thomassen apparut brusquement devant lui, barrant le passage. C'était un gaillard de bonne stature, aux larges épaules. Ils demeurèrent un instant stupéfaits, puis le visage de Daryl Thomassen se contracta violemment. « POLICE ! hurla-t-il à pleins poumons. POLICE ! ». Le cri ne trouva écho nulle part ; réglé en mode *maintenance,* le système d'alarme ne réagit pas à sa commande vocale. Et son appel à l'aide demeura sans réponse.

Tandis que Daryl déverrouillait l'écran de son bracelet pour composer manuellement le 9-1-1, Adel reprenait ses esprits. Il faut absolument l'en empêcher, quitte à jouer le tout pour le tout, raisonna-t-il froidement, mesurant la gravité de la situation. Il se rua sur Thomassen pour lui

209

sauter au cou, mais se buta contre une armoire à glace. Daryl parvint d'un geste habile à repousser son assaillant, mais l'autre rappliqua aussitôt pour l'empêcher de passer son appel : c'était une question de vie ou de mort.

Les coups fusèrent de part et d'autre, dans ce bref affrontement qui opposa des forces à peu près égales. D'un côté, la fougue d'une jeunesse bouillante et survoltée. De l'autre, l'expérience d'un sportif discipliné. Expérience et discipline l'emportèrent au final. Un coup de poing bien dirigé contre la mâchoire d'Adel le jeta au tapis. Le plancher vibra sous l'intensité du choc. Un son aigu résonna dans ses tympans. Adel se passa la main sur le front et remarqua avec horreur que sa cagoule n'y était plus. Elle avait été éjectée lors de l'impact et gisait maintenant au bas de l'escalier.

L'agresseur venait d'être démasqué.

Audrey eut un pincement au cœur. Il fallait être fou pour se jeter ainsi dans le néant. Elle ne pouvait abandonner Adel à lui-même. Il avait été humilié par sa faute, c'était évident. Elle se sentait coupable. La nostalgie la gagna quand elle le vit entrer dans la maison aussi facilement que s'il y habitait. Quelle bravoure ! Elle repensa à leurs premiers moments d'amour quand, plus jeunes, ils fomentaient leurs premiers actes de dissidence. Adel était un gars brillant, curieux, assoiffé de justice. Autant de qualités qui l'avaient conquise et qui, aujourd'hui encore, la séduisaient.

Elle s'était attachée à lui beaucoup plus qu'elle n'osait se l'admettre.

Plongée dans ces réminiscences, elle tenta de mettre un mot sur ses sentiments. Aimait-elle Adel d'un amour fraternel ou d'un amour charnel ? Ou encore, passionnel ? Vrai, elle était tombée un moment pour Maximus – une aventure comme ça. Un feu de paille. En contrepartie, Adel et elle avaient un passé ensemble, une histoire. Peut-être, justement, qu'il était l'homme de sa vie ?

Elle chassa ces divagations d'un mouvement de la main et, braquant ses yeux sur la résidence de Thomassen, elle se concentra de nouveau sur sa tâche de surveillance. Elle jeta un œil sur son portable. Mine de rien, ça commençait à faire un petit bout qu'Adel se trouvait à l'intérieur. Il ne devrait pas tarder à en ressortir avec son butin, songea-t-elle. Elle se rassurait à cette idée quand les lumières de la maison s'allumèrent subitement. Que se passait-il ? Pourquoi diable Adel avait-il allumé les lumières ?

Elle n'eut pas le temps de digérer cette information que, déjà, un nouvel imprévu surgissait : les phares d'une voiture s'avançaient dans la nuit. Elle reconnut l'auto de Daryl Thomassen, qui se stationna devant chez lui. L'homme en descendit, puis remarquant les lumières de sa maison allumées, la considéra d'un air étonné. Il s'en approcha, perplexe, puis décida d'y rentrer. Audrey retint un cri. « *Shit de shit de shit* », pesta-t-elle. Vite, il faut rejoindre Adel avant qu'il ne soit trop tard. Peut-être avait-il encore une chance de s'échapper par-derrière. Elle saisit son portable, lança la composition automatique, mais l'appel ne passa pas. « Crisse de 7G à marde ! grommela-t-elle entre les dents. » Elle tenta une deuxième fois, puis une troisième : peine perdue. Et Adel qui ne sortait toujours pas ! Et si elle s'y rendait pour voir ? « Non, impossible », songea-t-elle, comme pour se rappeler à la raison. Elle ne pouvait risquer de se compromettre. En même temps, elle ne pouvait abandonner Adel à son sort. Elle pesa le pour et le contre et, dans un élan de solidarité, elle sortit de sa cachette et se précipita à l'intérieur de la maison, sans masque ni cagoule. Son cœur fit un tour complet dans sa poitrine lorsqu'elle vit ce qu'elle vit.

Armé d'un pistolet semi-automatique, Adel tenait en joue Daryl Thomassen.

L'arme trouvée sur les lieux du crime fut un pistolet semi-automatique de type Glock 17. Salem l'aurait assemblé lui-même avant de s'en servir pour faire feu sur Thomassen. L'enquête effectuée par la section des crimes majeurs permit de confirmer que l'engin fut confectionné à partir de pièces détachées conçues à même des dessins d'atelier disponibles sur le net. Leur fabrication aurait été possible grâce à l'une des imprimantes 3D de la bibliothèque de l'École Polytechnique de Montréal.

La présence de cette arme mit à rude épreuve la défense qui s'est avérée à court d'arguments pour réfuter les accusations de tentative de meurtre. D'autant plus que l'accusé avait tiré à trois reprises en direction de la victime.

La défense a plaidé que le geste d'Adel Salem ne fut pas délibéré, et qu'il avait agi sous le coup de l'émotion.

Pourquoi alors était-il en possession d'une arme à feu au moment des faits, si ce n'était pour s'en servir ? avait demandé la Couronne. Adel avait répondu qu'il ne le savait pas lui-même. Que la réussite de cette mission lui semblait capitale et que le port d'une arme le rassurait quant à sa capacité à mener à bien ses objectifs, avait-il bredouillé au terme d'un échange musclé avec l'avocat de la poursuite.

Canon braqué sur la figure, Daryl Thomassen leva les mains en l'air ? Il toisa son agresseur avec un mélange de méfiance et de mépris, tandis que l'autre évita de croiser son regard. Daryl Thomassen avait déjà vu cette tête-là quelque part. Mais où ? À cet instant précis, il n'aurait su dire.

Soudain, la porte d'entrée s'ouvrit avec fracas. Apparut alors une femme, dans la jeune vingtaine qui poussa un cri d'horreur à la vue de la scène. Son arrivée suscita tout un émoi, comme si l'assaillant ne s'était pas attendu à son arrivée. L'un et l'autre commencèrent à se disputer. Elle avait enfreint une règle qu'ils s'étaient donnée : celle de ne pas intervenir. Ainsi donc, ils étaient deux à avoir planifié ce coup. À les entendre, les évènements ne s'étaient pas déroulés comme prévu. La jeune femme n'arrêtait pas de crier : « Qu'est-ce tu câlisses avec un *gun* ? Mais qu'est-ce tu câlisses avec un *gun ?* »

Son complice peinait à la calmer. Ils se querellaient comme un couple. Daryl Thomassen déduisit que ces deux-là avaient une histoire ensemble. À qui avait-il affaire, au juste ? se demanda-t-il pendant que ses ravisseurs se chamaillaient. À de vulgaires cambrioleurs ? À un gang de rue ? spécula-t-il. Que lui voulait-on, au juste ?

Le jeune homme n'avait pas trouvé ce qu'il cherchait. Daryl l'avait manifestement pris sur le fait. N'eût été son ex-femme, il ne serait jamais revenu avant la fin de sa baignade. Par conséquent, il n'aurait jamais croisé ses malfaiteurs. C'était donc des gens qui connaissaient bien son emploi du temps. Du moins, étaient-ils parvenus à le déduire, peut-être en l'observant depuis quelque temps ? Conjuguant ces différents éléments, Thomassen tenta d'établir le niveau d'organisation criminelle auquel il avait affaire. Les avait-on payés ou agissaient-ils de leur propre chef ? Allaient-ils demander une rançon ? Faisaient-ils partie d'une organisation internationale ? Le Service canadien du renseignement l'avait prévenu ; ses activités d'entreprises l'exposaient à un risque accru en matière de sécurité personnelle. Mais ces deux malfrats semblaient beaucoup trop brouillons pour être des professionnels. Il avait probablement affaire à de vulgaires voyous venus pour cambrioler un riche. Il se remémora les formations et les ateliers qu'il avait suivis. Surtout, ne pas négocier, ne pas parler, gagner du temps, attendre l'arrivée des secours. Seulement, quelqu'un était-il au courant de sa situation ? Mis à part Ashley, qui l'attendait, il n'existait pratiquement personne qui, informé de sa détresse, puisse venir lui prêter secours, songea-t-il.

Daryl proposa de l'argent en échange de sa libération. Leur promit son silence. Le jeune homme ne voulut rien entendre. L'extorqueur l'interrogea plutôt au sujet de ses appareils informatiques. Il semblait étonné de ne pas en voir ici. Il cherchait sûrement à mettre la main sur des ordinateurs, des disques durs, des clés ou même des cryptoactifs. La jeune femme alla vérifier dans la voiture et revint bredouille avec son maillot de bain.

Daryl Thomassen leur répondit que son psychologue lui déconseillait formellement le télétravail et que, par surcroît, depuis sa séparation, celui-ci l'avait incité à évacuer tout appareil électronique de sa sphère privée. Qu'il devait – pour son bien-être – apprendre à compartimenter sa « bulle personnelle » de sa « bulle professionnelle ». Il en allait de même pour ses cryptoactifs qu'il ne conservait plus à portée de main, mais plutôt dans un coffret de sûreté à la banque. Quant à son bracelet électronique, c'était un modèle compact qui ne lui servait qu'à entrer en communication. En entendant ces justifications, et après avoir examiné le bracelet, le ravisseur tomba dans une colère noire. Il ne voulait pas y croire. Le menaçant de son arme, le bandit l'exhorta à lui fournir une autre réponse. À son grand regret, Daryl Thomassen n'en avait pas à lui offrir.

Ses agresseurs savaient donc à qui ils avaient affaire et ce qu'ils voulaient. Ils étaient au courant de ses recherches, de l'entreprise qu'il dirigeait, de la nature de ses projets, et de sa fortune. Envisageaient-ils, par hasard, de lui subtiliser une propriété intellectuelle ? Daryl Thomassen n'osa pas leur poser la question. Or, son silence les incita malgré lui à chercher de ce côté...

Posant le canon contre sa nuque, le jeune homme lui ordonna de descendre au sous-sol. La jeune femme implorait son complice de laisser tomber. Mais l'autre persistait. À un moment donné, il lui cria : « Ta gueule ! » Il n'allait pas repartir sans ce qu'il était venu chercher. Toute sa vie était « en jeu ».

Arrivés en bas, ils firent asseoir l'otage par terre, adossé contre le mur. Ce dernier remarqua les romans de sa femme, jetés au sol. C'est à ce moment qu'il commença à avoir peur pour sa vie. Vraiment.

Audrey n'en crut pas ses yeux : un pistolet semi-automatique vacillait entre les mains d'Adel. Que s'était-il passé ? Adel avait-il désarmé Thomassen ? Un coup d'œil dans sa direction lui fit écarter cette hypothèse ; l'homme était tout aussi ahuri qu'elle. Était-il possible qu'Adel fût armé depuis le... début ?

Cette pensée lui glaça le sang, comme un poignard dans le dos. Comment avait-il osé le lui cacher ? À elle, qui lui avait fait confiance depuis le début. Qui en plus, s'était sentie redevable envers lui. Adel argua, pour sa défense, que son arme l'avait sauvé. Sans quoi, il était « fini ». Il avait ensuite retourné la question contre elle. Que faisait-elle ici ? N'était-elle pas censée être à l'extérieur ? Pourquoi ne l'avait-elle pas avisé du danger ?

Ils se renvoyèrent la balle, mais comprirent rapidement qu'ils empiraient leur situation. Le temps était à la solidarité. Ils devaient joindre leurs efforts pour trouver une solution. Ne sachant par où commencer, ils verrouillèrent la porte d'entrée, puis descendirent leur otage au sous-sol, où ils l'isolèrent dans un coin. Ils s'entretinrent à voix basse.

À son grand malheur, la maison ne contenait pas ce qu'ils cherchaient. Visiblement, Thomassen n'entendait pas coopérer. Adel était tombé des nues à entendre son histoire : un psychologue ? Lui interdisant le télétravail ?! Se foutait-il à ce point de sa gueule ? Et pourtant, Adel avait fouillé la piaule de fond en comble, en vain. Son téléphone mobile, un bracelet aux fonctions bien limitées, n'était d'aucune utilité. Que faire ? Repartir, tout simplement ? Dans ce cas, comment garantir que Thomassen ne les dénonce pas à la police. Qu'est-ce qui l'empêcherait de le faire ?

Leurs discussions menaient à un cul-de-sac. « Foutus, on est foutus ! » n'arrêtait pas de répéter Audrey, en s'arrachant les cheveux. L'autre, moins exubérant, s'était enfermé dans le mutisme. Il lorgnait son otage du coin de l'œil. L'échec était manifeste, mais Adel persistait dans le déni. Il devait bien exister un moyen de se tirer d'embarras. *Penser en dehors de la boîte... En dehors de la boîte... en dehors de la boîte,* se répétait-il comme un mantra. Ses yeux s'éclairèrent soudain d'une lueur étrange.

— E-et si... si on le t-tuait ? bégaya-t-il, comme si les garde-fous de sa raison venaient de céder.

Le mot fit bondir Audrey.

— *Tuer* ? reprit-elle.

— Oui...

— Comment ?

— Bah, d'une... une balle dans la tête, pensa à voix haute Adel, en désignant son fusil, les yeux hagards. Il se gratta la tête. Son front arborait une sale piqûre de maringouin.

Le sol se déroba sous les pieds d'Audrey qui passa près de s'évanouir. L'autre la prit par le bras et serra très fort pour lui redonner contenance : mais avaient-ils seulement le choix ?

— De toute façon, c'est un criminel, argua Adel, dont le regard s'était subitement endurci.

— Un criminel ? s'étonna Audrey.

— Oui, renchérit Adel. Il conçoit des armes intelligentes, pour tuer des gens.

— On va quand même pas le tuer pour ça ! C'est pas à nous de...

— Pourquoi pas ? Mieux vaut en tuer un, que d'en laisser mourir mille autres à cause de lui, non ? défendit-il, avec conviction.

Adel promenait ses yeux, autour de lui.

— Regarde, fit-il en visant l'opulente œuvre abstraite, regarde comme il profite des guerres et s'enrichit sur le dos des pauvres ! Tu penses pas que le monde serait meilleur, sans lui ?

— OK, mais ça ferait de nous des meurtriers, non ?

— Mais non, mais non ! dit-il en balayant l'argument du revers de sa main. Écoute, soit on le tue tout de suite ; soit on se fait choper plus tard, à toi de choisir, poursuivit-il encore, comme pour clore le débat. Il rongeait son frein.

Audrey se dégagea de son emprise et trébucha. Elle n'arrivait pas à croire ce qu'elle entendait ; elle se sentit défaillir. Elle croisa le regard de Thomassen, qui semblait avoir deviné le sujet de leur conversation. Audrey vacilla en direction de l'escalier, puis monta à l'étage, se traînant les pieds. Les pensées se bousculaient dans sa tête. S'y entremêlaient colère, incompréhension et résignation. Elle vit le sofa, s'affala dessus. Son téléphone indiquait 23 heures précises. Un texto de sa mère la priait de lui passer un coup de fil. L'idée de l'appeler à l'instant traversa son esprit. Audrey était prête à tout avouer. La main tremblante, elle vint pour lancer la composition automatique, hésita puis changea d'idée. Elle n'avait pas envie d'entendre ses reproches. Elle appuya sur le bouton latéral pour verrouiller l'écran et fourra le téléphone dans sa poche. Inutile d'inquiéter tout le monde avec ça, songea-t-elle. Audrey pouvait encore partir, sortir d'ici pendant qu'il était encore temps. Elle se leva pour atteindre la porte, en déverrouilla la serrure, puis se ravisa, verrouilla de nouveau. Elle revint s'effondrer sur le sofa. La fatigue l'accablait. Elle ne savait plus ce qu'elle voulait. Ses yeux errèrent à travers les lignes de l'œuvre abstraite suspendue devant elle. Elle avait mérité son sort, songea-t-elle. Tout était de sa faute. Comme elle se sentait bête ! Ne restait plus qu'à assumer les conséquences, accepter son destin. Telle était sa volonté... Il lui sembla d'ailleurs que c'était la seule chose sur quoi elle eut encore un pouvoir et qui ne relevait pas du hasard : sa volonté. Elle considéra avec dédain l'exécrable tableau brossé à coups dans le vide. Laissé à lui-même, Adel était capable du pire. Elle l'en empêcherait. Quitte à y laisser sa vie.

Alors que sa cagoule tombait au bas de l'escalier, le monde basculait sur un fatidique pivot. En dégainant son arme, Adel Salem changeait à jamais le cours de sa vie. Le point de non-retour avait été franchi, seulement il n'en était pas encore conscient. Son cerveau n'avait jamais été confronté à l'insoluble équation qui était sur le point de se présenter à lui, et qui régirait le nouvel ordre des choses. Tuer ou ne pas tuer Daryl Thomassen ? Rien, ni la raison, ni son humanité, ni la terreur dans le regard d'Audrey n'allaient pouvoir le soustraire à ce dilemme. Comment dénouer l'impasse ? Thomassen était capable de les reconnaître et de les dénoncer. Sa vie au complet était foutue ! *Leurs* vies à tous les deux étaient foutues. Audrey ne le réalisait pas ? Mais où avait-elle disparu ?

Il entendit des pas venant du haut. C'était elle qui descendait les marches. Quelque chose, dans son attitude et son regard, avait changé. Il ne la reconnaissait plus. Ce n'était plus une amoureuse, une amante ou une amie. Adel avait devant lui une étrangère. Plus rien ne les unissait désormais mis à part cette merde dans laquelle ils s'étaient enfoncés jusqu'au cou. Ni l'un ni l'autre n'était prêt à faire de la prison, c'était évident. Mais, de là à assassiner Thomassen ? Adel se heurtait à un refus catégorique. Or, l'épargner posait un autre problème.

Audrey voulut interroger Daryl Thomassen, au grand dam d'Adel. Peut-être pouvaient-ils s'entendre, s'en faire un allié, présuma-t-elle. Le délire avait pris des proportions tellement gigantesques. Le dialogue lui apparaissait comme leur seule voie de salut. Elle lui demanda s'il savait pourquoi on le séquestrait, s'il était conscient des torts qu'on lui reprochait.

Daryl, qui s'était résigné au silence, réclama un verre d'eau. Audrey vint pour lui apporter à boire quand Adel lui barra le chemin et l'empoigna par le bras.

— À quoi tu joues ? fulmina-t-il.

— Laisse-moi ! rétorqua Audrey en se dégageant.

Elle revint vers l'otage. Il était assis sur le sol, contre le mur, les jambes allongées vers l'avant, le visage éraflé. Audrey lui tendit l'eau. Thomassen but à grandes lampées.

— Savez-vous pourquoi vous êtes séquestré, Daryl Thomassen ? lui demanda Audrey.

— Ainsi donc, vous connaissez mon nom... répliqua Thomassen avec un fort accent.

Daryl déposa son verre, remarqua les yeux braqués sur lui.

— On vous a pas choisi au hasard, reprit Audrey.

Adel jura entre ses dents.

— Puis-je savoir à qui j'ai affaire, alors ? répliqua Thomassen.

— J'ai peur que ce soit impossible, répondit Audrey.

— Ça suffit ! interrompit Adel. Arrête de parler à ce criminel !

— Criminel, moi ? s'insurgea Daryl Thomassen.

— Oui ! Vous développez des armes intelligentes pour tuer des populations civiles ! renchérit Adel qui s'était rapproché d'eux. Vous vous apprêtez à les vendre au Canada et aux États-Unis. Vous croyez qu'on l'ignorait ? vociféra-t-il encore. Il exhiba de nouveau son arme à la vue de tout le monde. Mais au moment où il la pointa de nouveau vers l'otage, Audrey intervint aussitôt et se planta devant lui. Daryl Thomassen sourcilla.

— Oui, c'est vrai, répondit calmement Thomassen. Je conçois des armes intelligentes. Elles servent justement à éviter les erreurs humaines, et à rendre les guerres plus éthiques. Mais toi, qui nous tiens en joue avec ton arme, toi qui es entré par effraction chez moi, qui m'as attaqué et qui menaces de me tuer, n'es-tu pas toi-même un criminel ? À qui je n'ai rien fait ?

— M-moi j-je me bats pour la liberté, bégaya Adel, en faisant un pas de côté pour se remettre face à lui. Il bouscula Audrey au passage. M-mais aussi, reprit-il, contre tous ceux qui fabriquent des m-machines de guerre pour tuer des innocents ! Et vous, Daryl Thomassen, v-vous êtes un... un rouage de ce système !

— La liberté ? répéta ironiquement Thomassen, en levant ses mains en l'air.

Il pointa l'arme d'Adel.

— Comment peux-tu affirmer combattre au nom de la liberté, alors que tu séquestres des gens ? enchaîna-t-il, perplexe.

Le visage d'Adel se tendit. Ses yeux s'écarquillèrent de colère. Il leva son arme vers l'otage pour l'exécuter. Le geste fit bondir Audrey, qui s'interposa de nouveau entre les deux hommes, et s'écria :

— Non !

Elle posa la main sur le canon pour l'abaisser.

— Nous, on se bat pour que tout le monde soit libre !

— Tuons-le maintenant. Finissons-en tout de suite, qu'on puisse enfin foutre le camp ! rétorqua Adel, tentant de la dégager de sa ligne de tir. Audrey se dressait devant lui, se servant de son corps comme d'un bouclier pour protéger Daryl Thomassen.

— Jamais de la vie ! répliqua-t-elle.

Adel se prit sa tête dans les mains et soupira d'exaspération. C'était un homme pragmatique, après tout, peu enclin aux débats, aux dilemmes éthiques, aux questions insolubles, à tout ce qui ne pouvait se résoudre par une ligne de code.

Il fit les cent pas, gardant son otage à l'œil. Bien que sa mort réglât tous ses problèmes, il ne pouvait l'envisager en la présence d'Audrey, estimait-il. Eut-il été seul qu'il l'aurait déjà achevé. La présence d'un témoin le gênait. En outre, il n'avait jamais tiré sur quelqu'un, dans la « vraie vie ». En fait, il n'avait jamais utilisé son flingue. Quelle idée ridicule, d'ailleurs, de l'avoir apporté. D'en posséder un, de prime abord. Il maudissait le jour où il était tombé sur des dessins d'atelier du Glock. Il affectionnait particulièrement ce modèle qui, sous sa menace, enjoignait une stripteaseuse à se déshabiller dans *Game of death*. Il en avait développé une obsession maladive. Les pièces étaient faciles à usiner à partir d'une imprimante 3D. Il n'avait eu aucun mal à pirater celle de la bibliothèque de l'école Polytechnique. Le pistolet assemblé, il avait réussi à se procurer quelques munitions, pour en vérifier la qualité d'usinage. Il avait posé avec le fusil, s'était donné à quelques activités onanistes, sans plus. D'ailleurs, l'examen du canon démontra bien que le fusil n'avait jamais servi auparavant. Hypothèse confirmée de l'aveu même d'Adel Salem, qui assura n'en avoir jamais fait usage ni projeté de le faire... avant de se retrouver nez à nez avec Thomassen. L'idée d'apporter une arme chargée en vue d'un cambriolage avait donc relevé, à l'origine, beaucoup plus du fantasme, que de la raison, ou du projet d'en faire usage, aussi étrange et glauque que puisse paraître son alibi. Car en cet instant précis, il regrettait amèrement sa décision et se sentait idiot. Il devait bien exister une solution pour se sortir du pétrin dans lequel il s'était fourré, et ce, sans avoir à *tuer* quelqu'un. Pour ça, il devait mettre la main sur quelque chose de suffisamment cher aux yeux de Thomassen pour garantir son silence. Seulement, rien ici ne pouvait jouer ce rôle.

Tandis qu'il ruminait ces pensées, un petit voyant lumineux caché entre les livres de la bibliothèque attira son attention et le fit bondir. Il s'approcha et dégagea les livres qui entouraient le dispositif. C'était bel et bien un modem. Il se tapa le front. Un modem, nom de Dieu ! Comment n'y avait-il pas pensé plus tôt ? Comment aurait-il pu désactiver la domotique de Thomassen, si celle-ci n'était pas connectée via modem ?

Il fouilla son sac à dos, en sortit le micro-ordinateur et l'alluma, sous le regard médusé des deux autres. L'appareil reconnut aussitôt le signal wifi. Adel s'approcha de Daryl et lui demanda de s'authentifier à l'aide de sa e-Claw. Thomassen obtempéra à contrecœur. Ne manquait plus qu'à configurer le VPN pour se connecter aux serveurs de Skyline Solutions. Thomassen refusa. Les deux ravisseurs échangèrent un coup d'œil approbateur, puis Adel arma le chien de son fusil et braqua l'arme sur la tempe de Thomassen. Quand Adel reprit son ordinateur, un serveur venait de s'ajouter à son répertoire, en vertu du protocole EES. Il double cliqua dessus. Une fenêtre s'ouvrit, avec une douzaine de fichiers, ordonnancés par année, selon une structure de découpage assez simple. Adel sourit à la vue de ce petit pactole. Dans le champ recherche, il tapa le mot-clé « Flyborg ». L'ordinateur se mit à fureter. Cinq dossiers apparurent. Il compara leur taille ; l'un d'eux pesait 18,5 téraoctets : tout le code et les images vidéo ayant servi à l'entraînement des réseaux de neurones de HiOS, songea Adel. Il vérifia l'espace disponible sur son disque dur. C'était tout juste. Il fit un glisser-déposer. L'ordinateur estima le temps de transfert. Il en avait pour trois héures.

Le téléchargement débuta.

Au moment où Daryl Thomassen raccrocha, Ashley Jones ne put réprimer un sourire nostalgique. C'était bien lui, ça. Toujours serviable, loyal et dévoué. Plus tôt, en couchant le petit Angus, le doute s'était emparé d'elle. Elle avait été excessive à son endroit. Daryl ne méritait pas un tel sort. C'était une mère indigne. Son fils ne lui pardonnerait jamais d'avoir quitté son père. Lui qui était pourtant si courageux au moment de se battre contre des ennemis imaginaires, ne passait plus une nuit sans se lever en panique, demandant à voir son papa. Il fondait alors en larmes. Et le cœur d'Ashley, rempli de culpabilité, chavirait à ce triste spectacle.

Telles étaient les pensées qui traversèrent son esprit tandis qu'elle vérifiait d'un œil averti que son garçon s'était bel et bien endormi. Elle ne voulait pas qu'il vît son père. Il en serait beaucoup trop excité ; sa nuit en serait gâchée. Elle se posta à la fenêtre du salon, attendant l'arrivée de Daryl Thomassen. Elle irait le rejoindre en bas, une fois sa Volvo garée.

Elle attendit une demi-heure, comme Daryl avait promis. Une heure plus tard, il n'était toujours pas passé. Elle s'abstint de lui envoyer un message de reproche. Au bout de deux heures, elle finit par lui écrire : « Ça va ? »

Pas de réponse.

Avait-il finalement décidé d'aller à la piscine ? Dans ce cas, il l'aurait prévenu, songea-t-elle.

À moins qu'il fît exprès de l'ignorer ? Non, ce n'était pas son genre.

Elle se brossa les dents, gagna son lit, mais ne parvint pas à fermer l'œil, consultant son téléphone aux quinze minutes, espérant y voir une notification rassurante.

Vers minuit, elle se leva d'un bond, et décida de l'appeler pour en avoir le cœur net. Encore une fois, pas de réponse. Là, ce n'était plus normal. Daryl avait l'habitude de dormir près du téléphone, ignorant les conseils de son psychologue. Une habitude qu'il avait prise, et dont il ne pouvait se défaire depuis que ses affaires prospéraient outre-Atlantique. Les contacts d'urgence, auxquels elle appartenait, pouvaient le joindre 24/7.

Ashley laissa deux messages vocaux. Quelque chose ne tournait pas rond. Plusieurs incidents étaient survenus, dernièrement, impliquant des entrepreneurs qui avaient maille à partir avec des groupes extrémistes. Chaque semaine, une nouvelle victime faisait les manchettes. Dernièrement, le président d'une compagnie de forage avait vu ses bureaux vandalisés. La résidence d'un promoteur immobilier était partie en fumée. Un architecte avait été battu et laissé pour mort par des anarchistes.

Dans la tourmente, Ashley tenta de joindre les voisins situés au 15 rue Summit. Elle n'y parvint pas ; il était beaucoup trop tard. Ils devaient être couchés, la sonnerie de leurs téléphones, éteinte.

Ashley s'habilla pour aller vérifier d'elle-même ce qu'il en était, mais se ravisa. Et si Angus se réveillait pendant son absence ? Elle abandonna le projet.

Après mûre réflexion, elle décida d'appeler la police pour leur expliquer la situation. La répartitrice du 9-1-1 lui posa les questions d'usage. M. Thomassen consommait-il des drogues ? Avait-il des problèmes de santé ? Possédait-il des armes ? « Non, non et non », répondit Ashley Jones. L'opératrice remplit la carte d'appel et l'achemina au centre de communications du SPVM, qui lui attribua une priorité moyenne.

Vers 3 h 30 du matin, soit deux heures après qu'Ashley ait communiqué avec les services d'urgence, l'appel fut transféré aux unités du poste de quartier 12, dans Westmount, qui firent dépêcher une patrouille de reconnaissance au 13, rue Summit.

Le constable de classe 7, agent Youri Akoulov, matricule 274, était de garde en cette nuit du jeudi 17 au vendredi 18 juin 2032. Il était affecté, ce soir-là, au poste de quartier 12 de Ville-Marie Ouest | Westmount et remplaçait l'agente Noémie Lapointe, en congé de maladie. Il patrouillait avec l'agent Phong Dang, recrue qui en était seulement à sa première semaine au sein du service. Un cas de force majeure, car d'ordinaire, les duos de soir peuvent toujours compter sur un policier d'expérience parmi eux. Or, face à un effectif réduit, le sergent de garde en cette nuit fatidique ne pouvait faire autrement.

Le quart des deux flics avait commencé à 22 h. Le secteur Westmount était plutôt tranquille, comparativement à ses quartiers périphériques. On y observait peu d'activités liées aux gangs de rue. La prostitution n'y était pas apparente. On avait plutôt affaire, dans ce secteur, à des entrées par effraction et à des vols qualifiés. Ceux-ci survenaient surtout les fins de semaine, en l'absence des propriétaires partis pour leurs luxueux chalets. Mais en ce jour de semaine, les deux patrouilleurs s'attendaient à une nuit plutôt tranquille. L'appel d'un homme en détresse qui menaçait de se défenestrer du quatrième étage les avait surpris. Le client les avait occupés une bonne partie de la nuit. Les policiers étaient parvenus, après négociations, à convaincre le malade d'éviter le pire. Ils l'avaient ensuite conduit à l'hôpital où il reçut les soins psychiatriques appropriés.

Vers 3 h 30, la patrouille se rendit donc au 13 rue Summit, pour une vérification d'usage, suite au signalement d'un homme manquant à l'appel. Arrivés sur place, les policiers se garèrent devant la maison et procédèrent à l'inspection des lieux. A priori, tout semblait normal. La voiture du propriétaire était garée devant sa demeure, comme le confirma la plaque d'immatriculation relevée par Colombus. Les lumières étant allumées, les deux constables décidèrent de sonner à la porte. Ils n'obtinrent aucune réponse. La porte était barrée. Ils sonnèrent à nouveau ; toujours rien. Le silence leur sembla étrange. Les deux policiers firent le tour de la maison, espérant déceler d'autres indices pouvant les éclairer sur la situation. Ils regardèrent par les fenêtres, inspectèrent le boisé en face de la maison, arpentèrent la cour. Rien. L'agent Dang proposa d'appeler du « *back-up* », mais Akoulov tempéra les ardeurs de la nouvelle recrue. Il n'y avait, pour l'instant, aucune raison d'appeler le « *back-up* ». Ils revinrent à la porte principale, et sonnèrent à nouveau. Toujours rien.

Soudain, un coup de feu retentit à l'intérieur de la maison. Puis un autre et encore un autre, à quelques secondes d'intervalle. Des cris fusèrent du sous-sol. Les deux agents dégainèrent aussitôt leur arme. L'agent Dang contacta la centrale pour rapporter la situation, et demanda du même coup des renforts. L'indomptable agent Akoulov décida quant à lui d'intervenir sur-le-champ, quitte à défoncer la porte. Colombus lui déconseilla cette manœuvre hors protocole.

Se servant de son pied droit comme d'un bélier, Akoulov parvint à faire sauter le verrou du portail, après trois assauts. Il pénétra à l'intérieur, et fut arrosé de toutes parts par les brumisateurs anti-cambriolage à la fluorescéine disposés sur le cadre de porte autour de lui, tandis que Dang demeura à l'extérieur.

Au même moment, venant de l'intérieur, une personne tomba face à face avec Akoulov.

Colombus analysa la situation, à partir d'une caméra embarquée 8 K. La fluorescéine dont elle était désormais imprégnée nuisit à la visibilité. Les capteurs, réputés très sensibles, réussirent quand même à évaluer un certain nombre de facteurs tels que la vitesse du sujet fonçant dans leur direction et ses caractéristiques faciales. Le tout fut compilé et interprété par un savant algorithme, qui conclut en 0,8 seconde et avec un taux de confiance supérieur à 99 % que l'agent Akoulov courait un grand danger. Colombus suggéra de « tirer » immédiatement, ce qu'Akoulov fit, à bout portant. Un corps s'effondra subitement devant lui.

Audrey Lavoie venait d'être atteinte d'une balle en plein cœur.

Il n'y avait plus aucun doute. Ses deux ravisseurs connaissaient tous les détails de sa vie, déduisit Daryl Thomassen en s'adressant à la jeune femme, dont la voix trahissait la peur. Son visage était plutôt joli. Il nota sa coupe de cheveux à la garçonne, les innombrables anneaux qui ornaient son oreille, le petit diamant incrusté dans son nez. Il n'aurait aucun mal à la replacer, s'il sortait d'ici vivant. Même chose pour son compagnon, dont les traits et l'allure lui semblèrent toutefois plus grotesques. Une immense boursouflure ornait son visage, sans doute une vilaine piqûre de moustique. Le malfaiteur avait poussé l'audace jusqu'à le traiter, lui, de « criminel ». « Criminel... », songea encore Thomassen, retournant le mot plusieurs fois dans sa tête. Des dizaines de milliers d'heures et autant de millions de dollars investis pour perfectionner une arme afin de – justement, se martelait-il à lui-même, justement – prévenir les erreurs. Protéger nos soldats. Défendre notre territoire. Promouvoir la paix dans le monde. Tenir en respect les bandits, les envahisseurs, les terroristes et les anarchistes. Et voilà qu'on le traitait de « criminel » ! Reproche qui le mettait dans une fureur noire, d'autant plus qu'il n'était pas en position de discuter ni d'avancer ses arguments.

De toute évidence, il avait affaire à de fanatiques *wokes*, des profanes, des justiciers radicaux enclins, voire déterminés, à l'abattre au moindre faux pas. À la moindre parole qui ne fit pas leur affaire. En outre, ils ne semblaient pas venus pour dialoguer avec un scientifique de son calibre. Tous ses soupçons se confirmèrent d'ailleurs, lorsque l'extorqueur sortit un ordinateur pour lui demander de configurer un VPN afin de se connecter aux serveurs locaux de Skyline Solutions. Inutile de résister ou de faire le malin, conclut Thomassen. C'étaient des gens organisés qui avaient à leur disposition tous les outils nécessaires à l'atteinte de leurs objectifs, en plus d'être armés et dangereux.

Fusil contre la tempe, Daryl Thomassen obtempéra, conscient qu'il donnait accès à tous ses secrets d'affaires, et même, à des documents classifiés « secrets d'État ». Le programme Flyborg était classé ultracondientiel par la Défense nationale, non sans raison. La divulgation non autorisée de son code ou des données servant à l'entraînement de son réseau de neurones portait atteinte à l'intérêt national. Ses agresseurs cherchaient à s'en emparer en gage de son silence, conclut-il, compte tenu du préjudice considérable que pouvait lui causer leur dévoilement. Ses contrats seraient résiliés, sa carrière terminée. Tout le travail d'une vie, anéanti. C'était ça ou une balle dans la tête. Bien honnêtement, lorsque la connexion s'établit effectivement avec les serveurs de Skyline Solutions, et que le ravisseur commença d'en télécharger des fichiers, Thomassen n'aurait su dire s'il préférait la vie ou la mort. Il ne pouvait s'imaginer annoncer à ses clients que leurs projets de développement d'armes éthiques et intelligentes, au coût de plusieurs millions de dollars, avaient été compromis par de vulgaires anarchistes.

Mais qui étaient ces gens ? Comment avaient-ils fait pour le repérer ? Qui leur avait fourni des informations clés à son sujet ? Il fouilla sa mémoire de fond en comble, à la recherche de visages qui puissent correspondre à celui de ses agresseurs. Celui de la jeune femme ne lui disait absolument rien. L'autre, pourtant... L'autre... Il avait déjà vu cette tête-là quelque part. Mais où ? Il n'aurait pas su dire.

Le téléchargement avait débuté depuis une bonne demi-heure. Thomassen était maintenant seul avec le brigand. Où était donc passée la femme ? Depuis tout à l'heure, elle n'arrêtait pas de faire les cent pas, passant de l'étage au sous-sol, du sous-sol à l'étage. Elle semblait nerveuse, agitée. Demandait tout le temps à l'autre « combien de temps encore ? ».

— Deux ou trois heures, répondait-il toujours, exaspéré.

« Deux ou trois heures », songeait Thomassen. C'était donc du gros. Helios-Athéna, à n'en pas douter. Avec toute sa librairie de données servant à engager des cibles humaines de manière éthique et autonome. Banque d'images non traitées de militaires et de combattants rebelles, toutes nationalités et allégeances confondues. Et que dire des civils apparaissant sur les lieux du combat : hommes, femmes et enfants, filles et garçons de tous âges. De quoi faire un scandale international, si ces documents devaient être éventés. Il voyait déjà les redoutables manchettes : « *UNE*

ARME CANADIENNE CONÇUE POUR ABATTRE DES MINEURS » ou encore : « *CIVILS, FEMMES ET ENFANTS DANS LA MIRE DU CANADA !* »

Thomassen demeura bouche bée devant la brutalité de ce sabotage. C'était, pour lui, comme voir son enfant violé sous ses yeux. L'insolence de son agresseur le rendait fou, le remplissait d'une rage aussi furieuse que le profond sentiment d'impuissance l'accompagnant. Le fruit de toute une vie de travail se piratait impunément sous ses yeux. Si seulement il avait le courage d'intervenir pour empêcher ce carnage. En même temps, l'autre le tenait en joue, prêt à tirer au moindre faux pas. Valait-il la peine de risquer sa vie ? Il pensa à Angus, son fils, qu'il laisserait orphelin. À Ashley Jones, qui tôt ou tard, finirait par renouer avec lui et demander pardon pour ses fautes. Il fallait s'accrocher, coûte que coûte. Tout n'était pas perdu. La situation pouvait encore tourner à son avantage, espérait-il toujours avec ferveur. Mais au fur et à mesure que les minutes s'écoulèrent, que deux heures passèrent et que la troisième s'entama, Daryl Thomassen en vint à abandonner tout espoir. Et tandis qu'il s'imaginait déjà faire faillite après avoir tout perdu – fortune, clientèle et crédibilité – on entendit soudain sonner à la porte, comme si Dieu lui-même avait entendu ses prières, appuyé sur le timbre et patientait dehors.

Le ravisseur sursauta, laissant tomber son ordinateur qu'il heurta accidentellement d'un coup de pied. Un juron sortit de sa bouche à la vue de son écran fracassé. Inquiet, il s'avança prudemment en direction de l'escalier, fusillant Daryl Thomassen du regard : attendait-il quelqu'un sans l'avoir mentionné ? L'otage fit non de la tête. Qui cela pouvait-il bien être ? La jeune femme descendit en catastrophe, les yeux écarquillés comme des trous de balle.

— L... La... po... poli... ce, parvint-elle à articuler, à bout de souffle. Son complice grimaça.

— Ils sont combien ?

— Je sais pas... un ou deux..., répliqua l'autre, paniquée.

Le visage de l'assaillant se crispa jusqu'à le défigurer complètement. Daryl Thomassen remarqua l'étrange étoile à l'oreille du bourreau et un déclic s'opéra. Il le reconnut enfin : celui-là même que la voiture avait renversé, une semaine plus tôt. Il cligna des yeux. C'était lui, pas de doute. Il pourrait toujours vérifier dans l'historique de navigation de sa voiture qui avait certainement conservé les images de l'accrochage.

Thomassen lâcha un cri de soulagement. De sa vie, il n'avait jamais connu de moment plus joyeux. La jouissance, toutefois, fut éphémère. Son agresseur devint fou de rage, et ordonna à tout le monde de se la fermer. La jeune femme supplia son compagnon de se rendre, mais se buta contre une sourde oreille. Elle se précipita vers l'escalier avec l'intention de se livrer aux policiers, mais l'autre dirigea son arme contre elle et la somma d'y renoncer. « Tu es fou... fou... », ne cessait-elle de répéter. À son tour, Daryl Thomassen tenta de le raisonner, en lui promettant sa clémence et celle des autorités. Ces prières ne firent que l'énerver davantage et, craignant d'être la victime d'une balle perdue, Thomassen se tut et attendit.

Un silence inquiétant régnait désormais entre eux. Impossible de savoir si la police attendait toujours à la porte ou si elle était partie, car du sous-sol, on ne pouvait rien voir de l'extérieur. Cinq minutes s'écoulèrent ainsi.

La tension atteignait son paroxysme quand soudain, ils entendirent sonner une deuxième fois à la porte. Cette fois, les agents crièrent : « Police ! ». Daryl reconnut plusieurs voix et songea qu'ils étaient au moins deux. Cette fois, il ne se fit pas prier et se leva pour se diriger vers l'escalier, ignorant le danger mortel pointé vers lui et les menaces de son tortionnaire.

Paniqué, Adel tira un premier coup dans sa direction, espérant le dissuader d'aller plus loin. Une giclée de sang éclaboussa le mur derrière. Un deuxième et un troisième coup suivirent.

Traversé par deux projectiles, Daryl Thomassen s'effondra au sol. Les évènements qui suivirent demeurent encore flous dans sa mémoire. Il se souvint pourtant de quelques vagues images. Il crut entendre des coups à la porte, des cris retentir, et la jeune femme s'échapper à son tour en montant les escaliers. Puis, il crut entendre un gros « CRACK » – c'était la porte d'en haut qui venait de céder. Enfin, un autre coup de feu ; l'effondrement d'un corps à l'étage. Celui de la jeune femme, sans doute.

Puis plus rien. Noir.

Le matin du drame, les médias rapportèrent qu'un homme reposait entre la vie et la mort, après avoir été la victime d'un violent cambriolage, à sa résidence. Une opération policière devant lui porter secours aurait mal tourné. Parmi les suspects, une jeune femme, déjà connue des milieux policiers, aurait été abattue sur place. L'autre, un individu sans histoire, serait détenu.

Selon le rapport de police, deux agents du SPVM se seraient présentés au domicile de la victime vers 4 h 30, après que le 9-1-1 ait été signalé. Un homme manquait à l'appel. Des traces d'activités suspectes avaient alors été repérées aux abords de sa maison.

C'est après avoir entendu des coups de feu, à l'intérieur, que les deux constables auraient convenu d'intervenir. D'emblée, l'opération tourne à la débâcle et fait deux victimes. La première, identifiée comme l'un des suspects, est abattue dans la résidence par l'agent Akoulov qui affirmera plus tard que, craignant pour sa vie, il aurait fait feu sur elle. La deuxième victime, le propriétaire des lieux, est découverte au sous-sol de sa maison, gisant dans son sang ;

deux projectiles de 9 mm tirés à bout portant par le second suspect l'auraient atteint ; ce dernier allait se rendre aux autorités sans opposer de résistance.

L'agression survenue aurait surpris les résidents de la rue du Summit Circle, voie bordée de luxueuses demeures au sommet du Mont-Royal. « Le quartier est tranquille, ici. C'est inquiétant qu'on s'en prenne encore une fois aux riches. On lit de plus en plus d'histoires de vols, de grabuges, d'incendies criminels [...] Vraiment, on ne sait plus quoi penser ! », s'était plaint un résident, interrogé par Radio-Canada, étonné par la présence policière inhabituelle dans ce secteur de la ville plutôt calme.

L'identité des victimes dévoilée, on réfuta la thèse du cambriolage : une employée de Eagle Eyes Systems, qui avait retracé l'adresse de la descente policière, confirma qu'elle coïncidait avec celle de Daryl Thomassen, bénéficiaire du service Harmony+, censé lui conférer une protection accrue à domicile, au travail et sur la route. Aucune alarme n'avait pourtant retenti pendant la soirée ni dans la matinée, ce qui n'augurait rien de bon. D'autant plus que le principal suspect fut à l'emploi de la firme.

Dans la foulée de cette révélation, Skyline Solutions, compagnie fondée par Thomassen et entretenant des liens étroits avec la Défense nationale, confirma à son tour qu'une brèche avait été repérée sur son réseau. Un fichier « classé top secret » avait été téléchargé vers une adresse IP inconnue. La nature du fichier, de même que les liens contractuels unissant Thomassen avec l'Aviation royale du Canada laissaient présager le pire. Tout portait à croire que la fraude et le vol survenus n'étaient pas si banals. Le crime s'apparentait davantage à un cas d'espionnage industriel, ou même, un vol de secrets d'État.

Quels étaient les réels motifs d'Adel Salem, un homme apparemment sans histoire ? Et surtout : quels liens l'unissaient à Daryl Thomassen et Audrey Lavoie ? Seule la suite de l'enquête allait le révéler.

Au total, une dizaine d'enquêteurs de l'unité des Crimes majeurs, accompagnés de membres de la Section de l'identification judiciaire, inspectèrent les lieux. On mobilisa un camion-laboratoire pour étudier et comprendre les circonstances du drame. Les agents Akoulov et Dang furent considérés comme les témoins principaux de la scène. Les images captées par leurs caméras corporelles furent saisies, de même que toutes les données historiques conservées par l'assistant numérique d'Akoulov.

Le corps d'Audrey Lavoie fut confié au coroner Samuel Ferland, qui dirigea les investigations entourant les circonstances de sa mort. À la demande du ministre de la Sécurité publique, le Bureau des enquêtes indépendantes déclencha aussi sa propre enquête, afin d'établir si des charges criminelles devaient être retenues ou non contre les deux policiers.

Des deux projectiles qui atteignirent Daryl Thomassen, l'un s'était logé dans son épaule et l'autre avait effleuré son aorte. Une importante hémorragie allait le plonger dans un profond coma. Le prélèvement de ses cellules souches allait permettre l'impression d'une nouvelle aorte. Ce n'est que dix jours plus tard qu'il put être interrogé, à l'Institut de Cardiologie de Montréal.

Il fallut attendre le mardi suivant, soit le 22 juin 2032, avant d'en savoir davantage sur le suspect, ses motifs, et connaître l'ensemble des chefs d'accusation portés contre lui. Le ministre public et le Directeur des poursuites avaient demandé à disposer de quelques jours supplémentaires, le temps d'effectuer les perquisitions et d'analyser tous les éléments de preuve. Au nombre des pièces à conviction figuraient notamment l'arme du crime, des enregistrements vidéo, un ordinateur portable laissé sur les lieux, deux téléphones – l'un appartenant à Lavoie et l'autre à Salem. Items auxquels s'ajoutèrent également une vingtaine d'appareils électroniques en tous genres, provenant des fouilles et perquisitions domiciliaires menées chez Salem, ses parents et dans les bureaux de EES.

Les résultats d'autopsie, la transcription des témoignages, l'extraction des appareils informatiques, de même que le code source du logiciel HiOS, avec toute sa base de données, furent téléversés dans le Module d'assistance judiciaire intégré aux systèmes des Tribunaux automatisés du Québec – MajisTraQ –, par l'action d'un greffier. Dix heures d'analyse suffirent au logiciel pour compiler les données et générer les chefs d'accusation.

Fruit d'une collaboration internationale impliquant près d'une soixantaine de chercheurs, mais conçu et développé à Montréal grâce au soutien financier de la Fondation canadienne à l'innovation, la plateforme modulaire MajisTraQ peut, selon sa configuration, remplir plusieurs fonctions. Cette puissance lui est conférée par son noyau logiciel « Cyberjustice », qui comprend l'ensemble des services nécessaires au fonctionnement d'un tribunal classique. Ceux-ci incluent, sans s'y limiter, la gestion des dossiers judiciaires et des documents d'audience, l'authentification et l'identification des témoins, les agendas du personnel, les horaires de réunion, le registre des incidents, etc.

MajisTraq peut ainsi modéliser rapidement les principales fonctions d'une chaîne judiciaire criminelle, civile ou administrative. En mode automatique, l'application opère comme une plateforme en ligne pour régler les litiges de faible gravité, peu complexes. En mode plus « manuel », l'outil peut offrir à chaque acteur de la chaîne un assistant numérique intelligent personnalisé, capable d'exécuter de façon autonome certaines tâches de nature administrative ou procédurale, et ce, à l'intérieur de délais réduits. Un avocat peut ainsi, grâce à MajisTraQ, analyser d'importants volumes de documents à partir du greffier électronique, et établir des recoupements en un tour de main. Le greffier peut aussi archiver les actes de procédure, les retranscriptions de déclaration par saisie vocale, réviser les qualifications de preuves et leur dépôt dans le cadre d'une audience, et ainsi de suite. Quant au juge – et c'est là l'une des fonctions les plus intéressantes – il peut, grâce à un compilateur, modéliser différents jugements à partir des textes de loi, des preuves et des témoignages. Un rapport généré automatiquement retrace, avec exactitude, la pondération allouée à chaque critère ayant mené à la sentence. Les résultats, rendus publics, garantissent la formulation de jugements transparents, impartiaux, objectifs et exempts de biais. Une technologie de chaîne de blocs sécurise les opérations.

Lancé en tant que projet pilote au tournant de 2025, MajisTraQ fut d'abord testé dans les Cours municipales et la Cour du Québec, en support aux audiences civiles. Une étude compara les jugements obtenus par la Cour, aux jugements modélisés par l'application. Les résultats, sur près de 1000 procès, furent stupéfiants ; non seulement les verdicts étaient sensiblement identiques (à 98 % près), mais MajisTraQ y parvenait en quelques heures à peine – fort d'un rapport étalant toutes les étapes de son raisonnement, depuis l'énoncé des faits jusqu'au jugement, en passant par l'évaluation des preuves et l'analyse des plaidoiries. Véritable tour de force que les tribunaux classiques ne parvenaient à accomplir qu'au terme de plusieurs mois, voire des années.

Devant l'impressionnante efficacité de l'application, on commença à introduire MajisTraQ dans les chambres criminelles, pour encadrer les poursuites pénales relatives aux infractions sommaires : conduites avec facultés affaiblies, cas de violence conjugale, d'agressions sexuelles, les méfaits publics... Bref, les délits de masse. La Commission des libérations conditionnelles en fit bientôt l'acquisition pour ses membres. La Cour fédérale, le Tribunal des droits de la personne et les tribunaux d'appel emboîtèrent le pas.

Les constats étaient sans appel et parlaient d'eux-mêmes. Face à un système judiciaire complexe, engorgé, ralenti par des coûts exorbitants et la longueur des procédures, plombé de surcroît par une grave pénurie de personnel et une augmentation des demandes d'aide, force était de constater que les plus vulnérables étaient privés d'un accès équitable à la justice. Combien d'affaires impliquant des violences à caractère sexuel avaient été suspendues pour cause de délais déraisonnables ? Combien de pauvres, de femmes et d'enfants subissaient, chaque jour, les affres d'une justice onéreuse, laxiste, contrôlée, manipulée par une élite corrompue ? La justice s'était démocratisée, grâce à l'IA et aux mégadonnées. Tout citoyen, peu importe sa couleur, sa classe, son orientation sexuelle et son rang, pouvait désormais aspirer à une meilleure défense de ses droits, à un coût réduit.

LES ÉVÈNEMENTS ENTOURANT
LE PROCÈS D'ADEL SALEM

JUIN 2032 À JUIN 2033

*Qui a mis la sagesse dans le cœur,
qui a donné l'intelligence à l'esprit ?*

Job 38, 36

La salle du Palais de justice dans laquelle Adel Salem se présenta était minuscule. La pièce était munie d'une dizaine de caméras, disposées tout autour de lui. Plusieurs capteurs, intégrés à même le box des accusés, relevaient ses données biométriques. Toutes réactions physiologiques suscitées pendant cette audience allaient être consignées.

Le visionnement de la séance fut disponible en ligne pour qui détenait un compte sur le site web du Tribunal virtuel. Le nombre de connexions étant limité, il fallut en faire la demande au préalable. Les membres de la famille Salem s'étaient déplacés au Palais de justice pour assister à la comparution, mais faute d'espace, seulement le père put pénétrer dans la salle d'audience, la mère et la sœur devant y assister à partir d'une autre salle.

Vêtu d'une ample combinaison blanche, Adel Salem apparut menotté, les cheveux en broussailles et le corps traversé d'innombrables tics nerveux. Escorté par deux constables, il buta à la vue de son père, M. Salem, qui du haut de ses soixante-dix ans, le fusillait du regard. L'échine courbée, il paraissait lutter contre l'effondrement de son être. Père et fils se regardèrent l'un l'autre, sans pourtant s'échanger une parole, leur bouche entrouverte comme des poissons morts. Les agents forcèrent la marche, malgré les gesticulations de l'accusé. Son agitation redoubla lorsque les préposés lui enfilèrent l'oxymètre au doigt et lui indiquèrent la position des caméras. Le juge Momodou Samba fit alors son entrée pour lui faire la lecture des faits et gestes reprochés, conservant tout au long de l'audience un ton protocolaire.

« Le 17 juin 2032, Adel Salem :

a eu en sa possession une arme à feu prohibée, chargée ;

a eu en sa possession des renseignements identificateurs sur la personne de M. Daryl Thomassen, dans des circonstances qui permettent de conclure qu'ils étaient destinés à commettre une fraude ;

s'est introduit par effraction dans sa résidence dans le but d'y perpétrer un vol qualifié ;

s'est livré à des voies de fait à son endroit et lui a infligé des lésions corporelles ;

a séquestré, emprisonné et saisi de force M. Daryl Thomassen ;

a tenté d'obtenir des éléments relevant de la propriété intellectuelle, contre sa volonté,

a tenté de lui causer la mort en utilisant une arme à feu ;

s'est livré à des dommages matériels considérables qui, compte tenu du contexte, et des motifs idéologiques évoqués, ont fait craindre que des activités terroristes soient menées ;

a, par négligence criminelle, causé la mort d'Audrey Lavoie en l'incitant à perpétrer des actes criminels avec lui et en son nom, contre sa volonté. »

Adel étouffa un sanglot. « A-Audrey... A-Audrey » balbutia-t-il plusieurs fois, s'infligeant des coups à la tête. Les constables vinrent pour le maîtriser. Toute la procédure n'aura duré que quelques minutes. Suite à quoi, le juge Momodou Samba ordonna qu'une évaluation psychiatrique soit menée afin de déterminer si Adel Salem était apte à subir un procès.

Il comparut une deuxième fois, et ce, quelques minutes plus tard, pour que la couronne puisse s'opposer à sa remise en liberté. Cette fois, Adel apparut la mine abattue, flanqué de ses deux sbires. Il fixa le sol durant la quasi-totalité de la séance, sauf pour jeter un coup d'œil nerveux vers son avocat, Me Chatura Sultana. Celui-ci proposa une remise en liberté sous caution. Le juge Momodou Samba s'y opposa, compte tenu de la gravité des crimes présumés. Adel Salem devait comparaître à nouveau devant le tribunal pour la suite des procédures. D'ici là, il devait être placé en détention.

La version MajisTraQ qui mit en examen Adel Salem fut la v. 10.15.4, une version bêta lancée en décembre 2031. Logiciel dont le module « Gestion de preuves » fut amélioré pour inclure dans sa portée les programmes informatiques et autres applications d'usage.

L'accusation de terrorisme stupéfia tant la communauté judiciaire que les journalistes. Le dépôt, par un logiciel, d'un acte d'accusation dans une affaire de terrorisme était une véritable première... Du moins, au Canada. Il s'agissait après tout d'une charge relevant d'un champ de compétence qui, jusqu'alors, était strictement réservé à du personnel judiciaire.

Il existait quelques cas peu médiatisés en Chine, en Iran et en Russie. Les interpellations s'avéraient aléatoires et les preuves, jamais divulguées ou soumises à un examen plus minutieux de la part de vrais procureurs, totalement impartiaux. De sorte que les verdicts – et cette pratique en général – demeurèrent contestés par les différentes ligues de droits de la personne à travers le monde. En Amérique comme en Europe, toutefois, ce domaine judiciaire avait été, jusque-là, entièrement réservé à l'analyse rationnelle des êtres humains.

Comme l'écrivait un chroniqueur judiciaire du journal *Le Devoir* :

> « *Le code source de MajisTraQ aurait dû l'inciter à s'en tenir à ses attributions. C'est-à-dire, la modélisation de chefs d'accusation classiques généralement admis par le système. Mais il semble que son algorithme d'apprentissage, basé sur une jurisprudence de plus d'un million de cas mis en mémoire, et de tous les verdicts rendus dans les pays de l'OCDE depuis 1969, l'ait conduit à outrepasser cette directive. Comme si, le logiciel obéissant à son éthique interne*

devait absolument révéler quelque chose, ne pouvant s'astreindre au silence en regard d'une possible infraction à la loi antiterroriste canadienne. Ainsi, pressentant que ni les policiers ni le procureur de la Couronne ne se dirigeaient vers une accusation de terrorisme, MajisTraQ a cru bon d'ajouter, de sa propre initiative, ces chefs (en s'appuyant sur l'analyse des éléments de preuve probants admis dans le module Preuves), craignant que l'humain n'ait commis une erreur qui puisse mettre le pays en danger. Initiative que le procureur et le juge ont approuvée, après examen approfondi, en entérinant l'ensemble des accusations portées contre Adel Salem. »

Confronté à ce sujet, l'avocat de la poursuite avait argué que : « Les accusations portées se révélèrent conformes à la preuve policière recueillie. »

À la demande de l'avocat représentant le consortium médiatique, on rendit publics plusieurs éléments de ladite preuve. L'extraction informatique des appareils d'Adel Salem révéla des historiques de navigation compromettants. On découvrit, en l'occurrence, qu'il exploitait une ribambelle de faux profils pour faire l'apologie d'un « militantisme ultra-radical », selon l'expression employée par MajisTraQ. Le logiciel avait établi un recoupement avec la boucle d'oreille en forme d'étoile anarchocommuniste que l'accusé portait sur son oreille gauche au moment de son arrestation. Essentiellement, ces groupes critiquaient les politiques gouvernementales, la consommation de masse, le patriarcat, les guerres « injustes », et incitaient leurs partisans aux actions directes et à la désobéissance civile, notait le rapport rendu par le programme.

La situation personnelle de Daryl Thomassen, ses liens étroits avec le Gouvernement du Canada et, plus particulièrement, sa fonction stratégique auprès de la Défense nationale, en tant que développeur de systèmes logiciels pour armes létales autonomes, pesa pour beaucoup dans le jugement de MajisTraqQ. Mais la preuve la plus percutante demeura cet enregistrement trouvé sur la messagerie vocale de Mme Sylvie Lavoie, mère de la victime. Le fichier audio aurait été envoyé à l'insu d'Audrey Lavoie des suites d'un appel involontaire, communément appelé « *pocket call* ». L'extrait de trois minutes sur lequel on put entendre la voix d'Adel Salem allait comme suit : « [...] M-moi j-je me bats pour la liberté, et contre tous ceux qui fabriquent des m-machines de guerre pour tuer des innocents ! Et vous, Daryl Thomassen, v-vous êtes un... un rouage de ce système ! [...] »

Ces paroles se répandirent comme une traînée de poudre. Les médias firent jouer l'extrait en boucle. Des mèmes en d'innombrables langues pullulèrent sur le web, en référence à ce passage.

Pour ce qui est des autres éléments de preuve, les procureurs aux poursuites criminelles et pénales firent savoir qu'ils en compléteraient la divulgation, une fois Daryl Thomassen interrogé. La victime demeurait toujours dans le coma, mais depuis son opération, on ne craignait plus pour sa vie.

Près d'un mois après le drame, soit le mercredi 21 juillet 2032, une nouvelle audience se tint au palais de justice de Montréal pour permettre à la Couronne de divulguer toute la preuve. La défense, représentée par Me Chathura Sultana, en avait obtenu copie une semaine plus tôt.

Daryl Thomassen, qui reprit connaissance le 27 juin, put enfin être interrogée par les policiers. Suite à un malaise, son interrogatoire fut ajournée au lendemain. Sa déposition vint corroborer la validité des accusations portées contre Adel Salem.

En guise de compléments de preuve sont venus s'ajouter différentes expertises médico-légales et un rapport faisant état de tous les déplacements effectués par Adel Salem. Ce document démontra bien qu'il s'était rendu à la maison de Daryl Thomassen, quelques jours avant les faits, pour y installer une caméra de surveillance à l'orée du bois Summit, confirmant ainsi la préméditation de ses crimes.

Avant que ne débute la séance, la rumeur laissait entendre qu'Adel Salem consentait à plaider coupable à l'ensemble des chefs d'accusation, hormis ceux de terrorisme et de négligence criminelle ayant causé la mort d'Audrey Lavoie. Visage affaissé, l'accusé apparut à la séance du tribunal, quelque peu assommé par les médicaments. Il prit place dans le box des accusés et suivit péniblement l'audience, qui dura douze minutes. Son avocat plaida pour lui.

Le défenseur soutint qu'en vertu de l'*actus reus* et du *mens rea*, on ne pouvait tenir son client responsable d'un acte de terrorisme en se basant uniquement sur des preuves circonstancielles. Pris un à un, ces éléments de preuve ne démontraient pas, hors de tout doute raisonnable, qu'Adel Salem était coupable d'un tel crime. Le plaideur fit remarquer qu'Adel Salem présentait des troubles de santé mentale liés à une dépression non traitée. Mieux encore, il rappela qu'Adel Salem avait agi en son nom personnel (non en tant que membre d'une organisation), et qu'à ce titre, tout portait à croire qu'il était émotionnellement instable au moment des faits reprochés. Quant à la négligence criminelle ayant causé la mort d'Audrey Lavoie, Me Sultana fit remarquer que la victime avait agi en tant que complice, et que conséquemment, elle avait pris des risques en toute connaissance de cause. Son décès, des suites de l'opération policière, ne pouvait être imputable, d'aucune manière, à Adel Salem. Par conséquent, il demanda que soient rejetées ces accusations, ce que la Couronne refusa de faire.

La défense demanda alors à ce que soit tenue une enquête préliminaire afin de vérifier l'admissibilité des preuves. Le juge Momodou Samba accepta la requête, et ajourna la séance au 6 septembre 2032.

L'enquête préliminaire se déroula sur près de huit jours. La Couronne fit entendre près de dix-sept témoins, parmi lesquels figurèrent des experts en informatique, les policiers qui effectuèrent des perquisitions, des anciens collègues et amis d'Adel Salem. Et le dernier, mais non le moindre, Daryl Thomassen.

Maximilien Caron, alias Maximus, vint témoigner à la barre. Il exposa en détail la nature des relations qu'il entretenait avec la victime et l'accusé. Il raconta minutieusement la soirée du 7 juin, ainsi que la nuit qui s'en suivit, où il s'était pris une raclée, suivant l'incendie de la boutique La Grange. Il imputa l'agression d'Adel à sa mégalomanie qui les avait entraînés, le Resco et lui-même, dans une action aux proportions démesurées. C'était Adel qui avait proposé d'incendier le local, lui qui en avait assuré la logistique, lui qui avait allumé et balancé la torche malgré les réserves exprimées par le groupe. Son tempérament impulsif et revanchard les avait conduits, malgré eux, à s'associer avec lui, sous peine de subir ses représailles. Maximilien avait payé les frais pour avoir osé le critiquer. Son témoignage fut corroboré par les autres membres du Resco, y compris Manon « Sœur » Bouchard, qui abondèrent dans le même sens et qui se présentèrent comme des victimes d'Adel Salem.

En dépit des efforts déployés par la Défense, Me Chathura Sultana ne put remettre en doute ni la validité des preuves ni la crédibilité des témoins de la poursuite. Il donna ainsi l'aval à la tenue d'un procès. La Cour supérieure ayant l'habitude de prévoir un nombre supplémentaire de jurés pour pallier les défections, quatorze citoyens plutôt que douze furent sélectionnés pour ce procès hors norme.

C'est un algorithme de hasard qui, dans la région de Montréal, se chargea de convoquer près de deux cents citoyens candidats à ce poste. Les critères de sélection reposèrent entre autres sur l'âge, l'état de santé, le sexe, l'occupation professionnelle et les responsabilités familiales des participants. On posa les questions d'usage pour vérifier leur impartialité.

« Connaissez-vous personnellement Adel Salem, ou entretenez-vous des relations avec un membre de sa famille, proche ou éloignée ? »

« Entretenez-vous un préjugé favorable ou défavorable à l'égard des personnes d'une ethnie ou d'une croyance religieuse différente de la vôtre ? »

« Êtes-vous capable de mettre de côté votre opinion sur la culpabilité d'Adel Salem et de rendre un verdict en vous basant uniquement sur la preuve et les directives du juge ? »

L'algorithme consigna les réponses et les réactions physiologiques des candidats, sur la base desquelles il sélectionna le jury du procès en moins de trois secondes.

Adel Salem fut incarcéré au centre de détention Laval dans l'attente de son procès. C'était un bâtiment nouvellement inauguré, flanqué d'écocertifications, témoignant des efforts réalisés en construction durable. Outre les systèmes d'énergies renouvelables hautement performants, l'ouvrage intégrait une forte proportion de contenu régional et de matériaux recyclés grâce au béton québécois et à l'acier ontarien des barreaux, relevait le rapport d'audit environnemental.

Accusé de terrorisme, Adel Salem fut détenu dans la zone à sécurité maximale du pénitencier. Il put ainsi jouir d'une cellule individuelle, avec fenêtre, lavabo, toilette, lit et table de travail à sa disposition. Ce qui, en fin de compte, fut tout à son avantage, car son intégration en milieu carcéral n'avait pas été de tout repos. Diagnostiqué de dépression sévère avec troubles psychotiques, Adel nécessita un suivi attentif, tant son risque de suicide fut important. Ces troubles se présentèrent sous plusieurs formes, ce qui en fit un cas d'école pour la formation clinique. Son déni de la mort d'Audrey captiva les stagiaires. Les psychologues eurent beau lui énoncer les évidences, son décès lui était inconcevable. Il interprétait ces déclarations comme une machination ourdie contre sa personne, même si, le matin fatidique du 18 juin, il avait bien vu Audrey, morte, quittant les lieux du drame sur une civière. Il persistait à croire qu'elle poursuivait une lente convalescence et qu'elle communiquerait avec lui, d'un jour à l'autre, mais que sa colère l'empêchait, pour un temps, tout rapprochement. Les jours passèrent toutefois sans qu'aucun signe de vie ne vienne supporter sa conviction. Il mit sa mauvaise fortune sur le dos de l'agent Akoulov qui avait tiré sur son amie par erreur. Il réclamait que justice soit faite. Il s'en prit ensuite à Daryl Thomassen à qui il imputa tous ses malheurs. Ce fut ensuite contre « le système » qu'il manifesta sa hargne. Puis les psychothérapies et l'introspection aidant, il en vint finalement à accepter l'inacceptable, à réaliser ses torts et à retourner sa colère contre lui-même, ouvrant ainsi la voie à une nouvelle phase de psychose aiguë, avec délires hallucinatoires. Les traitements prouvèrent leur efficacité, le laissant par ailleurs dans un état aboulique.

C'est vers cette période qu'il fit la rencontre de Mostapha Bousmina, un récidiviste du même âge, incarcéré dans une zone du pénitencier adjacente à la sienne. Mostapha Bousmina purgeait une peine de dix ans pour fraude, vol de cryptomonnaie et piratage informatique d'institutions fédérales. Le codétenu avait réussi, durant les heures de repas et les récréations, à aborder Adel Salem, à se lier d'amitié avec lui et le sortir de son apathie. Ensemble, ils partagèrent leurs techniques de piratage, leurs ressentiments face « au système », ce qui n'était pas sans apporter un peu de réconfort au présumé criminel.

Quelle ne fut la surprise d'Adel lorsque, deux semaines plus tard, il retrouva Mostapha Bousmina au tribunal, dans le cadre de son enquête préliminaire. Pour l'occasion, il s'était vêtu d'un complet veston-cravate et portait un badge de police. Il se présenta comme un agent double de la GRC, venu dévoiler à la cour toutes les confidences livrées par l'accusé. Son témoignage allait servir de preuve contre Adel Salem, venant renforcer les accusations de terrorisme.

Les couloirs du centre de détention Laval arboraient des décorations de Noël à l'épreuve des suicides, en ce vendredi 24 décembre 2032. Le menu régulier avait cédé la place à un menu un peu plus festif. Ce soir, les détenus avaient droit à un bœuf Stroganoff servi avec pâtes, et à des tartelettes au citron en guise de dessert. Rien, pour aiguiser l'appétit d'Adel qui préféra la triste froideur de sa cellule à la compagnie des codétenus.

Plus tôt cet après-midi, Adel Salem et son avocat, Me Chatura Sultana, avaient passé en revue sa défense. La rencontre s'était déroulée en vidéoconférence. Le plus important, martelait le juriste, était de laisser planer un doute raisonnable à l'endroit du « motif idéologique » de son crime. Or, en l'absence de manifeste, sans déclaration d'intention, bref, sans preuve claire que son crime était motivé par une cause politique ou religieuse « en vue d'intimider toute ou une partie de la population », l'accusation de terrorisme – la plus grave – avait de fortes chances de tomber, selon lui.

Il restait l'enregistrement découvert sur la messagerie vocale de Mme Lavoie. Me Sultana persistait à croire qu'à lui seul, cet élément ne pouvait constituer une preuve hors de tout doute raisonnable de la motivation du crime, et qu'à cet égard, il était même possible de plaider la folie passagère. Le rapport médical d'Adel Salem ne manquait pas d'arguments. L'accusé faisait d'ailleurs l'objet d'innombrables thérapies et d'une médication neuroleptique.

Adel Salem avait écouté son avocat sans sourciller, sans faire de commentaire, sans montrer une quelconque émotion. Ses forces l'avaient quitté.

Il n'attendait plus que son procès.

Sa téléconférence terminée, Me Chatura Sultana s'empressa de compléter sa toilette afin de se rendre au centre-ville, où se déroulait, dans un bistrot de la rue Crescent, une petite réception de Noël organisée par son cabinet d'avocats. Une section du restaurant avait été réservée pour le groupe d'une quinzaine de personnes. Un menu des fêtes avait été concocté pour l'occasion.

L'ambiance était festive, les convives de bonne humeur. Chatura Sultana avait choisi le buisson d'écrevisses en entrée, suivi du filet mignon poêlé avec sauce au poivre. Un savoureux Bordeaux accompagnait le tout.

Un des associés principaux du cabinet, Me Justin Le Roux, avait fait tinter son verre avant de prendre la parole. Il tenait à exprimer sa fierté d'être parmi ses collègues. L'année 2032 en avait été une de croissance exceptionnelle. L'équipe s'était agrandie. Le public leur vouait une confiance grandissante pour défendre des dossiers en matière de droit criminel, et ce à la grandeur du Québec. Passion, conviction, amour de la justice et dévouement demeuraient les valeurs fondamentales sur lesquelles devait se bâtir la pratique du droit : « notre pratique du droit ».

Le recours aux systèmes automatisés, de plus en plus courant, ne devait pas soustraire l'avocat à ses tâches et responsabilités. « Tout le contraire, même », ajouta-t-il. S'il fut une époque où le rôle de l'avocat se cantonnait principalement à la recherche et à l'analyse, aujourd'hui, il était davantage axé sur l'explication des résultats générés par l'IA, afin d'aider ses clients à mieux comprendre leurs droits.

Il est vrai que les technologies juridiques automatisées permirent aux avocats de se libérer de plusieurs tâches administratives. Toutefois, elles ne pouvaient ni ne devaient les réduire au simple rôle d'opérateurs. Aucune machine ne pourra remplacer les plaidoiries. Ni s'adapter à l'air du temps et à ses subtils enjeux en matière de politiques publiques. Les dossiers délicats nécessiteront toujours « du doigté », fit-il en mimant subtilement un geste obscène, ce qui lui valut quelques éclats de rire. Le contact humain et la confiance auprès des clients – deux dimensions hors d'atteinte des technologies d'IA – devaient demeurer la pierre d'assise du rôle de l'avocat.

Mᵉ Chatura Sultana écouta le discours, bien qu'il ne fut que partiellement d'accord avec les propos de Mᵉ Le Roux. À ses yeux, le problème avec l'IA était qu'elle pipait les dés d'avance, tant elle pouvait prédire l'issue du procès avec exactitude. Bien sûr, il existait quelquefois des surprises ; il y a toujours eu (et il y aura toujours) des avocats consciencieux, intelligents, capables, par leurs plaidoiries et, contre toute attente, de gagner des causes indéfendables. Mais, de manière générale, la qualité de la défense avait toujours été fonction des honoraires prévus, qui eux-mêmes dépendaient du budget de l'accusé, qui dans le cas d'Adel Salem, était plutôt limité, en dépit de la somme considérable que ses parents avaient été en mesure d'amasser. Or, la preuve recueillie par la Couronne était solide, et la réfuter n'allait pas être une mince affaire.

En dressant le profil du prévenu, la poursuite avait réussi à démontrer qu'Adel Salem était bien connu des milieux anarchogauchistes, et qu'il avait réussi à cacher son jeu, au fil des ans. Plusieurs croisements obtenus grâce à des archives de caméras permirent d'établir avec un taux de certitude quasi parfait la présence d'Adel Salem à un rassemblement prokurde survenu à Montréal en 2030, tout comme sa participation à une kyrielle de manifs antiracistes, anticapitalistes, antipolicières entre 2027 et 2029, ainsi que lui-même l'avait admis aux enquêteurs, il y a quelques années, dans le cadre de son embauche chez EES.

En outre, le public semblait en faveur d'un verdict de culpabilité pour l'ensemble des chefs d'accusation. Le tout, assorti d'une condamnation exemplaire. Personne n'avait manqué d'ajouter son grain de sel pour exprimer son opinion sur cette affaire. Évoquant la séquestration de Daryl Thomassen, le premier ministre du Québec avait parlé d'une atteinte à la liberté fondamentale des individus. Le vice-premier ministre et le ministre de la Sécurité publique avaient abondé dans le même sens, tout en promettant de nouvelles ressources pour lutter contre la fraude et l'usurpation d'identité. De son côté, le ministre de la Défense nationale du Canada évoqua une dangereuse atteinte à la sécurité. La présidente de la Chambre de commerce avait, elle aussi, effectué une sortie pour parler de la peur qui régnait chez ses membres.

Compte tenu du montant forfaitaire limitant ses honoraires, Me Chatura Sultana pouvait d'ores et déjà prédire l'issue du procès. Du reste, l'associé directeur du cabinet ne semblait pas faire de cette cause une priorité. D'autres dossiers, au rapport risques/bénéfices plus avantageux, accaparaient son attention et l'énergie de ses meilleures ressources. N'empêche, Adel Salem pouvait compter sur la meilleure défense pénale que l'argent fut en mesure d'acheter, se gratifia Chatura Sultana, en savourant le dernier morceau de son steak qu'il rinça d'une généreuse lampée de rouge.

Le procès d'Adel Salem s'étala sur un peu plus de trois semaines, entre le 4 et le 28 janvier 2033, au Palais de justice de Montréal.

Parmi les témoins de la Couronne qui se succédèrent à la barre, Daryl Thomassen retint la plus grande attention. À lui seul, il fallut compter deux jours pour sa comparution, le juge Momodou Samba ayant donné comme directive que – de tous les témoignages – celui de Thomassen ne devait être écourté. L'homme d'affaires raconta la séquestration qu'il vécut dans la nuit du 17 au 18 juin 2032. Il ne lésina pas sur les détails, rapportant un récit des plus horrifiants aux oreilles de ceux qui l'entendirent. Durant sa déclaration, Daryl Thomassen aura toutefois eu un mot tendre pour Audrey Lavoie ; sans elle, il n'aurait probablement pas survécu à la « folie meurtrière » d'Adel Salem. Selon Thomassen, Audrey Lavoie était une victime de son ex-copain qui l'encouragea, malgré elle, à perpétrer cette agression. Il écarta la responsabilité du policier qui, rappela-t-il, lui a sauvé la vie.

Plus encore, la Couronne avança quantité de preuves pour établir qu'Adel Salem avait sciemment commis des actes susceptibles de faire craindre que des activités terroristes soient menées. Le fichier code source du logiciel HiOS, propriété de Skyline Solution, fut de ce nombre. Le contenu du fichier étant classé « très secret », un arrêt de la Cour interdisait sa divulgation. Mais un rapport d'expert rendu public en décrivait le contenu, soulignant l'importance stratégique de cette propriété intellectuelle pour le Canada.

Le logiciel développé par M. Daryl Thomassen, écrivait l'expert, devait servir à équiper une nouvelle flotte de drones FEMALE (flotte étendue de moyenne altitude et de longue endurance) pouvant repérer des cibles, les identifier et les abattre sans intervention humaine, dans le strict respect du droit international et de l'éthique militaire. Ces armes à la fine pointe de la technologie devaient notamment servir dans la guerre contre le terrorisme que menait le Canada en Iran. L'expert mentionnait aussi, dans son rapport, les répercussions désastreuses encourues par la divulgation publique de son code source. Parmi ces conséquences, l'expert souligna le préjudice économique et financier irréparable porté à Skyline Solutions. Mais il insista surtout sur les menaces que cette fuite entraînerait sur la vie des Canadiens.

Le psychiatre embauché par la Couronne rejeta d'emblée la thèse de la psychose pour réfuter les arguments en faveur de la non-responsabilité criminelle. Bien que l'accusé éprouvât effectivement des troubles de santé mentale, le médecin spécialiste conclut qu'il était « fort improbable » qu'il ait été aux prises avec des idées délirantes le soir de son crime. En étudiant le parcours de l'assaillant, l'expert n'arriva pas à percevoir le « glissement » ou le « prodrome », communs aux schizophrènes. Tout en admettant que son sujet fût bel et bien en proie à des visions hallucinatoires, le psychiatre soutint que celles-ci ne se manifestèrent qu'après les évènements tragiques dont il fut à la fois le témoin et le précurseur ; c'est donc la mort d'Audrey et la prise de conscience de sa responsabilité qui induisirent le traumatisme à l'origine de sa schizophrénie. La préméditation du crime, de même que son entêtement à persister dans le refus de voir son erreur démontrent qu'Adel Salem comprenait très bien le caractère illégal de ses actes et leurs conséquences dommageables pour le pays. Le criminel s'était lancé, selon lui, dans une quête narcissique lui permettant d'exprimer ses ressentiments face « au système », tout en démontrant sa supériorité par un acte spectaculaire.

La défense, quant à elle, s'efforça principalement de soulever un doute dans l'esprit du jury quant à la culpabilité d'Adel Salem, en regard des chefs de terrorisme et de négligence criminelle. Pour ce faire, la stratégie de Me Chathura Sultana fut de dépeindre Adel Salem sous les traits d'un esprit tourmenté. De sorte que ses gestes traduisirent une erreur de jugement plutôt qu'un complot terroriste. Il comptait ainsi gagner la sympathie des jurés.

À cette fin, Me Chathura Sultana ne ménagea aucun argument, soulignant à maintes occasions la névrose identitaire du jeune informaticien. Il s'attarda longuement sur les liens étroits entre l'accusé et la victime. Il écorcha celle-ci au passage par l'étalage peu glorieux de ses antécédents. Tablant sur leur relation fusionnelle, c'est Audrey Lavoie qui, selon lui, aurait initié Adel Salem à un militantisme radical et violent – aveux qu'il parvint à arracher d'un ancien membre du Resco, suite à un interrogatoire des plus musclés. Le plaideur mit également en lumière « la blessure intérieure » de son client, qui souffrait d'un triangle amoureux impliquant son ex-compagne et Maximilien Caron – déchirement douloureux qui aurait fait dérailler sa raison, comme en témoignent les comportements inhabituels qui suivirent ce « choc émotionnel ». Ici, Me Chatura Sultana fit référence à la tentative de suicide de son client sur le boulevard Crémazie (images qui furent diffusées en cour). Tout portait donc à croire que les crimes commis par d'Adel Salem – le vol de données, l'usurpation d'identité, l'entrée par effraction chez Daryl Thomassen – auraient été la résultante d'une crise existentielle, provoquée par le désir désespéré de se racheter auprès du groupe qui l'aurait rejeté et humilié. C'est ainsi que, prenant le blâme de leurs récents déboires amoureux, et percevant le danger pour son compagnon qui ne voulait entendre raison, Audrey Lavoie aurait décidé de l'accompagner dans son crime. Un acte de solidarité qui lui a coûté la vie. Les choses tournèrent en tragédie à la suite du retour inattendu de Daryl Thomassen. Scénario qui, à la base, n'avait été envisagé ni par Salem ni par Lavoie. Considérant ce qui précède, comment alors évoquer l'idée même d'un *acte de terrorisme* ? Sans parler de cette dette de plus de trente mille dollars, contractée par l'achat, sur marge de crédit, d'un cryptoactif – le Comet coin – dont le cours s'effondra en l'espace d'une semaine, affligeant Salem d'une dette abyssale. L'espoir de tomber, chez Daryl Thomassen, sur une propriété intellectuelle de valeur, dont la vente illégale sur le *dark web* aurait pu lui permettre d'éponger ce déficit, devrait être considéré comme le principal motif des gestes de l'accusé, concluait son avocat.

La psychiatre embauchée par la défense pour déterminer si Adel Salem avait bel et bien été motivé par des idéaux terroristes avait rencontré le détenu pendant une douzaine d'heures. Elle corrobora les propos de son collègue à l'effet que l'accusé ne fut pas sous l'emprise d'une psychose au moment des faits et qu'il poursuivait une quête narcissique. Toutefois, pour sa part, les gestes d'Adel Salem auraient été principalement alimentés par la nécessité de prouver à Audrey qu'il était « digne de son amour ». Selon elle, Salem ne portait aucune cause idéologique ou religieuse ; il n'agissait qu'en fonction de sa propre personne, sous l'emprise de ses blessures psychiques. En ce sens, Adel Salem présentait tous les attributs d'un jeune homme ordinaire, avec ses zones d'ombres, dans toute sa normalité et sa fragilité : « Comme spécialiste, nous ouvrons une fenêtre sur l'esprit des gens. Nous nous servons d'une grille d'analyse pour comprendre l'incompréhensible et trouver des repères. Reste que l'esprit est un magma. La nature humaine est complexe » tint-elle à rappeler humblement, à la défense de l'accusé.

L'un des temps forts du procès fut le témoignage inattendu d'Adel Salem. Une décision in extremis de la défense, car il n'était pas prévu que l'accusé témoigne à son procès. Compte tenu des allégations et des preuves accablantes qui pesaient contre lui, cette stratégie semblait porteuse d'espoir, quant à l'impression favorable qu'Adel Salem aurait pu avoir sur le jury. Enfin, Me Chatura Sultana évalua que son client n'avait pas le choix, s'il souhaitait s'en tirer avec une peine plus clémente. De sa pénible et peu convaincante déclaration, qu'il est impossible de rendre compte tellement elle fut décousue et inintelligible, Adel termina par cette émouvante proclamation : « elle est morte, par ma f-faute... J'ai perdu l'amour de ma vie... » avait-il lancé d'une voix criblée de sanglots.

Loin de l'aider, son témoignage le nuisit. Le contre-interrogatoire de la Couronne le mit en échec à plusieurs reprises. Les questions portèrent sur son passé, sur les idées politiques qu'il partageait avec Audrey Lavoie, sur son militantisme qu'il avait longtemps réussi à cacher aux autorités. Que pensait-il « du système » ? Est-il vrai qu'il le dénonçait ? Comment, lors de ses entretiens d'embauche chez Eagle Eyes Systems, avait-il pu déjouer les recruteurs et les enquêteurs de la GRC, au point de se faire accréditer une cote fédérale de fiabilité 3, communément appelée cote *secret* ? Le procureur en rajouta une couche en le questionnant sur son « militantisme radical » : participation à des manifs illégales, méfaits contre les biens publics, collaboration à un incendie criminel... Et comme pour planter le dernier clou dans son cercueil, il le confronta sur le Glock qu'il réussit à répliquer de manière remarquable et qu'il utilisa contre sa victime. Le coup de grâce.

Tout au long de cette période de questions qui n'offrit au tribunal que quelques bribes incohérentes, un appareil sophistiqué releva et consigna les caractéristiques biométriques singulières de l'accusé. Le buste entre autres, qui ne cessait d'opérer un mouvement de l'avant vers l'arrière, comme un pendule, traduisait un comportement compulsif. Un oxymètre de pouls évalua la vitesse des battements du cœur, une caméra thermique enregistra sa température corporelle, des capteurs mesurèrent l'intensité de ses tremblements et sa conductance cutanée. Toutes ces manifestations psychophysiologiques démontrèrent, avec un taux de certitude élevé, qu'Adel Salem éprouvait un niveau de stress supérieur à la normale, laissant présager, aux yeux du tribunal et des jurés, qu'il cherchait à inventer des mensonges. Ce qui n'aida en rien à sa cause.

Faisant suite aux directives du juge Momodou Samba, les quatorze membres du jury se retirèrent et entamèrent leurs délibérations à huis clos, le matin du vendredi 28 janvier de l'an 2033. Une heure ne s'était pas écoulée que les jurés rendirent déjà un verdict unanime : Adel Salem, reconnu coupable de participation à des activités terroristes et de négligence criminelle ayant entraîné la mort d'Audrey Lavoie. Ces chefs s'ajoutaient aux huit autres, soit : fraude, vol d'identité, possession d'arme, vol qualifié, voies de fait, séquestration, extorsion et tentative de meurtre sur Daryl Thomassen. Adel Salem faisait face à l'emprisonnement à perpétuité, sans libération conditionnelle avant vingt-cinq ans.

Les plaidoiries sur sentence se déroulèrent sur près de deux jours, en juin 2033, pour fixer la peine du contrevenant. Daryl Thomassen fut appelé encore une fois à témoigner. Il évoqua de nouveau sa séquestration, et rappela au tribunal à quel point ses traumatismes continuaient d'affecter sa vie. Il s'épancha sur ses craintes d'une libération anticipée de son agresseur. Mêmes préoccupations du côté d'Ashley Jones qui fit une brève déclaration en ce sens. La présidente de la Chambre de commerce réclama une peine exemplaire pour rasséréner les membres de la communauté d'affaires et décourager les activistes anticapitalistes de s'en prendre aux dirigeants.

La sœur d'Adel, Myriam Salem, soutint qu'une peine maximale annihilait toute chance de réhabilitation pour son frère, un jeune homme pourtant intelligent, et aimant, qui aurait pu contribuer à la société, par son talent.

Pour ce qui est d'Adel Salem, il montra des remords sincères. Il s'adressa à Daryl Thomassen, pour lui demander pardon. Le vibrant témoignage qu'il rendit à la famille d'Audrey, « l'amour de sa vie » le fit éclater en sanglots. Les données biométriques enregistrées lors de sa déclaration confirmèrent effectivement qu'il éprouvait une très grande tristesse et de sincères remords.

Il fut très difficile au système MajisTraQ de pondérer les émotions d'Adel Salem : la peine d'amour et la jalousie de l'accusé, par exemple, furent des paramètres, en fin de compte, complètement ignorés par l'algorithme du Module d'assistance judiciaire, qui dût les reléguer sur le plan des troubles mentaux. Ses remords, quant à eux, sentiments connus et interprétables, furent considérés comme des circonstances atténuantes. Aussi sincères fussent-ils, ses regrets ne purent faire contrepoids à l'ensemble des charges qui pesaient contre lui, en particulier l'accusation de terrorisme, la négligence criminelle, la possession d'une arme à feu illégale et surtout, le caractère prémédité évident de tous ces crimes. En foi de quoi, le rapport généré automatiquement par MajisTraQ recommanda la peine maximale, soit l'emprisonnement à perpétuité, sans libération conditionnelle avant 25 ans, pour Adel Salem.

Le juge Momodou Samba prit la chose en délibéré et fixa le prononcé de la sentence au 15 novembre 2033.

LE 15 NOVEMBRE 2033

Les évènements tragiques qui coûtèrent la vie à Audrey Lavoie plongèrent le constable de classe 7, l'agent Akoulov, au cœur d'une tempête médiatique. En attendant les conclusions de l'enquête indépendante, le matricule 274 avait été muté à l'unité du métro. Bien que le rapport fît état de plusieurs manquements aux règles, Akoulov fut disculpé des accusations criminelles qui pesaient contre lui. L'enquêteur responsable du dossier arriva à la conclusion que la force utilisée par le policier lorsqu'il tira sur Audrey Lavoie était légitime, étant donné qu'il craignait réellement pour sa vie, ainsi que l'ont démontré les données biométriques extraites de son assistant intelligent Colombus.

De son côté, le coroner qui prit en charge la dépouille d'Audrey Lavoie et qui enquêta sur les circonstances de sa mort examina lui aussi les composantes logicielles de l'assistant intelligent Colombus. Rappelons que c'est une directive de cette application qui enjoignit Akoulov à faire feu sur Audrey Lavoie. Examinant les données historiques, et revoyant les images captées par la caméra embarquée de l'appareil optique de l'agent, le coroner put reconstituer l'arbre de décision fatidique qui mena Colombus à interpréter comme un danger mortel l'irruption soudaine d'Audrey Lavoie dans son champ de vision. À un nœud bien précis de cet arbre, le coroner remarqua la distribution inhabituelle des variables « armer », « désarmer », et « tirer ». Il constata qu'à cet embranchement-ci, un degré d'incertitude inhabituel embrouillait l'intelligence artificielle, qui tentait de décoder la scène. Comparant ces données avec les images filmées par la caméra, le coroner conclut que c'est le nuage de fluorescéine formé par les brumisateurs du dispositif anti-cambriolage, déclenché par l'entrée fracassante d'Akoulov, qui brouilla la vision de l'appareil et qui provoqua la suite de décisions funestes que nous connaissons. Colombus préférant ne pas courir de risques quant à la sécurité de son partenaire, l'enjoignant ainsi à « tirer » devant un sujet fiché dans sa base de données et reconnu comme étant « criminel » – sujet fonçant vers lui, de surcroît, à une accélération supérieure à sa plage de tolérance. Ici, l'incertitude relative à la sécurité du policier avait primé sur l'incertitude relative à la dangerosité de la situation. La pondération accordée à la variable « tirer » fut de loin supérieure à celle accordée à la variable « désarmer », entraînant par suite logique le drame que nous connaissons.

Le coroner conclut, dans son rapport, que c'est un malheureux concours de circonstances qui entraîna la mort violente d'Audrey Lavoie, et que l'assistant intelligent Colombus n'était pas en cause. Il recommanda toutefois qu'une mise à jour soit effectuée sur le logiciel, afin d'en raffiner le calcul, par l'ajout de la variable « sommer » qui offrirait au policier le choix d'une force d'intervention moindre que la force létale. La mise à jour fut effectuée selon ses recommandations.

L'agent Akoulov n'avait d'ailleurs rien à craindre au sujet de son avenir au sein du service de police, qui souffrait d'une pénurie de main-d'œuvre historique. Le syndicat planchait activement sur son dossier : ce n'était qu'une question de temps avant qu'il ne réintègre ses anciennes fonctions.

En ce matin, donc, du 15 novembre 2033, le constable de classe 7, agent Youri Akoulov, matricule 274, patrouillait seul sur le quai de la station Champ-de-Mars. La matinée avait été plutôt éprouvante avec tous ses itinérants déboussolés que la nuit avait malmenés. Le policier achevait de remettre son cinquième constat d'infraction. Son dernier client, un Arabe, lui avait donné le haut-le-cœur. Le clochard empestait d'une odeur nauséabonde. Ses vêtements, infestés de grillons. Akoulov poursuivit sa ronde, espérant se changer les idées. Son regard se perdit sur l'écran mural annonçant l'arrivée du prochain métro dans trois minutes. Il faisait 24 °C sur le Grand Montréal. Le Bitcoin franchissait le seuil historique des 1,2 million de dollars US. Une Lavalloise remportait la 21ᵉ saison de *Canada's Got Talent*. Les Canadiens avaient perdu 3-2 contre les Bruins de Boston.

Les statistiques firent place aux affaires judiciaires. Akoulov sursauta en reconnaissant le visage d'Adel Salem. La sentence était tombée. Le terroriste était condamné à l'emprisonnement à perpétuité, sans libération conditionnelle avant vingt-cinq ans. Akoulov contempla les images défilant devant ses yeux. Daryl Thomassen s'adressait aux médias. Des manifestants défilaient avec des pancartes *#freeAdelSalem* devant les marches du Palais de justice. Un sentiment de soulagement envahit le policier. Justice avait été rendue. L'air se mit à vibrer, le quai d'embarquement s'anima, le métro fit son entrée à la station, déversant ses passagers et en avalant d'autres. En l'espace de quelques minutes, le quai se vida. Akoulov erra le long de la plateforme. Soudain, il entendit une sorte de stridulation venant de sa droite. Il s'approcha pour mieux voir quel pouvait en être la source, et vit un gros insecte à la jonction du mur et du sol. Il se pencha et fit une grimace de dégoût à la vue de l'orthoptère. Un grillon suintant agitait ses longues antennes dans sa direction. « Le métro au complet serait-il infesté ? » se demanda le policier. Akoulov ne fit ni une ni deux, et écrasa le malheureux insecte de sa lourde botte. « Scrounch » entendit-il en écrabouillant le fragile exosquelette. Il se pencha pour voir à nouveau, et admira les élytres nervurés, quoique broyés, du cadavre. Une notification de Colombus, lui annonçant sa pause de midi dans quinze minutes, le rappela à l'ordre. Akoulov se redressa, reprit sa ronde.

NOTE DE L'AUTEUR

Le plaidoyer des systèmes d'armes létales autonomes (SALA) livré par le gouvernement canadien est, en fait, inspiré d'une conférence donnée par Marco Sassòli, Directeur de l'Académie de droit international humanitaire et droits humains à Genève, professeur à l'Université de Genève. L'évènement, organisé par la Croix-Rouge canadienne, s'est tenu à l'Université du Québec à Montréal, le 14 mars 2019.

DANS LA COLLECTION ROMAN

Gouverneurs de la rosée, Jacques Roumain
Trilogie tropicale, Raphaël Confiant
Brisants, Max Jeanne
Une aiguille nue, Nuruddin Farah
Mémoire errante (coédition avec Remue-Ménage), J. J. Dominique
Dessalines, Guy Poitry
L'allée des soupirs, Raphaël Confiant
Je ne suis pas Jack Kérouac (coédition avec Fédérop), Jean-Paul Loubes
Saison de porcs, Gary Victor
Traversée de l'Amérique dans les yeux d'un papillon, Laure Morali
Les immortelles, Makenzy Orcel
Le reste du temps, Emmelie Prophète
L'amour au temps des mimosas, Nadia Ghalem
La dot de Sara (coédition avec Remue-Ménage), Marie-Célie Agnant
L'ombre de l'olivier, Yara El-Ghadban
Kuessipan, Naomi Fontaine
Les latrines, Makenzy Orcel
Vers l'Ouest, Mahigan Lepage
Soro, Gary Victor
Les tiens, Claude-Andrée L'Espérance
L'invention de la tribu, Catherine-Lune Grayson
Détour par First Avenue, Myrtelle Devilmé
Éloge des ténèbres, Verly Dabel
Impasse Dignité, Emmelie Prophète

La prison des jours, Michel Soukar

Coulées, Mahigan Lepage

Maudite éducation, Gary Victor

Je ne savais pas que la vie serait si longue après la mort,
collectif dirigé par Gary Victor

L'amant du lac, Virginia Pésémapéo Bordeleau

La nuit de l'Imoko, Boubacar Boris Diop

Les chants incomplets, Miguel Duplan

La dernière nuit de Cincinnatus Leconte, Michel Soukar

Cures et châtiments, Gary Victor

Des vies cassées, H. Nigel Thomas
(traduit par Alexie Doucet)

Le testament des solitudes, Emmelie Prophète

Première nuit : une anthologie du désir,
collectif dirigé par Léonora Miano

La maison des épices, Nafissatou Dia Diouf

L'enfant hiver, Virginia Pésémapéo Bordeleau

Quartz, Joanne Rochette

Fuites mineures, Mahigan Lepage

Les brasseurs de la ville, Evains Wêche

Le vieux canapé bleu, Seymour Mayne

Volcaniques : une anthologie du plaisir,
collectif dirigé par Léonora Miano

Le bout du monde est une fenêtre, Emmelie Prophète

Manhattan Blues, Jean-Claude Charles

Le parfum de Nour, Yara El-Ghadban

Le jour de l'émancipation, Wayne Grady
(traduit par Caroline Lavoie)

Le petit caillou de la mémoire, Monique Durand

Bamboola Bamboche, Jean-Claude Charles

Nuit albinos, Gary Victor

Le bar des Amériques, Alfred Alexandre

De glace et d'ombre, H. Nigel Thomas
(traduit par Christophe Bernard et Yara El-Ghadban)

Le testament de nos corps, Catherine-Lune Grayson

La femme tombée du ciel, Thomas King
(traduit par Caroline Lavoie)

Sans capote ni kalachnikov, Blaise Ndala

Adel, l'apprenti migrateur, Salah El Khalfa Beddiari

Phototaxie, Olivia Tapiero

Écorchées vivantes, collectif dirigé par Martine Fidèle

Manikanetish, Naomi Fontaine

Sainte dérive des cochons, Jean-Claude Charles

160 rue Saint-Viateur Ouest, Magali Sauves

Masi, Gary Victor

Je suis Ariel Sharon, Yara El-Ghadban

Cartographie de l'amour décolonial, Leanne Betasamosake Simpson
(traduit par Arianne Des Rochers et Natasha Kanapé Fontaine)

Le rossignol t'empêche de dormir, Steven Heighton
(traduit par Caroline Lavoie)

Le chant de Corbeau, Lee Maracle
(traduit par Joanie Demers)

Les enfants du printemps, Wallace Thurman
(traduit par Daniel Grenier)

Ben Aïcha, Kebir Ammi

La balançoire de jasmin, Ahmad Danny Ramadan
(traduit par Caroline Lavoie)

Jonny Appleseed, Joshua Whitehead
(traduit par Arianne Des Rochers)

Débutants, Catherine Blondeau

Mère à Mère, Sindiwe Magona
(traduit par Sarah Davies Cordova)

On se perd toujours par accident, Leanne Betasamosake Simpson
(traduit par Arianne Des Rochers et Natasha Kanapé Fontaine)

Boat-People, Sharon Bala
(traduit par Véronique Lessard et Marc Charron)

Ayiti, Roxane Gay
(traduit par Stanley Péan)

Balai de sorcière, Lawrence Scott,
(traduit par Christine Pagnoulle)

Laisse folie courir, Gerda Cadostin

Les villages de Dieu, Emmelie Prophète

Dans le ventre du Congo, Blaise Ndala

Annie Muktuk et autres histoires, Norma Dunning
(traduit par Daniel Grenier)

Tisser, Raharimanana

Le K ne se prononce pas, Souvankham Thammavongsa
(traduit par Véronique Lessard)

Le chant de Celia, Lee Maracle
(traduit par Joanie Demers)

Noopiming. Remède pour guérir de la blancheur,
Leanne Betasamosake Simpson
(traduit par Arianne Des Rochers)

Ferdinand je suis à Paris, Jean-Claude Charles

Maisons vides, Brenda Navarro
(traduit par Sarah Laberge-Mustad)

Le testament des solitudes, Emmelie Prophète

Difficult Women, Roxane Gay
(traduit par Olivia Tapiero)

Tomber, Carlos Manuel Álvarez
(traduit par Éric Reyes Roher)

Seuil de tolérance, Thomas King
(traduit par Daniel Grenier)

Neige des lunes brisées, Waubgeshig Rice
(traduit par Yara El-Ghadban)

Jamais l'oubli, Wayne Grady
(traduit par Catherine Ego)

Hors-Sol, Philippe Yong

L'or des mélèzes, Carole Labarre

Mon cœur bat vite, Nadia Chonville

La sirène de Black Conch, Monique Roffey
(traduit par Gerty Dambury)

Le violon d'Adrien, Gary Victor

Édition — Rodney Saint-Éloi, Yara El-Ghadban
Révision — Jean-François Létourneau
Correction — Laurence Poulin
Direction artistique et design graphique — Julie Espinasse
Atelier Mille Mille
Œuvre en couverture — © Philippe Mayaux

Fantôme de l'autorité, dit le dictator, 2011-2017
Impression 3D, lecteur mp3, tissus et perruque
Courtesy galerie Loevenbruck, Paris
© ADAGP, Paris. Photo tous droits réservés.

Mémoire d'encrier reconnaît l'aide financière du Gouvernement
du Canada par l'entremise du Conseil des Arts du Canada,
du Fonds du livre du Canada et du Gouvernement du Québec
par le Programme de crédit d'impôt pour l'édition de livres, Gestion Sodec.

Mémoire d'encrier est diffusée et distribuée par:
Harmonia Mundi livre — Europe
Gallimard Diffusion — Canada

Dépôt légal: 3ᵉ trimestre 2023
© Mémoire d'encrier, 2023 pour l'édition française
Jean-Pierre Gorkynian, 2023

Catalogage avant publication de Bibliothèque et Archives nationales
du Québec et Bibliothèque et Archives Canada

ISBN (PAPIER) : 978-2-89712-942-2
ISBN (EPUB) : 978-2-89712-943-9
ISBN (PDF) : 978-2-89712-944-6

CIP : LCC PS8613.O746 D57 2023 I CDD C843/.6—dc23

L'ouvrage *Dissident* de Jean-Pierre Gorkynian
est composé en Stanley regular, d'Optimo.
Il est imprimé sur du papier Enviro en juillet 2023
au Québec (Canada), par Marquis Imprimeur pour le compte
des Éditions Mémoire d'encrier Inc.